INDIGENOUS PEOPLES AND THE LAW

Indigenous Peoples and the Law provides an historical, comparative and contextual analysis of various legal and policy issues affecting Indigenous peoples. It focuses on the common law jurisdictions of Australia, Canada, New Zealand and the US, as well as relevant international law developments. Edited by Benjamin J Richardson, Shin Imai and Kent McNeil, this collection of new essays features 13 contributors including many Indigenous scholars, drawn from around the world. The book provides a pithy overview of the subject-matter, enabling readers to appreciate the seminal issues, precedents and international legal trends of most concern to Indigenous peoples.

The first half of *Indigenous Peoples and the Law* takes an historical perspective of the principal jurisdictions, canvassing, in particular, themes of Indigenous sovereignty, status and identity, and the movement for Indigenous self-determination. It also examines these issues in an international context, including the Inter-American human rights regime and the 2007 UN Declaration on the Rights of Indigenous Peoples. The second part of the book canvasses some contemporary issues and claims of Indigenous peoples, including land rights, mobility rights, community self governance, environmental governance, alternative dispute resolution processes, the legal status of Aboriginal women and the place of Indigenous legal traditions and legal theory.

Although an introductory volume designed primarily for readers without advanced understanding of Indigenous legal issues, *Indigenous Peoples and the Law* should also appeal to seasoned scholars, policy-makers, lawyers and others who are knowledgeable of such issues in their own jurisdiction and wish to learn more about developments in other places.

Series: Osgoode Readers

The Osgoode Readers offer interdisciplinary and cosmopolitan treatments of the essential elements of a variety of legal fields. Each chapter in an Osgoode Reader takes the form of a critical synthesis providing a succinct, engaging overview and analysis of contemporary issues and problems that are both shaping and being shaped by the law. The core of each Osgoode Reader consists of newly written chapters that build on each contributor's recent field-leading work, alongside chapters that are revised versions of recently published articles that have been thoroughly reworked to suit the focus and flow of the reader.

Osgoode Readers are distinguished by their attention to fresh perspectives dealing not only with traditional legal concerns but also with newer challenges posed by changes in social, ethical, economic and political environments. Osgoode Readers are organised and their analysis framed in ways that are alert to comparative-law insights and are intended to be relevant across legal jurisdictions.

Each Osgoode Reader is primarily aimed at upper-year LLB and JD, as well as graduate law courses as either companion volumes or core prescribed readings. Most readers will also appeal to law scholars interested in keeping abreast of current developments in their own field, as well as researchers new to the field in question.

Indigenous Peoples and the Law

Comparative and Critical Perspectives

Edited by
Benjamin J Richardson
Shin Imai
and
Kent McNeil
Professors at Osgoode Hall Law School of York University in Toronto

• HART •
PUBLISHING

OXFORD AND PORTLAND, OREGON
2009

Published in North America (US and Canada) by
Hart Publishing
c/o International Specialized Book Services
920 NE 58th Avenue, Suite 300
Portland, OR 97213-3786
USA
Tel: +1 503 287 3093 or toll-free: (1) 800 944 6190
Fax: +1 503 280 8832
E-mail: orders@isbs.com
Web Site: www.isbs.com

Hart Publishing Ltd, 16C Worcester Place, Oxford, OX1 2JW
Telephone: +44 (0)1865 517530 Fax: +44 (0)1865 510710
E-mail: mail@hartpub.co.uk
Website: www.hartpub.co.uk

British Library Cataloguing in Publication Data
Data Available

ISBN: 978-184113-795-7

Typeset by Hope Services Ltd, Abingdon
Printed and bound in Great Britain by
TJ International Ltd, Padstow

ACKNOWLEDGEMENTS

A book project of this size and scope requires the assistance and co-operation of many people. We wish to thank the Indigenous and non-Indigenous people who have shared their views with us over the years and helped inform our understanding of this area of law. We are grateful as well for the good humour with which the contributors to this volume received our advice and prodding. We appreciate the support and patience of Richard Hart and his staff, and their efficiency in preparing the book for timely publication. Three Osgoode Hall students also contributed ably to the completion of this book. Benjamin J Richardson would like to thank Rami Shoucri and Sarah Robicheau for their editorial and research assistance. Likewise, Shin Imai would like to thank Jessica Di Federico for work on his chapter. Kent McNeil is grateful to his partner Kathy Simo for reviewing his chapter and providing helpful suggestions. Kent is also indebted to the Social Sciences and Humanities Research Council of Canada for grant money and the Killam Trusts for research leave time. We are all grateful to our faculty colleague Craig Scott for establishing the Osgoode-Hart Reader series, which provided the initial motivation to write this book. Finally, we would like to thank Dean Patrick Monahan and our other colleagues at Osgoode for providing a supportive and stimulating research environment in which to work.

CONTENTS

COMMON ABBREVIATIONS

Aboriginal and Torres Strait Islander Commission	ATSIC
Aborigines' Progressive Association	APA
Alaska Native Claims Settlement Act	ANCSA
Alternative dispute resolution	ADR
Australian Aborigines' League	AAL
Bureau of Indian Affairs	BIA
British Columbia Treaty Commission	BCTC
Centre for Indigenous Environmental Resources	CIER
Comprehensive Land Claims Process	CLCP
Convention on Biological Diversity	CBD
Convention on the Rights of the Child	CRC
Convention on the Elimination of All Forms of Racial Discrimination	CERD
Convention on the Elimination of Discrimination Against Women	CEDAW
Critical Race Theory	CRT
Economic and Social Council	ECOSOC
Equator Principles	EPs
Expert Mechanism on the Rights of Indigenous Peoples	EMRIP
General Allotment Act	GAA
Human Rights Commission	HR Commission
Human Rights Council	HR Council
Indian Civil Rights Act	ICRA
Indian Reorganization Act	IRA
Indigenous Land Use Agreement	ILUA
Indigenous legal theory	ILT
Inter-American Commission on Human Rights	IACHR
International Court of Justice	ICJ
International Covenant and Committee on Economic, Social and Cultural Rights	ICESCR
International Covenant on Civil and Political Rights	ICCPR
International Labour Organization	ILO
Indian Claims Commission	ICC
Indian Claims Commission Act	ICCA
Indian Specific Claims Commission	ISCC
National Aboriginal Consultative Committee	NACC
National Native Title Tribunal	NNTT

Native Title Representative Body	NTRB
Native Title Act	NTA
New South Wales	NSW
New Zealand	NZ
New Zealand Law Commission	NZLC
Non-governmental organisation	NGO
Northern Territory	NT
Organization of American States	OAS
Special Rapporteur	SR
Specific Claims Tribunal Act	SCTA
Traditional environmental knowledge	TEK
Treaty of Waitangi Act	TWA
United Nations	UN
United Nations Educational and Scientific Organisation	UNESCO
United Nations Permanent Forum on Indigenous Issues	UNPFII
United States	US
Working Group on Indigenous Populations	WGIP
World Intellectual Property Office	WIPO

CONTRIBUTORS

John Borrows, BA, MA, LLB, LLM (Toronto), DJur (Osgoode), is Anishinabe and a member of the Chippewa of the Nawash First Nation. He was appointed to the Faculty of Law of the University of Victoria, Canada, as Professor and Law Foundation Chair of Aboriginal Justice and Governance in 2001. Previously, he taught at the University of Toronto; the University of British Columbia as the Director of the First Nations Law Program; Osgoode Hall Law School as the Director of the Intensive Program in Lands, Resources and First Nations Governments; and was a visiting professor at Arizona State University and Executive Director of the Indian Legal Program. His research interests are in Aboriginal law, constitutional law, and natural resources/environmental law.

Claire Charters, BA LLB(Hons) (Otago), LLM (NYU), is a Senior Lecturer at the University of Victoria, Wellington, New Zealand. Prior to joining its Law Faculty, Claire worked at Bell Gully law firm and for Ngati Whakaue. She is an active advocate in indigenous peoples' rights in various international fora, and is a member of the International Law Association's Committee on Indigenous Peoples' Rights. She has also advised the New Zealand Law Commission and the Human Rights Commission on domestic and international issues involving Maori and indigenous peoples' rights.

Gordon Christie, LLB (Victoria), PhD (California, Santa Barbara), is a law professor at the University of British Columbia's Faculty of Law. He is originally from Inuvik, in the Northwest Territories of Canada, and his mother's family is Inupiat/Inuvialuit. Gordon has taught in various universities in Canada and the United States, in Faculties of Law, and Departments of Philosophy and Indigenous Studies. Most recently he was an Assistant Professor at Osgoode Hall Law School (1998–2004), where he also acted as Director of the Intensive Program in Aboriginal Lands, Resources and Governments. Among his publications, he has edited *Aboriginality and Governance: A Multidisciplinary Perspective* (Theytus 2007).

Jennifer Clarke works in the ANU College of Law at Australian National University. She was previously an Aboriginal land claims solicitor in Australia's Northern Territory. Jennifer is co-author (with Peter Hanks and Patrick Keyzer) of a constitutional law casebook, and has taught property and constitutional law, a range of subjects relating to indigenous legal issues and a comparative 'race and the law' course with Prof Bryan Fair of the University of Alabama. Her research includes articles on native title and other forms of indigenous land rights, the 'stolen generations' and mining law.

Michael Coyle, LLB (Western Ontario), LLM (Osgoode), is a law professor at the University of Western Ontario's Faculty of Law. His primary research interests relate to aboriginal rights and dispute resolution theory. He has also been active in public service. In 2004 he was commissioned by the Ipperwash Inquiry to write its background research paper on Aboriginal land claims and treaty rights in Ontario. In recent years he has been invited by the Canadian Senate Standing Committee on Aboriginal Peoples to present submissions to the Committee on land claims reform. Michael has also considerable experience in settling complex disputes as Director of Mediation at the Indian Commission of Ontario.

Christine Zuni Cruz is a law professor at the University of New Mexico's School of Law, where she established the Southwest Indian Law Clinic in 1993. In her research and teaching, Zuni Cruz, a member of Isleta Pueblo, focuses on the traditional and modern law of Indigenous peoples, as well as the impact of law and the practice of Indian Law and lawyering on native communities. She is editor-in-chief of the Tribal Law Journal, and presently serves as an associate justice on the Isleta Appellate Court. Previously, she held other judicial appointments including as tribal court judge with the Pueblo of Taos, and as an appellate judge with the Southwest Intertribal Court of Appeals.

James Hopkins, BA, LLB (Toronto), LLM (Harvard), is an Associate Clinical Professor in the University of Arizona's Indigenous Peoples Law and Policy Program and is Chief Justice of the Pascua Yaqui Court of Appeals. His teaching includes US Indian Law, Indigenous Economic Development, and he participates in the University's law clinic. Previously, James held appointments at the University of Alberta's Faculty of Law and was a judicial clerk in the Ontario Superior Court of Justice. He has published and spoken extensively on legal issues concerning Indigenous peoples. He has also participated in many community service projects concerning tribal land use and tribal public health.

Shin Imai, a law professor at Osgoode Hall, is Co-Director of the Intensive Program in Aboriginal Lands, Resources and Governments and Co-Director of the Latin American Human Rights Research and Education Network. He has also served as Academic Director of the Intensive Program in Poverty Law at Osgoode's Parkdale Community Legal Services, and as Director of Clinical Education for the Law School. His research interests are Aboriginal law in Canada, indigenous rights in Latin America, alternative dispute resolution and clinical legal education. Prior to joining Osgoode Hall in 1997, Professor Imai held positions with the Ontario Ministry of the Attorney General and worked as a staff lawyer at Keewaytinok Native Legal Services in Moosonee, Ontario.

Kent McNeil has been a faculty member at Osgoode Hall Law School since 1987, and was formerly the Research Director of the University of Saskatchewan Native Law Centre. In 2006, he was awarded a prestigious Killam Fellowship to pursue research on the legality of European assertions of sovereignty in North America

Kent's primary research interest is the rights of Indigenous peoples, particularly in Canada, Australia, and the United States. He has written a book, *Common Law Aboriginal Title*, and numerous monographs and articles on this subject, some of which are collected in *Emerging Justice? Essays on Indigenous Rights in Canada and Australia*. He has acted as a consultant and expert witness on land rights, treaty rights and self-government issues.

Val Napoleon is from north-eastern British Columbia (BC) and is of Cree and Dunneza heritage. She worked as a community activist and consultant in north-western BC for over 25 years, specialising in health, education, and justice issues. Val received her LB from the University of Victoria and was called to the bar in 2002. Val is completing a PhD at the Faculty of Law, University of Victoria. Since 2005, Val has been an assistant professor with the University of Alberta teaching in the faculties of law and native studies. She has published in areas of indigenous law, cultural heritage, indigenous feminism, oral histories, restorative justice, and governance. Her current research interests include indigenous legal theory, indigenous legal orders, indigenous feminism, real property issues on reserve, conflict and conflict management, and governance.

Benjamin J Richardson has been a law professor at Osgoode Hall Law School since 2003. Previously, he lectured at the law schools of the Universities of Manchester (UK) and Auckland (New Zealand). Passionate about environmental law, he also worked for the National Parks and Wildlife Service in Australia and the IUCN (International Union for Conservation of Nature) in Kenya and Nepal. He also teaches and researches Aboriginal law, and previously was co-director of Osgoode's Intensive Program in Aboriginal Law. His most recent major book is *Socially Responsible Investment Law* (Oxford University Press, 2008).

Jacinta Ruru is a senior law lecturer at the University of Otago, New Zealand where she teaches Maori land law, comparative Indigenous peoples law and property law. Her research interests are predominantly in comparative Indigenous peoples' rights relating to national parks and matrimonial property. She has published numerous articles exploring the legal experiences and rights specific to Maori, and presented at major international conferences throughout the world.

Mark D Walters, BA (Western Ontario), LLB (Queen's), DPhil (Oxford), is an Associate Professor and Associate Dean (Graduate Studies and Research) in the Faculty of Law at Queen's University. He researches and publishes in the areas of constitutional law, legal history, and legal theory, and he has a particular interest in legal issues relating to Aboriginal peoples. In 2002 he was awarded the Jules and Gabrielle Léger Fellowship, in 2005 he was the Herbert Smith Visitor in the Faculty of Law, University of Cambridge, and in 2006 he was given the Canadian Association of Law Teachers Award for Academic Excellence.

Introduction

1

Indigenous Peoples and the Law—Historical, Comparative and Contextual Issues

BENJAMIN J RICHARDSON, SHIN IMAI AND KENT MCNEIL

A. Aims and Scope

Indigenous Peoples and the Law provides an historical, comparative, and contextual analysis of various legal and policy issues concerning Indigenous peoples. It focuses on the principal common law jurisdictions, namely Australia, Canada, New Zealand, and the United States (US), as well as relevant international law developments.[1] Although an introductory book designed primarily for students and other readers without advanced knowledge of Indigenous legal issues, *Indigenous Peoples and the Law* should also appeal to seasoned scholars, policy-makers, lawyers, and others with greater knowledge of such issues in their own jurisdiction, and wishing to learn more about other places. While we may know a lot about the struggle for Indigenous rights in our home country, we may be insufficiently informed of similar struggles and valuable legal precedents elsewhere. Certainly, there is a plethora of fine scholarship on Indigenous peoples and the law, yet for various reasons it is often unsuitable for readers seeking a broad overview of the main issues, challenges, and future directions facing Indigenous communities worldwide. Frequently, the extant scholarship assumes too much prior knowledge, is too theoretically oriented, or dwells on only one jurisdiction or a particular case study to the exclusion of broader issues. This book seeks to

[1] This book builds on other comparative law scholarship concerning Indigenous peoples, such as A Fleras and JL Elliott, *The 'Nations Within': Aboriginal–State Relations in Canada, the United States and New Zealand* (Oxford University Press, 1992); P Havemann (ed), *Indigenous Peoples' Rights in Australia, Canada and New Zealand* (Oxford University Press, 1999); LA Knafla and H Westra (eds), *Aboriginal Title and Indigenous Peoples: Comparative Essays in Canada, Australia, and New Zealand* (UBC Press, 2009); K McNeil, *Emerging Justice? Essays on Indigenous Rights in Canada and Australia* (Native Law Centre of Canada, 2001); S Wiessner, 'Rights and Status of Indigenous Peoples: A Global Comparative and International Legal Analysis' (1999) 12 *Harvard Human Rights Journal* 57; S Young, *The Trouble with Tradition: Native Title and Cultural Change* (Federation Press, 2008).

overcome these limitations to learning about Indigenous legal issues in a broad historical, comparative, and contextual way. Thereby, it is hoped that the pursuit of justice for Indigenous peoples will be advanced.

Indigenous Peoples and the Law is an edition of the Osgoode Hall–Hart Publishing series of 'readers'. Each provides a collection of pithy essays of new scholarship on topical, complex, and dynamic areas of law.[2] Unlike a reader in the traditional sense, reproducing excerpts from classic published works, the chapters in this book are fresh writings, each drawing on the authors' earlier scholarship. Yet, like other readers, this one provides a broad overview of the subject-matter, enabling a snapshot of major issues, trends, and precedents, and is generously referenced to provide a gateway for further research and enquiry. Also, as with many readers, this multi-author collection of essays provides diverse and contrasting perspectives on a topical subject area rife with controversy. Importantly, this book offers perspectives from a number of Indigenous scholars, including John Borrows (Canada), Gordon Christie (Canada), Val Napoleon (Canada), Claire Charters (New Zealand), Jacinta Ruru (New Zealand), James Hopkins (US/Canada), and Christine Zuni Cruz (US). Their voices are mixed with those of other experts on Indigenous legal issues.

Indigenous Peoples and the Law, particularly the essays in Part 1, takes an historical perspective, canvassing themes of Indigenous sovereignty, status and identity, and the movement for self-determination. It covers the main common law jurisdictions with Indigenous populations, namely Canada (chapter by Mark Walters), the US (Benjamin Richardson), New Zealand (Ruru) and Australia (Jennifer Clarke), and examines regional and international legal standards pertaining to Indigenous peoples (chapters by Hopkins and Charters respectively). This book does not explore in any detail Indigenous legal traditions and history in the pre-colonial period.

Although these common law jurisdictions shared the traditions of British imperial power, the application of that power and the response of Indigenous populations varied in each case. Nominally, the general policy was to claim empty lands in the name of the Crown and negotiate for acquisition of any occupied lands. In practice, the immense geographic distance between Britain and its colonies meant that those on the frontier had the strongest voices regarding native relations, leading to divergent policies and practices. Yet, often regardless of the means of colonisation, in nearly all cases Indigenous peoples were severely displaced by the economic and political forces of empire-building.[3] Although the colonies have long since become independent states, their policies have recently begun to face common pressures to accommodate new international norms concerning human

[2] See the inaugural volume of this series, BJ Richardson and S Wood (eds), *Environmental Law for Sustainability* (Hart Publishing, 2006).

[3] S Banner, *How the Indians Lost Their Land: Law and Power on the Frontier* (Belknap Press of Harvard University Press, 2005) and *Possessing the Pacific: Land, Settlers, and Indigenous People from Australia to Alaska* (Harvard University Press, 2007): JC Weaver, *The Great Land Rush and the Making of the Modern World, 1650–1900* (McGill-Queen's University Press, 2003).

rights and Indigenous peoples, such as the United Nations (UN) Declaration on the Rights of Indigenous Peoples of 2007 (as detailed in chapters by Charters and Hopkins).[4]

We should nonetheless be vigilant of the historical context to Indigenous rights, as failure to make the connection between the continuing impact of past government policies and the contemporary plight of Indigenous peoples can foster antagonism in wider society towards necessary remedial and special measures. Moreover, some people wrongly regard the Indigenous struggle for rights as a recent phenomenon, assuming it to have only emerged in the heady days of the 1960s during the civil rights movement that swept Western societies. In fact, Indigenous resistance to colonialism and its legal machinery has been waged for centuries, and continues today, as the essays in Part 2 of the book focusing on contemporary claims remind us.[5] 'History' clearly matters in understanding and advancing these claims, as highlighted in the seminal reports of the Canadian Royal Commission on Aboriginal Peoples[6] and the Australian Human Rights Commission,[7] pointing to the unresolved nature of many historical grievances.

Among the individual chapters in Part 1 of this book, Ruru focuses on the continuing impact of the Treaty of Waitangi of 1840 which, although for many years dismissed by New Zealand authorities as an historical anachronism, has since the 1970s critically framed Māori political activism and legal strategies.[8] In the US, Richardson's chapter highlights the dyadic qualities of law, having provided both a means to suppress and empower Native Americans. The resurgence of tribal self-governance on many Indian reservations has been anchored to doctrines of inherent tribal sovereignty, as recognised historically by the Marshall decisions of the 1830s.[9] While Clarke and Walters' chapters highlight many differences between the Australian and Canadian legal histories, most notably the absence or reliance on treaty-making, in both jurisdictions a complex jurisprudence on Aboriginal title claims to land has flourished in recent decades.[10] At the international level, several legal instruments, including the UN Declaration, the

[4] UN Doc A/61/L 67, 7 September 2007; see further SJ Anaya, *Indigenous Peoples in International Law* (2nd edn, Oxford University Press, 2004).

[5] See also PH Russell, *Recognizing Aboriginal Title: The Mabo Case and Indigenous Resistance to English-settler Colonialism* (University of Toronto Press, 2005); C Wilkinson, *Blood Struggle: The Rise of Modern Indian Nations* (WW Norton, 2005).

[6] Canada, *Report of the Royal Commission on Aboriginal Peoples* (Supply and Services Canada, 1996).

[7] Human Rights and Equal Opportunity Commission, *Bringing Them Home*, report of the National Inquiry into the separation of Aboriginal and Torres Strait Islander Children from their Families (Australian Government Publishing Service, 1996).

[8] See also M Belgrave, M Kawharu and D Williams (eds), *Waitangi Revisited: Perspectives on the Treaty of Waitangi* (Oxford University Press, 2005); P McHugh, *The Māori Magna Carta: New Zealand Law and the Treaty of Waitangi* (Oxford University Press, 1991).

[9] MLM Fletcher, 'The Iron Cold of the Marshall Trilogy' (2006) 84 *North Dakota Law Review* 628; Wilkinson, above n 5.

[10] Eg *Mabo v Queensland (No 2)* (1992) 175 CLR 1; *Wik Peoples v Queensland* (1996) 121 ALR 129; *Members of the Yorta Yorta Community v Victoria* (2002) 214 CLR 422; *Delgamuukw v British Columbia* [1997] 3 SCR 1010; *Tsilhqot'in Nation v British Columbia* [2007] BCSC 1700.

International Labour Organisation's (ILO) Convention No 169, and regional initiatives in the Inter-American human rights system, have provided another layer of rights and tools for Indigenous peoples. Charters and Hopkins trace the historical development of these international and regional regimes, finding that practical redress for Indigenous peoples has tended to lag behind the considerable normative advances in the definition of Indigenous rights.

Shifting focus, Part 2 of the book canvasses some of these contemporary issues and claims of Indigenous peoples. It begins with Christie's investigation of the challenges to developing a distinct and vibrant body of scholarship identifiable as 'Indigenous legal theory', and the general place of legal theory in relation to Indigenous people. Christie stresses the need for more 'theorising' by Indigenous scholars in order to advance the struggle for Indigenous rights. Such theorising can help us understand the importance of recognising and reasserting Indigenous legal traditions, as explored by Zuni Cruz. Her chapter focuses on the presence of these traditions in tribal courts in Native American communities, highlighting the importance of both 'internal' recognition within Indian nations and 'external' recognition and affirmation by wider society.

Land rights and self-governance are perhaps the two most controversial and weighty issues in the Indigenous policy agenda today, and Kent McNeil and Shin Imai respectively examine these topics by comparing the main common law jurisdictions. These issues are closely intertwined, as self-governance commonly involves authority to manage land and resources. Territorial rights and self-governance have also been frequently dealt with together through a process of negotiation of claims, as explored in Michael Coyle's chapter. Canada's comprehensive land claims settlements have involved perhaps the most complex negotiations of Indigenous claims anywhere.[11] Richardson examines the relationships between Indigenous rights and environmental management, a topic that has also attracted intense scholarly interest.[12] Again, land rights and concomitant powers of self-government over territory are crucial to the Indigenous stake in environmental management.

However, issues of land, natural resources, and governance are not the only legal concerns of Indigenous peoples. In her chapter, Napoleon discusses the importance of gendered and feminist analysis in Indigenous discourse, and how this relates to Aboriginal rights jurisprudence and Indigenous legal orders. Applying this analysis in a community case study, she relates actual experiences and discusses issues of power, authenticity, membership, citizenship, and identity in a local setting. In the concluding chapter, 'Physical Philosophy: Mobility and

[11] See BJ Richardson, D Craig and B Boer, *Regional Agreements for Indigenous Lands and Cultures in Canada* (Australian National University, 1995); T Penikett, *Reconciliation: First Nations Treaty Making in British Columbia* (Douglas and McIntyre, 2006); A Woolford, *Between Justice and Certainty: Treaty Making in British Columbia* (UBC Press, 2005).

[12] Eg J Borrows, 'Living Between Water and Rocks: First Nations, Environmental Planning and Democracy' (1997) 47 *University of Toronto Law Journal* 417; LM Shields, 'Are Conservation Goals and Aboriginal Rights Incompatible?' (2001) 10 *Journal of Environmental Law and Practice* 187l; L Watters, *Indigenous Peoples, the Environment and Law* (Carolina Academic Press, 2004).

the Future of Indigenous Rights', Borrows explores future prospects for Indigenous peoples, and argues that removal of inappropriate legal restraints on Indigenous peoples' mobility must be a priority, as mobility rights are crucial to maintaining Indigenous connections to the land and relationships among increasingly dispersed Indigenous populations.

Indigenous Peoples and the Law covers many but certainly not all of the potential topics that one could imagine in a book on this subject. It focuses on some of the most salient issues for Indigenous peoples, judged by the volume of case law and other legal activity, the demands of Indigenous peoples, and academic commentary. Other topics, though undoubtedly important, could not be covered in detail in a single book. The intellectual property rights of Indigenous peoples, for instance, are only considered briefly, such as in Charters' chapter.[13] The criminal justice system is another topic only briefly touched on, although it has been a source of great hardship for Indigenous peoples, as revealed, for example, by Australia's Royal Commission into Aboriginal Deaths in Custody.[14] Many other issues in the realm of social policy, such as restorative justice for the victims of the residential schools and public health issues in Aboriginal communities, are canvassed only briefly.[15] Also, this book does not cover non-common law jurisdictions with Indigenous populations, although some relevant examples are referred to in chapters by Hopkins and Richardson.[16]

[13] See further R Coombe, 'Intellectual Property, Human Rights, and Sovereignty: New Dilemmas in International Law Posed by the Recognition of Indigenous Knowledge and the Conservation of Biodiversity' (1998) 6 *Indiana Journal of Global Legal Studies* 59; S von Lewinski and AV Hahn, *Indigenous Heritage and Intellectual Property: Genetic Resources, Traditional Knowledge, and Folklore* (Kluwer Law, 2003); I Mgbeoji, *Global Biopiracy: Patents, Plants, and Indigenous Knowledge* (UBC Press, 2005).

[14] Royal Commission into Aboriginal Deaths in Custody, *Royal Commission into Aboriginal Deaths in Custody National Report: Overview and Recommendations (Commissioner Elliott Johnson)* (Australian Government Publishing Service, 1991). See also C Cunneen, 'Racism, Discrimination and the Over-Representation of Indigenous People in the Criminal Justice System: Some Conceptual and Explanatory Issues' (2005) 17 *Current Issues in Criminal Justice* 329; AC Hamilton and CM Sinclair, *Report of the Aboriginal Justice Inquiry of Manitoba* (Queen's Printer, 1991).

[15] See A Buti, 'The Removal of Indigenous Children from their Families—US and Australia Compared' (2004) 6 *University of Western Sydney Law Review* 125; J Cassidy, 'Best Interests of the Child? The Stolen Generations in Canada and Australia' (2006) 15 *Griffith Law Review* 111; JL Llewellyn, 'Dealing with the Legacy of Native Residential School Abuse in Canada: Litigation, ADR, and Restorative Justice' (2002) 52 *University of Toronto Law Journal* 253.

[16] See further M Kearney and S Varese, 'Latin America's Indigenous Peoples: Changing Identities and Forms of Resistance' in S Halebsky and RL Harris (eds), *Capital, Power, and Inequality in Latin America* (Westview Press, 1995) 207; P Korsmo, 'Claiming Territory: The Saami Assemblies as Ethno-Political Institutions' (1996) 20(3) *Polar Geography* 163; L Sillanpaa, 'A Comparative Analysis of Indigenous Rights in Fennoscandia' (1997) 20 *Scandinavian Political Studies* 197; KB Warren and JE Jackson, *Indigenous Movements, Self-representation, and the State in Latin America* (University of Texas Press, 2002).

B. Synopsis of Key Jurisdictions

This book aims to provide a framework for critical and comparative evaluations of laws, policies and state practices affecting Indigenous peoples in selected jurisdictions. Although it focuses on common law jurisdictions, some examples in other regions are discussed, including Scandinavia, Latin America and Southeast Asia. Comparative methods of legal analysis have several benefits, as noted by other scholarship on Indigenous rights.[17] They can broaden the perspective of one's own circumstances by learning about developments elsewhere. They also enable us to understand general patterns and relationships, and to assess the scope and limits of generalisations possible from one situation to another. Comparative research also assists policy analysis, enabling us to learn from the successes and failures of other jurisdictions, and thereby improve the conditions for legal reform.

In the common law jurisdictions, Indigenous peoples remain on the frontier as visible minorities and often as inhabitants of remote, forbidding environments. Yet, their ongoing struggle for justice raises doubts about the moral legitimacy of the nation-states that were founded on denial of their prior ownership.[18] These predominantly Anglo-Saxon states experienced similar patterns of nation-building, including a history of prejudice against Indigenous peoples who were perceived as obstacles to colonisation and the dissemination of the economic and cultural traditions of the British metropole. The thirst for land and natural resources to power the colonial economies quickly brought conflict with Indigenous inhabitants, who were expected to be assimilated into the white settler societies. The legal and political institutions imported by the colonialists, notably liberal-democratic governance for the enfranchised and the dogma of the rule of law, gave a semblance of order and legitimacy to these brutal processes of nation-building. Although wars and massacres sometimes occurred, more often pacification was undertaken under a legal veneer that included formal treaties ceding land, paternalist assimilation such as the schooling of Indigenous children in missionary schools, and the absorption of Indigenous, subsistence livelihoods into commercial, market-based economies. The colonial legal systems commonly left only crumbs for the dispossessed. In common law jurisdictions other than the US, Indigenous rights have been trivialised by authorities 'as a *sui generis* category of usufructuary lifestyle rights and/or a municipalised version of self-management powers, rather than as sovereign rights for nations within'.[19] However, the inequalities between the colonised and coloniser endemic in these societies are gradually being challenged as Indigenous peoples seek to reclaim their identities,

[17] P Havemann, 'Comparing Indigenous Peoples' Rights in Australia, Canada and New Zealand' in Havemann, above n 1, 2.

[18] See P Keal, *European Conquest and the Rights of Indigenous Peoples. The Moral Backwardness of International Society* (Cambridge University Press, 2003); L Robertson, *Conquest by Law: How the Discovery of America Dispossessed Indigenous People of Their Lands* (Oxford University Press, 2005).

[19] Havemann, above n 17, 7.

lands, and institutions. But while Indigenous peoples often seek the protection of state law today, they fiercely resist it when it serves as a means for their assimilation or persecution. As will be shown throughout this book, non-Indigenous law has a capricious, dyadic character, variously providing a means both to empower and control them. Although discriminatory government policies and laws are often thought to be relics of the past, the effects of dispossession of land, removal of children, and a cycle of poverty continue to reverberate through many Indigenous communities. Current social and economic problems are rooted in historical injustice.

In each of the common law colonies, early settlement was predicated upon the imperialist doctrine of discoverers' rights, giving colonising European nations 'title' and exclusive authority to deal with Indigenous peoples and their lands. Except in Australia, however, this assertion was mollified by a limited theoretical respect for existing Indigenous rights and recognition of the necessity of treaties to formalise relationships and facilitate the orderly acquisition of Indigenous lands and imposition of governance arrangements over them. In the US, the Marshall trilogy of cases, which advanced the doctrine of 'Indian title', provided the most comprehensive legal enunciation of this aspect of colonisation.[20] They provided important precedents for the other Anglo-Saxon jurisdictions that eventually would also have to accommodate Indigenous rights. While the Marshall cases were marginalised by executive and legislative actions in the US for 100 years, they underpinned the conceptual foundations for later policy shifts in the 1930s and post-1970 to promote Native American interests.[21]

The Canadian story, at least initially, also reveals a pattern of treaty-making and white settlement not unlike that which occurred in the US.[22] Similar economic and social pressures necessitated military and trading alliances with First Nations, later the acquisition of their lands through treaties of cession, and later still increasingly paternalistic governance of First Nations for the purposes of their assimilation into the dominant European society. There was, however, only limited judicial recognition of Aboriginal title in Canada until the early 1970s, when the *Calder* decision opened the way for recognition of more comprehensive Aboriginal claims to land.[23] The constitutional amendments in 1982 that recognised and protected 'existing' Aboriginal and treaty rights made the accommoda-

[20] Fletcher, above n 9.

[21] See V Deloria Jr, *American Indian Policy in the Twentieth Century* (University of Oklahoma Press, 1985); ED Lemont (ed), *American Indian Constitutional Reform and the Rebuilding of Native Nations* (University of Texas Press, 2006).

[22] See generally M Asch (ed), *Aboriginal and Treaty Rights in Canada: Essays on Law, Equality, and Respect for Difference* (UBC Press, 1997); J Borrows, *Recovering Canada: The Resurgence of Indigenous Law* (University of Toronto Press, 2002); S Imai, K Logan and G Stein, *Aboriginal Law Handbook* (Carswell, 1999); RW Johnson, 'Fragile Gains: Two Centuries of Canadian and United States Policy Toward Indians' (1991) 66 *Washington Law Review* 643; J Miller, *Compact, Contract, Covenant: Aboriginal Treaty-Making in Canada* (University of Toronto Press, 2009).

[23] *Calder v Attorney General of British Columbia* [1973] SCR 313; See H Foster, H Raven and J Webber (eds), *Let Right Be Done: Aboriginal Title, the Calder Case and the Future of Indigenous Rights* (UBC Press, 2008).

tion of Indigenous interests in Canada stronger—at least in theory—than any other jurisdiction. Yet, the seminal 1996 *Report of the Royal Commission on Aboriginal Peoples* revealed that many systemic economic, social, and governance problems continue to hinder the self-determination of Indigenous peoples.[24] The Canadian Prime Minister's apology to its Indigenous peoples in June 2008 for Canada's role in the infamous residential school system,[25] and the concomitant establishment of the Truth and Reconciliation Commission to examine the legacy of that system,[26] highlight an ongoing process of reconciliation and critical reflection.[27]

A similar process of reconciliation is occurring in Australia, evident in Prime Minister Kevin Rudd's national apology in February 2008 for his country's role in its equivalent system of residential schools and removal of Aboriginal children from their families.[28] The earlier 1996 report of the Australian Human Rights Commission, *Bringing Them Home*, highlighted the dreadful legacy of the policies that led to the so-called 'Stolen Generation'.[29] In many respects, owing partly to greater legal disadvantages, Indigenous Australians have faced more hurdles than their counterparts in other countries.[30] Unlike Indigenous groups in New Zealand and North America, Aborigines and Torres Strait Islanders do not have treaty rights. Nor have they been accorded constitutional recognition of their native title rights.[31] Australian courts only acknowledged a common law basis for Indigenous land and resource rights in the 1990s, long after their recognition in comparable jurisdictions.[32] Further, Australia has not provided for Indigenous representation in legislatures, unlike New Zealand, where seats are formally designated for Māori. And Australian legislative initiatives, such as the Native Title Act of 1993, have proven to be two-edged swords that are vulnerable to hostile political forces.[33]

The relevant New Zealand legal history differs somewhat from the other common law jurisdictions for several reasons. One seminal factor is the relatively larger Indigenous population sharing a common language, enabling Māori to coordinate

[24] Above n 6.

[25] 'Harper "Sorry" for Native Residential Schools' (June 12, 2008) *Toronto Star*. The apology can be viewed at www.thestar.com/News/Canada/article/441820.

[26] 'LaForme to Lead Residential Schools Commission' (28 April 2008) *CBC News*.

[27] See also A Lokan, 'From Recognition to Reconciliation: The Functions of Aboriginal Rights Law' (1999) 23 *Melbourne University Law Review* 65.

[28] For the text of the apology, see S Peatling, 'Rudd's Apology Revealed' (13 February 2008) *Sydney Morning Herald*, at www.smh.com.au/news/national/rudds-apology-revealed/2008/02/12/1202760286861.html.

[29] R Atkinson, 'Denial and Loss: The Removal of Indigenous Australian Children from their Families and Culture' (2005) 5 *QUT Law and Justice Journal*, at www.law.qut.edu.au/ljj/editions/v5n1.

[30] For an important historical perspective, see H Reynolds, *The Other Side of the Frontier: Aboriginal Resistance to the European Invasion of Australia* (Penguin Books, 1982).

[31] See generally C Cunneen, *Indigenous People and the Law in Australia* (Butterworths, 1996).

[32] See P Butt, RD Eagleson and P Lane, *Mabo, Wik and Native Title* (Federation Press, 2001); H McRae, G Netheim, L Beacroft and L McNamara (eds), *Indigenous Legal Issues: Commentary and Materials* (3rd edn, Lawbook Co, 2003); RH Bartlett, *Native Title in Australia* (2nd edn, LexisNexis Butterworths, 2004).

[33] L Behrendt, *Mabo: Ten Years On*, Occasional paper (Australian National University, Faculty of Law, 2002).

greater resistance. Today, they constitute at least 15 per cent of the New Zealand populace. Colonised later, the lessons of earlier British colonial policy mistakes could be avoided in Aotearoa. The Treaty of Waitangi of 1840 was more accommodating of Indigenous interests than treaties of a similar era in other jurisdictions.[34] Yet, as elsewhere, in subsequent decades the Māori were under siege by governmental policies and laws that sought to dispossess and marginalise them as the colony gained strength. In the notorious *Wi Parata* judgment of 1877, the New Zealand court dismissed the Treaty of Waitangi 'as a simple nullity'.[35] Yet, as in other jurisdictions, from the late 1960s a resurgent Indigenous voice in New Zealand politics ushered in various reforms, including the establishment of the Waitangi Tribunal in 1975, the comprehensive settlement of Māori claims to commercial fisheries in the 1992 'Sealords' deal, and greater judicial sensitivity to Māori interests.[36]

It would be misleading, however, to imply an inevitable drift towards more enlightened and just policies for Indigenous peoples. Legal setbacks in all jurisdictions have occurred. Some courts have become less receptive to or more ambivalent about some Indigenous claims. In the US, the Supreme Court has been 'backtracking on Indian sovereignty',[37] as is evident in cases such as *Nevada v Hicks*[38] and *Rice v Cayetano*.[39] In New Zealand, the government controversially overturned judicial recognition of Māori proprietary interests in coastal areas through the Foreshore and Seabed Act of 2004.[40] In Australia, even more regressive steps occurred under the former Howard government, such as its amendments to water down protections in the Native Title Act.[41]

We should be mindful that there are perhaps as many similarities as differences between the relevant legal histories for Indigenous peoples worldwide. The growth in regional and international legal standards pertaining to Indigenous peoples, as canvassed in chapters by Hopkins and Charters, is helping to harmonise

[34] N Cox, 'The Treaty of Waitangi and the Relationship between the Crown and Maori in New Zealand' (2002) 28 *Brooklyn Journal International Law* 123.

[35] *Wi Parata v Bishop of Wellington* (1877) 3 NZ Jur (NS) SC 72, 78.

[36] See, eg, *New Zealand Maori Council v Attorney-General* (1987) 1 NZLR 641; *Attorney-General v Ngati Apa* (2003) 3 NZLR 643; HK Guth, 'Dividing the Catch: Natural Resource Reparations to Indigenous Peoples—Examining the Maori Fisheries Settlement' (2001) 24 *Hawaii Law Review* 179.

[37] P McHugh, *Aboriginal Societies and the Common Law: A History of Sovereignty, Status and Self-Determination* (Oxford University Press, 2005) 330. However, there have been exceptions to this trend, notably *California v Cabazon Band*, 480 US 202 (1987) (concerning the rights of Indian tribes to operate gaming facilities on Indian reservations), and *US v Lara*, 541 US 193 (2004) (tribal jurisdiction over non-member Indians).

[38] 533 US 353 (2001). In this case the Supreme Court held that state officers could enter an Indian reservation uninvited to investigate or prosecute an off-reservation violation of state law. It further held that tribal courts are not empowered to hear civil rights cases under federal law because they are not courts of general jurisdiction.

[39] 528 US 495 (2000). Here the Supreme Court struck down the state's Hawaiian-only restriction for voting in elections for a state agency that administered millions of dollars earmarked exclusively for Indigenous Hawaiians. The court ruled that the racial restriction violated the Fifteenth Amendment.

[40] See C Charters and A Erueti (eds), *Māori Property Rights in the Foreshore and Seabed: The Last Frontier* (Victoria University Press, 2007).

[41] Behrendt, above n 33.

standards globally.[42] Even though Australia, Canada, New Zealand and the US each have shunned the principal legal instruments enunciating Indigenous rights, international law at least is becoming a point of reference for discerning best practice. Another commonality is reliance on similar methods for advancing and resolving Indigenous claims, as detailed in Coyle's and other chapters. For example, Indigenous peoples often look to the courts to prove their historical claims and challenge those of the state. Notable examples are the recognition of Aboriginal title to land in the *Calder* and *Mabo* cases in Canada and Australia.[43] Negotiation has also been widely used as another method to settle Indigenous claims. Historically, treaties were 'negotiated' during the early periods of colonisation (except in Australia) to provide for the orderly acquisition of Indigenous lands. Since the early 1970s, negotiations have become a more seriously used technique to settle grievances and claims of Indigenous peoples, resulting in settlement of Aboriginal title claims and natural resource-sharing agreements. Finally, national leaders in several countries have recently offered public, official apologies to acknowledge past wrongs and open dialogue to address larger issues, such as cultural integrity, national memory, and the future of Indigenous communities.[44] Thus, in a global legal environment, the practices and reforms of one jurisdiction can readily be duplicated in others.

C. Some Key Issues and Terminology

This book is about 'Indigenous peoples', yet who are they? There is no authoritative or incontrovertible definition, as Indigenous identity and membership can be defined in myriad ways.[45] According to the United Nations' Working Group on Indigenous Populations (WGIP), they are the 'descendants of the original inhabitants of conquered territories possessing a minority culture and recognizing themselves as such'.[46] However, this definition does not completely encompass all

[42] See also SJ Anaya, 'International Human Rights and Indigenous Peoples: The Move Toward the Multicultural State' (2004) 21 *Arizona Journal of International and Comparative Law* 13; J Gilbert, *Indigenous Peoples' Land Rights Under International Law* (Transnational Publishers, 2006); F MacKay, *A Guide to Indigenous Peoples' Rights in the Inter-American Human Rights System* (Aksant Academic Publishers, 2002); S Pritchard, *Indigenous Peoples, the United Nations and Human Rights* (Zed Books, 1998).

[43] *Calder*, above n 23; *Mabo*, above n 10.

[44] See generally D Mellor, D Bretherton and L Firth, 'Aboriginal and Non-Aboriginal Australia: The Dilemma of Apologies, Forgiveness, and Reconciliation' (2007) 13 *Peace and Conflict: Journal of Peace Psychology* 11.

[45] T Schouls, *Shifting Boundaries: Aboriginal Identity, Pluralist Theory, and the Politics of Self-Government* (UBC Press, 2003).

[46] UN Working Group on Indigenous Populations, *Preliminary Report on the Study of the Problem of Discrimination against Indigenous Populations* (UN Doc E/CN4/Sub2/L 566, 1982), cited in JJ Corntassel and TP Primeau, 'Indigenous "Sovereignty" and International Law: Revised Strategies for Pursuing "Self-determination"' (1995) 17 *Human Rights Quarterly* 343, 345.

nuanced differences in the position of the some 250–300 million Indigenous people worldwide.[47] First, in some states Indigenous people are not a minority of the population, as in some countries in Latin America and the South Pacific where they are numerically the majority. Also, the WGIP's definition speaks of the descendants of the 'original inhabitants'. Yet, because such descendants evolve and may change racially and culturally, should they be defined as Indigenous on the basis of self-identification, biological affinity, cultural traits or some other standard? A further difficulty with the WGIP definition, note Corntassel and Primeau, is that it is so expansive that it could cover many stateless groups around the world, including Basques, Kurds, Tibetans, and numerous other communities.[48]

International law has not resolved these definitional issues. The ILO Convention of 1989 states that peoples are considered Indigenous if they are:

(a) tribal peoples in independent countries whose social, cultural and economic conditions distinguish them from other sections of the national community, and whose status is regulated wholly or partially by their own customs or traditions or by special laws or regulations;
(b) peoples in independent countries who are regarded as indigenous on account of their descent from the populations which inhabited the country, or a geographical region to which the country belongs, at the time of conquest or colonisation or the establishment of present State boundaries and who, irrespective of their legal status, retain some or all of their own social, economic, cultural and political institutions.[49]

However, the UN Declaration on the Rights of Indigenous Peoples, adopted in 2007, does not define Indigenous peoples.[50]

The contributors to this book have not attempted to formulate a uniform, detailed definition of Indigenous peoples, although in many chapters the issues of Indigenous status and identity are discussed with reference to government policies and Indigenous demands.

'Self-determination' is another concept that features prominently in contemporary policy-making on Indigenous affairs and has become the dominant motif in the articulation of Indigenous claims and rights.[51] Generically, it may be defined as the right of a people to determine their own political status and control their economic, social, and cultural development, without external compulsion. While self-determination has become a normative standard internationally for all peoples, it has particular significance for Indigenous peoples in their struggles to achieve recognition and autonomy, as Charters explains in her chapter. It is

[47] See J Burger, *The Gaia Atlas of First Peoples: A Future for the Indigenous World* (Doubleday, 1990) 18–19, 180–85.

[48] Corntassel and Primeau, above n 46.

[49] Art 1, International Labor Organization (ILO) Convention Concerning Indigenous and Tribal People in Independent Countries, No 169, June 27, 1989; (1989) 28 ILM 1382.

[50] It does, however, state in Art 32 that 'Indigenous peoples have the right . . . to select the membership of their institutions in accordance with their own procedures': UN Doc A/61/L 67, 7 September 2007.

[51] See A Daes, 'Some Considerations on the Right of Indigenous Peoples to Self-Determination' (1993) 3 *Transnational Law and Contemporary Problems* 1; MC Lâm, *At the Edge of the State: Indigenous Peoples and Self-Determination* (Transnational Publishers, 2000).

included as a central provision in UN Declaration on the Rights of Indigenous Peoples, which states emphatically that 'Indigenous peoples have the right to self-determination. By virtue of that right they freely determine their political status and freely pursue their economic, social, and cultural development'.[52]

However, 'self-determination' remains a contested legal concept with politically controversial ramifications, and all four of the key common law jurisdictions with Indigenous populations voted against the UN Declaration in the General Assembly. Among the views of distinguished international scholars, Antonio Cassese contends that, while the right to self-determination is an important principle of international law that extends to all peoples, including cultural and ethnic minorities of an existing state, in general only existing states are entitled to the full panoply of rights to self-determination.[53] By contrast, according to Cassese, a minority within the general population of a state is entitled only to 'internal' self-determination, without a right of secession. In this legal analysis, therefore, Indigenous peoples would ordinarily be entitled under international law to only some autonomy over their local affairs.[54] However, many groups engaged in anti-colonial struggles, such as the Tibetans and Tamils, seek more than local autonomy.[55]

James Anaya rejects the contention that self-determination should be equated with the decolonisation process, commonly associated with the emergence after World War II of new states in Africa and other regions formerly under European rule. Anaya asserts that it is a right of all people, capable of being exercised in an array of contexts and ways, including the possible formation of new states.[56] Anaya argues that 'self-determination gives rise to remedies that tear at the legacies of empire, discrimination, oppression of democratic participation, and cultural suffocation'.[57] While such remedies are being pursued vigorously with some success domestically, such as community ratification of comprehensive land claims agreements, there has been little headway internationally. Indigenous nations have periodically fought with little success to have historic treaties made with colonial powers recognised as prescriptions of international law.[58] Nonetheless, in the 1975 *Western Sahara* case the International Court of Justice did reject the notion that areas occupied by Indigenous peoples were *territoria nullius*.[59]

Self-determination is closely related to another theme of this book, namely 'sovereignty'. Like self-determination, sovereignty is a nebulous concept that can be understood in various ways. A political entity that has the capacity to act without

[52] Art 3, above n 50.

[53] A Cassese, *Self-determination of Peoples* (Cambridge University Press, 1995) 57–62.

[54] Cassese concedes, however, that secession for such minorities may be permissible when a state is 'irremediably oppressive and despotic': *ibid*, 359.

[55] D Otto, 'Subalternity and International Law: The Problems of Global Community and the Incommensurability of Difference' (1996) 5 *Society and Legal Studies* 337, 343.

[56] Anaya, above n 4.

[57] *Ibid*, 98.

[58] There have been some limited successes before the UN Human Rights Committee, such as for the Lubicon Cree who complained of human rights violations by Canada: see J Goddard, *Last Stand of the Lubicon Cree* (Douglas and McIntyre, 1991).

[59] *Western Sahara* (1975) ICJ 4 (Advisory Opinion).

subjugation to any other entity is generally regarded as having sovereignty. In international law, states are thus deemed to be sovereign.[60] However, the term has also come to be used in relation to the legal status of specific groups within states, including Indigenous peoples.[61] This has fuelled legal disputes that raise questions about the legitimacy of colonial authority, as when Aboriginal lawyer Paul Coe unsuccessfully challenged the 'discovery' basis for British sovereignty over Australia in the High Court.[62]

In the US, Chief Justice Marshall decided in *Cherokee Nation v Georgia* in 1831 that the Indian tribes enjoy residual sovereignty as 'domestic dependent nations'.[63] While determining that tribes within the US are not foreign nations, he found they were nonetheless 'a distinct political society, separated from others, capable of managing [their] own affairs and governing [themselves]'.[64] In the 1978 case of *United States v Wheeler*, the Supreme Court described Indigenous sovereignty as authority wielded by Indian tribes that is not delegated by the US government but, rather, is traceable to the sovereignty they enjoyed prior to colonisation.[65] However, while tribes enjoy inherent sovereignty as nations within the US, the Supreme Court has also held that their residual authority can be unilaterally taken away by Congress.[66]

In New Zealand, as Ruru explains in her chapter, the status of Māori sovereignty is central to debates about the significance of the Treaty of Waitangi of 1840, signed by dignatories of the British Crown and various Māori chiefs from the north island of Aotearoa. However, the English and Māori language versions of the Treaty differ, and disagreements linger as to the terms agreed to. The Crown maintains that it was entitled to colonise the islands and their peoples because the Treaty gave Britain sovereignty over all of Aotearoa. Conversely, the Māori contend that their version of the Treaty guaranteed their *te tino rangatiratanga* (self-determination or sovereignty), while simply acknowledging the need for British governance of Aotearoa's peoples.[67] Although the Treaty of Waitangi was marginalised in the legal history of New Zealand over the ensuing century, since the early 1970s it has reacquired great significance. While the extent to which the Crown is bound by the Treaty remains fiercely contested, courts have increasingly given weight to the 'principles of the Treaty' in interpreting legislation.[68]

60 However, all nations are subject to overriding norms of international law. States today accept more attenuated jurisdictional entitlements in a world of environmental and economic interdependency: C Schreuer, 'The Waning of the Sovereign State: Towards a New Paradigm for International Law' (1993) 4 *European Journal of International Law* 447.

61 J Cassidy, 'Sovereignty of Aboriginal Peoples' (1998) 9 *Indiana International and Comparative Law Review* 65; F Lenzerini, 'Sovereignty Revisited: International Law and Parallel Sovereignty of Indigenous Peoples' (2006) 42 *Texas International Law Journal* 155.

62 *Coe v Commonwealth* (1979) 53 ALJR 403.

63 30 US (5 Pet) 1, 17 (1831).

64 *Ibid*, 15.

65 435 US 313, 323 (1978).

66 *Lone Wolf v Hitchcock*, 187 US 553 (1903); *Wheeler*, *ibid*, 323.

67 McHugh, above n 37, 415; see also C Orange, *The Treaty of Waitangi* (Allen and Unwin/Port Nicholson Press, 1987); McHugh, above n 8.

68 Eg *New Zealand Maori Council*, above n 36.

In practice, Indigenous aspirations for self-determination and sovereignty have focused on achieving a measure of self-governance and autonomy within the existing framework of nation-states. As Imai documents in his chapter, self-governance can take forms falling short of outright secession and political independence.[69] Many governance systems have been designed specifically to promote land use planning and resource management on Indigenous territories, as Richardson details in his chapter on environmental governance. Compared to Indigenous communities in other common law jurisdictions, Indian tribes in the US enjoy substantially more powers of self-governance. On their reservations, tribal powers commonly include determination of tribal membership, authority over tribal property, and the administration of justice.[70]

Along with self-governance, the struggle for recognition of Indigenous land rights has been one of the most dominant issues in their legal history. Land is central to Indigenous cultures and livelihoods, and without it their powers of self-governance would be much less meaningful. Indigenous land rights can derive from many sources, including custom, the common law, treaties, and legislation. As early as the 17th century, Britain recognised that Native Americans had rights to the land, and major treaties were signed across Canada as settlement expanded.[71] The US government also entered into treaties up to 1871.[72] In Australia, where no treaties have been acknowledged, legislation enacted from the 1960s has provided land to specific Aboriginal communities, albeit usually only 'vacant' Crown land.[73]

Only in recent decades, however, have authorities in common law countries generally acknowledged the legal nature of Aboriginal property rights and their status independent of treaty or legislation, as McNeil outlines in his chapter.[74] Aboriginal title has been recognised as a common law property interest in land in Canada, Australia, New Zealand, and increasingly in other common law jurisdictions such as Malaysia and Belize.[75] Indigenous peoples have often looked to the

[69] See also G Nettheim, GD Meyers and D Craig, *Indigenous Peoples and Governance Structures* (Aboriginal Studies Press, 2002).

[70] JD Green and S Work, 'Inherent Indian Sovereignty' (1976) 4 *American Law Review* 311; Wilkinson, above n 5.

[71] Eg Treaties 1 to 11, 1871–1921: see A Morris, *The Treaties of Canada with the Indians of Manitoba and the North-West Territories* (Belfords, Clarke and Co, 1880); Asch, above n 22.

[72] FP Prucha, *American Indian Treaties: The History of a Political Anomaly* (University of California Press, 1994).

[73] Eg Aboriginal Land Rights Act 1983 (NSW).

[74] Although the US Supreme Court acknowledged the legal existence of Indian title early on in *Fletcher v Peck*, 10 US (6 Cranch) 87, 142–43 (1810), and *Johnson v M'Intosh*, 21 US (8 Wheat) 543 (1823), in *Tee-Hit-Ton Indians v US*, 348 US 272 (1955), the court decided that unrecognised Indian title is a right of occupancy, not a right of property that is compensable under the Fifth Amendment to the US Constitution.

[75] See *Adong bin Kuwau and 51 Ors v The Government of Jahore* (1997) 1 MLJ 418 (confirmed by the Court of Appeal, (1998) 2 MLJ 158); *Cal v Attorney General of Belize; Coy v Attorney General of Belize*, Claim Nos 171 and 172 of 2007, SC of Belize. Among the vast literature, see J Cassidy, 'Aboriginal Title: An Overgrown and Poorly Excavated Archaeological Site?' (1988) 10 *International Legal Perspectives* 39; B Donovan, 'The Evolution and Present Status of Common Law Aboriginal Title in Canada: The Law's Crooked Path and the Hollow Promise of Delgamuukw' (2001) 35 *University of British Columbi*

courts to prove many of their historical claims and to challenge those of the state. Outside of the common law systems, Indigenous land claims have also been considered; in Central America, the Inter-American Human Rights system has been used to seek recognition and protection of Indigenous rights, as Hopkins discusses in his chapter.[76]

D. Conclusions

Since the late 20th century, nation-states considered in this book have generally sought to be more accommodating to Indigenous interests than they were in the past. Yet, it would be dangerous to assume that legal policies can readily correct the past and make the future. The horrific experiences of Indigenous peoples over recent centuries certainly will not be purged by the avowed policies of reconciliation, compensation, land rights, and other measures that purport to make amends. Moreover, just as law by itself was not responsible for the racist effects of colonial power, nor will current legal reforms alone likely be able to engineer sweeping changes in the condition of Indigenous peoples.

Legal scholars in other areas of social affairs have highlighted the limits of law. The enormous extension and intensification of legal standards worldwide in such fields as environmental protection, human rights, health care, and other domains has often failed to improve conditions.[77] Social inequality, poverty, racism, climate change and environmental degradation, among many other seemingly intractable problems, continue to beset societies around the globe. For reasons canvassed in other literature, it is increasingly doubtful that the methods of grand social engineering and detailed, prescriptive regulation can provide comprehensive answers to such problems, thus prompting some legal scholars to envision a more subdued and modest role for law reform.[78]

In relation to Indigenous affairs, such arguments could, however, provide reasons to enhance Indigenous self-determination. If the modern state, suffering from its fragmented power, bureaucratic inefficiencies, and fiscal constraints, cannot be relied upon as a means of social reform, then all the more reason to allow

Law Review 43; P McHugh, 'Aboriginal Title in New Zealand: A Retrospect and Prospect' (2004) 2 *New Zealand Journal of Public and International Law* 139; B Slattery, 'Understanding Aboriginal Rights' (1987) 66 *Canadian Bar Review* 727, and 'The Metamorphosis of Aboriginal Title' (2006) 85 *Canadian Bar Review* 255; K McNeil, *Common Law Aboriginal Title* (Oxford University Press, 1989); Young, above n 1.

[76] See also SJ Anaya and C Grossman, 'The Case of *Awas Tingni v Nicaragua*: A New Step in the International Law of Indigenous Peoples' (2002) 19 *Arizona Journal of International and Comparative Law* 1.

[77] R Susskind, *The Future of Law: Facing the Challenges of Information Technology* (Clarendon Press, 1996); PC Yeager, *The Limits of Law: The Public Regulation of Private Pollution* (Cambridge University Press, 1991).

[78] G Teubner, 'After Legal Instrumentalism?' in G Teubner (ed), *Dilemmas of Law in the Welfare State* (Walter De Gruyter, 1986) 222.

Indigenous communities to govern themselves. There is also a challenge here for Indigenous peoples, who must reform and revitalise internal institutional structures to take on responsibilities that formally were carried out by the state. While the difficulties of contemporary public governance cannot be an excuse for denying justice to Indigenous peoples, they can be good reasons to change course entirely, and allow such peoples the autonomy and resources to manage their own affairs. The seminal Harvard Project on American Indian Economic Development has documented how communities that exercise more self-governance and independence often enjoy higher social and economic well-being.[79]

In this book, readers will learn more about the intersection between the historical experiences of Indigenous peoples, their contemporary concerns, and the role of the law in subjugating, defining, channelling and empowering their interests. Hopefully, by acquiring a better understanding of these issues from the perspectives of many different contributors from various parts of the world, we can help to facilitate a more beneficial and enlightened role for law in advancing the interests of Indigenous peoples.

[79] The Harvard Project on American Indian Economic Development, *The State of the Native Nations: Conditions under US Policies of Self-Determination* (Oxford University Press, 2007).

Part 1

Sovereignty, Status and Self-Determination in Historical Perspective

2

Promise and Paradox: The Emergence of Indigenous Rights Law in Canada

MARK D WALTERS

A. Introduction

Visitors to the Museum of Anthropology at the University of British Columbia will find a sculpture by Gitxsan artist Eric Robertson, completed in 2000, consisting of two large cedar poles that may be turned by pushing carved wooden hands that extend from each pole. Wrapped around one pole is a copper plate covered in small, antique lettering. Those who stop to read the plate will find at the top the words, 'A Proclamation . . . George the Third, by the Grace of God, King of England', and, at the end, after a long passage of legal language, the words, 'Given by my hand at St. James Palace, October 7th, 1763'.[1]

The placement of the copper plate upon the polished cedar wood is incongruous: the cold pomposity of colonial power contrasts starkly with the organic grain of the aboriginal carving. But once the visitor learns that the copper lettering reproduces a king's promise to protect Indian land rights, the effect of the image is to upset preconceptions about power in colonial and post-colonial settings. In this sculpture, the sovereign will of a long-dead European monarch comes alive as a bold, ironic assertion of modern aboriginal rights. The words of George III are worked into a piece of art that draws inspiration from a traditional aboriginal game involving outstretched hands, and the artist thus imagines—and asks us to imagine—the possibility that the words represent a transcendent voice of justice that is *both* aboriginal and non-aboriginal in essence.

The sculpture captures artistically the promise and paradox of law for indigenous peoples in Canada. It celebrates law's promise of reconciliation. It embodies the aspiration of Canadian judges of identifying a basis for aboriginal rights within 'a form of intersocietal law' arising from the 'reconciliation of the different legal cultures of aboriginal and non-aboriginal peoples . . .'.[2] It reminds us too of the

[1] E Robertson, 'Shaking the Crown's Bone', sculpture completed in January 2000, Museum of Anthropology, University of British Columbia, Collection ID No Nb7.346a–b.

[2] *R v Van der Peet* [1996] 2 SCR 507, per Lamer CJC, para 42 and McLachlin J, para 310.

paradox underlying this aspiration. Canadian judges also say that indigenous traditions only count if they can be 'framed in terms cognizable to the Canadian legal and constitutional structure.'[3] Reconciling legal cultures may, in other words, mean submitting indigenous traditions to non-indigenous control, and this raises the possibility that aboriginal peoples will end up 'housed inside the constitutional compound of the settler-state.'[4] Pushing the hands on the cedar pole of the sculpture, the Royal Proclamation of 1763 spins in and out of view—its promise real but unrealised, its legacy still uncertain.

That an 18th-century legal instrument could have normative force today for indigenous peoples in Canada is itself something of a paradox. As a British parliamentary committee reported in 1837, European colonisation represented a 'calamity' for aboriginal peoples producing 'evil' and 'misery' in their lives.[5] Many of these evils, including the loss of territories and independence, were seemingly perpetrated through the instrumentality of law. Why, then, do indigenous peoples in Canada sometimes turn to laws of the colonial past when developing arguments about rights today? Why does the placement of the Royal Proclamation in Robertson's sculpture inspire—as good art often does and good legal arguments always do—such powerful sensations of indignation and hope?

The answer may have something to do with the universal appeal of legality as a human value, and with the ways in which legality is instantiated between peoples through the efforts they make to honour their commitments to one another over time. It may be that law is not so much a thing proclaimed into existence as a dynamic interpretive process in which normative standards are articulated through a constant cycle of reminders. 'We have always had in mind Brother', the Algonquins and Nipissings said in 1841 when defending claims to their traditional territory along the Ottawa River, 'the promises & commands of Our Great & Good Father King George the Third . . . [expressed] in His Proclamation of 1763 of which our Father Sir William Johnson gave our ancestors a writing in parchment which we still hold . . .'.[6] Even in the midst of the 'calamity' of colonialisation, it seems that people never stopped seeking to articulate ideals of justice in legal forms that bridged cultural differences. They never stopped searching for an intersocietal law of national coexistence.

Of course this search has not succeeded—not fully, not yet. As we shall see, the law of indigenous rights in Canada is really an on-going process of intersocietal discourse and engagement. This interpretive process is guided by, and results in, diverse manifestations of law—not just proclamations, but also intercultural custom, historic and modern treaties, evolving common law narratives, and statutory and constitutional texts. A thorough examination of these various sources of law

[3] *Ibid*, per Lamer CJC, para 49.

[4] PG McHugh, *Aboriginal Societies and the Common Law: A History of Sovereignty, Status, and Self-Determination* (Oxford University Press, 2004) 609.

[5] Great Britain, Parliamentary Select Committee, 'Report From the Select Committee on Aborigines (British Settlements)', *Parliamentary Papers* 1837, VII, no 425, 74, 75.

[6] Council held at the Lake of the Two Mountains, Lower Canada, 4 Sept 1841, National Archives of Canada, RG 10, vol 78: 43072–76.

is not possible here. However, by attending to some of the ways in which indigenous claims have been expressed, and denied, within legal discourses over time we may at least gain a general sense of the shape and content of indigenous rights law in Canada today.

The discussion is divided into three main parts. I shall begin with an overview of early Crown-Indian treaty relations. I shall then review how the objectives of Canadian aboriginal policy shifted from assimilation to accommodation and reconciliation over the course of the 20th century. And, finally, I shall consider the emergence of a distinctively legal discourse on aboriginal rights by examining some central themes that have characterised the judicial approach to this subject in Canada. The opinions expressed will necessarily be tentative and contingent and coloured by my own non-aboriginal cultural perspective. Exploring intersocietal legal ideas implies a process of intercultural learning that prohibits definitive statements of meaning in essays like this one.

B. Empires, Nations and Identity

Canada's identity as a nation-state is often defined by reference to the rival imperial claims to North America pressed by Britain and France long ago. These claims were resolved in Britain's favour by a series of 18th century wars and treaties. In the Treaty of Utrecht, 1713, France agreed that 'Nova Scotia or Acadie', 'Newfoundland', and 'the bay and streights of Hudson' were British, but it claimed 'Canada' for itself.[7] Canada then consisted of the settlements of the St Lawrence River valley and (in French eyes at least) the vast, undefined *pays d'en haut* that stretched through the Great Lakes region and beyond. French efforts in the mid-18th century to secure the fur trade with the indigenous inhabitants of this upper country met with opposition from British traders and settlers who were beginning to spill over the mountains that divided the British colonies of the eastern seaboard from the continental interior. British victories during the ensuing Seven Years' War—culminating with Wolfe's dramatic defeat of Montcalm at Quebec—effectively ended the French regime in North America.[8] On 10 February 1763, the Treaty of Paris was signed and the King of France formally ceded to the King of Great Britain 'in full right, Canada with all its dependencies'.[9] British Crown sovereignty over the eastern half of North America was, from the European perspective at least, confirmed. After the American Revolution and the loss to the Crown of its older colonies to the south, Canada's story becomes one of how the Crown's remaining North American territories were carved into provinces, how

[7] Treaty of Utrecht 1713, Arts X, XII, XIII, XV, in WPM Kennedy (ed), *Statutes, Treaties and Documents of the Canadian Constitution, 1713–1929* (2nd edn, Oxford University Press, 1930) 5–6.

[8] See, eg, F Anderson, *Crucible of War: The Seven Years' War and the Fate of Empire in British North America, 1754–1766* (Vintage Books, 2001).

[9] Treaty of Paris, 1763, Art IV, in Kennedy, above n 7, 32.

the reach of Crown sovereignty was extended westward to the Pacific coast, how boundaries and laws were reconfigured from time to time to accommodate the needs of English and French-speaking settlers, and, finally, how the various provinces and territories joined together to form a federal union under the Crown known as the Dominion of Canada.[10]

But where were indigenous peoples in this story? For a long time, they were—much like the tattooed and feathered warrior in West's famous painting of Wolfe's death on the Plains of Abraham—at the margins of the unfolding imperial and national drama.[11] The legal account of this version of the story was described in blunt terms by a judge in 1929: the 'savages' rights of sovereignty [and] even of ownership were never recognized', he said, and thus large parts of the country passed to Britain 'not by gift or purchase from or even by conquest of the Indians but by treaty with France, which had acquired it by priority of discovery and ancient possession; and the Indians passed with it'.[12] Other parts of the country, this judge would no doubt have said, were acquired by the Crown's *own* acts of discovery and possession. The characterisation of a colonial possession as a discovery had significant legal implications. Judges assumed that English law flowed across the legally empty terrain automatically to provide the newly arrived settlers with their law.[13] Territories gained by conquest or cession from other peoples, in contrast, were presumed at common law to be governed by the local laws already existing, at least until the Crown took steps to provide alternative laws.[14]

The standard accounts of the discovery and conquest doctrines and their respective corollaries on the reception and continuity of laws were not designed to address the status of aboriginal peoples and their laws in North America, nor do they fit with what actually happened there.[15] The version of the story given by the judge in 1929 is erroneous, and the errors begin with a failure to grasp how indigenous identity was constructed and interpreted in the past. The famous assertion by Hobbes, that the Indians of North America were a 'savage people' living without arts, letters, society or government in a 'brutish' state of nature, reflected the popular European view of indigenous peoples, and this view clearly infected later judicial reasoning.[16] But Europeans who lived and worked with indigenous peoples knew better. It was an 'injustice', wrote Joseph Lafitau in 1724, to describe

[10] For a standard account, see D Creighton, *Dominion of the North: A History of Canada* (Macmillan Co, 1962).

[11] B West's painting, 'The Death of General Wolfe' (1770), is in the collection of the National Gallery of Canada. See V Green Fryd, 'Rereading the Indian in Benjamin West's "Death of General Wolfe"' (1995) 9(1) *American Art* 72.

[12] *Rex v Syliboy* [1929] 1 DLR 307 (NS Co Ct) 313.

[13] *Blankard v Galdy* (1693) 2 Salk 411.

[14] *Campbell v Hall* (1774) Loft 655.

[15] MD Walters, 'British Imperial Constitutional Law and Aboriginal Rights: A Comment on *Delgamuukw v British Columbia*' (1992) 17 *Queen's Law Journal* 350; PG McHugh, 'The Common-Law Status of Colonies and Aboriginal 'Rights': How Lawyers and Historians Treat the Past' (1998) 61 *Saskatchewan Law Review* 393.

[16] T Hobbes, *Leviathan or the Matter, Forme and Power of a Commonwealth Ecclesiasticall and Civil* [1651], M Oakeshot (ed) (Basil Blackwell, 1957) 82, 83.

Indians as 'barbarians without laws', and he proceeded to explain the matriarchal clan system of law and government that he had observed among the Iroquois communities near Montreal.[17]

It was this more realistic view of things that seemed to inform the first constitutional instrument made by Britain for North America after its conquest of Canada. In the Royal Proclamation of 1763, we find the King recognising the land rights of 'the several Nations or Tribes of Indians, with whom We are connected'.[18] Issued in haste, the Proclamation was short on details. The imperial Lords of Trade were thus charged with the task of developing a more thorough set of laws to regulate relations with Indian nations. In 1764, they drafted a bill to supplement the terms of the Proclamation, and although it was never enacted by Parliament it reveals much about official attitudes then prevailing. According to the Lords of Trade, the manner in which Indians 'regulate their civil Concerns' demonstrated that 'a steady and uniform attachment to and Love of Justice and Equity is one of their first Principles of Government'; the proposed statute, which would have established a framework in positive law for future treaty relations, was, the Lords of Trade insisted, designed 'to conform . . . to their Inclinations and Disposition in this Respect'.[19] There was no talk of claims based on discovery here, no references to a Hobbesian state of nature or absolute Crown sovereignty. Rather, the assumption seems to have been that indigenous inhabitants had polities and laws that were to be acknowledged and accommodated within territories over which the Crown asserted exclusive rights vis-à-vis other European states.

The authors of the Proclamation, in referring to the Indians as constituting a series of distinct 'Nations or Tribes', appreciated that 'Indians' were not all the same. In fact, indigenous societies in the territories that now form Canada were, and are, as varied as the country's geography. They represented over 50 different languages or dialects. Algonquian speakers were found between the Atlantic coast and the Rocky Mountains; Athapaskan speakers occupied much of the northwestern interior; Inuktitut speakers covered the far north; Salishan, Haida, Tsimshian, and Tlingit speakers lived along the Pacific coast.[20]

[17] Father JF Lafitau, *Customs of the American Indians Compared with the Customs of Primitive Times* [1724], WN Fenton and EL Moore (eds and trans), (Champlain Society, 1974) vol I, 283.

[18] Royal Proclamation of 7 October 1763, in Kennedy, above n 7, 35–38; also reproduced at RSC 1985, App II, no 1.

[19] Lords of Trade to Sir W Johnson, Supt Gen Indian Affrs, 10 July 1764, in EB O'Callaghan (ed), *Documents Relative to the Colonial History of the State of New York* (Weed, Parsons and Co, 1856–1861) vol III, 634–36.

[20] The general description of aboriginal nations in this and following paragraphs is drawn from the following works in history, ethnohistory and anthropology: D Jenness, *The Indians of Canada* (6th edn, National Museum of Canada, 1963); AD McMillan, *Native Peoples and Cultures of Canada: An Anthropological Overview* (2nd edn, Douglas and McIntyre, 1995); OP Dickason, *Canada's First Nations: A History of Founding Peoples from Earliest Times* (3rd edn, Oxford University Press, 2002); WN Fenton, *The Great Law and the Longhouse: A Political History of the Iroquois Confederacy* (University of Oklahoma Press, 1998); BG Trigger, *The Children of Aataentsic: A History of the Huron People to 1660* (McGill-Queen's University Press, 1987); DK Richter, *The Ordeal of the Longhouse: The Peoples of the Iroquois League in the Era of European Colonization* (University of North Carolina Press, 1992); ES Rogers and DB Smith (eds), *Aboriginal Ontario: Historical Perspectives on the First Nations*

And with these different languages came distinctive cultural practices. The Iroquoian speakers of the lower Great Lakes region, including the Wendat or Huron and the Haudenosaunee or Five (later Six) Nations Iroquois, cultivated fields around palisaded villages consisting of substantial longhouses. In contrast, the Algonquian-speaking Anishnaabeg of the upper Great Lakes gathered at village sites near fisheries during spring and summer and broke into smaller groups that dispersed inland to hunt during autumn and winter. Differences in patterns of settlement and resource use were reflected in legal and political structures. The matrilineal clans from which hereditary chiefs were selected among the Iroquoians of the Great Lakes and the Haida, Tlingit, and Tsimshian of the Pacific coast, for example, contrasted with the patrilineal groups and more fluid systems of leadership found among Athapaskan and Algonquian speakers of the central plains, northern boreal forests and eastern woodlands.

These diverse societies did, however, share some common perspectives that distinguished them from Europeans and that helped shape responses to intercultural contact. Wendat historian Georges Sioui observes that indigenous peoples tended to see all beings as 'equal and interdependent'.[21] They tended to regard the world around them—the animals they hunted, the waters they travelled, the plants they harvested—as animated by spirits or manitous (as the Anishnaabeg called them), and through fasting, dreaming, and ceremonial gift-giving they integrated themselves into this natural-spirit world. Family and clan identities were often associated with animal spirits that provided clan crests or totems, and ties of spiritual-kinship secured broader forms of political organisation.

These peoples were not *states* in the European sense. Individual liberty and collective solidarity were celebrated within structures that avoided formal coercion or command. Coalitions negotiated between family or clan groups secured order within bands and villages, and clan relations often linked bands and villages together to form larger national identities. Gift giving—like the *potlatch* ceremonies of the west coast—was important for both coordinated action and spiritual balance. To exchange presents was to enter a relationship of spiritual-kinship, a normative world of rights and duties of care and respect. In this world, political leaders were not authoritarian figures, but providers and mentors. The law was not issued from above and imposed below, but was a narrative woven through stories and songs at the council fire, places where 'tears were wiped away' through condolence ceremonies that secured the conditions for dialogue and sound judgment.[22]

Almost as soon as they arrived in North America, Europeans were invited to these council fires. Indeed, it was through submission to the customary forms of council discourse followed by indigenous peoples that Europeans became, to use

(Dundurn Press, 1994); D Murray, *Indian Giving: Economies of Power in Indian-White Exchanges* (University of Massachusetts Press, 2000).

[21] GE Sioui, *For an Amerindian Autohistory: An Essay on the Foundations of a Social Ethic* (Queen's-McGill University Press, 1992) 8.

[22] MD Walters, 'The Morality of Aboriginal Law' (2006) 31 *Queen's Law Journal* 470, 482–89.

the expression found in the Royal Proclamation of 1763, 'connected' to them.[23] As the following description of a treaty council held between the governor of Canada and Iroquois, Huron and Algonquin representatives at Trois Rivières in 1645 suggests, there was initially a considerable cultural gap to bridge at these councils:

> [i]n the centre was a large space, somewhat longer than wide, in which the Iroquois caused two poles to be planted, and a cord to be stretched from one to the other on which to hang and tie the words that they were to bring us,—that is to say, the presents they wished to make us, which consisted of seventeen collars of porcelain [wampum] beads, a portion of which were on their bodies. . . . When all had assembled and taken their places, Kiotsaeton who was high in stature rose and looked at the Sun, then cast his eyes over the whole Company; he took a collar of porcelain beads in his hand and commenced to harangue in a loud voice. . . . [He said] '. . . I have only good songs in my mouth . . .'. Thereupon he began to sing; his countrymen responded; he walked about that great space as if on the stage of a theatre; he made a thousand gestures; he looked up to Heaven; he gazed at the Sun; he rubbed his arms as if he wished to draw from them the strength that moved them in war. . . . In a word, I have never seen anything better done than this acting.[24]

Of the wampum strings given as presents at this council, the observer noted that each had its own message or meaning, expressed through some metaphor. Presents of wampum were given, for example, to wipe tears away in condolence of past losses, to remove clouds over the council, to open navigation between nations, and to bind peoples together in a knot. After the French had reciprocated with their own presents, Kiotsaeton stated: 'Adieu my brothers; I am one of your relatives'.[25]

French and British representatives made treaties like this one with indigenous peoples throughout the 17th and 18th centuries.[26] In such councils, the British forged the famous 'silver covenant chain' treaty relationship with the Six Nations Iroquois and other nations.[27] These treaties are sometimes described now as peace and friendship treaties to distinguish them from the land-surrender treaties that followed. Yet somehow this label fails to capture fully the essence of the legal relationship established. The records we have of these treaty encounters hint at a deeper meaning that was almost impossible for scribes to capture on paper. 'Everyone admitted that this man was impassioned and eloquent', the observer stated of Kiotsaeton's oratory, '[but] I gathered only some disconnected fragments, taken from the mouth of the interpreter'.[28] Yes, peace and friendship were established. But Kiotsaeton must have intended something much more complex

[23] See, in general, WN Fenton, 'Structure, Continuity, and Change in the Process of Iroquois Treaty Making' in F Jennings (ed), *The History and Culture of Iroquois Diplomacy: An Interdisciplinary Guide to the Treaties of the Six Nations and Their League* (Syracuse University Press, 1985) 3–36.

[24] RG Thwaites (ed), *The Jesuit Relations and Allied Documents* (Burrows Bros, 1896–1901) vol 27, 253, 255.

[25] *Ibid*, 273.

[26] See, in general, RA Williams Jr, *Linking Arms Together: American Indian Treaty Visions of Law and Peace, 1600–1800* (Oxford University Press, 1997).

[27] F Jennings, *The Ambiguous Iroquois Empire: The Covenant Chain Confederation of Indian Tribes with English Colonies* (WW Norton, 1984).

[28] Thwaites, above n 24, 265.

and rich than this by his words, songs, actions and presents. Through the ceremony that day, and through the countless treaty councils that would follow over the next two-and-half centuries, a form of spiritual-kinship emerged. Indigenous peoples worked Europeans into the web of kinship relations that defined their own political and legal orders. They became, as the interpreter described Kiotsaeton's words, 'relatives'. European identities and roles came to be defined by aboriginal laws. In 1645, Kiotsaeton's songs may have been difficult for Europeans to understand. By 1756, however, we find the Crown's superintendent of Indian affairs, Sir William Johnson, on his way to affirm the covenant chain treaty at Onondaga, 'march[ing] on at the Head of the Sachems singing the condoling song which contains the names, laws & Customs of their renowned ancestors'.[29]

European sovereigns were, by this means, redefined in indigenous terms. The French King and his representative, the governor of Canada, were adopted by aboriginal nations. Bearing his adoptive name, *Onontio*, the governor became for them an ally, a protector, a provider, an arbitrator—one might even say a chief. He became, in short, their *father*.[30] Similarly, British colonial governors became brothers, and the British king they represented a father. The Crown-as-father was not a *sovereign*. The legal tradition that clothed the Crown with its constitutional identity of father did not and could not acknowledge sovereigns in the European sense.[31] What the British Crown gained by its victory over the French in Canada was, from the indigenous legal perspective, merely an opportunity to assume the status of father vacated by Onontio—a status long on duty and short on power.[32]

Sir William Johnson knew this, but other British officials did not. When military authorities ordered a stop to the customary giving of presents, and troops took possession of forts within Indian territory in 1763, Indian nations feared that the Crown had repudiated its role as father and assumed the mantle of sovereign—and war resulted. The Royal Proclamation of 1763 was quickly issued to reassure them of the Crown's goodwill, but its promise to protect Indian land rights under Crown 'Sovereignty' and 'Dominion', when read literally, appeared to assert precisely what aboriginal nations feared. Johnson appreciated this fact. In his view, coexistence with Indian nations in Canada necessitated a 'Treaty' with them, conducted 'according to their own forms'.[33]

[29] 'Journal of Sir William Johnson's Proceedings with the Indians' (1756) in O'Callaghan, above n 19, vol VIII, 130–5.

[30] R White, *The Middle Ground: Indians, Empires, and Republics in the Great Lakes Region, 1650–1815* (Cambridge University Press, 1991) 175–85; G Havard, *Empire et métissages: Indiens et Français dans le Pays d'en Haut* (Septentrion, 2003) 205–39, 359–414; G Havard, *The Great Peace of Montreal of 1701* (McGill-Queen's University Press, 2001) 15–45.

[31] Sir W Johnson to T Gage, 31 October 1764, in J Sullivan (ed), *The Papers of Sir William Johnson* (State University of New York, 1921–65) vol XI, 394–6: '. . . it is necessary to observe that no Nation of Indians have any word which can express, or convey the Idea of Subjection . . . [T]hey often say, we acknowledge the great King to be our Father . . . for which our People too readily adopt & insert a Word [i.e., sovereign] very different in signification, and never intended by the Indians . . .'.

[32] See, in general, GE Dowd, *War under Heaven: Pontiac, the Indian Nations, and the British Empire* (The Johns Hopkins University Press, 2002).

[33] Sir W Johnson, Supt Gen Ind Affrs, to T Gage, Commander in Chief, 19 Feb 1764, in Sullivan, above n 31, vol IV, 328–33.

With copies of the Proclamation that he distributed to Indian nations, Johnson therefore included an invitation to attend a treaty council at Niagara. The resulting council, held in the summer of 1764, was the largest such council ever held, attracting nations from around the Great Lakes and beyond.[34] It was here, John Borrows argues, that the Proclamation was effectively incorporated into the Crown-Indian treaty relationship, being transformed in the process from unilateral to intersocietal law.[35] It was here that Crown rights in Canada were established—and limited rights they were. At the council, Johnson gave the assembled chiefs 'the great belt of the *Covenant Chain*', an elaborate wampum belt '23 Rows broad, & the Year 1764 worked upon it', knowing that the relationship that it affirmed was far more complicated and nuanced than the text of the Proclamation might suggest.[36] The royal sovereign had become, once again, an indigenous father. We may say, then, that the process of reconciling legal traditions began a long time ago.

C. From Assimilation to Reconciliation

The memory of the Niagara covenant chain council would soon fade in non-aboriginal Canada. Writing in 1861, the Mississauga chief Peter Jones observed that 'the old chiefs' still mentioned the silver chain in their councils, recalling that the treaty 'placed them as allies' and 'not subjects' of the Crown; but, he continued, once the 'influx of emigration completely outnumbered the aborigines', the government 'assumed a parental authority over them, treating them in every respect as children'.[37] The Crown essentially appropriated the label 'father' and gave it a European meaning, one that implied an unyielding sense of paternalism. Aboriginal peoples in Canada are still recovering from the effects of the oppressive way in which this paternal power was exercised from the mid-19th to the mid 20th centuries.

Just over one million people in Canada, or about 4 per cent of the population, now identify as aboriginal. The number of aboriginal people as a percentage of the

[34] Sir W Johnson to the Lords of Trade, 30 August 1764, in O'Callaghan, above n 19, vol VII, 648–50.

[35] J Borrows, 'Wampum at Niagara: The Royal Proclamation, Canadian Legal History and Self-Government' in M Asch (ed), *Aboriginal and Treaty Rights in Canada: Essays on Law, Equality and Respect for Difference* (UBC Press, 1997) 155–72. The argument was accepted in *Chippewas of Sarnia Band v Canada (Attorney General)* (2001), 51 OR (3d) 641 (CA), 703; leave to appeal denied [2001] SCCA No 63.

[36] 'Conference with Indians', Niagara, July 9–Aug 14, 1764, in Sullivan, above n 31, vol XI, 309–10. Johnson would afterwards deny that the Niagara treaty established 'sovereignty' over Indian nations: Sir W Johnson to the Lords of Trade, 30 October 1764, in O'Callaghan, above n 19, vol VII, 670–4. See MD Walters, 'Brightening the Covenant Chain: Aboriginal Treaty Meanings in Law and History after Marshall' (2001) 24 *Dalhousie Law Journal* 75.

[37] P Jones (Kah-ke-wa-quo-na-by), *History of the Ojebway Indians; with Especial References to their Conversion to Christianity* (AW Bennett, 1861) 216–17.

general population is highest in the northern territories of Nunavut (85 per cent), the Northwest Territories (50 per cent), and the Yukon (25 per cent), and in the prairie provinces of Manitoba and Saskatchewan (15 per cent).[38] The cultures and circumstances of aboriginal peoples vary dramatically across the country today as they did in times past, and their legal relations with federal and provincial authorities are not uniform either.

Canada is established as a federal state by the Constitution Act 1867, and that Act provides in section 91(24) that the federal Parliament of Canada has exclusive legislative authority in relation to 'Indians, and Lands reserved for the Indians'.[39] Provincial authority over Indians is therefore limited. Constitutional reforms in 1982 introduced new provisions concerning human rights and freedoms generally, and aboriginal rights in particular.[40] Section 25 of the Constitution Act 1982 provides that general rights and freedoms are not to be construed so as to derogate from the aboriginal and treaty rights of aboriginal peoples, including 'any rights or freedoms that have been recognised by the Royal Proclamation of October 7, 1763'. Section 35(1) of the Act provides: 'The existing aboriginal and treaty rights of the aboriginal peoples of Canada are hereby recognized and affirmed'. The 'aboriginal peoples of Canada' who hold these rights are defined in section 35(2) as including 'the Indian, Inuit and Métis peoples of Canada'. Over 700,000 people in Canada identify as Indians, almost 400,000 identify as Métis and about 50,500 identify as Inuit.[41]

The 1982 constitutional affirmation of aboriginal and treaty rights did not serve to sweep away older laws relating to aboriginal peoples in Canada. Many of those older laws remain in force, at least insofar as they are not inconsistent with the new constitutional regime. The result is a patchwork of laws for indigenous peoples across the country. Thus, for example, a distinction is made between status and non-status Indians. Status Indians are registered as 'Indians' under the federal Indian Act, an antiquated statute first enacted in 1876.[42] These aboriginal peoples are generally members of Indian 'bands' (or First Nations) that possess 'reserves' and exercise limited powers of self-government through 'band councils' under the terms of the Indian Act. There are 615 bands and over 2,000 reserves across the country.[43] As of 2004, there were 719,496 registered Indians, 60 per cent of whom lived on reserves.[44] In comparison to Indian reservations in the United States, Canadian Indian reserves are small: they could all fit into an area half the size of

[38] Statistics Canada, *Aboriginal Peoples in Canada in 2006: Inuit, Métis and First Nations, 2006 Census* (Minister of Industry, 2008) 6–8, 11.

[39] Constitution Act 1867, 30 and 31 Vic, c 3 (UK).

[40] Constitution Act 1982 (enacted as Sch B to the Canada Act 1982 (UK), c 11).

[41] Statistics Canada, above n 38, 6–8, 11.

[42] Indian Act, RSC 1985, c I–5 (first enacted as An Act to amend and consolidate the laws respecting Indians, SC 1876, c 18).

[43] Indian and Northern Affairs Canada, *2007–08 Report on Plans and Priorities* (INAC, 2007) 9.

[44] Indian and Northern Affairs Canada, *Basic Departmental Data, 2004* (Department of Indian Affairs and Northern Development, December 2005) 3–4.

the Navajo reservation in Arizona[45] (though in many cases band members retain rights to natural resources and lands in territories surrounding their reserves[46]). Unlike American tribal governments, which have long been acknowledged as enjoying powers of residual sovereignty, Indian band councils in Canada are commonly—but wrongly—considered to have only those powers that are conferred by the Indian Act.[47] Finally, whereas state laws are largely excluded from American Indian reservations, since 1951 the Indian Act has provided that provincial laws of general application apply to Indians (but not necessarily lands) within Indian reserves, unless inconsistent with federal legislation or a treaty.

The Indian Act represents the primary statutory manifestation of the Crown's paternal authority over aboriginal peoples in Canada. Its origins lay in the decision by colonial officials in the early 19th century to civilise and assimilate Indians—a decision, as the Secretary of State for the Colonies wrote in 1830, to overcome the 'disposition in the Aboriginal inhabitants to cling to their original habits and mode of life'.[48] Officials appreciated that Indian chiefs would resist any attempt 'to withdraw the people from under their authority' and that Indians themselves would resist any attempt 'to do away with the nationality of each separate tribe'.[49] They therefore designed the civilisation policy accordingly. They accepted the idea of 'perpetuating th[e] influence . . . [of] chiefs',[50] and they balanced the goal of 'attaching the Indians to their farms' with the Indian refusal 'to intermix with the white population'.[51] The solution, they concluded, was to encourage Indian settlement within separate national or tribal communities, where 'their antipathy to associate with other people . . . w[ould] be gradually overcome; and their amalgamation with the mass of the population [would] be most effectively promoted'.[52] Small tracts of land, or 'reserves', were thus set aside for this purpose, in some cases by reserving lands out of treaty surrenders of traditional territories, and in other cases by unilateral government act. Traditional aboriginal laws and governments continued, in modified and limited ways, within these reserves, but under the

45 *Report of the Royal Commission on Aboriginal Peoples*, vol II: *Restructuring the Relationship* (Canada Communication Group, 1996) 422–23.

46 Eg, aboriginal rights to fish (*R v Sparrow* [1990] 1 SCR 1075), treaty rights to hunt over surrendered lands (*R v Badger* [1996] 1 SCR 771), and rights to hunt and fish for food secured by the Natural Resources Transfer Agreements, affirmed by the Constitution Act 1930, 20 and 21 Geo V c 26 (UK), for Indians in Alberta, Saskatchewan and Manitoba.

47 On American Indian sovereignty: DE Wilkins, *Uneven Grounds: American Indian Sovereignty and Federal Law* (University of Oklahoma Press, 2001). The common Canadian view: *Heron Seismic Services Ltd v Muscowpetung Indian Band* [1991] 2 CNLR 52 (Sask QB), 55 (an Indian band council is a 'creature of statute' exercising delegated powers). A sounder approach is reflected in *Bone v Sioux Valley Indian Band No 290* [1996] 3 CNLR 54 (Fed TD) (bands have certain 'inherent' powers relating to governance that the Indian Act 'interferes with').

48 Sir G Murray, Sec of State for the Colonies, to Sir J Kempt, Gov Gen, 25 January 1830, UK Parliamentary Papers, *Imperial Blue Books on Affairs Relating to Canada; Reports, Returns and Other Papers, Presented to the Imperial Houses of Parliament of Great Britain and Ireland Relating to Canada*, vol 5 *Papers Relative to the Aboriginal Tribes in British Possessions*, 1834, No. 617, 87–89.

49 *Ibid.*

50 *Ibid.*

51 Kempt to Murray, 20 May 1830, above n 48, 95–97.

52 *Ibid.*

watchful eye of Indian department agents.[53] Gradually the system of reserves and band governments was given statutory recognition, and in 1876 these statutes were consolidated in the Indian Act.

Assimilation proved a difficult objective to achieve. Officials resorted to increasingly aggressive measures to 'civilise' Indians, the most intrusive being the Indian residential school system. The objective of 'weaning' Indians 'from the habits and feelings of their ancestors', it was concluded, required removing children 'from the injurious influence of their homes'.[54] From the late-19th century until the latter half of the 20th century, thousands of aboriginal children were separated from their families and sent to church-operated residential schools where conditions were often appalling, native languages and cultures were suppressed, and many students were subjected to physical and sexual abuse.[55] The policy helped to create serious social problems within aboriginal communities, including high rates of poverty, substance abuse and disease, but it did not result in assimilation.

In the end, it must be acknowledged, as the Royal Commission on Aboriginal Peoples did in its 1996 report, that the Indian Act was, and remains, a 'paradox': designed as a tool of assimilation, its ultimate effect was to provide space within which aboriginal identities survived.[56] Of course, the Act's rationale and much of its detail became increasingly difficult to justify in light of the discourse of tolerance and human rights that emerged globally after World War II. Some of the more oppressive provisions, such as criminalisation of the potlatch ceremony, were repealed, and Indians were finally granted the right to vote in federal elections in 1960; but the Indian Act remained, and remains, largely unchanged from its original form. The 1969 decision of the Supreme Court of Canada in *R v Drybones*, which held Indian Act provisions making it an offence for Indians to be intoxicated off reserve as contrary to the right to 'equality before the law' in the Canadian Bill of Rights 1960, was just one vivid illustration of the conflict between Canada's colonial laws and its commitment to human rights.[57] Still, governments did not know how to square rights to equality with respect for indigenous difference. In the same year, the federal government released a White Paper on Indian policy in which it denounced the objective of assimilation, insisting that Indians in Canada were 'entitled to an equality which preserves and enriches Indian identity and distinction'.[58]

[53] See, eg, MD Walters, '"According to the Old Customs of Our Nation": Aboriginal Self-Government on the Credit River Mississauga Reserve, 1826–1847' (1999) 30 *Ottawa Law Review* 1; MD Walters, 'The Extension of Colonial Criminal Jurisdiction over the Aboriginal Peoples of Upper Canada: Reconsidering the *Shawanakiskie* Case (1822–26)' (1996) 46 *University of Toronto Law Journal* 273.

[54] 'Report on the Affairs of the Indians in Canada, Laid Before the Legislative Assembly, 20th March, 1845', Sec III, 3, 4, *Journals of the Legislative Assembly of Canada* (1847) appendix T.

[55] JS Milloy, *A National Crime: The Canadian Government and the Residential School System, 1879 to 1986* (University of Manitoba Press, 1999).

[56] *Report of the Royal Commission on Aboriginal Peoples*, vol I: *Looking Forward, Looking Back* (Canada Communication Group, 1996) 258–59.

[57] *R v Drybones* [1970] SCR 282.

[58] Canada, *Statement of the Government of Canada on Indian Policy* (Presented to the First Session of the Twenty-eighth Parliament by the Honourable Jean Chrétien, Minister of Indian Affairs and Northern Development, 1969).

But the government assumed that honouring equality meant repealing the Indian Act, and, indeed, abolishing 'the separate legal status' of aboriginal peoples entirely, including ending recognition of their historic treaty rights.[59] Aboriginal leaders were outraged. The plan was, wrote Harold Cardinal, 'a thinly disguised programme of extermination through assimilation'.[60]

Over time, a more nuanced conception of equality would emerge in Canada, one capable of embracing legal as well as cultural pluralism. The civilisation and assimilation policy has now been firmly repudiated and steps have been taken to address the painful legacy of the residential school system, including financial compensation to former students, the creation of a Truth and Reconciliation Commission to further the healing process, and a formal apology by the Prime Minister on behalf of the government of Canada.[61] But while its original purpose has been gutted, the legislative hulk of the Indian Act remains. First Nations continue to oppose its repeal until they agree to acceptable alternative arrangements for their territories and governments. In the early 1980s, aboriginal organisations lobbied for a constitutional commitment by federal and provincial governments to make further amendments that would define the constitutional expression of 'aboriginal rights' as including broad rights to self-government, and they opposed the wording of section 35 of the Constitution Act 1982 because that commitment was not made.[62] A decade later, federal and provincial governments did agree to entrench in the constitution 'the inherent right of [aboriginal] self-government within Canada', but the proposal, along with a host of unrelated proposals, was defeated in a national referendum.[63] Work towards establishing aboriginal self-government has since focused on treaty-making rather than constitution-writing. In 1995, the federal government conceded that the 'inherent right of aboriginal self-government' is already an implicit part of the aboriginal rights protected by section 35 of the Constitution Act 1982, and it set forth a policy for negotiating the terms of that right through modern treaties.[64] As the Royal Commission on Aboriginal Peoples would conclude in 1996, only by pursuing 'the goal of equal, co-existing, and self-governing peoples' would Canada 'preserve and enhance the values of liberal

[59] *Ibid.*

[60] H Cardinal, *The Unjust Society: The Tragedy of Canada's Indians* (MG Hurtig, 1969) 1.

[61] *Gathering Strength—Canada's Aboriginal Action Plan* (7 January 1998), including 'Statement of Reconciliation'. The Indian Residential Schools Settlement Agreement, signed on 8 May 2006 by the federal government, aboriginal organisations, and churches, provides for financial compensation and the establishment of a Truth and Reconciliation Commission. On 11 June 2008, the Prime Minister of Canada made a formal apology in the House of Commons to aboriginal peoples for the residential school policy.

[62] D Sanders, 'The Indian Lobby' in K Banting and R Simeon (eds), *And No One Cheered: Federalism, Democracy and the Constitution Act* (Methuen, 1983) 301–32.

[63] Charlottetown Accord, Draft Legal Text, 9 October 1992, s 35.1(1). See ME Turpel, 'The Charlottetown Discord and Aboriginal Peoples' Struggle for Fundamental Political Change' in K McRoberts and P Monahan (eds), *The Charlottetown Accord, The Referendum, and the Future of Canada* (University of Toronto Press, 1993) 117–51.

[64] Department of Indian Affairs and Northern Development, *Federal Policy Guide, Aboriginal Self-Government: The Government of Canada's Approach to Implementation of the Inherent Right and the Negotiation of Aboriginal Self-Government* (Public Works and Government Services, 1995).

democracy in a manner appropriate to a multinational society'.[65] An increasing number of First Nations are now negotiating self-government agreements to escape the confines of the Indian Act, though progress towards this end has been very slow.

It is important to note that not all aboriginal peoples fall within the Indian Act regime. Long ignored by federal and provincial governments, so-called 'non-status' aboriginal communities—bands not registered under the Indian Act—have, in recent years, begun to press for the recognition of their aboriginal rights to land and self-government.[66] Métis peoples—the descendants of fur traders and indigenous peoples who developed their own sense of national identity—have also occupied an ambiguous legal status. Despite 'rebellions' in 1869 and 1885 during which provisional Métis governments were established on the prairies, the Canadian government historically refused to acknowledge Métis peoples as national groups or as bands under the Indian Act, and it generally dealt with Métis land claims by issuing 'scrip', or certificates for individual land allotments, rather than by treaty.[67] Only recently have Métis rights been recognized by the courts and by treaty.[68] Finally, the Inuit peoples of Canada's Arctic have occupied a distinct status. Although the Supreme Court of Canada ruled in 1939 that 'Indians' in section 91(24) of the Constitution Act 1867 means 'aborigines' and therefore includes 'Eskimos' or Inuit, and hence matters relating to the Inuit fall within the federal Parliament's exclusive legislative authority, the Inuit were not subjected to the terms of the federal Indian Act.[69] Inuit rights to land and self-government have only recently been acknowledged judicially and through land-claim settlements.[70] As a result of these settlements, for example, a new territory, Nunavut, was created in 1999 (where Inuit are a majority), and an agreement to establish a regional Inuit government for Nunavik within the province of Quebec was reached in 2007.[71]

These land-claim settlements carry forward the long tradition of treaty-making in Canada described in I. above. The nature of the treaty relationship has evolved considerably over time. The peace and friendship, or covenant chain, treaties of the sort negotiated at Niagara in 1764 were followed in the 19th and early 20th centuries by a series of land-surrender treaties.[72] The Royal Proclamation of 1763 affirmed that lands needed for settlement were to be acquired by the Crown from

[65] *Report of the Royal Commission*, above n 56, 679, 681.

[66] Eg, *Lovelace v Ontario* [2000] 1 SCR 950.

[67] See in general J Weinstein, *Quiet Revolution West: The Rebirth of Métis Nationalism* (Fifth House, 2007).

[68] Eg, *R v Powley* [2003] 2 SCR 207 and Sahtu Dene and Métis Land Claim Settlement Act, SC 1994, c 27.

[69] *Re Eskimos (sub nom Re Term 'Indians')* [1939] 2 DLR 417 (SCC), 430.

[70] *Hamlet of Baker Lake v Minister of Indian Affairs and Northern Development* (1979), 107 DLR (3d) 513 (FCTD).

[71] Land-claim settlements with Inuit include: Western Arctic (Inuvialuit) Claims Settlement Act, SC 1984, c 24; Nunavut Land Claims Agreement Act, SC 1993, c 29; Labrador Inuit Land Claims Agreement Act, SC 2005, c 27. See also, The Agreement in Principle Concerning the Amalgamation of Certain Public Institutions and Creation of the Nunavik Regional Government, signed by Makivik Corporation, Canada and Quebec, 5 December 2007.

[72] Canada, *Indian Treaties and Surrenders*, vols I and II (Brown Chamberlin, 1891); vol III (CH Parmelee, 1912).

Indian nations in public meetings held for that purpose. But these rules were not followed everywhere. The Crown made a series of land-surrender treaties—the so-called 'numbered' treaties—with indigenous nations from Ontario to the Rocky Mountains.[73] But land-surrender treaties were not generally made in the far north, Quebec, the Atlantic provinces, or British Columbia.

With the signing of the Williams Treaty in Ontario in 1923, treaty-making came to a temporary halt. It would not start again until 1973, when the modern land-claims settlement process began. Since then, aboriginal claims to lands, resources and self-government have been addressed by the federal government through two policies. Negotiations to resolve claims that concern historic treaties are governed by a *specific claims* policy. In 25 years, 282 specific claims have been resolved, with an average award of $6.5 million; 800 claims are still outstanding.[74] Negotiations to resolve claims where no historic treaties were made are governed by a *comprehensive* claims process.[75] So far 20 comprehensive land-claim agreements have been signed, mostly in the far north.[76] These agreements typically recognise aboriginal ownership of designated tracts of land, and provide for financial compensation, mechanisms for co-managing natural resources, and, more recently, powers of self-government.[77] Under the 1998 Nisga'a Treaty, for example, the Nisga'a Nation in British Columbia received $190 million in compensation, recognition of ownership rights in 1,900 square kilometres of land, and self-government powers in relation to such things as land and resource use, culture and language, education, health services, child and family services, and adoption.[78] By virtue of section 35(3) of the Constitution Act 1982 new land-claims agreements, including self-government provisions, are constitutionally protected as treaty rights. At present, 12 comprehensive claims are being negotiated.[79] This number does not include claims in British Columbia, where since 1995 negotiations have taken place under the auspices of the British Columbia Treaty Commission.[80] So far, two comprehensive land and self-government treaties have been signed and ratified under that process.[81] There are presently 58 First Nations involved in 48 sets of negotiations in British Columbia.[82]

[73] See, eg, A Morris, *The Treaties of Canada with the Indians of Manitoba and the North-West Territories* (Belfords, Clarke and Co, 1880); R Fumoleau, *As Long as This Land Shall Last: A History of Treaty 8 and Treaty 11, 1870–1939* (McClelland and Stewart, 1973); R Price (ed), *The Spirit of the Alberta Indian Treaties* (Pica Pica Press, 1987).

[74] Indian and Northern Affairs Canada (INAC), *Specific Claims: Justice at Last* (INAC, 2007) 3.

[75] INAC, *Comprehensive Claims Policy and Status of Claims* (Public Works and Governments Services, 2003).

[76] Comprehensive Claims Branch, Indian Affairs and Northern Development, *General Briefing Note on the Comprehensive Land Claims Policy of Canada and the Status of Claims* (March, 2007).

[77] JE Dalton, 'Aboriginal Title and Self-Government in Canada: What is the True Scope of Comprehensive Land Claims Agreements?' (2006) 22 *Windsor Review of Legal and Social Issues* 29.

[78] Nisga'a Final Agreement, signed 4 August 1998.

[79] *General Briefing Note,* above n 76, 14–31.

[80] See in general T Penikett, *Reconciliation: First Nations Treaty Making in British Columbia* (Douglas and McIntyre, 2006).

[81] Tsawwassen First Nation Final Agreement, signed 8 December 2006; Maa-nulth First Nations Final Agreement, signed 9 December 2006.

[82] British Columbia Treaty Commission (BCTC), *Treaty Commission Annual Report 2007* (BCTC, 2007) 4.

Even where land-claims and self-government agreements have been reached, aboriginal peoples in Canada remain citizens with rights and responsibilities under Canadian law. And so, for example, the federal government has insisted that the Criminal Code of Canada as administered by regular Canadian courts (directly or at least on appeal) continues to govern aboriginal peoples. The complex social problems within many aboriginal communities that are the legacy of Canada's colonial past have been manifested, in part, by disproportionately high rates of criminal conviction and incarceration of aboriginal peoples. To address this problem, the Criminal Code was amended in 1996 to require that sentencing judges consider alternatives to incarceration for all offenders, 'with particular attention to the circumstances of aboriginal offenders'.[83] The point of this direction, the Supreme Court of Canada ruled in 1999, is to allow aboriginal 'customs and traditions' on criminal justice, in particular 'innovative sentencing practices, such as healing and sentencing circles' and other 'community-based' responses to crime, to guide judges in the exercise of their sentencing powers.[84]

D. Judicial Narratives on Indigenous Rights in Canada

1. Overview

To summarise, then, a process of political reconciliation between indigenous and non-indigenous peoples in Canada is unfolding that embraces specific and comprehensive claims to land, natural resources and self-government. At bargaining tables across the country, the terms of national coexistence are being negotiated through intersocietal dialogue.

But what does *law* have to do with this process? On one level, reconciliation is a matter of political power: political actors take positions on behalf of their constituencies and adjust those positions to achieve accommodation only when political conditions demand it. Because political power generally favours majoritarian interests, however, indigenous peoples occupy a disadvantaged position within this process. Federal and provincial governments participate in settlement negotiations only grudgingly, and aboriginal frustration over lack of progress has often led to direct action in the form of demonstrations, occupations, protests, and blockades. Sadly, these acts of confrontation have sometimes resulted in violence, injuries and, in two instances, loss of life. In his report into the fatal shooting by police of native protester Dudley George at Ipperwash, Justice Sidney Linden concluded that the land-claims process in Canada is 'largely ineffective, painfully slow, and unfair' and the frequency of aboriginal protests and blockades will likely

[83] *Criminal Code*, RSC 1985, c C–46, s 718.2(e).
[84] *R v Gladue* [1999] 1 SCR 688, paras 73–74.

increase in the future because of 'our collective and continuing inability' to address aboriginal claims in a timely and just way.[85]

On another level, reconciliation is about principle not power. To view the process solely in terms of political manoeuvring is to ensure its failure. The reality is that political positions are expressed by native and non-native actors alike, whether at bargaining tables or across barricades, within the context of a larger discourse about political and constitutional morality. It is possible, for example, for someone like Bob Lovelace, jailed for his part in a native protest against uranium exploration within traditional Algonquin territories, to say (as he did at his sentencing hearing) that courts are often 'used to oppress indigenous people' and that participation in court proceedings is often 'a waste of time', while at the same time defending, in eloquent terms, a vision of the 'rule of law' based on 'respect [for] Canadian law as well as Algonquin law', and insisting that conflict 'can be resolved . . . by all parties attorning to the law'.[86] Indigenous and non-indigenous people may disagree about what the law is, or what the rule of law implies, but there appears to be a shared commitment to the idea that legality disciplines, or should discipline, power.

But if there is a legal narrative that informs the political narrative on indigenous rights in Canada, whose 'narrative' is it? How do we identify it? Is it simply a matter of reading the case reports to see what judges say? If the law of indigenous rights in Canada really is an intersocietal interpretive process, then looking to the statements of judges, who are overwhelmingly *non*-aboriginal, in an effort to understand that law may seem counterintuitive. Still, the courtroom today is one place—perhaps the most important one—where power must be justified according to principle. It is here where reasoned arguments about indigenous rights are made, and it is here where a distinctively legal narrative on these rights is unfolding.

Since 1982, the judicial narrative on indigenous rights in Canada has focused upon the meaning of 'existing aboriginal and treaty rights' in section 35 of the Constitution Act 1982.[87] The narrative is, the judges say, a story about reconciliation: section 35 is to be understood in light of the general objective of reconciling the pre-existence of indigenous societies in Canada with the reality of Crown sovereignty. The story builds upon ideas and perspectives drawn from both indigenous and non-indigenous legal traditions. It is, according to the courts, an intersocietal legal narrative. In terms of substantive content, the courts identify three principal strands of rights: aboriginal title to land, non-title aboriginal rights,

[85] *Report of the Ipperwash Inquiry*, Sidney B Linden, Commissioner, 30 May 2007, vol 2: *Policy Analysis*, 77, 15.

[86] *Frontenac Ventures Co v Ardoch Algonquin First Nation et al*, Ontario Superior Court of Justice, File 395/07, Transcript of Proceedings at Contempt Motion, 12 February 2008, Kingston, Ontario, vol II, 116, 108, 120, 121.

[87] See in general P Macklem, *Indigenous Difference and the Constitution of Canada* (University of Toronto, 2001); J Borrows, *Recovering Canada: The Resurgence of Indigenous Law* (University of Toronto Press, 2002); K McNeil, *Emerging Justice?: Essays on Indigenous Rights in Canada and Australia* (University of Saskatchewan Native Law Centre, 2001); B Slattery, 'Making Sense of Aboriginal and Treaty Rights' (2000) 79 *Canadian Bar Review* 196.

and treaty rights. Aboriginal title to land, we are told, exists in relation to those lands that indigenous nations held exclusively (either *de facto* or *de jure* according to their own legal traditions) at the time when the Crown asserted sovereignty, and where it continues to exist today it represents a *sui generis* communal property right that, although inalienable except to the Crown, permits title-holders to use the land for any purpose that does not destroy their cultural attachment to it.[88] Aboriginal title is distinguished from non-title aboriginal rights.[89] Aboriginal rights in this narrower sense are, according to the judges, specific practices, customs or traditions that may be traced back to practices, customs or traditions that were integral to distinctive aboriginal cultures existing prior to contact with Europeans—such as, for example, non-exclusive rights of hunting or fishing.[90] Aboriginal title and non-title aboriginal rights, together with treaty rights, are woven together to provide a constitutional doctrine of aboriginal rights. As constitutional rights, they are protected from governmental and legislative interference. However, judges have ruled that legislative limits on these rights are permissible if legislation pursues an important public interest in a proportionate way and the Crown abides by the fiduciary or trust-like duty that it owes to aboriginal peoples (for example, by consulting them about the manner and extent of proposed limitations on their rights).[91] The fiduciary duty is an aspect of a more general 'honour of the Crown' interpretive principle that permeates the law in this area, informing treaty interpretation[92] and mandating government consultation with aboriginal nations about land and resource use even before aboriginal claims have been settled or judicially determined.[93]

This is, of course, only a superficial overview of the judicial narrative on indigenous rights in Canada. It is beyond the scope of this essay to consider the law in detail. However, by focusing upon four related themes that characterise this narrative—namely, the role of the courts in identifying indigenous rights, the contested relationship between law, morality and policy in this area, the challenge of translating indigenous conceptions of territory into non-indigenous law, and the question of how indigenous rights relate to indigenous cultures—we may gain a better sense of the shape of indigenous rights law in Canada.

[88] *Delgamuukw v British Columbia* [1997] 3 SCR 1010.

[89] K McNeil, 'Aboriginal Title and Aboriginal Rights: What's the Connection?' (1997) 36 *Alberta Law Review* 759.

[90] *R v Van der Peet* [1996] 2 SCR 507. For critical commentary see RL Barsh and J (Sákéj) Youngblood Henderson, 'The Supreme Court's *Van der Peet* Trilogy: Naïve Imperialism and Ropes of Sand' (1997) 42 *McGill Law Journal* 993; Borrows, above n 87, 56–76; MD Walters, 'The "Golden Thread" of Continuity: Aboriginal Customs at Common Law and under the Constitution Act, 1982' (1999) 44 *McGill Law Journal* 711.

[91] *R v Sparrow* [1990] 1 SCR 1075; *R v Gladstone* [1996] 2 SCR 723.

[92] *R v Marshall* [1999] 3 SCR 456. See G Christie, 'Justifying Principles of Treaty Interpretation' (2000) 26 *Queen's Law Journal* 143.

[93] *Haida Nation v British Columbia (Minister of Forests)* [2004] 3 SCR 511. For a critical view: G Christie, 'A Colonial Reading of Recent Jurisprudence: *Sparrow, Delgamuukw* and *Haida Nation*' (2005) 23 *Windsor Yearbook of Access to Justice* 18.

2. Canadian Courts and Aboriginal Peoples

In the unfolding story about indigenous rights in Canada, the year 1973 is clearly a turning point. As seen, it was in that year that the 50-year hiatus in treaty-making came to an end. This was a remarkable turn of events given that just a few years before, in 1969, the federal government had stated that aboriginal claims to land were too 'general and undefined' to be recognised.[94]

In a way, the law on aboriginal title to land in Canada *was* relatively general and undefined—or 'shadowy',[95] as one judge put it—at that time. The courts had said little about the topic since the 1880s, when 'Indian title' had been described as a mere personal right to occupy Crown land dependent upon the goodwill of the Crown. The leading case on this point, *St Catherine's Milling and Lumber Co v The Queen*, was essentially a dispute between federal and provincial authorities, and aboriginal peoples were not parties or represented.[96] The emergence of the law on indigenous rights in Canada is partly a story about how indigenous peoples made the transition from being pawns to being participants in the litigation affecting their concerns. The significance of the year 1973 is that the Supreme Court of Canada finally had the opportunity in that year to consider an argument about aboriginal rights presented by an aboriginal nation. In *Calder v British Columbia*, the Nisga'a nation argued that their title to land in British Columbia existed at common law, independent of recognition by treaty, grant or proclamation.[97] Six of seven justices agreed, and although they disagreed on whether that title had been lawfully extinguished in British Columbia, the case prompted the federal government to begin the modern land-claims settlement process.[98]

Why did it take so long for indigenous people to put their claims before the courts? To begin with, for much of the 19th century, officials thought that Indians were 'minors under the guardianship of the Crown' and therefore 'not competent to sustain actions (collectively) in Courts of Law'.[99] This notion was eventually rejected, and by the early 20th century courts were entertaining occasional suits by chiefs on behalf of their communities to enforce rights under treaty or grant.[100] However, such lawsuits were not frequent in the first half of the 20th century, for several reasons. First, the Crown was immune from lawsuits unless it agreed to be

[94] Canada, above n 58.

[95] *Province of Ontario v Dominion of Canada* (1909), 42 SCR 1, per Idington J, 107.

[96] *Regina v The St Catharines Milling and Lumber Company* (1885), 10 OR 196 (Ch Div), aff'd (1886), 13 OAR 148 (CA), aff'd *sub nom St Catharines Milling and Lumber Co v The Queen* (1886), 13 SCR 577, aff'd *sub nom St Catherine's Milling and Lumber Co v The Queen* (1889), 14 App Cas 46 (JCPC).

[97] *Calder v Attorney General of British Columbia* [1973] SCR 313.

[98] See, in general, H Foster, H Raven and J Webber (eds), *Let Right Be Done: Aboriginal Title, the* Calder *Case, and the Future of Indigenous Rights* (UBC Press, 2007).

[99] S Chesley, Indian Dept Agent, to LH Lafontaine, Att Gen, 28 March 1843, National Archives of Canada, RG 10 vol 7: 3353–4.

[100] Eg, *Henry et al v The King* (1905), 9 Ex CR 417 (Exch Ct Can); *Corinthe et al v Seminary of St Sulpice* (1912), 5 DLR 263 (JCPC).

sued. For some 20 years, between 1908 and 1928, the Nisga'a petitioned and lobbied to have their land claim judicially determined, but the provincial, federal and imperial governments refused to co-operate.[101] Second, efforts to litigate aboriginal title were frustrated by Indian Act provisions in force between 1927 and 1951 making it unlawful to raise money to pursue Indian land claims.[102] Until the second half of the 20th century, then, access to the courts was effectively denied to aboriginal peoples who wanted to assert title to their traditional territories.

But even had the courtroom doors been open, at least some aboriginal communities would have refused to enter. Not all aboriginal leaders thought it was appropriate to recognise the jurisdiction of Canadian courts over their claims. Indeed, colonial officials initially shared these concerns. For example, William Dummer Powell, a justice of the Upper Canada King's Bench, concluded that the Crown's relationship with the Six Nations Iroquois, who occupied lands on the Grand River located in the heart of Upper Canada (Ontario), was 'a Compact of one nation with another, to be governed by general rules and not by the provisions of the common Law of England', and therefore 'a Council, a Treaty, a [wampum] Belt' was sufficient to define their land rights; if they were granted a fee simple estate in their lands (as some of them wanted), their rights would be 'subjected to the cognizance of the Kings Courts', and surely, he concluded, the government 'cannot wish to constrain them or to introduce our Laws among them as long as they continue a people apart'.[103] It was, in other words, inconsistent with the nation-to-nation relationship between Crown and Indians to suggest that one nation submit to the courts and laws of the other nation. It is for this reason that the Six Nations later pressed their claims before international bodies, including the League of Nations in 1924.[104]

Justice Powell's concern was not just about the jurisdiction of domestic courts. It was also about choice of laws. He assumed that Canadian courts would apply English law rather than the 'general rules' that defined the nation-to-nation relationship between Crown and Indians, and this was one reason for denying judicial jurisdiction. He seemed not to have considered the possibility that judges might take a broad view of the common law and incorporate elements of aboriginal custom into the law that they applied in order to establish a set of general legal principles appropriate to the unique relationship involved. This attitude was put bluntly by Sir John Beverley Robinson CJ in 1852: judges 'cannot recognize any peculiar law of real property applying to the Indians—the common law is not part savage and part civilized'.[105] As late as 1991 we find the trial judge in the leading aboriginal title case in Canada, *Delgamuukw v British Columbia*, insisting that

[101] H Foster, 'We Are Not O'Meara's Children: Law, Lawyers, and the First Campaign for Aboriginal Title in British Columbia, 1908–28' in Foster, Raven and Webber, above n 98, 61–84.

[102] *Indian Act* RSC 1927, c 98, s 149A.

[103] WD Powell to P Russell, 3 January 1797, in EA Cruikshank and AF Hunter (eds), *The Correspondence of the Honourable Peter Russell* (Ontario Historical Society, 1932–36) vol I, 120–123.

[104] 'Appeal of the Six Nations to the League' (June 1924) 6 *League of Nations Official Journal* 829.

[105] *Doe dem Sheldon v Ramsay et al* (1852), 9 UCQB 105 (UCQB) 123.

although the aboriginal plaintiffs in that case considered 'aboriginal laws' relevant, he was bound to apply what they called 'the white man's law'.[106]

We know that the early treaty relationship between Crown and Indians did involve the integration of legal traditions. The council fire was a place where diverse societies built relationships through synthesising diverse customs and legal values. Perhaps the most significant development in modern aboriginal rights law in Canada, then, is the rejection by judges of the idea that aboriginal rights are defined by *non*-aboriginal law and the acceptance of an idea of intercultural legal synthesis. The doctrine of aboriginal rights, the Supreme Court of Canada ruled in the 1996 case of *R v Van der Peet*, is not aboriginal or non-aboriginal in essence, but rather it an 'intersocietal law' (borrowing Brian Slattery's phrase) that somehow draws upon and reconciles indigenous and non-indigenous legal traditions.[107] Gone are the references to 'white man's law': in overturning the trial judgment in *Delgamuukw* in 1997, Chief Justice Antonio Lamer, writing for a majority of the Supreme Court of Canada, asserted that aboriginal title to land arises from the 'relationship between common law and pre-existing systems of aboriginal law',[108] and therefore trial judges must give due weight to oral history evidence concerning aboriginal cultures and legal traditions relating to the lands and territories claimed.[109]

The articulation by (non-aboriginal) judges of an intersocietal law of indigenous rights is ambitious and controversial. It has been said that it is 'almost oxymoronic to talk of non-Aboriginal conceptions of Aboriginal justice'.[110] Given cultural differences, it will be no easy task for judges to integrate indigenous legal traditions into their understanding of the law. Still, as Professor Borrows writes, if we are to take judges seriously in their pledge to articulate an intersocietal law relating to aboriginal rights—and he thinks we should—then people of all cultures must be encouraged to engage in an inter-cultural dialogue about what indigenous laws are and what they mean for Canadian law today.[111]

Aside from challenges associated with intercultural jurisprudential fit, monumental logistical problems confront the judge charged with adjudicating a comprehensive land claim. The *Tsilhqot'in* case is illustrative. The Tsilhqot'in nation began legal proceedings in 1989 to secure title to their traditional territory in British Columbia. The trial took 339 days between 2002 and 2007 at which extensive ethnographical and oral history evidence, the sort of evidence needed if an intersocietal legal approach is to be taken, was admitted. In the end, however, the trial judge held that problems in the way the case was pleaded prevented him from

106 *Delgamuukw v British Columbia* (1991), 79 DLR (4th) 185 (BCSC), per McEachern CJBC 201.

107 *Van der Peet*, above n 2, para 42 (quoting B Slattery, 'The Legal Basis of Aboriginal Title' in F Cassidy (ed), *Aboriginal Title in British Columbia: Delgamuukw v The Queen* (Oolichan Books, 1992) 120–1).

108 *Delgamuukw*, above n 88, para 114.

109 *Ibid*, paras 114, 92–108.

110 T Palys and W Victor, '"Getting to a Better Place": Qwi:qwelstóm, the Stó:lō, and Self-Determination' in Law Commission of Canada, *Indigenous Legal Traditions* (UBC Press, 2007) 14.

111 Borrows, above n 87, 26.

making a binding determination on aboriginal title.[112] In an 'ideal world', DH Vickers J wrote in his judgment, the process of reconciliation would take place 'outside the adversarial milieu of a courtroom', for judges are 'ill equipped to effect a reconciliation of competing interests' that are best left to 'treaty negotiation'.[113] These sentiments echo statements from the highest judicial levels that 'the treaty process' and 'negotiation' represent the 'ultimate route to achieving reconciliation between aboriginal societies and the Crown'.[114]

This is no doubt true. But it is also true that the treaty process in Canada today exists only because of judicial rulings on aboriginal rights.

3. Law, Morality and Policy

'We say that there is no Indian title at law or in equity. The claim of the Indians is simply moral and no more'.[115] These were the words of the Attorney General (and Premier) for Ontario, Oliver Mowat, who personally argued Ontario's case in the *St Catherine's Milling* litigation of the 1880s.[116] The trial judge, Chancellor John Alexander Boyd, agreed: the Crown made treaties with Indians, but (citing a 1675 legal opinion) only for reasons of 'prudence and Christian charity'.[117] At the Supreme Court of Canada, Sir Henri-Elzear Taschereau J also agreed: the 'general policy' of treaty-making was based upon 'motives of humanity and benevolence', not law; in the performance of its 'sacred political obligation' to deal justly with Indian interests 'the state must be free from judicial control'.[118]

Legal positivists tell us that law and morality do not always connect, and maybe they are right; but a flourishing legal order cannot permit deep fissures between the two to persist indefinitely. Indeed, the tendency within the common law towards coherence and equality usually serves to close any distance that may develop between particular legal rules and the principles of political morality that animate the law generally. The emergence of a distinctively *legal* discourse on indigenous rights in Canada is essentially this sort of correction. Officials acknowledged from an early time that it was right and prudent—or, in the words of the Royal Proclamation of 1763, 'just and reasonable, and essential to our Interest, and the Security of our Colonies'—to acknowledge aboriginal rights. But a virulent strain of legal positivism seems to have infected judges for a long time, and morality and custom relating to aboriginal rights were thought to have no legal dimension. Once officials concluded that Indians were subjects of the Crown

[112] *Tsilhqot'in Nation v British Columbia* [2007] BCJ No 2465 (BCSC).
[113] *Ibid*, para 1357.
[114] *Van der Peet* above n 2, per McLachlin J, para 313 and *British Columbia (Minister of Forests) v Okanagan Indian Band* [2003] 3 SCR 371, per LeBel J, para 47.
[115] *St Catharines Milling*, above n 96, 10 OR 199.
[116] SL Harring, *White Man's Law: Native People in Nineteenth Century Canadian Jurisprudence* (University of Toronto Press, 1998) 132.
[117] *St Catharines Milling*, above n 96, 10 OR 206–07.
[118] *Ibid*, 13 SCR 648–649.

(which they had done by the mid-19th century), and therefore protected from any acts of war or extra-legal aggression by the state,[119] the idea that their rights might be left wholly to the discretion of the Crown seems, now at least, like a troubling failure of the rule of law. Furthermore, the judges' claim that they were just upholding law in this respect rather than policy or morality is unconvincing. After stating that 'sentimental and philanthropic considerations' must not interfere with 'legal and constitutional principles', Taschereau J let slip the real basis for his reasoning: if judges were to recognise Indian title 'all progress of civilization and development in this country' would be 'at the mercy of the Indian race'.[120] The reason for refusing to see the Crown's treaty-making policy as legally mandated was not some objective rule of law after all, but just another policy objective, namely, the goal of facilitating the colonial settlement of the country.

It was not impossible for judges in the 19th century to contemplate a different relationship between law, policy and morality. In the famous cases on Indian title and self-government from the United States, Chief Justice John Marshall examined Crown-Indian practice closely and then concluded that Indians 'were admitted to be the rightful occupants of the soil, with a *legal* as well as just claim to retain possession of it, and to use it according to their own discretion', even though 'their rights to complete sovereignty, as independent nations, were necessarily diminished'.[121] At the Supreme Court of Canada in *St Catherine's Milling*, Justice Samuel Strong, in dissent, considered these cases and agreed that 'colonial policy' relative to Indians had 'ripened into well established rules of law', and thus Indians held their lands 'as their rightful though inalienable property'; indeed, Strong J insisted that even if there had been an 'entire absence of any written legislative act ordaining this rule as an express positive law' (even, that is, had the Royal Proclamation of 1763 never been made), it would still have been right for Canadian judges to hold, as their American counterparts had already held, 'that it nevertheless existed as a rule of the unwritten common law'.[122]

Eventually, it was this argument that won out. In *Calder*, Justice Emmett Hall showed little patience for the old argument that treaties made by the Crown with aboriginal nations were unnecessary in law. He noted that Treaty 8, which was signed in 1899, provided that the relevant aboriginal nations ceded to the Crown '*all their rights, titles and privileges whatsoever, to the lands*'. If this treaty did not relate to pre-existing legal rights, he stated, then it was nothing but a 'gross fraud' perpetrated by the Crown on the aboriginal signatories—and that, he added, cannot be assumed.[123]

[119] Eg, *Sanderson v Heap* (1909) 11 WLR 238 (Manitoba KB) 240 ('Unlike the Indians of the United States, who are aliens, the Indians of Canada are British subjects and entitled to all the rights and privileges of subjects . . .').

[120] *St Catharines Milling*, above n 96, 13 SCR 648–49.

[121] *Johnson v M'Intosh*, 21 US (8 Wheat) 543 (1823) 574 [emphasis added]. See also *Worcester v State of George*, 31 US 515 (1832).

[122] *St Catharines Milling*, above n 96, 612, 613.

[123] *Calder*, above n 97, 202.

Like most groundbreaking common law decisions, *Calder* reflected trends in common law thinking that had already been evolving for some time. Indeed, the case is best seen as part of a gradual awakening of Canadian judges to the reality that aboriginal peoples enjoyed a whole set of rights and interests by virtue of their prior existence as 'organized . . . societies',[124] of which title to land was just an example. A significant moment in this awakening occurred in 1961 when Justice Jack Sissons of the Northwest Territories Territorial Court began enforcing Inuit marriage and adoption customs at common law. His reasoning, that 'Eskimos . . . are clinging to their culture and way of life' and they have 'a right to retain whatever they like of their culture until they are prepared of their own free will to accept a new culture', signalled a new judicial respect for equality between peoples.[125] But Sissons J did not rely upon abstract morality alone. For authority, he turned to the common law itself. He cited old Canadian cases—previously forgotten or ignored—in which 'Indian laws and usages' were acknowledged and enforced by judges, cases that drew upon the learning on Crown-Indian practice that Marshall CJ had developed in the American cases on Indian title and self-government in the 1820s and 1830s.[126]

The redemptive possibilities of Sissons' reasoning were explosive: from behind the texts of treaties, proclamations, statutes and constitutions there suddenly loomed the normative backdrop of a common law doctrine of aboriginal rights—an unwritten law that was older than all of these other sources of law; a law that recognised not just the prior occupation of aboriginal peoples, but their pre-existing legal orders; a law that derived from Crown-Indian usage and thus was, in origin and essence, distinctively *intersocietal*. In a sense, we are still struggling to appreciate what the full implications of this revelation are.

4. Aboriginal Title and Legal Translation

In the 17th century, Locke wrote that the 'wild woods and uncultivated wast[e] of America' represented a state of nature waiting to be appropriated by the first people to reduce it to a form of property through labour.[127] Vattel, writing in the 18th century, insisted that by the 'law of nature' each nation was under a duty to cultivate its lands, and nations who 'avoid labour . . . [and] live only by hunting' in North America could not complain if more industrious nations seized part of their lands; after all, hunters 'rather ranged through than inhabited' them.[128]

[124] *Calder*, above n 97, per Judson J, 156.

[125] *Re Adoption of Katie E7–1807* (1961), 32 DLR (2d) 686 (NWT Terr Ct) 687.

[126] *Re Noah Estate* (1961), 32 DLR (2d) 185 (NWT Terr Ct) 200, quoting *The Queen v Nan-E-Quis-A-Ka* (1889), 1 Terr LR 211, per Wetmore J, 212–13, relying upon the case of *Connolly v Woolrich and Johnson et al* (1867), 17 RJRQ 75 (Que Sup Ct), which, in upholding Cree customary laws on marriage, relied upon the American decisions by Chief Justice John Marshall (see note 121 above).

[127] J Locke, *Essay Concerning the True Original, Extent, and End of Civil-Government* in *Two Treatises of Government* (Black Swan, 1698) para 37.

[128] E Vattel, *The Law of Nations; or Principles of the Law of Nature Applied to the Conduct and Affairs of Nations and Sovereigns* [1756], J Chitty (ed) (S Sweet, 1834) book 1, ch vii, para 81.

These statements reflect a particular attitude about property and labour. But they do more than that. They are evocative expressions of an entire cultural tradition concerning humanity, a tradition with a complete set of associated social, political, legal, religious and philosophical assumptions.

Out this intellectual tradition colonialism emerged, and it was inevitable that Canadian judges would share its attitudes about land and people. Representative judicial statements from *St Catherine's Milling* include the following assertions: 'scattered bands of Ojibbeways, most of them presenting a more than usually degraded Indian type', could not have been legal owners of the vast territory they surrendered to the Crown; it was 'very startling' to suggest that 'a tract of country of over one hundred thousand square miles in extent . . . was owned by the small body of Indians, less than four thousand in number, who were roaming over it at large in their primitive state, and occupying it merely as hunting or fishing grounds'; Indians had 'over-run . . . rather than inhabited' their hunting territories; Indians 'were not in possession of any particular portion of the land' because 'for years and years they might never be on certain portions of it'.[129] To the question—can highly mobile indigenous peoples claim title to large expanses of territory that they use seasonally or cyclically for hunting and fishing?—the answer given by these judges was clearly, no. The implication, of course, was that, as Locke and Vattel had argued, a European state was perfectly justified in taking the lands for itself and exploiting them for its own profit.

It would not be going too far to suggest that the position just summarised is now taken by many people to represent everything that was morally bankrupt about the colonial experience in North America. But this is hardly a recent revelation. As seen, the same judges who said roaming Indians had no title to their hunting lands, proclaimed in no uncertain terms that morality demanded that the Crown make treaties with them before seizing those lands. We have already seen how the emergence of indigenous rights in Canada involved a judicial awakening to the fact that these moral rights were also legal rights. But this leaves open a question that is only now being addressed in Canadian law: just how much hunting territory can an indigenous nation claim? If some requirement of physical possession is imposed that cannot be met by mobile hunting societies, then we are, in effect, back at the morally bankrupt position set forth by the judges in *St Catherine's Milling.*

Again, this issue is not new. On the question of whether hunting societies might claim title to their territories, Strong J in his *St Catherine's Milling* dissent quoted with approval a summary of the United States Supreme Court decision in *Mitchel v United States.*[130] In that case, Baldwin J concluded that 'Indian possession or occupation was considered with reference to their habits and modes of life; their hunting grounds were as much in their actual possession as the cleared fields of the whites; and their rights to its exclusive enjoyment in their own way and for their

[129] *St Catharines Milling*, above n 96, 10 OR 227–28 (Boyd C); 13 OAR 159 (Burton JA); 13 SCR 641 (Henry J).

[130] *St Catharines Milling*, above n 96, 13 SCR 612.

own purposes were as much respected'.[131] Looking at possession or occupation from the perspective of 'their habits and modes of life' precluded the sort of reasoning the other judges followed, for it turned attention away from common law assumptions about possession and towards indigenous perceptions.

If we move forward a century, we find judges still seeking to reconcile indigenous and common law views about land. In *Calder*, the trial judge engaged in close questioning of an expert anthropological witness, seeking to determine if the Nisga'a nation had a conception of property that met the minimum indicia for property at common law. At the Supreme Court of Canada, however, Hall J concluded that this attempt to 'relate' Nisga'a concepts of landholding to the 'conventional common law elements of ownership' ignored the admonition of Viscount Haldane, made in a Privy Council appeal in 1921, that in 'interpreting the native title to land' there is a 'tendency . . . to render that title conceptually in terms which are appropriate only to systems which have grown up under English law', and this tendency 'has to be held in check closely'.[132]

By defining aboriginal title as the product of the 'relationship between common law and pre-existing systems of aboriginal law',[133] Lamer CJC in *Delgamuukw* seemed to have avoided the erroneous tendency identified by Viscount Haldane. But in the 2005 decision of *Bernard and Marshall*, the Supreme Court of Canada seemed to resurrect (using gentler language, of course) the approach to aboriginal title articulated by judges in the late-19th century. Chief Justice Beverley McLachlin, writing for a majority of the Court, said that 'reconcil[ing] the aboriginal and European perspectives' on land ownership requires that judges must identify the aboriginal practice relating to land prior to the assertion of Crown sovereignty and then 'translate' that practice into a 'modern right' by 'seek[ing] a corresponding common law right'.[134] Although this process of legal translation is supposed to represent a 'process of reconciliation', the result is that no aboriginal nation can assert aboriginal title to land unless prior to the Crown's assertion of sovereignty their relationship to land amounted to property as defined by 'common law property rules'[135]—which may mean that seasonal patterns of resource use are not sufficient to found a title claim. The court does say that if a group's seasonal hunting and fishing practices are not sufficient to establish aboriginal title to land, they may claim non-exclusive aboriginal rights to access Crown lands for hunting and fishing. But this seems to take us right back to the way judges thought in the 1880s: aboriginal peoples only have a non-proprietary, non-exclusive right to use their hunting territories, which otherwise belong to the Crown.

[131] *Mitchel v United States*, 34 US 711 (1835), per Baldwin J for the court.
[132] *Amodu Tijani v The Secretary, Southern Nigeria* [1921] 2 AC 399 (PC) 402–3.
[133] *Delgamuukw*, above n 88, para 114.
[134] *R v Marshall; R v Bernard* [2005] 2 SCR 220, para 51.
[135] *Ibid*, paras 52, 54.

5. Aboriginal Rights and Distinctive Cultures

Law is an interpretive enterprise, and its interpretive life is in language. Law's texts initiate narratives of normative meaning, and sometimes they obscure normative meaning. Nowhere is this more obvious than in the interpretation of 'aboriginal rights' in Canada. Section 35 of the Constitution Act 1982 does not protect the rights of aboriginal peoples; it protects the *aboriginal* rights of aboriginal peoples. Chief Justice Antonio Lamer thus concluded that section 35 must be defined in a way that 'captures both the aboriginal and the rights in aboriginal rights'.[136] The result is one of the more puzzling aspects of the judicial view of aboriginal rights in Canada: the limitation of aboriginal rights (of the non-title variety) to specific customs, traditions and practices that were integral to pre-European contact aboriginal cultures—thus apparently ruling out of bounds a general right of aboriginal self-government meaningful for modern aboriginal communities.[137] According to the court, section 35 protects 'the distinctive cultures of aboriginal peoples', with culture defined by reference to 'the pre-contact culture or way of life of an aboriginal society'.[138] Aboriginal rights thus protect 'the means by which an aboriginal society traditionally sustained itself'.[139]

How did this legal narrative about aboriginality emerge? Is it the right narrative? Grammatically, the adjective 'aboriginal' does qualify 'rights' in 'aboriginal rights'. But can 'rights', as opposed to peoples, be 'aboriginal'? When the expression 'aboriginal rights' was used in the late 18th century, it seems that the adjective 'aboriginal' *did* describe the character of the 'right' invoked rather than the people holding the right. 'Purchases [by private parties] from the Indian Natives, as of their aboriginal right', a colonial governor wrote in 1774, 'have never been held to be a legal Title in this Province . . . [for] the King is the Fountain of all real property'.[140] Here aboriginal right is synonymous with another expression occasionally used in the 18th century, 'aboriginal title'.[141] But 'aboriginal' in these expressions, as they were used then, had nothing to do with the character (or culture) of the people holding the right or title. When colonists wished to identify native people in cultural terms they tended to use the word 'Indian', not aborigine or aboriginal.[142] The terms 'aborigine' and 'aboriginal' were taken from the Latin *ab origine*—meaning *from the beginning* or *original*—and they were used literally in

136 *Van der Peet*, above n 2, para 20.

137 *R v Pamajewon* [1996] 2 SCR 821. A more principled conclusion, that a general right of aboriginal self-government exists as an unwritten constitutional principle in Canada, is articulated in *Campbell v British Columbia (Attorney General)* (2000), 189 DLR. (4th) 333 (BCSC). See K McNeil, 'Judicial Approaches to Self-Government since *Calder*: Searching for Doctrinal Coherence' in H Foster, Raven and Webber, above n 98.

138 *R v Sappier; R v Gray* [2006] 2 SCR 686, para 22.

139 *Ibid*, para 37.

140 'Governor William Tryon on the State of the Province of New-York' (1774) in EB O'Callaghan, *Documentary History of the State of New-York* (Weed, Parsons and Co, 1850–51) vol I, 751.

141 *Sims v Irvine*, 3 US (3 Dall) 425 (USSC 1799) ('aboriginal title of the Indian tribes').

142 Eg, Indian Act, SC 1876, s 4 (non-treaty Indian was defined as a person of Indian blood 'or who follows the Indian mode of life').

that sense. So, in relation to land rights, aboriginal right or title implied a right or title that existed from the beginning. A 1775 deed thus referred to the Indian grantors as 'the Cherokee nation, or tribe of Indians, being the aborigines and sole owners by occupancy from the beginning of time of the lands'.[143]

In colonial narratives, then, 'aborigines' or 'aboriginal occupants' were Indians who possessed land from the beginning, and they could be distinguished from Indians who did not. A distinction was thus made in 1764 between the Mohawks at Kahnawake, who 'were invited into Canada' by the French, and the '*aborigines*' of the country.[144] An extreme example of this literal use of 'aboriginal' is found in *Worcester v Georgia*, where Chief Justice Marshall stated that the principle of discovery regulated the competition between Europeans for territory in North America, 'but could not affect the rights of those [Indians] already in possession, either as aboriginal occupants, or as occupants by virtue of a discovery made before the memory of man'.[145] Indians who did not possess land from the beginning, but only from a later date (even if from time immemorial) were not 'aboriginal' occupants. Similarly, the 'Six Nations Indians' who were granted the Grand River tract in Upper Canada in 1784 in compensation for the loss of their territories in New York after the American Revolution were contrasted with 'the aboriginal Indians' from whom the Crown had purchased the tract.[146]

To summarise, then, the historic uses of 'aboriginal' were literally about locating people on land from the beginning, and implied nothing about their cultures. 'Aboriginal' in this sense could be, and was, used to describe the right or title that was thought to derive from original occupancy. But 'aboriginal' was not used to describe other sorts of rights, because there were no other rights that were justified temporally in this way. So, for example, when Justice James Monk in *Connolly v Woolrich* enforced Cree marriage custom in 1867 he did not use the expression 'aboriginal laws'; rather he referred to the 'laws of the Aborigines'.[147] In his view, the Cree were original occupants, but he had no reason to think or to care whether their laws—or their traditions, customs or practices—also dated back to the beginning and were 'aboriginal'. What mattered was the state of their law at the relevant time, which was when the contested marriage took place in 1803.

In the legal discourse on aboriginal rights in Canada today, the concept of aboriginality has moved well beyond the narrow, literal sense it had in the 18th and 19th centuries. Aboriginal title in Canada is now seen as a title derived from occupation and indigenous legal traditions from the beginning of Crown sovereignty, not from the beginning of time. But in relation to non-title aboriginal rights, the theory of pre-contact cultural rights developed by Canadian judges bears some of

[143] Quoted in *Kenny v Clark*, 43 US 76 (USSC 1844) 114.

[144] Thomas Gage, Comm in Chief of British Forces, to Sir William Johnson, Supt Genl Indian Affrs, 6 February 1764, in Sullivan, above n 31, vol IV, 318.

[145] *Worcester*, above n 121, 544.

[146] *Bown v West* (1846), 1 E & A 117 (UC Ex Council) 119; *Little et al v Keating* (1842), 6 UCQB (OS) 265 (UCQB) 268–69.

[147] *Connolly v Woolrich*, above n 126, 85, 87.

the marks of that narrow sense of 'aboriginal' once prevalent, and the paradoxical result is that 'aboriginal rights', at least when read through the interpretive eyes of judges, excludes general rights of self-government that were recognised historically and are now recognised politically through modern treaties.

E. Conclusion

The central themes or problems emerging from the judicial narrative on indigenous rights examined above suggest that judges are struggling to give proper expression to the ambitious ideal of an intersocietal law of aboriginal rights in Canada, and there are both accomplishments to celebrate and mistakes to correct within that narrative as it now stands. One thing that should be clear is that the law that judges are trying to identify and expound is not of their own making. They are merely participants in a process of interpretation that seeks to give shape and texture to an unwritten constitutional law of intercultural relations in Canada. Judges play a critical role in that process, but there are other participants too, and in the end the judicial contribution only serves to inform, not determine, our understanding of the law itself. If present judicial expressions of aboriginal rights exhausted our understanding of those rights, then we would have to say that many of the territorial and self-government rights secured by modern land-claim settlements like the Nisga'a Treaty—rights that would seem to fail to meet the cribbed judicial tests set for aboriginal rights—must be new rights created by the parties to these agreements. But the parties to these agreements do not see the law in that way: the Nisga'a Treaty, for example, purports to define pre-existing aboriginal rights that are 'modified, and continue as modified' under the agreement.[148] In short, the law of indigenous rights must be seen as a 'law' that transcends the positive legal expressions found in judicial decisions, or, indeed, in the positive expressions found in written legal texts generally, including constitutions, statutes, royal proclamations and even treaties. Seeing law in an interpretive rather than a positivist light is, in other words, one precondition for a genuinely intersocietal legal discourse. As an intersocietal law, the law of indigenous rights must lay beyond the control of any single writer or expounder of law. Judicial authority in this area of the law must therefore be tempered by a real sense of interpretive humility.

Judges began to talk openly about the intersocietal character of indigenous rights in 1996. But we are only just beginning to come to grips with the full implications of intercultural legal reconciliation in Canada. What would the Canadian constitution look like, reconceived through an indigenous legal perspective? What would the fundamental unwritten values of Canadian constitutionalism—the values associated with the rule of law, democracy, and human rights—mean if

[148] Nisga'a Final Agreement, Art 24. See in general *Campbell v British Columbia*, above n 137.

an aboriginal legal perspective helped shape their meaning? These are questions of a grand and abstract sort. But the answers, if they are to be convincing, will probably only emerge gradually at law's ground-level, so to speak, as self-government agreements are negotiated, as co-management boards decide on resource development, as elders advise judges in sentencing matters, and as local communities retake control over their own destinies. There is an intersocietal legal dynamic in Canada, paradoxical as it may seem, and it remains an open question whether and how it will live up to the promise that it holds for reconciliation between diverse peoples.

3

The Dyadic Character of US Indian Law

BENJAMIN J RICHARDSON

A. Some Major Issues

The story of US Indian law cannot be told without a clear perspective of the past, for it is immersed in dramatic historical events and complex, long-standing relationships between culturally distinct and sovereign peoples.[1] US Indian law has evolved into a labyrinth of legal doctrines and policies, often changeable, inconsistent, and ambiguous. It has been complicated by the often conflicting policies and rules of judicial, executive, and legislative authorities. Despite the formalities of the rule of law, the treatment of Native Americans has at times gravely tested the morality and constitutionalism of the US system of government.

Like several other jurisdictions canvassed in this book, US Indian law has straddled the contradictory tensions of serving both as an agent of colonisation and, more recently, the framework for policies of Indigenous sovereignty and self-determination. Yet, these dyadic qualities have tended to be much more pronounced in US legal history than in comparable jurisdictions. In exploring the oscillating, dyadic character of US Indian law, this introductory chapter concentrates on the most seminal patterns and issues of Native Americans' encounters with and influences on US Indian law, aiming to provide greater clarity of its motivations, evolution, and impacts. It canvasses issues relating to tribal sovereignty, jurisdiction over tribal reservations, and federal government power and

[1] For introductory readings, see S Banner, *How the Indians Lost Their Land: Law and Power on the Frontier* (Belknap Press of Harvard University, 2005); RN Clinton, CE Goldberg and R Tsosie, *American Indian Law: Native Nations and the Federal System: Cases and Materials* (LexisNexis Matthew Bender, 2007); MB Duthu, *American Indians and the Law* (Viking Penguin, 2008); LG Robertson, *Conquest by Law: How the Discovery of America Dispossessed Indigenous Peoples of their Lands* (Oxford University Press, 2005); DH Getches, CF Wilkinson and RA Williams Jr, *Cases and Materials on Federal Indian Law* (Thomson West, 2005); DA Rosen, *American Indians and State Law: Sovereignty, Race, and Citizenship, 1790–1880* (University of Nebraska Press, 2007); NJ Newton (ed), *Cohen's Handbook of Federal Indian Law* (LexisNexis, 2005); WE Washburn, *Red Man's Land/White Man's Law: The Past and Present Status of the American Indian* (University of Oklahoma Press, 1995); D Wilkins and KT Lomawaima, *Uneven Grounds: American Indian Sovereignty and Federal Law* (University of Oklahoma Press, 2001); RA Williams Jr, *The American Indian in Western Legal Thought: The Discourses of Conquest* (Oxford University Press, 1990).

responsibilities. The chapter does not examine the traditional customary laws and institutions of Native Americans; rather, it examines the legal issues that have shaped their livelihoods since the arrival of Europeans.[2] Distinctions in US law are often made between Native Americans, Native Alaskans, and Native Hawaiians, and this chapter focuses (although not exclusively) on the first group.

As David Getches, one of the leading scholars on US Indian law, has observed, '[t]he remarkable history of American tribes is not that they were victims of unrelenting attempts to change them. But it is truly astounding that they did manage to hold onto some land and that the core of their culture remains intact'.[3] US colonialism was in various ways arguably more violent and severe than other examples considered in this book, with warfare and massacres on a grander scale.[4] Today, however, the pioneering Harvard Project optimistically finds that 'the Indian voice is rising, the population is growing rapidly, economic progress is being made, and the winds of extermination and de-recognition are being weathered'.[5]

Among some specific indicators, the 2000 national census recorded that more than 4 million people, representing about 1.5 per cent of the US population, identified themselves as partly or wholly Native American (including Native Alaskans or Hawaiians).[6] About half live in urban areas, and the remainder mostly on some 310 tribal reservations or other Indian-related areas.[7] In total, Indian-controlled lands presently amount to about 4.5 per cent of all US territory, comprising 40 million acres held by Alaskan Natives and another 56 million acres of tribal lands in the rest of the US.[8] Not all tribes, however, have their own reservations. In 2008, there were at least 562 federally recognised tribes, of which some 230 are village groups in Alaska, and a further 200 tribes are seeking official imprimatur.[9] Despite concerted efforts to dispossess them, some tribes continue to retain substantial tracts of land. The largest reservation, of the Navajo, is nearly 16 million acres, and the large Sioux reservations collectively total some 5 million acres. Many other factors, however, shape the success and quality of life in tribal com-

[2] Certainly, customary law continues to play a role in tribal life, as detailed further in Christine Zuni Cruz's Chapter in this volume. See also MLM Fletcher, 'Rethinking Customary Law in Tribal Jurisprudence' (2007) 13 *Michigan Journal of Race and Law* 57.

[3] DH Getches, 'A Philosophy of Permanence: The Indians' Legacy for the West' (1990) 29(3) *Journal of the West* 54, 57.

[4] J Tebbel and K Jennison, *The American Indian Wars* (Phoenix Press, 2001); J Belich, *The New Zealand Wars* (Penguin, 1988). Although other places certainly experienced some bitter conflicts, such as New Zealand's 'Māori Wars'.

[5] The Harvard Project on American Indian Economic Development, *The State of the Native Nations* (Oxford University Press, 2008) 2.

[6] About 2.5 million people identified themselves as only Native American: US Census Bureau, *Census 2000*, at www.census.gov/main/www/cen2000.html.

[7] Harvard Project, above n 5, 6.

[8] Department of the Interior (DOI), *Lands under the Jurisdiction of the Bureau of Indian Affairs* (DOI, 1996). Many tribal reservations contain within their boundaries lands held by non-Indians, which are not counted in these figures.

[9] See statistics held by the Bureau of Indian Affairs (BIA), at www.doi.gov/bia. See also K Frantz, *Indian Reservations in the United States: Territory, Sovereignty, and Socioeconomic Change* (University of Chicago Press, 1999).

munities apart from land rights, including their degree of self-governance and the cultural paradigms which shape their lives.[10]

In deciphering the legal history of Native Americans, it is worthwhile to begin by sketching some of the distinctive legal issues, and to contrast them to other jurisdictions encountered in this book. Land rights and Indigenous self-governance are vital points of contrast, as explored more fully by Kent McNeil and Shin Imai in their Chapters. While Aboriginal peoples in the British Commonwealth jurisdictions have retained some land in the midst of the colonial onslaught, such as reservations in Canada held under the Indian Act, they have lacked the authority to govern their own affairs in ways that Native American tribes often enjoy.[11] In Australia, New Zealand, and Canada, Indigenous self-governance powers derive primarily from state legislation or treaties. In the US, by contrast, Indian tribes derive their governance powers primarily from their inherent sovereignty.[12] In the British Commonwealth, sovereignty is doctrinally conceptualised as entrenched in the Crown-in-parliament.[13] Tribal sovereignty, however, entitles Native Americans to be ruled by their own laws on their lands. The powers of inherent sovereignty have been recognised by US courts as including the power to determine tribal membership, power over tribal property, and administration of justice.[14] As long as sovereign tribal rights have not been voluntarily ceded by treaties or extinguished by the plenary powers of the US Congress, they ordinarily remain intact. A significant corollary to the principle that tribes retain sovereignty is that, absent congressional authorisation, the states lack authority over tribal lands and affairs.

A second significant attribute of the US experience is that, as in the Canadian legal system, US law recognises a fiduciary relationship between Native tribes and national governments.[15] However, the incidents of the fiduciary relationship are not identical in both systems, and American and Canadian understandings of the fiduciary relationship are hotly contested and constantly evolving.[16] In theory, it applies to both executive and legislative actions. Historically, the judiciary has recognised enforceable fiduciary obligations owed by the federal executive as a

[10] For an interesting study of these factors in relation to Indian gaming, see N Mezey, 'The Distribution of Wealth, Sovereignty, and Culture through Indian Gaming' (1996) 48 *Stanford Law Review* 711.

[11] Yet, tribal self-governance in the US is not without significant limitations, as tribes generally lack jurisdiction over non-Indians and non-Indian lands situated within reservation boundaries, whereas even Canada's much-deficient Indian Act gives Indian bands authority over non-Indians on reservations.

[12] JD Green and S Work, 'Inherent Indian Sovereignty' (1976) 4 *American Indian Law Review* 311.

[13] JD Goldsworthy, *The Sovereignty of Parliament: History and Philosophy* (Oxford University Press, 1999). Also, the Crown itself (executive branch) still retains significant prerogative powers in relation to foreign affairs.

[14] Green and Work, above n 12, 311.

[15] Getches *et al*, above n 1, 5.

[16] See P Manus, 'Indigenous Peoples' Environmental Rights: Evolving Common Law Perspectives in Canada, Australia, and the United States' (2005) 33 *Boston College Environmental Affairs Law Review* 1, for a general discussion on the difficulties of a comparative analysis of the jurisprudence of these common law countries.

source of Indian rights.[17] For example, courts have used the fiduciary duty to award damages for the mismanagement of Indian resources or assets in the custody of federal authorities assigned responsibility to manage them for the benefit of tribes.[18] The ongoing litigation in *Cobell v Kempthorne*,[19] a class action suit concerning mismanagement of trust fund accounts of individual Indians, suggests that the legal thresholds for succeeding in such a suit are high. As in Canadian law, consultation has become pivotal to the federal executive-tribal relationship. With a wide range of statutory,[20] executive,[21] and regulatory[22] procedures currently in place mandating some degree of consultation with Indian tribes, the most legally significant question is no longer whether there is a duty to consult but rather what is the content of that duty.[23]

Concomitantly, the Congressional-Indian relationship involves a fiduciary relationship which has often been characterised as a 'political' or even a 'moral' trust.[24] This trust relationship has typically not been a source of rights for Indians, but rather interpreted to augment the power accorded to Congress by the Constitution's 'Indian Commerce Clause' over tribal affairs.[25] It has underpinned legislation purporting to be in the 'best interests' of a tribe,[26] even if the legislation abrogates a treaty,[27] so long as there is a sufficient expression of congressional intent to do so.[28] The exact degree of clarity required and the evidence that would

[17] See, eg, *Lane, Secretary of the Interior, et al v Pueblo of Santa Rosa*, 249 US 110, 39 S Ct 185 (1919) where the court found no authority for the Secretary of the Interior to dispossess the Pueblo by administrative action. Such action would not be consistent with the special relationship.

[18] Eg, *US v Mitchell*, 463 US 206 (1983).

[19] See www.indiantrust.com.

[20] Many statutes require various degrees of substantive and procedural protections to Indians: eg, Energy Policy Act, Pub L No 102-486, 106 Stat 2776 (1992), s 2602.

[21] See, eg, Executive Order 13175 Consultation and Coordination with Indian Tribal Governments (2000) 65 FR 67249.

[22] See, eg, 25 CFR s 32.2 (1997) ('"Consultation" means a conferring process with Tribes, Alaska Native entities, and Tribal organizations on a periodic and systematic basis in which the Bureau and Department officials listen to and give effect, to the extent they can, to the views of these entities').

[23] See DC Haskew, 'Federal Consultation with Indian Tribes: The Foundation of Enlightened Policy Decisions or Another Badge of Shame?' (2000) 24 *American Indian Law Review* 21. Yet, the extent to which duty to consult is an aspect of the common law fiduciary obligation owed by the executive towards Native American independently from statutory and regulatory obligations remains debated: see *Pyramid Lake Paiute Tribe of Indians v United States Dep't of Navy*, 898 F 2d 1410, 1420 (9th Cir 1990).

[24] See S O'Brien, 'The Government-Government and Trust Relationships: Conflicts and Inconsistencies' (1986) 10(4) *American Indian Culture and Research Journal* 57; R Cross, 'Federal Trust Duty in an Age of Indian Self-Determination: An Epitaph for a Dying Doctrine?' (2003) 39 *Tulsa Law Review* 369.

[25] US Constitution, Art 1, s 8.

[26] See, eg, *United States v Kagama*, 118 US 375, 6 S Ct 1109 (1886) where the Supreme Court upheld application of the Major Crimes Act (making certain crimes committed on Indian land, federal crimes) on the grounds of the special relationship.

[27] *Lone Wolf v Hitchcock*, 187 US 553, 23 S Ct 216 (1903), where the Supreme Court held the trust relationship to be the source of the plenary power to dispose of assets as Congress saw fit. The Court stated that 'Congress possesse[s] a paramount power over the property of the Indians, by reason of its exercise of guardianship over their interests, and that such authority might be implied, even though opposed to the strict letter of a treaty with the Indians' (at 556).

[28] See *United States v Dion*, 476 US 734, 106 S Ct 2216 (1986).

suffice to establish such intention have been the key issues in the jurisprudence on treaty abrogation[29] and the justification of the standard has rested on the interpretation of the 'special relationship'. Despite the apparent inconsistency of this principle with tribal self-determination, some scholars believe that this jurisprudence has actually constitutionalised the authority of Congress to enact legislation to promote tribal self-determination that might not otherwise be within its authority.[30]

Yet, despite recognition of an inherent tribal sovereignty and the special fiduciary relationship, the constitutional protection given to Native Americans' interests is comparatively weaker than in Canada and possibly even New Zealand, but superior to that in Australia. Exercise of federal legislative power in this field stems mainly from the Indian Commerce Clause, which confers Congressional power 'to regulate commerce . . . with the Indian Tribes'. This authority has essentially allowed the federal government to monopolise land transactions with Indians, and to pre-empt the jurisdiction of the states. Unlike in Canada where constitutional protections for Aboriginal rights have been entrenched since 1982, in the US the Congress can unilaterally extinguish Native American rights, and can even abrogate treaty commitments, subject to judicial review, as noted above.

Another salient feature of the US is the absence of any significant Aboriginal land title claims today, as found in Canada and Australia. The US has no sensational equivalent of *Delgamuukw* or *Mabo*, although US courts have certainly recognised that Indian title can exist apart from any formal recognition by treaty or statute.[31] Yet in the notorious 1955 case of *Tee-Hit-Ton Indians v US*,[32] the Supreme Court held that Indian title that has not been formally recognised by the US is not a property right compensable under the American Constitution.[33]

The lack of Aboriginal title litigation in the US is because nearly all Indian land rights are now treaty or statute-based; the last major land claim was settled in the early 1970s through the Alaska Native Claims Settlement Act. The former Indian Claims Commission also considered some claims primarily concerning compensation for the extinguishment of title to Indian lands.[34] Some isolated land claims have since been settled with Congress, such as the Seminole Indian Land Claims Settlement Act of 1987.[35] Presently, most land on tribal reservations is known as tribal trust lands, being held in trust by the US government for the use of a tribe collectively. Native Americans nonetheless may still retain specific rights outside

[29] In *Menominee Tribe v United States*, 391 US 404, 88 S Ct 1705 (1968) the Supreme Court required an 'explicit statement' of the intent to abrogate treaty rights.

[30] SA Tallchief, 'Integrating the Indian Trust Doctrine into the Constitution' (2003) 39 *Tulsa Law Review* 247.

[31] See, eg, *Cramer v US*, 261 US 210 (1923).

[32] 348 US 272 (1955).

[33] The Fifth Amendment of the Constitution provides, inter alia, that private property shall not be taken by government without just compensation.

[34] CL Orlando, 'Aboriginal Title Claims in the Indian Claims Commission: *United States v Dann* and Its Due Process Implications' (1985) 13 *Boston College Environmental Affairs Law Review* 241.

[35] BS Monahan, 'Florida's Seminole Indian Land Claims Agreement: Vehicle for an Innovative Water Rights Compact' (1990) 15 *American Indian Law Review* 341.

of the treaty system that were not extinguished, as confirmed by cases concerning off-reservation tribal fishing rights.[36] Under the 'reserved rights doctrine', US courts have held that tribal hunting and fishing rights can be retained by a tribe even when treaties are silent on such practices.[37]

When considering tribal governance over land and natural resources, we should also note that geography matters. For many Indian reservations, tribal jurisdiction is frustrated by checkerboard land ownership patterns, which are a legacy of the General Allotment Act of 1887 which replaced some tribal lands with individual land tenures.[38] The boundaries of many reservations now encompass land held in freehold by non-Indians, in addition to tribally held land and lands owned in fee by individual tribal members. Apart from being the biggest land grab in US history, this Act set the stage for intense jurisdictional conflicts because of the resulting mosaic of land tenures within reservation boundaries. Another aspect of geography is that many reservations are too small to properly insulate Indian tribes from surrounding environmental problems and inappropriate development pressures.[39]

A final significant theme, as the rest of the Chapter emphasises, is that federal Indian policy has been strongly cyclical.[40] Policy changes have stemmed principally from the tensions between the dyadic forces of separatism and assimilation. These tensions reflect the interplay between governmental strategies and the demands of Native Americans. They also reflect conflicts between different arms of government—the executive, legislature and judiciary have often not acted in unison on Indian policy. The forces of separatism are evident in policies to establish homelands for tribes through the reservation system, and to safeguard tribal sovereignty from the incursions of the state governments. The forces of assimilation have spanned missionary indoctrination, military campaigns to pacify tribes, and policies to privatise tribal lands. The tensions between separatism and assimilation simmer today, evident in the tribal struggles against state governments' usurpations and an often acquiescent Supreme Court.

The rest of the Chapter will highlight these and other themes as it traces the evolution of US Indian law, beginning with the early colonial period.

B. Diplomacy, Trade and Hostilities

The early colonisation of North America drew on a theory, developed by the colonising nations of Europe, that gave to 'discoverers' the right to extend their

[36] FG Cohen, *Treaties on Trial: The Continuing Controversy over Northwest Indian Fishing Rights* (University of Washington Press, 1986).
[37] *Menominee Tribe v US*, 391 US 404 (1968).
[38] C 119, 24 Stat 388.
[39] Harvard Project, above n 5, 95–109.
[40] See generally LS Tyler, *A History of Indian Policy* (University Press of the Pacific, 2001).

dominion and sovereignty over Aboriginal peoples to the exclusion of other international powers.[41] In 1492, Columbus arrived on the shores of the Indigenous-populated Americas and claimed them for the Spanish Crown.[42] Thereafter, the process of acquiring Indian lands and containing the tribes was largely achieved by the European imperialists in the Americas through military pacification and negotiation of treaties with their representatives.[43] These policies were continued by the US after it became politically independent from Britain in the 1770s.

The Spanish and French were actively colonising parts of North America during this time.[44] The French, by the mid-17th century, were perhaps the strongest imperial power in North America, and as a result of the La Salle expedition in the 1680s had established settlements along the Mississippi and the Gulf coast, as well as extended their trading posts and territorial claims from Quebec south of the Great Lakes into the Ohio Valley.[45] Yet, by the 'Louisiana Purchase' of 1803, where the US purportedly bought some 2 million km? of territory from France, its presence in the region was eliminated. The Spanish, who had actually controlled Louisiana from 1762 to 1800, were more active in Central America and the Caribbean.[46] The Laws of Burgos of 1512–13, adopted for the 'Spanish Indies' in the Caribbean, were relatively mild compared to later versions of Spanish colonial rule.[47] Felix Cohen, who characterised much of the Spanish law towards the Indians as remarkably humane, cautions that '[t]his is not to say that Indians were not widely oppressed under Spanish rule but merely to suggest that it was in defiance of, rather than pursuant to, the laws of Spain'.[48] Spain ceded parts of its territories and claims in North America to the US in the 1819 Adams-Onís Treaty.[49]

European relations with Native Americans were often violent from the earliest moments of contact.[50] Skirmishes frequently erupted, and Indians were kidnapped

[41] B Slattery, 'Aboriginal Sovereignty and Imperial Claims: Reconstructing North American History' in F Cassidy (ed), *Aboriginal Self-Determination* (Oolichan Books, 1991) 197; J Muldoon (ed), *The Expansion of Europe: the First Phase* (University of Pennsylvania Press, 1977); RJ Miller, *Native America, Discovered and Conquered: Thomas Jefferson, Lewis and Clark, and Manifest Destiny* (Praeger, 2006).

[42] SH Venne, *Our Elders Understand our Rights: Evolving International Law Regarding Indigenous Peoples* (Theytus Books, 1998).

[43] See WW Abbot, *The Colonial Origins of the United States: 1607–1763* (Wiley, 1975); H Koning, *The Conquest of America: How the Indian Nations Lost their Continent* (Monthly Review Press, 1993).

[44] See C Daniels and MN Kennedy (eds), *Negotiated Empires: Centers and Peripheries in the Americas, 1500–1820* (Routledge, 2002).

[45] WJ Eccles, *France in America* (2nd edn, Godwit, 1990).

[46] See A Pagden, *Spanish Imperialism and the Political Imagination* (Yale University Press, 1990); DJ Weber, *The Spanish Frontier in North America* (Yale University Press, 1992).

[47] LB Simpson (trans and ed), *The Laws of Burgos of 1512–1513: Royal Ordinances for the Good Government and Treatment of the Indians* (John Howell Books, 1960).

[48] F Cohen, 'The Spanish Origin of Indian Rights in the Law of the United States' in LK Cohen (ed), *The Legal Conscience: Selected Papers of Felix S Cohen* (Yale University Press, 1960) 230, 243.

[49] Apart from Florida, this treaty drew the boundary between Spanish and American territory—Spain retained much of its North American possessions, including Texas, the Southwest, California and Mexico, though they all became part of Mexico when that country became independent in 1821.

[50] See DK Richter, *Facing East From Indian Country: A Native History of Early America* (Cambridge University Press, 2001); P Seed, *Ceremonies of Possession in Europe's Conquest of the New World, 1492–1640* (Cambridge University Press, 1995).

and sold into slavery.[51] Major wars also erupted, such as the Poquot War of 1636–37 in present-day New England. The English also brought with them epidemic diseases such as smallpox, which decimated native populations, with somewhere between 50 and 90 per cent of the population dying in infected regions.[52] In some situations, Indian tribes enjoyed peaceful relations with the Pilgrims and other settlers, even occasionally forming alliances to gain an upper hand against rivals.[53] By the end of the 1600s, Indians in the colonies of Virginia and New England had been pacified and the English had expanded their population and control of lands considerably.

Governance of settler-native relations was undertaken in a variety of ways. The first treaty, of several hundred that would eventually be 'negotiated' with Indian tribes, was signed in 1621 for maintaining peace.[54] Many treaties were subsequently bargained or imposed for purposes of trade, diplomacy and, in particular, acquiring tribal lands.[55] Treaty-making continued until 1871, when Congress banned their use, although other types of agreements were continued.[56] The chartered companies also had a role in colonial governance in the early period. For instance, the Massachusetts Bay Company took responsibility for supervising relations between settlers and Indians, with a view to opening up Indian lands for white occupation and to replace tribal life and culture with English customs and Protestant Christianity. The Company instructed settlers to purchase land from local chiefs and punished those who committed misdeeds against the Indians.[57] But Indians usually faced harsher punishment for their wrongs, and from the 1650s separate legal codes for controlling the activities of local Indians began to appear in the colonies.[58]

It would be misleading to imply that Native Americans were hapless and helpless victims of these patterns of European colonisation. Rather, they used trade, diplomacy, and warfare to manage the intrusions.[59] While they sought to avoid European domination, they often welcomed European technology such as guns and household utensils. During the 18th century the fur trade became a crucial means for many tribes to maintain their economic livelihoods. Population losses and reduced hunting grounds persuaded Indians to increase trade with Europeans. Trading relationships also unfortunately brought further unwanted

[51] RL Nichols, *Indians in the United States and Canada: A Comparative History* (University of Nebraska Press, 1998) 61; see also on enslavement: JE Chaplin, 'Enslavement of Indians in Early America: Captivity without the Narrative' in E Mancke and C Shammas (eds), *The Creation of the British Atlantic World* (Johns Hopkins University Press, 2005) 45.

[52] Nichols, *ibid*, 62, 97.

[53] *Ibid*, 66.

[54] The text of the 1621 treaty appears in N Saltonstall, 'A Continuation of the State of New England, 1676' in CH Lincoln (ed), *Narratives of the Indian War 1675–1699* (Barnes and Noble, 1941) 51, 68–9.

[55] See FP Prucha, *American Indian Treaties: The History of a Political Anomaly* (University of California Press, 1994); RA Williams Jr, *Linking Arms Together: American Indian Treaty Visions of Law and Peace, 1600–1800* (Oxford University Press, 1997).

[56] Prucha, above n 55, 17.

[57] Nichols, above n 51, 68.

[58] *Ibid*, 83.

[59] See IK Steele, *Warpaths: Invasions of North America* (Oxford University Press, 1994).

interferences. For example, according to Nichols, 'one tactic of the greedy traders was to extend nearly unlimited credit and, when the Indians could no longer pay their debts, to seize the women and children of a village people and take them [away] to be sold into slavery'.[60]

C. Indians' Retreat and Perseverance: 1770s–1850s

The seeds of the American War of Independence, which began in 1775, sprouted partly from tensions between the 13 colonies and the British Crown over policies to govern westward expansion into Indian lands. In 1763, King George III issued the famous Royal Proclamation, which sought to manage relations with Native Americans by restraining colonists from occupying or acquiring Indian lands west of the Appalachian Mountains. Further, the Crown gave itself a monopoly in acquiring land from Native Americans. The policy was unpopular with the colonists, as many were engaged in land speculation and some had already established settlements beyond the demarcation line. Historians have debated the influence of the Royal Proclamation in precipitating the American Revolution. While some believe that by 1768 the Proclamation was no longer of significant concern, since new treaties with Indians and adjustments to the boundary line had enabled more lands to be settled,[61] other historians contend that colonial resentment of the Proclamation lingered.[62] Certainly, during the War of Independence most Indian tribes allied with the British Crown.[63]

In the US, the Royal Proclamation ceased to have effect when Great Britain ceded the relevant territories to the US under the Treaty of Paris, 1783. Clinton and Hotopp, however, stress that Britain left a significant administrative and legal legacy in this field of law.[64] As the fledgling US government also encountered instability and violence on its western frontier, it came to rely on similar policies.[65] The Indian Intercourse Acts adopted from 1790 controlled trade and travel in Indian territory, and restricted conveyance of Indian lands without the consent of the US government.[66] The US Constitution of 1787 had given Congress broad power under the Indian Commerce Clause to regulate relations with Native Americans.[67] In practice, however, the federal government often struggled to

[60] Nichols, above n 51, 99.

[61] A Taylor, *Divided Ground: Indians, Settlers, and the Northern Borderland of the American Revolution* (Random House, 2006) 43–4.

[62] See JC Wahlke (ed), *The Causes of the American Revolution* (Heath and Company, 1973).

[63] Taylor, above n 61, 85.

[64] RN Clinton and MT Hotopp, 'Judicial Enforcement of the Federal Restraints on Alienation of Indian Land: The Origins of the Eastern Land Claims' (1979–80) 31 *Maine Law Review* 17, 19–23.

[65] See generally FP Prucha, *American Indian Policy in the Formative Years: Indian Trade and Intercourse Acts, 1790–1834* (University of Nebraska Press, 1962).

[66] Trade and Intercourse Act of 1790.

[67] Art 1, s 8.

assert its authority over the states, and some conveyances were made without federal imprimatur, such as by the State of New York with tribes of the Iroquois Confederacy.[68]

As the US gained greater military strength, from about 1815 we see a shift in national government policy to remove Indians and clear them from the land, through warfare or other means, to make way for white settlers and to facilitate economic development. To oversee federal activities, the Bureau of Indian Affairs (BIA) was established in 1824, and remains today the pre-eminent national body governing Indian matters.[69] The 'peaceful' removal policy faded by about the 1850s, as the designated Indian homelands became swamped by gold and land-hungry speculators and settlers. Often, the removal policy required the intervention of the US Army in the West to restrict the movements of various tribes. Along with other factors, including intrusion on Indian lands, decimation of the plains bison, and broken treaties, these actions contributed to the so-called 'Indian Wars'.[70]

The dyadic character of US Indian policy is also evident in how different arms of the state advocated conflicting policies. In contrast to the often belligerent approach taken by the executive and the legislative arms of the state, the US courts sometimes showed more sensitivity to Native American interests. The Supreme Court led by Chief Justice John Marshall laid the basis for tribal sovereignty and US Indian law in three key cases decided between 1823 and 1832 known as the 'Marshall Trilogy'. In *Johnson v McIntosh*, the Supreme Court concluded that Native Americans could not properly convey title to land because they had mere 'title of occupancy', a decision which thus acknowledged, but limited, tribal ownership and sovereignty.[71] In *Cherokee Nation v Georgia*, the court ruled that while Indian tribes were not foreign nations, they were nonetheless 'a distinct political society, separated from others, capable of managing [their] own affairs and governing [themselves]'.[72] By also characterising tribes as 'domestic dependent nations',[73] the Marshall ruling set a legal precedent for the trust relationship between the US government and Native Americans. In *Worcester v Georgia*, the court held that state laws were not applicable within the borders of tribal lands, thereby entitling the Cherokee (although not a party to the case) to federal protection from Georgia's laws.[74]

Increasing difficulties in the enforcement of treaties and the provisions of the various Indian Intercourse Acts in the late 18th and early 19th centuries[75] led many in the US government to believe that tribes and settlers could not co-exist

[68] Taylor, above n 61.
[69] See www.doi.gov/bia.
[70] See N Blackhawk, *Violence over the Land: Indians and Empires in the Early American West* (Harvard University Press, 2006).
[71] 21 US (8 Wheat) 543 (1823).
[72] 30 US (5 Pet) 1 (1831).
[73] *Ibid*, 17.
[74] 31 US (6 Pet) 515 (1832).
[75] See Prucha, above n 55.

under the contemporary arrangements. Considerable pressure for action came from the state governments, especially Georgia, and the federal executive, which was reluctant to enforce existing treaty provisions,[76] Acts of Congress and Supreme Court judgments.[77] The most drastic proposed 'solution', which ultimately prevailed, was the ejection of Indian tribes from areas under high pressure from settlers to areas mostly west of the Mississippi where the settler pressure was much lower.[78] The Indian Removal Act of 1830[79] was the federal legislative contribution to the issue. It authorised the federal executive to allocate portions of the newly acquired territory west of the Mississippi to Indian tribes who agreed to move. With the western expansion of European settlers, the reservations became 'islands of Indianness'.[80]

While the statutory policy was usually only to authorise relocations consented to by tribes, implementation of the legislation was somewhat more unilateral. The position of the Cherokee was one example, for Georgia agreed to cede its claims to westerly lands to the federal government in exchange for the removal of the Cherokee from their midst.[81] Despite Marshall's decision in *Worcester v Georgia*, a case that concerned the application of Georgia's law on Cherokee lands, the Cherokees were shortly forced to move west. President Jackson was a firm supporter of the removal policy,[82] and many of his actions, including the explicit refusal to intervene on behalf of the Cherokee Nation in their struggle with the State of Georgia, certainly furthered the objective. In the end, most tribes, including the Cherokee, signed treaties and relocated west.[83] The winter march of the Cherokees to the Indian Territory resulted in shocking loss of life (apparently more than one quarter of the Cherokee population of 16,000 died), and has become known as the 'Trail of Tears'.[84] Many were relocated into various reservations, although these in practice often offered little protection from the hordes of white settlers, and the reservations concomitantly shrunk over time, as the following section explains.

[76] Getches *et al*, above n 1, 101.

[77] See JC Burke, 'The Cherokee Cases: A Study in Law, Politics, and Morality' (1969) 21 *Stanford Law Review* 500.

[78] One of the earliest proposals was made by Henry Knox, Secretary of War, in a 1789 report to Congress (cited in Getches *et al*, above n 1, 93. Also see President Jefferson's 'unofficial and private letter' to Indiana Governor Harrison in 1803 (cited in Getches *et al*, above n 1, 94).

[79] C 148, 4 Stat 411.

[80] F Pommersheim, 'Is There a (Little or Not So Little) Constitutional Crisis Developing in Indian Law? A Brief Review Essay' (2003) 5 *University of Pennsylvania Journal of Constitutional Law* 271, 276.

[81] See WL Anderson (ed), *Cherokee Removal: Before and After* (University of Georgia Press, 1992).

[82] RN Satz, *American Indian Policy in the Jacksonian Era* (University of Nebraska Press, 1975).

[83] Those who refused to leave were granted small reservations but sometimes only after wars were fought. See Getches *et al*, above n 1, 127, for the size and description of the remaining lands of the 'Five Civilized Tribes' east of the Mississippi.

[84] V Rozema (ed), *Voices from the Trail of Tears* (John F Blair, 2003). The legitimacy of the leadership that signed the treaty created a civil war of sorts in the Cherokee Nation: see J Ehle, *Trail of Tears: The Rise and Fall of the Cherokee Nation* (Doubleday, 1988).

D. Surviving the Siege: 1860s–1920s

1. Assimilation by Force or the Word of God

By the 1850s, the US government had firmly adopted assimilation and removal as 'solutions' to the encroachment on Indian lands by white traders and settlers. The period from about the 1860s to the 1920s was one of the most difficult for Native Americans, as enormous economic expansion after the post-bellum period placed Indian tribes under siege.[85] Many had ignored the relocation orders, and often the policy required the continuing support of the US Army, leading to a series of battles on the Great Plains and further west that largely ended in the 1880s.[86] One of the most intense conflicts was the Sioux War between 1876 and 1881. In many cases, it would be more accurate to describe the conflicts as genocidal massacres committed by the US Army, such as the euphemistically labelled 'Battle of Wounded Knee'.[87]

The Homestead Act of 1862 was one of the principal mechanisms for settling Indian land.[88] It provided for the transfer of 160 acres of 'unoccupied' public land to each settler, subject to a nominal fee after five years of residence. Intended to relieve the concentration of settlers in the eastern states, the Homestead Act served to facilitate greatly the mass migrations to western Indian lands for non-Indian settlement.[89] While the Federal Land Policy and Management Act[90] ended homesteading in the mid-1970s, with the exception of parts of Alaska until 1986, it was essentially a symbolic gesture, as the Act had largely served its purpose by the early 1900s.

From the 1860s, US government policy also called for the replacement of government officials by religious men nominated by churches to oversee some public programmes on reservations and to teach Christianity to the Indians.[91] As in Canada and Australia, the churches also played a seminal role in implementing a US government policy to compel thousands of Native American children to attend Christian boarding schools.[92] The 'civilisation' policy was aimed at eventually

[85] See SL Cadwalader and V Deloria, Jr (eds), *The Aggressions of Civilization: Federal Indian Policy Since the 1880s* (Temple University Press, 1984); CF Wilkinson and ER Biggs, 'The Evolution of the Termination Policy' (1977) 5 *American Indian Law Review* 139.

[86] RM Utley *et al*, *The Indian Wars* (Mariner Books, 2002).

[87] D Brown, *Bury My Heart at Wounded Knee: An Indian History of the American West* (Holt, Rinehart and Winston, 1970).

[88] Pub L No 37-64, 12 Stat 392 (1862).

[89] TW Shanks, 'The Homestead Act: A Major Asset-Building Policy in American History' in MW Sherraden (ed), *Inclusion in the American Dream: Assets, Poverty, and Public Policy* (Oxford University Press, 2005) 20; PW Gates, *The Jeffersonian Dream: Studies in the History of American Land Policy and Development* (University of New Mexico Press, 1996).

[90] Pub L No 94-579, 90 Stat 2744 (1976).

[91] GE Tinker, *Missionary Conquest: The Gospel and Native American Cultural Genocide* (Fortress Press, 1993).

[92] DW Adams, *Education for Extinction: American Indians and the Boarding School Experience, 1875–1928* (University Press Kansas, 1995).

preparing tribal members for citizenship.[93] Missionaries, however, had not always been viewed by governments as allies; for instance, the Supreme Court case of *Worcester v Georgia* arose from a Georgian law that prohibited whites from living in Cherokee territory without a permit from the state. The law was intended to evict missionaries domiciled among the Cherokees who were believed to be encouraging their notions of tribal sovereignty and their resistance to relocation.[94]

2. General Allotment Act

One of the most abhorrent laws of this period, indeed ever in the US, was the General Allotment Act (GAA) of 1887 (also popularly known as the 'Dawes Act' after its principal sponsor).[95] Essentially, it was designed to destroy Native American governments, privatise tribal land, and assimilate Indians into American society. The GAA consolidated a paradigm shift in federal policy regarding Indians from one focused on 'removal and reservation' towards one dedicated to 'allotment and assimilation'. The shift was predicated on the assumption that more aggressive tactics were required for the successful integration of individual Indians into American society.

A core objective of the GAA was to eliminate the communal aspects of tribal conceptions of property, which were perceived as a major barrier to successful cultural and economic integration. Thus, the GAA provided the framework for the assignment of tribal lands to individual Indians, although initially beneficial title to allotted lands vested in the US as trustee for individual Indians, who would only be entitled to issuance of a fee patent after a period of many years. Lands determined by the Secretary of the Interior to be 'surplus' to the needs of the Indians were conveyed to white settlers.[96] As the tribes were barred from hunting or no longer able to do so in their customary manner, the Act's sponsors also believed it would provide the framework for Indians to be taught the rudiments of agriculture in order to sustain themselves on their individual plots.[97]

The GAA was not the first manifestation of the general policy goal of 'allotment', though it represented its apotheosis. Several previous treaties and Acts of Congress included provisions for the allotment of Indian land in severalty.[98] The

[93] It was not until 1924 that the Indian Citizenship Act (Pub L No 68-175, 43 Stat 253) deemed all non-citizen Indians born within the territorial limits of the US to be US citizens.

[94] See WG McLoughlin and WH Conser Jr, *The Cherokees and Christianity, 1794–1870: Essays on Acculturation and Cultural Persistence* (University of Georgia Press, 1994).

[95] 24 Stat 388 (1887); repealed by Pub L No 106-462. See E Greenwald, *Reconfiguring the Reservation: The Nez Perces, Jicarilla Apaches, and the Dawes Act* (University of New Mexico Press, 2002).

[96] Although one condition for the validity of disposal of 'surplus' lands was that it be 'in conformity with the treaty or statute under which such reservation is held' (s 5 of the Act), this requirement proved illusory in light of subsequent Supreme Court rulings which effectively rendered the entire process beyond the review of the courts: see *Lone Wolf v Hitchcock*, above n 27.

[97] See General Allotment Act, s 1.

[98] See, eg, Treaty between the US and the Oto and Missouri Indians, Art 6, cited in DS Otis, *The Dawes Act and the Allotment of Indian Lands*, edited by FP Prucha (University of Oklahoma Press, 1973) 86.

GAA applied to all lands reserved for Indians, howsoever reserved,[99] except those lands that were reserved for the tribes specifically enumerated in section 8 of the Act.[100] Overall, the legislation predictably resulted in a massive loss of tribal land.[101] By the calculations of the federal government, the total land holdings of Indians were reduced from 138 million acres in 1887 to 48 million acres in 1934, with 20 million of these remaining acres being arid areas.[102]

The acquiescence of the judiciary during this period was crucial in putting Native Americans under siege. In contrast to the activism of the Marshall Court, the court in *Lone Wolf v Hitchcock*[103] endorsed a virtually unreviewable congressional power and virtually standardless trust authority, which made it nearly impossible for tribes to obtain judicial protection in disputes with the federal government. In a case concerning a disputed allotment of tribal land in violation of an Indian treaty, the Supreme Court approved Congressional authority to abrogate Indian treaties, just as international agreements with other nations can be abrogated, subject only to compensation under the Fifth Amendment if Indian property rights recognised by the US were lost or harmed.

E. The Indian 'New Deal' and the Backlash: 1930s–1950s

1. The Indian Reorganization Act

The Indian Reorganization Act (IRA) of 1934,[104] also known informally as the centrepiece of the Indian 'New Deal', marked another turning point in US Indian policy away from forced assimilation. However, the impetus for reform arose earlier, in the 1920s. In response to the continued deterioration of the conditions experienced by the Native Hawaiians, in 1920 Congress passed the Hawaiian Homes Commission Act, designed to return some 200,000 acres to Native Hawaiians.[105] In 1928, the government-sponsored Meriam Report had documented deplorable living conditions on mainland Indian reservations, including poverty and ill health, and recommended reforms in Bureau of Indian Affairs (BIA) administration and Indian policy, including ending allotment.[106] In other

[99] This included by treaty, Act of Congress, or Executive Order.

[100] Eg, territories occupied by the Cherokee, Osage and Seneca nations.

[101] JV Royster, 'The Legacy of Allotment' (1995) 27 *Arizona State Law Journal* 1.

[102] J Collier, 'The Purposes and Operation of the Wheeler-Howard Indian Rights Bill', 73rd Cong, 2nd Sess, 15 (1934) cited in Getches *et al*, above n 1.

[103] 187 US 553 (1903); and see JV Royster, '*Lone Wolf v Hitchcock*: One Hundred Years Later, Foreword: Looking Back in Anger' (2002) 38 *Tulsa Law Review* 1; B Clark, *Lone Wolf v Hitchcock: Treaty Rights and Indian Law at the End of the Nineteenth Century* (University of Nebraska Press, 1999).

[104] Pub L No 73-383, 48 Stat 984 (1934).

[105] Pub L No 67-34, 42 Stat 108 (1921).

[106] *The Problem of Indian Administration* (Report of a Survey made at the request of Honorable Hubert Work, Secretary of the Interior, and submitted to him, 21 February 1928).

words, the Report was a formal recognition that the GAA and concomitant policies had been a disaster. After the election of Franklin Roosevelt as President, Congress responded by enacting the IRA, which reversed the allotment of lands, and provided for local self-government on a tribal basis.[107] As Getches and others explain its rationale, '[t]he reformers believed that the tribe itself, organized as a self-governing community, was better equipped to deal with the outside influences of the dominant society'.[108]

Though the IRA could not fully eliminate the checkboard system of land tenure within tribal areas created by the GAA, through its polices for the consolidation and reacquisition of tribal lands it led to the return of some 8,000 km^2 to various tribes within 20 years. Further restorations of tribal lands occurred many years later pursuant to the Indian Land Consolidation Act of 1983.[109] The IRA also contained provisions to foster economic development on tribal lands, such as to allow tribes to establish business corporations.

While pioneering for its time, especially compared to other common law jurisdictions, the IRA would not generally meet standards of tribal self-governance acceptable to Indigenous peoples today, as canvassed further in Shin Imai's chapter. Tribes were able to adopt a Western-style constitution detailed in the IRA for their local governance, which was not necessarily adaptable to their customary methods of decision-making. Tribal reservation governments constituted under the IRA often lacked widespread community support. According to one study, 'most reservations came to have the feel of a branch office of the federal government, with decision-making dominated by the Bureau of Indian Affairs (BIA) and . . . with tribal governments typically totally dependent on BIA programs and funds'.[110] While the IRA reduced federal government oversight, it still empowered the Secretary of the Interior to review many actions of the tribal governments.

The influence of the IRA still lingers, for many tribes possess governmental forms that remain heavily influenced by this Act. While 77 tribes rejected the boiler-plate IRA constitutions, a total of 181 tribes adopted them (by choice or pressure). Getches and others, however, also suggest that the IRA created an opportunity for 'resurrecting and revitalizing'[111] older tribal forms of self-government, a trend which has been intensified greatly since the 1970s.

2. Indian Claims Commission

The Indian Claims Commission (ICC), as Coyle examines in his Chapter in this book, was another institutional innovation that provided a new process outside the courts for resolution of outstanding Indian grievances. The Meriam Report

[107] GD Taylor, *The New Deal and American Indian Tribalism: The Administration of the Indian Reorganization Act, 1934–1945* (University of Nebraska Press, 1980).
[108] Getches *et al*, above n 1, 188.
[109] Pub L No 97-459, 96 Stat 2517 (1983).
[110] Harvard Project, above n 5, 4.
[111] Getches *et al*, above n 1, 192.

had recommended establishment of a new procedure,[112] which eventually happened in 1946 through the Indian Claims Commission Act (ICCA).[113] While the Commission set a precedent that would later inspire similar reforms in Canada and New Zealand, it arguably failed to do enough to bring closure to many injustices and claims.[114]

Prior to the ICC, Native Americans had few legal options for making claims against the federal government, owing to the core American constitutional principle that gave it sovereign immunity against suit in a US court. The government had, however, selectively waived its sovereign immunity pursuant to various legislative enactments.[115] Indian tribes with a grievance against government agents could also petition Congress directly for a remedy.[116] This procedure was nonetheless unsatisfactory to all concerned for a variety of reasons, including long delays, excessive complexity, and the inappropriateness of monetary relief for land claims.

The ICCA provided for the basic structure and operations of the ICC, its jurisdiction, and procedures for filing tribal claims. The Commission was originally authorised to hear only claims relating to events before 1946 that were filed within five years of the date that the Act came into force.[117] Subsequently, the ICC was able to consider claims filed later, as the life of the commission was extended by Congress until the ICC was finally abolished in 1978. The ICC had jurisdiction to hear and determine various claims, primarily involving: (i) any general claims in law or equity; (ii) claims stemming from treaties and agreements between tribes and the US based on fraud, duress, unconscionable consideration, and mutual or unilateral mistake; and (iii) claims arising from the taking of Indian lands without compensation.

Overall, the ICC completed over 500 dockets, issuing 274 monetary awards, totalling some US$818 million.[118] Section 22 of the Act provided that '[t]he payment of any claim, after its determination in accordance with this Act, shall be a full discharge of the United States of all claims and demands touching any of the matters involved in the controversy'. Beyond the numbers, the Commission's accomplishments can also be assessed by the degree to which its work fulfilled the expectations of several perspectives, including the stated objectives, the tribal

[112] W Churchill, 'Charades, Anyone? The Indian Claims Commission in Context' (2000) 24(1) *American Indian Culture and Research Journal* 52.

[113] Pub L No 726, 60 Stat 1049 (1946). Churchill (*ibid*, 53) suggests that the primary impetus for the ICCA was related to the impending Nuremberg Trials. The initiative was meant to distance the US from Hitler's well publicised comments about using the American approach of dealing with the Indian tribes as his model for his own march across Europe.

[114] D Wishart, 'Belated Justice? The Indian Claims Commission and the Waitangi Tribunal' (2001) 25(1) *American Indian Culture and Research Journal* 81.

[115] Eg, An Act to establish a Court for the Investigation of Claims against the United States (1855) 10 Stat 612.

[116] Between 1881 and 1946, Congress passed 146 special laws in response to such petitions, by waiving sovereign immunity to allow suit in the Court of Claims: see HD Rosenthal, *Their Day in Court: A History of the Indian Claims Commission* (Garland, 1990).

[117] Section 12. This date was 13 August 1951.

[118] ICC, *Final Report*, 96th Congress, 2nd Sess, 1978 (House Document No 96, 383) 125.

claimants, and international legal norms.[119] Rosenthal notes that President Truman's pithy speech when the Act was signed, with its connotations of termination, assimilation and 'final settlements', revealed that the Act was 'government-oriented rather than Indian-oriented'.[120]

The two most significant and interrelated concerns of native peoples were the issues of accepting monetary compensation in lieu of land and the legitimacy of the parties who presented the claim to the ICC in generally representing the interests of the tribe. One claim that cast doubt on the legitimacy of the ICC process was the *Dann* case, which was appealed to the Inter-American Commission on Human Rights (IACHR).[121] The Dann sisters challenged the validity of an ICC settlement ostensibly agreed to by their tribe. After their case was unfavourably decided by the Supreme Court,[122] the sisters took their case to the IACHR, which held that the US had violated their human rights under international law. The IACHR commented that:

> the ICC Act permitted an individual or small group of Indians to present a claim on behalf of a whole tribal group without requiring proof of consent of that tribe, the absence of rules permitting the intervention of interested persons in the proceedings before the ICC, and the narrowing of the ICC jurisdiction to award only monetary compensation and accordingly to preclude claimants from recovering land.[123]

Another live issue concerned the effect of not filing a claim that was within the jurisdiction of the ICC. In a highly controversial case, the 10th Circuit Court of Appeals held that the failure of the Navajo Nation to file a claim with the ICC for an issue within its jurisdiction had the effect of extinguishing the Aboriginal title underlying the claim.[124]

3. Public Law 280 and the Backlash of the 1950s

Whatever we might think of the limitations of the IRA and the ICC for Native Americans, their aspiration for self-determination was jolted when Congress passed Public Law 280 in 1953.[125] In a return to assimilationist policies, the law provided for the transfer of some federal jurisdiction to state governments, which dramatically altered the partition of legal authority among tribal, federal and state governments.[126] Public Law 280 gave six states[127] broad civil and criminal

[119] See generally SC Danforth, 'Repaying Historical Debts: The Indian Claims Commission' (1979) 49 *North Dakota Law Review* 359.

[120] Rosenthal, above n 116, 48.

[121] *Mary and Carrie Dann v United States* (2002), IACHR No.75/02.

[122] *United States v Dann*, 470 US 39 (1985).

[123] Above n 121, para 113.

[124] *Navajo Tribe of Indians v New Mexico*, 809 F 2d 1455 (10th Cir 1987).

[125] Pub L No 83-280, 67 Stat 588 (1953).

[126] For background to its adoption, see VJ Jiménez and SC Song, 'Concurrent Tribal and State Jurisdiction Under Public Law 280' (1998) 47 *American University Law Review* 1627, 1656–67.

[127] Initially, they were California, Minnesota, Nebraska, Oregon, and Wisconsin; and later Alaska upon statehood. Within these states, a few specific tribal reservations were kept under federal jurisdiction.

jurisdiction over tribal lands. Other states could also opt to acquire some of this jurisdiction, without the need for tribal consent.[128] Nine states elected to. Thus, in practical terms Public Law 280, for instance, allowed state law enforcement officers to apprehend tribal members for prosecution in state courts for criminal matters within reservation boundaries. Yet, many tribal governments already had their own codes and court systems to adjudicate violations. Public Law 280 ultimately failed to meet its own goals, because the states were handed jurisdiction without the federal funds necessary to finance it, and the resulting jurisdictional gaps contributed to more lawlessness, which the legislation was supposedly to stem.[129]

Public Law 280 was part of a wider backlash against tribal interests, which included several other draconian federal initiatives.[130] One was the adoption in 1953 of House Concurrent Resolution 108, which established tribal termination as an official government policy and singled out specific tribes for termination.[131] Over 100 tribes had their relationships with the federal government terminated by Congressional laws before the policy was repudiated in 1970.[132] Termination generally ended all federal protection of tribal lands and sovereignty from state and local authorities, and it disqualified the group from receiving any federal programmes based on the trust relationship. The termination policy was complemented by another austere policy, implemented by the BIA, which was a 'relocation' programme to encourage Indians to leave the reservations and seek to make a living in mainstream society.[133] Begun in 1948, BIA's Indian Relocation Program contributed to thousands of Native Americans migrating to the cities, and by the mid-1970s more Indians lived in urban areas than on reservations.

F. Tribal Self-Determination and Governance

1. Introduction

Despite strenuous efforts to dismantle Indian tribes and confiscate their territories in the 19th and 20th centuries, in recent decades Native Americans in the US have

[128] CE Goldberg, 'Public Law 280: The Limits of State Jurisdiction over Reservation Indians' (1975) 22 *UCLA Law Review* 535.

[129] C Goldberg-Ambrose, *Planting Tail Feathers: Tribal Survival and Public Law 280* (UCLA American Indian Studies Center, 1997) 12.

[130] See F Cohen, 'The Erosion of Indian Rights, 1950–53' (1953) 62 *Yale Law Journal* 348.

[131] US, HR Cong Res 108, *House Resolution* 108, 83rd Cong 1953.

[132] KR Philip, 'Termination: A Legacy of the Indian New Deal' (1983) 14(2) *Western Historical Quarterly* 165.

[133] LW Burt, 'Roots of the Native American Urban Experience: Relocation Policy in the 1950s' (1986) 10(2) *American Indian Quarterly* 85; DL Fixico, *Termination and Relocation: Federal Indian Policy, 1945–1960* (University of New Mexico Press, 1986).

regained territories and concomitant authority to govern their own affairs.[134] The civil rights movement of the 1960s and 1970s provided fertile ground for advancing these trends. As in other jurisdictions, US governmental policy on Indian affairs and, conversely, tribal demands, have increasingly been framed around themes of Indigenous 'self-determination' and 'self-governance'.[135] However, these terms are understood within the American system somewhat differently from in other countries. They derive from the inherent sovereign status of tribal entities and it is from this extra-constitutional source that a tribe's powers of self-governance emanate.[136] In *US v Wheeler*, the Supreme Court explained that tribal sovereignty

> exists only at the sufferance of Congress and is subject to complete defeasance. But until Congress acts, the tribes retain their existing sovereign powers. In sum, Indian tribes still possess those aspects of sovereignty not withdrawn by treaty or statute, or by implication as a necessary result of their dependent status.[137]

This tribal sovereignty has come to acquire more respect in an era where US government policy has had to respond to an increasingly politically resurgent Native American people, evident by such events as the 1969 occupation of Alcatraz and the 1972 'Trail of Broken Treaties' march.[138] Political activism by Indians, however, did not just begin in the 1960s.[139] The Society of American Indians was formed in 1911, marking the first step in the direction of pan-Indian unity.[140] It campaigned principally for better health care and citizenship for Indians. Later, in 1944 the National Congress of American Indians was established to monitor federal policies.[141] Today, over 250 member tribes through the National Congress collaborate to preserve rights under treaties and to further the common welfare of Native Americans. In 1968, the American Indian Movement was founded,[142] comprising mainly young urban Indians who favoured more direct and militant methods to achieve change. Its involvement in the Pine Ridge Reservation shootout of 1975 made the Movement one of the most controversial actors in the Indian civil rights movement in the eyes of federal authorities.

These and other tactics helped to leverage policy changes in the US government. Since the late 1960s, policies of self-determination and economic self-sufficiency,

[134] For some examples, see ED Lemont (ed), *American Indian Constitutional Reform and the Rebuilding of Native Nations* (University of Texas Press, 2006).

[135] V Deloria Jr, *American Indian Policy in the Twentieth Century* (University of Oklahoma Press, 1985); TM Johnson and J Hamilton, 'Self-Governance for Indian Tribes: From Paternalism to Empowerment' (1995) 27 *Connecticut Law Review* 1251.

[136] The reality of tribal control, however, can often be rather different: see JA Casey, 'Sovereignty by Sufferance: The Illusion of Indian Tribal Sovereignty' (1994) 79 *Cornell Law Review* 404.

[137] 435 US 313, 323 (1978).

[138] T Johnson, 'The Occupation of Alcatraz Island: Roots of American Indian Activism' (1994) 10(2) *Wicazo Sa Review* 63.

[139] For recent history, see PC Smith and RA Warrior, *Like a Hurricane: The Indian Movement from Alcatraz to Wounded Knee* (New Press, 1997).

[140] JW Larner, *The Papers of the Society of American Indians* (Society Resources, 1987).

[141] See www.ncai.org.

[142] See www.aimovement.org.

redolent of the IRA—but going further—have dominated federal Indian policy. Among the first initiatives, the 1968 Indian Civil Rights Act[143] revised Public Law 280 by requiring states to obtain tribal consent prior to extending any legal jurisdiction over an Indian reservation. It also gave most protections of the Bill of Rights and the Fourteenth Amendment to tribal members in dealings with their tribal governments—although these involved human rights standards not derived from tribal traditions.[144] Reforms continued in the 1970s, with President Nixon calling for the cessation of policies of termination and greater scope for tribal self-determination,[145] and more specific policy reforms being recommended by the American Indian Policy Review Commission in 1977.[146]

A flurry of laws ensued, including the Indian Health Care Improvement Act[147] (to improve funding and delivery of health programmes to tribal and urban Indian), the Indian Self-Determination and Education Assistance Act[148] (to establish procedures by which tribes could negotiate contracts with the BIA to administer their own education and social service programmes), and the Indian Child Welfare Act[149] (upholding tribal jurisdiction over children in the wake of some states' policies of removing Indian children to non-Indian foster homes). Also, in 1977, the Senate Committee on Indian Affairs was re-established (it had been disbanded in 1946), with jurisdiction including into proposing legislation to deal with such issues as Indian education, economic development, health care, and claims against the US government.[150] Other legislative reforms continued, although with somewhat less intensity, in the ensuing years, such as the Native American Graves Protection and Repatriation Act,[151] the Native American Languages Act,[152] and the American Indian Religious Freedom Act.[153] Specific reforms to recognise land rights and allow for a measure of self-governance were also adopted for Indigenous communities in Alaska and Hawaii.[154] The following sections concentrate on those reforms related to the reassertion of tribal status and self-governance.

143 Pub L No 90-284, 82 Stat 73 (1968).

144 It has been pointed out that Indians did not lobby for the Indian Civil Rights Act. According to McSloy, 'it was a state's rights issue. It was introduced by Sam Ervin, Senator from North Carolina, to take the heat off civil rights violations by southern states by pointing at tribal governments as allegedly more egregious violators': SP McSloy, 'A Bird's Eye View of American Indian Law and its Future' (26 September 2003) *Indian Country Today*, at www.indiancountry.com.

145 President RM Nixon, 'Message from the President of the United States Transmitting Recommendations for Indian Policy', HR Doc No. 91-363, 91st Congress (2d Sess, 1970).

146 American Indian Policy Review Commission, *Final Report* (US Government Printing Office, 1977).

147 Pub L No 94-437, 90 Stat 1400 (1976).

148 Pub L No 93-638, 88 Stat 203 (1975).

149 Pub L No 95-608, 92 Stat 3069 (1978).

150 See indian.senate.gov/public.

151 Pub L No 101-601, 104 Stat 3048 (1990).

152 Pub L No 101-477, 104 Stat 1153 (1990).

153 Pub L No 95-341, 108 Stat 3125 (1994).

154 JM van Dyke, CD Amore-Siah and GW Berkley-Coats, 'Self-determination for Nonself-governing Peoples and for Indigenous Peoples: The Cases of Guam and Hawaii' (1996) 18 *University of Hawaii Law Review* 623; for Alaska, see references below 212–24.

2. Tribal Recognition and Indian Identity

The reassertion of tribal status has been one the central political and legal issues in US Indian affairs in recent decades. The tribe is the primary social and political unit of Indian communities. It is the vehicle for their cultural, economic and political self-determination. The question of which communities enjoy 'tribal status' therefore carries enormous significance, and has often triggered intense political struggles.[155] Today, almost every federal department and agency delivers programmes and services specifically for Indian tribes. Recognition of the tribal status of a group is a prerequisite for these programmes and services, but the source and exercise of the power *to recognise* has been the subject of much debate. Self-identification as a tribe is necessary but insufficient in federal law. Congress, the executive, and the judiciary have each historically assumed some authority to regulate the recognition of the tribal status of a group, sometimes in conflict with each other.

The role of the judiciary in the recognition of tribal status has been limited by earlier judicial classification of the issue as a political question, left solely to Congress.[156] However, litigation stemming from ambiguities in Congressional enactments and the actions of the executive has generated significant jurisprudence on the issue. The *Mashpee* case[157] affirmed the definition of a tribe as 'a body of Indians of the same or similar race united in one community under one leadership or government, and inhabiting a particular though sometimes ill-defined territory'.[158] The method of judicial determination, especially by jury, and the standard utilised for the determination of tribal status have been criticised for, among other reasons, encouraging the recognition of an Indian tribe based on dominant culture assumptions of what it means to be an Indian.[159]

Coinciding with the demise of the termination era, the BIA began identifying 'recognised' tribes in the 1960s, but the process was not governed by adequately comprehensive and publicly available rules until 1978.[160] These rules[161] were substantially modified in the 1990s in the wake of congressional efforts to assert authority over the recognition of Indian tribes. The resulting Federally Recognized Indian Tribe List Act[162] of 1994 identified the following legitimate methods of

[155] Eg, the efforts of the Lumbee Indians to gain federal recognition in recent years: 'Lumbees Testify Before US House for Federal Recognition' (14 May 2007), *Indian Country Today*, at www.indiancountry.com. See also M Miller, *Forgotten Tribes: Unrecognized Indians and the Federal Acknowledgment Process* (University of Nebraska Press, 2004).

[156] *United States v Holliday*, 70 US 407, 18 L Ed 182 (1865).

[157] *Mashpee Tribe v New Seabury Corp* 592 F 2d 575 (1st Cir 1979) certiorari denied 444 US 866 (1979).

[158] *Montoya v United States*, 180 US 261, 266 (1901)

[159] See, eg, Getches *et al*, above n 1, 311.

[160] See, eg, the struggle of the Stillaguamish Tribe to secure federal executive recognition of tribal status in the cases *United States v Washington*, 520 F 2d 676 (9th Cir 1975) certiorari denied 423 US 1086 (1976) and *Stillaguamish Tribe v Kleppe*, No 75-1718 (DDC 24 August 1975).

[161] *Procedures for establishing that an American Indian Group Exists as an Indian Tribe* 25 CFR Part 83 (1978).

[162] Pub L No 103-454, 108 Stat 4791 (1994).

recognition; (i) by an act of Congress, (ii) by the BIA's administrative rules, or (iii) by a decision of a US court. The Act also obligated the Secretary of the Interior to publish an annual list of the federally recognised Indian tribes to harmonise the approach of all federal departments.[163] The present criteria for BIA listing include that the petitioning group comprises a distinct community and has existed as a community historically until the present, and that it has during this time maintained political influence or authority over its members as an autonomous entity.[164] As of April 2008, there were 562 tribes identified in the BIA list,[165] with numerous groups in the various stages of petitioning the Secretary for recognition under the Bureau's rules.[166]

Regarding the determination of the status of individual Indians, no single tribal or federal criterion defines a person's identity as an Indian. A tribe establishes its own membership criteria, although government agencies also use differing criteria to determine who is an Indian eligible to participate in their programmes.[167] Yet, while the federal government allows federally recognised tribes to decide who their proper members are, the BIA's procedures make reference to how tribes determine membership.[168] Since these criteria are part of the evaluation of federal tribal recognition, the government is not as removed from the process as it might seem. Membership requirements are often outlined in tribal constitutions, which are scrutinised by the BIA.[169] Although each tribe identifies a mix of criteria which entitle one to membership, they are often a combination of historical and cultural ties to the tribe, as well as satisfying some blood quantum.[170]

Tribal membership policies can give rise to tensions between tribal authority and individual civil rights, as has occurred in other jurisdictions such as Canada, as Val Napoleon notes in her Chapter in this book. The Supreme Court decision of *Santa Clara Pueblo v Martinez* was one case involving such tensions, when a challenge was made to the Santa Clara tribe's policy of denying membership to the children of women who married outside the tribe.[171] The claimants argued that this policy violated the Indian Civil Rights Act (ICRA). The court did not decide

[163] Significantly, however, Congress reasserted its exclusive authority to terminate the special relationship between the US and a particular tribe, while expressing its position that termination was no longer the prevailing Congressional policy. This emphasised that exclusion from the BIA list did not constitute termination of the federal-tribal special relationship.

[164] See s 83.7 of Procedures for establishing that an American Indian Group exists as an Indian tribe, in Title 25 of the Code of Federal Regulations.

[165] Department of the Interior, 'Indian Entities Recognized and Eligible to Receive Services from the United States Bureau of Indian Affairs' (4 April 2008) 73(66) *Federal Register* 18553.

[166] For the most up-to-date status of these proceedings see www.doi.gov/bia/federal_acknowledgment_decisions.html.

[167] S Wiessner, 'Rights and Status of Indigenous Peoples: A Global Comparative and International Legal Analysis' (1999) 12 *Harvard Human Rights Journal* 57, 65.

[168] Sections 83.7(d)(e)–(f), above n 164.

[169] R Thorton, 'Tribal Membership Requirements and the Demography of "Old" and "New" Native Americans' (1997) 16 *Population Research and Policy Review* 33, 35.

[170] *Ibid*, 36–37.

[171] 436 US 49 (1978). The tribe's policy, however, allowed tribal membership to children of male members who married outside the tribe.

this issue, deciding instead that it was a tribal matter and that federal courts lacked jurisdiction to enforce the ICRA unless habeas corpus was an issue. The court believed that 'Congress, in passing the ICRA, did not intend to intrude on tribal sovereignty by authorizing a civil action against a tribe or its officers in federal court for its alleged violations of the ICRA, and it refused to imply a federal cause of action'.[172]

Some commentators have argued that policies such as those of Santa Clara Pueblo are not based on historical reality (contending, for example, that tribal membership was historically matrilineal). Rather, they suggest that such policies represent 'modern, federally guided, male supremacist law disguised as an artefact of traditional tribal culture'.[173] This debate thus raises questions that are not unfamiliar to Aboriginal rights debates internationally. What is the source of a tribe's right to set its own membership criteria? Are they bound by the caveat that they follow 'traditional' cultural practice? This may also raise vital human rights questions, particularly for many of the organisations that seek to further the interests of Indigenous populations, while concurrently they may be complicit in ongoing violations of the rights of women within the larger tribal community.

3. Tribal Self-Governance

Determination of tribal membership is just one aspect of many powers in contemporary tribal self-governance. Other powers include to levy taxes, plan land use, control hunting and to administer courts, among various examples of tribal civil and criminal jurisdiction.[174] While tribal governance of reservations is widely seen as derived from the inherent sovereignty of tribes, the structure of self-governance has often been shaped by federal assignment of programmes and services to tribes for management.

One of the important federal government responses to the movement for tribal self-determination was the Tribal Self-Governance Act.[175] It was enacted within the context of a series of significant executive acts regarding Indian affairs during the Clinton Administration.[176] The Act was designed to build upon the Tribal Self-Governance Demonstration Project (TSGDP) begun in 1988.[177] The lessons learned from the TSGDP were incorporated into the Tribal Self-Governance Act, which

[172] LA Curry, 'A Closer Look at *Santa Clara Pueblo v Martinez*: Membership by Sex, by Race, and by Tribal Tradition' (2001) 16(2) *Wisconsin Women's Law Journal* 161, 162.

[173] *Ibid*, 161.

[174] ZK Synder-Joy, 'Self-Determination and American Indian Justice: Tribal versus Federal Jurisdiction on Indian Lands', in DF Hawkins (ed), *Ethnicity, Race, and Crime: Perspectives Across Time and Place* (SUNY Press, 1995) 310.

[175] Pub L No 103-413, 108 Stat 4250 (1994).

[176] Memoranda of President, *Government-to-Government Relations with Native American Tribal Governments*, 29 April 1994, 59 FR 22951. Memoranda of President, *Distribution of Eagle Feathers for Indian Religious Purposes*, 29 April 1994, 59 FR 22953. Ex Ord No 13007, *Indian Sacred Sites*, 24 May 1996, 61 FR 26771.

[177] Indian Self-Determination Amendments. Pub L No 100-472, 102 Stat 2296 (1987), s 301.

established a federal agency that was separate from the BIA, the Office of Self-Governance, which would help any federal organisation within the Department of the Interior or the Indian Health Service, which provides services to Indian tribes, to negotiate self-administration. The negotiated agreements aim to enhance tribal control over how federal funds are spent, and programmes and services delivered. In 2006, 91 compact agreements covering 231 tribes were operational.[178] Tribal self-governance has also been bolstered by various special legislative delegations in different areas of economic, environmental and social policy. For instance, the federal Environmental Protection Agency (EPA) in 1984 adopted a policy that recognised Indian tribal governments as the appropriate non-federal party in setting environmental standards and managing environmental programmes within reservation boundaries.[179] Delegation of regulatory powers to tribes pursuant to various environmental statutes has since ensued, although most tribes cannot effectively utilise such powers without additional financial and technical support.[180]

The development of tribal courts has been another seminal aspect of the tribal self-governance agenda, as detailed further in Zuni Cruz's Chapter in this book. Sovereignty implies control of internal affairs, including the maintenance of a system of law and order.[181] Tribal courts can help to provide such a system, by drawing on tribal customary and traditional law 'in a manner that speaks to Indian people'.[182] The perceived need, mostly by non-Indian agents and administrators, to have what was recognised in the mainstream American system as a formal dispute resolution system motivated the Secretary of the Interior to authorise the establishment of Courts of Indian Offenses in 1883.[183] Formal court systems were further encouraged by the IRA after 1934.[184] Within this context, a sophisticated and diverse set of tribal court systems were developed to adjudicate a wide variety of disputes on reservations.

The Indian Tribal Justice Act (ITJA) of 1993[185] was meant to reorganise the federal interface with tribal justice systems and support their development through funding and technical assistance. The ITJA made provision for the establishment of an Office of Tribal Justice Support (OTJS) within the BIA. The Act authorised new functions for the OTJS, including the distribution of federal funds for infrastructure and training costs, and the provision of technical assistance and train-

[178] See website of the Office of Self-Governance at 64.58.34.34/osg.

[179] WD Ruckelshaus, American Indian Environmental Office, *EPA Policy for the Administration of Environmental Programs on Indian Reservations* (EPA, 8 November 1984).

[180] For example, JA Milford, 'Tribal Authority under the Clean Air Act: How is it Working?' (2004) 44 *Natural Resources Journal* 213.

[181] See, eg, the landmark court decision regarding tribal courts in *Williams v Lee*, 358 US 217, 79 S Ct 269 (1959) where Justice Black in a case regarding the jurisdiction of Navajo courts stated: 'absent governing acts of Congress, the question has always been whether the state action infringed on the right of reservation Indians to make their own laws and be ruled by them'.

[182] Fletcher, above n 2, 96.

[183] Code of Federal Regulations, Title 25, part 11.

[184] Getches *et al*, above n 1, 415.

[185] Pub L No 103-176, 107 Stat (2004); see also JA Myers and E Coochise, 'Development of Tribal Courts: Past, Present and Future' (1995) 79 *Judicature* 147.

ing.[186] Notably, the Act also explicitly prohibited the OTJS from imposing 'justice standards' on tribal justice systems as a condition of funding approval or in any other form. No funds were actually appropriated under the authority of the ITJA within the time frame addressed in the Act.[187] Congress enacted the Tribal Justice Technical and Legal Assistance Act[188] to, among other things, 'assist in the development of tribal judicial systems by supplementing prior congressional efforts such as the Indian Tribal Justice Act'.[189]

These initiatives, however, are being undermined by federal courts, highlighting again the dyadic quality of US Indian law where different arms of the state can act at cross-purposes. Tribal jurisdiction has been sorely tested by a series of Supreme Court rulings since the 1970s that have pegged back tribal authority over non-Indians or non-Indian lands within reservation boundaries. Owing principally to the historic allotments made under the GAA, in many reservations much land was transferred from tribal ownership to individuals, including non-Indians. For example, 48 per cent of land within the Swinomish Reservation, in the state of Washington, is owned by non-Indians.[190] Supreme Court decisions, such as *Oliphant v Suquamish Indian Tribe*,[191] *Montana v US*,[192] *Duro v Reina*,[193] and *Brendale v Yakama Nation*,[194] have significantly curbed the criminal and civil jurisdiction of tribal governments. The dominant judicial reasoning is that as the tribes are 'domestic dependent nations', they lack inherent jurisdiction over non-Indians and can only acquire it by a Congressional grant of authority, which has not occurred.[195] More recent decisions since 2000, notably *Nevada v Hicks*[196] and *Atkinson Trading Co v Shirley*,[197] suggest that the Supreme Court remains inclined to peg back tribal jurisdiction over the conduct of non-Indians or even non-tribal members within tribal territory.[198] In *Atkinson*, for instance, it held that the Navajo Nation could not levy an occupancy tax on a hotel located on non-Indian fee land within the reservation, thus depriving the Navajo of a valuable source of

186 Section 101.

187 See www.naicja.org/legislation/house_testimony.asp.

188 Pub L No 106-59, 114 Stat 2779 (2000).

189 *Ibid*, preamble of stated statutory purposes.

190 Getches *et al*, above n 1, 22.

191 435 US 191 (1978).

192 450 US 544 (1981).

193 495 US 676 (1990). The effect of this decision, denying tribal criminal jurisdiction over non-member Indians on tribal land, was reversed by an amendment to the ICRA, which was upheld by the Supreme Court in *US v Lara* 541 US 193 (2004): see AB Roberts, 'Reservations on Tribal Sovereignty: How *United States v Lara* Will Affect Indians, Tribes, and the Fight to Regain Independence' (2006) 43 *Houston Law Review* 527, 544.

194 492 US 408 (1989).

195 *Oliphant*, above n 191, 208–9. See also DE Wilkins, *American Indian Sovereignty and the US Supreme Court* (University of Texas Press, 1997).

196 533 US 353 (2001).

197 532 US 645 (2001).

198 K Radermacher, 'The Ongoing Divestiture by the Supreme Court of Tribal Jurisdiction Over Nonmembers, On and Off the Reservation' (2002) 78 *Nevada Law Review* 126; RA Williams, *Like a Loaded Weapon: The Rehnquist Court, Indian Rights, and the History of Racism in America* (University of Minnesota Press, 2005).

revenue. We should be mindful, however, that limitations to tribal self-governance in relation to federal authority have much deeper historical roots than the recent Supreme Court jurisprudence; the erosion began as early as 1817 with the enactment of the General Crimes Act, which gave federal authorities jurisdiction over crimes involving non-Indians committed on tribal land.[199]

Defenders of this jurisprudence would probably point out that tribal jurisdiction has been upheld in some key areas, most notably over Indian gaming activities. In an effort to stimulate economic activity in Indian country, many tribes exercised their tribal sovereignty and launched commercial gaming operations on their lands in the 1970s.[200] The Department of the Interior often supported the tribal ordinances that sanctioned the activities.[201] In many instances, however, states contended that the gaming operations violated state laws, which they believed applied to tribal gaming operations pursuant to Public Law 280. The validity of this proposition was rejected by the Supreme Court in the context of a dispute between the State of California and the Cabazon Band of Mission Indians.[202] The majority decision was based on the classification of California gaming laws as 'civil or regulatory' in nature and thus not within the scope of Public Law 280.[203] The decision was also informed by the salient tribal and federal interests at stake in promoting economically viable initiatives in tribal communities.

The Indian Gaming Regulatory Act[204] was enacted by Congress in 1988 in response to such disputes. It provided for the establishment of the National Indian Gaming Commission to implement and supervise three classes of gaming activity, each with its own regulatory scheme, ranging from those activities wholly within tribal jurisdiction to those that must be 'conducted in accordance with a Tribal-State compact entered into by the Indian Tribe and the State'.[205] The IGRA obligated states to bargain in 'good faith' for the development of tribal-state compacts and created a cause of action in the federal court for its breach.[206] This Congressional initiative, however, did not entirely settle the issue, with some states continuing to make challenges on constitutional or other legal grounds.[207]

While casinos have flourished on some reservations since the late 1980s,[208] their overall social and economic effects and benefits have been heavily debated. Cornell

[199] Ch 92, 3 Stat 383. Later, the Major Crimes Act of 1885, 23 Stat 385, subjected Indians to federal prosecution for some enumerated crimes, even if committed in Indian country.

[200] See JG Jorgensen, 'Gaming and Recent American Indian Economic Development' (1998) 22(3) *American Indian Culture and Research Journal* 157; TL Wilson, 'Indian Gaming and Economic Development on the Reservation' (1989) 68 *Michigan Bar Journal* 380.

[201] WC Canby Jr, *American Indian Law in a Nutshell* (4th edn, Thomson-West, 2004) 303.

[202] *California v Cabazon Band of Mission Indians* 480 US 202, 107 S Ct 1083 (1987).

[203] The majority interpreted Public Law 280's distinction between 'criminal' and 'civil' matters in light of the jurisprudence, especially *Bryan v Itasca County*, 426 US 373, 96 S Ct 2102 (1976).

[204] Pub L No 100-497, 102 Stat 2467 (1988).

[205] IGRA s 11(d). Camby notes: 'in practice, Class III includes the staples of the typical casino, such as slot machines, craps, roulette, and banked card games such as blackjack' (above n 201, 308).

[206] IGRA s 11(7)(A).

[207] *Seminole Tribe of Florida v Florida*, 517 US 44, 116 S Ct 1114 (1996).

[208] See SA Light and KRL Rand, *Indian Gaming and Tribal Sovereignty: The Casino Compromise* (University Press of Kansas, 2005).

conducted an analysis of Indian gaming in Arizona, and found they had made a significant contribution not only to the tribes but also to the state's economy.[209] The Harvard study on Indian economic development downplays their economic significance for Native Americans generally. It found that 'during the first full decade of Indian gaming, real household income actually grew more rapidly in Indian areas without gaming (33 per cent) than in areas with gaming (24 per cent)'.[210] As of 2006, 224 of the 561 federally recognised tribes operated gaming facilities.[211] The Harvard study thought that robust tribal self-government and culturally appropriate institutions were more salient ingredients for the economic health of tribal communities.

4. Tribal Governance in Alaska

Another special approach to tribal governance arose in Alaska. Native Alaskans have long experienced somewhat different legal arrangements from that of other Native Americans south of the 49th line of latitude.[212] In the face of threats from mining and oil industries, nature conservationists' demands and other interests, the Alaska Federation of Natives was formed in 1966 to help unite Indigenous Alaskans to secure protection of their lands and compensation for any losses.[213] Most Federation leaders were strongly opposed to the idea that the 1930s-era IRA be the means to achieve their empowerment. Yet, the governance structure that they negotiated with the federal government ultimately proved quite unsatisfactory.

In the context of the policy shift towards Indigenous self-determination, the Alaska Native Claims Settlement Act (ANCSA) was enacted in 1971.[214] The legislation marked the culmination of apparent federal government concern for Indigenous rights. This was a distinct departure from American Indian policy in other parts of the US, though perhaps because of slow economic development rather than a rejection of Indian policy adopted elsewhere.[215] The ANCSA extinguished native claims to almost all of Alaska in exchange for approximately one-ninth of the state's land (over 40 million acres) and US $962.5 million in compensation, both to be managed by 12 new regional corporations, each region reflecting common culture wherever possible. The regional corporation was to be a profit-making mechanism, comprised of resident Native shareholders. Further, individual village corporations could be set up under the auspices of the regional

209 S Cornell, *An Analysis of the Economic Impacts of Indian Gaming in the State of Arizona* (Udall Center for Studies in Public Policy, 2001).

210 Harvard Project, above n 5, 6.

211 *Ibid*, 148.

212 For background, see DS Case, *Alaska Natives and Alaska Laws* (University of Alaska Press, 1984); JG Jorgensen, *Oil Age Eskimos* (University of California Press, 1990).

213 See www.nativefederation.org.

214 Pub L No 92-203, 85 Stat 339 (1971).

215 RA Cooley, 'Evolution of Alaska Land Policy' in T Morehouse (ed), *Alaskan Resources Development: Issues of the 1980s* (Westview Press, 1983) 13.

bodies to administer some of the lands and settlement monies, and over 200 were subsequently established.

Though the ANCSA appeared progressive for Native rights at the time, and provided the model for Canada's comprehensive land claims agreements, eventually the ANCSA came to be seen as a flawed model. In 1983, the Inuit Circumpolar Conference appointed Mr Justice Thomas Berger, formerly of the Supreme Court of British Columbia, to review ANCSA. The result of his review was a landmark study, which made a searing critique of ANSCA from the Indigenous perspective.[216] It identified problems and conflicts centred on land selection and use, money management, the high administrative costs the system has imposed on Native communities, and the nature of the corporate structure itself.[217] In the latter, the identity of tribal members is reduced to shareholders in for-profit corporations, whose purpose is to invest in the cash economy rather than to invest in the real social and economic needs of their communities.[218] Moreover, Native shareholders in the corporation could freely sell their shares after 1991, and thus Berger feared control would pass into non-Indigenous hands. He was also critical of the lack of a governmental mechanism prepared to defend the Native livelihoods including subsistence hunting against the predatory demands of corporate America seeking access to its oil and mineral riches.

Successive amendments to ANCSA over the decades attempted to alleviate some of these problems,[219] but Berger's core proposals for reconstituting tribal governments were not adopted, and ANCSA remains mired by some fundamental problems. One set of amendments provided for continued restrictions on shareholding to maintain Indigenous control and ownership of the corporations.[220] In 1994 the Alaska Natives Commission, created by Congress to conduct the first comprehensive assessment of the social, cultural, and economic condition of Alaska's Natives, reported its findings.[221] It made recommendations on self-governance, substance abuse and expanding job opportunities, which were moderately successfully implemented.[222] While the ANCSA is generally seen as providing Alaskan Natives with rights superior to those of Indians in other parts of the US, this is not always so. In the 1998 case of *Alaska v Native Village of Venetie Tribal Government*,[223] the Supreme Court ruled that ANCSA lands are not 'Indian

[216] TR Berger, *Village Journey: The Report of the Alaska Native Review Commission* (Hill and Wang, 1985).

[217] ME Thomas, 'The Alaska Native Claims Settlement Act: Conflict and Controversy' (1986) 23(142) *Polar Record* 27.

[218] NE Flanders, 'The Alaska Native Corporation as Conglomerate: The Problem of Profitability' (1989) 48 *Organization* 299.

[219] JF Walsh, 'Settling the Alaska Native Claims Settlement Act' (1985) 38 *Stanford Law Review* 227.

[220] T Morehouse, 'Sovereignty, Tribal Government and the Alaska Native Claims Settlement Act Amendments of 1987' (1989) 25(154) *Polar Record* 197.

[221] Alaska Natives Commission, *Final Report*, 3 vols (Joint Federal-State Commission on Policies and Programs Affecting Alaska Natives, 1994).

[222] See Alaska Natives Commission, *Achieving Alaska Native Self-Governance: Toward Implementation of the Alaska Natives Commission. Final Report* (Institute of Social and Economic Research, University of Alaska, 1999).

[223] *Alaska v Native Village of Venetie Tribal Government*, 522 US 520, 118 S Ct 948 (1998).

country' as understood in US law generally, and therefore the tribe in question did not have jurisdiction to tax non-tribal members doing business on that land.[224]

G. Conclusions

Many tribes today are enjoying new-found economic prosperity, cultural vitality, and greater self-governance.[225] The period since the late 1960s is widely characterised as one of tribal self-determination, in place of the assimilationist or genocidal policies of the past. Yet, accompanying these strides linger threats to tribal sovereignty. It would be misleading to imply that the history of Native Americans in the US has been of ongoing improvement in their legal status and rights. Certainly, the large-scale territorial dispossessions and physical expiration of the 19th century are no longer practised. Yet, tribal authority sometimes remains precarious. The relatively benign reforms of the Indian New Deal in the 1930s were back-tracked somewhat by Public Law 280 in the 1950s. More recently, the Supreme Court has effectively been making federal Indian policy, which is problematic because 'the Court's policy choices are frequently uneducated in terms of their on-the-ground impacts'.[226] The Supreme Court is increasingly accommodating the interests of state governments and non-Indians at the expense of Indian tribes. The US government has also shunned landmark international standards for Indigenous rights, including the UN Declaration on the Rights of Indigenous Peoples,[227] as explained in Claire Charters' Chapter in this book.

US Indian law thus can be seen to have a strongly dyadic character, having both been a means to give effect to and rationalise painful colonial policies, as well as to empower Native Americans. The permeations in US Indian law have reflected many factors and interests, not least of which have been policy divisions at the federal level and between federal and state authorities. Native Americans have also played a crucial role in the story of US Indian law, even defeating some anti-tribal legislation.[228] The future direction of US Indian law remains debatable, but seminal studies such as the Harvard Project on American Indian Economic Development remain optimistic. It recently concluded that, '[i]f the challenge of the last 50 years was to catch the vision of self-determination, then the challenge of the next 50 years will be to enact it'.[229]

224 See GD Strommer and SD Osborne, '"Indian Country" and the Nature and Scope of Tribal Self-Government in Alaska' (2005) 22 *Alaska Law Review* 1.

225 For some case studies, see RH White, *Tribal Assets: The Rebirth of Native America* (Henry Holt, 1990).

226 MLM Fletcher, 'The Supreme Court and Federal Indian Policy' (2006–07) 85 *Nebraska Law Review* 121, 128.

227 UN Doc A/61/L 67, 7 September 2007.

228 C Wilkinson, *Blood Struggle: The Rise of Modern Indian Nations* (WW Norton, 2005) 267–8.

229 Harvard Project, above n 5, 374.

4

Australia: The White House with Lovely Dot Paintings whose Inhabitants have 'Moved on' from History?

JENNIFER CLARKE

A. Introduction: Responsibility in the 'Age of Apology'

On 13 February 2008, Australian Prime Minister Kevin Rudd moved that the Commonwealth Parliament[1]:

> apologise for the laws and policies of successive parliaments and governments that have inflicted profound grief, suffering and loss on [Indigenous] Australians . . . especially for the removal of . . . children from their families, their communities and their country. For the pain, suffering and hurt of these stolen generations, their descendants and for their families left behind . . . [a]nd for the indignity and degradation thus inflicted on a proud people and a proud culture, we say sorry.[2]

This was an historic moment, long sought and profoundly felt by many Australians, including indigenous people.[3] However, such occasions are also troubling for their emphasis on national redemption and transcendence, without altering in any fundamental way the allocation of resources produced by colonisation.[4] The 2008 apology primarily concerned the approximately 40,000 surviving

[1] A parliamentary apology is not actionable in Australian courts: Parliamentary Privilege Act 1987 (Cth) s 16. On the international phenomenon of apologies, see RL Brooks, *When Sorry Isn't Enough: The Controversy over Apologies and Reparations for Human Injustice* (New York University Press, 1999); M Gibney *et al*, *The Age of Apology: Facing Up to the Past* (University of Pennsylvania Press, 2007).

[2] See House of Representatives 'Apology to Australia's Indigenous Peoples', www.aph.gov.au/house/index.htm.

[3] Australia's lead was soon followed in Canada: 'Canada Apology for Native Schools' *BBC News*, 11 June 2008.

[4] See A Moran, 'The Psycho-Dynamics of Australian Settler-Nationalism' (2002) 23 *Political Psychology* 667.

members of the 'stolen generations'[5]—Aboriginal children, especially so-called 'mixed race' progeny, forcibly removed from their families, in particular under 20th-century race-specific laws. But by failing to include a commitment to compensate these people or their descendants,[6] the apology highlighted the significant ground that remains to be covered in addressing (legacies of) historical wrongs to indigenous Australians.[7] At the same time, discussion of such legacies raises pressing questions about the relationship between colonial history and contemporary indigenous disadvantage—including the position of people who(se ancestors) were *not* 'stolen'. While the United Nations Development Program recently ranked Australia third in the world on its Human Development Index (a basket of various socio-economic criteria),[8] on telling indicators such as life expectancy,[9] Aboriginal Australians fare *worse* than people of many 'Third World' countries. These problems particularly afflict people who(se ancestors), rather than being targeted for removal as children, were expected to stay living in poverty, segregated from wider Australia.[10] The increasingly populous remote 'communities' which have grown out of those segregated enclaves have been likened to a 'failed state' because of their low socio-economic status, high levels of interpersonal violence, and poor government service delivery.[11]

This chapter analyses some of the main legal and public policy developments that have affected indigenous people in Australia, putting these into an historical, geographical and institutional context. It does not explore in any detail indigenous legal traditions and history in the continent before European colonisation. The aim is to inform unfamiliar readers with some of the most salient institutional, political, legal and policy developments. Many such issues, such as land rights, however, will be canvassed only briefly, as they are examined more fully in other parts of this book. An important message of this Chapter is that the current treatment of indigenous Australians is heavily shaped by the legacies of the past. For example, the states in Australia have traditionally been pre-eminent in indigenous affairs, and even a constitutional amendment to empower federal law-making in this area has not yet led to the kind of national leadership found in other countries. This Chapter also seeks to convey that the laws and policies affecting Aboriginal people and Torres Strait Islanders are deeply immersed in a cultural and geo-

[5] This was the Howard government's estimate: Senate Legal and Constitutional Affairs Committee, *Healing: A Legacy of Generations* (Commonwealth of Australia, 2000) 8.30.

[6] 'Macklin Rules Out Compensation for Stolen Generation' *ABC Radio (AM)*, 13 February 2008.

[7] Some state governments have taken modest steps towards compensating either former 'stolen' Aboriginal children or former institutionalised or abused children generally: see, eg, Stolen Generations of Aboriginal Children Act 2006 (Tas).

[8] United Nations Development Program (UNDP), *Human Development Report 2006: Beyond Scarcity: Power, Poverty and the Global Water Crisis* (UNDP, 2006) 283–6.

[9] See *Deaths Australia 2005*, at www.abs.gov.au.

[10] The most disadvantaged indigenous people are these populations of remote areas: Commonwealth Grants Commission, *Report on Indigenous Funding* (2001), at www.cgc.gov.au/IFI_Pages/ifi_final_report_vol1.htm.

[11] M Dillon and N Westbury, *Beyond Humbug: Transforming Government Engagement with Indigenous Australia* (Seaview Press, 2008).

graphical context in many ways distinctive to Australia, such as the remoteness of many small inland Aboriginal communities from the majority of the 'mainstream' population, which hugs the urbanised east, south-east and south-west coasts.[12]

This Chapter also serves to provide a point of contrast with other jurisdictions examined in this book. Although Australia shared many traditions of British imperial power experienced in North America and New Zealand, the effectiveness of that power and the response of indigenous populations varied dramatically from place to place because of the immense geographic distance between Britain and its colonies.[13] Yet in all settler colonies, including Australia, indigenous people were severely displaced to accommodate the political and economic growth of Empire.[14] In recent decades, legal policy in Australia has also faced global pressures to accommodate movements for indigenous self-determination, reflected in international legal instruments such as the United Nations Declaration on the Rights of Indigenous Peoples of 2007.[15] Yet, again, the manner and form by which those pressures have been addressed in Australia is somewhat distinctive, as this Chapter shows.

B. Geography and Culture

1. A Fragile Continent Populated by Small, Flat Societies

Australia has been inhabited for perhaps as long as 60,000 years, making indigenous Australians' probably the oldest continuous human cultures in the world. Despite its size,[16] unlike North America, Australia cannot support large human populations. Two-thirds of the continent is arid, and much of the remainder prone to drought. While some indigenous Australians explain their origins or essence in international terms,[17] a more common traditional account has particular groups of Aboriginal people formed locally as part of the natural world,[18] a

[12] About 85% of Australians live within 50 km of the coast, in cities or towns of more than 1,000 people. By contrast, about two-thirds of the indigenous population lives outside of major cities, although only about one-quarter lives in remote areas.

[13] See A Doukakis, *The Aboriginal People, Parliament and 'Protection' in New South Wales 1856–1916* (Federation Press, 2006), for an example of 'local colonial' policies.

[14] B Slattery, 'Aboriginal Sovereignty and Imperial Claims' (1991) 29 *Osgoode Hall Law Journal* 681.

[15] UN Doc A/61/L 67, 7 Sept 2007.

[16] Continental Australia is slightly smaller than the 48 mainland US states, excluding Alaska.

[17] Accounts of ancestors arriving from, or departing upon death to, another place are found where traditions accommodated arrivals of outsiders (eg 'Macassans' from Sulawesi into Arnhem Land). See T Swain, *A Place for Strangers: Towards a History of Aboriginal Being* (Cambridge University Press, 1993) ch 4.

[18] These processes are attributed to creator beings known in Aboriginal English as 'Dreamings', which remain active in the natural environment, often manifesting as totemic species. Human relationships to them are transmitted by inheritance or (in the 'Western Desert' cultural region) by birth or conception close by.

process which laid down religious norms (eg ceremonial obligations towards creator beings), social protocols associated with kinship systems, and environmental norms (eg periodically burning the landscape to promote biological diversity and abundance).[19] Science holds that human beings entered Australia (then joined with Papua New Guinea as the continent Sahul) through Southeast Asia via land bridges caused by sea levels considerably lower than present.[20] After European colonisation of Indonesia, Dutch and possibly Portuguese explorers (or even slavers) and 'Macassan'[21] trepangers landed in Australia, but full colonisation began in 1788 when Britain's 'First Fleet' arrived to establish a penal colony. At the time, the Aboriginal inhabitants numbered somewhere between 300,000 and 1.5 million.[22]

Eighteenth-century cultures in Australia were as different from European ones as those of any colonised people. Continental Australian economies were based on hunting and gathering, supplemented by trade and obligations of reciprocity.[23] Except in well-resourced areas, nomadism was necessary.[24] Agriculture was practised in the eastern Torres Strait,[25] and Torres Strait Islanders engaged in long-range ocean trade.[26] As nomadic societies cannot afford material abundance, Aborigines valued environmental, social and ritual skills and knowledge.[27] Societies were small-scale, with no universal institutions monopolising law and violence—these functions were embedded in the social order.[28] While there was considerable local resistance to invasion,[29] Australia had no Iroquois Confederacy and lacked the linguistic commonality which supported Māori political action. More than 250 territorially associated indigenous languages were spoken, but these 'language-owning groups' were not political units.[30] Outside of the 'Western

[19] DB Rose, *Nourishing Terrains* (Australian Heritage Commission, 1996).

[20] See generally J Mulvaney and J Kamminga, *Prehistory of Australia* (Allen and Unwin, 1999).

[21] Ie, people from Makassar in south Sulawesi and other parts of what is now Indonesia.

[22] See 'Aboriginal and Torres Strait Islander Population', *Year Book Australia 2006*, at www.abs.gov.au; RL Smith, *The Aboriginal Population of Australia* (Academy of the Social Sciences in Australia, 1980).

[23] Mulvaney and Kamminga, above n 20, 93–7; F McCarthy, '"Trade" in Aboriginal Australia, and "Trade" Relationships with Torres Strait, New Guinea and Malaya' (1939) 9 *Oceania* 80, 171.

[24] The people of the Murray River valley and western Victoria were relatively sedentary, living in stone houses and planting crops. In better-watered areas (eg south-east or Arnhem Land coasts), nomadism occurred within smaller territories than in the desert.

[25] A Shnukal, 'Torres Strait Islanders' in M Brandle (ed), *Multicultural Queensland 2001: 100 Years, 100 Communities, a Century of Contributions* (Queensland Department of Premier and Cabinet, 2001).

[26] N Sharp, *Stars of Tagai: The Torres Strait Islanders* (Aboriginal Studies Press, 1993).

[27] I Keen, *Knowledge and Secrecy in an Aboriginal Religion* (Oxford University Press, 1994).

[28] In Australia's first (failed) native title case, Blackburn J of the Northern Territory (NT) Supreme Court described Yolngu (eastern Arnhem Land) traditions as 'a subtle and elaborate system highly adapted to the country in which the people led their lives, which provided a stable order of society and was remarkably free from the vagaries of personal whim or influence . . . "a government of laws, and not of men"': *Milirrpum v Nabalco* (1971) 17 FLR 141, 267.

[29] For example, Darug warrior Pemulwuy speared the NSW Governor's gamekeeper and led raids on settlers at the end of the 18th century, Tiwi opposition helped to close a Melville Island colonial outpost in 1826, and former police tracker Tjandamarra organised an armed defence of Bunuba country at Windjana Gorge in the East Kimberley in the 1890s.

[30] Mulvaney and Kamminga, above n 20, 75–6.

Desert'—a cultural region encompassing inland Western Australia, South Australia and the Northern Territory (NT) in which tenure is based on multiple factors—primary responsibility to and for relatively small land estates was exercised by, and transmitted through, small groups defined by kinship.[31] Some Torres Strait traditions recognised individual property rights and clear boundaries,[32] but no indigenous Australian culture contemplated permanent alienation of land. In Aboriginal societies, religious authority accrued to qualified people as they aged. However, the secular domain, organised largely on gender lines, was fairly egalitarian: 'Australia lacked the environmental and resource conditions for the development of enduring inequality'.[33]

Because of their small population,[34] isolation and occupation of lands and climates considered suitable for European settlement,[35] Aboriginal Australians were vulnerable to invaders. It has been estimated that 20,000[36] died directly as a result of violence—perpetrated by settlers[37] or the state[38]—but many more succumbed to diseases such as smallpox carried by European invaders or 'Macassans'.[39] Cultural differences also rendered the Aboriginal civilizations 'backward' in European eyes, justifying legal rules as diverse as the constitutional treatment of Australia as unoccupied for the purposes of colonial acquisition,[40] and the colonial courts' refusal to admit Aboriginal testimony (discussed below).

[31] In *Milirrpum v Nabalco*, above n 28. Blackburn J misunderstood the proprietary dimensions of this relationship, but accurately characterised its wider nature, finding that the evidence suggested that 'the clan belongs to the land [rather] than that the land belongs to the clan': at 270–1.

[32] See factual findings of Moynihan J of the Queensland Supreme Court, discussed in *Mabo v Queensland (No 2)* (1992) 175 CLR 1, 12, 19.

[33] I Keen, 'Constraints on the Development of Enduring Inequalities in late Holocene Australia' (2006) 47 *Current Anthropology* 7, 18.

[34] In pre-colonial times, inadequate diet, nomadism and lengthy breast-feeding kept Aboriginal women's ovulation irregular, imposing a natural limit on birth rates: see G Cowlishaw, 'The Determinants of Fertility among Australian Aborigines' (1981) 13(1) *Mankind* 31.

[35] The tropical Torres Strait Islands and northern Australia were colonised much later than temperate zones.

[36] H Reynolds, *The Other Side of the Frontier* (UNSW Press, 2007 (first published in 1983)) 9.

[37] Violence was so condoned that some convicts hanged for the 1838 massacre of Aboriginal people at Myall Creek in northern NSW reportedly confessed that they had not known that killing Aborigines was unlawful. For reports of these trials—the only hangings of settlers for such killings—see, eg, *R v Kilmeister (No 1)*, *R v Kilmeister (No 2)* (1838), and *R v Lamb, Toulouse and Palliser* (1839), reproduced by Bruce Kercher at www.law.mq.edu.au/scnsw.

[38] Typical of state violence were reprisal expeditions against whole 'tribes', eg the 'Battle of the Pinjarra' in Western Australia (1834), led by Governor Stirling, and a massacre of 30 Aboriginal people by a party led by their 'Protector', Matthew Moorhouse, at Rufus River in South Australia (1841).

[39] A 1789 smallpox outbreak around Sydney reduced the Aboriginal population by half, but it is possible that the disease entered northern Australia in precolonial times: J Campbell, *Invisible Invaders: Smallpox and Other Diseases in Aboriginal Australia 1780–1880* (Melbourne University Press, 2002).

[40] According to ME Lindley, *The Acquisition and Government of Backward Territory in International Law* ((1926), republished Negro Universities Press, 1969), in Australia 'there appeared to be no political society to be dealt with', and such a society meant one in which 'a considerable number of persons . . . are permanently united by habitual obedience to a certain and common superior, or whose conduct in regard to their mutual relations habitually conforms to recognised standards' (40–1, and 23).

Today, Australia's indigenous population remains small, with fewer than 500,000 people[41] identifying as indigenous in a country of some 21 million. Australian legislation counts as 'indigenous' anyone with an Aboriginal or Torres Strait Islander ancestor who identifies as indigenous, and is accepted as such, by *an* indigenous 'community'.[42] Statutory Aboriginality was historically vulnerable to utilitarian policy calculations. It was defined and redefined[43] to reflect what governments wanted to do with Aborigines or resources allocated to them, in ways which regularly moved the colour bar between those entitled to full citizenship rights and those denied them.[44] The expansive contemporary definition of Aboriginality, adopted 30–40 years ago as a response to this arbitrariness, primarily filters claims to limited affirmative action benefits—some inadequate substitutes for inaccessible 'mainstream' citizenship entitlements—or distinctive land rights. Because the definition is statutory, not tribal, courts play a central role in defining indigeneity, often with limited deference to local indigenous opinion. Controversy has arisen from court decisions considered over-inclusive because they recognise as 'Aboriginal' people of limited or contested indigenous descent who have discovered this pedigree fairly recently.[45] Although indigenous people constitute only 2.3 per cent of Australia's population, and Australia has no Nunavut—a territory in which indigenous people are a majority population[46]—they have long been conspicuous for several reasons, as the following section explains.

2. Conspicuous Brown Minorities in a 'White' Nation

One reason is that Australia has no other historically significant cultural minorities. It had no chattel slavery.[47] Nineteenth-century experiments with 'blackbirding' (importing mostly Melanesian labour, including through trickery and kidnappings) ended in deportation,[48] as did pre-federation[49] admissions of

[41] Thus there are fewer 'indigenous' people in Australia than in Canada, New Zealand, the state of California, or two US Indian tribes (Cherokee and Navajo) combined.

[42] Eg Aboriginal Land Rights Act 1983 (NSW), s 4(1); and see *Shaw v Wolf* (1998) 83 FCR 113.

[43] By 'Aboriginal protection' or 'Aboriginal welfare' laws: see text to nn 63 and 65 below.

[44] J Clarke, '*Cubillo v Commonwealth*' (2001) 25 *Melbourne University Law Review* 218 at n 87 and text thereto. See also S Weaver, 'Struggles of the Nation-state to Define Aboriginal Ethnicity: Canada and Australia' in G Gold (ed), *Minorities and Mother Country Imagery* (Memorial University of Newfoundland, 1984), and the discussion of 'Aboriginal protection' laws below.

[45] See, eg, *Shaw v Wolf*, above n 42; *Patmore v Independent Indigenous Advisory Committee* [2002] FCAFC 316.

[46] Aboriginal people constitute 28% of the NT's population: *2006 Census Quickstats: Northern Territory*, at www.abs.gov.au.

[47] *Somersett's case* (1772) 98 ER 509, became Australian law upon colonisation; the Slavery Abolition Act 1833 (Imp) prevented inconsistent Australian legislation. While labour provisions in 'Aboriginal Protection' Acts are sometimes compared with US slave codes, none reduced Aboriginal Australians to a form of property with 'no rights which the white man was bound to respect' (cf *Dred Scott v Sandford*, 60 US 393 (1857)).

[48] 50,000 Pacific Islanders were imported into Queensland in the second half of the 19th century to work in the sugar industry, and most were later expelled after 1901.

[49] Ie, before the Australian colonies federated into the Commonwealth of Australia in 1901.

Indonesian traders and Chinese miners. Australia's colonisation by a single power, its long history of trade protection, and a determined pursuit of a '"whites"-only' migration policy from the late 19th century,[50] deprived it of non-indigenous minorities. Recent increases in immigration from Asia, Africa and other regions have only begun to dent this monoculture, in which indigenous Australians have always stood out and race relations taken a simplistic, binary ('indigenous'–'non-indigenous') form.[51]

Another factor in the conspicuousness of indigenous people in Australia is the country's majoritarian political culture. Australia was colonised, and matured politically, in the era of Benthamism. The sense of legitimate regional or inherited differences and interests found in the United States is much less pronounced in Australia,[52] where it is usually necessary to present self-interest in utilitarian terms[53] in order to press it politically. Decisions by 'the ethnic majority' to privilege their own interests are typically cast as neutral, and minority grievances with them presented as unhelpfully sectional.[54] Continued sacrifice of Aboriginal interests to 'majority' ones in cases of conflict is perceived as essential and inevitable, even if it is necessary politically to mask this unpalatable truth, sometimes with law.[55] Thus Australia's trademark egalitarianism[56] is not customarily extended to Aboriginal people—because their humanity or political citizenship has been denied or, in recent years, their cultural difference over-emphasised.[57] Paradoxically, appeals to formal egalitarianism also often prevent recognition of Aboriginal-specific rights or affirmative action measures.[58] Australia lacks the constitutional infrastructure for judicial enforcement of minority rights: few

[50] Australia's capricious use of a 'European language' dictation test *to exclude* people of colour between 1901 and 1958 is notorious.

[51] A Curthoys, 'An Uneasy Conversation: The Multicultural and the Indigenous' in J Docker and G Fischer (eds), *Race, Colour and Identity in Australia and New Zealand* (UNSW Press, 2000).

[52] Although Western Australia threatened to secede (unconstitutionally) from the federation in the 1930s.

[53] On utilitarianism in Australian majoritarianism, see P Kildea, 'The Bill of Rights Debate in Australian Political Culture' (2003) 9(1) *Australian Journal of Human Rights* 7.

[54] G Hage, *White Nation: Fantasies of White Supremacy in a Multicultural Society* (Pluto Press, 1998).

[55] Eg, the Native Title Act 1993 (Cth) (NTA), which allows land held under this Aboriginal property right to be allocated to other people without the consent of native title holders, contains a provision (s 7) designed to suggest that those allocations are consistent with the Racial Discrimination Act 1975 (Cth) (RDA), which implements the International Convention on the Elimination of All Forms of Racial Discrimination, 1965, 660 UNTS 195. However, s 7 cannot overcome other provisions of the NTA which expressly authorise discriminatory treatment of native title land, impliedly repealing the RDA's protection of its holders.

[56] See Kildea, above n 53.

[57] Valorised, as well as stigmatised, difference justifies fewer or weaker rights. In Australia, the inferior property right native title takes its content from what a court perceives of traditional laws and customs, which can severely limit its scope. See S Young, *The Trouble with Tradition* (Federation Press, 2008).

[58] M Goot and T Rowse, *Divided Nation? Indigenous Affairs and the Imagined Public* (Melbourne University Press, 2007).

constitutions refer to human rights or Aborigines[59]; rights protections in the Commonwealth Constitution tend to be ineffective and inapplicable to the states[60]; and the rare state provisions are unentrenched.[61] Only two jurisdictions with small indigenous populations (the Australian Capital Territory and Victoria) have recently prohibited racial discrimination and guaranteed respect for minority cultures in statutory charters.[62]

Indigenous Australians' physical appearance also carried lasting political and cultural significance under the 'caste' provisions of 'Aboriginal protection' legislation. Known as 'Aboriginal Welfare Acts' after World War II,[63] and colloquially among Aboriginal people as 'Dog Acts', these were the colonial, state and (in the territories) Commonwealth laws that inter alia authorised removal of 'stolen generations' children from their families. When Australia was first colonised, dark skin had marked Aboriginal Australians out from the invaders, but things became more complicated as the overwhelmingly male invading population began to father Aboriginal children. For the next one and a half centuries, governments struggled in different and sometimes contradictory ways with 'the Aboriginal problem' and, particularly in frontier regions, 'the half-caste problem'.[64] 'Protection' laws segregated people of 'full', and at different times people of fractional ('half-caste', 'quadroon', etc), indigenous descent from other Australians (and often from one another), imposing on them discriminatory controls and allowing discriminatory state intervention in their family and personal affairs. An official decision that a person did or did not[65] fall under a 'protection' statute—including because he or she had been exempted from it as a result of assimilationist life choices[66]—had profound consequences for his or her privacy, family relationships, reproduction, choice of residence, freedom of movement and

[59] The Constitution Act 1975 (Vic), s 1A, inserted in 2004, 'recognises' the 'unique status' of Aboriginal people as 'original custodians' of land in the state, their distinctive relationships with land and their contribution to the state, and 'acknowledges' that events leading up to the Constitution's enactment occurred without consultation with the indigenous population. This provision is only a symbolic one—in its own terms, it has no operative effect.

[60] An exception is the implied freedom of political communication, which may incorporate a freedom of movement. However, this protects the system of government established by the Constitution, not communication generally.

[61] Eg, s 46 Constitution Act 1934 (Tas), which protects religious freedom. Generally speaking, state constitutions are ordinary Acts which can be amended by state legislatures.

[62] The Human Rights Act 2004 (ACT) s 27, and the Charter of Rights and Responsibilities Act 2006 (Vic) s 19 (which contains an Aboriginal-specific provision), protect minority cultural rights.

[63] See www1.aiatsis.gov.au/exhibitions/removeprotect/index.html.

[64] Examples of this anxiety include former Western Australian Protector of Aborigines Auber Octavius Neville's book, *Australia's Coloured Minority* (Currawong Publishing, 1947), and NB Tindale, 'Survey of the Half-caste Problem in South Australia' (1940–41) 42 *Proceedings of the Royal Geographical Society of Australasia, South Australia* 66.

[65] Internationally famous Aranda artist Albert Namatjira was one of few people of 'full' Aboriginal descent not reclassified as falling on the Aboriginal side of the line under the 1957 NT 'protection' regime.

[66] Aboriginal people call the exemption certificates issued under 20th-century 'protection' statutes most of which were revocable if the holder associated with unexempted relatives, 'dog licences'.

association, working conditions, access to social security,[67] leisure choices, control of personal property, and (in the 20th century) right to vote, yet officials charged with applying these laws were often permitted to determine a person's racial caste visually.[68] Consequently, and in the absence of recognised 'tribal' institutions,[69] while the public cultures of New Zealand, Canada and the United States have understood indigeneity at least partly in terms of 'tribal' citizenship, Australian public culture still sometimes defines, and posits 'degrees' of, 'Aboriginality' by reference to skin colour, without adequately acknowledging the law's contribution to construction of these distinctions.[70]

Several other factors have contributed to the conspicuous and inferior status of Australia's indigenous people. Economic globalisation has drained population, wealth, services and cultural capital from much of rural Australia, but significant numbers of Aboriginal people remain.[71] Many still live in 'communities' to which their ancestors were once confined under 'Aboriginal protection' laws, while in northern Australia about 20,000 others have moved to more remote 'outstations' on the same land or land to which titles were subsequently acquired.[72] The 'outstation movement' aimed to provide an escape from the overcrowding of indigenous townships and the alcohol abuse, racial discrimination and financial costs associated with earlier attempts 'to assimilate' Aborigines into 'white'-majority towns. However, most outstation communities are tiny, averaging 20 residents, and lack state services like police and schools.[73] Outstations have therefore compounded remote Aborigines' pre-existing segregation from wider Australian society, while their size and distance have been used to excuse continuing government under-spending on remote Aborigines.[74] This population distribution also rein-

[67] State and (later) Commonwealth child endowment payments, introduced in the 20th century, were paid to missions or other authorities that ran reserves on which Aboriginal children resided, rather than to their mothers. Aborigines were excluded from receipt of other social security payments until the 1960s and sometimes 1970s. Before then, it was thus necessary to seek exemption from 'protection' laws and move off Aboriginal reserves to qualify for these payments.

[68] Eg, s 26 of Aboriginals Protection and Restriction of the Sale of Opium Act 1897 (Qld), treated a police averment as prima facie evidence of Aboriginality; s 60 of the Aboriginals Ordinance 1918 (NT), allowed a judge, 'having seen the person, to determine the question'.

[69] See below, text to ns 202–19.

[70] A tendency recognised by Weaver, above n 44.

[71] High mobility can mean that many 'urban' indigenous families' commitments to the city are temporary or partial: J Taylor, *Population and Diversity: Policy Implications of Emerging Indigenous Population Trends*, Research discussion paper 283 (ANU Centre for Aboriginal Economic Policy Research, 2006).

[72] Titles granted under 'land rights' legislation are discussed below at text to nn 229–39. In Western Australia, many 'outstations' have been established on small blocks excised from pastoral leases on inferior tenures, making them inadequate to provide economic support for their residents. For 1970s advocacy of outstations, see HC Coombs, *The Outstation Movement* (Centre for Resource and Environmental Studies, Australian National University, 1979). For a fierce (but often inaccurate) recent critique, see H Hughes, *Lands of Shame* (Centre for Independent Studies, 2007).

[73] J Altman, *In Search of an Outstations Policy for Indigenous Australians*, Working paper 34/2006 (ANU Centre for Aboriginal Economic Policy Research).

[74] This under-spending has a long history: in the 'protection' and 'welfare' eras, many former Aboriginal reserves or institutions were run by churches or missions on underpaid or volunteer labour. To this day, some Aboriginal 'communities' are still referred to colloquially as 'missions'.

forces the stereotypical association of 'real' Aboriginality with 'the Outback', and its corollary: the idea that Aboriginal people do not belong in mainstream (increasingly affluent, urban) Australia.[75] The population profile of indigenous Australians also diverges from that of mainstream Australia. After precipitous declines during the 19th and early 20th centuries, in recent decades the Aboriginal population has recovered due to higher fertility and greater willingness to self-identify. This gulf has profound policy implications: for example, higher crime rates for the Aboriginal population stem partly from it containing many more people in the main criminal offending age group (18–25 years),[76] and conversely (because of low life expectancy compared to other Australians), very few old people (responsible for minimal crime).

The legal system and government policy have played other prominent roles in preventing or distorting interactions between most indigenous and other Australians. Barriers to normal dealings have included land dispossession for the purposes of transfer to 'whites' (an ongoing practice)[77] and the *de facto* spatial segregation which ensues, the selective and discriminatory use and payment of indigenous labour[78] and other legal, illegal and practical constraints on indigenous wealth acquisition and transmission.[79] The law has imposed constraints on inter-racial friendships, political relationships, sexual encounters and marriages,[80] thereby encouraging suppression of indigenous identities in families whose

[75] This idea has a long history. 'Protection' laws declared towns off-limits to statutory 'Aboriginals' and 'half-castes', other than those with special (labour-related) entry permits, at least at night. During World War II, similar curfews applied to northern army towns.

[76] Bureau of Crime Statistics and Research, 'Who are the Offenders?', at www.lawlink.nsw.gov.au/lawlink/bocsar/ll_bocsar.nsf/pages/bocsar_offenders_stats.

[77] Many Aboriginal reserves in Australia were revoked so that the land could be granted to others, including 'selectors' (homesteaders) and (non-Aboriginal) soldier settlers: see, eg, West Australian Department of Indigenous Affairs, *Lost Lands* (Department of Indigenous Affairs, 2004). Among the discriminatory land dealings authorised by the NTA is compulsory acquisition of native title land so that the Crown can re-grant it to another private owner: *Griffiths v Minister for Lands, Planning and Environment* [2008] HCA 20.

[78] 'Protection' and 'welfare' laws authorised unpaid and underpaid use of Aboriginal labour for more than a century, including remuneration in kind long after other workers became subject to Truck Acts. 'Equal wages' for men in the northern pastoral industry were awarded by the industrial Conciliation and Arbitration Commission in 1966, just when the industry was becoming mechanised and jobs were being cut. Other laws authorising unequal wages on racial grounds were rendered invalid by the Racial Discrimination Act 1975 (Cth).

[79] Most 20th-century 'Aboriginal protection' laws authorised garnishment of Aboriginal wages, sometimes to fund other Aborigines' segregation—a practice first contemplated by the Aborigines Protection Act 1869 (Vic), s 2(III). At least two states mishandled funds withheld from Aboriginal wages on employees' behalf: R Kidd, *Trustees on Trial: Recovering the Stolen Wages* (Aboriginal Studies Press, 2006).

[80] Northern 'Aboriginal protection' laws required official consent for marriages between Aboriginal women and 'white' men (marriage between 'white' women and Aboriginal men being unthinkable). Most 'Aboriginal protection' laws prevented egress from Aboriginal reserves by those consigned to them, and entry by others without official permission (see, eg, Northern Territory Ordinance, 1918, ss 16, 19–20, 45). Of course, these controls did not prevent widespread sexual intimacy between, and reproduction by, 'white' men and Aboriginal women. In 1940s Western Australia, a priest who supported an Aboriginal labour strike was forced to appeal to the High Court against a conviction for going too close to a native camp without a protector's permission: *Hodge v Needle* (1946) 20 ALJ 499.

interests lay in 'passing' as 'white'[81] or as new migrants.[82] As noted above, 'land rights' legislation and outstation policy have compounded segregation, in part because entry permit systems developed during the 'protection' era have been retained to protect small communities from violent or voyeuristic outsiders.[83]

Despite this separateness, indigenous Australians have often been allocated a morally symbolic role in Australian nationalism that masks the contributions of law and policy to their predicament. There was intense international, 'scientific' interest in these 'Stone Age ancestors of modern Man' in the late 19th and early 20th centuries,[84] but in 'settled' Australia the typical policy response before about 1920 was to 'smooth the dying pillow' of a race whose demise highlighted the inevitability and advancement of European colonisation.[85] These themes, and associated guilt and potential for international embarrassment, have echoed through Australian history since. There were 19th-century controversies with Britain over the consequences of settler violence towards Aborigines for the colonies' political maturation.[86] The 1960s featured a huge outpouring of inclusive sentiment towards indigenous people via a constitutional referendum purportedly on their 'citizenship'[87]—sentiment very similar to that associated with the 2008 Commonwealth apology.[88] From the 1980s, the state and public culture have appropriated increasingly enthusiastically the cultural motifs of 'our indigenous peoples' as markers of national identity,[89] and obsessed about 'reconciliation' with them.[90] While preferred forms of indigeneity are performed through officially sanctioned or majority-desired forms of exoticised cultural difference,[91] other cultural differences (eg 'promise marriages' of adolescent girls to much older

[81] Eg, S Morgan, *My Place* (Freemantle Arts Press, 1989).

[82] In X Herbert's novel of the NT, *Capricornia* (Publicist Publishing, 1938), 'half-caste' Aboriginal people are encouraged to pass themselves off as (descendants of) Javanese royalty.

[83] See, eg, Aboriginal Land Act (NT).

[84] See A Kuper, *The Invention of Primitive Society: Transformations of an Illusion* (Routledge, 1988) ch 5.

[85] R McGregor, *Imagined Destinies: Indigenous Australians and the 'Doomed Race' Theory 1880–1939* (Melbourne University Press, 1997).

[86] The evangelically dominated British House of Commons Select Committee on the Condition of Aborigines (British Settlements) 1837 proposed Imperial oversight of settler-indigenous relations: Reynolds, above n 36. Britain initially withheld control of Aborigines from self-governing Western Australia: *Yougarla v Western Australia* (2001) 207 CLR 344.

[87] The referendum is discussed at text to nn 183–5.

[88] B Attwood and A Markus, *The 1967 Referendum, or When Aborigines Didn't Get the Vote* (Aboriginal Studies Press, 1997, 2nd edn, 2007).

[89] Eg, the Aboriginal and Torres Strait Islander flags are proclaimed as indigenous and official flags under the Flags Act 1953 (Cth), and indigenous Australians (particularly dancer Djakapurra Munyarryun and middle distance athlete Cathy Freeman) were major players in the opening ceremony for the Sydney 2000 Olympic Games.

[90] In the 1990s, 'reconciliation' as Commonwealth government policy was pursued by a statutory Council—the Council for Aboriginal Reconciliation. The Council's successor is the private company Reconciliation Australia, see www.reconciliation.org.au.

[91] Indigenous art is worth at least A$100 million annually: Senate Environment, Communications, Information Technology and the Arts Committee, *Australia's Indigenous Arts and Crafts Sector* (20 June 2007).

men)[92] remain beyond tolerance.[93] Persistent resort to indigenous symbols probably reflects collective insecurity about the legitimacy or permanence of the 'white' population's hold on the continent, a desire to embellish and distinguish local 'white' identity in a globalised world, or the commercial exploitability of these anxieties.[94] It is not a reliable barometer of the quality of indigenous human rights.

C. Colonisation and its Consequences

1. Assertion of Sovereignty over the Land and its People

More than in other British colonies, Australia's colonisation (initially as a penal colony) was an exercise in public power—then, as now, the state played a central role in society. Three main assertions of Crown sovereignty, starting in the east, accounted for the entire continent. When Governor Phillip's Commission was read at Sydney Cove on 7 February 1788, the local Eora people and others as far away as the Yolngu of eastern Arnhem Land officially fell under British control. In just over 40 years, the remaining inhabitants of 'New Holland' followed, with six colonies (later states, alongside three mainland territories) being carved out of these boundaries. The Torres Strait Islands in Australia's far north remained formally uncolonised for another 50 years until the 1870s, making them an ideal base for the first successful 'native title' test case.

These assertions of British sovereignty were initially supported by very limited occupation, although by the 1860s most fertile (and many arid) regions were held on some kind of pastoral tenure.[95] Colonisation was funded initially by the Imperial government (rather than by charter or joint stock companies), then by sales of indigenous land to subsidise further immigration.[96] By the mid-19th century, the pastoral and mining economy founded on this dispossession provided (non-indigenous) Australians with the highest GDP per capita in the world.[97] When Britain began to grant the colonies self-government from the 1850s, power to alienate 'waste' lands and resources was vested in colonial (later state)

[92] This Aboriginal tradition (applicable when girls have reached puberty) was tolerated by the *Criminal Code* (NT), in a manner recommended by the Australian Law Reform Commission (see n 149 below), until 2004, when it was abolished due to pressure to 'protect' Aboriginal 'children' from 'sexual abuse'.

[93] E Povinelli, *The Cunning of Recognition: Indigenous Alterities and the Making of Indigenous Multiculturalism* (Duke University Press, 2002).

[94] The latter two themes in particular are explored by Povinelli, *ibid.*

[95] M Gumbert, *Neither Justice Nor Reason: A Legal and Anthropological Analysis of Aboriginal Land Rights* (University of Queensland Press, 1984) 13.

[96] Under the Australian Waste Lands Act 1842 (Imp), half the proceeds of colonial land sales were used to fund British immigration. The colony of South Australia had been established on this basis in 1834.

[97] A Maddison, *The World Economy*, vol 2 (Historical Statistics) (OECD, 2005).

legislatures[98]—an arrangement undisturbed by federation in 1901.[99] Those colonial legislatures continued the Imperial practice of creating new statutory titles to land,[100] including pastoral leases containing access and subsistence reservations in favour of Aboriginal people.[101] By the early 20th century, most state governments had added *in situ* minerals to their wealth, without compensating any prior owners.[102]

Not only were Aboriginal lands confiscated to fuel the settler colony, but Aboriginal people were increasingly conscripted as a source of cheap labour. In the eastern colonies of New South Wales (NSW) and Van Diemen's Land (Tasmania), the availability of convict labour to government and private masters[103] reduced demand for indigenous labour, initially fostering racial segregation.[104] However, rising social inequality in the early 20th century fuelled demand for servants, including teenage Aboriginal girls removed from NSW 'reserves' and placed in 'suitable situations' to 'save them from the camps' and stop them reproducing.[105] By contrast, in Western Australia, which received convicts later and only for public works, early Aboriginal policy sought *to attract* indigenous labour into Perth rather than to banish it.[106] In northern WA, where deployment of convicts was prohibited, Master and Servant Act-style labour laws[107]—with their sanctions of imprisonment for servant breaches and police powers to return convicted runaways—were retained well into the 20th century, long after their abolition for the general population,[108] guaranteeing pastoralists and pearlers an Aboriginal labour supply, even during wars and gold rushes.[109]

[98] Eg s 3 of the Western Australia Constitution Act 1890 (Imp) and s 30 of the Constitution Act 1867 (Qld).

[99] See ss 106–107 of the Commonwealth Constitution.

[100] Including pastoral leases, the 'ranch' tenure under which much of Australia outside the cities is held. See *Wik Peoples v Queensland* (1996) 187 CLR 1.

[101] See *Wik* case, *ibid*, but compare *Wilson v Anderson* (2002) 213 CLR 401, regarding smaller NSW leases.

[102] *Western Australia v Ward* (2002) 213 CLR 1 [376]–[385]; and *Wik Peoples v Queensland* [1996] 63 FCR 450 (Drummond J) paras 115–50.

[103] A system of convict assignment to private employers operated in NSW between 1788 and 1841.

[104] See generally J Hagan, 'Settlers and the State: The Creation of an Aboriginal Workforce in Australia' (1988) 22 *Aboriginal History* 11.

[105] V Haskins, *One Bright Spot* (Palgrave Macmillan, 2005) ch 3.

[106] Eg An Act to prevent the enticing away of Aboriginal girls 1844 (WA). See P Hasluck, *Black Australians: A Survey of Native Policy in Western Australia, 1829–1897* (Melbourne University Press, 1942); P Hetherington, *Settlers, Servants and Slaves: Aboriginal and European Children in Nineteenth Century Western Australia* (University of Western Australia Press, 2002).

[107] See generally D Hay and P Craven (eds), *Masters, Servants and Magistrates in Britain and the Empire 1562–1955* (University of North Carolina Press, 2004).

[108] Discrimination introduced by the Aborigines Protection (Amendment) Act 1892 and repealed in 1954.

[109] Gold was discovered at Coolgardie in 1892. 39% of Australia's male population aged 18–44 enlisted during World War I, including 32,000 men from WA. Northern Australia's 'white' populations were evacuated during World War II, but WA 'Aboriginal protection' laws forbade Aborigines leaving their employment or district, or travelling south of a latitudinal 'leprosy line' which bisected the state.

Doubts about the status of Australia's Aboriginal population and the appropriateness of extending British law to them lingered for half a century after 1788.[110] (In the late 20th century, the courts were still hearing claims that Australia had been acquired by conquest, not settlement.)[111] However, as the settler and convict population increased, the convenient wisdom, in law and policy, hardened into a view that the Aborigines lacked laws, land relationships and political institutions deserving respect or recognition.[112] Ignoring the authoritarian convict period, the courts declared that British settlers had imported a universal legal heritage: instead of indigenous legal systems, the law of an Australian colony had become, from the moment sovereignty was asserted over it, the common law of England—to the extent applicable to local conditions, and as amended by statute.[113] British subjecthood was assumed to have been extended to Aboriginal Australians upon their colonisation under the rule in *Calvin's Case.*[114] Not until the 1990s did Australian courts recognise the Aboriginal title to land first recognised by the United States[115] and New Zealand[116] courts in the first half of the 19th century[117]—and then only in an ersatz form.[118]

The contrast with the position of indigenous people in North America reflects important differences of history and geography. The creation of the Australian colonies, and their eventual political independence, occurred in the absence of territorial claims by other European sovereigns against whom indigenous allegiances could have been forged.[119] Also, there was no contiguous Aboriginal territory on which the new Australian nation might focus expansionist ambitions. The neigh-

[110] Despite multiple proclamations and directives that Aborigines were equal before the law and/or not entitled to settle disputes by 'custom', courts struggled with the application of criminal laws to them for offences *inter se* into the 1840s: see P Hanks, P Keyzer and J Clarke, *Australian Constitutional Law: Materials and Commentary* (7th edn, Butterworths, 2004) 71–73; H Reynolds, *Aboriginal Sovereignty: Three Nations, One Australia* (Allen and Unwin, 1996) ch 3.

[111] *Milirrpum v Nabalco*, above n 28; *Coe v Commonwealth* (1979) 24 ALR 118. Municipal law orthodoxy—that Australia was a settled colony—was re-emphasised in *Mabo*, above n 32, despite conflicting with international law orthodoxy that only uninhabited territories could be so acquired: see G Simpson, 'Mabo, International Law, Terra Nullius and the Stories of Settlement: An Unresolved Jurisprudence' (1993) 19 *Melbourne University Law Review* 195. It seems unlikely, however, that classifying Australia as a 'conquered' colony would alter the position of Aboriginal Australians today: in such colonies, indigenous norms can be displaced by the Crown exercising *prerogative* powers, as well as by parliaments enacting legislation.

[112] In *Cooper v Stuart* (1889) 14 App Cas 286, the Privy Council described NSW as 'a tract of territory practically unoccupied, without settled inhabitants or settled law' (at 291).

[113] Before representative government, this meant British statutes intended to apply to the colonies. This position was reinforced by the Australian Courts Act 1828 (Imp), 9 Geo IV c 83, s 24.

[114] (1608) 7 Co Rep 2a.

[115] *Johnson v M'Intosh*, 8 Wheat 543 (1823).

[116] *R v Symonds* [1840–1932] (1847) NZPCC 387.

[117] *Mabo*, above n 32.

[118] As noted later in this Chapter, native title in Australia takes its contours from what can be proven of traditional laws and customs. The High Court in *Mabo (No 2)* was also forced to accommodate some 200 years of land alienation by declaring *obiter dicta* that native title could be extinguished obliquely by the grant of an inconsistent interest in the same land by the Crown. See also this book's Chapter by Kent McNeil.

[119] The French sailed into Sydney immediately after Governor Phillip, but did not assert territorial claims.

bouring island of Papua, populated by Melanesians like the Torres Strait Islanders, fell partly under British control in the late 19th century (and Australian control in the 20th), but its extreme topography and tropical climate offered European settlers fewer attractions than Alta California or Nuevo México.

This cultural and political hegemony made unnecessary some of the innovations and distinctions of Imperial policy in North America and New Zealand. For example, Australian courts have never recognised indigenous sovereignty, over territory or people[120]: the only laws, citizenship and institutions on offer to indigenous subjects were British (later Australian) ones. Nor was there an Australian equivalent of the Imperial Royal Proclamation of 1763 over the American colonies, which withheld from the settlers lands for the use of the Indigenes.[121] Also, there was no Australian tradition (not even a flawed one) of the state negotiating treaties to acquire indigenous land.[122] Further, the Australian courts have never recognised a general trust relationship between the state and its indigenous inhabitants,[123] unlike in Canada where the Crown owes special fiduciary responsibilities to First Nations. This is not simply because of the traditionally limited role of the national government in indigenous affairs, as discussed below, but also due to the absence of treaty relationships between indigenous people and government institutions upon which such relationships might be founded, the narrow scope of fiduciary principles in Australian law, the strength of the doctrine of parliamentary supremacy, and the existence of comprehensive land alienation statutes.[124] Even had the Australian courts been prepared to impose trust obligations on Australian *executive* governments, such obligations would have been overridden by unilateral, inconsistent statutory powers like those which have authorised dispossession and child removal.

2. The Exclusion of Indigenous People from Public Institutions

The assertion of British sovereignty also led, as a practical matter, to the effective exclusion of indigenous people from the institutions of the emerging Australian state—its legislatures, courts and executive agencies. The settlers constructed Australian institutions in their own image. Once Britain transferred power to alienate land to the new colonial parliaments, local settlers' control of Aboriginal land and affairs intensified. Despite early universal male suffrage for the lower

[120] See *Walker v New South Wales* (1994) 82 CLR 45; *Coe v Commonwealth (No 2)* (1993) 118 ALR 193.

[121] An attempt to reserve lands for Aborigines in the Letters Patent establishing the colony of South Australia was overtaken by new British legislation conferring the power to grant land on the colonial legislature: see Hanks, Keyzer and Clarke, above n 110, ch 2 at [2.3.15].

[122] Land transfers from Aborigines to private citizens were declared invalid by Governor Bourke in 1835, in response to John Batman's fraudulent attempt to acquire by 'treaty' a large area of Port Phillip around what is now Melbourne: A Campbell, *John Batman and the Aborigines* (Kibble Books, 1987).

[123] *Director of Aboriginal and Islanders Advancement v Peinkinna* (1978) 17 ALR 129; compare Toohey J in *Mabo*, above n 32, 203.

[124] Hanks, Keyzer and Clarke, above n 110.

houses of colonial legislatures, their upper houses were nominated or elected on a property franchise, sometimes one allowing plural voting,[125] giving considerable power to *propertied* settlers. These privileges survived federation; most were not reformed until the mid- to late 20th century.[126]

The problem was compounded by formal exclusion of Aboriginal voters from the franchise in Western Australia, Queensland, NT and at the federal level[127] for most of the 20th century, and less explicit disenfranchisement of many Aboriginal people in other states because of their receipt of charitable aid.[128] Beneficiaries of cheap Aboriginal labour and land also enjoyed unequal say in indigenous policy via electoral gerrymandering favouring rural electorates in several states. Thus the historical relationship of Aboriginal Australians to legislatures bears some similarities to the disenfranchisement of African-Americans before the 1960s.[129] Historically, the property franchise also affected Aboriginal people at local levels, such as through racial segregation of public facilities like swimming pools[130] by municipal councils, elected by ratepayers. A mixed popular and propertied franchise still applies to municipal elections in most states at a time when 75 per cent of indigenous Australians live in rental accommodation.[131]

Unsurprisingly, then, only a handful of Aboriginal people have ever been elected to Australian parliaments.[132] While several Australian jurisdictions have recently flirted with the idea of designated seats for indigenous people on the model first adopted in New Zealand in 1867, no such seats have been created.

Aborigines have also been excluded from meaningful participation in the justice system, except as defendants (a role in which they are presently, and have been historically, seriously over-represented).[133] Unlike convict evidence,[134] Aboriginal

[125] See J Winter, 'English Democracy and the Example of Australia' (1966) 35(1) *Pacific Historical Review* 67.

[126] South Australia was the last state to abandon the property qualification, in 1973.

[127] The NT and Commonwealth franchises were open to people of less than 'preponderant' indigenous descent, and exceptions were made in these and some other jurisdictions for ex-servicemen and holders of 'dog tickets' (certificates of exemption from the 'protection' laws). However, many of these eligible people were prevented from voting by electoral officers.

[128] A Twomey, *The Constitution of NSW* (Federation Press, 2004) 324–7.

[129] Ie, before the Supreme Court's 'one vote, one value' decisions and enactment of the Voting Rights Act 1965. Neither the Australian Constitution nor state constitutions guarantee equal voting power: *Attorney-General (Cth); ex rel McKinlay v Commonwealth* (1975) 135 CLR 1; *McGinty v WA* (1996) 186 CLR 140.

[130] See N Landers and R Perkins, 'Freedom Ride', episode in series *Blood Brothers* (Australian Broadcasting Corporation and Australian Film Finance Corporation, 1993).

[131] M Sawer, *Property Votes—OK?* (Democratic Audit of Australia, 2006) and Productivity Commission, *Overcoming Indigenous Disadvantage: Key Indicators* (Productivity Commission, 2007) ch 3.7.

[132] See Hanks, Keyzer and Clarke, above n 110, ch 2, 90. Notably, in late 2007, Tiwi Aboriginal woman Marion Scrymgour was elected deputy Chief Minister of the NT. She was one of five Aboriginal members elected to the 25-seat NT Parliament in 2005.

[133] Indigenous adults are 13 times more likely than others to be imprisoned. For juveniles, the rate is 17 times: Productivity Commission, above n 131, ch 3.12.

[134] Which was inadmissible in England but accepted by colonial courts: see *R v Gardner and Yems*, Supreme Court of NSW, 1829, reproduced at www.law.mq.edu.au/scnsw/Cases1829-30/html/r_v_gardener_and_yems__1829.htm.

evidence was inadmissible in Australian courts before the 1840s[135]—in some colonies as late as the 1880s—making prosecution of frontier violence difficult.[136] Western Australia operated separate, inferior systems of summary justice for Aboriginal people for most of the 19th and early 20th centuries.[137] Well into the last century in some states, the practical treatment of Aboriginal witnesses in court cases was virtually indistinguishable from that of defendants.[138] Lack of availability of adequately trained interpreters who speak indigenous languages,[139] and lack of understanding of indigenous communication techniques by judges and lawyers, risks compromising the evidence of people whose first language is not English.[140] Even in the NT, an Aboriginal Interpreter Service was established as late as 2000.[141]

Aborigines have also been excluded from jury pools because of their historical exclusion from electoral rolls, their criminal records, or the lack of extension to remote or rural areas of jury districts.[142] It is unusual for a judge to rule that a 'white' jury cannot try an Aboriginal defendant fairly.[143] Not only are indigenous Australians rarely tried by juries of their peers in cultural terms, but it is assumed that non-Aboriginal juries try 'whites' accused of crimes against Aboriginal victims fairly.[144] The relationship between Aborigines and police has long been an antagonistic one, not simply because of discriminatory enforcement of criminal laws,[145]

[135] A Bill to permit Aboriginal evidence was passed in NSW in 1838 (following the Myall Creek massacre), but disallowed as 'contrary to the principles of British jurisprudence'. After a change of government in Britain, the Imperial Parliament legislated to permit such initiatives in 1843: R Smandych, 'Contemplating the Testimony of Others' (2004) 8 *Australian Journal of Legal History* 237.

[136] See N Wright, 'The Problems of Aboriginal Evidence in Early Colonial New South Wales' in D Kirkby and C Coleborne (eds), *Law, History, Colonialism: The Reaches of Empire* (Manchester University Press, 2001).

[137] See Hasluck, above n 106; K Auty, *Black Glass: Western Australian Courts of Native Affairs 1936–1954* (Freemantle Arts Centre Press, 2005).

[138] Eg by 'bringing them in on the [neck] chain' to town and keeping them incarcerated before court hearings, a practice which was still used in mid-20th century Western Australia.

[139] This is despite statutory guarantees of the provision of interpreters, eg s 36 of the Evidence Act 1995 (Cth).

[140] See M Cooke, *Indigenous Interpreting: Issues for Courts*, www.aija.org.au/ac01/Cooke.pdf, and D Eades, *Aboriginal English and the Law: Communicating with Aboriginal English Speaking Clients: A Handbook for Legal Practitioners* (Queensland Law Society, 1992).

[141] See www.dlghs.nt.gov.au/ais.

[142] In 1985, the NSW Law Reform Commission discovered that 10% of electoral rolls (notably those in the state's west, which has a sizeable indigenous population) had not been allocated to any jury district: *Discussion Paper 12 (1985): Criminal Procedure: The Jury in a Criminal Trial* (NSW Law Reform Commission, 1985).

[143] The Queensland District Court did order, on the basis of a survey of 400 Townsville residents, that the trial of accused 2004 Palm Island rioter Lex Wotton be moved from Townsville to Brisbane because an unbiased jury could not be found in Townsville: *Wotton v Director of Public Prosecutions* [2006] QDC 202.

[144] Despite the survey evidence (see previous note), the police officer whose conduct precipitated the Palm Island riot was tried and acquitted of manslaughter in Townsville by an all-'white' jury: T Koch, 'Another Black Stain', *The Australian*, 21 June 2007.

[145] For a classic study, see E Eggleston, *Fear, Favour or Affection: Aborigines and the Criminal Law in Victoria, South Australia and Western Australia* (ANU Press, 1976). See also the 1991 findings of the Royal Commission into Aboriginal Deaths in Custody, available at www.austlii.edu.au/au/other/IndigLRes.

but also because of the historical role of police as Aboriginal 'protectors' in enforcing discriminatory 'protection' laws (for example, those authorising removal of children). Today, police are still accused of failing to investigate or prosecute crimes against Aboriginal victims earnestly,[146] and police conduct has precipitated major Aboriginal riots.[147] At the same time, some remote 'communities' suffer intolerable levels of violence in part because of lack of adequate local policing.[148]

As in Canada and the United States, there have been several late investigations (for example, by law reform commissions) into the possibility of Australian legal systems 'recognising' Aboriginal customary laws, particularly as a measure to address indigenous over-representation in the criminal justice system. The recent tendency is towards recommendations facilitating more effective Aboriginal participation in the justice system, rather than changes in the substantive (criminal) law to reflect 'customary' norms.[149] There are obvious problems with the latter type of reform where Aboriginal societies do not retain effective power to generate norms.[150] Meanwhile, however, Parliament under the Howard government abolished judicial discretion to take account of customary and cultural factors when bailing and sentencing federal and NT offenders.[151] Useful reform measures in recent years include establishment of Aboriginal sentencing courts—sometimes known by the wider regional names for particular indigenous populations, that is, as Koori, Nunga or Murri[152] courts—or sentencing circles on the Canadian model.[153] While the inclusive nature of these proceedings is resource-intensive, they appear to have contributed to a drop in recidivism in some jurisdictions.[154]

[146] R Coulthart, 'Black and White Justice', *Sunday* (Channel 9 TV), 26 February 2006, at sunday.ninemsn.com.au/sunday/cover_stories/article_1938.asp.

[147] At Redfern in Sydney in February 2004, and on Palm Island off east Queensland in November 2004.

[148] B Stoll and J Valentin, *A Review of the Operational and Corporate Implications Arising from the Alleged Activities of Certain Police Secondees to the Former National Crime Authority and Australian Crime Commission During the Period 28 February 2000 to 18 February 2004* (Australian Crime Commission, 2004).

[149] Eg, the 1986 Australian Law Reform Commission's report no 31, *The Recognition of Aboriginal Customary Laws*, and the 2006 Law Reform Commission of Western Australia's report on *Aboriginal Customary Laws*.

[150] See C Cunneen and M Schwartz, *Customary Law, Human Rights and International Law: Some Conceptual Issues*, Background Paper 11 (Law Reform Commission of Western Australia, 2005); *Walker*, above n 120.

[151] See, eg, amendments to the Crimes Act 1914 (Cth), ss 15AB and 16A, which prevent bail and sentencing courts taking account of 'any form of customary law or cultural practice' in mitigation or aggravation of an offence.

[152] For Victoria, South Australia and Queensland respectively.

[153] Eg, in Nowra and other parts of NSW.

[154] I Potas *et al*, *Circle Sentencing in NSW: A Review and Evaluation* (Judicial Commission of NSW, 2003) pandora.nla.gov.au/pan/40232/20040206-0000/circle+sentencing+report.pdf.

3. Indigenous Policy, Politics and Governance in the Federal Context

For most of Australian history, indigenous policy was the domain of the self-governing colonies, later the Australian states. Between federation and 1967, the Commonwealth's indigenous affairs role was limited to its territories—although some states referred powers over Aborigines to it during World War II,[155] the Commonwealth did not use them.[156] This is a fundamental difference from the North American federations, in which administration of indigenous affairs has primarily (especially in Canada) been the task of national governments. The Commonwealth's record in NT indigenous affairs, while not distinguished,[157] had been in the Australian vanguard.[158] Further, by the 1960s it was apparent that some states were virtually leaving their indigenous people to die, and that to address these problems it was necessary to harness the Commonwealth's far more substantial financial resources.[159]

This is not to say that Aboriginal people simply tolerated government policies and laws affecting them. The armed resistance campaigns against Australia's early colonisation[160] gave way to diverse political objections to discriminatory government policies and dispossession. Before the 1960s, the small size of Australia's indigenous population, the absence of other people of colour,[161] and many Aborigines' incarceration meant that these campaigns often involved 'white' supporters[162] and risked entanglement in wider political agendas.[163] The fact that past protests and demands were expressed in the language and aspirations of the day can also present problems for contemporary demands for an essential, enduring indigeneity or tradition.[164]

[155] Eg Commonwealth Powers Act 1942 (NSW) and Commonwealth Powers Act 1943 (Vic).

[156] The Migration Act 1958 (Cth) did prevent Aborigines from leaving Australia until 1973.

[157] Eg it spent more on the Governor-General's salary than it did on NT Aboriginal protection in the years before World War II: A Markus, *Governing Savages* (Allen and Unwin, 1990) 9–10.

[158] The largest Aboriginal reserves had been proclaimed in the NT, and Former Minister for Territories Paul Hasluck had introduced a relatively enlightened version of the assimilation policy in the 1950s.

[159] The Commonwealth dominates Australian 'fiscal federalism'. This position has been achieved by a combination of a Commonwealth monopoly over customs and excise revenues under the Constitution, Commonwealth income taxation laws driving the states from that field, and the Commonwealth's power to make conditional grants to the states under s 96 of the Constitution.

[160] See n 29 above.

[161] A notable exception being the FCAATSI campaigner, Faith Bandler, whose ni-Vanuatu father escaped the early 19th century deportation of Pacific Island labourers.

[162] There were, of course, also 'white' humanitarian organisations pressing similar agendas, eg those which grew out of the British Anti-Slavery Society in the early 19th century.

[163] See B Attwood, *Rights for Aborigines* (Allen and Unwin, 2003).

[164] Eg in the Yorta Yorta native title claim to the Murray River region of Victoria and NSW, Justice Olney interpreted a petition to Queen Victoria from Aboriginal people living near Cumeragunja, including the claimants' ancestors, in which they asked for a land grant and expressed desire to assimilate, as evidence of loss of the tradition on which native title is founded: see *Members of the Yorta Yorta Community v Victoria* [1998] FCA 1606, paras 119–21, upheld on appeal by the High Court (2002) 214 CLR 422.

Kulin people from Coranderrk outside Melbourne, who had worked hard to meet the colonisers' demands that they become agriculturalists, organised an early 'rebellion' against closure of their Aboriginal reserve for reallocation to covetous 'whites' in the 1870s.[165] Cumeragunja reserve in NSW, just across the Murray River from Victoria, received Coranderrk refugees when Victoria redefined 'Aboriginality' to evict 'half-castes' from its reserves in the 1880s, but evicted them when NSW introduced similarly restrictive legislation in 1909.[166] Cumeragunja residents walked off the reserve for nine months to protest authoritarian management in 1939.[167]

Out of events like these emerged the Aborigines' Progressive Association (APA), founded in 1825 by Aboriginal activists and 'white' supporters,[168] and the Australian Aborigines' League (AAL), founded by Yorta Yorta man William Cooper. In 1938, Cooper led a delegation to Prime Minister Joe Lyons arguing for the constitutional amendment allowing the Commonwealth to enter the indigenous affairs field which was eventually adopted in 1967. The AAL also advocated increased parliamentary representation for Aboriginal Australians and other citizenship rights,[169] and its members were involved in trying to improve 'protection' regimes from within.[170] The APA and the AAL staged a 'Day of Mourning' protest in 1938 while the rest of Australia celebrated the country's sesquicentenary of the arrival of the first convict ships.[171] Between the 1930s and the 1960s, Aboriginal and Torres Strait Islander protests extended to labour conditions; for example, in 1946 (two decades before the famous Gurindji walkoff from Wave Hill station in the NT),[172] many Aboriginal station hands in the Pilbara region of Western Australia struck for three years over employment conditions.[173] There were many acts of individual or family resistance: mothers hiding 'half-caste' children from those who sought to remove them, families moving around or women marrying 'white' men (where this was permitted) to avoid incarceration, and reserve housing residents protesting its poor quality via rent strikes. With the growth of social

[165] The 'Coranderrk Rebellion', led by William Barak, kept the reserve in Aboriginal hands until it was depopulated as a result of eviction of 'half-castes' (see text to next note). It was closed in the 1920s. See Attwood, above n 163, ch 1.

[166] See the definition of 'Aboriginal' in s 3 of the Aborigines Protection Act 1909 (NSW), available on www1.aiatsis.gov.au/exhibitions/removeprotect/leg/nsw_leg.html; Attwood, above n 163; H Goodall, *Invasion to Embassy: Land in Aboriginal Politics in New South Wales 1770–1972* (Allen and Unwin, 1996).

[167] Goodall, above n 166, ch 18.

[168] J Maynard, 'Vision, Voice and Influence: The Rise of the Australian Aboriginal Progressive Association', (2003) 34 *Australian Historical Studies* 91.

[169] A Markus, *Blood from Stone: William Cooper and the Australian Aborigines' League* (Allen and Unwin, 1998).

[170] Eg activist Pearl Gibbs was the only woman ever appointed to the NSW Aborigines Welfare Board.

[171] J Horner, *Seeking Racial Justice: An Insider's Memoir of the Movement for Aboriginal Advancement, 1938–1978* (Aboriginal Studies Press, 2004) 3–7.

[172] D Rose, *Hidden Histories* (Aboriginal Studies Press, 1991).

[173] See generally J McCorquodale, 'The Myth of Mateship: Aborigines and Employment' (1985) 27(1) *Journal of Industrial Relations* 3.

movements in the 1960s, Aboriginal protests took a greater lead from developments like the US civil rights movement. In 1965, Aranda man Charles Perkins[174] and more than 30 non-indigenous university students toured northwest NSW in a bus to publicise and challenge entrenched segregation in access to local government services (for example, swimming pools) and discrimination in supply of other services (for example, bans on Aborigines drinking in local hotels).[175]

By the 1960s, an increasingly multinational mining industry was seeking to establish large extraction projects where landowner negotiations and protests could be avoided.[176] Mineralisation and lack of recognition of indigenous title in Australia made its northern remote areas ideal locations. Discoveries of bauxite on the Gove and Cape York Peninsulas in the 1950s led Commonwealth and Queensland governments to propose that Aboriginal reserves (previously closed to outsiders) be opened to mining without Aboriginal consent.[177] This ignited protests by local Aboriginal people and missionaries. In 1963, Yolngu people from Yirrkala on the Gove Peninsula sent a petition protesting mining, attached to bark paintings depicting their traditional land ownership motifs, to the Commonwealth Parliament.[178] Although the Yolngu lost their campaign to prevent mining, and their subsequent 'native title' court case,[179] these events precipitated the Whitlam government's proposals for NT land rights legislation, eventually enacted under the conservative Fraser administration.[180] Opening of Queensland reserves to bauxite miners from the 1950s, and retention of 'Aboriginal protection' laws into the 1970s and even 1980s,[181] by the maverick and authoritarian Bjelke-Petersen state government led to increasing calls for federal leadership on indigenous affairs and national anti-discrimination laws.

In 1967, sustained campaigning by the multi-racial Federal Council for the Advancement of Aborigines and Torres Strait Islanders[182] helped produce a landslide constitutional referendum vote,[183] extending the Commonwealth Parliament's existing, anomalous power—to make 'special laws' for 'the people of any race, other than the aboriginal race in any state' which Parliament has 'deemed

174 Perkins went on to head the Commonwealth Department of Aboriginal Affairs in the 1970s.

175 A Curthoys, *Freedom Ride: A Freedom Rider Remembers* (Allen and Unwin, 2002). Supply of alcohol to Aboriginal people had been decriminalised in NSW two years earlier.

176 See generally D Mercer, *A Question of Balance: Natural Resources Conflict Issues in Australia* (3rd edn, Federation Press, 1995) ch 4.

177 The Aboriginals Benefit Account which funds NT land councils (see note 209) is a legacy of the compromise which allowed mining on reserves in return for 'royalty equivalent' payments.

178 The bark petition, by which the Yirrkala expected to convince Parliament of the validity of their 'title deeds', hangs in Parliament House in Canberra. See National Archives of Australia, at www.foundingdocs.gov.au/item.asp?sdID=100.

179 *Milirrpum v Nabalco*, above n 28.

180 Land rights are discussed below at text to n 229–46.

181 G Nettheim, *Victims of Law: Black Queenslanders Today* (International Commission of Jurists, 1981).

182 S Taffe, *Black and White Together: FCAATSI The Federal Council for the Advancement of Aborigines and Torres Strait Islanders 1958–1973* (University of Queensland Press, 2005).

183 Under s 128 of the Constitution, which requires the support of a majority of electors in a majority of states.

necessary'—to Aborigines.[184] Unfortunately, the constitutional amendment appears to have allowed Commonwealth laws discriminating *against* Aboriginal people as well as laws which single them out for benign discrimination or affirmative action.[185] Because the referendum did not remove concurrent state powers, the Commonwealth (especially under conservative governments) has been surprisingly reluctant to flex its muscles in this field, at least on behalf of indigenous people. For example, the new power was not used to enact regulatory (as opposed to grants and loans) legislation until Parliament under the Whitlam Labor government legislated to override remnants of Queensland 'protection' laws—eg those allowing exile of 'trouble-makers'[186] from reserves in 1975.[187] After 1967, Whitlam's conservative predecessors had appointed Ministers of Aboriginal Affairs and a (non-indigenous) advisory Council,[188] but established no federal Aboriginal Affairs department.

This inaction, and the conservative McMahon government's decision to permit mining at Gove without addressing the land rights question, precipitated the establishment on Australia Day, 1972,[189] of one of the more poignant symbols of Australian indigenous protest: the 'tent embassy' outside the (then) Parliament House in Canberra.[190] Originally modelled on the 1969 American Indian takeover of Alcatraz, the embassy succeeds[191] as political theatre because its sprawling, outdoor untidiness continues to evoke at least some Aboriginal living conditions or Aboriginal ways of using public space,[192] particularly by contrast with the order of Canberra's parliamentary triangle, which now includes an official 'Reconciliation Place'. The embassy existed on and off during the 1970s, was re-established in 1992 and remains, despite multiple attempts to remove or institutionalise it.

The most significant Commonwealth legislation enacted under the power conferred by the 1967 referendum has been the Native Title Act 1993 (Cth) (hereafter NTA), which came about only after the courts had recognised indigenous titles to land (as discussed below, proposals to use the power to enact national 'land rights'

[184] This was achieved by deleting the words 'other than the aboriginal race in any state'.

[185] See, eg, *Koowarta v Bjelke-Petersen* (1982) 153 CLR 168; *Kartinyeri v Commonwealth* (1998) 195 CLR 337.

[186] The power to exile seems to have been widely used in Queensland. Eddie Mabo was exiled from Mer as a teenager.

[187] Aboriginal and Torres Strait Islanders (Queensland Discriminatory Laws) Act 1975 (Cth).

[188] The Council for Aboriginal Affairs was chaired by economist Herbert Cole 'Nugget' Coombs, credited with influencing the Whitlam government's decision to replace the official policy of 'assimilation' with one of 'self-determination'. See T Rowse, *Obliged to be Difficult: Nugget Coombs' Legacy in Indigenous Affairs* (Cambridge University Press, 2000).

[189] Since this date, 26 January, has nothing to do with federation—it is the anniversary of the First Fleet's arrival in Sydney Cove, NSW—it is commonly referred to by Aborigines as 'Invasion Day'.

[190] Goodall, above n 166, ch 24. Parliament House moved to a new building in 1988, but the embassy remains outside 'old' Parliament House.

[191] Of course, such protests tend to attract followers who find it difficult to compromise with the state, and inevitably also attract other marginalised people, so that they are easily discredited as 'fringe' operations.

[192] For example, there have been ongoing disputes about camp fires at the embassy, as well as what appear to have been acts of arson against it.

legislation in the 1980s foundered on federalism). The power has also supported 'last resort' national Aboriginal heritage legislation.[193] The Keating Labor government's use of this legislation in the 1990s to block development proposals which had been cleared under state Aboriginal heritage laws—which generally have not left the question of significance for indigenous determination and have allowed it to be offset by development considerations[194]—generated heated controversy.[195]

Over the 220 years since Australia's colonisation, government policies towards indigenous people have varied in their motivations, design and impact, in part depending on preferences for segregation, 'assimilation', 'integration' or limited self-determination.[196] However, as occurs in other inter-racial contexts,[197] it is surprising how often these choices resolve into binary oppositions about whether Aboriginal people really can (or should be permitted to) live among other Australians as equals, when they won't always conform to other Australians' ideas about how they should behave, or whether (since they won't conform) they would be better off removed some distance away. Further, what appear to be policy choices are often driven by economic forces (as the examples of the opening of segregated northern reserves to bauxite mining cited above show), or by the desire to avoid significant government expenditure.[198] And as the operation of racist 'protection' laws and the Racial Discrimination Act 1975 (Cth) in 1970s Queensland illustrated,[199] overlapping federal and state responsibility has also sometimes seen competing tendencies operating in the same jurisdiction.

The absence of a tradition of treaty-making in Australia leads to regular suggestions that indigenous affairs would be improved by having one. Labor Prime Minister Bob Hawke raised the possibility of a national treaty or 'compact'[200] between Aboriginal and non-Aboriginal Australians after being presented with yet another petition for land rights, self-determination and civil rights on a bark painting at the Barunga sports and cultural festival in the NT in the country's bicentennial year.[201] Yet, even leaving aside the obvious problems with treaties in

[193] Aboriginal and Torres Strait Islander Heritage Protection Act 1984 (Cth).

[194] See E Evatt, *Review of the Aboriginal and Torres Strait Islander Heritage Protection Act 1984*, www.austlii.edu.au/au/other/IndigLRes/1996/1/index.html.

[195] Eg, see the cases relating to the proposed Hindmarsh Island bridge near Goolwa in South Australia: *Norvill v Chapman* (1995) 55 FCR 316; *Wilson v Minister for Aboriginal and Torres Strait Islander Affairs* (1996) 189 CLR 1; *Kartinyeri v Commonwealth* (1998) 195 CLR 337; *Chapman v Luminis (No 5)* (2001) 123 FCR 62.

[196] See P McHugh, *Aboriginal Societies and the Common Law* (Oxford University Press, 2004), 276–84, 337–46, 396–414.

[197] Eg, those of the increasingly re-segregated US.

[198] For example, Jeremy Beckett has argued that moves in the 1960s away from policies of assimilation were driven by the massive likely cost of properly housing, educating and caring for the health of Aboriginal people; under policies of 'integration' and 'self-determination', 'their poverty . . . [was] rendered exotic and so no longer comparable to other forms of poverty': 'Aboriginality, Citizenship and Nation State' (1988) 24 *Social Analysis* 3, 12.

[199] Conflicts of laws are resolved by the federal supremacy clause under s 109 of the Constitution, but conflicts of policy are often much less easily identified by those not affected by them.

[200] This terminology easily lent itself to comparisons (humorous and serious) with cosmetic products.

[201] The Barunga Statement also hangs in Parliament House in Canberra.

other jurisdictions, it is far from clear how a treaty would achieve anything that cannot presently be achieved by either legislation or constitutional change in Australia, and how it could protect Aboriginal rights to land in a country where most land was alienated long ago.

There have been multiple recent experiments with regional and pan-Aboriginal representation in Australia. In this area, history repeats itself on a short cycle. In 1973, the Whitlam government introduced a 41-member National Aboriginal Consultative Committee (NACC), elected by indigenous people Australia-wide.[202] This 'black parliament' immediately voted to change its name to 'National Aboriginal Congress' and its advisory status to one of controlling government policy and expenditure, provoking a showdown with the Minister and the departmental head. Despite a review proposing its retention, the NACC was abolished by the Fraser government in favour of a smaller 'forum for the expression of Aboriginal views', the National Aboriginal Conference (NAC), in 1977.[203] The Hawke Labor government abolished the NAC in 1985, and, after lengthy consultations, replaced it four years later with a statutory authority (the Aboriginal and Torres Strait Islander Commission (ATSIC)) overseen by an elected indigenous board.[204] ATSIC was elected on a tiered system through regional councils, many of which proved to be its most effective element. However, it was deprived of control over Aboriginal health by the Keating government in the mid-1990s, and the conservative Howard government increasingly established other offices from which to take its indigenous affairs advice. The Howard government disbanded ATSIC (despite a review proposing its reform)[205] in 2004–05[206] because of leadership flaws and government claims that it had taken wrong policy directions.[207] The successor to ATSIC, the nominated and advisory National Indigenous Council, was swiftly disbanded by the Rudd government upon its 2007 election.[208] However, the Rudd government has indicated that it intends to establish a new national indigenous representative body.

A variety of other institutions have been created to 'represent' indigenous interests, with mixed results. Among the more successful are statutory corporations with limited mandates tied to indigenous instructions which don't depend on annual government funding—for example, large land councils established by the

[202] A collection of newspaper articles on the former NACC appears on Garry Foley's history website, www.kooriweb.org/foley/images/history/1970s/nacc74/naccdx.html.

[203] See *Establishment, Role and Functions: National Aboriginal Conference*, www1.aiatsis.gov.au/exhibitions/treaty/nac/r000004579678_a.pdf.

[204] Aboriginal and Torres Strait Islander Commission Act 1989 (Cth).

[205] J Hannaford, J Huggins and R Collins, *In the Hands of the Regions: A New ATSIC*, Report to the Minister for Immigration and Multicultural and Indigenous Affairs, www.atsicreview.gov.au/ATSIC%20Review%20report.pdf.

[206] A Pratt, *The End of ATSIC and the Future Administration of Indigenous Affairs* (Australian Parliamentary Library Current Issues Brief, 2004–05).

[207] 'Fed Govt Plans to Abolish ATSIC', ABC Radio (PM) 15 April 2004, www.abc.net.au/pm.

[208] 'Govt Scraps National Indigenous Council', *ABC News (online)*, 15 January 2008.

Aboriginal Land Rights (Northern Territory) Act 1976 (Cth).[209] By contrast, the tightly regulated, budget-funded Native Title Representative Bodies (NTRBs) and other entities responsible for bringing claims and conducting negotiations over native title land[210] often struggle to meet expectations. While this under-performance reflects poor funding, high staff turnover, the inferior property rights involved, and unduly complex regulatory environment, there are more fundamental cross-cultural problems of institutional design.[211] NTRBs are essentially not-for-profit corporations[212] approved[213] to discharge public functions consistently with Australian public law (which reflects Anglo-Australian political norms of universalism, representativeness, objectivity and finality of decision-making). But Aboriginal political culture is fundamentally participatory—even 'anarchist'[214]—and often based in prior social categories or interests (for example, those of kinship). Its open-ended decision-making processes[215] and strong resource distribution traditions (for example, of 'demand sharing')[216] do not sit easily with other land users' or public demands for transactional certainty and financial accountability.

NTRBs are just one example of Australia's widespread use of voluntary corporations as 'representative' and service-delivery bodies. This development began in the 1970s (as the Commonwealth moved to exercise its new indigenous affairs powers) with incorporation of co-operatives, associations or companies under state law to satisfy demands that the legal persons receiving government resources 'represented' 'communities', and accelerated thereafter as a shrinking state outsourced more government functions. Since 1976, the Commonwealth has maintained an indigenous-specific incorporation statute,[217] under which about 2,500 entities[218] (most very small) have been formed. However, the officially 'voluntary' nature of these institutions can mask patterns of their use to represent prior social categories like families or traditional landowners. This Act was recently overhauled to make it more like the mainstream Corporations Act; it now

[209] NT land councils derive their funding from the Aboriginals Benefit Account, into which the Commonwealth pays the equivalent of royalties received by it and the NT from mining on Aboriginal land: see Part VI of the Act. Because of this funding base for their 'land rights' activities, the NT land councils also discharge their dual role of NTRBs (see next note) more effectively than many other bodies accredited for this purpose.

[210] For maps showing these bodies' areas of responsibility and other aspects of native title, see www.nntt.gov.au/Publications-And-Research/Maps-and-Spatial-Reports/Pages/National-Maps.aspx.

[211] See generally C Mantziaris and D Martin, *Native Title Corporations: A Legal and Policy Analysis* (Federation Press, 2000).

[212] Ie, under the Corporations (Aboriginal and Torres Strait Islander) Act 2006 (Cth).

[213] See Part 11, NTA (Cth).

[214] L Hiatt, *Arguments about Aborigines: Australia and the Evolution of Social Anthropology* (Cambridge University Press, 1996) ch 5.

[215] N Williams, 'On Aboriginal Decision-making' in D Barwick, M Reay and J Beckett (eds), *Metaphors of Interpretation: Essays in Honour of WEH Stanner* (ANU Press, 1986). Such 'relational' approaches to contract are of course common outside of cultures derived from northern Europe.

[216] N Peterson, 'Demand Sharing: Reciprocity and the Pressure for Generosity among Foragers' (1993) 95 *American Anthropologist* 860.

[217] Originally the Aboriginal Councils and Associations Act 1976 (Cth).

[218] See www.oratsic.gov.au.

allows 'indigenous corporations' a minority (up to 49 per cent) of non-indigenous members.[219]

4. Aboriginal Land and Natural Resource Rights

There is a long Australian history of governments reserving, under statute,[220] land for use by Aboriginal people and Torres Strait Islanders. However, these reservations did not vest property rights in Aboriginal people. Further, as discussed above, in 'settled' Australia there is an equally long history of reserves being revoked where settlers wanted property rights in, or access to, the land.[221] As explained in Kent McNeil's Chapter in this book, it was not until the *Mabo (No 2)*[222] decision in 1992 that Australian common law recognised indigenous title of a kind which might relate to these reserves.

Native title certainly has its limitations—notably, its content is limited by what can be proven of tradition, and it can be acquired by governments for reallocation to others.[223] Further, once extinguished, it cannot revive.[224] However, native title is also capable of co-existing with limited statutory rights to land, like pastoral leases,[225] and the introduction by Parliament under the Keating government of a special negotiation procedure for the grant of mining tenements over native title land[226] has seen some native title holders and claimants make significant private royalty arrangements with miners, including over pastoral leasehold land.[227] There is also the occasional lucrative land settlement resulting from native title—for example, the 2007 allocation of about $100 million worth of real estate in the up-market NSW resort town of Byron Bay to traditional owners.[228]

Before *Mabo (No 2)*, the only prospect of Aboriginal title to land was via 'land rights' statutes, which usually related to vacant Crown lands of limited economic value. South Australia legislated in the mid-1960s to invest title to Aboriginal reserves in the state's south in an indigenous body, the Aboriginal Lands Trust.[229] While the area of land transferred was relatively small, much larger central Australian reserves were later transferred under separate legislation in the 1980s.[230] The Commonwealth followed suit in the NT in 1976, converting existing reserves to 'Aboriginal land' for the benefit of their 'traditional Aboriginal

[219] Corporations (Aboriginal and Torres Strait Islander) Act 2006 (Cth).
[220] Such reservations were authorised by the Australian Waste Lands Act 1842 (Imp).
[221] See text to n 77 above.
[222] *Mabo*, above n 32.
[223] See n 77 above.
[224] *Fejo v Northern Territory* (1998) 195 CLR 96; NTA, s 237A.
[225] *Wik Peoples*, above n 100.
[226] The 'right to negotiate': see NTA, Part 2 Div 3 Subdiv P.
[227] See Deputy President Chris Sumner of the National Native Title Tribunal's paper, 'Getting the Most Out of the Future Act Process', AIATSIS Native Title Conference (Cairns, June 2007).
[228] J Lyons, 'Secret Native Title Deal Divides Byron', *The Australian*, 6 October 2007.
[229] Aboriginal Lands Trust Act 1966 (SA).
[230] Anangu Pitjantjatjara Yankunytjatjara Land Rights Act 1981 (SA) and Maralinga Tjarutja Land Rights Act 1984 (SA).

owners', and introducing a system under which further lands could be claimed on this basis.[231] Under this regime, almost 50 per cent of the Territory has become Aboriginal land or remains under claim.[232] The NT regime is also among the most supportive of Aboriginal control of land use, and allows traditional owners to receive 'mining royalty equivalent' and compensation payments.[233]

The impact of land rights reforms in other states has been less dramatic, at least in spatial terms. For instance, beginning in 1983, NSW transferred former reserves for the benefit of residential populations to a tiered system of local, regional and state land councils, allowed further claims to surplus Crown land, and established a fund to receive a percentage of state land taxes to purchase more.[234] However, the fund was not well invested, small land councils were inefficient, and these and other aspects of the regime—such as land sales and development joint ventures[235]—were affected by illegality or corruption.[236] Statutory amendments in 1996 complicated the picture by allowing certain nature parks to be claimed on the basis of traditional affiliation rather than residence.[237] This is not the only jurisdiction in which the land claims of 'traditional' and 'historical' people[238] are in competition, but in NSW the law exacerbates that competition. By contrast, Western Australia has never gone further than the first step taken in South Australia in 1966: transferring title to reserves to an Aboriginalised statutory lands trust.[239]

In addition to recognition of indigenous property rights, some Aboriginal communities have also acquired rights to participate in natural resource management regimes, as detailed further in Benjamin Richardson's Chapter on environmental issues in this book. Two distinctive legal techniques have been deployed in this area in Australia. One approach has been to institutionalise consultation mechanisms, such as the Aboriginal Cultural Liaison Unit created in 1995 under the Greater Barrier Reef Marine Park Authority, or the Indigenous Advisory Committee established under the Environmental Protection and Biodiversity Conservation Act 1999 (Cth) to advise the Minister on the operation of the legislation.[240] The other technique is the use of leasehold or contractual arrangements between Aboriginal organisations, public agencies and even developers relating to

231 The Aboriginal Land Rights (Northern Territory) Act 1976 (Cth) implemented many recommendations of the Woodward Aboriginal Land Rights Commission.

232 However, because of a sunset clause (s 50(2A)), no new claims could be filed after June 1997.

233 See Aboriginal Land Rights (Northern Territory) Act 1976 (Cth), Parts IV and VI.

234 Aboriginal Land Rights Act 1983 (NSW).

235 See, eg, *Koompahtoo Local Aboriginal Land Council v Sanpine* [2007] HCA 61, and the Independent Commission on Corruption's report on this development of 2005, available on www.icac.nsw.gov.au.

236 See the NSW Independent Commission on Corruption's 1999 and 2000 reports on *Aboriginal Land Councils in NSW*, available at www.icac.nsw.gov.au.

237 See also National Parks and Wildlife Act 1974 (NSW), Part 4A.

238 The latter term refers to the large numbers of people resident on other Aborigines' traditional land, sometimes for many generations, as a result, for example, of their past dispossession, diaspora, incarceration under 'protection' laws, or intermarriage with traditional owners.

239 See Aboriginal Affairs Planning Authority Act 1972 (WA).

240 Section 505A.

land and resource management.[241] It is most strongly evident in the philosophy of 'joint management', which has often been presented by federal and state governments as a means for sharing resource governance between national park authorities and the traditional owners or custodians of conservation areas. The large Commonwealth national parks in the NT, Kakadu and Uluru-Kata Juta, with their Aboriginal-majority Boards of Management, provide the most sophisticated examples of the joint management model[242] and a striking contrast with limited indigenous involvement in similar parks (for example, the Grand Canyon) overseas. Indigenous Land Use Agreements (ILUAs) under the NTA[243] can also provide a framework for co-management, as under the Arakwal ILUA in the Byron Bay area.[244] However, joint management schemes may limit indigenous management, use and economic development of traditional lands.[245] Depending on the legislative framework, a joint management regime can also require that the traditional owners permit tourist access to traditional lands, which can threaten ecosystems and cultural sites.[246]

D. Beyond International Bias and Policy Without History?

History's role in Australian indigenous policy remains strong, but for reasons different from those which explain indigenous policy in some other common law jurisdictions. Australia's lack of constitutional protection for indigenous rights or against racial discrimination is one obvious contrast with Canada, for instance; another is the prominent role played by state governments. Less noticeable are the multiple ways in which Australia, perhaps more than any other former British settler colony, has been built on indigenous dispossession and exclusion. While the historical treaties and tribal institutions of other nations have many inherent problems—as discussed in other Chapters in this book—Australia's experience of negotiating indigenous rights is limited to a few flawed examples in the 20th and 21st centuries.

[241] See G Nettheim, GD Meyers and D Craig, *Indigenous Peoples and Governance Structures: A Comparative Analysis of Land and Resource Management Rights* (Aboriginal Studies Press, 2002) ch 14.

[242] See Environment Protection and Biodiversity Act 1999 (Cth) Part 15 Div 4 Subdiv F. See B Richardson and D Craig, 'Indigenous Peoples, Law and the Environment' in BJ Richardson and S Wood (eds), *Environmental Law for Sustainability* (Hart Publishing, 2006) 195, 220–1.

[243] ILUAs are contracts which, by force of the Act, bind all native title holders (whether or not they are parties) once registered: see NTA Part 2, Div 3, Subdivs B–E.

[244] For details, see www.atns.net.au/agreement.asp?EntityID=506.

[245] D Smyth, 'Joint Management of National Parks in Australia' in R Baker, J Davies and E Young (eds), *Working on Country—Contemporary Indigenous Management of Australia's Lands and Coastal Regions.* (Oxford University Press, 2001) 75.

[246] *Ibid.*

At the time of writing, Prime Minister Rudd was proposing to negotiate meaningfully with indigenous Australians about their appropriate 'recognition' in the Commonwealth *Constitution*, but advice proposing such 'recognition' has been ignored before,[247] and it is not always clear what the practical outcomes of 'recognition' might be. While Indigenous aspirations are easily accommodated in northern nature parks or up-market tourist towns, the outcomes of other land dealings are often limited by the poor quality of indigenous property rights or weaknesses in the governance arrangements under which those rights are held. The most economically valuable benefits to flow from native title have been extracted from miners or other developers seeking to avoid transaction costs in a boom economy. Where boom conditions do not prevail, indigenous people are often limited to asking governments to give them something back, without any constitutional guarantee of being able to hold it indefinitely if 'majority' interests later see fit to renege on the deal. Perhaps because so many of them are migrants, each generation of non-indigenous Australians tends to approach 'the Aboriginal problem' afresh, ignorant of broken promises made by the state (on behalf of their predecessors in colonization) to Aborigines or Torres Strait Islanders. Thus the goal posts move frequently, without public acknowledgment of the state's role as protagonist, rather than umpire, in dealings between the small indigenous population and the rapidly expanding number of other people who want their land.[248]

Recent policy rhetoric, as in other jurisdictions canvassed in this book, has emphasised 'reconciliation' and 'partnerships' without fundamentally altering these underlying structural relationships; meanwhile, past policy experiments (like those in national Indigenous representation) are recycled with alarming frequency. The 2007 Commonwealth emergency 'intervention' in the NT, ostensibly to curb alcohol-related problems in indigenous communities, illustrates yet another problematic tendency: to characterise indigenous affairs as a set of crises caused by old 'policy failures' which demand immediate, unreflective, unproven and unilateral action.[249] While indigenous social problems are in the national spotlight for good reason, there is a need to ensure that any 'solutions' devised emerge from processes which adequately involve Aboriginal people and organisations, and that policy changes (particularly radical ones) are backed by adequate resources and personnel.

[247] See the former Council for Aboriginal Reconciliation's *Final Report*, chapter 10, recommendation 3, at www.austlii.edu.au/au/other/IndigLRes/car/2000/16/text10.htm.

[248] S Curry, *Indigenous Sovereignty and the Democratic Project* (Ashgate, 2004).

[249] See Northern Territory National Emergency Response Act 2007 (Cth).

5

The Māori Encounter with Aotearoa: New Zealand's Legal System

JACINTA RURU

Ko Papatuanuku to tatou whaea
Ko ia to matua atawhai
He oranga mo tatou
I roto i te moengaroa
ka hoki tatou ki te kopu o te whenua
The land is our mother
She is the loving parent
She nourishes and sustains us
When we die she enfolds us in her arms[1]

A. Introduction

This Chapter tells the story of the Māori encounter with the state legal system in Aotearoa New Zealand. At one level, it resonates strongly with Indigenous peoples' experiences in Canada, Australia and the United States. British colonisation undeniably shattered who Māori were: disease and warfare decimated the population, and legislation criminalised the Māori way of life. But the tools for colonisation and the recent remedies to overcome the disasters of colonisation are in many ways unique to this South-West Pacific island country. There exists a single treaty of cession, the Treaty of Waitangi, and legal institutions with counterparts not found elsewhere: the Māori Land Court and the Waitangi Tribunal. Today, Māori, as a significant and visible component of Aotearoa New Zealand's population (currently constituting over 15 per cent of Aotearoa New Zealand's 4 million people), are rebuilding their communities and ways of knowing. Self-described as tangata whenua (the people of the land), this Chapter focuses on the experiences of how the law was used to turn the Māori world upside down and the role of law in seeking amends.

[1] This whakatauki (proverb) is reproduced in M Roberts *et al*, 'Kaitiakitanga: Māori Perspectives on Conservation' (1995) 2 *Pacific Conservation Biology* 7, 10.

There are many different descriptors that can be used to categorise this story.[2] The five chosen here are: 1) tangata whenua law; 2) recognising one another; 3) 'civilising' tangata whenua; 4) 'reconciling' with tangata whenua; and 5) tangata whenua and the law. The first is a brief insight into the Māori world pre-European contact. The second is a glimpse into what happened when the Europeans arrived and why, in 1840, the Treaty of Waitangi was signed. The third part discusses how, between 1840 and 1960, the newcomers seized power and began a destructive assimilationist quest to 'civilise' Māori. The fourth part explains how Parliament and the courts, since the 1970s, have sought to rectify the past injustices. The last part considers the Māori response, and new issues the law might present for Māori in the 21st century.

B. Tangata Whenua Law

The legal history of Aotearoa New Zealand began when the first peoples settled on these shores (some put it at about AD 800,[3] others at about AD 1200[4]). The place—a mountainous landscape, densely forested with a cool climate—swarmed with birds (many flightless) and teemed with fish. Māori had found the last part of the ancient Gondwanaland continent; they had found 'the last habitable land mass of any size to remain unpeopled'.[5] Grouped into distinct peoples, they became, literally, the people of the land. The common language (with regional dialectal differences) captured this literal interrelationship. For instance, hapu means sub-tribe and to be pregnant; whanau means family and to give birth; and whenua means land and afterbirth. The approximately 40 distinct iwi (tribes), and hundreds of hapu, each derived their identity from the mountains, rivers and lakes.[6] For example, at the tribal level the people of Ngai Tahu (the largest tribe in the South Island, the fourth largest tribe overall), state: Ko Aoraki taku mauka (Aoraki is my mountain), Ko Waitaki taku awa (Waitaki is my river), Ko Tahupotiki te tupuna (Tahupotiki is the ancestor), Ko Kai Tahu taku iwi (Kai Tahu is my tribe).[7] They then further define themselves by their hapu, providing a local statement such as: Ko Poutaiki taku mauka (Poutaiki is my mountain), Ko Waihemo taku

[2] For example, see P Havemann, 'Introduction. Comparing Indigenous Peoples' Rights in Australia, Canada, and New Zealand. Some Signposts' in P Havemann (ed), *Indigenous Peoples' Rights in Australia, Canada and New Zealand* (Oxford University Press, 1999) 1.

[3] R Walker, *Ka Whawahi Tonu Matou. Struggle without End* (Penguin Books, 2004) 24.

[4] M King, *The Penguin History of New Zealand* (Penguin Books, 2003) 48.

[5] B Biggs, 'In the Beginning' in K Sinclair (ed), *The Oxford Illustrated History of New Zealand* (2nd edn, Oxford University Press, 1996). See the appendix for a map illustrating the contemporary territory of iwi.

[6] For an introduction to Māori mythology, see R Calman and AW Reed, *Reed Book of Māori Mythology* (Reed NZ, 2004).

[7] All tribes have their own geographically located descriptors, identifying with regional mountains and waterways. For example, I personally relate to the Maungatautari mountain and the Waikato river in the North Island.

awa (Waihemo is my river), Ko Matiaha Tiramorehu te takata (Matiaha Tiramorehu is the man), Ko Kati Rakiamoa te hapu (Kati Rakiamoa is the hapu).[8]

The Māori legal system is predominantly values, not rules, based. It encapsulates a certain way of life that depends on the relationships between all things, including between people and gods, different groups of people, and people and everything in the surrounding world.[9] Integral values thus include whakapapa (genealogy), whanaungatanga (family relationships), mana (authority), mauri (spiritual life-principles), tapu (sacredness), rahui (prohibition or conservation), and manaaki (hospitality).[10] For example, to expand briefly the latter concept, manaakitanga is mainly about establishing one's status and authority by acts of kindness and caring.[11] Another key concept, utu, played a regulatory role because it established that everything given or taken required a return of some kind in order to maintain harmony and balance, ensuring reciprocal acts of continued generosity.[12] Kaitiakitanga (guardianship), as a further example, is about 'more than managing relations between environmental resources and humans; it also involves managing relationships between people in the past, present and future'.[13]

The Māori phrase for law—tikanga Māori—involves an 'obligation to do things in the "right" way'[14] or 'way(s) of doing and thinking held by Māori to be just and correct'.[15] Tikanga are said to be 'tools of thought and understandings . . . They help us to differentiate between right and wrong'.[16] To illustrate in a specific context, contracts concerned not the transfer of rights for a prescribed consideration or immediate return as is typical in Western transactions, but the establishment of a permanent and personal relationship with reciprocal obligations where the main benefit to both sides would come in the course of time.[17] This law and way of knowing came under threat in the nineteenth century.

[8] See H O'Regan, *Ko Tahu, Ko Au. Kai Tahu Tribal Identity* (Horomaka Publishing, 2001).

[9] See E Durie, 'Ethics and Values' (1999) 7, at www.knowledge-basket.co.nz/oldwaitangi/press/98massey.HTM. This website and all subsequent sites referenced in this Chapter were last accessed on 2 April 2008.

[10] See New Zealand Law Commission (NZLC), *Study Paper 9. Māori Custom and Values in New Zealand Law* (NZLC, 2001) 30–1; M Kawharu, '*Kaitiakitanga:* A Māori Anthropological Perspective on the Māori Socio-Environmental Ethic of Resource Management' (2000) 109 *Journal of the Polynesian Society* 349, 349.

[11] ET Durie, 'Will the Settlers Settle? Cultural Conciliation and Law' (1996) 8 *Otago Law Review* 449.

[12] *Ibid*, 455.

[13] Kawharu, above n 10, 352.

[14] NZLC, above n 10, 16, citing Bishop Manuhuia Bennet.

[15] *Ibid.*

[16] *Ibid.* See also HM Mead, *Tikanga Maori. Living by Māori Values* (Huia Publishers, 2003).

[17] See Durie, above n 11, 455. For other examples, see E Durie, 'Te Hono ki Hawai'iki: The bond with the Pacific' in M Wilson and P Hunt, *Culture, Rights, and Cultural Rights Perspectives from the South Pacific* (Huia Publishers, 2000); A Erueti, 'Māori Customary Law and Land Tenure: An Analysis', in R Boast, A Erueti, D McPhail, and NF Smith (eds), *Māori Land Law* (2nd edn, LexisNexis, 2004); P Tohe, 'Māori Jurisprudence: The Neglect of Tapu' (1998) 8 *Auckland Universities Law Review* 884; M Jackson, 'The Colonization of Māori Philosophy' in G Oddie and RW Perrett (eds), *Justice, Ethics, and New Zealand Society* (Oxford University Press, 1992).

C. Recognising One Another

Following the British explorer James Cook's first visit to Aotearoa in 1779, European explorers, whalers and sealers began arriving, bringing with them their own distinct worldview, technology, goods and animals. Trade between the two peoples quickly evolved: Māori wanted the nails, blankets and potatoes; the Europeans needed Māori local knowledge for survival, land for settlement, and labour for their business ventures. During these early years of contact, Māori sovereignty, law and justice continued unthreatened by the European arrivals.[18] Relations between the two peoples were relatively good, boding well for a promising future relationship. Many of the tribes were eager for Pakeha (as Māori described the British settlers) to settle nearby because 'they were useful for their goods and skills and for enhancing the mana of their patron chief'.[19]

The British Crown formally acknowledged the independent sovereignty of the tribes in 1835,[20] and again five years later. In 1840, Captain William Hobson, representing the Crown, and over 500 Māori chiefs signed te Tiriti o Waitangi / the Treaty of Waitangi.[21] It is a short document, consisting of three articles expressed in English and Māori. The controversy lies in the translation of the first two articles.[22] According to the English version, Māori ceded to the Crown, absolutely and without reservation, all the rights and powers of sovereignty (Article 1), but retained full exclusive and undisturbed possession of their lands and estates, forests, fisheries and other properties (Article 2). In contrast, in the Māori version, Māori ceded to the Crown governance only (Article 1), and retained tino rangatiratanga (sovereignty) over their taonga (treasures). Article 2 granted the Crown a pre-emptive right to purchase property from Māori, and Article 3 granted Māori the same rights and privileges as British citizens living in Aotearoa New Zealand.

The bilingual Treaty of Cession was a unique contractual agreement not replicated elsewhere.[23] Humanitarian interests, along with the need to control the

[18] See C Wickliffe, 'Te Timatanga: Māori Women's Access to Justice' (2005) 8 *Yearbook of New Zealand Jurisprudence Special Issue—Te Purenga* 217, 226.

[19] C Orange, 'The Māori People and British Crown (1769–1840)' in Sinclair, above n 5, 21, 30.

[20] Declaration of Independence. To view the Declaration and read some commentary about it: see C Orange, *An Illustrated History of the Treaty of Waitangi* (Bridget Williams Books, 2004) 13–16.

[21] To view a copy of the Treaty: see First Schedule of the Treaty of Waitangi Act 1975 or the Government's official Treaty website: www.treatyofwaitangi.govt.nz.

[22] For an analysis of these textual problems, see B Biggs, 'Humpty-Dumpty and the Treaty of Waitangi' in IH Kawharu (ed), *Waitangi: Māori and Pakeha Perspectives of the Treaty of Waitangi* (Oxford University Press, 1989) 300–12; RM Ross, 'Te Tiriti o Waitangi. Texts and Translations' (1972) 6(2) *New Zealand Journal of History* 129 (reprinted in J Binney (ed), *The Shaping of History. Essays from the New Zealand Journal of History* (Bridget Williams Books, 2001)).

[23] See W Renwick, 'A Variation of a Theme' in W Renwick (ed), *Sovereignty and Indigenous Rights. The Treaty of Waitangi in International Contexts* (Victoria University Press, 1991) 199, 207, where he explains that, by the time the treaties were signed on Vancouver Island, BC, Canada (a mere decade later), 'British imperial policy was determined by strategic considerations not humanitarian intentions'. See also C Wickliffe, who asserts that '[t]he Treaty of Waitangi is fundamentally different to treaties in the Americas . . . [as it] did not deal with the sovereign status of indigenous polities': above n 18, 229 n 70.

unruly behaviour of some of the new settlers, and to keep at bay the interests of France and the United States of America, contributed to the British desire for a signed treaty.[24] Māori chiefs signed for similarly numerous reasons. On the face of it, the Treaty looked as if it was asking little of them and offering them much in return.[25] They expected trade to increase, to receive assistance in handling the new changes occurring in society, and 'not least, the possibility of manipulating British authority in inter-tribal rivalries'.[26]

In an early judicial decision considering whether the Queen had the *exclusive* right of pre-emption to purchase land from Māori as articulated in the Treaty, Justice Chapman observed that the 'intercourse of civilised nations'[27] (namely, Great Britain) with Indigenous communities (especially in North America) had led to established principles of law. This law, encapsulated in the common law doctrine of native title, stipulates that the Queen's right is exclusive. He explained:

> it cannot be too solemnly asserted that [native title] is entitled to be respected, that it cannot be extinguished (at least in times of peace) otherwise than by the free consent of the Native occupiers. But for their protection, and for the sake of humanity, the government is bound to maintain, and the Courts to assert, the Queen's exclusive right to extinguish it.[28]

The Justice observed that, in guaranteeing Native title and the Queen's pre-emptive right, 'the Treaty of Waitangi . . . does not assert either in doctrine or in practice any thing new and unsettled'.[29] While this observation could be disputed, especially on reading the Māori version,[30] the decision marked a positive start to the building of a new nation. It was to take another 150 years before a court was to describe the common law as applicable to Māori in quite the same way.

D. 'Civilising' Tangata Whenua

The initial British Governors in Aotearoa New Zealand exerted a distinct colonialist policy based on the assumption that 'Māori were unusually intelligent (for blacks) and that intelligence translated into the desire to become British'.[31] Between 1840 and 1860, the tools for this evangelism—God, money, law and

[24] Note that, although the British were pursuing cession, a mindset of discovery still permeated the negotiations: see RJ Miller and J Ruru, 'An Indigenous Lens into Comparative Law: The Doctrine of Discovery in the United States and New Zealand' (Lewis and Clark Law School Legal Studies Research Paper Series No 2008–7).

[25] C Orange, *The Treaty of Waitangi* (Allen and Unwin NZ, 1987) 58.

[26] *Ibid*, 58. Note that Colonial government was established in 1852 pursuant to the Constitution Act 1852.

[27] *R v Symonds* [1847] NZPCC 387, 388.

[28] *Ibid*, 390.

[29] *Ibid*, 390, 395 per Martin CJ.

[30] See E Durie, 'The Treaty in Māori History' in Renwick, above n 23, 156.

[31] J Belich, 'The Governors and the Māori (1840–72)' in Sinclair, above n 5, 78.

land—sought to convert Māori from 'savages' to 'civilisation' via assimilation by the '[m]ixing of the two peoples geographically'.[32] But the early evangelism had few complete successes. While many Māori did embrace Christianity, it was not to the exclusion of their own religion: 'Māori religion had always been open, able to incorporate new gods'.[33] Similarly, while many Māori tribes became commercialised (they dominated the food supply market from growing crops, to transporting and selling to the Pakeha), individualism did not flourish.[34]

By the late 1850s, however, the worlds of some tribes had been radically changed by land deals that have today been cast as shady and in some instances in breach of the Treaty of Waitangi. Less than 20 years after the Treaty was signed, the British Crown had acquired most of the land in the South Island and the lower part of the North Island (constituting about 60 per cent of Aotearoa New Zealand's land mass and where about 10 per cent of Māori lived).[35] In most instances the tribes had been duped. First, there was controversy about the actual land included in the purchase agreements, and secondly, there was disquiet in that the Crown had not set aside land for reserves for them as pursuant to the agreements.[36] Deeply disturbed by the correlation between selling land and loss of independence, the North Island tribes that still had land began turning against land sales. Importantly, the pan-tribal sentiment saw the emergence of the Māori King Movement.[37] Perturbed that land selling would come to an end, and thus the amalgamation of Māori would come to a halt, the British concluded that the 'law of nature' required help. A new colonial tool was endorsed in the form of warfare. In underestimating tribal resistance, the New Zealand wars, which began in March 1860, did not abate until a decade later.[38] A tougher new evangelism emerged during this time, with law becoming the central tool in destroying the Māori way of life.

Large tracts of Māori land in the North Island were confiscated pursuant to legislation.[39] Legislation also stipulated that native schools could only receive funding if the curriculum was taught in the English language,[40] a policy which led to the near extinction of the Māori language and culture, and marginalised Māori 'by a deliberate policy of training for manual labour rather than the professions'.[41] Further legislation ensured that any person practising traditional Māori healing

[32] J Belich, 'The Governors and the Māori (1840–72)' in Sinclair, above n 5, 80.

[33] *Ibid*, 78.

[34] See *ibid*, 80.

[35] See *ibid*, 84.

[36] See, eg, Waitangi Tribunal, *The Ngai Tahu Report* (Wai 27, 1991) and T O'Regan, 'The Ngai Tahu Claim' in Kawharu, above n 22, 234.

[37] For a discussion of Māori resistance movements, including the Māori King Movement, see L Cox, *Kotahitanga. The Search for Māori Political Unity* (Oxford University Press, 1993).

[38] See J Belich, *The New Zealand Wars* (NZ Penguin, 1998).

[39] See New Zealand Settlements Act 1863, and Suppression of Rebellion Act 1863. See also later public works legislation, eg, Public Works Act 1928.

[40] See Native Schools Act 1858; Native Schools Act 1867 and the Native Schools Act 1871.

[41] S Milroy and L Whiu, 'Waikato Law School: An Experiment in Bicultural Legal Education' (2005) 8 *Yearbook of New Zealand Jurisprudence. Special Issue, Te Purenga* 173, 175.

could became liable for conviction,[42] a policy that led to the loss of much traditional knowledge.[43]

At the heart of the new cultural genocide[44] crusade was the establishment of the Native Land Court. The Crown waived its right of pre-emption, as endorsed in the Treaty of Waitangi and common law doctrine of native title, in favour of Māori being able to freely alienate their land, the catch being that they first had to obtain a certificate of title. The system sought to transform land communally held by whanau and hapu (Māori customary land) into individualised titles derived from the Crown (Māori freehold title). The preamble to the Native Lands Act 1862 explained:

> whereas it would greatly promote the peaceful settlement of the Colony and the advancement and civilization of the Natives if their rights to land were ascertained defined and declared and if the ownership of such lands . . . [was] assimilated as nearly as possible to the ownership of land according to British law.

The legislation ensured 'Māori could participate in the new British prosperity only by selling or leasing their land'.[45] Or, as Honourable Sewell, a Member of the House of Representatives in 1870, reflected, the Act had two objects. One was 'to bring the great bulk of the lands of the Northern Island which belonged to the Natives . . . within the reach of colonization'.[46] The other was

> the detribalisation of the Natives—to destroy, if it were possible, the principles of communism which ran through the whole of their institutions, upon which their social system was based, and which stood as a barrier in the way of all attempts to amalgamate the Native race into our own social and political system.[47]

The Court was extraordinarily effective in freeing up Māori land for private purchase. In the early years,

> a predatory horde of storekeepers, grog-sellers, surveyors, lawyers, land-agents and money-lenders made advances to rival groups of Māori claimants and recouped the costs in land. Rightful Māori owners could not avoid litigation and expensive surveys if false claims were put forward, since Fenton [the Chief Judge], seeking to inflate the status of the Court, insisted that judgments be based only upon evidence presented before it.[48]

[42] See the Tohunga Suppression Act 1908.

[43] See M Solomon, 'The Wai 262 Claim: A Claim by Māori to Indigenous Flora and Fauna: *Me o Rātou Taonga Katoa*', in M Belgrave, M Kawharu and D Williams (eds), *Waitangi Revisited. Perspectives on the Treaty of Waitangi* (Oxford University Press, 2005) 213.

[44] For a discussion of this term, see D Williams, 'Myths, National Origins, Common Law and the Waitangi Tribunal' (2004) 11 *Murdoch University Electronic Journal of Law,* at www.murdoch.edu.au/elaw/issues/v11n4/williams114_text.html.

[45] Waitangi Tribunal, *Turanga Tangata. Turanga Whenua. The Report on the Turanganui a Kiwa Claims.* Vol III (Wai 814, 2004) 444.

[46] 29 August 1870, NZPD, vol 9, at 361 as quoted in D Williams, *'Te Kooti Tango Whenua'. The Native Land Court 1864–1909* (Huia Publishers, 1999) 87–88.

[47] *Ibid.*

[48] A Ward, *A Show of Justice: Racial 'Amalgamation' in Nineteenth Century New Zealand* (Auckland and Oxford University Presses, 1974) 185–6. See also Williams, above n 46; R Boast, 'Māori and the Law, 1840–2000', in P Spiller, J Finn and R Boast (eds), *A New Zealand Legal History* (2nd edn,

By the 1930s, very little tribal land remained in Māori ownership (today it amounts to 5 per cent of Aotearoa New Zealand's total landmass). The court's early work has been described as a 'veritable engine of destruction for any tribe's tenure of land',[49] and 'a scandal'.[50]

By the late 1870s, the now-named High Court, in line with the new evangelism, began to rewrite history, deeming the Treaty of Waitangi a 'simple nullity', because '[n]o body politic existed capable of making cession of sovereignty' because Māori were 'primitive barbarians'.[51] At the turn of the century the Privy Council deemed such reasoning as going 'too far',[52] yet the judiciary ignored the Privy Council—'the only recorded instance of a New Zealand court's publicly avowing its disapproval of a superior tribunal'.[53] Later, in 1941, the Privy Council reinterpreted the Treaty as enforceable in the courts if recognised in legislation.[54] This did not occur until 1975, and, in regard to the status of the doctrine of native title, it was not fully reinstated into Aotearoa New Zealand's common law until 2003, as is discussed later in this Chapter.

In summary, in the years following the signing of the Treaty of Waitangi, the policy of 'civilising' had led to a 'shattered'[55] Māori world. Yet, it had also created some interesting variations on the experiences of colonisation. For example, the new Māori freehold land status had created unique 'problems'. One was that more Māori males now satisfied the property qualification (individual tenure) to vote. In 1867, the legislature fixed this by providing Māori with four electoral districts. While the four Māori seats (Southern, Western, Eastern, Northern) ring-fenced Māori participation, they still gave Māori a political voice, and, from the 1930s until recently, the seats have been linked with the Labour Party.[56] Another problem was that the English inheritance law (eldest son inherits) made no sense on determining succession to Māori freehold land (most Māori children were 'illegitimate'). The legislature recognised this and directed the Native Land Court to ascertain intestate succession 'according to law as nearly as it can be reconciled

Brookers, 2001) 122; R Boast, *Buying the Land, Selling the Land: Governments and Māori Land in the North Island 1865–1921* (Victoria University Press, 2008): P Meredith, 'Pakeha by Law: The Europeanisation of Māori 1912–1931' (2006) 22 *New Zealand Universities Law Review* 103.

[49] IH Kawharu, *Māori Land Tenure: Studies of a Changing Institution* (Oxford University Press, 1977) 15. See also BD Gilling, 'Engine of Destruction? An Introduction to the History of the Māori Land Court' (1994) 24(2) *Victoria University of Wellington Law Review* 115.

[50] MPK Sorrenson, 'The Purchase of Māori Lands, 1865–1892' (MA thesis, Auckland University College, 1955) 146, citing a newspaper report in the *New Zealand Herald* (2 March 1883) 4.

[51] *Wi Parata v Bishop of Wellington* (1877) 3 NZ Jur (NS) 72, 78.

[52] *Nireaha Tamaki v Baker* [1901] AC 561, 577–8 (Lord Davey).

[53] Sir R Cooke, 'The Nineteenth Century Chief Justices' in R Cooke (ed), *Portrait of a Profession. The Centennial Book of the New Zealand Law Society* (Reed, 1969) 36, 46. One of the more well known cases to assert the *Wi Parata* precedent was *In Re Ninety Mile Beach* [1963] NZLR 461. See R Boast, '*In Re Ninety Mile Beach* Revisited: The Native Land Court and the Foreshore in New Zealand Legal History' (1993) 23 *Victoria University of Wellington Law Review* 145.

[54] *Hoani Te Heuheu Tukino v Aotea District Māori Land Board* [1941] AC 308. See A Frame, 'Hoani Te Heuheu's Case in London 1940–1941: An Explosive Story' (2006) 22 *New Zealand Universities Law Review* 148.

[55] Mead, above n 16, 306.

[56] Famous Māori MPs in the early 1900s included Apirana Ngata and James Carroll.

with Native custom'.[57] In 1867, the court decided that Māori male *and* female children (whether legitimate or not) could succeed equally to their deceased parent's interests in Māori freehold land.[58] Other examples of problems associated with Māori land status include legislative and judicial recognition of iwi ownership of lakes and river beds[59]; various attempts to make right the perceived wrongs endured in the South Island land purchases[60]; and confiscation of lands in the North Island[61] (albeit described now as unjust to the tribes involved[62]). In the 1960s, the government became more aggressive with its efforts to 'integrate' Māori, and this, along with the fact that most tribes had already lost nearly everything dear to them (their land and language), tangata whenau began to mobilise in new ways.[63]

E. 'Reconciling' with Tangata Whenua

In 1972, the Labour political party, for the first time since 1957, came into government with more willingness than the previous National governments to listen to Māori concerns. Labour appointed Hon Matiu Rata (Member for Northern Māori) as Minister of Māori Affairs, and he became instrumental in responding to Māori protests, establishing the Waitangi Tribunal and initiating a review of the Māori Land Court. However, Labour's stint in power was short-lived. During the National Party's term of office (1975–1984), Māori protests became prominent, including one that lasted 507 days and ended after police and the army forcibly removed the occupants and destroyed the buildings involved.[64] However, since the mid-1980s both the Labour and National governments, when in power, began enacting legislation referencing the principles of the Treaty of Waitangi and certain components of tikanga Māori, and the courts began to reintroduce the doctrine of native title into the common law of Aotearoa New Zealand. A new age dawned, but whether it amounts to reconciliation proper remains to be seen.

57 Native Lands Act 1865, s 30.

58 *Papakura—Claim of Succession. New Zealand Gazette* (12 April 1867) 19. The precedent led to extreme fragmentation of interests in Māori land. For commentary, and other examples of legislative recognition of Māori succession law, see J Ruru, 'Implications for Māori: Historical Overview' in N Peart, M Briggs and M Henaghan (eds), *Relationship Property on Death* (Brookers, 2004) 445.

59 Eg, *Tamihana Korokai v Solicitor-General* (1912) 32 NZLR 321 (CA) and Poukawa Native Reserve Act 1903. See Boast, 'Māori and the Law 1840–2000', above n 48, 178–79.

60 Eg, South Island Landless Natives Act 1906, and Ngai Tahu Claims Settlement Act 1944.

61 Eg, Taranaki Claims Settlement Act 1944.

62 For an excellent insight into the experiences of four iwi, see M Belgrave, *Historical Frictions. Māori Claims and Reinvented Histories* (Auckland University Press, 2005).

63 J Hunn, *Report on Department of Māori Affairs, with Statistical Supplement* (Government Printer, 1961); I Prichard and H Waetford, *Report of Committee of Inquiry into the Laws Affecting Māori Land and the Jurisdiction and Powers of the Māori Land Court* (Department of Māori Affairs, 1965). For commentary on this era, see also PG McHugh, *Aboriginal Societies and the Common Law. A History of Sovereignty, Status, and Self-Determination* (Oxford University Press, 2004) 264–76.

64 See Merata Mita's film *Bastion Point: Day 507* (Awatea Films, 1980).

1. The Waitangi Tribunal and Treaty Settlement Process

The Waitangi Tribunal was established in 1975 as a permanent commission of inquiry empowered to receive, report and recommend on alleged Crown breaches of the principles of the Treaty of Waitangi post-1975.[65] During Labour's next term in government (commencing in 1984), parliament passed legislation granting the Tribunal retrospective powers to investigate claims dating back to 1840.[66] The Tribunal's jurisdiction is to consider claims by Māori that they have been prejudicially affected by legislation, Crown policy or practice, or Crown action or omission, on or after 6 February 1840. The Tribunal generally can only make non-binding rather than binding recommendations to the Crown on redress for what it considers to be valid claims.

The establishment of the Tribunal signified that the Crown now accepted that 'the historical grievances of Māori about Crown actions that harmed whanau, hapu and iwi are real'.[67] Its work has been 'at the forefront of a nation coming painfully to terms with its past for the first time'.[68] It is symbolic of biculturalism, appointing both Māori and Pakeha as members, and comfortable in both Māori and Pakeha environments. Its quarter-century work has been immense. It has released numerous reports on iwi-region specific claims alleging historical breaches in the South Island, North Island and Chatham Islands, and has reported on an array of generic issues, including the use of the Māori language, customary fishing, the allocation of radio frequencies, petroleum and aquaculture.[69] Of those generic claims where it has recommended government action, in some instances the government has accepted such claims and enacted appropriate legislation (for example, the Māori Language Act 1987 and the Māori Commercial Aquaculture Claims Settlement Act 2004), but denied several others (for example, the reports on petroleum, and the foreshore and seabed).

In regard to historical claims pursued in the Waitangi Tribunal, the Crown's response has been to engage in a 'fair and final' settlement process. The Crown does not require claimants to have first gone to the Tribunal, but many claimants find value in doing so. The settlement process itself is conducted through the Office of Treaty Settlements as a separate unit within the Ministry of Justice. The Office has the mandate to resolve historical Treaty claims (defined as claims arising from actions or omissions by or on behalf of the Crown or by or under

[65] Treaty of Waitangi Act 1975, s 6.

[66] *Ibid*, as amended by the Treaty of Waitangi Amendment Act 1985. For commentary, see J Hayward and NR Wheen (eds), *The Waitangi Tribunal. Te Roopu Whakamana I te Tiriti o Waitangi* (Bridget Williams Books, 2004); A Ward, *An Unsettled History: Treaty Claims in New Zealand Today* (Bridget Williams Books, 1999).

[67] Office of Treaty Settlements, *Ka tika a muri, ka tika a mua. Healing the Past, Building a Future* (2nd edn, Office of Treaty Settlements, 2002) 3. Available from the Office of Treaty Settlements' website, www.ots.govt.nz.

[68] P Hamer, 'A Quarter-century of the Waitangi Tribunal. Responding to the Challenge', in Hayward and Wheen, above n 66, 6.

[69] To view the reports, see the Tribunal's website at www.waitangi-tribunal.govt.nz/reports.

legislation on or before 21 September 1992). There are five steps in the claims process encompassing several preliminary agreements, often including 'terms of negotiation', 'agreement in principle', 'deed of settlement' and finally 'settlement legislation'.[70] The settlements aim to provide the foundation for a new and continuing relationship between the Crown and the claimant group based on the Treaty of Waitangi principles. Settlements thus contain Crown apologies of wrongs done, financial and commercial redress, and redress recognising the claimant group's spiritual, cultural, historical or traditional associations with the natural environment.

The most significant pan-tribal settlement concerns commercial fisheries, which included cash compensation, 50 per cent shareholding in Sealord Products Limited, 10 per cent of fish stocks introduced into the quota management system in 1986, and 20 per cent of all new stock brought into the system thereafter (now valued at around NZ$750 million).[71] This deal was negotiated in 1992 and dubbed the 'Sealord deal'. Today, an even more financially significant pan-tribal settlement for several North Island tribes is on the verge of being legislated, labelled the 'treelord' deal. The April 2008 signed agreement will return ownership of 170,000 hectares of forest valued at between NZ$170,000 million and NZ$190,000 million to Māori, and about NZ$248,000 million paid to the claimant tribes. It is also thought that the tradable carbon credits could be valued at between NZ$50 and NZ$70 million.[72]

In regard to legislated tribal settlements, more than 18 groups have received redress, amounting to a total value of more than NZ$718 million (with the largest cash compensation paid to single tribes being NZ$170 million).[73] Nonetheless, several parameters determine the scope of the negotiations: the Crown 'strongly prefers to negotiate claims with large natural groupings rather than individual whanau and hapu',[74] and it is attempting to settle all grievances within a tight budget and timeframe.[75]

[70] See Office of Treaty Settlements, above n 67. For an insight into tribal governance entities, see New Zealand Law Commission, *Waka Umanga: A Proposed Law for Māori Governance Entities*, Report 92 (NZLC, 2006) available at www.lawcom.govt.nz; the Waka Umanga (Māori Corporations) Bill 2007; M Gibbs, 'What Structures are Appropriate to Receive Treaty of Waitangi Settlement Assets?' (2004) 21 *New Zealand Universities Law Review* 197; R Joseph, 'Contemporary Māori Governance: New Era or New Error?' (2007) 22 *New Zealand Universities Law Review* 628.

[71] See Treaty of Waitangi (Fisheries Claim) Settlement Act 1992 and Māori Fisheries Act 2004. For commentary on the settlement and legislation, see Te Ohu Kaimoana's website, teohu.Māori.nz/index.htm, and comments below at n 141.

[72] For newspaper coverage, see www.stuff.co.nz/4505192a8153.html.

[73] See the Government's official Treaty website, www.treatyofwaitangi.govt.nz/settlements/summary.php?i=8; but note these figures are conservative, as they have not been updated since April 2005.

[74] Office of Treaty Settlements, above n 67, 32. Note, cross-claim boundary disputes are often at issue. For example, see *NZ Māori Council v Attorney-General* [2007] NZCA 269 and *Te Runanga o Ngai Tahu v Waitangi Tribunal*, High Court, Wellington C97/01, 2001; and see Waitangi Tribunal reports, such as: *The Report on the Impact of the Crown's Treaty Settlement Policy on Te Arawa Waka* (2007) and *Tamaki Makarau Settlement Process Report* (2007).

[75] See Māori Purposes Bill (No 55-1), cl 18 (tabled June 2006).

2. Statutory Incorporation of the Treaty of Waitangi

The Treaty of Waitangi Act 1975 was the first statute to use the term 'the principles of the Treaty of Waitangi' and the Waitangi Tribunal, by 1986, had begun creating a Treaty jurisprudence. The courts entered this terrain post-1986 via the opening provided in the State Owned Enterprises Act 1986.[76] Section 9 of the latter Act states: 'Nothing in this Act shall permit the Crown to act in a manner that is inconsistent with the principles of the Treaty of Waitangi'. The provision allowed Māori to advance a Treaty argument in the courts, and the Court of Appeal's decision, in 1987, became the founding judicial authority on the Treaty principles. The Court specifically stated that the Treaty can no longer be treated as a 'dead letter',[77] and to do so 'would be unhappily and unacceptably reminiscent of an attitude, now past'.[78] Partnership, reasonableness and good faith are the hallmarks of the expression 'the principles of the Treaty of Waitangi'. As the then Cooke P concluded: '[Treaty] principles require the Pakeha and Māori Treaty partners to act towards each other reasonably and with the utmost good faith. That duty is no light one. It is infinitely more than a formality'.[79] All five judges in the case elaborated to include among the Treaty principles such notions as active protection, acting in an honest manner to ascertain facts before a decision is made, consulting each other, and recognising the right of the Crown to govern and the right of Māori to exercise, in certain circumstances, tino rangatiratanga. The court also stressed the importance of not freezing Treaty principles in time: 'What matters is the spirit ... The Treaty has to be seen as an embryo rather than a fully developed and integrated set of ideas'.[80] Subsequent judicial decisions, including decisions from the Privy Council, have confirmed the underlying tenor of this landmark decision, including respectfully not construing a finite list of Treaty principles.[81]

Today, government departments, regional government bodies, and many other decision-making boards must have some level of regard to Treaty principles. The Department of Conservation, for example, must 'give effect to'[82] and education

[76] The courts have defined the relationship by stating that the Tribunal's opinions 'are of great value to the Court' (*NZ Māori Council v A-G* [1987] 1 NZLR 641, 662) and 'are entitled to considerable weight' (*Moana Te Aira Te Uri Karaka Te Waero v The Minister of Conservation and Auckland City Council* (HC, Auckland, M360-SW01, 19 February 2002, Harrison J), para 59), but can be freely dismissed.

[77] *NZ Māori Council v A-G* [1987] 1 NZLR 641 (CA), 661.

[78] *Ibid*, 661.

[79] *Ibid*, 667.

[80] *Ibid*, 663. To better understand the significance of this case, see J Ruru (ed), '*In Good Faith. Symposium Proceedings Marking the 20th Anniversary of the Lands Case* (New Zealand Law Foundation and University of Otago, 2008).

[81] For example, see *Attorney-General v New Zealand Māori Council (No 2)* [1991] 2 NZLR 147 (CA); *New Zealand Māori Council v Attorney-General* [1992] 2 NZLR 576 (CA); *New Zealand Māori Council v Attorney-General* [1994] 1 NZLR 513 (PC); *New Zealand Māori Council v Attorney-General* [1996] 3 NZLR 140 (CA); *Takamore Trustees v Kapiti Coast District Council* [2003] 3 NZLR 496 (HC); *Carter Holt Harvey Ltd v Te Runanga o Tuwharetoa ki Kawerau* [2003] 2 NZLR 349 (HC).

[82] Conservation Act 1987, s 4. This is the strongest legislative threshold: see J Ruru, 'Managing Our Treasured Home: The Conservation Estate and the Principles of the Treaty of Waitangi' (2004) 8 *New Zealand Journal of Environmental Law* 243.

institutions have a duty to 'acknowledge',[83] the Treaty principles. All persons exercising functions and powers under the Crown Minerals Act 1991,[84] the Resource Management Act 1991,[85] the Hazardous Substances and New Organisms Act 1996,[86] and the Energy Efficiency and Conservation Act 2000[87] must 'take into account' or 'have regard to' Treaty principles. More recently the Crown has recognised its responsibility to 'take appropriate account of the principles of the Treaty of Waitangi' by explicitly providing in legislation the avenues for Māori contribution in the decision-making processes of local government, land transport, and health and disability services.[88] Government departments, local councils and so on have since developed comprehensive Treaty of Waitangi policy statements.[89] However, in recent years these references have come under political opposition.[90]

3. Statutory Incorporation of Tikanga Māori

Since the 1980s many decision-makers have had to have some level of regard to tikanga Māori. A notable example is the Resource Management Act 1991. Under this Act, regional and local governments are primarily responsible for regulating the natural and physical resources in Aotearoa New Zealand, including the use of land, air and water. Persons wishing to use these resources must comply with district, regional and coastal plans and policy statements. Often this requires applying for special resource consents. Those acting under the Act must have some level of regard to a list of factors concerning, for example, the preservation and intrinsic value of these resources.[91] As part of this balancing act, the decision-makers must also 'recognise and provide for . . . the relationship of Māori and their culture and traditions with their ancestral lands, water, sites, waahi tapu, and other taonga' as a matter of national importance, and they must 'have particular regard to . . . kaitiakitanga'.[92] The Act does not define 'wahi tapu', but it means, in simple terms, a sacred place, and 'taonga', also not defined, means a treasure.

[83] Education Act 1989, s 181.
[84] Crown Minerals Act 1991, s 4.
[85] Resource Management Act 1991, s 8.
[86] Hazardous Substances and New Organisms Act 1996, s 8.
[87] Energy Efficiency and Conservation Act 2000, s 6(d).
[88] See New Zealand Public Health and Disability Act 2000, s 4; Local Government Act 2002, s 4; and Land Transport Management Act 2003, s 4.
[89] Eg, see Environment Waikato Regional Council website, www.ew.govt.nz/enviroinfo/profile/Māoriperspective.htm#Bookmark_tura. See also McHugh, above n 63, 414–22, 509–13. The Government has also commissioned research by Māori to be conducted in accordance with kaupapa Māori. See, eg, D Pitama, G Ririnui and A Mikaere, *Guardianship, Custody and Access: Māori Perspectives and Experiences* (Ministry of Justice, 2002); F Cram *et al*, *Evaluation of Programmes for Māori Adult Protected Persons under the Domestic Violence Act 1995* (Ministry of Justice and Department for Courts, 2002).
[90] See Treaty of Waitangi Deletion Bill 2006 (Member's Bill, Winston Peters, Leader of NZ First) and Treaty of Waitangi (Principles) Bill (Member's Bill 2006, Rodney Hyde, Leader of ACT).
[91] Resource Management Act 1991, ss 5–7.
[92] *Ibid*, ss 6(e) and 7(a).

Kaitiakitanga is defined to mean 'the exercise of guardianship by the tangata whenua of an area in accordance with tikanga Māori in relation to natural and physical resources; and includes the ethic of stewardship'.[93] The Act uses several other Māori concepts with accompanying definitions, including tangata whenua ('the iwi, or hapu, that holds mana whenua over that area'); mana whenua ('customary authority exercised by an iwi or hapu in an identified area'); maataitai (food resources from the sea); taonga raranga (plants which produce material highly prized for use in weaving); tauranga waka (canoe landing sites); and tikanga Māori ('Māori customary values and practices').[94]

A new trend is for Treaty settlement legislation to include tribal worldviews. These statutes often describe iwi, hapu, and whanau cultural, spiritual, historical, and traditional associations with sites ranging from mountains, lakes, rivers and wetlands. For example, Schedule 12 of the Ngaa Rauru Kiitahi Claims Settlement Act 2005 explains how the people of Ngaa Rauru Kiitahi have

> a spiritual and physical relationship through whakapapa to its taonga. It is espoused within mana atua, mana whenua, and mana tangata. These taonga encompass the expanses of Ranginui (sky), the vastness of Tangaroa (sea), and the immensity of Papa-tua-nuku (land).

Schedule 10 of the Ngati Awa Claims Settlement Act 2005 describes how Ngati Awa named the Whakatane River and the taniwha (spiritual guardians) that live in the river. Schedule 3 of the Pouakani Claims Settlement Act 2000 describes part of the creation story of the mountains Titiraupenga and Pureora, including how Ranginui (sky father) turned these once ancestors into stone and later how their guardians, the Patupaerehe (fairy people) and Te Ririo (a forest guardian) care for its native flora and fauna and streams, and tolerate no disrespect. Schedules in the Ngai Tahu Claims Settlement Act 1998 recount the deaths of two taniwha that now lie as islands in a lake,[95] and the travels of Parekiore, a giant, whose footsteps represent lakes.[96]

Recent case law, however, illustrates the remaining vulnerability of tangata whenua in protecting their environment. For example, the Takamore Trustees were unsuccessful in stopping the building of a road over a wahi tapu site alleged to be an old burial ground; and Ngati Rangi and Ngapuhi were unsuccessful in stopping the building of a prison upon land where an alleged taniwha lives.[97] Moreover, some politicians and academics have been highly critical of the references to Māori concepts, arguing that they pose serious issues for the rule of law and notions of equality.[98]

[93] Resource Management Act 1991, s 2 'Kaitiakitanga'.

[94] *Ibid*, s 2.

[95] Sch 25.

[96] Sch 62.

[97] For commentary on the case law: see J Ruru and J Stephenson, 'Wahi Tapu and the Law' (March 2004) *New Zealand Law Journal* 58, and NR Wheen, 'Belief and Environmental Decision-making: Some Recent New Zealand Experience' (2005) 15 *Journal of Environmental Law and Practice* 297.

[98] See Honourable Don Brash (leader of the National Party, New Zealand, Orewa Speech 'Nationhood' (27 January 2004) at the National Party's website, www.national.org.nz/; and Honourable Bill English's (National Party MP) speeches, including his Chapman lecture on educators

4. A New-look Māori Land Court

In the 1970s several Māori land protests caught the attention of the mainstream public. One of the more prominent protests included a walk from the north of the North Island to Wellington supporting a 'not one more acre of Māori land' stance. Led by Whina Cooper, the land march was an expression of the 'rising resentment over the relentless alienation and control of the remaining 1.2 million hectares of Māori land by Pakeha laws'.[99] Accepting that a new Māori land policy had to be formulated, Hon Rata introduced a new Māori Land Bill into the House in 1978. It had a long gestation. It was initially delayed in order for a Royal Commission to consider the future of the Māori Land Court.[100] The arguments presented to the Commission reflected a wider debate occurring at that time, namely whether institutions set up specifically for Māori should continue or be disbanded because they are products of paternalism.[101] By 1993, when the Bill became law, the court was envisaged as a permanent part of the judiciary, empowered with the special but complex role of assisting owners to better utilise their land.[102]

Te Ture Whenua Māori Act 1993 (the Māori Land Act) recognises that land is a taonga tuku iho (a gift handed down through generations) of special significance to Māori people and, for that reason, retention of it should be promoted, and occupation, development and utilisation of it should be facilitated for the benefit of its owners, their whanau, and their hapu.[103] The court must 'assist the Māori people to achieve the implementation of these principles'.[104] It thus operates in an entirely different fashion than in the past. It is now affectionately referred to as 'the people's court'. It often conducts hearings on marae, and welcomes the use of Māori culture and language. More than half the bench are Māori (total 10 judges), including the Chief Judge Joe Williams.[105]

and the Treaty of Waitangi on his personal website, www.billenglish.co.nz; and 'Treaty of Waitangi and New Zealand Citizenship' (2002) *New Zealand Law Journal* 254. See also D Round, 'Here Be Dragons' (2005) 11 *Otago Law Review* 31. For a wider debate on these issues, see G Huscroft and P Rishworth (eds), *Litigating Rights. Perspectives from Domestic and International Law* (Hart Publishing, 2002).

[99] Walker, above n 3, 212. Assimilationist legislation enacted in the 1960s had fuelled the specific resentment: for example, see Māori Affairs Amendment Act 1967 and Rating Act 1967.

[100] Report of the Royal Commission of Inquiry, *The Māori Land Courts* (Government Printer, 1980).

[101] *Ibid*, ch 12.

[102] See NZLC, *Report 85. Delivering Justice for All. A Vision for New Zealand Courts and Tribunals* (NZLC, 2004). Note, however, recent statements from the now Māori Labour MP Shane Jones, questioning the Court's future. See, eg, F O'Sullivan, 'Who Runs NZ? All Eyes on Williams and Whakatohea' *New Zealand Herald* (31 March 2005) at www.nzherald.co.nz/feature/story.cfm?c_id=1500896&ObjectID=10117881.

[103] See preamble, and ss 2 and 17. Note, about 5% of Aotearoa New Zealand's total land mass is classified as Māori freehold land (land in which the Māori Land Court has determined the ownership by freehold order), and most of it is owned in common with small blocks having many owners. For current statistics on Māori land, see J Grant, *Māori Land Development: Survey and Title* (Department of Courts, 2000).

[104] Preamble. See also ss 6, 17 and 18.

[105] For information on the court, see www.courts.govt.nz/Māorilandcourt/; and Judge C Wickliffe, 'Te Ao Māori Mai I Te Tairawhiti' in *Te Nupepa o Te Tairawhiti* (4 February, 2004).

The bulk of the court's work concerns succession orders and orders relating to establishing and administering Māori land trusts and, to a lesser extent, alienation applications (for example, to sell, gift, lease or mortgage Māori land).[106] A major challenge is to find ways for the owners to utilise the land themselves. Some barriers include reluctance by commercial lending institutions to lend on Māori land because it is often multiply owned and has a low valuation (few wish to purchase Māori land because of the restrictions imposed by Te Ture Whenua Māori Act),[107] and some portions remain landlocked.[108]

Te Ture Whenua Māori Act aspired to reform previous Māori land law by creating a new way of viewing Māori land: recognising retention as paramount, and past use, for example, of public works legislation to take Māori land as unacceptable. There has been concern expressed that while the Māori Land Court has adapted to this new role, the higher courts have not. Where there is conflict between the aspirations of Te Ture Whenua Māori Act and other statutes, such as the Resource Management Act 1991 or the Land Transfer Act 1952, the Court of Appeal has favoured giving effect to the principles of other statutes.[109] The most recent Court of Appeal decision concerning the Māori Land Court's jurisdiction, in the context of the foreshore and seabed, is in contrast to these decisions, as is discussed below.

5. Common Law Doctrine of Native Title

The High Court reintroduced part of the doctrine of native title into Aotearoa New Zealand's common law in 1986. *Te Weehi* held that a Māori person has a right to take undersized paua, or abalone, a type of shellfish, even though this was in contravention of legislation, because no statute had plainly and clearly extinguished the customary right.[110] Williamson J distinguished earlier case law which had adopted a *Wi Parata* type reasoning (namely the Court of Appeal's decision *In re the Ninety-Mile Beach*) because this case was 'not based upon ownership of land or upon an exclusive right to a foreshore or bank of a river'.[111] Subsequent case law

[106] See Boast *et al*, above n 17, T Bennion, 'Māori Land' in T Bennion, R Muir and K Palmer (eds), *New Zealand Land Law* (Brookers, 2005) 293; J Ruru, 'Implications for Māori: Contemporary Legislation' in Peart *et al*, above n 59. To keep abreast of Māori Land Court decisions, see T Bennion (ed), *Māori Law Review*, back copies available at www.bennion.co.nz/mlr/.

[107] For recent case law, see *Re Papamoa 2 A1* (2003) 20 Waikato Maniopoto District APWM 167; *Re Orokawa 3 B Lot 14* (2004) Taitokerau 6 APWH 240; *Kaiapoi MR 873 Blk XI Sec 71B* (2005) Te Waipounamu MB 110 SI 85–90.

[108] See J Ruru and A Crosbie, 'The Key to Unlocking Landlocked Māori Land: The Extension of the Māori Land Court's Jurisdiction' (2004) 10 *Canterbury Law Review* 318.

[109] See *Attorney-General v Māori Land Court* [1999] 1 NZLR 689; *McGuire v Hastings District Council* (2002) 2 NZLR 577; *Bruce v Edwards* [2003] 1 NZLR 515. For commentary, see N Tomas, 'Jurisdiction Wars. Will the Māori Land Court Judges Please Lie Down' (2000) 9 *Butterworths Conveyancing Bulletin* 33; N Tomas, 'Māori Land: Te Ture Whenua Māori Act and the Resource Management Act' (2002) 10 *Butterworths Conveyancing Bulletin* 22; J Ruru, '*Bruce v Edwards*: The Court of Appeal's Latest Ruling on Māori Land' (2003) 15 *Lexis Nexis Conveyancing Bulletin* 169.

[110] *Te Weehi v Regional Fisheries Officer* [1986] 1 NZLR 680.

[111] *Ibid*, 692.

in the 1990s reinforced the existence of the common law doctrine of native title in Aotearoa New Zealand, but did not accept the arguments posed under it. For example, the Court of Appeal, in 1994, concluded that Māori do not have a right under the doctrine (or under the Treaty of Waitangi) to generate electricity by the use of water power.[112] Further, in 1999, by majority, the Court of Appeal held that Māori cannot claim under the doctrine (or under the Treaty) a customary right to fish for introduced species.[113]

In 2003, the Court of Appeal, in *Attorney-General v Ngati Apa*,[114] reintroduced the full spectrum of the doctrine, even accepting the possibility that native title could encompass land either permanently or temporarily under salt-water.[115] Chief Justice Elias CJ stated:

> The common law as received in New Zealand was modified by recognised Māori customary property interests. If any such custom is shown to give interests in foreshore and seabed, there is no room for a contrary presumption derived from English common law. The common law of New Zealand is different.[116]

The court did not proceed to answer the question of whether Māori customary land rights to the foreshore and seabed exist, as the case had been brought on whether the Māori Land Court has jurisdiction to determine this matter (a land status rather than a native title issue). All five judges held that the Māori Land Court did have the necessary jurisdiction to consider such an application.

Before the Māori Land Court had an opportunity to do so, the Labour-led government announced its intention to enact clear and plain legislation asserting Crown ownership of the foreshore and seabed. In response to the government's position, outlined in a report released in December 2003, many Māori groups who protested the policy lodged an urgent claim with the Waitangi Tribunal.[117] There they argued that the policy, if enacted, would constitute a serious breach of the principles of the Treaty of Waitangi and wider norms of domestic and international law. The Tribunal agreed. It stated, in its March 2004 report, that the policy gave rise to serious prejudice which, by 'cutting off their access to the courts and effectively expropriating their property rights, puts them in a class different from and inferior to all other citizens'.[118] Despite the Tribunal's strong recommendations for continued consultation between government and Māori, the government rejected the report's central conclusions as based on 'dubious or

[112] *Te Runanganui o Te Ika Whenua Inc Society v Attorney-General* [1994] 2 NZLR 20, 25.
[113] *McRitchie v Taranaki Fish and Game Council* [1999] 2 NZLR 139. Note that Justice Thomas gave a strong dissent. The third case to discuss the doctrine in the 1990s was *Te Runanga o Muriwhenua Inc v Attorney-General* [1990] 2 NZLR 641.
[114] [2003] 3 NZLR 643.
[115] But note that the court assumed Crown sovereignty: see R Dawson, 'Doing Justice in Property "Taking" Cases: From Coal to Sand' (2006) 12 *Canterbury Law Review* 292.
[116] *Ngati Apa*, above n 114, 668.
[117] *Summary of the Foreshore and Seabed Framework* (2003) at www.beehive.govt.nz/foreshore/summary.cfm.
[118] Waitangi Tribunal, *Report on the Crown's Foreshore and Seabed Policy* (Wai 1071, 2004) xiv–xv.

incorrect assumptions'.[119] The government stressed the notion of parliamentary sovereignty—the idea that Aotearoa New Zealand's Parliament is supreme and is unhindered in its law-making abilities.

Section 3 of the Foreshore and Seabed Act 2004 states its object as to:

> preserve the public foreshore and seabed in perpetuity as the common heritage of all New Zealanders in a way that enables the protection by the Crown of the public foreshore and seabed on behalf of all the people of New Zealand, including the protection of the association of whanau, hapu, and iwi with areas of the public foreshore and seabed.

First, the Act vests the land in Crown ownership. Then, it replaces the Māori Land Court's jurisdiction to issue land status orders with a new jurisdiction to issue customary rights orders, and replaces the High Court's jurisdiction to hear and determine the common law doctrine of native title with a new jurisdiction to determine territorial customary rights.[120]

The government's handling of the foreshore and seabed issue angered many Māori. Protests included a successful claim to the United Nations;[121] a hikoi (march) of about 20,000 Māori on Parliament grounds; and the resignation of a Māori Labour Cabinet Minister, Tarina Turia, and her re-election to Parliament as a representative of the newly formed Māori Party. The issue also sparked discussion about reforming New Zealand's constitutional order and, in any such reform, the place of the Treaty of Waitangi.[122]

F. Tangata Whenua and the Law

Aotearoa New Zealand's state legal system has undergone a dramatic transformation in the past two decades. The remaining issue is whether the efforts by the

[119] Deputy Prime Minister Michael Cullen's official speech, 'Waitangi Tribunal Report Disappointing' (8 March 2004) at www.beehive.govt.nz/ViewDocument.cfm?DocumentID=19091.

[120] For commentary on this Act and its background, see R Boast, *Foreshore and Seabed* (LexisNexis, 2005); N Tomas and K Johnston, 'Ask that Taniwha Who Owns the Foreshore and Seabed of Aotearoa' (2004) 1 *Te Tai Haruru/Journal of Māori Legal Writing* 10; FM Brookfield, 'Māori Claims and the "Special" Juridical Nature of Foreshore and Seabed' [2005] *New Zealand Law Review* 179; PG McHugh, 'Aboriginal Title in New Zealand: A Retrospect and Prospect' (2004) 2 *New Zealand Journal of Public and International Law* 139; C Charters and A Erueti (eds), *Māori Property Rights and the Foreshore and Seabed: The Last Frontier* (Victoria University Press, 2007); J Ruru, 'What Could Have Been: The Common Law Doctrine of Native Title in Land Under Salt Water in Australia and Aotearoa/New Zealand' (2006) 32 *Monash University Law Review* 116.

[121] The United Nations Committee on the Elimination of Racial Discrimination on the New Zealand Foreshore and Seabed Act 2004. See also C Charters and A Erueti, 'Report from the Inside: The CERD Committee's Review of the Foreshore and Seabed Act 2004' (2005) 36 *Victoria University of Wellington Law Review* 257.

[122] See B Harris, 'The Treaty of Waitangi and the Constitutional Future of New Zealand' [2005] *New Zealand Law Review* 189; C James (ed), *Building the Constitution* (Institute of Policy Studies, 2000); M Palmer, 'Constitutional Realism about Constitutional Protection: Indigenous Rights under a Judicialized and a Politicized Constitution' (2006) 29 *Dalhousie Law Journal* 1.

legislature and the courts towards reconciliation have delivered what tangata whenua have sought. Most iwi and hapu groups want what the Treaty of Waitangi guaranteed to them—tino rangatiratanga.[123] Despite the new look of the legal system, the courts cannot deliver this—be it through the doctrine of native title, the principles of the Treaty of Waitangi jurisprudence, or the Māori Land Court jurisdiction—because they derive their authority from the Crown.[124] But, even so, in this new environment, tangata whenua are rebuilding. This part provides a comment on contemporary Māori, and the role of the law in defining that identity.

Today, most Māori have some non-Māori ancestry due to more than 200 years of genetic mixing.[125] Ethnic intermarriage remains common. Legislation reflects this reality in that it defines 'Māori' to mean a person of the Māori race of Aotearoa New Zealand, and includes any descendant of such a person.[126] This is consistent with how Māori define themselves. Descent, in terms of whakapapa (genealogy), is the essence of being Māori: 'When children are born with whakapapa they are grandchildren or "mokopuna of the iwi". They are Māori'.[127] The legislative consequence for identifying as Māori gives that individual the option of enrolling on the Māori electoral roll or the general electoral roll.[128] Since 1993, when Aotearoa New Zealand changed from a first-past-the-post voting system to a mixed-member proportional electoral process, the Māori seats have become proportionate to the number of Māori on the Māori roll. There are currently seven Māori seats, and an increasing number of Māori being elected to Parliament on party lists, representing the spectrum of political ideologies. Today, 21 of the 121 Members of Parliament identify as being Māori, putting Māori representation at 17.4 per cent in the House; a slightly higher figure than the Māori population.[129]

[123] See, eg, M Durie, 'Tino Rangatiratanga' in Belgrave *et al*, above n 43, 3; McHugh, above n 63; R Maaka and A Fleras, 'Engaging with Indigeneity: Tino Rangatiratanga in Aotearoa' in D Ivison, P Patton and W Sanders (eds), *Political Theory and the Rights of Indigenous Peoples* (Cambridge University Press, 2000) 89.

[124] See, eg, the scholarship of M Jackson, A Mikaere and J Kelsey. For an excellent recent articulation and summary of their arguments, see A Mikaere, 'The Treaty of Waitangi and Recognition of Tikanga Māori' in Belgrave *et al*, above n 43, 330. See also the contributions made in Belgrave's book on the wider question of how far Aotearoa New Zealand has come. Some believe gains have been made (see R Walker, D Williams, P McHugh, S Jones and M Durie); some are optimistic for potential gains (see H Kawharu and M Kawharu); some are extremely hesitant about the overall direction or even hostile to it (see A Mikaere and J Kelsey); and others remain highly sceptical about how the gains will impact positively on their own communities (see E Tuuta and M Mutu). More recent discussion is being advanced concerning the possibilities of the Treaty: see D Williams, 'The Treaty of Waitangi: A 'Bridle' on Parliamentary Sovereignty' (2007) 22 *New Zealand Universities Law Review* 596; H Wilberg, 'Judicial Remedies for the Original Breach' [2007] *New Zealand Law Review* 173; P Keal, *European Conquest and the Rights of Indigenous Peoples: The Moral Backwardness of International Society* (Cambridge University Press, 2003) 174.

[125] See P Callister, 'Ethnicity Measures, Intermarriage and Social Policy' (2004) 23 *Social Policy Journal of New Zealand* 109.

[126] See Electoral Act 1993, s 3 'Māori'.

[127] M Jackson, 'The Part-Māori Syndrome' (2003) 52 *Mana* 62, 62.

[128] For further discussion of Māori individual advantage in legislation, see M Durie, *Nga Tai Matatu. Tides of Māori Endurance* (Oxford University Press, 2005) 205–6.

[129] See Parliament's website at www.ps.parliament.govt.nz/schools/texts/Māorimp.shtml.

The continued existence of the Māori seats is causing controversy in the political arena, with increasing calls to abolish them.[130]

The issues concerning Māori identity in the courts mostly relate to who has the proper standing as a group to be recognised as an iwi or hapu. While Māori are still tribal, and identify themselves by their whanau, hapu and iwi (and speak of, for example, Taranakitanga),

> [w]e have moved so very far from the situation where, really little more than fifty years ago, most Māori were living in their own tribal regions, and were left by the rest of New Zealand to deal with their own issues in a sort of parallel universe. It is no wonder that, given the extent and pace of the change that has occurred, the situation today, as to who represents whom and as to what, is frequently unclear and unsettled. It is also unsurprising that, given the importance of some of the issues confronted by the various groups, and the value of the resources at stake, representation issues end up before the courts.[131]

Representation issues are particularly prevalent when hapu and iwi are seeking historical redress from the Crown, or when a particular group or groups assert status as mana whenua and therefore have rights to be consulted and responsibilities to practise, for example, kaitiakitanga. The courts have been asked to determine which tribal group has the correct standing, which group or groups hold mana whenua status over a particular area, and where the boundary lines between groups should be drawn on the landscape.[132]

Another contentious identity issue concerns those Māori who no longer know their ancestral identity; 17 per cent of those responding to the question on iwi affiliation did not know in the 2006 census—but down from 26 per cent in 1996 census.[133] Rapid urbanisation, beginning in the 1940s, is the source of this dislocation. More than 80 per cent of the Māori population now live in cities. Since the 1980s, several Māori urban authorities have been established to help provide a range of social and economic initiatives to urban-dwelling Māori.[134] A litigious issue has been whether these urban authorities constitute new 'iwi', and this has been most contentious in the reallocation of sea fishery assets.[135] In an attempt to stem ancestral dislocation and reconnect Māori with their tribal ancestry, a new website, Tuhono, is encouraging Māori to register their details. The project aims to chan-

[130] For a comprehensive insight into the history and contemporary issues of the Māori seats, see A Geddis, 'A Dual Track Democracy? The Symbolic Role of the Māori Seats in New Zealand's Electoral System' (2006) 5 *Election Law Journal* 347.

[131] C Wainwright, 'Māori Representation Issues and the Courts' (2002) 33 *Victoria University of Wellington Law Review* 603, 610.

[132] See M Hond, 'Resort to Mediation in Māori-to-Māori Dispute Resolution: Is it the Elixir to Cure all Ills?' (2002) 33 *Victoria University of Wellington Law Review* 579. See also McHugh, above n 63, 505–29; M Stephens, 'Kaumatua, Leadership and the Treaty of Waitangi Claims Settlement Process; Some Data and Observations' (2002) 33 *Victoria University of Wellington Law Review* 321.

[133] See Statistics New Zealand website, www.stats.govt.nz/census/2006-census-data/quickstats-about-Māori.

[134] Eg, see the Manakau Urban Māori Authority at www.muma.org.nz/flash.html.

[135] For the most recent of these cases, see *Thompson v Treaty of Waitangi Fisheries Commission* [2005] 2 NZLR 9. See also Māori Fisheries Act 2004 and Te Ohu Kaimoana (Māori Fisheries Commission) website at teohu.Māori.nz. For commentary, see Durie, above n 128, ch 5.

nel information between iwi and individuals and essentially foster whanau, hapu and iwi links.[136]

New advances in biological and medical technology are posing some particularly interesting issues for Māori identity in the 21st century. Legislation contemplates Māori participation in navigating these new realms. Decision-makers acting under the Hazardous Substances and New Organisms Act 1996 must take into account a series of issues, such as the sustainability of all native flora and fauna and public health, and including 'the relationship of Māori and their culture and traditions with their ancestral lands, water, sites, waahi tapu, valued flora and fauna, and other taonga', and the Treaty of Waitangi principles.[137] Yet, in the two most significant cases to date concerning this Act and Māori, the Environmental Risk Management Authority appeared 'uncomfortable with evaluating and counting the matters of Māori spiritual belief'.[138] Likewise, while the Human Assisted Reproductive Technology Act 2004 now makes it mandatory for those acting under the Act to consider and treat with respect 'the needs, values, and beliefs of Māori',[139] the Law Commission's reports on legal parenthood issues have not even been able to sufficiently grasp the issues as they relate to Māori.[140]

The most significant change occurring in Māori identity, however, is not being played out in the courts, but in the communities. A major cultural revival is empowering Māori individual and group identity. Current Crown settlements of historical wrongs with iwi and hapu are injecting large amounts of cash and assets into these communities. This development is re-empowering tribal governance—tino rangatiratanga. For example, in regard to one of the first iwi to settle with the Crown in the late 1990s, Te Runanga o Ngai Tahu's commercial arm, Ngai Tahu Holdings Group, is now a formidable business player in the South Island, with investments in property, seafood and tourism. It is a major advocate in the education sector, having developed, for example, Memorandums of Understanding with the South Island tertiary institutions. It publishes a quarterly news magazine, Te Karaka, has its own radio station, Tahu FM, and has developed more than 30 health and social services programmes specifically designed for groups ranging from youth through to those with gambling addictions.[141]

[136] See www.tuhono.net.

[137] Sections 4, 6(d) and 8. See also *Report of the Royal Commission on Genetic Modification* (Wellington, 2001) at www.mfe.govt.nz/publications/organisms/royal-commission-gm/index.html; and the Bioethics Council's publications, including *Whakapapa and Xenotransplantation: Animal-to-Human Transplantation* (Bioethics Council, 2005) at www.bioethics.org.nz/publications/xeno-whakapapa-jan05/index.html.

[138] Wheen, above n 97, 310.

[139] Section 4.

[140] See its *Preliminary Paper 54: New Issues in Legal Parenthood. A Discussion Paper* (NZLC, 2004), and *Report 88. New Issues in Legal Parenthood* (NZLC, 2005). For commentary, see J Ruru, 'Indigenous Peoples and Family Law: Issues in Aotearoa New Zealand' (2005) 19 *International Journal of Law, Policy and the Family* 327. See also Human Genome Research Project, *Choosing Genes for Future Children: Regulating Preimplantation Genetic Diagnosis* (Human Genome Research Project, 2006). Climate change is another new issue affecting Māori: see, eg, the discussion on the Climate Change (Emissions Trading and Renewable Preference) Bill 2007.

[141] See Te Runanga o Ngai Tahu's website at www.ngaitahu.iwi.nz/Home.

At the heart of the cultural revival has been the resurgence in the use of te reo Māori (the Māori language). According to the 2001 census, 42 per cent of Māori can now speak and understand Māori to some degree. Nearly half of these speakers are young—under 25 years.[142] This is attributed to the hard work of those Māori who established kohanga reo (early childhood education centres) in the early 1980s.[143] In 1987, te reo Māori became an official language of Aotearoa New Zealand and confers the right to speak Māori in certain legal proceedings.[144] This new era differs remarkably from the past where te reo Māori was essentially banned from use for all purposes.[145] There are now Māori immersion pre, primary and secondary schools, several Wananga (Māori tertiary providers), and university and polytechnic degrees and diplomas are attainable in te reo and tikanga Māori. In March 2004, Māori TV, a free-to-air Māori television channel was launched, with a Māori language content of at least 50 per cent.[146] These arenas, including language development, and the expression of language and culture in literature and arts, have effectively captured the revival of a proud Māori identity.[147]

G. Conclusion

The future concerns for tangata whenua in the legal realm will most certainly relate to 'how Māori self-governance can be advanced within the confines of a unitary state'.[148] Pressing and tricky issues have some way to evolve before lasting resolutions are found. Throughout these journeys, Papatuanuku, our earth mother, as captured in the proverb at the beginning of this chapter, continues to offer us her nourishment and sustainment. In these lands, appropriate answers will eventually unfold, and the story here told will continue to meander along, with luck towards more respectful relations between the two Treaty of Waitangi signatory peoples.

[142] See Te Puni Kokiri website at www.tpk.govt.nz/Māori/language/default.asp.

[143] For a current insight, see New Zealand Crown/Kohanga Reo National Trust Joint Working Group, *Review of the Relationship between the Crown and Te Kohanga Reo National Trust* (Government Printer, 2001).

[144] See Māori Language Act 1987, s 4. Note that this right has attracted controversy. In regard to criminal proceedings, the Crown opposed a request to translate into Māori questions put in cross-examination (*R v Hillman* [1991] DCR 68); opposed any delay to the start of a trial by jury so that an interpreter could be found for the defendant (he asked for the interpreter on the day his trial was to begin) (*R v Cooper* [1997] DCR 632); and alleged that a defendant had been obstructive when he stated his name and address in Māori to an inquiring police officer (*Wharepapa v Police* unreported, High Court, Tauranga, 11 March 2002, AP 73/02, Priestly J). In all three cases, the court did not accept the Crown's arguments.

[145] See M Durie, *Te Mana, Te Kawanatanga. The Politics of Māori Self-Determination* (Oxford University Press, 1998) 59.

[146] See Māori Television (Te Aratuku Whakaata Irirangi Māori) Act 2003. See also Durie, above n 128, 47–49.

[147] Examples are numerous, including the internationally acclaimed film the 'Whale Rider' and P Grace's latest novel 'Tu', which won the top 2005 literary prize in Aotearoa New Zealand.

[148] Durie, above n 128, 15.

Appendix 1

Map of contemporary iwi territory

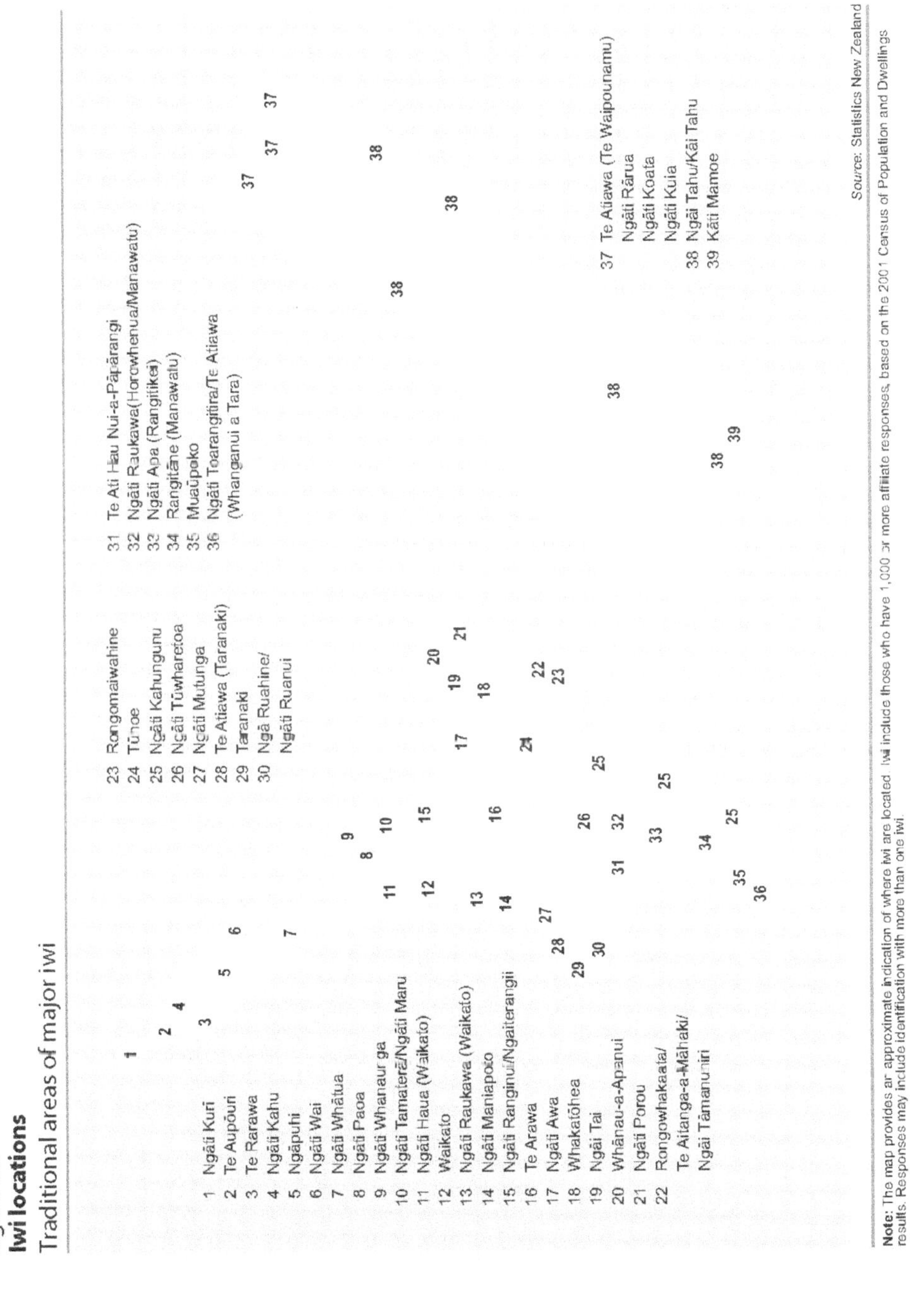

Source: Statistics New Zealand, New Zealand Official Yearbook 2002

6

The Inter-American System and the Rights of Indigenous Peoples: Human Rights and the Realist Model

JAMES HOPKINS

A. Introduction

How do Indigenous peoples and Indigenous communities effectively claim title to their traditional lands and resources? In Central and South America, the focus of this Chapter, the response to this question has resulted in dramatic developments in international human rights law, with profound consequences affecting the normative legal framework of nation-states, particularly states that have historically barred consideration of this very question and those that have systemically and violently trammelled upon the rights of Indigenous peoples. Increasingly, member states to multilateral agreements and international organisations are being scrutinised by international decision-making bodies with respect to their failure to meet international human rights standards in their treatment of Indigenous communities. These international bodies draw from a broad range of progressive sources of international human rights law that have developed over the past 50 years within the context of adjudicating Indigenous claims. Remedies are context-specific, and frequently seek the demarcation, delineation and titling of Indigenous customary lands as a way forward. These striking normative developments arise from precedent-setting claims ushered along by Indigenous claimants,[1] their counsel, and a network of non-governmental organisations (NGOs) who have all worked tirelessly to create an avenue of international recourse where domestic avenues for redress and justice have failed or broken down.[2]

[1] See especially SJ Anaya, 'Indian Givers: What Indigenous Peoples Have Contributed to International Human Rights Law' (2006) 22 *Washington University Journal of Law and Policy* 107.
[2] See RC Blitt, 'Who Will Watch the Watchdogs? Human Rights Nongovernmental Organizations and the Case for Regulations' (2004) 10 *Buffalo Human Rights Law Review* 261.

At first blush, these developments may seem natural, given the broad and descriptive language employed by human rights law, whose underlying norms are equally broad in definition and scope. It is understandable that this field has generated criticism, and to some extent cynicism, on account of its moorings to Western-based legal principles.[3] Yet, critiques of the aspirational nature of human rights overlook a critical capacity-building aspect of international decision-making bodies that use context-specific remedies as a means to both challenge and invigorate the way nation-states approach Indigenous populations. This exciting development may also tamp down the human rights critique by narrowing the scope of human rights law to alleged infringements on a case-by-case basis.

International decision-making bodies also play an important role in domestic law and policy reforms by guiding and assisting nation-states in fulfilling their obligations under international human rights law. In this respect, the remedial aspects affirm the prescriptive nature of human rights law—giving it the transitory teeth from 'soft' to 'hard' law.[4] Further, human rights are not mere abstractions existing in a theoretical vacuum: the articulation of human rights by international decision-making bodies sheds new meaning on the universal limits to cruelties and hardships humankind has visited upon Indigenous peoples, a group historically characterised by inadequate protections under domestic legal systems, including substantive, procedural and administrative shortcomings.[5]

In Latin America, the capacity and sophistication of international decision-making bodies to apply new interpretative models of human rights law offers enormous possibilities to address the dilemma Indigenous communities habitually face: in practical terms, it confronts the hardships and atrocities of the colonial past and the expanding demand for Indigenous resources in the global marketplace. Responding to this dilemma with great interest are the Organization of American States (OAS) and the two international decision-making bodies under its jurisdiction: the Inter-American Commission on Human Rights (IACHR) and the Inter-American Court of Human Rights. These two OAS decision-making bodies are at the forefront in deconstructing the post-colonial dilemma and challenging member-state practices that have long favoured nation-state interests in absolute terms.

As well, a sophisticated network of information exchange exists among Indigenous groups, NGOs, international advisory groups, and international moni-

[3] See especially KD King-Hopkins, 'The Inter-American Commission on Human Rights: Is Its Bark Worse than Its Bite in Resolving Human Rights Disputes?' (2000) 35 *Tulsa Law Journal* 421, 440. See also J Gordon, 'The Concept of Human Rights: The History and Meaning of its Politicization' (1998) 23 *Brooklyn Journal of International Law* 689.

[4] 'Soft law' refers to a legal instrument that attracts compliance solely on a voluntary basis. By contrast, 'hard law' creates clear obligatory rights that bind a sovereign nation. See C Joyner, 'Recommended Measures under the Antarctic Treaty: Hardening Compliance with Soft International Law' (1998) 19 *Michigan Journal of International Law* 401, 402.

[5] See *Cherokee Nation v Georgia*, 30 US 1 (5 Pet) (1831). This seminal decision by Chief Justice Marshall of the United States Supreme Court established the doctrine of tribal sovereignty. However, its remedial impact on the Cherokee claimants was breached and flouted by the State of Georgia, which proceeded with its Indian removal policy despite the landmark decision.

toring agencies. With respect to the OAS, this has had a significant positive effect on the ability of the IACHR to receive petitions involving allegations of human rights violations against Indigenous communities. This information network empowers a broad spectrum of human rights actors, including universities, NGOs, local Indigenous governments, and legal counsel. For example, NGOs can readily publicise internationally the plight of Indigenous peoples.[6] Moreover, an important feedback loop exists within the IACHR, as it publishes a wide array of findings, reports, cases and other information of value through a variety of accessible mediums that were not available to the general public before the 1990s. For example, IACHR is empowered under Article 40 of the Rules of Procedure, Inter-American Commission on Human Rights, to carry out on-site, fact-finding investigations pursuant to the receipt of a petition and where the Commission deems it 'necessary and advisable'.[7] The findings are readily available through the IACHR website in both Spanish and English, allowing for NGOs, human rights advocates, Indigenous groups and others to utilise such findings and recommendations in advancing new international human rights norms. Thus, these integrated information exchange networks—whether they are formalised under international agreement, or function informally through accessible mediums like the Internet—create awareness and inform the emerging discourse on human rights so that Indigenous peoples do not simply fade from public consciousness.

Natural resources are often closely linked to Indigenous human rights, including cultural identity and property rights. These resources are becoming highly desirable and sought after, giving rise to human rights disputes in Latin America. This dynamic was prevalent in the landmark 2001 decision by the Inter-American Court of Human Rights in *The Case of the Mayagna (Sumo) Awas Tingni Community v Nicaragua*.[8] Following the issuance of a timber lease by the Nicaraguan government in favour of SOLCARSA, a Korean-based logging company, the Mayagna (Sumo) Awas Tingni Community succeeded in stalling the logging when the court decided that the government of Nicaragua must delimit, demarcate and title the community's communal land holdings that were affected by the logging concession. Such developments have given the Indigenous peoples of the Americas a refreshing hope that human rights law can be applied to create a new regime where none had previously existed—either *de jure* or through custom.

In my view, human rights law in this context is understood through the substantive and procedural dialogue between the parties to a claim and the subsequent directions of the international decision-making body. As well, the emphasis on substance and procedure interconnects with other significant international

[6] NGOs can do so by placing digital streamed recordings online through web domains that are open to the public, blog sites, and web pages (eg, online video of the forcible removal of Indigenous communities by paramilitary groups through YouTube).

[7] Approved by the Commission at its 109th special session, OAS Res 448 (IX-0/79), vol 1, 98. Reprinted in Basic Documents Pertaining to Human Rights in the Inter-American System, OAS/Ser.L/V/I.4 Rev 7, 153 (2000), Art 40 (IACHR Rules of Procedure).

[8] Inter-Am Ct HR (Ser C) No 79 (31 August 2001), reprinted in (2002) 19 *Arizona Journal of International and Comparative Law* 395 (*Awas Tingni*).

bodies, namely, non-state actors like the World Bank and the International Monetary Fund whose own actions can undermine Indigenous communities and their rights to land and natural resources.[9] With respect to the inter-American system, the jurisprudence further illustrates this dynamic and emerging model of human rights.

This Chapter examines the decisions of the IACHR and the Inter-American Court in an effort to demonstrate the emerging model of human rights law and the significance this has with respect to the status of Indigenous rights. Particular attention is paid to the process as well as the remedial awards available to each inter-American body. These developments will illustrate a significant doctrinal shift within the human rights discourse that reinforces the capacity of international decision-making bodies to squarely address the claims of Indigenous communities, particularly concerning Indigenous lands and resources.[10]

Further, this Chapter analyses and discusses how this doctrinal shift marks a divergence away from the original theoretical anchor of strict positivism, or legal formalism, towards a new theory of realism. I will argue that this 'realist approach' to human rights interpretation is vital to the continuance of capacity-building within institutions like the inter-American system in expanding a normative sphere that addresses the rights of Indigenous peoples to land and natural resources.[11] The response by the international human rights system is a much-needed normative change to the long-established historical model that has played a dramatic role in shaping the status quo response of domestic legal systems throughout the Americas. Indeed, S James Anaya observes that the Indigenous experience seeks a unifying theme, defined along shared experiences of conquest:

> As empire building and colonial settlement proceeded from the sixteenth century onward, those who already inhabited the encroached-upon lands and who were subjected to oppressive forces became known as indigenous, native, or aboriginal. Such designations have continued to apply to people by virtue of their place and condition within the life-altering human encounter set in motion by colonialism. Today, the term *indigenous* refers broadly to the living descendants of preinvasion inhabitants of lands now dominated by others. Indigenous peoples, nations, or communities are culturally distinctive groups that find themselves engulfed by settler societies born of the forces of empire and conquest.[12]

[9] See, eg, F MacKay, 'Universal Rights or a Universe unto Itself? Indigenous Peoples' Human Rights and the World Bank's Draft Operational Policy 4.10 on Indigenous Peoples' (2002) 17 *American University International Law Review* 527; see also JC Hopkins, 'Therapeutic Lending in a Post-Colonial World' (2006) 14 *Michigan State Journal of International Law* 439.

[10] D Shelton, 'Improving Human Rights Protections: Recommendations for Enhancing the Effectiveness of the Inter-American Commission and Inter-American Court of Human Rights' (1988) 3 *American University Journal of International Law and Policy* 323, 329.

[11] See also SJ Anaya, 'Divergent Discourses about International Law, Indigenous Peoples, and Rights Over Lands and Natural Resources: Towards a Realist Trend' (2005) 16 *Colorado Journal of International Environmental Law and Policy* 237.

[12] SJ Anaya, *Indigenous Peoples in International Law* (2nd edn, Oxford University Press, 2004) 3.

This Chapter will explore the transition and evolution of human rights law away from a formalist model and towards a realist model in the context of claims made by Indigenous communities before the inter-American system. In section B it will be observed that formalism and classical colonial doctrine provided the rationale for state expansion, including the displacement and unfettered exploitation of Indigenous peoples, their lands, and their resources. This discussion of the inter-American system and its role in the evolution of human rights law will be analysed in relation to the realist model of interpreting human rights. This will further illustrate the changes in human rights discourse and the interpretative framework applied by the decision-making bodies within the inter-American system.

Section C of this Chapter will demonstrate the practical application of the realist model and the importance procedural aspects play in the inter-American system in developing context-specific remedies to claims by Indigenous communities to traditional lands and natural resources. It is contended that the realist model is not a panacea unto itself: it relies on the capacity of decision-making bodies to properly weigh and interpret the details of each case in concert with broadly prescribed principles of international human rights law. And yet, if one focuses on the remedies that address the nature of the problem at hand, the realist model raises the challenge of enlightenment—the very kind presented by Bartolomé Clavero—in a genuinely pragmatic manner. He states:

> If you seek real enlightenment, that is, self-knowledge and mutual understanding, mistrust European Enlightenment. Work in the plural. Do not permit any text to be cancelled. You need all or at least most of both.[13]

Thus, an IACHR recommendation requiring a member state to demarcate, delineate and title customary Indigenous land holdings in the member state's de jure system—a system that entrenched itself on the denial of Indigenous title—is a remarkable transition, as it forces the state to search deeper into the meaning behind Indigenous values in relation to lands and resources. It also changes the role of law schools in the Americas, the manner in which property and human rights law is taught, and the strategic approach pursued by Indigenous groups and NGOs.[14]

[13] B Clavero, *Freedom's Law and Indigenous Rights: From Europe's Oeconomy to the Constitutionalism of the Americas* (Robbins Collection Publications, University of California at Berkeley, 2005) 45–6.

[14] See DR Hurwitz, 'Lawyering for Justice and the Inevitability of International Human Rights Clinics' (2003) 28 *Yale Journal of International Law* 505.

B. Realism and the Protection of Indigenous Lands and Resources

1. The Realist Model of Interpreting Human Rights

To appreciate the protective role that international human rights can play in preserving Indigenous claims to land and natural resources, one must understand the relationship between classical international law and international human rights law, as the latter has emerged from the former. With its penchant for prescribed rules and doctrines, classical international law's historical context provides important insights into the contemporary legal status of Indigenous communities, and demonstrates the evolving nature of human rights norms from the classical moorings of this body of law. As Anaya observes, the modern analysis given to international human rights law is 'more aptly about process in connection with norms and values than about rules alone'.[15] An appreciation of international law's historical backdrop demonstrates how over the past 500 years it has evolved to include human rights and the recognition of Indigenous peoples. International law's chronology, its normative structure, and overarching themes reflected the colonial aspirations of European powers and set the stage for subsequent changes to the governing framework between nation-states and the Indigenous communities who collided with mercantilist expansion over their lands and natural resources.

In the ideal human rights model, norms change and emerge as a result of member states adhering to their international obligations as well as the decisions of international decision-making bodies that interpret these obligations. The reality, however, is a changing international landscape where non-state actors increasingly exert their legal claims against nation-states before international decision-making bodies. The process of asserting Indigenous claims to title and natural resources becomes plural: nation-states may not adhere to the findings of an international decision-making body in every instance, but they acknowledge the institution or face the risk that their legitimacy within the international community will suffer. Likewise, specific directions by international decision-making bodies to delineate, demarcate and title Indigenous lands deepens the legitimacy crisis on the part of nation-states seeking to avoid their international obligations within their own territorial boundaries.

This changing landscape in international law has engendered a spectrum of human rights law developments. Traditionally, international law interpreted the rights of Indigenous peoples with fixed rules and positive applications. This approach, one end of the spectrum, is known as 'formalism', and its development in the common law has produced doctrines such as domestic dependent nations,

[15] Anaya, above n 12, 6.

terra nullius and sui generis legal status. It provides a context for explaining the subordination of Indigenous peoples' rights to resources and land.[16]

At the other end of the spectrum, international law has pursued a model that emphasises a contextual interpretation of human rights norms as it applies and relates to a specific set of problems. An international decision-making body that orders a nation-state to demarcate, delineate and title Indigenous lands does so with reference to a larger bundle of international human rights instruments, with the intent of advancing respect for human rights. According to Anaya, the realist model establishes three interpretative maxims that international decision-making bodies widely accept:

> terms in international human rights instruments are to be interpreted (1) keeping in mind the overall context and object of the instrument of which they form a part; (2) in light of the larger body of relevant existing or developing human rights standards; and (3) in the manner that is most advantageous to the enjoyment of human rights (the pro homine principle).[17]

The realist model of interpreting human rights invigorates an important intellectual discussion over the methodology used by international decision-making bodies in the face of alleged human rights violations. On the one hand, human rights can be viewed as too broad, or lacking formal positive structure in claims by Indigenous communities against nation-states. On the other hand, human rights interpretation should not be overly simplified by its application to specific actions of government and it necessitates a larger inquiry into the state of Indigenous affairs. Realism's emphasis on the context of a claim or dispute avoids the limitations of legal formalism, and more accurately accounts for the prevalence of failed domestic legal systems that impact on Indigenous peoples' rights.[18] True to Clavero's cause of pluralism, the absence of a domestic structure to recognise Indigenous peoples' land rights reflects the general assumptions made regarding values and uses of Indigenous lands and resources. In practical terms, the success of Indigenous communities in establishing human rights violations before the inter-American system suggests that human rights law is now articulating a normative discourse around their claims and demands—one that we have not seen before.

2. Domestic Status: Classical–Colonial Origins

This change in discourse is in stark contrast to the legacy of colonisation throughout the Americas. Characterised by a systemic rejection of Indigenous civilisation as inferior, the onset of European sovereignty through conquest and subsequent colonisation caused irreparable upheaval to inherent systems of property rights

[16] Anaya, above n 11, 238.
[17] *Ibid*, 257.
[18] *Ibid*.

and Indigenous customary laws. As Robert A Williams Jr observes, in the case of Spain, the 'Iberian genesis' empowered a discourse of conquest under a unified vision of law 'discoverable by reason' and entirely dependent upon Christian subjugation for legitimacy.[19] Spanish exploration and the unilateral extension of its sovereignty in the New World was secured by the legal legitimacy of the Roman Catholic empire—whose constituents did not include the vast populations of Indigenous peoples at the time of contact—and was prescribed by canon law, referred to by Williams as the 'the perfect instrument of empire'.[20]

In contrast to the aspirations of the realist model, the colonial framework drew upon the assumption that European nations could unilaterally extend their sovereignty in the New World by discovery and conquest. Rejection of Indigenous identity as a legitimate body politic was closely linked to the moral imperative of Spanish wardship over Indigenous populations—an idea first introduced in 1532 by the eminent scholar and theologian Francisco de Vitoria.[21] Vitoria asserted that Indigenous peoples were capable of rational thought and, accordingly, held political autonomy and limited rights to land; however, this assertion was based on racial stereotypes, including inherent limitations with respect to Indigenous society because of their cultural beliefs. Anaya observes the future ramifications of this paternalistic approach by stating that '[t]his early affirmation of rights also can be seen reflected in the ensuing pattern of treaty making between the European powers and Indigenous peoples'.[22]

In the case of Spanish colonial law, the incorporation of Indigenous peoples into the corpus of the body politic as domestic wards had transparent assimilationist goals. Clavero states that domestic status was a doctrine that 'assimilated Indigenous peoples—all Indigenous people—to the status of minors in need of guardianship that would be provided for by both the Spanish Monarchy and the Roman Church'.[23] Throughout colonial history, the rejection of Indigenous customary law and property rights remained steadfast, with limited recognition tied to pejorative presuppositions. As Luis Rodriguez-Pinero remarks,

> [a] 'humanitarian' concern for the fate of 'indigenous' peoples has had a presence in . . . helping to bridge the moral gap existing between idealistic principles of 'civilisation' and the brutish practice of colonial conquest, ultimately contributing to legitimize that conquest. Grounded on the same social evolutionist and Eurocentric assumptions that underlie the notion of trusteeship, the class concept of indigenousness [presents] . . .

[19] RA Williams Jr, *The American Indian in Western Legal Thought: The Discourse of Conquest* (Oxford University Press, 1990) 59.

[20] *Ibid.*

[21] F Victoria, *De indis et de ivre belli relectiones*, trans by J Bate (Carnegie Institution of Washington, 1917).

[22] Anaya, above n 12, 19. See also E Kades, 'The Dark Side of Efficiency: *Johnson v M'Intosh* and the Expropriation of American Indian Lands' (2000) 148 *University of Pennsylvania Law Review* 1065. The author applies a similar analysis using law and economics to explain the pattern of development in the United States.

[23] Clavero, above n 13, 163.

> a normative location that simultaneously entailed a duty to 'civilize' on the part of the civilized and the ejection of 'indigenous' peoples to the margins of international law.[24]

Indeed, the development of international law as the law of nations made direct reference to the care of Indigenous populations in obtaining the requisite criteria for nation-state status. In 1758, Emmerich de Vattel drew upon the actions of emerging European superpowers and posited the entrenched idea of nation-state sovereignty whose powers included the care of Indigenous peoples and their lands.[25] Again, the consequence of this approach was to relegate Indigenous peoples to an inferior status within the nation-state system.

For example, during Vattel's era, emerging Latin American states experienced a constitutional reformation by extending full citizenship to Indigenous people. According to Clavero, this was an empty promise, as Indigenous people remained excluded from civic and democratic life. As well, the institutional practices around the constitutional traditions would inevitably lead 'back to the law of nations and thus to an exclusive, even racist culture'.[26] He asserts that '[c]onstitutionalism was born colonial between Europe and America and did not go native in the Americas'.[27] He describes a constitutional reality affecting millions of Indigenous people during this era as one with '[n]o checks, no balances, no rights, no freedoms, no constitutional achievements provided by the State'.[28]

Based on the foregoing, Indigenous customary legal systems and property rights were excluded in two possible ways. First, a nation-state could enter into a treaty for the express purpose of extinguishing Indigenous identity. Second, a nation-state could attempt to assimilate Indigenous identity by conferring citizenship on the entire population. Fortunately, international law has transitioned in a very different direction, away from its classical origins. Anaya observes:

> just as international law once moved away from natural law thinking that was to some extent supportive of indigenous peoples' survival as distinct autonomous communities, international law is again shifting. But this time the shift is in retreat from the orientation that would divorce law from morality and deny international rights to all but states, or that would regard non-Westernized peoples as necessarily inferior.[29]

International law's historical approach has been to limit notions of Indigenous land tenure to something other than full ownership. Indeed, this dilemma carries enormous consequences for Indigenous peoples who seek to articulate the cultural meaning of their land rights (including inalienable traits in certain instances) in a legal formula that is capable of bearing out a just and equitable equation.[30]

[24] LR Pinero, *Indigenous Peoples, Postcolonialism, and International Law: The ILO Regime (1919–1989)* (Oxford University Press, 2005) 5.

[25] E Vattel, *The Law of Nations, or the Principles of Natural Law* trans by CG Fenwick (Carnegie Institution of Washington, 1916).

[26] Clavero, above n 13, 161.

[27] *Ibid*, 169.

[28] *Ibid*, 161.

[29] Anaya, above n 12, 34.

[30] See S Wiessner, 'Rights and Status of Indigenous Peoples: A Global Comparative and International Legal Analysis' (1999) 12 *Harvard Human Rights Journal* 57, 93.

The evolving international approach requires nation-states to find an equitable middle ground, where traditional indigenous land tenure can be equated with full ownership.

The following section assesses the practical application of this evolving international approach in the context of the inter-American system for protection of human rights. It highlights the importance of procedural mechanisms in developing context-specific remedies to claims by Indigenous communities to traditional lands and natural resources.

C. The Inter-American System: Evolving Norms and Capacity

1. The Legal Framework Pertaining to the IACHR

In 1948, the Ninth International Conference of American States convened in Bogotá, Colombia, to formally proclaim the establishment of the Organization of American States.[31] The OAS, comprising 35 member states of the Americas, was established to promote regional solidarity and social and economic co-operation. Two significant legal instruments were advanced at this Conference that directly shaped the legal framework of the IACHR. First, OAS member states approved the constituting document of the OAS—the Charter of the Organization of American States.[32] With respect to the IACHR framework, the 1967 protocol to the Charter adopted by the General Assembly was significant in formally establishing the aspirations of the OAS to promulgate the IACHR. It reads in part:

> There shall be an Inter-American Commission on Human Rights, whose principal function shall be to promote the observance and protection of human rights and to serve as a consultative organ of the Organization in these matters.
>
> An inter-American convention on human rights shall determine the structure, competence, and procedure of this Commission, as well as those of other organs responsible for these matters.[33]

Moreover, the IACHR is an officially recognised organ of the OAS pursuant to Article 53(e) of the OAS Charter. The Commission has special powers to promote, protect, and consult on human rights. And yet, despite its prominent role within the OAS framework, the pith and substance of early cases involving human rights

[31] See further www.oas.org.

[32] Charter of the Organization of American States, concluded at Bogotá, 30 April 1948. Entered into force, 13 December 1951. 119 UNTS 3. Signed (15 June 1951) and ratified (13 December 1951) by the United States. Amended by four protocols: Buenos Aires (1967), Cartagena de Indias (1985), Washington (1992), and Managua (1993) (OAS Charter).

[33] *Ibid*, Art 106.

abuses against Indigenous peoples illustrate that the Commission initially emphasised its consultative role.

For example, one of its first cases on Indigenous rights, the 1970 *Guahibo* case in Colombia, reflected a Commission that had to reconnoitre its broad mandate within the general human rights framework in the first instance and, as a consequence, the decision suffered. Jurisdictional inquiries overshadowed the need for a normative discourse, development of which by the Commission has since made it a vanguard institutional actor and key decision-making body. In *Guahibo*, the Commission spent several years addressing its jurisdictional capacity to investigate a complaint by an Indigenous group in Colombia, and ultimately overlooked the intricate connections between customary communal land tenure, systematic abuse by the Colombian government, and human rights.[34] Similarly, a complaint arose in the 1977 *Ache* case out of Paraguay, and, in the face of systematic violence against the Ache community, the Commission requested that the Paraguayan government take 'vigorous measures'[35] to correct the violence.

By contrast, over 30 years later the human rights vision—promotion, protection and consultation—set forth by the OAS Charter has been more fully taken up by the Commission, providing it with a more ambitious agenda to respond to the increasingly complex situations that affect the rights of Indigenous communities within the OAS. An example of this progression is the 2005 global warming petition filed by the Inuit Circumpolar Conference against the United States on behalf of all Inuit of the Arctic Regions of the United States and Canada.[36] The ICC Petition ties together some of the most pressing environmental issues in conjunction with the rights of the Inuit throughout the Arctic regions of Canada and the United States. The allegations raise important issues about the scope of human rights protections conferred by OAS legal instruments and other instruments in the larger sphere of international human rights law, as the Inuit's traditional way of life is under direct threat from the effects of global warming.[37] The backdrop to this claim is the documented environmental changes that have affected their territory and are, according to the ICC Petition, causally connected to greenhouse gases emitted principally by the United States. At the very least, the ICC Petition strongly suggests that the Commission is viewed as a dynamic forum for creating public awareness and potential redress for Indigenous groups that face increasing environmental impacts transcending nation-state boundaries.

[34] Case No 1690 (Colombia), *Report on the Work Accomplished by the Inter-American Commission on Human Rights During Its Thirtieth Session*, OAS Doc OEA/Ser.L/V/II.30, doc 45, rev 1 at 21 (1973) (*Guahibo* case).

[35] Case No 1802 (Paraguay), *Annual Report of the Inter-American Commission on Human Rights, 1977*, OAS Doc OEA/Ser.L/V/II.43, doc 21 (1978) (*Ache* case).

[36] Petition to the Inter-American Commission on Human Rights Seeking Relief from Violations Resulting from Global Warming Caused by Acts and Omissions of the United States, submitted by Sheila Watt-Cloutier, with the support of the Inuit Circumpolar Conference, 7 December 2005 (ICC Petition).

[37] See HM Osofsky, 'Inuit Petition as a Bridge? Beyond Dialectics of Climate Change and Indigenous Peoples' Rights' (2007) 31 *American Indian Law Review* 675.

With respect to the second legal instrument promulgated by the 1948 Conference of American States, the IACHR's legal framework was additionally defined by the American Declaration of the Rights and Duties of Man.[38] Applied by the Commission to all OAS member states, this foundational instrument acts as an essential safe-harbour for Indigenous peoples in member states of the OAS who are not parties to the American Convention on Human Rights.[39]

This was the case before the Commission in *Mary and Carrie Dann v United States*, where the petitioners of the Dann band, as members of the Western Shoshone people, lodged a case against the United States citing numerous violations of the American Declaration based on the United States' ongoing infringement of their right to use and occupy their ancestral lands.[40] Their claim specified violations under Article II (the right to equality before the law), Article XVIII (the right to a fair trial), and Article XXIII (the right to property, which guarantees every person 'a right to own such private property as meets the essential needs of decent living and helps to maintain the dignity of the individual and of the home').[41]

The decision is significant because of the Commission's clear and instructive language on the normative framework regarding the American Declaration and its compatibility with developing international human rights norms outside of the inter-American system. In the *Dann* case, the Commission held the United States to be in violation of the foregoing articles, stating that the 1948 instrument should be 'interpreted and applied in the context of Indigenous petitioners with due regard to the particular principles of international human rights law governing the individual and collective interests of Indigenous peoples'.[42] The Commission acknowledged that its interpretation was not only consistent with several developments in international human rights law, but that safeguarding the 'integrity, livelihood and culture of Indigenous peoples through effective protection of their individual and collective human rights' reinforced the foundational purpose to the American Declaration as prescribed in the Declaration's preamble.[43] Lastly, the Commission's decision is relevant because it demonstrates the safe-harbour effect against OAS members such as the United States who are not parties to the American Convention on Human Rights.

[38] American Declaration of the Rights and Duties of Man, Adopted by the Ninth International Conference of American States, Bogotá, 30 March–2 May 1948. OAS Res XXX, reprinted in Basic Documents Pertaining to Human Rights in the Inter-American System, OAS/Ser.L/V/I.4 Rev 9 (2003) (American Declaration).

[39] American Convention on Human Rights, concluded at San Jose, 22 November 1969 (American Convention). Entered into force, 18 July 1978. 1144 UNTS 123; OASTS 36. Signed (1 June 1977), but not ratified by the United States.

[40] *Mary and Carrie Dann, Case No 11.140 (United States)*, Inter-Am CHR Report No 75/02 (merits decision of 27 December 2002) (*Dann* case).

[41] *Ibid*, para 2.

[42] *Ibid*, para 131.

[43] *Ibid*, citing the Preamble's recognition that, '[s]ince culture is the highest social and historical expression of that spiritual development, it is the duty of man to preserve, practice and foster culture by every means within his power'.

In conclusion, the two legal instruments that resulted directly from the 1948 Ninth International Conference of American States, along with the combined efforts of OAS member states, form a cornerstone to the inter-American system, greatly enhancing its role as a UN-recognised regional agency.[44] With respect to the IACHR, the Commission's legal framework is viewed as a source of international human rights law that is capable of evolving to meet the new challenges and articulations of human rights along contextual paradigms. This is perhaps one reason why the IACHR is at the forefront of establishing international human rights' norms, rules of conduct, and monitoring practices for the advancement of human rights.

2. The IACHR Statute and IACHR Rules of Procedure

As a direct result of the IACHR's role within the inter-American system, as it was originally envisioned in OAS Charter, the Commission's statutory framework was further enhanced by the Statute of the Inter-American Commission on Human Rights, which directs the Commission's overall function, composition, governance and regulation.[45] Article 1 to Chapter I of the IACHR Statute, titled 'Nature and Purposes', affirms the Commission's direct link within the OAS, and defines human rights by referring to the American Convention on Human Rights for ratifying member states (the United States has not ratified) and the American Declaration for all other member states. Subparagraphs (1) and (2) of Article 1 to the IACHR Statute provide:

1. The Inter-American Commission on Human Rights is an organ of the Organization of the American States, created to promote the observance and defense of human rights and to serve as consultative organ of the Organization in this matter.
2. For the purposes of the present Statute, human rights are understood to be:
   a. The rights set forth in the American Convention on Human Rights, in relation to the States Parties thereto;
   b. The rights set forth in the American Declaration of the Rights and Duties of Man, in relation to the other member states.[46]

Significantly, the American Convention on Human Rights directly sets out the means to protect the rights applicable by the Commission and the Inter-American Court of Human Rights, pursuant to Chapter II, Article 33. The significance of these enforcement provisions is further heightened by the reference to the special property rights protections conferred by Part I, 'States Obligations and Rights Protected', where, under the American Convention, Indigenous communities can

[44] The OAS is listed as a regional agency within the definition of Art 52 of the United Nations Charter.

[45] Statute of the Inter-American Commission on Human Rights, approved by Res 447, taken at the 9th Regular Session of the General Assembly of the OAS, La Paz, Bolivia, in October 1979, as amended by Res 508 at the 10th Session in 1980 (IACHR Statute).

[46] *Ibid.*

allege violations of their communal property rights and rely on the following protections, provided in Article 21:

1. Everyone has the right to the use and enjoyment of his property. The law may subordinate such use and enjoyment to the interest of society.
2. No one shall be deprived of his property except upon payment of just compensation, for reasons of public utility or social interest, and in the cases and according to the forms established by law.
3. Usury and any other form of exploitation of man by man shall be prohibited by law.[47]

In addition to the enforcement provisions provided by the American Convention, the Commission has a broad range of powers, conferred by Chapter IV of the IACHR Statute, titled 'Functions and Powers', to encourage and promote adherence to human rights standards by all member states as prescribed in Article 18. These include power to develop human rights awareness,[48] make recommendations to the governments of member states with respect to specific progressive measures that favour human rights (for example, constitutional reform),[49] prepare reports and request reports from governments on measures they adopt in matters of human rights,[50] and conduct on-site investigations with consent of the member state.[51]

Member states that have ratified the American Convention consent to additional powers of the Commission under it, specifically allowing primary enforcement at the OAS level to be carried out by the Commission. Most notable is the power of the Commission to act on petitions made pursuant to the American Convention on Human Rights and to appear before the Inter-American Court of Human Rights to seek immediate provisional measures in urgent matters. These additional powers, enumerated under Article 19 of the IACHR Statute, include the authority

a. to act on petitions and other communications, pursuant to the provisions of Articles 44 to 51 of the Convention;
b. to appear before the Inter-American Court of Human Rights in cases provided for in the Convention;
c. to request the Inter-American Court of Human Rights to take such provisional measures as it considers appropriate in serious and urgent cases which have not yet been submitted to it for consideration, whenever this becomes necessary to prevent irreparable injury to persons;
d. to consult the Court on the interpretation of the American Convention on Human Rights or of other treaties concerning the protection of human rights in the American states.[52]

[47] American Convention, above n 39, Art 21.
[48] IACHR Statute, above n 45, Art 18(a).
[49] *Ibid*, Art 18(b).
[50] *Ibid*, Art 18(c) and (d).
[51] *Ibid*, Art 18(h).
[52] *Ibid*, Art 19.

In addition, the Commission can make recommendations to states to bring about more effective human rights standards and, in doing so, consider 'whether the domestic legal procedures and remedies of each member state not a Party to the Convention have been duly applied and exhausted'.[53] Lastly, the Commission's legal framework is buttressed by the Rules of Procedure, Inter-American Commission on Human Rights. In particular, Article 58 empowers the Commission to prepare a 'general or special report on the status of human rights in a specific State',[54] and, more generally, Article 57 provides that the Commission, in its annual report, may analyse the 'human rights situation in the hemisphere [and make] recommendations to the States and organs of the OAS as to the measures necessary to strengthen respect for human rights'.[55]

3. Country Reports as a Strategic Role of the Commission

Within human rights scholarship, much attention has been given to the importance of precedent-setting findings and decisions made by the IACHR and the Inter-American Court respectively.[56] It is, however, important to also consider the Commission's complementary and equally significant role of raising human rights standards and compliance within the OAS community as a whole by acting as a monitoring body on the status of human rights conditions of Indigenous peoples within OAS member states. In this regard, the Commission has made a seminal contribution to the documentation of human rights conditions, formalising the process in 1993 by including specific chapters on Indigenous rights within the annual reports of member states.[57] This process was carried out several years prior to the drafting of the OAS Proposed American Declaration on the Rights of Indigenous Peoples in 1997, and reflected a growing consensus within the OAS with respect to the paramount nature of Indigenous rights in international law.[58] The consensus, as reflected in the Proposed Declaration, was a significant factor in the Commission's decision in the *Dann* case, where it expressly extended its interpretation of international human rights to legal instruments outside the inter-American system.[59]

[53] *Ibid*, Art 20(c).

[54] IACHR Rules of Procedure, above n 7, Art 58.

[55] *Ibid*, Art 57(1)(a).

[56] See SJ Anaya and RA Williams Jr, 'The Protection of Indigenous Peoples' Rights over Lands and Natural Resources Under the Inter-American Human Rights System' (2001) 14 *Harvard Human Rights Journal* 33.

[57] See LM Graham, 'Resolving Indigenous Claims to Self-Determination' (2004) 10 *International Law Student Association Journal of International and Comparative Law* 385, 409.

[58] *Proposed American Declaration on the Rights of Indigenous Peoples*, approved by the Inter-American Commission on Human Rights on 26 February 1997, at its 133rd session, 95th regular session, published in *Annual Report of the Inter-American Commission on Human Rights*, OAS Doc OEA/Ser.L/V/II.95.Doc 7 Rev (14 March 1996). See also *United Nations Declaration on the Rights of Indigenous Peoples*, 13 September 2007, online: www.ohchr.org/english/issues/indigenous/declaration.htm (adoption of the Declaration by the UN General Assembly).

[59] *Dann* case, above n 40, para 131.

To be sure, documenting the human rights conditions of Indigenous peoples is not merely about playing the role of passive witness to perilous situations: these fact-finding exercises have produced weighty documents that establish continuous monitoring of the human rights practices of member states. The annual country reports not only provide important evidentiary documentation of problems that member states face in complying with international human rights law, but they also carry a potent message to the OAS community, to both those member states who are making efforts to comply and those who simply ignore their obligations. These strategic facets of monitoring are illustrated in the Commission's 1997 report, titled *Report on the Situation of Human Rights in Ecuador*, which focused on widespread acts of violence directed against numerous Indigenous communities.[60] Citing the demise of several such communities caused directly by oil exploration and development, the Commission recommended that Ecuador take the necessary measures to guarantee the 'lives and physical integrity' of the affected Indigenous communities, 'such as the establishment of some form of legal protection for the lands they inhabit, as their very extinction as peoples is at issue'.[61] The Commission noted that the inter-American and international legal systems recognise the need to confer special protections for Indigenous peoples 'to ensure their physical and cultural survival'.[62]

Monitoring can also link specific petitions to the Commission's oversight role, involving the most egregious human rights violations, such as systematic massacres of Indigenous populations. For example, the Commission's 1993 Annual Report on Colombia documented the ongoing massacre of rural Indigenous peoples by Colombian paramilitary groups, and used the petition of a particular Indigenous village to illustrate the relentless violence and ongoing human rights violations.[63]

In this strategic capacity, the Commission plays an important advisory role to member states by addressing the degree of state compliance with the OAS framework and taking into account the full panoply of international human rights instruments that bear directly upon the status of Indigenous human rights. Of the country report concerning Ecuador, Anaya concluded that the Commission's report

> shed important light on problems that had gone without adequate attention by state authorities, raised those problems to a higher place in the hierarchy of governmental priorities, and provided guidance on how the problems should be addressed in accordance with contemporary norms.[64]

[60] *Report on the Situation of Human Rights in Ecuador*, OAS Doc OEA/Ser.L/V/II.96, Doc 10, rev 1 (1997). See ch IX, 'Human Rights Issues of Special Relevance to the Indigenous Inhabitants of the Country'.

[61] *Ibid.*

[62] *Ibid.*

[63] Inter-American Commission on Human Rights, *Second Report on the Situation of Human Rights in Colombia*, OAS Doc OEA/Serv.L/V/II.84, Doc 39, Rev (1993); see ch IX, 'The Rights of Indigenous Peoples in Colombia', part F.

[64] Anaya, above n 12, 234.

It is in this capacity that the member states are afforded the opportunity to progressively embrace a new regulatory discourse on the status of Indigenous rights. At a practical level, having the OAS Commission document and monitor the human rights status of Indigenous populations serves as an important reminder to its member states of their duties and obligations under the OAS Charter and international law generally. Finally, the country reports are consistent with the emerging discourse on Indigenous rights to traditionally held resources, as the reports deepen the normative backdrop from which OAS member states can develop their own laws and policies in a manner consistent with the OAS human rights requirements and international human law more generally.

D. Decision-Making Bodies: The Inter-American Commission and the Inter-American Court of Human Rights

An interesting facet to the IACHR process is the use of petitions to formally engage the Commission's jurisdiction over alleged human rights violations. On the one hand, the petition and related procedural aspects to the complaints process demonstrates the dynamism of the Commission's fact-finding role and the utility of generating dialogue between the parties through document exchange. In the long term, there is a transformative institutional aspect that parallels the normative discourse on emerging human rights protections for Indigenous communities. That process offers hope to Clavero's cause of seeking enlightenment by engaging in institutional pluralism. On the other hand, as Anaya observes,

> the effectiveness of these procedures remains constrained by the inherent weakness of the international human right system due to configurations of authority that favor state discretion especially in relation to matters deemed within the primary jurisdiction of states.[65]

1. Originating Process: The Petition

Title II of the IACHR Rules of Procedure sets forth several chapters and articles that prescribe the substantive requirements of the initiating petition. In recent years, the IACHR has focused on access by prospective petitioners, with the submission of the petition itself now tailored in a user-friendly format through the Commission's website.[66] Nonetheless, several important factors must be satisfied for the IACHR to make a positive finding on the admissibility of a petition before it can investigate the merits. With respect to standing, Article 23 of the IACHR Rules of Procedure governs the presentation of petitions:

[65] *Ibid*, 248.
[66] See www.cidh.oas.org/Basicos/basic20.htm.

> Any person or group of persons or nongovernmental entity legally recognized in one or more of the Member States of the OAS may submit petitions to the Commission, on their own behalf or on behalf of third persons, concerning alleged violations of a human right . . . The petitioner may designate an attorney or other person to represent him or her before the Commission, either in the petition itself or in another writing.[67]

The explicit reference to non-governmental entities is quite significant, as the emerging jurisprudence on Indigenous human rights within the OAS has been greatly assisted by the presence of NGOs and outreach educational programmes throughout the Americas. Moreover, under the provision in Article 23 of the IACHR Rules of Procedure the Commission is able to hear petitions alleging violations by states that have ratified the American Convention on Human Rights. As well, the Commission has jurisdiction to hear petitions that allege violations by OAS member states under the American Declaration pursuant to Article 49 of the IACHR Rules of Procedure.[68]

The Executive Secretariat to the IACHR is responsible for the initial processing of the petition and ensuring that petitions satisfy the admissibility criteria set forth under article 28 of the IACHR Rules of Procedure.[69] And yet, a significant substantive threshold is the requirement that the petitioner demonstrate steps taken to exhaust domestic remedies, or the impossibility of doing so, as prescribed under Article 28(h). The determination of admissibility on this issue, however, rests squarely with the Commission pursuant to Article 31 of IACHR Rules of Procedure, which provide:

1. In order to decide on the admissibility of a matter, the Commission shall verify whether the remedies of the domestic legal system have been pursued and exhausted in accordance with the generally recognized principles of international law.
2. The provisions of the preceding paragraph shall not apply when:
   a. the domestic legislation of the State concerned does not afford due process of law for protection of the right or rights that have allegedly been violated;
   b. the party alleging violation of his or her rights has been denied access to the remedies under domestic law or has been prevented from exhausting them; or,
   c. there has been unwarranted delay in rendering a final judgment under the aforementioned remedies.
3. When the petitioner contends that he or she is unable to prove compliance with the requirement indicated in this article, it shall be up to the State concerned to demonstrate to the Commission that the remedies under domestic law have not been previously exhausted, unless that is clearly evident from the record.

[67] IACHR Rules Procedure, above n 7, Art 23.
[68] *Ibid*, Art 49. See also Anaya and Williams, above n 56, n 23.
[69] *Ibid*, Art 29, 30.

The Commission may engage the member state through requests for information to determine whether or not domestic remedies have been exhausted, or, alternatively, to commence fact-finding through an on-site investigation or convening a hearing on the matter. This reflects a rich range of possibilities, and, thus, the response by the member state is critical in shaping the discourse with the Commission in the first instance. For example, if a member state refuses to provide information and if other evidence does not lead to a 'different conclusion', Article 39 of the IACHR Rules of Procedure permits the Commission to presume the alleged facts in a petition to be true.

Alternatively, a member state may not respond or implement recommendations in a timely manner, and, in so doing, attract further liability to the violations alleged in the petition. For example, in 1985, the Commission decided the *Yanomami case*, which involved violent encounters between the Brazilian Yanomami and the onslaught of speculators and criminal elements that besieged their ancestral lands, beginning with the construction of a large highway through their traditional territory in 1973. In this case, the Brazilian government was aware of the violence at the outset, and yet it did not respond with protective measures until 1983, three years after the petition had been filed before the Commission. The Commission found that Indigenous villages near the highway had been abandoned following several epidemics (for example, influenza), and the remaining inhabitants 'were changed into beggars or prostitutes'.[70] The Commission's resolution found Brazil to be in violation of the American Declaration as it concerned the rights to life, liberty and personal security, the right to residence and movement, and the right to the preservation of health and well-being, as the Brazilian government had 'failed to take timely and effective measures to protect the human rights of the Yanomamis'.[71]

By contrast, a member state may agree to mediation and the Commission may be in a position to invoke its friendly settlement regime, as was the situation in the 1999 *Lamenxay and Riachito* case. This settlement resulted in the Paraguayan government purchasing lands claimed by the Lamenxay and Riachito communities from third parties, and included titling the lands and resettling the displaced community members.[72] The friendly settlement provisions are contained in Article 41 of the IACHR Rules of Procedure:

1. On its own initiative or at the request of any of the parties, the Commission shall place itself at the disposal of the parties concerned, at any stage of the examination of a petition or case, with a view to reaching a friendly settlement of the matter on the basis of respect for the human rights . . .

[70] Case No 7615 (Brazil), Inter-Am CHR Res No 12/85 (5 March 1985), *Annual Report of the Inter-American Commission on Human Rights, 1984–1985*, OAS Doc OEA/Ser.L/V/II.66, doc 10, rev 1 (1985), para ix.

[71] *Ibid.*

[72] *Enxet-Lamenxay and Kayleyphapopyet (Riachito) Indigenous Communities*, Case No 11.713 (Paraguay), Inter-Am CHR Report No 90/99 (friendly settlement) (1999), *Annual Report of the Inter-American Commission on Human Rights 1999*, OAS Doc OEA/Ser.L/V/II.106, doc 6, rev, para 2 (2000).

2. The friendly settlement procedure shall be initiated and continue on the basis of the consent of the parties. . . .
4. The Commission may terminate its intervention in the friendly settlement procedure if it finds that the matter is not susceptible to such a resolution or any of the parties does not consent to its application, decides not to continue it, or does not display the willingness to reach a friendly settlement based on respect for human rights.[73]

And yet, as Anaya observes, 'the friendly settlement process may act more frequently as a mechanism for the state to delay a determination of its responsibility than as a means of genuine conciliation'.[74] Thus, while attempts at friendly settlement failed in the *Miskito* case, the Commission's 1983 recommendations included great sensitivity towards the facets and contexts of Nicaragua's Indigenous populations and the embittered civil war, and ordered the Nicaraguan government to negotiate a new constitutional and legislative regime.[75] Efforts at friendly settlement nonetheless deepened the exchange of information between the parties and ultimately enriched the Commission's findings.

The Commission's report would be revisited in a petition filed by another Indigenous community in Nicaragua several years later in the *Awas Tingi* case, presenting an opportunity for the Commission to interweave its depth and knowledge of the context directly into the findings as a way of further demonstrating the failure by the Nicaraguan government to adhere to the Commission's recommendation with respect to Indigenous land tenure. Paragraph 3 of the petition states:

> [I]n response to complaints of human rights abuses against the indigenous peoples of the Atlantic Coast, the Commission conducted an investigation which included an on-site visit and published its findings in its *Report on the Situation of a Segment of the Nicaraguan Population of Miskito Origin* . . . Among the problems identified by the Commission in its report was that of unsecured land tenure for the Miskito and other indigenous groups of the region. The Commission recommended that the government take steps to remedy this problem. However, over a decade later, the land rights of Awas Tingni and other indigenous communities remain vulnerable to violations in the persistent absence of effective government protections.[76]

Note, however, that a state may attract greater scrutiny and accountability by the Commission where it systematically hampers and delays attempts at friendly settlement in specific reference to time-limited requests by the Commission. In these instances, the Commission may invoke precautionary measures under Article 25 of the IACHR Rules of Procedure, which provides:

[73] IACHR Rules of Procedure, above n 7, Art 41.

[74] Anaya, above n 12, 265.

[75] Inter-American Commission on Human Rights, *Report on the Situation of Human Rights of a Segment of the Nicaraguan Population of Miskito Origin and Resolution on the Friendly Settlement Procedure Regarding the Human Rights Situation of a Segment of the Nicaraguan Population of Miskito Origin*, OAS Doc OEA/Ser.L/V/II.62, doc 10, rev 3 (1983), OEA/Ser.L/V/II.62, doc 26 (1984) (Case No 7964 (Nicaragua)).

[76] Petition of the Mayagna Indian Community of Awas Tingni and James Castillo Felipe, on his own behalf and on behalf of the Community of Awas Tingni, against Nicaragua, 2 October 1995.

1. In serious and urgent cases, and whenever necessary according to the information available, the Commission may, on its own initiative or at the request of a party, request that the State concerned adopt precautionary measures to prevent irreparable harm to persons.
2. If the Commission is not in session, the President, or, in his or her absence, one of the Vice-Presidents, shall consult with the other members, through the Executive Secretariat, on the application of the provision in the previous paragraph. If it is not possible to consult within a reasonable period of time under the circumstances, the President or, where appropriate, one of the Vice-Presidents shall take the decision on behalf of the Commission and shall so inform its members.
3. The Commission may request information from the interested parties on any matter related to the adoption and observance of the precautionary measures.
4. The granting of such measures and their adoption by the State shall not constitute a prejudgment on the merits of a case.

The leading Commission case on this set of circumstances is the *Maya* case, whose petition was initiated by the Toledo Maya Cultural Council against Belize in an effort to stop logging and oil development on their traditional lands.[77] The Commission's initial decision to admit the petition was accompanied soon after by the issuance of precautionary measures against the government of Belize for the protection of communal lands occupied and used by the Maya Communities in the District of Toledo. The response by member states is critical to my argument that the inter-American system is engaged in developing a new voice with respect to the normative framework that governs Indigenous rights to communal lands and natural resources. The model interconnects the space conferred by international decision-making bodies and the possibility of new domestic discourse on human rights that includes new institutions that fulfil the international obligations of the nation-state.[78]

2. Cases before the Inter-American Court of Human Rights

Unique to the OAS system is the ability of the Commission, in limited circumstances, to refer a matter that they have adjudicated to the Inter-American Court. If the member state elected to accept the Inter-American Court's jurisdiction under the American Convention on Human Rights, and the Commission finds the state to effectively be in non-compliance with its recommendations, the Commission is empowered to refer the case to the Court pursuant to Article 44 of the IACHR Rules of Procedure, which provides in part:

[77] *Maya Indigenous Communities*, Case No 12.053 (Belize), Inter-Am CHR Report No 96/03 (merits, preliminary version, 24 October 2003).

[78] See LC Reif, 'Building Democratic Institutions: The Role of National Human Rights Institutions in Good Governance and Human Rights Protection' (2000) 13 *Harvard Human Rights Journal* 1. The author discusses the role of domestic human rights institutions in building a national discourse on international human rights compliance.

2. The Commission shall give fundamental consideration to obtaining justice in the particular case, based, among others, on the following factors:

   a. the position of the petitioner;
   b. the nature and seriousness of the violation;
   c. the need to develop or clarify the case-law of the system;
   d. the future effect of the decision within the legal systems of the Member States; and,
   e. the quality of the evidence available.

As the court's decision is binding, Article 44 anticipates a high level of consultation between the Commission, the petitioners and the member state prior to referring a matter to the court. The watershed case in this instance was the *Case of Mayagna Community of Awas Tingni v Nicaragua*, where the Inter-American Court dramatically reshaped the legal landscape by validating and upholding the communal land tenure of the Awas Tingni people in the face of competing claims conferred by the state to a multinational logging company.

From a practical standpoint, the *Awas Tingni* decision demonstrates the capacity of contemporary decision-making bodies to synthesise two competing visions of property law into a coherent, principle-based model that focuses on process, reconciliation, fairness and trust. In this regard, the realist model discussed earlier in the Chapter reveals itself to have important progressive implications for the rights of Indigenous peoples. The decision in *Awas Tingni* illustrates the court's adherence to an OAS interpretive provision prescribed under Article 29 of the American Convention on Human Rights. Article 29(b) provides that no provision of the Convention shall be interpreted as 'restricting the enjoyment or exercise of any right or freedom recognized by virtue of the laws of any State Party or by virtue of another convention to which one of the said states is a party'.[79] In effect, Article 29 opened the door for the court to consider a less restrictive test in defining the scope of property rights under Article 21, as it was required to take into account both the state law and any other binding convention.

Thus, in the court's opinion, 'Article 21 of the Convention protects the right to property in a sense which includes, among others, the rights of members of the Indigenous communities within the framework of communal property, which is also recognized by the Constitution of Nicaragua'.[80] This was an important factor when the court considered the scope of property under Article 21 of the Convention. The court carefully crafted a broad definition of property to encompass Indigenous communal land tenure as being consistent with the aims and objects of Article 29, and held:

> Given the characteristics of the instant case, some specifications are required on the concept of property in indigenous communities. Among indigenous peoples there is a communitarian tradition regarding a communal form of collective property of the land,

[79] American Convention, above n 39, Art 29.
[80] *Awas Tingni*, above n 8, para 148.

> in the sense that ownership of the land is not centered on an individual but rather on the group and its community. Indigenous groups, by the fact of their very existence, have the right to live freely in their own territory; the close ties of indigenous people with the land must be recognized and understood as the fundamental basis of their cultures, their spiritual life, their integrity, and their economic survival. For indigenous communities, relations to the land are not merely a matter of possession and production but a material and spiritual element which they must fully enjoy, even to preserve their cultural legacy and transmit it to future generations.[81]

The importance of this decision is highlighted by the fact that, despite the legislative and constitutional efforts by Nicaragua, the clear inability of the government to effect and give meaning to Indigenous land tenure played an important role in the court's determination that Nicaragua had violated Article 21. The decision succinctly connected the government's failure to meet its obligations under the Convention with the harm and infringement experienced by the Awas Tingni communities in the use and enjoyment of their property. In its decision, the court held that the state must 'carry out the delimitation, demarcation, and titling of the territory belonging to the Community', and it must concomitantly abstain from actions taken by itself or third parties at its behest or tolerance that may 'affect the existence, value, use or enjoyment of the property located in the geographical area where the members of the Community live and carry out their activities'.[82]
On the issue of remedies for abrogations of property rights, the Commission unanimously required that the State of Nicaragua delimit, demarcate and title the petitioners' communal land holdings. These remedial aspects further illustrate the need for member states to offer substantive solutions to the problems experienced by Indigenous communities in trying to protect their traditional lands and resources. From an interpretative standpoint, it demonstrates the need to assess underlying state action, its legitimacy and its intent, all of which plays an important role in the court's assessment of the Commission's case.

The court's scrutiny and ruling on title imposes a level of moral legitimacy, which, as Paul Keal observes, seeks to establish a paradigm where states 'negotiate mutually agreed reconciliation' to secure the rights of Indigenous peoples and to 'ensure survival of indigenous cultures in accordance' with international law.[83] The importance of this decision is that it offers a way to reconcile the constraints imposed by legal formalism, with its bias towards state sovereignty, with solutions presented by a realist approach to interpreting human rights.[84]

81 *Ibid*, para 149.
82 *Ibid*, para 153.
83 P Keal, *European Conquest and the Rights of Indigenous Peoples: The Moral Backwardness of International Society* (Cambridge University Press, 2003) 174.
84 Anaya, above n 11, 238.

E. Conclusion

Indigenous peoples are not merely the beneficiaries of an equitable evolution within international law. Rather, they are active proponents who have found an international system of rights adjudication that gives voice to their long-established claims. The fundamental principle of recognising group rights to lands and natural resources is a critical element in the ongoing protection of the Indigenous cultural identity. The capacity of the IACHR and the Inter-American Court to apply a realist model of interpreting human rights to context-specific cases is cause for genuine optimism. The perceived threat of an inter-American system trammelling upon the laws of nation-states is substantially mediated by the length of the process itself and the individualised nature of each case. More promising still, with exhaustive detail to the international process, Anaya offers hope and an alternative to the dead-end arguments over relevancy and indeterminacy:

> international procedures are . . . capable of promoting the realization of indigenous peoples' rights in accordance with contemporary norms. They shed light on problem situations that might otherwise go unnoticed by all but the indigenous peoples concerned; they provide conduits for indigenous peoples to confront state authorities with their grievances where inadequate channels exist at the domestic level; and they provide the possibility of changing the terms of dialogue so that it is grounded in the language of human rights, rather than being constrained by the existing and often oppressive parameters of legality at the domestic level.[85]

The hope of a synthesis between international law and realism as a distinct domestic process is echoed by Clavero: 'All in all, for indigenous peoples, a better future may be offered by international law than constitutional grant. Or maybe the future belongs to both of them in this precise order, beginning with the equal and fair recognition of rights, of human rights of course'.[86]

Recall as well the connection between the historical exclusion of Indigenous property rights and customary law and the limited recognition of Indigenous peoples as wards or dependants under the colonial model. As a societal discourse, legal principles evolve and adapt to meet the context and circumstances demanded of them. From this perspective, the role of the Indigenous petitioners before the inter-American system is pivotal. Law is an evolutionary discipline, and within the analysis of Anaya and Clavero one can foresee the emergence of an interpretative model that gives new meaning to the rights of Indigenous communities, and yet is consistent with the social paradigm of institutional change.

By close analogy, Carol Rose has made important observations about the nature of the common law's system of possessory rights and its relationship to federal Indian law in the United States. On the right of first possession generally, she states

[85] Anaya, above n 12, 271.
[86] Clavero, above n 13, 179.

that it 'begins to look even more like something that requires a kind of communication, and the original claim to the property looks like a kind of speech, with the audience composed of all others who might be interested in claiming the object in question'.[87] With respect to the realist model, the inter-American system's interpretation of international human rights law in relation to the historical and current struggles of Indigenous communities provides a new venue for previously ignored claims, and an opportunity to synthesise those claims to property within the framework of a pluralist nation-state system.

In the end, the realist model of human rights changes the way we think about culture, identity and property, providing a new voice that resonates within the existing international and domestic institutions, with a focus on the scope and meaning of Indigenous rights to land and resources.

[87] C Rose, *Property and Persuasion* (Westview Press, 1994) 14.

7

Indigenous Peoples and International Law and Policy

CLAIRE CHARTERS

A. History of the Indigenous Peoples in International Law

Indigenous peoples are now firmly a subject of international law and policy.[1] Various international instruments deal with Indigenous peoples' rights, including widely ratified international human rights treaties, United Nations' (UN) declarations, UN special rapporteurs' reports, and international tribunals' decisions. Similarly, many international institutions focus exclusively on Indigenous peoples' issues or address international law and policy relevant to Indigenous peoples as part of their broader mandates. Nonetheless, some norms remain hotly contested, including Indigenous peoples' rights to self-determination, and land, and the status of treaties between Indigenous peoples and states. This Chapter outlines international law and policy, and international institutions, relevant to Indigenous peoples.

International law and Indigenous peoples have a long history, dating from the 1400s. Initial contact between Indigenous peoples and Europeans in the Americas engendered what many consider to be the foundations of international law.[2] After the European plunder of Indigenous peoples' land and mass-murder in the 'New World', 'concerned European theologians and jurists questioned the legality and morality of the onslaught'.[3] Francisco de Vitoria, based on European natural law ideals, maintained that Indigenous peoples owned their lands, and then detailed the

[1] See RL Barsh, 'Indigenous Peoples in the 1990s: From Object to Subject of International Law' (1994) 7 *Harvard Human Rights Journal* 33.

[2] SJ Anaya, 'Indigenous Rights Norms in Contemporary International Law' (1991) 8 *Arizona Journal of International and Comparative Law* 1, 2.

[3] *Ibid*, 1. As is cited by Anaya in that article, Spanish theologian Bartoleme de las Casas famously documented atrocity against Indigenous peoples in the Americas in the early 1500s: see Bartoleme de las Casas, *The Devastation of the Indies* (1542) in RS Leiken and B Ruben (eds), *The Central American Crisis Reader: The Essential Guide to the Most Controversial Foreign Policy Issue Today* (Summit, 1987) 51.

means by which Europeans could take land and assert authority.[4] This is not to say that colonisers then followed more humanist precepts in their early involvement with Indigenous peoples. As Wiessner quips, '[Vitoria's] view of the essential humanity of Indians and their natural rights . . . did not fit nicely with the atrocities committed by these self-invited guests'.[5] Indigenous peoples in former colonies often suffer from the loss of their sovereignty and dispossession of lands and resources.[6]

The rise of positivism in international law, especially in the 19th century, displaced Indigenous peoples from the international legal lens, as it shifted the focus of international law to European state behaviour.[7] Thus, despite Indigenous peoples' appeals to the League of Nations in the 1920s, international law in the early 20th century largely ignored Indigenous peoples.[8] In the *Island of Palmas Case* of 1928, the Permanent Court of Arbitration: did not consider treaties between Indigenous and the Dutch East India Company as binding international treaties; recognised the Spanish had original title over the islands derived from 'discovery', although the islands were inhabited by 'natives' at the time of supposed discovery; and did not consider whether, as a result of Spanish failure to cement its sovereignty through occupation, those same 'natives' had sovereignty over their islands throughout.[9] The arbitrator simply focused on the legal consequences of European assertions of authority over the lands. Similarly, Indian tribes were not recognised as having a legal personality in international law in the 1926 *Cayuga Indian Claims* arbitration.[10]

International law underwent an ideological sea-change in response to the atrocities of the world wars of the 20th century. The new focus on human rights opened a door to greater legal protections for non-state actors, including Indigenous peoples. Key early developments include the first convention to deal exclusively with Indigenous peoples' rights in the form of International Labour Organisation Convention 107 on Indigenous and Tribal Populations in 1957 (ILO Convention 107).[11] Within the UN, the voluminous early 1980s *Study of the Problem of*

[4] Vitoria influenced other pre-eminent founding fathers of international law such as Hugo Grotius and Emmerich de Vattel in their later writings: Anaya, above n 2, fns 6–11.

[5] S Wiessner, 'Rights and Status of Indigenous Peoples: A Global Comparative and International Legal Analysis' (1999) 12 *Harvard Human Rights Journal* 57, 59.

[6] *Ibid.* See also P McHugh, *Aboriginal Societies and the Common Law: A History of Sovereignty, Status and Land* (Oxford University Press, 2004); RA Williams, *The American Indian in Western Legal Thought: The Discourses of Conquest* (Oxford University Press, 1990).

[7] In Anaya's words, 'international law moved to embrace what the "civilized" states had *done*, and what they had done was to invade foreign lands and peoples and assert sovereignty over them': Anaya, above n 2, 3 (emphasis in the original).

[8] Representatives of Haudenosaunee in 1923, and Māori in 1926, appealed to the League of Nations. See UN Permanent Forum on Indigenous Issues, www.un.org/esa/socdev/unpfii/en/history.html.

[9] *Island of Palmas Case (United States v Netherlands)* 2 RIAA 829 (1928).

[10] *Cayuga Indians (Great Britain) v United States* 6 RIAA 173, 176 (1926).

[11] ILC 40th Session 26 June 1957 (entry into force 2 June 1959). For analysis of this earlier regime, see L Rodriguez-Pinero, *Indigenous Peoples, Postcolonialism and International Law: The ILO Regime (1919–1989)* (Oxford University Press, 2005). The ILO had also adopted earlier conventions relating to Indigenous peoples, including, for example, the Contracts of Employment (Indigenous Workers) Convention (No 64) ILC 25th Session, 27 June 1939.

Discrimination Against Indigenous Populations precipitated the establishment of the UN Working Group on Indigenous Populations (WGIP) in 1982 and, ultimately, the newly minted UN Declaration on the Rights of Indigenous Peoples (the Indigenous Peoples' Declaration).[12] Similarly, international regional bodies, such as the Organization of American States, discussed in James Hopkins' Chapter in this book, and the African Commission on Human and Peoples' Rights are developing their own jurisprudence relevant to Indigenous peoples.[13]

B. Contentious Issues

Several contentious issues unsettle all the institutions and instruments discussed in this Chapter. The difficulty is that the international legal system remains inherently opposed to many Indigenous peoples' demands. States, often responsible for the actions leading to Indigenous peoples' claims, largely control international law and policy: states sign on to treaties, adopt declarations, determine the content of customary international law and general principles of international law, and have standing before the International Court of Justice (ICJ).[14] As Wiessner notes,

> The traditional doctrine of state sovereignty, with its corollaries of territorial integrity, exclusive jurisdiction and non-intervention in domestic affairs, has hobbled the capacity of the international legal order to affirm Indigenous peoples' rights and to limit accordingly the action of states within their asserted spheres of control.[15]

Self-determination is a controversial subject in its own right, with a long history and much academic commentary.[16] It becomes more volatile when associated with Indigenous peoples living within the borders of independent states.[17] In negotiations on the Indigenous Peoples' Declaration, states tended to argue that Indigenous peoples are not 'peoples' as understood in international law, and do

[12] UN Doc E/CN.4/Sub.2/1986/7 and Adds 1–4 (1986).

[13] For information about the Organisation of African Commission on Human and Peoples' Rights Working Group on Indigenous Populations/Communities in Africa, see IWGIA www.iwgia.org/sw2073.asp.

[14] Treaties, international customary law, and general principles of international law are the three principal sources of international law, at least from a formal perspective: Statute of the ICJ, 1945, Art 38(1)(d).

[15] Anaya, above n 2, 5.

[16] Including, to name a few of the more well-known authors on this topic, A Cassese, *Self-Determination of Peoples: A Legal Reappraisal* (Cambridge University Press, 1995); J Crawford (ed), *The Rights of Peoples* (Oxford University Press, 1988); H Hannum, *Autonomy, Sovereignty and Self-Determination: The Accommodation of Conflicting Rights* (University of Pennsylvania Press, 1990); M Moore (ed), *National Self-Determination and Secession* (Oxford University Press, 1998).

[17] Authors dealing with this issue include A Huff, 'Indigenous Land Rights and the New Self-Determination' (2005) 16 *Colorado Journal of International Environmental Law and Policy* 295, 313; C Foster, 'Articulating Self-Determination in the Draft Declaration on the Rights of Indigenous Peoples' (2001) 12 *European Journal of International Law* 141; C Iorns, 'Indigenous Peoples and Self Determination: Challenging State Sovereignty' (1992) 24 *Case Western Reserve Journal of International Law* 199.

not have the right to secession. Some argued that Indigenous peoples' right to self-determination is qualitatively different from other peoples' right to self-determination, and should be explicitly confined to concepts of self-management and constrained by states' territorial integrity.[18] Indigenous peoples' responses included: that they are clearly 'peoples' in the natural understanding of the word; that it is discriminatory to differentiate between the peoples who do and do not have the right to self-determination or to give it a different meaning when applied to Indigenous peoples; and that self-determination best encapsulates what Indigenous peoples seek, namely to live as they wish without outside interference.

International law now clearly acknowledges that Indigenous peoples have the right to self-determination. The Indigenous Peoples' Declaration, accepted by most states, explicitly recognises this, as do other international institutions and instruments. When Indigenous peoples' circumstances are such that they meet certain established international law criteria, such as they are under colonial domination or subject to alien subjugation, they have the right to choose to secede.[19] Otherwise, the right to self-determination entitles Indigenous peoples, as the natural meaning of the word suggests, the freedom to determine their own destinies, including through self-government and autonomy.

Some robust Indigenous peoples' rights standards are sourced in international human rights instruments. However, a tension between human rights and Indigenous peoples' rights remains. For example, human rights are individualistic and are portrayed as universal in application. Indigenous peoples' rights are collective. Some also criticise human rights as Western cultural-specific, which underpins the ongoing dispute between universalists and cultural relativists. Haunani-Kay Trask describes the conundrum vividly:

> Ideologically, 'rights' talk is part of the larger, greatly obscured reality of American colonialism . . . [B]y entering legalistic discussions wholly internal to the American system, Natives participate in their own mental colonisation. Once Indigenous peoples begin to use terms like language 'rights' and burial 'rights', they are moving away from their cultural universe, from the understanding that language and burial places come out of our ancestral association with our lands of origin . . . When Hawaiians begin to think otherwise, that is, to think in terms of 'rights', the identification as 'Americans' is not far off.[20]

Overlaying this is the disquiet about potential conflicts between human rights and Indigenous peoples' rights.[21]

[18] Statement by Clive Pearson, Representative of New Zealand, on behalf of Australia, New Zealand and the United States of America, on the Declaration on the Rights of Indigenous Peoples at the United Nations Permanent Forum on Indigenous Issues (17 May 2006), available at New Zealand Ministry of Foreign Affairs and Trade: www.mfat.govt.nz/speech/minspeeches/17may06a.html.

[19] I am influenced here by the writings of Anaya and Huff.

[20] HK Trask, *From a Native Daughter: Colonialism and Sovereignty in Hawaii* (University of Hawaii Press, 1999).

[21] An excellent discussion of this issue in the Pacific context is found in the New Zealand Law Commission (NZLC), *Converging Currents: Custom and Human Rights in the Pacific* (Study Paper 19, NZLC, 2006).

Other issues with specific rights remain: land rights are contentious, with states fearing that international obligations concerning Indigenous peoples' traditional lands could upset non-Indigenous property rights, or create new injustice. On redress for loss of Indigenous peoples' control of their territories, states reject full restitution or comprehensive compensation. A current hot topic is the question of Indigenous peoples' rights to free, prior and informed consent, especially to development projects on or involving their territories and resources.[22]

Another contentious issue is the ongoing discussion about who is 'Indigenous', that is, which groups have a sufficient Indigenous quality necessary to enjoy Indigenous peoples' rights.[23] This has arisen in debates about which Asian and African groups were 'first', or, indeed, whether a group must be the original occupant of territories to qualify.[24] Other suggested 'criteria', not yet conclusively authoritative, include:[25] an attachment to land; 'tribal' characteristics; cultural distinctiveness; the experience of colonisation or dispossession; and self-identification, with the latter considered the most important.[26] Distinctions between ethnic minorities and Indigenous peoples can be difficult to make on the ground. The question of 'indigeneity' also plays out at the level of individuals. What qualifies an individual to call herself Indigenous—tribal membership, cultural attachment, blood quantum, or something else?

More generally, international law on Indigenous peoples suffers from incoherence, as international institutions and instruments apply different standards on Indigenous peoples' rights; for example, in relation to land, culture and self-governance. Institutions with the authority to determine issues involving Indigenous peoples' rights, such as human rights treaty bodies and the International Labour Organization (ILO), are at times influenced by other bodies' jurisprudence, but do not necessarily have the explicit mandate to do so.[27] Greater inter-institutional dialogue might go some way to facilitating greater coherence in the standards set by Indigenous peoples' rights. Compounding this issue is the fact

[22] R Barsh, 'Indigenous Peoples and the UN Commission on Human Rights: A Case of the Immovable Object and the Irresistible Force' (1996) 18 *Human Rights Quarterly* 782, 791–96.

[23] There is a good summary of this issue in J Firestone, J Lilley and I Torees de Noronha, 'Cultural Diversity, Human Rights, and the Emergence of Indigenous Peoples in International and Comparative Environmental Law' (2005) 20 *American University International Law Review* 219, 223–31.

[24] See B Kingsbury, '"Indigenous Peoples" in International Law: A Constructivist Approach to the Asian Controversy' (1998) 92 *American Journal of International Law* 414; J Waldron, 'Indigeneity? First Peoples and Last Occupancy' (2003) 1 *New Zealand Journal of Public and International Law* 55.

[25] See, eg, JR Martinez-Cobo, *The Study of the Problem of Discrimination Against Indigenous Populations* UN Doc E/CN.4/Sub.2/1986/7/Add 4, 379 (1983).

[26] As indicated by EI Daes, 'Standard-Setting Activities: Evolution of Standards Concerning the Rights of Indigenous Peoples' UN Doc E/CN.4/Sub.2/AC.4/1996/2. Indigenous peoples themselves have argued that they have the right to determine indigeneity.

[27] An ILO Committee, aware of this issue, stated '[t]he documentation of the United Nations bodies comes from bodies responsible for supervising treaties . . . and can be taken into account as indicative of the general framework. In effect, the ILO collaborates with United Nations on specific issues, although ILO supervisory bodies are responsible for its own instruments': ILO, 'Report of the Committee Set Up to Examine the Representation Alleging Non-Observance by Mexico of the Indigenous and Tribal Peoples Convention, 1989 (No 169), made under Art 24 of the ILO Constitution by the Authentic Workers' Front (FAT)', ILO ILOLEX Doc 162004MEX169.

that Indigenous peoples' rights are found in instruments with diverse levels of legally binding character—from treaties and customary international law to good practice standards drafted by non-governmental entities. Where they differ, which one trumps, when and how?

As mentioned above, Indigenous peoples have participated at an international level for some time, enhancing the legitimacy of the resulting norms and the processes. But Indigenous participation raises questions, such as should there be a mechanism to ensure adequate representation of Indigenous peoples, and what impact does participation have on Indigenous organisations?[28]

Finally, which international Indigenous peoples' rights have reached the threshold of customary international law? The ICJ has defined customary international law as 'settled practice' by states and as being 'carried out in such a way as to be evidence of a belief that this practice is rendered obligatory by the rule of law requiring it'[29] (opinio juris). Scholars diverge on how much practice is necessary and what counts as evidence of states' belief that a practice is obligatory.[30] Customary international law is significant because it is directly applicable under domestic law in many states. Some cogently argue that at least some Indigenous peoples' rights are customary international law.[31]

The ICJ has played a seminal role in the evolution of customary international law. But Indigenous peoples have hardly been involved in that process; they do not have standing to bring cases to the ICJ because they are not recognised as states.[32] The ICJ's advisory opinion on the legality of South Africa's occupation of Namibia confirmed a people's right to self-determination is *erga omnes*, meaning of universal application, which was reinforced in its 1995 decision involving East Timor.[33] Possibly the most significant ICJ case for Indigenous peoples is its advisory opinion in *Western Sahara*, which held that the Western Sahara was not terra nullius (belonging to no-one) at the time of Spanish colonisation in 1884.[34] Thus, the ICJ did not deny the fact of prior Indigenous occupation, as occurred in the *Island of Palmas case*.[35] Further, and of equal importance, the ICJ recognised that

[28] EB Bluemel, 'Separating Instrumental from Intrinsic Rights: Towards an Understanding of Indigenous Participation in International Rule-Making' (2005) 30 *American Indian Law Review* 55.

[29] *North Sea Continental Shelf (FRG/Den; FRG/Neth)* (1969) 169 ICJ Rep 3, 44.

[30] See, in particular, AE Roberts, 'Traditional and Modern Approaches to Customary International Law: A Reconciliation' (2001) 95 *American Journal of International Law* 757.

[31] Anaya adds that '[t]his is not to say that the consensus on Indigenous peoples' rights is entirely satisfactory or that there is sufficient commitment by authoritative actors to implementing that consensus': SJ Anaya, 'The Emergence of Customary International Law Concerning the Rights of Indigenous Peoples' (2005) 12 *Law and Anthropology* 127, 127–8.

[32] Statute of the ICJ, 1945, s 34(1).

[33] The ICJ found that it could not determine the legality of Australia's negotiations with Indonesia involving the Timor gap because Indonesia had not consented to the ICJ's competence in the dispute, and the ICJ could not decide the merits without determining Indonesia's legal rights and obligations: *Case Concerning East Timor (Portugal v Australia)* [1995] ICJ Reports 90, para 34.

[34] K Knop provides an excellent analysis in *Diversity and Self-Determination in International Law* (Cambridge University Press, 2002).

[35] Famously used in the seminal Australian aboriginal title case to belatedly recognise that Australia was inhabited prior to colonisation: *Mabo and Another v State of Queensland (No 2)* (1992) 175 CLR 1.

legal consequences flowed from the existence of pre-colonial Indigenous occupation of their territory: the colonial state could not then rely on discovery to found sovereign title. However, the ICJ did not go so far as to recognise that the Indigenous inhabitants had, at that time, their own sovereign authority as states over their territories. Similar findings in another ICJ decision led Reisman to conclude that 'a juridical value for Indigenous rights was denied, even in a case where the parties had authorised the court to take account of them'.[36]

C. The ILO and Indigenous Peoples

1. ILO Convention 169

The ILO Convention 107, drafted in the 1950s, was assimilationist in tenor,[37] leading the ILO to eventually draft the Convention Concerning Indigenous and Tribal Peoples in Independent Countries 1989 (ILO Convention No 169). It has entered into force with 19 ratifications to date.[38]

While ILO Convention 169 refers to 'peoples' as opposed to populations when describing Indigenous peoples, Article 1(3) explicitly states that 'the use of the term "peoples" in this Convention shall not be construed as having any implications as regards the rights which may attach to the term under international law'. This means that ILO Convention 169 is neutral on whether Indigenous peoples have the right to enjoy self-determination—the use of 'peoples' neither recognises nor undermines any Indigenous peoples' right to self-determination as a matter of international law.[39] The ILO has stated that 'self-identification as Indigenous or tribal shall be regarded as a fundamental criterion for determining the groups to which the provisions of this Convention apply'.[40]

[36] See WM Reisman, 'Protecting Indigenous Rights in International Adjudication' (1995) 89 *American Journal of International Law* 350, 356, referring to *Land, Island and Maritime Frontier Dispute (El Salvador v Honduras, Nicaragua Intervening)* 1992 ICJ Rep 351.

[37] Eg, the preamble to ILO Convention 107 states concern that 'there exist in various independent countries Indigenous and other tribal and semi-tribal populations which are not yet integrated into the national community'.

[38] See www.ilo.org/ilolex/english/convdisp1.htm.

[39] Swepston states that '[t]he ILO was attempting to find a way to designate these human groupings as "peoples" without entering into the international legal thicket of self-determination': L Swepston, 'A New Step in the International Law on Indigenous and Tribal Peoples: ILO Convention No 169 of 1989' (1990) 15 *Oklahoma City University Law Review* 677, 692. Barsh argues, however, that by respecting Indigenous 'institutions' the Convention indirectly acknowledges a right to self-determination: R Barsh, 'An Advocate's Guide to the Convention on Indigenous and Tribal Peoples' (1990) 15 *Oklahoma City University Law Review* 209, 215. See also his discussion at 231–34.

[40] ILO, 'Report of the Committee set up to Examine the Representation Alleging Non-Observance by Denmark of the Indigenous and Tribal Peoples Convention, 1989 (No 169), made under Article 24 of the ILO Convention by the National Confederation of Trade Unions of Greenland (Sulinnermik Inuussutissarsiutqartut Kattuffiat-SIK) (SIK)' (2001) para 32(2).

The Indigenous and tribal peoples' rights the ILO Convention 169 details include: economic, social and cultural rights (Article 2(2)(b)); 'special measures' (Article 4); participation in decision-making (Article 6(1)(b)); control over development that affects them (Article 7(1)); customs and customary law (Articles 8 and 9); protection in employment (Article 20); social security and health (Article 25); and education and means of communication (Articles 26–31). The land rights articles are relatively strong. They affirm the special importance of land for Indigenous peoples (Article 13). Further, Indigenous peoples have the right to own and possess the lands that they traditionally occupy (Article 14(1)). Article 15(2) requires states to establish and maintain procedures to consult with Indigenous peoples before exploring or exploiting mineral or sub-surface resources. Article 16 provides that, if relocated, Indigenous peoples are entitled to equivalent lands and compensation 'in all possible cases'. Article 17 deals with customary legal regulation of Indigenous peoples' lands and, in particular, alienation, while Article 18 requires the imposition of penalties for unauthorised intrusions on Indigenous peoples' lands.

It appears that not all Indigenous peoples support ILO Convention 169, partly because it does not explicitly refer to an Indigenous people's right to self-determination.[41] Lack of Indigenous backing may have negatively impacted on states' decisions to ratify, or not ratify, ILO Convention 169. Nonetheless, the Convention has provided a key benchmark from which Indigenous peoples have been able to argue for higher standards.[42] Anaya considers that Convention 169 'implies a convergence of subjectivities of obligation and expectation . . . regardless of any treaty ratification or other formal act of assent to the articulated norms'.[43] His point is that it is indicative of customary international law on Indigenous peoples' rights, and especially opinio juris.[44]

2. ILO Monitoring of States' Compliance with ILO Conventions

The ILO monitors states' compliance with ILO Conventions 107 and 169 in three ways. First, the ILO Committee of Experts on the Application of Conventions and Recommendations (ILO Committee of Experts) reviews reports from states on their compliance with ILO conventions. Workers' and employers' organisations, which can represent Indigenous peoples' interests, can communicate their concerns about a state's compliance to the ILO Committee of Experts. The Committee has published hundreds of comments on states' treatment of Indigenous peoples

[41] As recorded in Swepston, above n 39, 678.

[42] Eg, for negotiations on the UN Human Rights Council Declaration on the Rights of Indigenous Peoples: *ibid.*

[43] Anaya, above n 2, 13.

[44] It was adopted by a vote of 328 in favour, 1 against, and 49 abstentions. Report of the Committee on Convention No 107, Provisional Record 32, International Labour Conference, 75th Session (1988) 32/17–32/19. The members of the International Labour Conference include states, workers' organisations, and employers' organisation representatives.

under ILO Conventions 107 and 169, and also under other treaties. For example, concerning the ILO convention on forced labour, the Committee of Experts urged the Congo to repeal legislation on prisons in Indigenous districts that permit forced labour from detainees who have not been convicted.[45] Concerning Conventions 107 and 169, the ILO Committee of Experts, in 2006, examined several issues, including mining exploration activities in Bolivia,[46] displaced tribal peoples as a result of a dam project in India,[47] and the existence of Indigenous or tribal groups in Ghana.[48] The International Labour Conference Committee on the Application of Conventions and Recommendations (ILO Conference Committee) can, on the basis of ILO Committee of Experts' reports, request states to appear before it to discuss any issues raised. It, too, has issued a number of reports relating to Indigenous peoples. For example, it published a report on Brazil's compliance with ILO Convention 107 in 1999 commenting on the intrusion of gold-miners in Yanomami territory, the demarcation of Indigenous lands, and health services to Indigenous communities.[49]

Second, in response to either employers' or workers' association petitions, the ILO Governing Body 'may communicate this representation to the government against which it is made, and may invite that government to make such statement on the subject as it may think fit'.[50] Indigenous peoples have invoked this procedure through workers' associations (the association in question does not need to be directly affected by the petition). When a petition is considered 'receivable', the ILO Governing Body establishes a tri-partite committee, with workers', employees' and state representatives, to consider the petition, which then makes recommendations to be adopted by the ILO Governing Body. Some states have been the subject of such petitions involving Indigenous peoples' rights, including Mexico, Peru, Colombia, Denmark, Ecuador and Bolivia.

Third, the ILO has a more formal procedure: ILO delegates, which include workers' and employers' representatives, can file complaints that a state is not complying with an ILO convention it has ratified.[51] Alternatively, the ILO Governing Body may initiate the procedure. The ILO Governing Body will then set up a commission of inquiry, which holds legal proceedings and publishes a report. The state can appeal the decision to the ICJ. It seems Indigenous peoples have not yet invoked this procedure.

[45] ILO, 'CEACR: Individual Observation Concerning Forced Labour Convention, 1930 (No 29) Democratic Republic of Congo (ratification: 1960)' (2006) ILOLEX Doc 062006COD029, para 3.

[46] ILO, 'CEACR: Individual Observation Concerning Indigenous and Tribal Peoples Convention, 1989 (No 169) Bolivia (ratification: 1991)' (2006) ILOLEX Doc 062006BOL169.

[47] ILO, 'CEACR: Individual Observation Concerning Indigenous and Tribal Populations Convention, 1957 (No 107) India (ratification 1958)' (2006) ILOLEX Doc 062006IND107.

[48] ILO, 'CEACR: Individual Direct Request Concerning Indigenous and Tribal Populations Convention, 1957 (No 107) Ghana (ratification: 1958) Submitted: 2006' (2006) ILOLEX Doc 092006GHA107.

[49] ILO, 'ILCCR: Examination of Individual Case Concerning Convention No 107, Indigenous and Tribal Populations, 1957 Brazil (ratification: 1965)' (1999) ILOLEX Doc No 131999BRA107.

[50] Art 24, ILO Convention 169.

[51] Set out in Arts 22–31, ILO Convention 169.

There are some significant and unique aspects of ILO supervision mechanisms. Anaya notes that the majority of ILO decisions 'generally have focused on the convention's requirements of Indigenous consultation and participation' and, further, that the mechanism 'has not . . . provided for exacting scrutiny of state behaviour under the convention's substantive standards'.[52] The ILO complaint mechanisms are also significant, as the ILO does not require the exhaustion of local remedies before a group can raise an issue before it, as is required, for example, before bringing complaints to the UN Human Rights Committee.[53] Finally, the ILO has determined that while ILO conventions do not apply retroactively, that is, to actions preceding a state's ratification of a particular convention, they do apply where the effects of state action pre-ratification continue post-ratification.[54]

D. UN Human Rights Fora: The Charter Bodies

1. Human Rights Council and its Predecessors

The UN's human rights fora as established under the UN Charter were reformed over 2006 and 2007. This led to changes in the structure of the UN's human rights institutions focused on Indigenous peoples. The Economic and Social Council (ECOSOC) formerly parented the UN human rights institutions, with the Human Rights Commission (HR Commission), and its junior body, the Sub-Commission on the Protection and Promotion of Human Rights (HR Sub-Commission), sitting under it. In 2006 the HR Commission was replaced by the Human Rights Council (the HR Council) and moved to sit alongside rather than under the ECOSOC.[55]

While the HR Council was mandated to 'assume, review and, where necessary, improve and rationalise all mandates, mechanisms, functions and responsibilities of the Commission on Human Rights'[56] it also continues many of the functions of the former HR Commission. For example, it has continued to authorise the work of a number of special rapporteurs and independent experts, including the Special Rapporteur on the Situation of Human Rights and Fundamental Freedoms of Indigenous People (SR on Human Rights and Indigenous Peoples).

The Council, albeit utilising different procedure, continues the HR Commission's mandate to hear and monitor specific human rights situations under ECOSOC

[52] SJ Anaya, *Indigenous Peoples in International Law* (2nd edn, Oxford University Press, 2004) 250–1. Anaya suggests that the ILO's reluctance to provide 'exacting scrutiny' can be explained by 'the predisposition toward non-interference in domestic affairs that still permeates the international system' and the ILO's 'institutional policy of favouring technical advisory services' (252).

[53] ILO, above n 40, para 30.

[54] *Ibid*, para 29.

[55] UN GA Resolution 60/251 Human Rights Council (3 April 2006) UN Doc A/Res/60/251.

[56] *Ibid*, para 6.

Resolutions 1235 and 1503.[57] The Resolution 1235 Procedure authorised the HR Commission and the HR Sub-Commission to consider 'information relevant to gross violations of human rights and fundamental freedoms', and to 'make a thorough study of situations which reveal a consistent pattern of violations of human rights'.[58] The HR Commission commented on some situations in which Indigenous peoples' rights were at stake using this procedure.[59] For example, the Commission monitored Guatemala throughout the 1980s and 1990s and commented on the 'grave situation' facing Indigenous populations there.[60] The HR Council can now convene special sessions and authorise special procedures to respond to such situations.

The Resolution 1503 Procedure enabled the HR Commission to deliberate on communications about allegations of 'situations which appear to reveal a consistent pattern of gross and reliably attested violations of human rights'.[61] The Sub-Commission also proved its responsiveness to Indigenous peoples' issues when it mandated two members to examine the relocation of Navajo and Hopi in Arizona after such action was initiated.[62] The 1503 Procedure has been replaced by another communication procedure. To be admissible, communications must not be simultaneously heard in other international human rights fora, and domestic remedies must have been exhausted. The communications are first vetted by independent human rights experts, and, if they pass this initial stage, are forwarded to a working group of states, which can make recommendations to the HR Council as a whole for action. The procedure is confidential, unless, after review, the HR Council decides to take up the matter publicly. Advantages of this procedure include that it is available even if the state in question has not ratified any human rights instruments.

The HR Council also has a number of new and innovative functions when compared to its predecessor. One is its power to undertake 'universal periodic reviews' of states' compliance with international human rights.[63] The UN Permanent Forum on Indigenous Issues has recommended that, in doing so, it examine the situation of Indigenous peoples.[64]

The dis-establishment of the HR Commission resulted in the de facto dis-establishment of the UN's WGIP in 2006, which had sat under the HR Sub-Commission. It has been substituted by the UN Expert Mechanism on the Rights of Indigenous Peoples (EMRIP), which met for the first time in October 2008.

[57] UN ECOSOC Resolution 1235, 42 UN ESCOR (No 1) 17 (1967) UN Doc E/4393 and UN ECOSOC Resolution 1503 48 UN ESCOR (No 1A) (1970) UN Doc E/4832/Add.1.

[58] *Ibid.*

[59] Anaya, above n 52, 225.

[60] UN Human Rights Commission Resolution 1991/51 (5 March 1991).

[61] UN ECOSOC Resolution 1503 48 UN ESCOR (No 1A) (27 May 1970) UN Doc E/4832/Add 1.

[62] Anaya, above n 52, 225.

[63] Above n 55, para 5(e).

[64] United Nations Permanent Forum 'Report of the Fifth Session' (15–26 May 2006) UN Doc E/C 19/2006/11, para 80.

The HR Sub-Commission, a body of independent experts on human rights, has been replaced by the 18-member Advisory Committee on Human Rights (the Advisory Committee). It is considerably smaller and, arguably, less powerful than the former HR Sub-Commission, which was in the habit of adopting decisions. Made up of only 18 experts, compared to the HR Sub-Commission's 26-plus alternates, the Advisory Committee's mandate is explicitly confined to providing expertise to the HR Council in areas within the mandate of the HR Council and at the HR Council's request.[65] The Advisory Committee is prohibited from adopting resolutions and decisions.

2. UN Working Group on Indigenous Populations (WGIP)

The WGIP was the longest-standing UN body dealing exclusively with Indigenous peoples. It comprised five experts from the HR Sub-Commission who met annually in Geneva, Switzerland, from 1982 until 2006. Hundreds of Indigenous peoples' and states' representatives attended, participated actively, and had significant influence. WGIP's mandate was to:

- review developments pertaining to the promotion and protection of human rights and fundamental freedoms of Indigenous peoples; and
- give attention to the evolution of international standards concerning Indigenous rights.[66]

The WGIP's best-known endeavour was to draft the Indigenous Peoples' Declaration in the first instance, in a form that was then adopted by the HR Sub-Commission in 1994. But that was not its only role. Indigenous peoples often used it as a venue to air their concerns with, and bring international attention to, worrisome domestic state practice, to network and to formulate strategies for the better recognition of Indigenous peoples' rights under international law.[67]

3. UN Expert Mechanism on the Rights of Indigenous Peoples

The EMRIP convened for the first time in 2008 for three days. In future, it will convene for five days each year. It is made up of five experts on the rights of Indigenous peoples, with due regard being given to experts of Indigenous

[65] UN Human Rights Council, 'Institution-Building of the United Nations Human Rights Council' Resolution 5/1 (18 June 2007) paras 65–84.

[66] UN Commission on Prevention of Discrimination and Protection of Minorities, Resolution 2 (XXXIV) of 8 September 1981.

[67] Anaya, above n 52, 222, notes that '[t]he working group, however, is not equipped to investigate or otherwise respond to the numerous statements it hears alleging violations of Indigenous peoples' rights, and hence whatever effect these communications may have is usually limited to the value of their utterance in an official public forum of the United Nations'.

origin.[68] Participation is open to, amongst others, states and UN bodies, and Indigenous peoples' and non-governmental organisations.[69] In a positive move for Indigenous peoples, the HR Council established the EMRIP directly under the HR Council rather than under the HR Sub-Commission's successor, the Advisory Committee. This means that it is higher up within the UN's human rights Charter body fora than the WGIP, its predecessor, which was under the HR Sub-Commission. Further, while considerably different from the WGIP, the EMRIP's mandate is similar to that of the Advisory Committee, and broad in scope. It is to provide the Council with expertise on the rights of Indigenous peoples, mainly using studies and research, and may suggest proposals to the Council.[70]

4. Special Rapporteurs

UN Special Rapporteurs (SRs) are independent experts appointed by the UN human rights institutions, initially by the HR Commission and the HR Sub-Commission and now by the HR Council, to report on and investigate country-specific or thematic human rights issues. While special rapporteurs' views are not binding, they undoubtedly contribute to emerging international legal jurisprudence on Indigenous peoples. In fact, given that special rapporteurs are experts in their areas, it might be legitimately argued that their reports constitute a source of international law under Article 38(1)(d) of the ICJ Statute, constituting the work of 'highly qualified publicists'. Further, because special rapporteurs present their reports to other UN bodies, they have the potential to embarrass relevant states into addressing concerns raised.

The SR on Human Rights and Indigenous Peoples has the mandate: to gather, request, receive and exchange information and communications on violations of Indigenous peoples' human rights; to formulate recommendations and proposals on appropriate measures and activities to prevent and remedy violations of human rights; and to work closely with other institutions focused on Indigenous peoples.[71] In practice, this SR has concentrated on thematic research on Indigenous peoples' issues, country visits, and communications with governments about alleged violations of Indigenous peoples' human rights.[72] Many of his reports pack a punch. For example, he recommended to Guatemala that it 'redouble its efforts to ensure the full participation of Indigenous people in public affairs, and instruct

[68] UN Human Rights Council, '6/36 Expert Mechanism on the Rights of Indigenous Peoples' Resolution 6/36 (14 Dec 2007) in UN Doc A/HRC/6/L.11/Add 1, paras 3, 4.

[69] *Ibid*, para 9.

[70] *Ibid*, para 1.

[71] UN Council on Human Rights, '6/12 Human Rights and Indigenous Peoples: Mandate of the Special Rapporteur on the Situation of Human Rights and Fundamental Freedoms of Indigenous Peoples' Resolution 6/12 (28 Sept 2007) UN Doc A/HRC/6/19, para 1.

[72] His country reports can be found at the Office of the High Commissioner for Human Rights, at www.ohchr.org/english/issues/Indigenous/rapporteur.

the authorities to take appropriate measures to ensure that Indigenous people participate at all levels of public administration'.[73]

5. UN Permanent Forum on Indigenous Issues (UNPFII)

The UNPFII was established in 2000 by the ECOSOC and met for the first time in 2002. It is an advisory body to the ECOSOC and has the mandate to advise on Indigenous issues related to economic and social development, culture, the environment, education, health and human rights. In particular, it is required to:

- provide expert advice and recommendations on Indigenous issues to the ECOSOC, as well as to programmes, funds and agencies of the United Nations, through the ECOSOC;
- raise awareness and promote the integration and coordination of activities related to Indigenous issues within the UN system; and
- prepare and disseminate information on Indigenous issues.[74]

The make-up of the UNPFII includes Indigenous peoples' representatives—eight of the 16 experts are essentially appointed by regional Indigenous peoples' groups. They meet every year, and Indigenous peoples, NGOs, states, academics and other international institutions attend.

While the UNPFII meetings have a general principal issue of concern each year, such as the UN Millennium Development Goals for poverty reduction in 2006, the breadth of its coverage of issues relevant to Indigenous peoples is remarkable. For instance, the UNPFII has made recommendations on land rights urging, for example, the UN Development Program to develop its policy on land tenure systems with Indigenous peoples' input.[75] It has also recommended that states 'ensure that all cultural and customary practices that negatively affect the rights of Indigenous women (for example, female genital mutilation) are eliminated'.[76]

Some Indigenous peoples and others were disappointed that the UNPFII's mandate did not include a state-monitoring function.[77] Its conclusions and recommendations are instead directed at the ECOSOC and other UN institutions. Nonetheless, the UNPFII has not shied away from commenting on state actions affecting Indigenous peoples and supporting other international institutions with state monitoring functions. For example, the UNPFII, in 2006, supported the SR on Human Rights and Indigenous Peoples' reports on South Africa and New

[73] UN Commission on Human Rights, 'Report of the Special Rapporteur on the Situation of Human Rights and Fundamental Freedoms of Indigenous Peoples, Rodolfo Stavenhagen submitted in accordance with Resolution 2001/57: Mission to Guatemala' (24 Feb 2003) E/CN.4/2003/90/Add 2, para 72.

[74] UN Economic and Social Council Resolution 2000/22 (28 July 2000) UN Doc E/2000/22.

[75] United Nations Permanent Forum on Indigenous Issues, 'Report on the Third Session' (10–21 May 2004) UN Doc E/C.19/2004/23, para 70.

[76] United Nations Permanent Forum, 'Report of the Fifth Session' (15–26 May 2006) UN Doc E/C19/2006/11, para 53.

[77] Wiessner, above n 5, 123.

Zealand, and encouraged the UN human rights treaty bodies, which monitor states' human rights compliance, to formulate recommendations and general comments on the rights of Indigenous peoples.[78]

E. UN Declaration on the Rights of Indigenous Peoples (Indigenous Peoples' Declaration)

The Indigenous Peoples' Declaration is the most comprehensive and progressive of international instruments dealing with Indigenous peoples' rights. A unique aspect of the Indigenous Peoples' Declaration is that, unlike ILO Convention 169, it has 'buy-in' from many of the Indigenous peoples who participated in the negotiations.[79]

The Indigenous Peoples' Declaration is the product of more than 20 years of negotiations, starting in the WGIP in the mid 1980s, moving to a UN Human Rights Commission working group (known as the WGDD) in the mid-1990s,[80] to adoption by the UN Human Rights Council in 2006,[81] and then the General Assembly in September 2007.[82] Not all the Indigenous Peoples' Declaration's wording was determined by consensus between states and Indigenous peoples—a few states prevented consensus. However, the language in non-consensus articles was selected from proposals for amendments by states and Indigenous peoples.

The significance of the Indigenous Peoples' Declaration lies not in its formal legal effect; declarations do not per se normally constitute formally binding international law. Nonetheless, its provisions reflect a degree of states' *opinio juris*, and thus go towards establishing customary international law. Further, the Indigenous Peoples' Declaration has been of some persuasive impact domestically, such as in the 2007 Belize Supreme Court case dealing with Mayan land rights.[83] Similarly, other international institutions, such as the HR Council, can use the Indigenous Peoples' Declaration as an informative benchmark against which to assess states' behaviour. Finally, Indigenous peoples can reference the Indigenous Peoples' Declaration to enhance their political leverage.

[78] United Nations Permanent Forum, above n 76, paras 70 and 77.

[79] K Knop remarks on this unique process in *Diversity and Self-Determination in International Law* (Cambridge University Press, 2002).

[80] Commission on Human Rights, 'Resolution Establishing a Working Group to Elaborate a Draft United Nations Declaration on the Rights of Indigenous Peoples' (3 March 1995) Report on the 51st Session UN ESCOR Supp (No 4) UN Doc E/1995/23, 110.

[81] UN Human Rights Council, 'Resolution 2006/2: Working Group of the Commission on Human Rights to Elaborate a Draft Declaration in Accordance with Paragraph 5 of the General Assembly Resolution 49/214 of 23 December 1994' Resolution 2006/2 (29 June 2006).

[82] United Nations General Assembly, Resolution 61/295 'Declaration on the Rights of Indigenous Peoples' UN Doc A/RES/61/295 (13 Sept 2007).

[83] *Cal and Ors v the Attorney General of Belize and Anor* (2007) Claim Nos 171 and 172 of 2007, Conteh CJ (Belize Sup Ct).

Article 3 of the Indigenous Peoples' Declaration states that 'Indigenous peoples have the right of self-determination. By virtue of that right they freely determine their political status and freely pursue their economic, social and cultural development'. The Declaration includes Indigenous peoples' rights to: spiritual relationships with traditionally owned, occupied and used lands (Article 25); lands, territories and resources traditionally owned, occupied and used (Article 26); own, use, develop and control lands, territories and resources currently possessed by Indigenous peoples, and state legal recognition of that ownership (Article 26); and redress for lands, territories and resources confiscated, taken, occupied, used or damaged without the consent of Indigenous peoples. Redress is to take the form of restitution or, where that is not possible, compensation in the form of equivalent lands, monetary redress, or other forms of appropriate redress, unless otherwise agreed by the Indigenous peoples in question (Article 28). The Indigenous Peoples' Declaration also includes: rights to culture, in areas including education, technology, traditional knowledge, cultural property, development, health and the law; the right to equality; and recognition of treaties between Indigenous peoples and states (both recognising their international quality and requiring their implementation).

F. UN Human Rights Treaties and Treaty Bodies

1. Introduction

International human rights treaties constitute formally binding international law on, among other things, Indigenous peoples' rights to self-determination, land and culture. States can enter reservations to treaties, providing they are not incompatible with the object and purpose of a treaty, and some have done so.[84] A salient example is the Cook Islands, which has reserved the right not to apply the Convention on the Elimination of Discrimination Against Women to the extent that the customs governing the inheritance of chief titles may conflict with women's rights to freedom from discrimination.[85]

International human rights treaty bodies have been established to monitor the respective human rights treaties. The principal means by which they monitor is through the review of state reports. As part of that process, non-government organisations (NGOs) and Indigenous peoples often submit 'shadow reports', which document alleged concerns about a state's compliance with human rights.

[84] Vienna Convention on the Law of Treaties, (1969) 1155 UNTS 331, art 19.

[85] UN Meeting of the State Parties to the Convention on the Elimination of All Forms of Discrimination Against Women, 'Declarations, Reservations and Objections and Notifications of Withdrawal of Reservations to the Convention on the Elimination of All Forms of Discrimination Against Women' (10 April 2006) UN Doc CEDAW/SP/2006/2.

States can also bring alleged breaches of human rights conventions by other states to the attention of the monitoring bodies. When separately authorised, treaty bodies have jurisdiction to decide on communications from individuals. For example, the Human Rights Committee can hear communications from individuals when a state has ratified the First Optional Protocol to the International Covenant on Civil and Political Rights and certain criteria are met.[86] Treaty bodies have also established their own procedures for monitoring states' compliance with human rights treaties.[87] Finally, treaty bodies also elaborate on their interpretation of the human rights treaties in general comments or recommendations. Some relate specifically to the rights and freedoms of particular importance to Indigenous peoples, such as self-determination,[88] or explicitly address Indigenous peoples.[89]

2. The International Covenant on Civil and Political Rights (ICCPR) and the Human Rights Committee

(a) The Right to Self-determination

The Human Rights Committee initially refused to hear communications from Indigenous peoples based on alleged state breaches of the right to self-determination, reasoning that as the right to self-determination is a collective right, only collectives can bring claims based on Article 1 of the ICCPR.[90] However, collectives do not have standing to bring communications under the ICCPR Optional Protocol. The Human Rights Committee appears to have back-tracked slightly in that, in a communication from Māori individuals against New Zealand, it held that Article 1 can be relevant in the interpretation of Article 27, which relates to minorities' rights to culture, language and religion.[91] The Committee appears to extend its jurisprudence on self-determination to Indigenous peoples most clearly in its comments on state reports. For example, it observed in relation to Canada that 'extinguishing aboriginal rights be abandoned as incompatible with Article 1 of the Covenant'.[92] Similarly, in 2006 it requested that the US 'take further steps in order to secure the rights of all Indigenous peoples under Articles 1 and 27 of the Covenant to give them greater influence in

[86] (1966) 999 UNTS 302.

[87] P Thornberry, 'Confronting Racial Discrimination: A CERD Perspective' (2005) 5 *Human Rights Law Review* 239, 248.

[88] UN Human Rights Committee, 'General Comment 12, Article 1' (1994) UN Doc HRI\GEN\1\Rev 1, 12.

[89] Eg, the UN Committee on the Elimination of Racial Discrimination, 'General Recommendation XXIII: Indigenous Peoples' (18 Aug 1997) A/52/18, annex V.

[90] *Bernard Ominayak, Chief of the Lubicon Lake Band v Canada* Communication No 167/1984; Report of the Human Rights Committee, vol II (1990), UN Doc A/45/40.

[91] *Apirana Mahuika et al v New Zealand* Communication No 547/1993; Report of the Human Rights Committee (15 Nov 2000) CCPR/C/70/D/547/1993, para 9.2, UN Doc A/56/40.

[92] UN Human Rights Committee, 'Concluding Observations of the Human Rights Committee: Canada' (7 April 1999) CCPR/C/79/Add.105, para 8.

decision-making affecting their natural environment and their means of subsistence as well as their own culture'.[93]

(b) Minorities' Right to Culture

Article 27 of the ICCPR establishes a right to culture for individuals from minority communities. The right belongs to minorities rather than Indigenous peoples per se. It is also expressed negatively, as in 'persons . . . *shall not be denied*'. Despite this, Article 27 has been interpreted by the Human Rights Committee to impose positive obligations on states. The Committee has also highlighted the breadth of meaning of 'culture'—that it can extend to 'a way of life which is closely associated with territory and use of its resources'.[94] It found Canada in breach of Article 27 when it allowed oil and gas exploration and other development in the Lubicon Lake Band's ancestral territories.[95] Similarly, the Committee, in observations on state reports from Mexico, Chile and Guatemala, has made recommendations for the protection of Indigenous peoples' land rights.[96] On the other hand, in *Diegarrdt*, the Human Rights Committee rejected a claim by the Rehoboth community against Namibia that Article 27 had been breached because they were not entitled to exclusive use of certain lands for cattle breeding. The Committee found that, '[a]lthough the link of the Rehoboth community to the lands in question dates back some 125 years, it is not the result of a relationship that would have given rise to a distinctive culture'.[97]

The right to culture extends to individuals' membership in their tribe.[98] Traditional activities similarly attract Article 27 protection, such as Saami reindeer husbandry, as can economic activity that is pivotal to a community's culture.[99] The Human Rights Committee has also permitted limitations on the right to culture in certain circumstances. In *Lansmann* the Committee found that the interference with culture must be serious to constitute an infringement, ruling that quarrying on Saami lands did not breach Article 27 where the state had taken some measures to accommodate Saami and environmental concerns. It also found that the exchange of Māori customary fishing rights for entitlements in New Zealand's modern fishing quota regime and some Māori regulation of non-commercial

93 UN Human Rights Committee 'Concluding Observations on the United States of America' (15 September 2006) UN Doc CCPR/C/USA/CO/3.

94 UN Human Rights Committee, 'General Comment 23: The Rights of Minorities' (8 April 1994) UN Doc CCPR/C/21/Rev.1/Add 5, paras 3.2 and 7.

95 *Bernard Ominayak*, above n 90.

96 UN Human Rights Committee, 'Concluding Observations on Mexico's Fourth Periodic Report' (27 July 1999) CCPR/C/79/Add 109, para 19; UN Human Rights Committee, 'Concluding Observations on Chile's Fourth Periodic Report' (30 March 1999) CCPR/C/79/Add 1094, para 22; UN Human Rights Committee, 'Concluding Observations of the Human Rights Committee: Republic of Guatemala' (27 August 2001) UN Doc CCPR/CO/72/GTM.

97 *JGA Diergaardt (late Captain of the Rehoboth Baster Community) et al v Namibia* Communication No. 760/1997 (2000) UN Doc CCPR/C/69/D/760/1997, para 10.6.

98 *Lovelace v Canada* Communication No 24/1977 ((30 July 1981) UN Doc CCPR/C/13/D/24/1977.

99 *Länsman et al v Finland* Communication No 511/1992 (1992) UN Doc CCPR/C/52/D/511/1992, para 9.2.

fishing was justified, relying particularly on evidence of state consultation with Māori and apparent majority Māori support for the settlement.[100]

(c) The Interpretation of Other ICCPR Rights

Importantly, the Human Rights Committee has interpreted other rights and freedoms in the ICCPR in a manner consistent with an Indigenous peoples' perspective. Indigenous Tahitians brought a communication to the Human Rights Committee alleging France breached their right to family under the ICCPR because there were no available legal avenues available to prevent hotel developers disrupting a burial site where their ancestors rested. The Committee stated that 'cultural traditions should be taken into account when defining the term 'family' in a specific situation'.[101] Consequently, family was interpreted to include the relationship between the Indigenous complainants and their ancestors, which is consistent with Indigenous Tahitian ideology, and France was found to have breached their right to family under the ICCPR.

2. The Convention on the Elimination of All Forms of Racial Discrimination (CERD)

The CERD does not explicitly mention Indigenous peoples.[102] It does, however, include wide-ranging provisions to eliminate discrimination in areas vital to Indigenous peoples, including political participation and property. The CERD Committee clearly takes the view that the CERD applies to Indigenous peoples and has interpreted it in their favour.[103] In this way, and through the equality lens, the CERD Committee has contributed significantly to the emergence of international legal norms on Indigenous peoples' rights.

While the CERD Committee has taken a relatively conservative approach to self-determination in its general recommendation on the subject,[104] it has called on states to 'respect Indigenous distinct culture, history, language and way of life as an enrichment of the State's cultural identity and to promote its preservation' and to '[e]nsure that members of Indigenous peoples have equal rights in respect of effective participation in public life and that no decisions directly relating to their rights and interests are taken without their informed consent'.[105] The CERD

[100] *Apirana Mahuika*, above n 91.

[101] *Hopu and Bessert v France* Communication No 549/1993 (29 July 1997) UN Doc CCPR/C/60/D/549/1993, para 10.3.

[102] (4 January 1969) 660 UNTS 195.

[103] Thornberry, a member of the Committee on the Elimination of Racial Discrimination, wrote: 'The Committee tends to take it as read that national, ethnic, linguistic and religious minorities or cultural groups of various kinds come within the frame of Article 1' (above n 87, 258).

[104] CERD Committee, 'General Recommendation XXI: Self-Determination' (23 August 1996) UN Doc A/51/18.

[105] CERD Committee, 'General Recommendation XXIII: Indigenous Peoples' (18 August 1997) UN Doc A/52/18, annex V.

Committee's general recommendation 31 on the prevention of racial discrimination in the administration and functioning of the criminal justice system also calls on states to 'ensure respect for and recognition of the traditional systems of justice for Indigenous peoples' and consideration of the 'cultural or customary background' of Indigenous individuals.

The CERD Committee has commented on situations facing Indigenous peoples from the San in Botswana to the Veddas in Sri Lanka and Mapuche in Chile. Consistent themes coming through the Committee's jurisprudence include the need for state recognition of Indigenous peoples' land rights and right to be consulted about matters impacting on them. It has also recommended implementation of ILO Convention 169.[106] Specific issues addressed include concern expressed at the incidence of rape and sexual violence experienced by American Indian and Alaska Native women.[107]

In early warning action and urgent action procedures instigated by Indigenous peoples, the CERD Committee usually recommends dialogue between Indigenous peoples and the state to remedy breaches of CERD. After finding that Australia's 1998 amendments to the Native Title Act 1993, in effect extinguishing aboriginal title rights, breached CERD, the CERD Committee requested Australia to suspend the amendments and discuss solutions with Aboriginal and Torres Strait Islanders.[108] On finding New Zealand's Foreshore and Seabed Act 2004 discriminated against Māori customary rights, it recommended New Zealand to resume a dialogue with Māori 'to seek ways of lessening its discriminatory effects'.[109] However, the CERD Committee has also recommended more specific action, such as a finding that the United States should stop imposing grazing fees on Western Shoshone people while they are using their ancestral lands.[110]

The CERD Committee has monitored particular issues utilising more than one of its procedures, illustrating that its respective functions can complement each other. Its recent three decisions on Surinam,[111] utilising the early warning and urgent action procedure and expressing concern with the impact of resource exploitation on Indigenous peoples, were preceded by similar concerns on earlier Surinam state reports.[112] The Committee has also encouraged other UN human rights institutions to take up issues it considers particularly serious. It recom-

[106] CERD Committee, 'Concluding Observations: Argentina' UN Doc CERD/C/65/CO/1 (August 2004) para 16.

[107] CERD Committee, 'Concluding Observations: United States of America' UN Doc CERD/C/USA/CO/6 (Feb 2008).

[108] CERD Committee, 'Decision 1(53): Australia' (11 Aug 1998) UN Doc A/53/18, para 22.

[109] CERD Committee, 'Decision 1(66): New Zealand Foreshore and Seabed Act 2004' (11 March 2005) CERD/C/66/NZL/Dec 1, para 7.

[110] CERD Committee, 'Decision 1(68): United States of America' (11 April 2006) UN Doc CERD/C/USA/DEC/1.

[111] CERD Committee, 'Decision 3(66) Surinam' UN Doc CERD/C/66/SUR/Dec 3 (March 2005); 'Decision 1(67) Surinam' UN Doc CERD/C/DEC/SUR/2 (18 August 2005); and 'Prevention of Racial Discrimination including Early Warning Measures and Urgent Action Procedures: Decision 1(69) Surinam' UN Doc CERD/C/Dec/Sur/3 (18 August 2006) para 1.

[112] CERD Committee, 'Conclusions and Recommendations of the Committee on the Elimination of Racial Discrimination: Surinam' UN Doc CERD/C/64/CO/9 (2004).

mended that Surinam invite the SR on Human Rights and Indigenous Peoples to visit its country, and drew the attention of the HR Council 'to the particularly alarming situation in relation to the rights of Indigenous and tribal peoples in Surinam'.[113]

3. International Covenant on Economic, Social and Cultural Rights (ICESCR)

Like the ICCPR, Article 1 of the ICESCR affirms the right to self-determination, which the CESCR Committee has applied to Indigenous peoples. In its concluding observations on the Russian Federation, it recalled the right to self-determination and then urged the state to intensify 'its efforts to improve the situation of the Indigenous peoples'.[114]

The remainder of the ICESCR covers rights to employment, family, health, food, education and culture. The CESCR Committee has honed in on issues facing Indigenous peoples in its observations on states' reports. It has voiced concern about: discrimination against Indigenous peoples in employment, housing, health and education;[115] failures to legally recognise Indigenous rights to hold land communally;[116] the negative impact of resource extraction on Indigenous peoples' land and cultural rights;[117] states' failures to ratify ILO Convention 169; forced evictions of Indigenous peoples;[118] and so on. Its general comment on the right to housing recognises that Indigenous peoples disproportionately experience forced eviction.[119]

4. The Convention on the Rights of the Child (CRC)

The Convention on the Rights of the Child is unique in that it explicitly makes reference to Indigenous individuals.[120] Article 30 emulates Article 27 of the ICCPR on minorities' cultural rights, including religion and language. Among other pertinent provisions, under Article 29(1)(d) the education of the child shall be directed to preparing the child for a responsible life 'in friendship among all peoples, ethnic, national and religious groups and persons of Indigenous origin'.

[113] CERD Committee, above n 112, paras 2 and 4.

[114] CESCR Committee, 'Concluding Observations: Russian Federation' (12 December 2003) UN Doc E/C.12/1/Add 94, para 39.

[115] CESCR Committee, 'Concluding Observations: Ecuador' (7 June 2004) UN Doc E/C12/1/Add 100, para 11.

[116] *Ibid*, para 12.

[117] *Ibid.*

[118] CESCR Committee, 'Concluding Observations: Bolivia' (21 May 2001) UN Doc E/C12/1/Add 60.

[119] See UN Economic and Social Council Permanent Forum on Indigenous Issues, 'Information Received from the United Nations System: Office of the United Nations High Commissioner for Human Rights' (16 March 2005) UN Doc E/C.19/2006/6/Add 8, para 7.

[120] (20 Nov 1989) 1577 UNTS 3.

Mass media is encouraged to have 'particular regard to the linguistic needs of the child . . . who is Indigenous' under Article 17(d).

The CRC Committee has been active in reviewing states' policies dealing with Indigenous children. Its observations on state reports have highlighted issues of low education opportunities[121] malnutrition,[122] access to education,[123] access to health care,[124] and youth suicide in Indigenous communities.[125]

The CRC Committee has also drawn states' attention to Indigenous children in special recommendations, prompted by the SR on Human Rights and Indigenous Peoples and the UNPFII. After acknowledging ILO Convention 169, the Indigenous Peoples' Declaration, and WGIP, it: calls on states to protect the human rights of Indigenous children; reaffirms its commitment to systematically address Indigenous children's issues in state reports; calls on UN institutions, banks and civil society to adopt a rights-based approach to Indigenous children based on the Convention and other relevant standards; recognises that the right to enjoy culture in Article 30 of the CRC 'may consist of a way of life which is closely associated with territory and use of its resources'; and recommends that states 'seek consensus [with Indigenous peoples] on development strategies, policies and projects aimed at implementing children's rights'.[126] It explicitly recommends greater co-operation between the UN mechanisms dealing with Indigenous issues and the UN human rights treaty bodies.

5. Convention on the Elimination of Discrimination Against Women (CEDAW)

The CEDAW Committee has focused on problems facing Indigenous women in its observations on state reports, though it is yet to receive a communication from an Indigenous woman.[127] The CEDAW Committee's observations of substance include concerns and recommendations concerning: poverty facing Indigenous women;[128] the situation of Indigenous women domestic workers;[129] sexual vio-

[121] CRC Committee, 'Concluding Observations: Brazil' (1 Oct 2004) UN Doc CRC/C/15/add 241, para 70.

[122] *Ibid.*

[123] CRC Committee, 'Concluding Observations: Panama' (30 June 2004) UN Doc CRC/C/15/add 233, para 51.

[124] CRC Committee, 'Concluding Observations: Rwanda' (4 June 2004) UN Doc CRC/C/15/add 234, para 75.

[125] CRC Committee, 'Concluding Observations: New Zealand' (21 October 2003) UN Doc CRC/C/15/add 216 para 37.

[126] CRC Committee, 'Day of General Discussion on the Rights of Indigenous Children: Recommendations' (3 Oct 2003), at www.ohchr.org/english/bodies/crc/docs/discussion/indigenouschildren.pdf.

[127] (18 Dec 1979) 1249 UNTS 13.

[128] CEDAW Committee, 'Concluding Observations: El Salvador' UN Doc A/58/38 (21 Jan 2003) para 261.

[129] CEDAW Committee, 'Concluding Observations: Costa Rica' UN Doc A/58/38 (9 July 2003) para 62.

lence against Indigenous women;[130] Indigenous women's 'employment, political participation, decision-making positions in the public and private sector, the judiciary and tertiary education and economic independence';[131] Indigenous women's lack of access to agricultural lands;[132] high rates of illiteracy among Indigenous women;[133] and the need to ensure Indigenous women have access to individual ownership of aboriginal land.[134]

Under Articles 2(f) and 5(a) of the CEDAW, state parties undertake to eliminate discrimination against women under custom or in accordance with customary practices, which could cover Indigenous custom. These provisions could rub up against collective Indigenous peoples' rights to practise their culture, which would surely include their customs. State abolition of custom, if requested by the CEDAW, could be perceived as inappropriate. Nonetheless, the CEDAW Committee's approach appears to contain some nuance, not directly and explicitly recommending the abolition of custom, but also prioritising freedom from discrimination. For example, it urged Canada to undertake 'awareness-raising programmes to sensitize aboriginal communities about women's human rights'.[135] It has also expressed concern with the Fijian bulu bulu custom in sexual violence cases.[136]

G. Indigenous Peoples and the Environment

Indigenous peoples can benefit from generic international laws and policies directed at sustaining the environment.[137] Increasingly, Indigenous peoples are also a focus of, and participate in the development of, international environmental law, a move described by some scholars as a 'paradigmatic shift'.[138] This reflects a growing appreciation that Indigenous peoples can be particularly negatively affected by environmental degradation, for example when dams are built and mineral extraction occurs on Indigenous peoples' traditional lands, and can also

[130] UN Committee on the Elimination of Discrimination Against Women, 'Concluding Observations: Brazil' UN Doc A/58/38 (7 July 2003) para 115.

[131] CEDAW Committee, 'Concluding Observations: New Zealand' UN Doc A/58/38 (14 July 2003) para 423.

[132] CEDAW Committee, 'Concluding Observations: Suriname' UN Doc A/57/38 (Part II) (13 June 2002) para 65.

[133] CEDAW Committee, 'Concluding Observations: Panama' UN Doc A/53/38/Rev 1 (21 July 1998) para 119.

[134] CEDAW Committee, 'Concluding Observations: Australia' UN Doc A/52/38/Rev 1 Part II (12 August 1997) para 119.

[135] CEDAW Committee, 'Concluding Observations: Canada' UN Doc A/58/58 (23 January 2003) para 362.

[136] CEDAW Committee, 'Report of the Committee on the Elimination of Discrimination Against Women' (7 May 2002) UN Doc A/57/38, para 58.

[137] See BJ Richardson, 'Indigenous Peoples, International Law and Sustainability' (2001) 10(1) *Review of European Community & International Environmental Law* 1.

[138] Firestone *et al*, above n 23, 262.

be a source of inspiration for devising means to protect the environment.[139] International human rights norms, especially regarding lands, territories and resources, overlap with international environmental law norms relevant to Indigenous peoples.[140]

The 1992 Rio Declaration on Environment and Development notes the 'vital role' of Indigenous peoples in environmental management because of their traditional knowledge, and requests states to 'enable their effective participation in the achievement of sustainable development'.[141] Similar sentiments appear in Agenda 21.[142] These statements were revisited and reinforced in the final Declaration of the World Summit on Sustainable Development (WSSD) in 2002, which, for example, recommended enactment of measures to protect Indigenous resource management systems.[143]

Indigenous peoples and/or their concerns are explicitly addressed in several international environmental instruments. The 1992 UN Forest Principles state that national forest policies should recognise and support Indigenous peoples' rights, and 'appropriate conditions should be promoted for these groups to enable them to have an economic stake in forest use'.[144] The 1994 Convention to Combat Desertification requires states to include local communities in the design and implementation of the Convention and to protect 'local and traditional knowledge'.[145] Regional environmental initiatives involving Indigenous peoples include that of the Arctic Council, which is made up of the eight Arctic states and six permanent Indigenous peoples' representatives. The primary goal of its environmental protection strategies is 'to act as a regional forum for sustainable development, and its concerns include environmental, social and economic issues'.[146] It has five working groups focusing on topics that include pollution, climate change, and biodiversity conservation.

Indigenous peoples have also utilised the US Alien Tort Claims Act, which enables foreign nationals to bring suit for damages that result from breaches of international law outside the US, in an attempt to pin liability for environmental

[139] For a description of some of the environmental issues facing Indigenous peoples, see JA Cohen, 'Environmental rights of Indigenous Peoples under the Alien Tort Claims Act, the Public Trust Doctrine and Corporate Ethics, and Environmental Dispute Resolution' (2002) 20 *UCLA Journal of Environmental Law and Policy* 133.

[140] See R Coombe, 'Intellectual Property, Human Rights and Sovereignty: New Dilemmas in International Law Posed by Recognition of Indigenous Knowledge and the Conservation of Biodiversity' (1999) 6 *Indiana Journal of Global Legal Studies* 59.

[141] Rio Declaration on Environment and Development (1992) 33 ILM 874, principle 22.

[142] UN Conference on Environment and Development (UNCED), *Agenda 21* (UNCED 1993) ch 26.

[143] *Report of the World Summit on Sustainable Development, Plan of Implementation*, UNDESA, UN Doc A/CONF 199/20 (2002).

[144] UN General Assembly, 'Report of the United Nations Conference on Environment and Development: Non-Legally Binding Authoritative Statement of Principles for a Global Consensus on the Management, Conservation and Sustainable Development of All Forests' (14 Aug 1992) UN Doc A/CONF 151/26 (Vol III) Art 5(a).

[145] (17 June 1994), 33 ILM 1328, Art 16(g).

[146] The Declaration on the Establishment of the Arctic Council (1996), available at www.arctic-council.org/en/main/infopage/190.

degradation of their lands on multilateral companies. Amazonian Indigenous peoples in Ecuador and Peru lodged claims in the US against Texaco in the early 1990s, alleging Texaco's oil exploration activities breached international legal environmental standards.[147] While the case was dismissed by the US Federal Court on forum non conveniens grounds,[148] and is now being heard in Ecuador, this avenue remains open to Indigenous peoples in the future. Similarly, Inuit have brought a claim to the Inter-American Commission on Human Rights against the US for a failure to control greenhouse gas emissions leading to climate change.[149]

Indigenous peoples have been active in promulgating their own international instruments calling for environmental protection of their lands, territories and resources in, for example, the Kari-Oca Declaration and the Indigenous Peoples Earth Charter of 1992,[150] which were reinforced in the Kimberly Declaration of 2002.[151]

The international legal framework has also accommodated Indigenous peoples' traditional practices, to some extent, in providing exceptions to prohibitions on hunting activities.[152] The 1976 Convention on the Conservation of North Pacific Fur Seals does not apply the ban on sealing to Indigenous peoples in some circumstances.[153] Under the 1946 International Convention for the Regulation of Whaling,[154] grey whales may be taken by or on behalf of aborigines where 'they will be used exclusively for local consumption by the aborigines whose traditional aboriginal subsistence and cultural needs have been recognised'.[155] Likewise, the International Agreement on the Conservation of Polar Bears does not prohibit polar bear hunting by 'local people using traditional methods in the exercise of their traditional rights and in accordance with the laws of that Party'.[156]

Some environmental treaties also touch on Indigenous peoples' traditional knowledge, as the following section explains.

147 For discussion, see JA Cohen, 'Environmental Rights of Indigenous Peoples under the Alien Tort Claims Act, the Public Trust Doctrine and Corporate Ethics, and Environmental Dispute Resolution' (2002) 20 *UCLA Journal of Environmental Law and Policy* 133.

148 *Aguinda v Texaco* 303 F 3d 470 (2d Cir, 2002).

149 R Black, 'Inuit Sue US Over Climate Policy' (8 December 2006), news.bbc.co.uk/2/hi/science/nature/4511556.stm.

150 Kari-Oca Villages, Brazil (May 1992), available at www.idrc.ca/en/ev-30141-201-1-DO_TOPIC.html.

151 See www.iwgia.org/sw217.asp.

152 See discussion in BJ Richardson and D Craig, 'Indigenous Peoples, Law and the Environment' in BJ Richardson and S Wood (eds), *Environmental Law for Sustainability* (Hart Publishing, 2006) 200.

153 (1976) 27 UST 3371, Art VII.

154 (2 Dec 1946) 161 UNTS 72.

155 International Whaling Commission Amendments to the Schedule of the International Convention for the Regulation of Whaling of 2 December 1946 (Monte Carlo, 24 October 1997), sch para 13(b)(2).

156 (15 Nov 1973) 13 ILM 13, Art 3(d).

H. Indigenous Peoples' Traditional Knowledge

Traditional knowledge 'takes the form of stories, songs, folklore, proverbs, cultural values, beliefs, rituals, community laws, local language, and agricultural practices, including the development of plant species and animal breeds'.[157] Commonly, traditional knowledge is holistic, transmitted orally, and 'rooted in a social context that sees the world in terms of social and spiritual relations between all life-forms'.[158] It is also commonly regulated by customary law.

Indigenous peoples are justifiably concerned that their traditional knowledge can be easily misappropriated because existing intellectual property regimes do not adequately protect it.[159] For example, Indigenous peoples may have difficulty patenting their traditional knowledge of a plant's medicinal aspect, as it lacks, by definition, 'novelty'. However, scientists who 'discover' the particular chemical make-up of the component of the plant that gives it its medicinal aspect, and subsequently modify it, can patent their 'invention'. Once patented, all benefits go to that patent-holder.[160] Copyrights and trademarks can be equally inadequate to protect traditional knowledge.[161] Conceptually, too, there are tensions between intellectual property regimes and traditional knowledge. Intellectual property rights are individualistic and are concerned with innovation, whereas traditional knowledge is collective and tradition-focused.

Building on the international concern to protect traditional knowledge in Agenda 21,[162] the Rio Declaration and then the WSSD Johannesburg Plan of Implementation,[163] a number of international institutions are now addressing Indigenous peoples' traditional knowledge issues. The Convention on Biological

[157] Convention on Biological Diversity: www.biodiv.org/programmes/socio-eco/traditional/default.aspx.

[158] G Dutfield, 'TRIPS-Related Aspects of Traditional Knowledge' (2001) 33 *Case Western Reserve Journal of International Law* 233, 241.

[159] See ML Quinn, 'Protection for Indigenous Knowledge: An International Law Analysis' (2001) 14 *St Thomas Law Review* 287. But note the comment that '[i]t is not that elements of TK [traditional knowledge] cannot be protected through patents, copyrights, and trade secrets, but that the exploitation of traditional peoples and communities, including holders of TK, is fundamentally due to a widespread failure to respect their basic rights, and not to the inadequacies of [intellectual property rights] to protect TK': *ibid*, 293.

[160] Dutfield, above n 158, 258, notes: 'traditional peoples and communities see the globalisation of patent regulations modelled on those of the United States and Europe as a form of neo-colonialism'. And, 'if traditional peoples and communities in WTO member states are required to accept the existence of patents, of which they are economically prevented from acquiring for themselves, why shouldn't their own knowledge-related regimes be respected by others'?

[161] *Ibid*, 248–60.

[162] Agenda 21 suggested that states could 'adopt or strengthen appropriate policies and/or legal instruments that will protect Indigenous intellectual and cultural property': Agenda 21, Adopted by the UN Conference on Environment and Development, Rio de Janeiro (1992) UN Doc A/CONF 151/26.4(b).

[163] *Report of the World Summit on Sustainable Development, Plan of Implementation*, UNDESA, UN Doc A/CONF 199/20 (2002).

Diversity (CBD)[164] institutions and the World Intellectual Property Office (WIPO) are the most active, but have not yet provided comprehensive legal protections.

Article 8(j) of the CBD obliges states to protect 'knowledge, innovations and practices of Indigenous and local communities embodying traditional lifestyles relevant for the conservation and sustainable use of biological diversity'. But the obligation is a soft one, given the references to 'as far as possible' and 'as appropriate' and 'subject to national legislation'.[165] Also, the CBD recognises states' sovereign rights to biological diversity.[166] Other provisions relevant to Indigenous peoples' traditional knowledge include: Article 10(c), encouraging customary use of biological resources; Article 17(2), facilitating the exchange of information on traditional knowledge and return of information important to Indigenous communities relevant for the conservation and sustainable use of biological diversity; and Article 18(4), encouraging use of technologies, including Indigenous technologies.

The CBD Conference of the Parties (COP), the biannual meeting of state parties to the CBD, after assessing a report from a workshop on traditional knowledge, established an ad hoc working group to address the implementation of Article 8(j). It provided for Indigenous peoples' participation and, most importantly, included in its mandate the 'development of legal and other appropriate forms of protection for the knowledge, innovations and practices of Indigenous and local communities'.[167]

The WIPO was responsible, with the United Nations Educational, Scientific and Cultural Organisation (UNESCO), for the adoption of Model Provisions for National Laws on the Protection of Expressions of Folklore Against Illicit Exploitation and Other Prejudicial Actions in 1982. Picking up the issue again in the late 1990s, again with UNESCO, it organised a World Forum on Folklore, which led to suggestions for an international agreement on the sui generis protection of folklore. Other WIPO treaties relevant to Indigenous peoples' traditional knowledge include the WIPO Performers and Phonograms Treaty of 1996, which provides protections of producers' and performers' work, including expressions of folklore.[168] The WIPO's Global Intellectual Property Rights Division has traditional knowledge as one of its foci. It has conducted significant research on the subject, and held consultations together with UNESCO, publishing a comprehensive report with its findings.[169] A WIPO Intergovernmental Committee on Intellectual Property and Genetic Resources, Traditional Knowledge and Folklore

[164] (5 June 1992) 31 ILM 818.

[165] Richardson and Craig, above n 152.

[166] See Bluemel, above n 28.

[167] Convention on Biodiversity Conference of the Parties, 'Decision IV/9: Implementation of Article 8(j) and Related Provisions' (1998) para 1(a).

[168] UNTS (entered into force 20 May 2002) available at World Intellectual Property Office www.wipo.int/treaties/en/ip/wppt/trtdocs_wo034.html.

[169] WIPO, *Intellectual Property Needs and Expectations of Traditional Knowledge Holders' WIPO Report on Fact-Finding Missions on Intellectual Property and Traditional Knowledge (1998–1999)* (WIPO, April 2001).

was established in 2001. It has developed, and is currently discussing, progressive draft international policy and principles for the protection of traditional knowledge and traditional cultural expressions/expressions of folklore.

Also relevant to the treatment of traditional knowledge is the World Trade Organization and its governance of the Agreement on Trade-Related Aspects of Intellectual Property Rights (TRIPS).[170] The TRIPS provides for protection of intellectual property under patents, trademarks, copyrights and so on at the international level. However, the TRIPS does not explicitly provide protection for traditional knowledge, and may in fact facilitate its misappropriation, given the Agreement's emphasis on 'Western' intellectual property protections. As Curci notes,

> [t]he CBD is far more favourable to conservation of biodiversity and preservation of rights for developing countries while TRIPS is far more aggressive about facilitating biological patentability and promoting private ownership and exploitation of such resources.[171]

Other UN and international agencies are addressing Indigenous traditional knowledge through their policies and programmes, thereby contributing to the normative development of international standards for its protection. For instance, the Food and Agricultural Organisation (FAO) has been involved in a project examining local knowledge in southern Africa, and has published materials relevant to traditional knowledge.[172] The FAO's Treaty on Plant and Genetic Resources for Food and Agriculture is also relevant, as it aims to ensure conservation, exchange and sustainable use of plants' genetic resources 'in harmony with the CBD'.[173] The World Bank's Indigenous Knowledge Program includes in its objectives 'addressing intellectual property rights' of Indigenous peoples and dissemination information on Indigenous knowledge.[174] Further, UNESCO has been active in, and is the source of a number of treaties relevant to, traditional knowledge, including the new Convention on the Protection and Promotion of the Diversity of Cultural Expressions[175] and the Convention concerning the Protection of the World Cultural and Natural Heritage.[176]

[170] (15 April 1994) 33 ILM 1197.

[171] J Curci, 'The New Challenges to the International Patentability of Biotechnology: Legal Relations between the WTO Treaty on Trade-Related Aspects of Intellectual Property Rights and the Convention on Biodiversity' (2005) 2 *International Law and Management Review* 1, 4.

[172] UN Food and Agricultural Organisation (FAO), *The Utilisation of Indigenous Knowledge in Range Management and Forage Plants for Improving Livestock Productivity and Food Security in the Maasai and Barbaig Communities* (FAO, 2005).

[173] UN Food and Agricultural Organisation, Resolution 3/2001 (entered into force 29 June 2004).

[174] See www.worldbank.org/afr.

[175] CLT-2005/Convention Diversite-Cult Rev (20 October 2005).

[176] (1972) 1037 UNTS 151.

I. Other Relevant International Institutions

There is a flurry of activity relevant to, and in many cases including the unique contributions of, Indigenous peoples within international institutions. This has led to a plethora of international policies on Indigenous peoples within the respective areas of concern of each international institution.

The multilateral development banks, which financially support economic projects in developing countries, have drafted policies to manage the potential impacts of their loans and policies on Indigenous peoples.[177] The World Bank issued its first operational policy on Indigenous peoples in 1982,[178] which led to Operational Directive 4.20 (OD 4.20) in 1991, and most recently the 2005 Operational Policy and Bank Procedure on Indigenous Peoples 4.10 (OP/BP 4.10). The latter posits a procedure for: screening of a proposed project's impact on Indigenous peoples; an assessment of the effects of a project on Indigenous peoples, utilising free, prior and informed consultation and permitting resettlement only with consent; preparation of an Indigenous Peoples Plan or an Indigenous Peoples Planning Framework; and, finally, clearance from the World Bank for the project to proceed.[179] Any ensuing loan agreement sets out the borrower's obligation to implement relevant instruments relating to Indigenous peoples.[180] The OP/BP 4.10 also envisages projects being contingent on the legal recognition of Indigenous peoples' land rights and cultural resources, enjoyment of equitable benefits of commercial development, and consent to the development of cultural resources and knowledge.[181] While OP/BP 4.10 does not expressly recognise Indigenous peoples' customary land rights and self-government, the World Bank can influence states' conformity to Indigenous peoples' rights. The loan and credit agreements it makes with states are binding, and they can be conditioned on compliance with World Bank operational standards.[182] The Bank can withhold funds if conditions are not met.[183] Thus, 'it can incorporate specific policy and institutional reforms into domestic legal

[177] See generally A Gray, 'Development Policy, Development Protest: The World Bank, Indigenous Peoples and NGOs' in JA Fox and LD Brown (eds), *The Struggle for Accountability: The World Bank, NGOs, and Grassroots Movements* (MIT Press 1998) 267; B Kingsbury, 'Operational Policies of International Institutions as Part of the Law-Making Process: The World Bank and Indigenous Peoples' in GS Goodwin-Gill and S Talmon (eds), *The Reality of International Law: Essays in Honour of Ian Brownlie* (Clarendon Press, 1999) 324.

[178] Tribal Peoples in Bank-Finances Projects, Operational Manual Statement 2.34 (February 1982). See discussion of it in F MacKay, 'The Draft World Bank Operational Policy 4.10: Progress or More of the Same?' (2005) 22 *Arizona Journal of International and Comparative Law* 65.

[179] World Bank, *Operational Policy and Bank Procedure 4.10 Indigenous Peoples* (World Bank, 2005) para 1. McKay, *ibid*, provides an excellent summary of an earlier draft of this policy, and related concerns.

[180] World Bank, *ibid*, para 11.

[181] Para 8(a).

[182] GA Sarfaty, 'The World Bank and the Internalisation of Indigenous Rights Norms' (2005) 114 *Yale Law Journal* 1791, 1796.

[183] Of course, this power has given rise to questions about incursions into a state's sovereignty. However, Sarfaty, *ibid*, 1799, notes that 'such a threat rarely materialises'.

systems'.[184] Yet, evidence suggests that implementation of World Bank Indigenous-related policies have been intermittent in the past. The 1982 Operational Manual policy appeared to be largely ignored, and OD 4.20 only intermittently implemented.[185] Impediments included questions about who is Indigenous and borrower state resistance.[186] However, the broader difficulty lies with the World Bank's Articles of Agreement—that the Bank 'shall not interfere in the political affairs of any member' and that '[o]nly economic considerations shall be relevant to their decisions'.[187]

Other international banks, such as the Asian Development Bank and the Inter-American Development Bank, also deal with Indigenous issues. The former adopted a Policy on Indigenous Peoples in 1998.[188] It requires initial project assessments for their impact on Indigenous peoples and, if significant, a specific Indigenous peoples' plan must be developed to mitigate impacts and/or to provide compensation.[189] There is no reference to Indigenous peoples' free, prior and informed consent in the policy. Similarly, the Inter-American Development Bank's 2006 Strategy for Indigenous Development aims to avoid or mitigate adverse impacts of Bank operations on Indigenous peoples and their rights.[190] The Bank's Operational Policy sets out, first, that it use its 'best efforts' to promote 'development with identity', through activities such as implementing Indigenous peoples' rights, and, second, 'safeguards' to prevent and mitigate adverse impacts on Indigenous peoples.[191]

In the UN community there are a variety of agencies whose work addresses or touches on Indigenous Peoples.[192] Co-ordination of their activities is fostered through the Inter-Agency Support Group on Indigenous Issues. These agencies include the United Nations Children's Fund, the UN Development Programme, the Food and Agricultural Organization, and the UN Development Fund for Women, among several others.

In addition, Indigenous issues are increasingly a concern for international trade bodies. Some states have negotiated exceptions in trade treaties allowing them to

[184] *Ibid*, 184.

[185] Sarfaty, *ibid*, 1802, concludes that the World Bank Operations Evaluation Department (OED) report in 2003 'found that only 55 of the 89 projects (or about 62% of the projects) that could have potentially affected Indigenous peoples (as determined by the OED's application of the policy's stated criteria) actually applied OD 4.20'.

[186] *Ibid.*

[187] Articles of Agreement of the International Bank for Reconstruction and Development, Art IV, S 10, 60 Stat at 1440. 1449 (1945), 2 UNTS 134 (1947) 158; see MacKay, above n 178, 543.

[188] Asian Development Bank (ADB), *The Bank's Policy on Indigenous Peoples* (ADB, 1998).

[189] *Ibid*, para 37.

[190] Inter-American Development Bank (IADB), *Strategy for Indigenous Development* (IADB, 2006) para 5.1.

[191] IADB, Indigenous Peoples and Community Development Unit, *Operational Policy on Indigenous Peoples* (22 February 2006) para 4.1.

[192] See UN High Commissioner for Human Rights (UNHCR), 'Indigenous Peoples and the Unite Nations System: An Overview', leaflet no 1 (UNHCR, undated).

take special measures in favour of Indigenous peoples,[193] and Indigenous peoples have become involved in a number of international trade-related disputes.[194]

J. Conclusion

Over the past 30 years Indigenous peoples have surfaced as a subject of international law and policy, with the emergence of a plethora of new international legal norms and dramatically increased institutional attention. This Chapter has attempted to map the existing landscape, highlighting some of the more vexed issues underlying this nascent and rapidly changing body of law and the various institutions that are engaged.

The trajectory of international law and policy on Indigenous peoples is as yet unknown, as is the most pressing question of all—whether Indigenous peoples' lives and experiences will materially benefit as a result of increased international legal attention. However, all interested parties, including states, international organisations, non-governmental organisations, civil society and, particularly, Indigenous peoples, can have considerable influence on the likelihood that these norms will be implemented. By utilising and referencing international law on the rights of Indigenous peoples—framing local, regional, national and international issues in terms of their conformity to international legal standards—that law will become embedded in international and domestic legal systems and legal psyches. At the same time, constant and iterative application of international norms on the rights of indigenous peoples will function to clarify their meaning in concrete situations. This strategy, of simultaneously engaging domestic and international institutions in Indigenous peoples' rights and before all kinds of legal fora, will, it is hoped, produce a mutually reinforcing and continuing transnational dialogue on the content of those rights. For example, Indigenous peoples should continue to frame their claims in terms of the international right to self-determination in domestic and international legal fora, before international human rights institutions and local planning tribunals. Over time the meaning of the right in the Indigenous context will be clarified, as will, one hopes, the level of comfort and acceptance of the norm. In this way, Indigenous peoples can themselves stimulate greater respect for their rights.

193 See, eg, Agreement between New Zealand and Singapore on a Closer Economic Partnership, Art 74.

194 See, eg, the claim lodged by Glamis Gold, a Canadian gold mining company, against the United States under the North American Free Trade Agreement in response to Californian regulation of mining and prohibition on the use of certain sites for mining. Indigenous interests are involved because one of the areas in question was close to an American Indian reservation and sacred sites. Oxfam America, 'A Case Study of Investing in Destruction', available at www.oxfamamerica.org/pdfs/glamis_en.pdf. See also the details of Indigenous involvement in a lumber dispute between Canada and the United States described in A Manuel and N Schabus, 'Indigenous Peoples at the Margin of the Global Economy: A Violation of International Human Rights and International Trade Law' (2005) 8 *Chapman Law Review* 229, 257.

Part 2

Contemporary Claims, Issues and Settlements

8

Indigenous Legal Theory: Some Initial Considerations

GORDON CHRISTIE

A. Introduction

There is as yet no distinct and vibrant body of scholarship identifiable as Indigenous Legal Theory (ILT). Compounding the lack of legal-theoretic discourse centred on Indigenous peoples (and by Indigenous scholars) is the lack of any sustained investigation into background questions around the place of legal theory in relation to Indigenous people. Few Indigenous scholars in Canada have broached the question of whether Indigenous peoples might not only have particular perspectives from which to critique the law, but also particular theoretical perspectives concerning the law. While some (for example, Mary Ellen Turpel-Lafond, John Borrows, Val Napoleon, Darlene Johnston and Lucy Bell[1]) have produced important work with theoretical undertones and implications, only James Youngblood (Sákéj) Henderson and Patricia Monture-Angus have taken the first steps towards a direct and systematic investigation into the question of whether Indigenous peoples inhabit a conceptual space from which emerge particular, distinct and essential theoretical understandings of the law.[2] In this

[1] See, eg, ME Turpel, 'Aboriginal Peoples and the Canadian Charter of Rights and Freedoms: Contradictions and Challenges' (1989) 10 *Canadian Woman Studies* 149, and 'Aboriginal Peoples and the Canadian Charter: Interpretive Monopolies, Cultural Differences' (1989–90) 6 *Canadian Human Rights Yearbook* 3; J Borrows, *Recovering Canada: The Resurgence of Indigenous Law* (University of Toronto Press, 2002); *Indigenous Legal Traditions* (Law Commission of Canada, 2006), and 'Creating an Indigenous Legal Community' (2005) 50 *McGill Law Journal* 153; V Napoleon, 'Aboriginal Self Determination: Individual Self and Collective Selves', in B Lawrence and K Anderson (eds), (2005) 29(2) *Atlantis: A Women's Studies Journal* 31, and (with R Overstall), 'Indigenous Laws: Some Issues, Considerations and Experiences', prepared for the Centre for Indigenous Environmental Resources, accessible online at www.cier.ca/building-sustainable-communities/current-initiatives.aspx?id=438; D Johnston, 'Native Rights as Collective Rights: A Question of Group Self-Preservation' (1989) 2(1) *Canadian Journal of Law and Jurisprudence* 19, and L Bell, 'Kwakwaka'wakw Laws and Perspectives Regarding Property' (2006) 5 *Indigenous Law Journal* 119.

[2] Patricia Monture-Angus makes a call for such an investigation, and begins to sketch out an Indigenous account of 'rights', in *Journeying Forward: Dreaming First Nations' Independence* (Fernwood Publishing, 1999), 55–61. Sákéj Henderson offers a sustained investigation into several

Chapter, I work through some questions that float around such a notion—that there should be a body of theorising that emanates from, and is focused on, Indigenous peoples in Canada.

After an introductory investigation of certain issues and problems around the nature of legal theory, further introductory remarks are made about the general forms Indigenous theory might take. This leads into a discussion around the question of the need for theorising by Indigenous scholars. That is, an exploration is launched into possible ways of justifying the deployment of time and energy by Indigenous scholars on projects focused on theorising about the law. What is the value in such endeavours, when so much other jurisprudential work seems pressing?[3] The response to this query pulls us back to discussions of the nature of theory and theorising, and the place of legal theory in the lives of those working within the field of law.

One concern that emerges in discussing the prospects for Indigenous legal theorising is the role that the use of mainstream theory might play in the construction of Indigenous legal theories. In a sense, this is a question about cultural appropriation—are there insights from non-Indigenous sources that should be pulled out of these other cultural contexts and incorporated into Indigenous legal theories?[4] When looking at the use of mainstream theory in the construction of ILT, the intent is not to exhaustively examine the many theories that might be put to such good use. Rather, the intent is to highlight the sorts of issues that can arise when Indigenous scholars think about engaging with various arguments and principles that seem to offer some promise of assisting with the project of theorising from an Indigenous perspective. What emerges from the discussion around this issue is the injunction that throughout investigations into the possible utility of non-Indigenous theoretical positions the Indigenous theorist has to exercise extreme caution and be highly critical as she carefully considers how these theories might intersect with the particular insights and objectives that might be put forth from an Indigenous perspective. Two levels of inquiry are at play in this discussion—one about insights that might be gleaned from non-Indigenous sources, and the other about fundamental questions concerning ways by which non-Indigenous sources should be approached and employed.

The final substantive section grows out of this exploration into what might be learned from mainstream legal theory, and proceeds by way of a brief look into two examples of legal theorising at work within the Indigenous legal academy. The hope is that this sort of discussion hints at possibilities for future directions of

fundamental questions faced by Indigenous legal scholars in JY Henderson, 'Post-Colonial Indigenous Legal Consciousness' (2002) 1 *Indigenous Law Journal* 1, and *First Nations Jurisprudence and Aboriginal Rights: Defining the Just Society* (Native Law Centre of Canada, 2006).

[3] Sákéj Henderson, for example, speaks of the essential need to 'decolonise' Canadian jurisprudence, a task that falls on the shoulders of Indigenous legal scholars: above n 2.

[4] These theories include positivism, legal liberalism, law and economics, critical legal studies, feminist legal theory, Marxist legal theory, critical legal pluralism, various post-modern positions, critical race theory, post-colonialism, and so forth.

research that the Indigenous legal scholar might find fruitful. Some suggestions are methodological (looking at recent work on Indigenous research methodologies, for example, but expanding to the realm of theoretical work), others are more content-based. The discussion around the possible utility of mainstream legal theory slides into these matters, for one of the key concerns lies in the need to keep the focus on the development of *Indigenous* legal theory—theory that may borrow from other sources, but which in some central way must be connected to Indigenous communities.

The Chapter ends with a few words about the challenges that face those who undertake this sort of enterprise. The concluding thought is that while the challenges are many and diverse, arguments about the necessity of the undertaking (reintroduced from the opening introductory section) clearly demonstrate that positive considerations outweigh the hardships, risks and pitfalls along the way to the construction of a vibrant theoretical discourse around Indigenous legal issues.

B. Theory and Legal Theory

Thinking about the emergence of a distinct ILT should begin with some consideration as to what might be imagined. We must discuss what we mean by 'theory' in the context of legal study, to think more clearly about what sorts of Indigenous theories could be imagined in relation to both Indigenous legal systems and Canadian law as it applies to Indigenous peoples. What are we saying Indigenous communities might articulate concerning their own systems and what are we saying would be constructed in relation to domestic Canadian law?

At a very general level we can say that a theory about x functions to explain x (and phenomena associated with x). Broadly speaking, a theory about x would comprise an interconnected set of statements, the result of studies into the body of phenomena implicated in or connected to x, a set of statements providing a deeper understanding of the nature of the phenomena in question. The physical or hard sciences offer exemplars of 'theory' in this sense: a physical theory (such as a theory of gravity) provides a set of statements (theorems, principles, definitions, sub-theorems, etc) meant to explain the nature of the physical systems under study (bodies acting under gravitational attraction, etc).

A number of things must come together for the emergence of a theory about some aspect of the physical realm—a body of observations of some phenomena must have built up over time, some process of delineating the subject matter of investigation must be ongoing (and have resulted in some sense of what the thing under study is), some hypothesis meant to provide an explanation for what has been observed must be put forth, some process must be at hand for testing the hypothesis both in relation to other claims and in relation to the observations (the scientific method plays this role in the physical realm), and mechanisms for carrying through with this process must be in place.

It might seem straightforward to apply this framework to the field of the law. For example, we could try to say that a legal theory is meant to say things of a general nature about the law, or an aspect or aspects of the law. The aim would be to explain the nature of the legal phenomenon in question. On a very general level, for example, positivists theorise that the law is properly understood as nothing beyond the positive expression of law-makers (the laws and regulations passed by legislators, and the pronouncements of the courts),[5] while natural law theorists, by contrast, theorise that the law is properly understood as resting on 'natural' principles (derived from such sources as divine will, the natural world, or a noumenal realm).[6]

A large body of literature constitutes the field of legal theory in the West, a body of literature with a long and storied history.[7] Do we see in the literature and in instruction around legal theory nothing more than the presentation of testable hypotheses meant to provide explanations for legal phenomena? Is that all there is to understanding the basic nature of legal theory?

1. Theorising and the Nature of the Law

There seem to be special features about the law that make this understanding problematic. First, the subject matter itself is notoriously unclear. One of the ongoing and vigorous debates within the field of legal theory is about the nature of 'the law' itself.[8] In order to say of any given society that it contains a legal system, is it essential that there be a centralised authority vested with the power of promulgating and enforcing the particular laws of this society?[9] On a more detailed level, thinking about things we might call 'laws', how are these things distinguished from other forms of social norms (religious edicts, rules governing associations, moral precepts, etc)? Boundary identification problems for the law and its substantive contents are intimately connected to the problem of identifying the nature of the law. Are we to say that a system of rules regulating the lives of

[5] See, eg, HLA Hart, *The Concept of Law* (Clarendon Press, 1961); and JL Austin, *The Province of Jurisprudence* (Noonsday Press, 1954) [originally published in 1832].

[6] See, eg, L Fuller, *The Morality of Law* (Yale University Press, 1969): St T Aquinas, *Summa Theologica*, I–II, q 95 (available online eg at www.ccel.org/ccel/aquinas/summa.html).

[7] My focus in this Chapter is on Western, or Euro-Canadian, legal theory (in contrast to Indigenous legal theory). Its roots can be traced back to Plato and Aristotle (though some would suggest that this route backwards was generated—rather than discovered—in the early stages of the modern era).

[8] See, eg, M Golding, *Philosophy of Law* (Prentice-Hall, 1975) 7–23.

[9] The legal pluralist challenges the state-centred picture of the law, arguing, for example, that citizens are subject to multiple, overlapping bodies of law. See, eg, GR Woodman, 'Legal Pluralism and Justice' (1996) 40 *Journal of African Law* 152. Critical legal pluralists go further, arguing that it is a mistake both to (a) prioritise the state, measuring other legal systems against its nature, and (b) miss the central *creative* role the citizen plays in generating, comprehending, and living through the law ['A critical element in a philosophical approach to comprehending the law is missing if the legal pluralist attempts to debate the web of legal normativity without also addressing questions about those who spin its filaments'. M Kleinhans and R Macdonald, 'What is Critical Legal Pluralism?' (1997) 12(2) *Canadian Journal of Law and Society* 25, 36–7.]

the citizens of a polity constitute laws when this system is made up of a special kind of rule, or is it enough that the rules be the product of law-makers?[10]

As interesting (and vexing) as discussions of these matters might be, to focus on these in a realm of study examining a social institution captures only one vector of debate, while other sorts of problems and issues remain merely suggested. For example, when we run up against such immense difficulties in determining criteria by which we could identify this global form of social phenomena, this suggests a split between different sorts of theory that may be constructed, depending on whether one is trying to explain the nature of some instantiated social system (that is, a particular legal system), or the general conceptual nature of the social system itself (that is, 'the law' itself, considered as a thing we think and talk about).

2. Descriptive and Prescriptive Theories and the Possibility of Perspectivism

That is, one sort of work may be carried out by a legal theorist conducting theoretic work entirely within a legal framework embedded within a society (for example, the dominant legal system in Canada). This theorist bypasses questions about the nature of the law by taking as her subject of inquiry the system around her, presuming it to be a legal system. She asks about how this system functions, about what ends it promotes, about how to explain broad developments, about roles individual and group actors play in the ongoing functioning of the system, and so forth. Such work develops a theory primarily meant to be descriptive (and as such, this sort of theorising would run more deeply parallel to the production of theories in the physical sciences, as its focus would more clearly be some 'thing' in the immediately given world).

Another legal theorist, by contrast, may be less concerned about how any particular legal system actually functions in the world, and more with the very idea of law.[11] She works on developing theories of law which tend naturally to be primarily prescriptive in nature, meant to paint pictures of an idealised system of social regulation (to which instantiated systems could or should aspire).[12]

Two important points emerge from this distinction between kinds of theorising in the legal context, both of which can be illustrated by way of contrast with the activity of theorising in the realm of the physical sciences. First, on reflection we can see that a general demarcation has already been made between theorising in these two contexts. For while it makes little sense to imagine theorists in the physical sciences contemplating thoughts about how the world should look or function, those engaged in investigations into the fundamental nature of the law are

[10] Once again, this hints at the debate between positivists and natural law theorists.

[11] See, in this regard, B Bix, *Jurisprudence: Theory and Context* (Sweet and Maxwell, 1999) chs 1 and 2. This theorist might, as well, argue that this notion is poorly instantiated in the world.

[12] Perhaps the theorist intends that her work would apply to all human contexts, or she has in mind something narrower in scope, a theory meant to apply to particular sorts of human communities.

often engaged in precisely this kind of enterprise.[13] This highlights how a thread of normativity weaves its way through the tapestry of legal theorising. The second distinction between theorising in these different contexts focuses on the extent to which the theorist herself is implicated in the content of developed theories. To see this we have to back up a step of two.

We have identified two different sorts of theoretical work with which the legal theorist can be engaged—work aimed at developing descriptive models from within particular legal systems, and work aimed at investigating deeper questions about the nature of law itself. Yet the line between these two sorts of theorising is not so sharp and clear, especially in how we have characterised it as dividing up theories in terms of descriptive versus prescriptive emphasis. While this may be so in terms of intent, in reality we would have to imagine that legal theories that aim to be descriptive have a strong underlying prescriptive current. Consider the project of theorising from within, and about, a particular legal system. The theorist engaged in this enterprise may think of herself as exploring an extremely complex and dynamic object or thing in the world. Her intent may simply be to model a descriptive account of the basic nature of this system (or, more likely, a model of some aspect of this system). To do so, however, she will have to rely on the conceptual apparatus she brings to the task, apparatus which impacts her approach to the investigation of phenomena, and the model of the phenomena she develops.

The world of 'legal phenomena' does not exist prior to the act of theorising, ready to serve as 'raw data' for the process of analysis. The world must be categorised and conceptualised before the explicit process of legal analysis begins, which means that any purportedly pure act of description is impure, admixed with some degree of prior structuring. It is arguable, however, that there exists a more troubling possibility, namely the realisation that it may very well be impossible to formulate purely descriptive theories of the law.

In the realm of the physical sciences, some maintain that the line between 'fact' and 'theory' is blurred. But even admitting this does not necessarily lead to the notion that the institution of scientific research is inherently 'cultural' or 'political'—that is, we are not necessarily led to the notion that the interests, upbringings, and concerns of scientists somehow infect the very theories they develop and propose. One could find quite reasonable the position that the general scientific enterprise is acultural and apolitical in outcome (that is, that in some meaningful sense of the term scientific theories succeed in being descriptive). On the other hand, in the realm of legal theorising it is quite possible that what the legal theorist brings to the task of theorising is not just prior conceptual apparatus that simply functions to 'cut up' the world, but also pre-existing ideological and political positions and agendas, all of which have a vital impact on the very sorts of theories developed by the theorist. More weakly, it might be argued that the prior conceptual apparatus in this realm of inquiry is necessarily normative in nature,

[13] See, in this regard, JL Mackie, *Ethics: Inventing Right and Wrong* (Penguin, 1977).

infected with valuations, disguised through various linguistic means. We could term such possibilities 'perspectivism'.[14]

3. Rules Regulating Social Behaviour

Though obliquely, this discussion has introduced the fact of agency. The act of legal theorising, we have suggested, may be infected by the presence of the theorist as agent, as a being making choices. The presence of choice, the exercise of the will around choice, leads into further discussions into the peculiar nature of the law and legal theory. We can move directly into a discussion of agency by noting that it is generally accepted that at a preliminary level of description all legal systems comprise rules meant to regulate the behaviour of people attempting to live together. Somehow out of this large collection of socially prescribed rules would be carved out the rules of law (or just 'the laws'). So we come face to face with one aspect of agency at play in the legal realm—the agency of the active subject of the law, the citizen acting within a world of rules.

How are we to come to a full understanding of any particular system of socially determined and socially prescribed rules, when these rules prescribe how people *ought* to act? Any explicitly articulated particular social rule will have the form: 'All x must (or should, or may) do y when in situation z'.[15] The normative content is clear. The rule sets out a socially prescribed norm of conduct, meant to inform specific (types of) actors in specific circumstances how they ought to act.

If we contemplate a theory meant to explain the nature of a particular legal system, how do we imagine the inquiry unfolding when the explanation must encompass not only a general account of how things are, but also purportedly some notion of how people *ought* to act? Furthermore, if we contemplate a theory meant to explore the conceptual nature of the law, how shall such a theory accommodate the notions of rule-generation and rule-following, when these seem to carry with them constitutive subjective and prescriptive elements?

Thus we see that this fact about the law—that in some fashion it is rule-based—quite quickly raises two general sorts of problems: one methodological, the other substantive. On the one hand we have difficulty in thinking about how we will get

[14] This is left as a *possibility*, for there are arguments on both sides of this position—that legal theories can be 'objective' and 'descriptive' in some meaningful sense of the term, and that legal theories are all necessarily infected with 'perspectival truth'. The notion of perspectivism is prominent in the works of Nietzsche (see, eg, SD Hales and R Welshon, *Nietzsche's Perspectivism* (University of Illinois Press, 2000). One could distinguish between a weak perspectival position (that all data about the world is initially embedded in or interpreted through a perspective, but theoretical knowledge can be developed removed from its perspectival grounding), and a strong version (that all theoretical knowledge is irreducibly tainted by its grounding in concept-determining perspectives). The interesting possibility under consideration employs a strong perspectival position. This distinction will be central to a later discussion in this Chapter.

[15] All permissive rules could be defined in relation to the set of controlling rules—that is, rules of the form 'all x may do y in situations z' may be understood as emerging out of the realm of exclusion established by the rules that dictate what x must or should do.

to a satisfactory account of the thing under examination. That is, we might wonder whether we can ever fully explain the nature of the thing being studied, since some degree of understanding may necessarily be tied to the meanings and understandings attached to the rules by both those who promulgate and those who fall under them. Does one understand the system of rules if one studies behaviour alone, or must one try to come to grips with what the rules *mean* to their promulgators, and why people behave the way they do within the rule-system?

On the other hand, the things explored—the rules meant to govern behaviour—are clearly not the kind of thing that the physical sciences have as their subject matter. When we speak of natural laws (like those of thermodynamics), we do not imagine rules which matter and energy may choose to follow (under threat, perhaps, of some sort of penalty or other). If a physical system under study does not act in accord with the laws as currently explicated, the natural reaction is to suppose that more empirical and/or theoretical work is required, as clearly science has not yet managed to provide in this arena a satisfactory account of the laws in place.[16] People, however, are agents in the world. People may choose to act irresponsibly (and so to act contrary to the law, just as they may choose to follow the law).

Agency in the legal realm, however, is not restricted to the actions of the subjects of the law. The law itself is a human construct. Choices were, and continue to be, necessary in its construction. The creators of law act in the world, imposing their will within the fabric of social and political life.[17] Beyond this, there is the matter alluded to earlier—the question as to the role played by the legal theorist, herself an agent in the world. While she may have a minor role to play in the actual generation of law, it is not at all clear that she can be divorced from the content of the theoretical model she develops.

Taken together, these matters underscore the complexity inherent in, and the difficulties attached to, the project of theorising about the law. The legal theorist works with contested meanings, about an ill-defined subject matter (at all levels of enquiry), in a subject matter carved out of the panoply of possible systems of socially regulating rules, where the systems that constitute the law would seem to be only fully understood with appreciation of what it might be to generate and meaningfully act under community-spanning rules.

4. Forms of Indigenous Legal Theorising—An Initial Taxonomy

What, then, might an ILT look like? Presumably, an ILT would present a theory about law issuing from an Indigenous conceptual universe. It would seem folly,

[16] At the sub-atomic level the laws might be probabilistic in nature—as laws of probability would then determine outcomes, this does not open the door to rampant randomness (or some notion of choice).

[17] This process of creation is understood broadly in this context, so as to capture all sorts of acts around the generation of law (the acts of legislatures, the acts of judges, the acts of lawyers, and so forth). This is meant to include not just the genesis, development and promulgation of statutes, reg'' lations and case law, but the various acts of interpretation that swirl around 'the law' once articulate

however, to imagine that there might be a single Indigenous theory about the law, since such a monolithic theory would require a single conceptual 'pan-Indigenous' universe. Certainly we are imagining a plurality of Indigenous legal theories, sitting parallel and in contrast to the myriad 'mainstream' legal theories that exist,[18] each Indigenous theory emanating from a particular Indigenous conceptual framework or world-view.

Further in this vein, we should consider the possibility that even within an Indigenous collective there will not be raised a simple homogenous voice, that Indigenous communities will naturally contain degrees of diversity of opinion and perspective, just as we see within non-Indigenous communities. Why would we assume, for example, that the Cree would speak with a single unified voice on theoretical matters, while non-Indigenous Euro-Canadian legal theorists produce many and varied theories about the law? We might venture to guess that the many varied Indigenous world-views would produce families of theories, resemblances between them justifying a general kinship label, where within each separate Indigenous collective (defined around a common world-view) would exist varied individual understandings of the law.

Furthermore, it would seem that a general divide would exist within the general family of Indigenous legal theories—there would be (a) Indigenous theories concerning Indigenous law (perhaps capable of extrapolation to law in general), and (b) Indigenous theories focused on the dominant Canadian legal regime.

Finally, we must imagine that this divide within Indigenous legal theories intersects with the distinction between types of theorising. That is, we should imagine the possibility of Indigenous scholars sometimes producing theories meant to provide deeper and richer explanations concerning how some particular legal system functions,[19] and sometimes producing theories meant to say something more general and abstract about the nature of 'the law', understood as an idea or concept. Equally or more importantly, the fact that theorising can be focused on both particular legal systems and how we think about the law, together speak to the need for the emergence of *Indigenous* legal theory, articulated by Indigenous scholars.

C. The Need for Indigenous Theorising About the Law

The need for this kind of theorising emerges from our look into the interesting permutations that arise within the arena of legal theory. We would expect ILT to encompass both (a) theorising that focuses on Indigenous and non-Indigenous legal systems (the latter in relation to how these systems have impacted on the lives

[18] In this context, the term 'mainstream' refers to those theories of the dominant system, those typically taught, for example, in Canadian law schools. It includes, then, a vast array of theory, including critical theories emergent over the last few decades.

[19] Or, perhaps the Indigenous legal theorist might attempt to provide explanations around how several systems of law interact, or could interact.

of Indigenous peoples), and (b) theorising about Indigenous legal orders and conceptions of law (theorising grounded in distinct and unique cultural histories). Whether engaged in a project meant to be primarily descriptive or one centred more directly on presenting essentially prescriptive outcomes, the Indigenous legal scholar will be building explanations of legal systems or concepts as these speak from and relate to Indigenous communities and individuals. The notion of ideas being expressed from a certain position leads to several arguments based in culture and experience, while the question of agency brings in arguments based in the activity of communities in the world.

1. Cultural and Experiential Groundings

(a) Experiential Grounding

The first argument for the need for *Indigenous* theorising comes from the experiential grounding of explanations meant to be more descriptive, and from the 'cultural' grounding of explanations in the prescriptive/normative realm.[20] Given what we have said about the interconnections between descriptive and prescriptive accounts, this is not a simple matter. Seeing how this spells out into the need for Indigenous theorising about the law will require that we detail the ways in which 'experience' can play out into unique and meaningful explanations of the nature of the law, as well as the ways that 'culture' can both colour experience and generate 'nationalist' arguments.

First, consider the role experience can play in affecting the generation of models of the law. Non-Indigenous legal theorists exploring the nature of dominant non-Indigenous legal structures in Canada focus on questions clearly grounded in the subjective experiences of the generalised Canadian public: how (for example) do 'average' Canadians think of laws governing their private interactions?[21] How do they function within these laws—how do they recognise legal obligations, how do they act in relation to these, how do they react to ruptures?

Second, non-Indigenous legal theorists explore dominant non-Indigenous legal structures on a more abstract level, asking, for example, about how the notion of the rule of law is founded, how it is understood, and its place in the proper struc-

[20] I am using 'cultural' as a marker for general differences in how peoples might come to construct and understand their social realities. I am not here focused on differences in how different peoples might sing, dance or hold eating instruments, but in how they conceptually build a world of meaning within which they live. In the field of legal theory, we see this notion at play in an article by Joseph Raz, wherein he asks whether there can be a theory of law, described as culturally grounded yet universalisable, that delves into the West's concept of law and yet has room to consider how it intersects with other cultures, peoples and times: J Raz, 'Can There Be a Theory of Law?' in M Golding and W Edmundson (eds), *The Blackwell Guide to the Philosophy of Law and Legal Theory* (Blackwell Publishing, 2005) 324–42.

[21] While some theorists might not see themselves working so completely within a world bounded by subjective experience, this may be due to their own failure to 'step back' from or out of the doxa structuring the social world they share with the society they study: see P Bourdieu, *Language and Symbolic Power* (Harvard University Press, 1991).

turing of a legal system embedded within a liberal democracy. The construction of answers to these queries may not be so clearly a function of the experiential grounding of scholars working within non-Indigenous society, but the lack of an obvious connection does not make the connection any less secure than for the former sorts of questions—notions such as the 'rule of law' arise in particular historical/social/political settings, and 'make sense' to societies for whom they are culturally meaningful intellectual constructs.

Indigenous legal scholars, in contrast, will explore the nature of Indigenous legal systems in much the same (bifurcated) fashion, but from different experiential/intellectual/cultural groundings. Let us begin by focusing on the notion of purely experiential groundings of models of law in society. Indigenous legal scholars will be able to provide generalised descriptive accounts, providing deeper and richer explanations, for such matters as why certain dominant state-centred laws and policies came to be, explanations built upon and around their experiences with non-Indigenous legal systems. These scholars will be able to highlight the vast gulf that exists between (a) much of the work of non-Indigenous scholars (and the understandings of officials, lawyers, judges, and others), the bulk of whom seem either ignorant of, or wilfully blind to, the shockingly oppressive role the Canadian legal system has played (and arguably continues to play) in Canada, and (b) the experiences of those subject to this history of legally buttressed—in some ways legally generated—oppression.

Additionally, some kinds of experiences—or rather the *felt* nature of some kinds of experiences—may themselves be culturally conditioned or informed, which *further* speaks to the need for Indigenous explanations of the nature of the law. This is not to say that pain and suffering (or for that matter joy and happiness) are necessarily felt differently, but rather to say that we must acknowledge that some experiences may be understood and felt differently or more deeply between cultures. For example, the trauma around a kind of event may be greater (or lesser) depending on one's way of thinking and feeling in relation to their world. An example here might involve the deeply spiritual sense of place that marks the cultural life of many Indigenous peoples, a sense of connection that deeply colours their experiences of colonial takings of lands, and subsequent desecration of these lands.

(b) Cultural Groundings

Beyond these ways in which one can understand experience as shaping what is felt or thought about how a legal system might impact on people (especially when the legal system in question oppressively targets the people in question), we can also note that cultural grounding can have an effect on the generation of theories about the law in general. Just as non-Indigenous legal scholars will explore the conceptual universe that their communities have constructed over generations, likewise will Indigenous scholars muse abstractly about the conceptual universes within which they live, in attempts to make richer sense of how they conceive of the nature of the rules by which they order their lives, abstract musings that, indeed, are likely to prove insightful about how non-Indigenous scholars think of the law. An earlier discussion, stemming from the blurred line between descriptive and prescriptive projects, is particularly germane in this context. There will be an interesting interplay between the nature of legal phenomena (those things to be studied) and the theoretical frameworks Indigenous legal theorists bring to the task of theorising. This is not to say that Indigenous legal theorists would be more 'political' in their work than others, but rather to note that whereas the work of non-Indigenous legal scholars often rests on cultural structures 'hidden' to the audience (which shares most of the assumed background conceptual baggage), the work of Indigenous legal theorists will bring right to the fore (for the primarily non-Indigenous audience at least) ways that Indigenous communities cut up the world.

For example, many Indigenous legal theorists are likely to have a much less narrow concept of a 'legal order', in the sense that decentralised, less formalised systems of social regulation will be seen as encompassing legal systems.[22] Such conceptualisations of the law will in turn have an impact on how the world of legal phenomena comes to be perceived and studied. Consider: Indigenous legal theorists are likely to understand the assertion of Crown sovereignty as questionable, and as posing immense theoretical concerns. The highest court in Canada begins with the simple assertion that the assumption of Crown sovereignty was never questioned,[23] while Indigenous legal scholars are likely to begin with the thought that the presumption of Crown power is a fundamental puzzle in need of explication.

Thus, Indigenous legal theorising is essential in bringing out just these sorts of oppositional understandings of the nature of legal phenomena, and of what constitutes the sorts of legal issues that need study. Looking at the world via different cultural and experiential groundings, Indigenous peoples will not only be able to articulate how their own systems are structured and understood, but also to cast new light on dominant legal orders. The existence of multiple spheres of law presupposed in this general picture yields ripe questions as to how different legal systems can meaningfully interact, raising further theoretical issues in need of further exploration. How do we measure legitimacy, for example, when two normative systems meet and conflict? Do we search for meta-legal rules, rules within one or the other system, or rules that seem to lie in or emerge from an area of overlap between the systems?

2. Legal Theorising as Acting in the World

The existence of multiple legal orders suggests another justification for the expenditure of time and energy on the project of Indigenous legal theorising. Earlier in

[22] See, eg, Napoleon and Overstall, above n 1.

[23] See, eg, *R v Sparrow* [1990] 1 SCR 1075, 1103: '[T]here was from the outset never any doubt that sovereignty and legislative power, and indeed the underlying title, to such lands vested in the Crown'.

this discussion we touched on the possibility that the act of legal theorising is itself potentially implicated in the production of law,[24] the idea that the legal theorist comes to the task of theorising with presumptions and conceptual understandings that go into the categorisation of legal phenomena, which then feed into how an understanding of the law emerges. Given this discussion, it would seem a mistake to adopt a naive view of the nature of the act of legal theorising, as the implication is that much of what has been said about 'the law' seemingly applies to theorising about the law. Just as the law is a complex social phenomenon caught up in matters of subjective understandings and meanings and purposive acts (carried along by the fact that all law is, in some fashion, a matter of rule-generation and following), theorising in this context is also a complex social phenomenon. While the aim is to develop and articulate principles and schema, rather than rules that bind, it is arguable that this is an essentially social process, one tied to particular purposes, and to particular understandings and experiences.[25]

The ends and understandings of particular legal theorists could impact significantly on the content of the legal theories they develop.[26] First, we can imagine that the fact that the theorist inhabits a particular conceptual universe might go some way towards explaining the sort of theory the theorist constructs when she examines a particular society. The history of anthropological research in the West seems to provide support for this notion, as there are countless examples of the ways in which the findings of an anthropologist wound up having as much to say about the cultural background of the anthropologist as they did about the nature of the society under supposedly 'scientific' scrutiny.[27] One might suggest that the current methods of the anthropologist, requiring careful immersion in the society under study, reflect recognition of this phenomenon, as the field of inquiry attempts to find ways to overcome the effects on the production of research by the researcher's own cultural biases and understandings.

The second way a theorist may bring herself to the work with which she is engaged is through the production of theories that reflect her political or ideo logical agendas, a suggestion we earlier put to one side. We may imagine this happening with more or less conscious direction. If the infusion of one's political

[24] This is what is implied in suggesting that it may be that the legal theorist always comes to the task of theorising with a political or ideological agenda. In theorising, the theorist would be advancing these underlying schema, either promoting the maintenance and strengthening of a certain form of political structure (what we tend to see in what is called 'doctrinal' analysis in mainstream legal study), or pushing for varied degrees of legal reform.

[25] Bix highlights the purpose-driven nature of legal theorising in *Jurisprudence*, above n 11.

[26] It is an interesting question (not extensively tackled in this discussion) whether it is even possible for a legal theorist to successfully adopt the stance of the scientist, a value-neutral position from which a purely objective explanation for legal phenomena (or legal concepts) may be developed. The suggestion at this point is that this seems at least problematic in any particular scenario, since it will often be at least possible in any particular situation for the theorist to influence the development of law and policy through the articulation of certain theories.

[27] Struggles over the last few generations in the field of anthropology around twin research pillars of 'participation' and 'distance' are extensively discussed in BM Knauft, *Genealogies for the Present in Cultural Anthropology* (Routledge, 1996). The cultural place of the researcher/observer plays a prominent role in this dynamic.

and ideological beliefs into the theory produced is unreflective, it is not clear that the process is different in kind from what we noted above—the theorist is simply bringing other aspects of her cultural background to the task of making sense of some social reality. If, however, she is more actively engaged in imposing her political and ideological beliefs onto the data she is presented with, this can clearly invite different sorts of issues.

In her ground-breaking work, *Decolonizing Methodologies*, Linda Tuhiwai Smith opened her analysis of research methodologies in relation to Indigenous peoples with an observation tied into this point.[28] Non-Indigenous theorists, she argued, have often deployed their theories to oppress and dispossess Indigenous peoples. This is a claim about a particular set of legal theories that links to a general possibility we touched on earlier—the possibility that legal theorists might bring to the project of theorising pre-existing political or ideological positions which function to determine the very content of the theories produced. We must note, however, that while there seems to be some conceptual connection between the idea that non-Indigenous theorists might have produced theories in order to dispossess and oppress and this more general notion about the political/ideological grounding of all legal theory, the link needs careful consideration.

When we earlier introduced the general notion we framed it as the possibility that no descriptive modelling is possible—that is, that it may well be that all legal theorising is deeply reflective of particular theorists' interests and agendas. Smith's claim can support this notion, but does not necessarily lead to it. To agree that while over the last few centuries non-Indigenous legal theorists have employed theory not to try to provide explanations but rather to facilitate oppression is not necessarily to discount the possibility that some theorists might be able to move outside their own perspectival grounding to produce legal theories with content that is 'objective' in some meaningful sense of the term. As we did earlier, we will take the general suggestion (that all legal theory is inevitably tied to a political agenda, and does not function to merely describe a social reality) and treat it as a possibility, one to be explored more fully in a later section.[29] It is a clearly contestable matter, one suggested by the nature of law and legal theorising, but open to challenge. In an upcoming section we look more closely at the possible content of Indigenous legal theories and raise this matter, for in itself it is a theoretical position, one with something of a theoretical nature to say about both the law and legal theory (at this point, then, we treat this as a possibility concerning the act of theorising).

3. ILT Produced by Indigenous Scholars

These varied ways by which Indigenous legal scholars can contribute an essentially unique set of understandings of the law do not capture central features of the pro-

[28] LT Smith, *Decolonizing Methodologies: Research and Indigenous Peoples* (Zed Books, 1999).
[29] See discussion in section headed 'Truth'.

ject of legal theorising that might suggest an essential need for the development of Indigenous legal theories *propagated by Indigenous legal scholars.* It is certainly open to non-Indigenous scholars, for example, to study how the legal system of dominant society impacted (and continues to impact) on the lives of Indigenous peoples in Canada, and even how Indigenous peoples may conceive of the surrounding world (including how Indigenous peoples conceive of their own legal orders, and underlying concepts of law and order).[30] It may even be contended that the results of these studies by non-Indigenous scholars can go into the composition of elements of ILT. For a number of reasons, however, great care must be exercised in this matter, reasons that all tie down at some point to one central fact—that the experiences, understandings, concepts and theories that go into the process of theorising in this context all relate to the collective wills and visions of Indigenous peoples. We arrive back at the fact of agency and the role it plays not only in how the law functions as a social institution, but the role it plays in the generation of law and indeed in theorising about the law.

The notion that experience and culture come together to point to a conception of ILT suggests quite a bit more when joined to the fact of agency. These experiences and understandings rest on the very notion of *communities*, communities which in the Indigenous context are as 'political' as they are cultural. In this context, the 'cultural' slides into the 'political'. Crucially, Indigenous peoples not only have distinct ways of understanding their worlds, but these distinct understandings reflect and rest upon the existence of distinct self-contained collectives with shared histories and visions. When one appreciates that Indigenous communities comprise active self-determining peoples, the fact crystallises that it must be from their voices that emerge articulations of their shared visions. These collective visions reflect the lives of peoples who have lived forever on their lands, and these visions express collective wills to continue, to maintain the vast social connections that interweave past and present into plans for movement into the future.[31]

So, we have several arguments for the development of ILT. Some arguments work outward from the core notion of what it is to theorise in this context. Given the natures of both law and legal theorising, it is incumbent on Indigenous scholars to articulate visions of the law,[32] as these will reflect experiences and cultural groundings that serve as foundations for Indigenous understandings of the law. Other arguments also build out from considerations around the nature of legal theorising, but less directly. What we have seen developing in the last part of this section is an argument we might term 'cultural nationalist'. This argument points to the need for Indigenous scholars to meet on the field of conflict that often seems

[30] I adopt a cautious agnostic position in relation to the last point—it may very well be that someone inhabiting a non-Indigenous conceptual universe may be incapable of actually understanding what the world looks like, seen through the eyes (or rather the mind) of an Indigenous person. The possibility that it might be possible to reach such levels of understanding is left open, for it is a contestable point.

[31] See, eg, Henderson, above n 2.

[32] These visions could be of either legal systems—their own or others that impact on Indigenous communities—or of the law itself.

to characterise the arena of theorising in this context. Arguably, non-Indigenous theories have historically served as central instruments in the ongoing colonial project (right up to the present moment), acting to entrap and dispossess Indigenous peoples.[33] Indigenous scholars must respond to this force, defending Indigenous communities and their relations, through the deployment of understandings of the law that both (a) reveal how dominant legal theory plays this role, and (b) illustrate how Indigenous understandings of the law might sit in contrast to these oppressive regimes.

On the margins of these arguments, tied as they are to cultural matters, lies a third form of justification. This form of justification speaks more directly to the question of self-determination, removed from questions around culture. Indigenous legal scholars should be free to engage with the process of theorising about the law in order to strategically further the goals and objectives of Indigenous communities. The project here obviously connects to the nationalist element alluded to earlier, as it envisions Indigenous scholars engaged in a struggle with non-Indigenous theories (and with law and policy makers). But for the strategist forms of resistance are determined principally in light of the struggle for self-determination itself. The strategist is tied to the community, and engages in the activity of theorising in order to advance whatever the goals of the community might be, in light of whatever dynamic forces might be at play in the larger context within which the community functions.

The line between the cultural nationalist and strategist might well be, in many particular situations, very fine or even practically indistinguishable. In some circumstances, these characterisations might apply to one and same theorist, thinking of herself in complementary ways. On the other hand, across the varied landscape of Canada one also encounters different Indigenous legal theorists engaged in the process of theorising for reasons that fall separately under these two umbrellas, generating quite different visions of what the enterprise is all about. Some cultural nationalists will aggressively assert an Indigenous identity, one that stands, in some regard, in direct opposition to that of the mainstream or non-Indigenous world, while strategists may be nationalists in a sense of the term, but fixed on objectives that are much less 'oppositional' in nature, as these theorists may be tied to communities primarily seeking a firm place within the Canadian landscape. A strategist would still function under an understanding of collective self-determination, but being removed from oppositional notions of 'indigeneity' (or at least removed from having a primary focus on particular forms of cultural revitalisation) she could readily conceive of choices that pull her community ever closer to the non-Indigenous world (with the only requirement being that the movement toward assimilation be driven by choices made by the community).

[33] See, eg, Henderson, above n 2.

D. Reluctance to Theorise?

Given these varied arguments for the development of Indigenous legal theorising, why the paucity of explicit ILT? Some scholars, looking at a similar situation in the United States, find the lack of theorising tied to an uncomfortable relationship to critical theory.[34] Linda Smith likewise notes discomfort with both post-colonial and post-modern thought—they can seem faddish, and suspicions can arise that these are merely the latest non-Indigenous theories to move into the role of oppression and domination.[35]

This discomfort may explain the reluctance of some Indigenous scholars to embark on projects of theorising, but only to the extent that these sorts of projects might somehow force them into mouthing positions that are antithetical to the aims and purposes that drive their work. This sort of argument, then, serves to illustrate a danger, not a road-block. There would seem to be at least two ways open to the Indigenous theorist to manage the danger: first, she might attempt the task of developing theories to explain the nature of the law that flow naturally out of her existence within a cultural/conceptual universe determined by her Indigenous community (while doing her best to assiduously avoid the use of non-Indigenous conceptual models), or second, she might make use of insights developed from within non-Indigenous theoretical models, while maintaining a constant vigil against the possibility that what she is espousing is ill-suited for the tasks her community has set her.

Linda Smith acknowledges the danger. Speaking of various elements of the package of academic discourse—reading, writing, talking, science, theories, methodologies and interpretation—she notes that '[o]ne problem of . . . learning to read this way over many years of academic study, is that we can adopt uncritically similar patterns of writing. We begin to write about ourselves as indigenous peoples as if we really were "out there", the "Other", with all the baggage this entails'.[36] She goes on, however, to spell out how to avoid this danger. Indigenous peoples have to be ever-cognisant of the act of writing, constantly aware of who they might be writing for, and continually thinking of their work in a political context. While 'Indigenous peoples have been, in many ways, oppressed by theory',[37] this is because this theorising has constructed frameworks of interpretation that

[34] See, eg, E Cheyfitz, 'The (Post)Colonial Predicament of Native American Studies' (2002) 4 *Interventions* 405.

[35] Smith, above n 28. One might also suspect that the act of theorising itself is viewed with some suspicion in many Indigenous communities, as it seems to privilege one aspect of the self over the others, in a way that runs counter to a common holistic vision of the self that undergirds many Indigenous communities. Privileging this aspect of the self, furthermore, might be seen as making a break with the life of the community, as one step along the path to integration into the life of the academy, a life distant from the concerns of the Indigenous world. The latter point may go some way to explaining why there has been so little theorising (about the law, literature, history, and so forth).

[36] Smith, above n 28, 36.

[37] *Ibid*, 38.

marginalise them. When Indigenous peoples take up the task of developing theories, they grasp the power to 'design the tools', the power to '. . . determine priorities, to bring to the centre those issues of our own choosing, and to discuss them amongst ourselves'.[38] Smith sees this as part of a process of 'decolonisation'.[39]

Smith's suspicions concerning post-modernism and post-colonial theory (noted earlier) must be tempered, then, with realisation that she is not advising Indigenous scholars to disregard the insights they might provide. In essence, she calls for recognition of a division between purpose and content: non-Indigenous theories may have been developed for any number of reasons (to impress the scholarly world, to feed into law and policy that further oppresses and dispossesses Indigenous peoples, to try to arrive at clear and sound explanations for social, political and economic phenomena, and so forth), but the theories themselves contain arguments and explanations that may speak to Indigenous scholars (and their communities).

There are at least two worrisome matters buried in these remarks concerning the use of non-Indigenous theories. On the one hand, there is concern over the possibility that Indigenous scholars might unreflectively or uncritically fall into thinking and writing in non-Indigenous ways. On the other hand, there is concern that an Indigenous scholar might lose sight of the concerns and interests that should drive their scholarship, concerns and interests tied to Indigenous peoples struggling to survive in ongoing colonial existences. Both concerns relate to the care with which an Indigenous scholar must 'ground' her theorising. The first speaks to the care the scholar must take in being eternally vigilant and meticulous in the use of non-Indigenous knowledges. The second speaks to the need for Indigenous scholars to be ever cognisant of the larger political struggles that frame their work.

Similar concerns, notes Leela Gandhi, are debated in the field of post-colonial studies.[40] Third World critics (Gandhi discusses Arif Dirlik and Aijaz Ahmad) decry such matters as the 'postcolonial preoccupation with questions regarding the formation of subjectivities',[41] what these critics see as essentially 'self-indulgent and solipsistic questions [that] abjure the "real" politics of the collectivity'.[42] Gandhi notes remarks by Spivak, to the effect that 'recent concessions within the first-world metropolitan academy inadvertently serve to identify, confirm, and thereby exclude certain cultural formations as chronically marginal'.[43] Gandhi reaches conclusions similar to those we noted from Smith: the postcolonial scholar must be engaged in a process of 'continually resisting the institutional procedures of co-option'.[44]

[38] Smith, above n 28, 38.
[39] *Ibid*, 39.
[40] L Gandhi, *Postcolonial Theory: A Critical Introduction* (Allen and Unwin, 1998).
[41] *Ibid*, 56.
[42] *Ibid*, 56–7.
[43] *Ibid*, 55. Gandhi is paraphrasing Spivak, from G Spivak, *Outside in the Teaching Machine* (Routledge, 1993) 55.
[44] Gandhi, above n 40, 59.

Clearly, the concerns around the use of non-Indigenous theories are multi-faceted. We find concerns with the elevation of Indigenous legal scholars into the world of academia, where they may slide into a higher socio-economic class, and so possibly become preoccupied with self-indulgent 'theorising' (to the detriment of the 'real' concerns, the concerns of the collective), and in ways that threaten to reinforce the very marginalisation that they purportedly strive to overcome.

The common response to these sorts of dangers can raise equally troubling concerns. While both Smith and Gandhi argue for a critical and cautious approach to theorising and the use of non-Indigenous/postcolonial theories, it is possible that Indigenous scholars are cautionary to an extreme, and we find ourselves back in the position we seem to be in today—faced with a dire lack of clear-minded theorising and useful theory. In the realm of postcolonial theory Gandhi also notes the emergence of individuals suspicious of the very idea of theorising, a group carrying a 'categorical mistrust of intellectual activity in and of itself'.[45] She responds in step with Smith: 'knowledge production', she notes, 'remains a crucial sphere of influence—a place from which it is possible both to agitate thought within 'stupid institutions' and also, as Foucault maintains, to propose 'an insurrection of knowledges that are opposed . . . to the effects of the centralising powers that are linked to the institution'.[46]

E. Making Use of Non-Indigenous Theory

1. Preliminary Considerations

We are left with at least one major concern largely unaddressed: how, precisely, Indigenous legal scholars are to effectively make use of mainstream (non-Indigenous) theories, when the suspicion is that in various forms and guises these very theories have historically played a major role in the marginalisation and colonisation of Indigenous peoples. Precisely how are Indigenous legal scholars to make safe and effective use of legal liberalism, law and economics, Marxist analysis, critical race theory, postcolonial theory, postmodernist analysis, feminist theory, or legal pluralism?

It is not a simple matter of agreeing with a theory whenever one notes that it seems to fit well with one's predilections in some fashion or other. For example, Critical Race Theory arose out of recognition that 'perspectives' (determined by one's race or ethnicity) have a crucial role to play in making sense of the deeper nature of the law (as essentially and inherently racist).[47] One might suppose that

[45] *Ibid*, 60.

[46] *Ibid*, 63. She is referencing M Foucault, *Power/Knowledge: Selected Interviews and Other Writings 1972–1977* (ed Colin Gordon) (Harvester Press, 1980) 84.

[47] See, eg, D Bell, 'Racial Realism', and G Peller, 'Race-Consciousness', both reproduced in K Crenshaw *et al* (eds), *Critical Race Theory: The Key Writings That Formed the Movement* (The New Press, 1995) 302 and 127 respectively. In *Race-Consciousness*, Peller traces the struggle between

it would make eminent sense to carve out a field of 'Tribalcrit', akin to the emerging fields of 'Latcrit' and 'Asiancrit', which would push Critical Race Theory in the direction of Indigenous concerns.[48]

An immediate problem with this move, noted by Indigenous scholars, is the risk in such a move of downgrading or overlooking the key political aspect of Indigenous struggles, tied to the vast and complex history of interactions between the Crown/state and Indigenous peoples.[49] Therein lays a larger problem, the potential existence of numerous other hidden implications in the adoption of a theoretical framework. Over-swift adoption of a theory with roots in another context may lead to numerous implications not as immediately obvious to the eye as those of an overtly political nature.

The Indigenous legal theorist faces challenging work. Not only is there a wealth of non-Indigenous theory to wade through, much of which is complex (sometimes because it borders on the incoherent, or because a label only indicates a movement, and not a tight body of thought), but the Indigenous legal theorist must also come to grips with each theory in light of the potential dangers attendant on adopting theoretical insights in the context of distinct and independent Indigenous aims.

The last two sections of this Chapter are meant to illustrate several matters tied to this vision of the work of the Indigenous legal scholar. The next section illustrates how presumptions and claims may lie buried in non-Indigenous theories, presumptions and claims that may be less than palatable to the Indigenous theorist seeking understandings and explanations that accord with her grounding in an Indigenous community. We will see, however, that there are features inherent in the project of theorising from the perspectives of Indigenous peoples that can turn some such dangers to the advantage of Indigenous scholars. The closing section then explores a few snippets of work from two prominent Indigenous legal scholars working in Canada, striving together to build mechanisms and frameworks that might work for Indigenous scholars searching for better explanations of the world around.[50]

integrationist and nationalist approaches to the race issue in the United States through the tumultuous 1960s and 1970s, and highlights the distinct impressions of the world that emanated from differing cultural/historical backgrounds: 'The black nationalist worldview was based on a fundamentally different set of beliefs and perceptual categories through which reforms that looked progressive to integrationists looked regressive to nationalists' (at 137).

[48] See, eg, RS Chang, 'Toward an Asian American Legal Scholarship: Critical Race Theory, Post-Structuralism, and Narrative Space', and IFH Lopez, 'Race and Erasure: The Salience of Race to Latinos/as', both reproduced in R Delgado and J Stefancic (eds), *Critical Race Theory: The Cutting Edge* (2nd edn, Temple University Press, 2000) 354 and 369 respectively.

[49] See, in this regard, BKJ Brayboy, 'Toward a Tribal Critical Race Theory in Education' (2005) 37 *The Urban Review* 425.

[50] See, eg, J Borrows, 'Creating an Indigenous Legal Community' (2005) 50(1) *McGill Law Journal* 153.

2. 'Truth': Thinking Through the Use of Non-Indigenous Theories

In some way or other all theories about the law rest on deeper visions about the notion of 'truth'. We can note on a simple level that, in saying that all theories are meant to provide explanations of phenomena, a link is forged between the existence of theoretical models and their bodies of subject matter. Some might invoke the notion of truth at this point, saying that a particular theoretical model is 'true' when it accurately portrays the subject matter under analysis. We earlier noted in passing a general statement made by positivists—that law is that which is positively appropriately asserted by either legislatures or courts. Is this statement 'true'? Some might see the appropriate metric to be the simple matter of the degree to which this statement captures a 'fact' about the world.[51]

We noted earlier as well, however, how quickly matters around the activity of legal theorising get complex and murky. In what sense are there legal 'facts' which legal theories might strive to capture? Is there an essential role in this arrangement played by the theorist (does the theorist inevitably contribute her own conceptual filters and other interpretative apparatus to the task of theory-generation)? Clearly some of these concerns can play out in reflections on the nature of 'truth' and its connection to the activity of theorising.

It is essential that the Indigenous legal theorist reflect on this point, carefully considering the fact that how one thinks about something as straightforward as 'truth' may indeed reflect aspects of the historical, cultural and social background of the scholar pondering these matters. It is essential, for example, that the Indigenous legal theorist note that non-Indigenous legal theorists have built up their own tangled webs of arguments and positions around questions circling the activity of legal theorising, all of which play an enormous role in determining the nature of the theories they have adopted. If the Indigenous legal theorist is to make use of non-Indigenous legal theories, she will have to keep this in mind, so she can ensure that her work speaks to the concerns and understandings of her community.

In this section one instance of the interconnections between non-ILT and deeper philosophical commitments is explored, so as to both illustrate the kinds of concerns that can arise in this context and make some suggestions about how the Indigenous scholar might respond to them. This analysis will track the notion of 'truth', and explore how varied non-Indigenous understandings of 'truth' can sit buried deep within varied non-Indigenous legal theories.

3. Putting to Use Varied Notions of Truth

Much of the wing of 'progressive' theorising—strains within the critical movement, and many working within the postmodern rubric—rest one pillar of their

[51] Or, the degree to which it captures something about the concept, if this is meant to be an assertion made in the context of conceptual analysis.

theoretic foundation on a denial of correspondence theories of truth and knowledge. Correspondence theories hold that the truth of any particular statement depends on its connection to a reality that exists independent of the statement (where the statement expresses a proposition that purports to correspond to this independent reality, through some process of 're-presentation'). Under this model of truth, the truth of the propositions making up a theory of law would depend on the degree to which these statements correspond to a mind-independent reality.[52]

Many critical and postmodern theorists, however, are sceptical that any such connection can be demonstrated, or even that it makes sense to engage in the project of assessing statements by the degree to which they correspond to some mind-independent reality. They decry efforts in the West over the last few centuries at arriving at a satisfactory theory of justification underlying this notion of language-reality correspondence. Reaching back to the arguments of Protagoras, strengthened in their resolve by the arguments of such luminaries as Hume, Nietzsche, James, Derrida, Foucault and Rorty, tired of the endless search for this Holy Grail, these theorists strive to build alternative understanding of what it is for a proposition to be 'true'. Some would follow Protagoras' lead and make 'man the measure of all things'. For some, a proposition's truth value would be seen as depending not on the extent to which it corresponds with a given reality, but on the extent to which it coheres within a system of beliefs, and/or the degree to which it may be considered useful, and/or the degree to which it may allow us to 'cope' and not 'copy'.[53] Folding back on itself, the very notion of truth comes to be seen as any other conceptual entity—something constructed within a historical/social setting, serving certain purposes.

These latter sorts of approaches to understanding 'truth' can be quite useful to the Indigenous legal theorist. They help in building up arguments around how non-Indigenous scholars have constructed conceptual structures in order to achieve certain ideological or political goals. The Indigenous scholar, for example, might argue that the theory of Social Darwinism, put to use in developing and maintaining many of the most harmful Crown polices and legal instruments from

[52] This is one way to formulate a correspondence theory of truth. I put it this way to avoid murkier metaphysical conundrums that can arise when the distinction is framed more as one between a perceptual world (of things as they are perceived) and a real world (of 'things-in-themselves', things that ontologically exist independent of the world perceived). The less metaphysically bound version I employ looks for correspondence between a statement about the world of our perceptions, and the things we perceive. So, for example, a statement like 'it is raining outside' would be true simply if it was in fact raining outside. The key distinction is between the statement or proposition and the state of the world, independent of how it *happens* to be perceived. That is, the challenge to this sort of theory is generally from the arena of subjectivity—how do we know that the world we experience is as experienced, when all we have to go by are *subjective* experiences, which may vary between subjects. See S Blackburn, *Truth: A Guide* (Oxford University Press, 2005), particularly at section 2.3 ('The Variation of Subjectivities') 32–6.

[53] See, again, Blackburn, *ibid.* The latter is an allusion to Rorty's position, laid out in R Rorty, *Philosophy and the Mirror of Nature* (Blackwell, 1980), and *The Consequences of Pragmatism (Essays: 1972–1980)* (University of Minnesota Press, 1982).

the late 19th century onward, was never meant to describe any aspect of 'reality', but to justify the pursuit of certain colonial goals and objectives.[54]

What may happen—and arguably ought to—when Indigenous scholars consider appropriating these sorts of theoretical insights is that they become adopted in a particularly circumscribed manner. The qualification is simple—such insights can be put to the task of making sense of some of the forces that have been deployed against Indigenous communities, but they need not—and often should not—be taken any further. When an Indigenous scholar makes use of an insight drawn from non-Indigenous worlds, there is no need to suppose that she has therefore adopted some aspect of the worldview of the West. There is no requirement, in particular, that making use of such an insight commits the Indigenous scholar to more far-reaching or universal overtones. For example, in making use of critical notions of truth in analysing the actions of legal actors in the non-Indigenous world, there is no implication that the Indigenous legal scholar is thereby automatically swept up in the sort of conceptual entanglements that threaten to strangle the postmodern/critical theorist.[55] In particular, finding that what critical scholars have to say about 'truth' is useful in making sense of how others have acted is not a jump to the adoption of a pragmatic approach to truth. The Indigenous legal theorist can make use of insights concerning the use of 'truth' by non-Indigenous forces to reveal the nature of the conflicts within which they find themselves enmeshed, and yet fall back on their own understandings of law and society (and their own conceptions of 'truth') to undergird their own political struggles.

Clearly, caution must be paramount. When making use of such a tool in such a context, is the Indigenous scholar being consciously strategic in its deployment? Or, has the Indigenous scholar made it clear to her audiences that she is describing non-Indigenous systems with the use of non-Indigenous tools? The very real possibility exists that the community the Indigenous theorist is from does not have ties to a cultural history that comfortably leads down a path toward postmodern or critical understandings of truth. Is the Indigenous legal theorist appropriately accommodating the possibility that these (essentially inter-subjective or pragmatic) theories of truth are yet further conceptual tools intended (by non-Indigenous powers) to achieve certain political goals? Does the Indigenous theorist, caught up working in the Western academy, realise that this may be so? The caution advocated by Smith and Gandhi must lead the way.

The implication, nevertheless, is not that Indigenous scholars should avoid the use of these sorts of conceptual tools. Rather, they should be careful in their use—either by deploying 'truth' strategically, or by making clear that the uses to which they are putting this conceptual tool may have little or nothing to say about

[54] See, in a related note, A Anghie, 'Francisco de Vittoria and the Colonial Origins of International Law' (1996) 5 *Social and Legal Studies* 321.

[55] See, eg, SM Feldman, 'Playing with the Pieces: Postmodernism in the Lawyer's Toolbox' (1999) 85 *Virginia Law Review* 151.

Indigenous understandings of truth that lie at the core of the lives of their particular Indigenous communities (if that be the case).

4. Re-Examining Arguments for ILT

Having stated and restated the extent to which the principle of caution must rule the lives of Indigenous legal scholars, it might be instructive to note how this principle plays out in the context of the sort of work being carried out in this Chapter. That is, the same degree of caution must be exercised in relation to arguments developed in support of the activity of Indigenous legal theorising (and not just the content of Indigenous legal theories, as they are being articulated). In the midst of thinking about arguments that support the development of Indigenous legal theories, perhaps we unwittingly fell into accepting buried presuppositions or deeper theoretical commitments that might run counter to the understandings contained within Indigenous communities.

This discussion nicely dovetails with our concerns over the appropriation of non-Indigenous theory, for one common thread weaving through these arguments lies at the core of the development of Critical Race Theory (CRT). One might suppose that an Indigenous scholar could be led to the notion of an ILT through consideration of the insights of CRT. Is this a dangerous path to tread? How can possible threats be identified and defused? To explore these questions we (a) look to how the earlier arguments in support of an ILT developed in relation to notions of 'truth', (b) briefly discuss how CRT ties into these notions, and then (c) consider how an Indigenous scholar could safely deploy elements of this non-Indigenous theory. Robert Williams provides one example of how this can be deftly accomplished.[56]

Let us return to the set of arguments presented in support of the notion of Indigenous legal theorising (as a process developing a body of theory emergent out of Indigenous communities), to see how the notion of 'truth' might be employed in that more abstract context. The focus of inquiry will be the extent to which using non-Indigenous theories and insights might pull Indigenous theorists into making commitments that potentially run counter to the beliefs and interests of Indigenous communities.

Three kinds of arguments were generated (or suggested) in support of the need for legal theory about and emanating from Indigenous communities: (a) arguments resting weight on the distinct cultural and experiential groundings of Indigenous peoples (and on the cultural impact on experience itself), (b) arguments that spoke to the idea of a collective voice, expressing the will of an Indigenous community, and (c) arguments that focused on the possibility that conceptual and normative frame-

[56] See, eg, R Williams Jr, 'Vampires Anonymous and Critical Race Practice' (1997) 95 *Michigan Law Review* 741, and 'Documents of Barbarism: The Contemporary Legacy of European Racism and Colonialism in The Narrative Traditions of Federal Indian Law' (1989) 31 *Arizona Law Review* 237, both reprinted in R Delgado and J Stefancic, above n 48, 614 and 94 respectively.

works, supplied by the distinct cultural world-views of Indigenous communities, could fundamentally structure the very theories themselves that Indigenous scholars might generate. In our original classificatory enterprise the position of the strategist (developing Indigenous legal theories with an eye to nothing more than the will of the community, regardless of the relationship of these theories to aims of cultural revitalisation) floated over toward the last kind of argument, for it was imagined that the aim of the strategist was not to attempt to present explanatory models of the law that emerged from Indigenous cultural perspectives, but simply to build *useful* theories (for whatever aim dictated by the collective). On the other hand, we also entertained the possibility that all theories in the social realm are indeed nothing more than expressions of situated theorists (individuals living in particular times and places, embedded in particular cultural milieus). If one accepts this latter view as capturing all social theorising, one could argue for the development of ILT as nothing more than the project of constructing a system of thought saying something about—indeed saying nothing beyond—the ideological/cultural position of the theorist.

All these arguments seem to derive support from, or rest upon, the notion of perspectival truth. That is, when searching for justification for the project of developing ILT we seemed driven to the notion of truth grounded in, or emanating from, the perspective of the truth-seeker. This is hardly surprising, given that we are investigating arguments for the development of *Indigenous* legal theories. Have we, however, committed ourselves to a picture of the development of ILT that comes tied to subjectivised or limited notions of truth and knowledge? We earlier noted[57] the possibility that all legal theory might be infected by the perspective of the theorist. This notion must be fleshed out, for only with a closer look into the matter can we lay bare—and hopefully provide paths around—potential dangers lurking for the Indigenous scholar.

A legal theory might be linked to notions of perspectival truth in several ways. We can begin by noting that one might suppose that any theory (no matter what the subject matter or realm of inquiry) will bear some traces of its origins in the human agent. This can be a contentious matter in the physical sciences.[58] In the realm of the social sciences—and even more so in the realm of legal theorising—this is not nearly so contentious an issue. The law itself is acknowledged by most to be a human construct.[59] How hard is it to imagine that the conceptual constructs used to make sense of this institutional/social construct will reflect the fact that the seeker of knowledge herself comes to the task with the limited tools supplied by her location in a particular time and place—the tools of her historically and culturally determined language, employed in the context of her particularity in a historical time, place and culture?

[57] This was towards the end of our discussion about the peculiarities of legal theorising, about those factors that seem to separate out the activity of legal theorising from theorising in the physical sciences.

[58] Eg, some with strong Kantian grounding might push this line, arguing that even space and time, themselves underlying the 'categories of the understanding', are inextricably tied to our human nature.

[59] Even Aquinas, for example, would acknowledge that human law is human-made, at best roughly approximating divine law: Aquinas, above n 6.

Acknowledging that a legal theorist comes to the task of theorising from a time, place and culture does not necessarily imply something substantive about the *content* of any theoretical model developed. There seems no reason to suppose that the mere fact the theoretician is limited in her conceptual tool chest to tools that reflect her situation in a particular time/place/culture will prevent her from saying something *truthful* about this way things are.[60] However, a legal theory may also reflect powerful ideological groundings, as a theorist may develop and present a theory that advances a certain political agenda. This may be done with different degrees of conscious intent, but whatever the explicit intent such a situation immediately calls into question the relationship between the theory propounded and the state of the world it purports to be about.[61] One might suspect that the theory is not really meant to relate to some given world, but rather to achieve some other end, only tangentially related to the idea of modelling the world (the theorist is not concerned so much with *modelling* the world as with *creating* the world).

The first two sorts of arguments for the development of ILT only commit us to the weak form of perspectivism. That is, we can imagine Indigenous scholars developing explanatory models of the law that bear some imprint tied to the theorists' positions in the world, flowing from the fact that they are working from particular cultural and experiential spaces, and/or from the fact they are working as agents of political collectives, but still imagine that the models developed can successfully relate to the world around (hopefully providing insights that say something meaningful about the way things actually are). The last sort of argument, meanwhile, envisions Indigenous scholars developing theoretical models that unavoidably call into question whether they are operating under critical or postmodern understandings of truth. Operating as if theories are constructed so as to advance certain ideological or cultural positions moves one away from objectives of description (and indeed of modelling).

The Indigenous scholar is not, however, entrapped in a nest of contradictory commitments to varied notions of truth. She can choose to work 'politically', pushing theoretical positions and arguments that work to advance the interests of her community. She can, alternatively, choose to push outward from Indigenous understandings, presenting to the world models that emerge from unique experiential and cultural groundings. Indeed, a single theorist could choose to work from either position, depending on the nature of her immediate project (though this could get messy over time).

Key to the promise of ILT is the way it sits in the contemporary world resting on an intellectual history with deep roots distinct from those of the West. That

[60] Here, reverting for the moment to a correspondence theory of truth.

[61] I have in mind here individual psychological idiosyncrasies, but also situations wherein a scholar is so deeply embedded in a cultural project, framed by a larger set of historical, political and social circumstances, that she is unaware of the fact that the work she is engaged with is meant to promote a particular political agenda (of which she may be quite unaware). Many non-Indigenous legal scholars, I would suspect, fall into this grouping—they may be unaware of the deeply colonial nature of their work (they may be quite unaware of Canada's deep colonial history and nature, and how they speak out of this).

history is now generations into an encounter with the West, but with an emphasis on revitalisation. Indigenous scholars can work from platforms that afford unique and insightful windows into legal phenomena. They also have the need to defend their nations from the continuing encounter with the West, a task that may press them into the sort of ideologically driven arguments and assumptions that historically marked much legal 'theorising' in the West. Waging the second sort of struggle—which may necessitate employing tools that come with their own histories in the West—does not preclude struggles of the first sort—which may include projects built around Indigenous notions of truth, wisdom, meaning and understanding.

Consider Robert Williams' embrace of CRT. This is a theory with a short but turbulent history. Born out of dissatisfaction with the direction taken by (or lack of direction of) Critical Legal Studies, this approach to the study of law retained certain elements of its progenitor, while focusing on the insights that emerge from study of the law from the position of those subject to its racist force. One element retained from Critical Legal Studies is its 'critical' stance, which in the world of the early 21st century unpacks as a commitment to certain positions that flow from a rejection of the project of Modernity. So, for example, CRT assumes a non-essentialist stance in relation to the meaning of terms. Language (along with all other aspects of our social world) is seen as localised in time and place, with words only having the meaning they have at the moment, in the game being presently played within a language community.[62]

This is at the core of Jayne Chong-Soon Lee's critique of Anthony Appiah's attempt to 'map race'.[63] While generally appreciative of Appiah's work, Lee takes him to task for not seeing that his argument for a shift from 'race' talk to 'culture' talk will prevent us from having meaningful discussions about the continuing impact of morphological features of race in contemporary society (the fact, for example, that skin-colour does indeed continue to have an impact on people's lives and experiences). Lee's critique, one might imagine, is grounded in facts embedded in the world—facts based in biology and perceptual matters. To an extent this is so, but given CRT's adherence to anti-essentialism the deeper argument has to do with the ability to *talk* in a certain way, which is something that must be constantly understood to be embedded in our dynamic world of ever-shifting meaning. In a sense, in eschewing any connection between race and biology Appiah ignores the over-arching theory of the social construction of meaning that he claims to work under. Lee asks that we keep the construction of meaning forever in the foreground of our analysis—we have to see that linking race to biology is itself a matter of the social construction of meaning, and as such it must be explored historically, and carefully considered in each context to

[62] This is not to say that meaning is a stable feature of all language communities. Some communities are terribly fractured, and the meanings of key terms are endlessly—and even violently—contested.

[63] YC Lee, 'Navigating the Topology of Race', in Crenshaw *et al*, above n 47, 441. The focus of her analysis is A Appiah, *In My Father's House: Africa in the Philosophy of Culture* (Oxford University Press, 1992).

determine its *usefulness.* Nonetheless, there may be 'raced' communities that wish to use their own constructions of meaning, likewise linking race to biology, in furtherance of their struggles. So, for example, black American communities may want to deploy such instruments as affirmative action programmes in a battle against the liberal ideology of absolute race neutrality, and in doing so they may find it necessary to use the term 'race' in a way that maintains some of its linkages to its troubling past.

In his use of CRT, Williams makes use of such notions as the social construction of meaning. He began to 'recover' as a law professor when he realised (and wrote about) the deep racist roots of federal Indian law and policy in the United States.[64] This form of writing, based in a theoretical framework supplied by such Western intellectuals as Foucault, Derrida and Nietzsche, gave him something meaningful to say about the law in the United States, something that centred on its use of legal discourse in dispossessing and oppressing Indian nations.

But CRT could only provide a first, small step on the way to recovery—to avoid becoming a vampire (a typical law professor, member of a coterie removed from the concerns of humanity, unconcerned with the suffering of others—especially Indians!) he had to move beyond a solitary existence putting together written work read by a handful of other similarly stunted individuals: he had to move to a world of 'Critical Race Practice'. Williams' move to a form of praxis is quite instructive—he does so on the basis of his Lumbee upbringing, on the basis of his understanding of what it is to be a Lumbee. 'Think independently and act for others' was a key injunction in his youth, capturing the heart of a way of living based on a core sense of responsibilities to family, tribe and people. Over time he makes service to others—in particular to the tribes around the University of Arizona—a defining element in his understanding of what it is to think about the world from a CRT stance.

CRT stands then as a way for Williams to intellectually deconstruct the nature of American law and policy, while living as a Lumbee requires that this be supplemented with truths that emanate from his Indian roots. Are these truths nothing more than 'social constructions'? Must Williams eschew any suggestion that his Lumbee nation could think of their ways of living as 'true'. Must he avoid suggesting that his people possess truths that say something deeply meaningful about how the Lumbee think it is right and proper to live in the world as good people?

Must the Indigenous scholar, in making use of non-Indigenous theory, succumb to charges that her theoretical work is all irreducibly infected with the assumptions and arguments that rest on the history of the West's struggle with modernity? No, for the argument in this section has been that the position of the Indigenous scholar is unique. It is the position of a scholar facing grave external threats that may only be met if non-Indigenous tools are picked up and wielded, but it is also the position of a person tied to a cultural community with its own

[64] Williams, above n 56. The description of his intellectual and moral growth comes from *Vampires Anonymous.*

distinct intellectual history. These distinct intellectual histories are not only capable of grounding distinct theories about the law, but also capable of supporting those theories with thoughts and ideas around such matters as 'truth', 'meaning', and 'knowledge'.

This early foray into the development of Indigenous legal theory concludes with a brief look at how two contemporary Indigenous legal scholars work with both theoretical and methodological matters as they both challenge the dominant system of law and hint at what their own Indigenous communities have to say about law.

F. Indigenous Theorising I: Borrows' Admonishment From the Margins

In 'Questioning Canada's Title to Land: The Rule of Law, Aboriginal Peoples, and Colonialism' (a chapter in the text *Recovering Canada: The Resurgence of Indigenous Law*[65]), John Borrows looks at the act in Canada of the assertion of Crown sovereignty (with underlying title). As we noted earlier, this is one of those tremendously significant events in the legal/political history of Canada-Indigenous relations viewed completely differently by the two sides to the event. Early in the chapter he makes a general point:

> Many people assume that since their experience of life in Canada is one of fairness and justice, most people must experience life in Canada in this way. However, Canada is a country that does not have an 'even' experience of justice.[66]

Borrows notes later that should the courts of Canada seriously question the validity of Crown title and sovereignty, '[m]ost Canadians would consider a decision to this effect unreasonable, impractical, unrealistic, unsound, and indicative of a lack of knowledge of the law or history of Aboriginal rights', while Aboriginal peoples would by and large 'consider such a conclusion reasonable, practical, realistic, sensible, and demonstrative of an understanding of the law and history of Aboriginal rights'.[67]

My intent in this section is to walk through some of the key arguments Borrows develops in this chapter, with an eye to seeing how one can place this selection from his text into the framework built up in the preceding sections of this Chapter. A fair amount of interpolation and extrapolation will be carried out, for this chapter from Borrows' text does not contain an explicit discussion of the place of theory in the debates over Aboriginal rights or Indigenous law in Canada. Nevertheless, it is quite clear that Borrows, as any legal scholar engaged in a sustained critique of some aspect of the law, makes heavy use of certain theoretical

[65] Borrows, *Recovering Canada*, above n 1.
[66] *Ibid*, 114.
[67] *Ibid*, 121.

positions, arguments and presuppositions. It is my intent to look at some of these to illustrate how complex and subtle the use of theory can be in the context of the interaction of the Crown and Indigenous peoples.

Borrows makes use of the notion of the rule of law, arguing that this pillar of the Canadian system of law, when exercised appropriately, necessarily calls into question the assertion (and subsequent acquisition) of Crown title and sovereignty in Canada (displacing, as these purportedly do, the prior valid claims of Indigenous peoples).

The 'rule of law' is not a clearly defined jurisprudential notion. Borrows takes its meaning primarily from what the Supreme Court of Canada has itself said about the nature and place of this principle in the Canadian legal and political landscape. The two key aspects of this notion highlighted by the court are its injunction against the exercise of arbitrary power by the state, and its abhorrence of legal and political chaos (its role, that is, in promoting a stable legal order).[68] Under the first aspect we find the notion that the state itself falls under the law (that, in some sense, the law is sovereign—a notion now encapsulated in Canadian law in section 52 of the Constitution Act 1982, which provides that the Constitution is the supreme law in Canada). This principle upholds the ideal, then, that state action must not reflect 'personal' goals, but rather such action must accord with the law of the land.

With many illustrations, Borrows details the many ways that the governments of Canada have often acted with clear bias against Aboriginal peoples in Canada. The one key (and fundamental) event, however, is the acquisition of title and sovereignty. In asserting title and sovereignty with little or no regard for the pre-existing status of Indigenous peoples, the state acted 'arbitrarily', in contradiction to the rule of law.

It is not obvious what theoretical positions Borrows adopts in making this argument—not only because Borrows does not make it so, but quite likely because it is possible that in relation to some theoretical or fundamental principles Borrows is not so much interested in the adoption of these principles but in their utility in making certain arguments. It may well be that he uses certain principles and arguments in order to reach certain conclusions. Nevertheless, whether or not Borrows adheres to these, we can identify certain theoretical claims about the nature of the law upon which the general argument rests.

The rule of law can be cast as an essentially procedural safeguard, preventing the state from acting without working its way through the appropriate stages of law-making (in many democratic systems this manifests in a system of checks and balances, with, for example, the executive branch prevented from acting in certain areas reserved to the purview of the legislative branch, with an independent judiciary overseeing all). Borrows, however, does not limit himself to such a notion of the rule of law (often criticised as being a hollow shell, since if this were all the rule

[68] Borrows, *Recovering Canada*, above n 1, 116.

of law amounted to there would be no limit to state action, so long as the government 'acted appropriately'[69]).

Borrows references remarks from Aristotle and the preamble to the Constitution Act 1982 to introduce the notion of 'right' laws (tied to the 'supremacy of God'), which would provide the sort of solid foundation upon which must rest the operation of the rule of law.[70] He appears to advocate, then, a natural law approach, with the state properly ruled over by—and so bound to follow—'right' laws (seemingly, those that emerge from a recognition of the supremacy of God).

Does Borrows, as an Indigenous legal theorist, accept a picture of the law as rightly resting on deeper moral precepts (perhaps themselves reflective of God's will)? Here, again, things get murky, for it is not necessary that Borrows commit to this picture, given his self-described task as a critic of the application of Canadian law to Indigenous peoples in Canada. He does not necessarily speak from within the dominant system of beliefs, a system purportedly built around an adherence to the ideal of the rule of law. It could quite well be that he stands outside this world-system, asking of the dominant system of law why, from within *its* web of principles, it fails to be consistent (an especially pressing point, as the principle at issue is one meant to oversee consistency!). Borrows might well be examining the dominant system from a point outside, querying what seems to be a matter of internal inconsistency.

This argument seems to function, then, without appeal to any measure of critical theory. Borrows does not seem to argue, for example, that the dominant system is essentially political in nature, that its legal system actually reflects nothing more than the particular interests of certain groups with power over the development and maintenance of the law. On the other hand, as the chapter progresses a subtle argument begins to emerge, one with a clear connection in this context to critical legal theorising.

Earlier we noted how Borrows highlights the way that the law in Canada appears in quite a different light depending on whether one enjoys its stability and other fruits or whether one lives within an Indigenous community, the beneficiary of generations of oppression and dispossession. With this book his primary audience is most assuredly non-Indigenous society, and his message: 'you live within a system that claims to be built around certain principles, but which seems quite removed from these, when seen from an Indigenous perspective'. Indeed, expanding on this notion of perspectival revelations, in the second half of the chapter Borrows goes on to examine how the set of fundamental (unwritten) constitutional principles that Canadian society rests upon look when 'interrogated' through a lens generated from a perspective that includes Indigenous legal orders. The general conclusion reached is that 'Aboriginal self-determination

[69] *Ibid*, 115. Borrows notes that some argue that the rule of law may be a 'hollow phrase' if it can be somehow 'used by those who want to govern others to accomplish their own purposes'. He here cites A Hutchinson and P Monahan (eds), *The Rule of Law: Idea or Ideology* (Carswell, 1987).

[70] He quotes sections from E Barker (ed), *The Politics of Aristotle* (Oxford University Press, 1958) 126–7.

should receive negotiated expression within Canada through an appropriate extension of the rule of law in matters of federalism, democracy, and minority protection'.[71]

Borrows' next line is telling: 'Otherwise, we might properly regard the Crown's treatment of Aboriginal peoples as 'colonial rule' that leads to their 'subjugation, domination and exploitation' and blocks their 'meaningful exercise of self-determination'.[72] One might see here a proposition embedded in a subtle argument about the nature of the dominant legal system, an argument that calls into question the purportedly apolitical nature of Canadian law.

Earlier Borrows had built up the central argument of the chapter around the notion that the rule of law functions to forbid 'arbitrary' state action. The meaning attributed to 'arbitrary' is fairly narrow, the term applying to 'personal' or 'biased' action, in some sense of these terms.[73] These two terms, however, can point to quite different phenomena, as one might say that a government body acts 'personally' when it has in mind promoting its own particular interests (as when a government official might take advantage of his position to make a small fortune), and one might say that a government body demonstrates 'bias' when it acts in a way that promotes the interests of a certain group (to which it may or may not be directly connected).

At a general level, then, we can say that Borrows' argument is meant to link up the notion of the rule of law with some generalised sense of equal and fair treatment (which would define what constitutes its opposite, 'biased' treatment). In providing an overview of state action in relation to Aboriginal peoples, Borrows notes many instances of unequal and unfair treatment. Through the long history of colonial rule, there are many instances of government actions that are 'arbitrary' only in this narrow sense, since these things were done for very specific reasons.

Thus the key question is whether we must characterise such state action as 'illegal'. Borrows' final suggestion seems to be that the answer is now in the hands of Canadian society. Two options are presented—either the rule of law is seen as more than a merely rhetorical device, so that Canadian society is forced to consider the possibility that there are serious problems with the very legitimacy of Crown title and sovereignty, or the rule of law is really a smokescreen, an empty principle masking deeper political forces and manoeuvrings (all of an essentially colonial nature).

Borrows' chapter, then, might be seen as presenting a test for the plausibility of the critical position—if the Canadian system continues to ignore what seem to be matters of clear bias in the very original acts that led to its creation, acts that should be open to legal analysis, then perhaps the law really is nothing more than a tool of oppression put to constant use to dispossess and subjugate Indigenous peoples.

[71] Borrows, above n 1, 136.

[72] *Ibid*, 136. Borrows is quoting from *Reference Re Secession of Quebec* [1998] 2 SCR 217, 284–6.

[73] One might also call an action arbitrary when it is non-directed, perhaps as the result of the flip of a coin.

So we might 'properly regard the Crown's treatment of Aboriginal peoples as "colonial rule"'.[74]

Interestingly, however, this interpretation of the general argument in Borrows' text has little to say of a direct nature about how Indigenous communities might think of 'the law'. Borrows is engaged in one particular form of legal analysis, an examination of the interaction of the dominant system of law and Indigenous peoples—an examination vastly enriched through his presentation of how the dominant system looks to Indigenous peoples, an examination removed from questions about how Indigenous communities themselves regulate their own social behaviour. It provides a locus for discussion around certain ways Indigenous scholars might think of using theoretical positions, principles and presuppositions, all in serious pursuit of both understanding better the nature of the dominant legal system, and of working out strategies to move the discourse around the dominant legal system in directions more fruitful for Indigenous communities (and more fruitful for those who think there might be strong connections between moral precepts and 'right' laws).[75]

G. Indigenous Theorising II: Monture-Angus on the Nature of Canadian Law

In the second chapter of her text *Journeying Forward*,[76] Patricia Monture-Angus examines what she takes to be a serious lack of theoretical underpinning for the vast sea-changes in Canadian constitutional law concerning Aboriginal rights that have occurred over the last few decades. This theoretical vacuum is the result not only of a lack of reasoning on the part of the courts, for '[l]egal academics are . . . equally responsible'.[77] Monture-Angus provides a theoretically descriptive backdrop to this lack of theorising, as she proceeds through an analysis of recent Canadian case law. In this last section of this collection of thoughts around the emergence of Indigenous legal theorising, the discussion turns to how explicit attempts at Indigenous theorising can open legal and political discourse in Canada to ways of going forward that promise an 'even' experience of justice for both Indigenous and non-Indigenous societies.

Monture-Angus is not concerned solely with a lack of Indigenous theorising about Aboriginal rights, but rather with a lack of theorising from all perspectives, and in particular with a lack of theorising that aims to integrate the world-views of both Indigenous and non-Indigenous society. Much of what passes for the context

[74] Borrows, above n 1, 136.

[75] It should be noted that much of the rest of Borrows' text, *Recovering Canada*, does rest on the articulation of Anishinabek understandings of law and society.

[76] Monture-Angus, above n 2.

[77] *Ibid*, 58.

in which Aboriginal rights are discussed and litigated is a simple wall of assumptions, presumptions and bald assertions, a wall entirely constructed by non-Indigenous authorities. Monture-Angus sees here not a simple lack of clear reasoning, but processes which are deeply troubling, especially when experienced from an Indigenous perspective.

She notes that as a Kanien'kehaka (Mohawk) woman she speaks from a particular perspective on the law, one based both in experience and cultural grounding. Her experience helps in revealing the nature of the law as it relates to Indigenous communities in Canada: 'I use my lived experience to help me accomplish this task of recognising mono-culturalism in Canadian law'.[78] This lived experience speaks to the dissonance between how non-Indigenous and Indigenous people experience the law.[79]

This is a lived experience passing through the lens of her cultural grounding as a Mohawk woman. It lays bare the myth of objectivity wielded by Canadian judges, those who work within systems built around such Western constructs as 'rights' and the 'public/private divide'. Unlike the grounds of Borrows' quieter admonishment to Canadian society (the admonishment to not merely acknowledge—but overcome—its colonial past), Monture-Angus looks at Canadian law in its historical interaction with Indigenous peoples and sees it built on racist assumptions (the assumption of the superiority of Euro-Canadian legal and political systems), the very same racist assumptions that seem to account for the blindness built into current jurisprudence.

The past flows into the present, and it seems incumbent on those of clear mind to acknowledge that the means and ways by which the law has been used to oppress and dispossess Indigenous communities continue to function. The focus of her book is the current development of jurisprudence around Aboriginal and treaty rights constitutionally recognised and affirmed in section 35 of the Constitution Act 1982. Monture-Angus sees in the way Canadian courts turn to the task of interpreting this constitutional instrument 'a dangerous potential for the judicial determination of rights to occur in such a way that the difference in meaning attached to this word by Aboriginal Peoples will be invisible and therefore excluded'.[80]

Her work goes to support points made earlier about the powerful need for Indigenous legal theorising. Indigenous scholars, grounded in their communities, must articulate how the dominant system presents itself to them, as this adds a layer of description of this legal system that enriches theoretical understandings of the nature of this particular legal system. These experientially grounded descriptions then feed into revelations about how the dominant system interacts with those it has attempted to displace (which goes to support the nationalist justification of the need for Indigenous legal theorising).

[78] Monture-Angus, above n 2, 49.
[79] *Ibid*, 54.
[80] *Ibid*, 55.

Around and through all of this can emerge Indigenous conceptions of their own systems of law, and indeed Indigenous conceptions of how their own understandings of law might inform cross-cultural conceptions of things like 'rights'. For example, understanding that concepts like 'rights' have meanings securely tied to the cultural worlds of Euro-Canadians—a connection between concept and culture that Euro-Canadians by and large fail to see (or acknowledge)—Monture-Angus sketches out in this chapter her vision of one form of an Aboriginal theory of 'rights', one that would make sense to a Kanien'kahaka woman.

This construction of a sketch of a Mohawk notion of rights is tied to Monture-Angus' vision of the deeper nature of the problems facing Indigenous peoples in Canada. She identifies obstacles to the development of a Canadian system of law experienced as 'just' by Aboriginal peoples to be (a) the present lack of articulation as to what the current 'status quo' is around Aboriginal legal claims, (b) an apparent inability (or unwillingness) of Canadian judges to recognise their own cultural grounding, manifest in their inability to see the cultural bias inherent in the decisions they reach, framed in legal terms that only make sense in the limited conceptual horizons constructed within Canadian jurisprudence, and (c) an unwillingness on the part of Canadian law and policy makers to hear the excluded voices of Aboriginal peoples. What ties all these together is a common process of exclusion, the key tool employed by Canadian authorities to maintain their control over Indigenous communities. Articulating alternative Indigenous legal conceptions works to chip away at this process of exclusion, and Monture-Angus has identified where the control over discourse and language is most serious: in the realm of theorising.

The way forward, then, is necessarily at the point of cultural interaction, where Indigenous and non-Indigenous societies meet on the level of meanings and understandings. Monture-Angus narrows her focus even further, noting that in the realm of jurisprudence the key point of cultural contact happens at the level of legal theorising, where Indigenous voices must go into a process of negotiation around the nature and meaning of the very legal terms that would go into a new realm of just jurisprudence.

As we noted at several points in our earlier discussions, this is not a path free of danger—in fact, it is fraught with enormous challenges, at times subtle and hidden. For example, Monture-Angus goes beyond questioning the emphasis on 'property' that goes into current jurisprudence around Aboriginal rights to suggest that an Indigenous perspective on Aboriginal rights would marry notions of property interests to Indigenous human rights, which she equates with rights tied to spiritual and social responsibilities. While this infusion of an Indigenous legal conceptualisation into the dialogue on Aboriginal rights is essential, one has to wonder about the dangers in adopting human rights discourse in this context.

Once again we are faced with questions about the appropriation of a complex legal regime, developed over centuries in the West (and under constant redevelopment), designed around culturally determined underlying epistemological, religious, ontological and political notions, and its application to the context swirling around and through Indigenous interests and concerns. With what presumptions and deeper theoretical principles and positions is the Indigenous scholar possibly becoming entangled?

Consider, for example, what the Supreme Court of Canada has already said about the notion of deploying human rights in the context of Aboriginal claims. In *R v Van der Peet*, the court expressed the view that 'Aboriginal rights' cannot fit into the larger container of 'human rights, as they are, by definition, Aboriginal'.[81] As rights held by a subset of a population, they are not universalisable, while a hallmark of human rights is their universality. This tension led the court to move on to develop the culturally identified rights now defined under the *Van der Peet* test (known colloquially as the 'integral to the distinctive culture' test).

Monture-Angus does not operate within such a narrow view of human rights—indeed, she equates human rights with rights of self-determination, rights recognised in several UN documents. The struggle is in understanding and application of concepts—the core of human rights discourse is still locked to the modernist focus on the individual, while more recent progressive theorising has pushed human rights discourse into the arena of the collective (in particular, of the political collective).

And so the battle is waged—clearly it can be dangerous to try casting Indigenous aspirations within Canadian law in ways that tie them to human rights, as doing so runs directly into an ongoing and vigorous debate over the nature of human rights, but if this is following through on an expression of Indigenous understandings (cast in a way that incorporates non-Indigenous concepts, so that they are understandable to dominant society), then this is a path to be seriously considered. It is a matter of appreciating the nature and scope of dangers that exist, and with caution to act accordingly. One can only hope that being pulled towards a form of discourse that employs the language of human rights (even when enriched with recognition of collective interests) is not itself diversionary, that powerful forces are not hoping that Indigenous scholars push this line detrimentally, so that truly revolutionary action is deflated.

H. A Few Concluding Thoughts

The intent in this work has been to say something about the nature of legal theorising, and how Indigenous legal theorising is possible and essential. The last few sections have focused on the dangers attendant on theorising, and on the promise that critical, yet cautious and wary, theoretical work holds for Indigenous communities.

[81] *R v Van der Peet* [1996] 2 SCR 507.

It is indisputable that much of the 'heavy work' of colonialism has been carried out by the law, and indeed by the construction of the dominant system on a foundation of racist and colonial theoretical presumptions and positions. Indigenous legal scholars in Canada have vital work to do in (a) revealing the ways in which the dominant system has functioned to trap Indigenous aspirations within webs of theory and 'principle', (b) building Indigenous theoretical perspectives on both the dominant legal system and Indigenous legal orders, and (c) articulating how Indigenous understandings and conceptualisations underpin the theoretical perspectives presented.

The tools of non-ILT can be put to these tasks—especially that of making sense of how the dominant system has functioned to oppress and dispossess—so long as Indigenous scholars (a) maintain their grounding in their communities, (b) carefully assess the web of conceptual relationships within which a non-Indigenous theoretical position or argument is embedded in relation to this grounded Indigenous existence, and (c) if necessary, excise the content of the non-Indigenous argument or position from these extraneous matters, so it can safely be implemented by and for Indigenous peoples.

9

Aboriginal Discourse: Gender, Identity, and Community

VAL NAPOLEON

> To remember this history is not for the sake of keeping alive the memories of old tyrannies, but to recognize present tyranny, for these patterns are in us still. It would be strange if they were not.
>
> It is these patterns that I believe we should study, become conscious of, and recognize as they emerge in us and in the societies we live in.
>
> Doris Lessing[1]

A. Introduction

As a young woman in Southern Rhodesia (now Zimbabwe), Doris Lessing rejected the repressive and unjust white-dominated society of Africa and embraced communism as the only possible way to build a better world. She imagined this new world as being founded on certain unquestionable axioms of faith:

> when the war was over and the world was restored to normality, [she said in her 1986 CBC Massey Lectures] everyone would recognize the blessings of communism, and the world would be Communist, and be without crime, race prejudice or sex prejudice . . . We believed that everyone in the world would be living in harmony, love, plenty and peace. For ever. This was insane. And yet we believed it.[2]

Lessing's early idealism has an uncomfortably familiar ring to it because it sounds like some of the rhetoric about future aboriginal[3] self-government in Canada—that once self-government is established, all will be well. This mantra includes additional refrains about sovereignty, self-determination, a return to culture and

[1] D Lessing, *Prisons We Choose to Live Inside* (House of Anansi, 1986) 30.

[2] *Ibid*, 32–3.

[3] This includes First Nations, Inuit, and Métis peoples as per s 35(2) of the Constitution Act 1982, being Schedule B to the Canada Act 1982 (UK), 1982, c 11. I will use 'aboriginal' when referring to ··-enous people in Canada, and 'indigenous' when referring to indigenous peoples elsewhere in the

tradition, spirituality, and the restoration of pre-contact balance and harmony.[4] In this future world, indigenous peoples will resume their former constant state of prayer and oneness with the Creator.[5] Men and women will once again fulfil their traditional, usually idealised, gendered roles according to their cultural mores.[6] Best of all, those aboriginal communities disjointed by colonisation will once again become orderly, safe, and peaceful places in which to raise future generations.

Given this imagined future, there is no present need to address aboriginal women's issues or oppression, because sexism and violence against women are simply the result of colonisation, residential schools, and loss of culture.[7] If with the return of self-government, sexism and its attendant violence will effortlessly disappear, why worry about sex discrimination or gender at all? In fact, raising the spectre of sexism within aboriginal groups is often considered a betrayal of aboriginal people. To suggest that sexism and power imbalances are problems is to actually hinder the achievement of a self-determining and self-governing world. Worse, to worry about sexism in contemporary aboriginal societies is to have been foolishly duped by white women's feminism, which is seen as another form of colonisation.[8] According to many aboriginal men and women, to be a feminist aboriginal woman is to be less aboriginal—inauthentic, colonised, and corrupted. Sold out.

Within the aboriginal discourse, there are some arguments to the effect that aboriginal people have to survive first and deal with sexism later (if it still exists). Aboriginal scholar Andrea Smith asks, 'Whose survival?' She argues that dealing with violence, sexual assault, and other forms of oppression is exactly about sur-

[4] For a critique of how harmony is used to stifle internal conflict and challenges to the status quo, see L Nader, *Harmony Ideology: Justice and Control in a Zapotec Mountain Village* (Stanford University Press, 1990).

[5] Variations of this view are surprisingly common and are advanced by a range of people in communities, social agencies, political organisations, academic institutions, and government.

[6] Compare JA Green, 'Cultural and Ethnic Fundamentalism: The Mixed Potential for Identity, Liberation, and Oppression' in C Schick, J Jaffe and A Watkinson (eds), *Contesting Fundamentalism* (Fernwood, 2004).

[7] There are many forms of violence against aboriginal women in Canada. Much of this violence is deadly and much of it is documented. I am writing from the assumption that the prevalence of such violence is an indicator of sexism in aboriginal societies as it is in Canadian society. See, eg, A McGillivray and B Comaskey, *Black Eyes All of the Time, Intimate Violence, Aboriginal Women, and the Justice System* (University of Toronto Press, 1999); Status of Women, 'Measuring Violence Against Women: Statistical Trends 2006', catalogue no 85-570-XIE (Statistics Canada 2006) www.statcan.ca; W Stewart, A Huntley and F Blaney, 'The Implications of Restorative Justice for Aboriginal Women and Children Survivors of Violence: A Comparative Overview of Five Communities in British Columbia' (Report of the Aboriginal Women's Action Network, Vancouver, July 2001).

[8] While a full discussion of feminism is beyond the scope of this paper, it is important to acknowledge that there are many different feminist theories. Regarding feminist approaches to culture, Maneesha Deckha helpfully categorises feminist scholarship into three groups: (1) universalist, (2) post-colonial, and (3) differentiated. She advocates ethical feminism as a framework to evaluate the treatment of cultural claims by the various feminist theories. See M Deckha, 'Gender, Difference, and Anti-Essentialism: Towards a Feminist Response to Cultural Claims in Law' in A Eisenberg (ed), *Diversity and Equality: The Changing Framework of Freedom in Canada* (UBC Press, 2006) 114.

vival—of aboriginal women.[9] How can aboriginal people survive if aboriginal women do not survive? How can that be survival of aboriginal people? Andrea Smith, Joyce Green, and many other indigenous feminists ask whether there can ever be indigenous self-determination or self-government if the internal oppression of indigenous women is maintained under indigenous regimes.[10]

After all, if aboriginal women are oppressed, who is the self-determining self? Green and a growing number of other indigenous feminist scholars are developing theories that encompass decolonisation and advancement of indigenous political goals nationally and internationally. According to Andrea Smith, '[j]ust because there might not have been sexism in some indigenous societies in 1492 does not mean that we do not have sexism in our societies now. Nor does it mean that we should not deal with the sexism that we now have in our societies'.[11]

Generally, the scholarship relating to aboriginal issues is divided by gender: On one hand, aboriginal women's issues are commonly framed as membership, marital property,[12] violence, family, health, culture, education, and poverty.[13] While these are important matters which have enormous impact on the lives (and deaths)[14] of aboriginal women across Canada and elsewhere, they are like intellectual black holes that capture the voices of aboriginal women and absorb much of their political energy. On the other hand, from my perspective, aboriginal women's issues extend far beyond the usual rubrics of 'women's matters'. There is a lack of academic literature that includes either a gendered or a feminist analysis of the broader indigenous issues of self-determination, self-government, and aboriginal rights. And, while the existing literature certainly includes scholarly articles written by indigenous women, these too usually lack a deliberate gendered or feminist analysis.[15] Why is it so difficult to write and speak as an indigenous woman,

[9] A Smith, 'The Future of Native Studies' (keynote address, 'Race/Culture Divide in Education and the Helping Professions', 5th Annual Canadian Critical Race Conference, Researchers and Academics of Colour for Equity/Centre for Social Justice and Anti-Oppressive Education, University of Regina, 4–6 May 2006).

[10] See J Green (ed), *Making Space for Indigenous Feminism* (Fernwood, 2007).

[11] Author interview on 5 May 2006 with Smith, above n 9.

[12] Issues of membership and marital property on reserve have primarily involved aboriginal (ie, First Nations, Indian) women who are registered under the Indian Act, RSC 1985, c I-5. The Indian Act does not apply to Inuit or Métis women, or to First Nations women who are not registered as status Indians under the Act.

[13] See, eg, B Jacobs, 'Review of Beijing from an Indigenous Perspective' (report, Secretariat Permanent Forum on Indigenous Issues, 3 March 2005) at www.un.org/esa/socdev/unpfii/documents/presentation_jacobs_en.doc; E LaRocque, 'Re-examining Culturally Appropriate Models in Criminal Justice Applications' in M Asch (ed), *Aboriginal and Treaty Rights in Canada: Essays on Law, Equality, and Respect for Difference* (UBC Press, 1997); Native Women's Association of Canada (NWAC), www.nwac-hq.org. NWAC and some other aboriginal women's groups are expressly 'anti-feminist'. While these groups are working to address violence against aboriginal women and other symptoms of sexist oppression, they generally do not recognise any feminist theory as useful to their mandates.

[14] For a powerful documentary treatment of the estimated 500 missing aboriginal women in Canada, see Christine Welsh's film, *Finding Dawn* (National Film Board, 2007).

[15] For thoughtful historical and contemporary perspectives, see generally C Miller and P Chuchryk (eds), *Women of the First Nations: Power, Wisdom, and Strength* (University of Manitoba Press, 1996); LF Klein and LA Ackerman (eds), *Women and Power in Native North America* (University of Oklahoma Press, 1995).

explicitly from an indigenous woman's experience, about the broader political issues of self-determination, indigenous legal orders and law, self-government, or aboriginal rights?[16]

In fact, social justice for aboriginal peoples will require a dual approach that encompasses both a gendered or feminist analysis of the broader political issues and the contextualisation of 'women's issues' in a broader analytical political frame. In other words, at both a practical and a theoretical level, the work of each approach must inform the other. Without such a dual political strategy, the appalling disconnect between the political rhetoric and the lives of aboriginal women will persist.

This discussion raises two troubling questions relating to the agency of aboriginal men and women. First, while sexism in aboriginal societies is often described as a legacy of colonialism, how are individual and collective agency factored in?[17] In other words, how does agency factor into the adoption and present-day continuance of sexist practices that are antithetical to the way many aboriginal peoples describe themselves?[18] While we must always situate agency within its larger political frame, how might we consider and learn from the critical interplay between agency, colonialism, and neo-colonialism? The second question is related to the first and is about cognitive dissonance.[19] When describing the multiple oppressions experienced by aboriginal women, there seems to be a natural tendency to focus on aboriginal women being victims. The question is: How does one validate the oppression and suffering of aboriginal women while at the same time appreciating the agency of aboriginal women, as demonstrated by the many ways in which they survived and continue to survive? In fact, this question also applies to aboriginal people generally. In other words, if we focus on colonisation, then do we dishonour all the ways that aboriginal peoples have survived—lifetimes of decisions and actions that represent agency? This is not about acts of resistance alone, but includes everyday living—the relentless demands of getting up each day, supporting families, building communities, and working.

There are two main parts to this Chapter. First, I will discuss the importance of gendered and feminist analysis in indigenous discourse, and how this applies to aboriginal rights jurisprudence and indigenous legal orders. I distinguish between legal systems and legal orders[20] as a constant reminder of the different forms

[16] See SD McIvor, 'Self-Government and Aboriginal Women' in E Dua and A Robertson (eds), *Scratching the Surface: Canadian Anti-Racist Feminist Thought* (Women's Press, 1999). McIvor argues at 169–72 that aboriginal women's rights are existing aboriginal rights and form part of the inherent right to aboriginal self-government.

[17] For a historical perspective, see J Barman, 'Taming Aboriginal Sexuality: Gender, Power, and Race in British Columbia, 1850–1900' (1997/98) 115/116 *British Columbia Studies* 21.

[18] See, eg, J Fiske and E George, *Seeking Alternatives to Bill C-31: From Cultural Trauma to Cultural Revitalization through Customary Law* (Status of Women Canada, 2006); Klein and Ackerman, above n 15.

[19] 'Cognitive dissonance' is used here to mean the inability of the mind to accept opposite concepts simultaneously. Consequently, one version eclipses the other.

[20] I use the term 'legal system' to describe state-centred legal systems in which law is managed by legal professionals in legal institutions that are separate from other social and political institutions. In contrast, I use the term 'legal order' to describe law that is embedded in social, political, economic, and spiritual institutions. See HJ Berman, *Law and Revolution* (Harvard University Press, 1983) 49–50.

and approaches to law, and to be mindful of how indigenous legal traditions are interpreted in western legal constructs. Of course, it is preferable to use aboriginal peoples' own language when referring to law and legal concepts. For example, the Gitksan people's word for law is *ayook*, which has been translated into English as law, custom, or precedent. In Western Australia, the Mardudjara have the word *julubidi*, which anthropologist Robert Tonkinson has described as 'a body of jural rules and moral evaluations of customary and socially sanctioned behaviour patterns'.[21] Second, I will describe a small community case study that explores at a local level some of the experiences and issues of power and authenticity, membership, citizenship, and identity.

B. Gender Analysis

> Native societies and the males in them have continued their attempts to restrict [Native] women. Phrased differently, Indian males are chauvinistic! They are the first to admit this fact. However, they justify their stance by saying that certain behavior and proofs of self-sufficiency in an Indian female is 'Not the Indian way!' Whatever that may mean! This flies in the face of fact, of reality . . . [so a scholarly] examination of sex roles is imperative.[22]

1. What is a Gendered Analysis?

Status of Women Canada defines gender as:

> the culturally specific set of characteristics that identifies the social behaviour of women and men and the *relationship* between them. Gender, therefore, refers not simply to women or men, but to the relationship between them, and the way it is socially constructed. Because it is a relational term, gender must include women *and* men. Like the concepts of class, race and ethnicity, gender is an analytical tool for understanding social processes.[23]

While there are different approaches to gender analysis,[24] it can basically be described as a 'systematic examination of the particular roles of women and men

[21] R Tonkinson, *The Jigalong Mob: Aboriginal Victors of the Desert Crusade* (Cummings, 1974) 7, quoted in K Maddock, 'Aboriginal Customary Law' in P Hanks and B Keon-Cohen (eds), *Aborigines and the Law* (Allen and Unwin, 1984) 212, 212.

[22] B Medicine, *The Native American Woman: A Perspective* (National Education Laboratory, 1978) 13, quoted in D Maltz and J Archambault, 'Gender and Power in Native North America' in Klein and Ackerman, above n 15, 244.

[23] Status of Women Canada (SWC), *Gender-Based Analysis: A Guide for Policy-Making* (rev'd ed, SWC, 1998) www.swc-cfc.gc.ca (emphasis in original).

[24] The literature regarding gender analysis is vast. For a useful discussion of gender and social change, and the differences in gender analysis frameworks, see C Bacchi *et al*, 'Gender Analysis and Social Change: Testing the Water' (2005) 24(4) *Policy and Society* 45; International Labour Organization and SEAPAT, 'Gender Learning and Information Module', www.ilo.org; Status of Women Canada, 'Gender-Based Analysis / Gender Mainstreaming Annotated Bibliography' (2002) www.swc-cfc.gc.ca.

within their economic, political, social and cultural context'.[25] Specifically, gender analysis is a tool for understanding the impacts of social (including legal) processes. Such an analysis would include a critical and comparative examination of the potentially differential effects of law and policies 'on women or men [that] can often be masked or obscured'.[26] In contrast, a deliberately feminist gender analysis would focus on 'the causes of the major differences in women's and men's lives relative to the quality of life, work hours, health and literacy levels, economic, political and social standing, decision-making, access to resources and other equality measures'.[27]

Gender is multidimensional, involving 'economic processes, authority, violence, discourses and ideologies, sexuality and emotional connections'.[28] Raewyn Connell has developed what, for the purposes of this paper, is a very useful model for systematic research and comparison of gendered relationships and transactions:

> *gender division of labour*, i.e., the way in which production and consumption are arranged on gender lines, including the gendering of occupations, the division between paid work and domestic labour, etc.
>
> *gender relations of power*, i.e., the way in which control, authority, and force are exercised on gender lines, including organisational hierarchy, legal power, collective and individual violence;
>
> *emotion and human relations*, i.e., the way attachment and antagonism among people and groups are organized along gender lines, including feelings of solidarity, prejudice and disdain, sexual attraction and repulsion, etc.
>
> *gender culture and symbolism*, i.e., the way gender identities are defined in culture, the language and symbols of gender difference, the prevailing beliefs and attitudes about gender.[29]

However, in the end, gendered analysis is 'open-ended, malleable and subject to continual political pressures'.[30] That is, these are not static frameworks, but rather can more aptly be described as 'fields of contestation in a continuing quest for gender justice' or 'unfinished business'.[31]

2. Why a Gendered Analysis?

To consider this question, it is necessary to step back and consider the larger aboriginal political project. This project is about imagining and building a future in

[25] M Riley, 'Gender Analysis' (Center of Concern, 2003) 1, at www.comitemujeresasc.org/documents/76_genderanalysis.pdf.
[26] SWC, above n 23, 3.
[27] Riley, above n 25, 1.
[28] R Connell, 'Advancing Gender Reform in Large-Scale Organisations: A New Approach for Practitioners and Researchers' (2005) 24(4) *Policy and Society* 6.
[29] *Ibid*, 7.
[30] Bacchi, above n 24, 50.
[31] *Ibid.*

which aboriginal peoples define themselves and relate to the world according to their overall legal, social, economic, and political systems. Within this political project, aboriginal peoples will continually contest legal and social norms—as peoples in all societies always have done, and will do, through time.[32] If the society is healthy, it will be able to withstand the ongoing process of change that derives from large groups of people engaging in the messy business of managing themselves—complete with conflicts and the exercise of both individual and collective agency.[33]

While decolonisation is imperative, it does not have to define the whole of aboriginal peoples' political and legal consciousness.[34] To be effective, the aboriginal political project must go beyond the struggle against colonisation and an unquestioning adoption of the problematic ideologies contained in the language of aboriginal rights, sovereignty, self-government, autonomy, and self-determination.[35] Such a political project is about aboriginal people discovering, imagining, and defining themselves beyond the confines of colonisation, and beyond their resistance to oppression.

As with many other societies, the dynamics of internal oppression and power imbalances are part of aboriginal peoples' experiences. Despite the rhetoric, sexism and other oppressions, such as homophobia and ageism, are realities in many aboriginal communities. Many aboriginal communities are not safe places for children and other vulnerable individuals.[36] In Canada, aboriginal women's efforts to challenge these oppressions are often taken to the courts or other advocacy forums.[37] Cases such as *Canada v Lavell* (membership/human rights),[38] *Lovelace v Canada* (membership/human rights),[39] *Derrickson v Derrickson* (marital property),[40] *Paul v Paul* (marital property),[41] and *Native Women's Association of Canada v Canada* (funding and recognition for equal political representation),[42] *Sawridge Band v Canada* (membership/self-government),[43] and *McIvor v Canada (Registrar, Indian and Northern Affairs)* (Charter challenge to membership)[44] reveal much about the gendered nature of some of the internal struggles

[32] See generally J Webber, 'Legal Pluralism and Human Agency' (2005) 44(1) *Osgoode Hall Law Journal* 167.

[33] *Ibid*, 195–7.

[34] For a similar approach in the United States, see DJ Dickerson, *The End of Blackness* (Pantheon, 2004). She challenges black Americans to consider who they are beyond racism and oppression.

[35] For a critique of the aboriginal rights framework and s 35 of the Constitution Act, 1982, above n 2; see J Tully, 'The Struggles of Indigenous Peoples for and of Freedom' in A Walkem and H Bruce (eds), *Box of Treasures or Empty Box: Twenty Years of Section 35* (Theytus, 2003) 271, 284–5.

[36] For the latest grim statistics on aboriginal victims and offenders, see *The Daily* (Statistics Canada, 6 June 2006) www.statcan.ca/Daily/English/060606/d060606b.htm; Statistics Canada, above n 7.

[37] On indigenous women's citizenship issues generally, see Fiske and George, above n 18.

[38] [1974] SCR 1349.

[39] [1981] HRC 36 UN GOAR Supp (no 40) Annex XVIII.

[40] [1986] 1 SCR 285.

[41] [1986] 1 SCR 306.

[42] [1994] 3 SCR 627.

[43] [1996] 1 FC 3 (TD) (hereafter *Sawridge* 1996); [1997] 3 FC 580 (CA); [2003] 3 CNLR 344 (TD) (hereafter *Sawridge* 2003).

[44] (2007) BCSC 827 (hereafter *McIvor*).

within aboriginal groups.[45] I will return to several of the key aspects raised by these cases later.

3. What Is a Feminist Standpoint Analysis?

Standpoint analysis is a useful tool for beginning a gendered analysis. Developed by Dorothy Smith, standpoint analysis starts with centring inquiries directly in the lives of actual women, and extends from there to examining the forces that shape their experiences and consciousness.[46] Smith's basic thesis is that we all come from *somewhere*—politically, economically, and culturally—and we need to pay attention to how this plays out in our work. Adele Mueller explains:

> [I]t is a powerful methodological tool with which to investigate the extended relations of gender, race, and class as they converge in ways which women experience as local and specific. The standpoint of women breaks through the formidable discursive barrier which separates the practices of sociology from the everyday world in which people make, and make sense of, their lives. This use of 'standpoint of women' as a methodological tool is distinguished from its more common treatment as an abstracted epistemological point which is taken as the basis for a restrictive focus on women or conflated with a feminist perspective.[47]

There is much debate about Smith's use of feminist standpoint theory.[48] For example, some have argued that it is preoccupied with subject position and power, while others have claimed that it privileges the oppressed and that it is ethnocentric. However, Smith currently advances a 'woman's standpoint' that is synthesised from many standpoints so that no one experience is taken as truth.[49] For the purposes of this paper, feminist standpoint theory, as redefined by Smith, is an effective way to begin the discussion about aboriginal women's experiences.

What might standpoint analysis look like applied to the lives of aboriginal women and the laws surrounding them? It would begin by ensuring that aboriginal women's actual experiences are the pivot for figuring out the power dynamics in their lives. What are the political, legal, economic, and social forces that are part of their worlds? What are their particular interests and specific perspectives? Given that aboriginal women share the political and cultural diversity of all aboriginal peoples in Canada, care has to be taken to be as geographically and culturally specific as possible.

[45] See generally JJ Borrows and LI Rotman, *Aboriginal Legal Issues: Cases, Materials and Commentary*, (2nd edn, Butterworths, 2003) ch 8. For other court challenges to the provisions of the Indian Act, above n 12; see S Imai, *The 2007 Annotated Indian Act and Related Aboriginal Constitutional Provisions* (Thomson, updated annually).

[46] See generally D Smith, *The Conceptual Practices of Power: A Feminist Sociology of Knowledge* (University of Toronto Press, 1990).

[47] A Mueller, 'Beginning in the Standpoint of Women: An Investigation of the Gap between Cholas and "Women in Peru"' in M Campbell and A Manicom (eds), *Knowledge, Experience, and Ruling Relations: Studies in the Social Organization of Knowledge* (University of Toronto Press, 1995) 96 (references omitted).

[48] For a useful summary, see A Cameron, 'Gender, Power and Justice: A Feminist Perspective on Restorative Justice and Intimate Violence' (LLM thesis, University of British Columbia, 2003).

[49] *Ibid.*

In reality, aboriginal women's experiences will cut across many standpoints. Standpoint analysis must start with the perspectives of many aboriginal women and from this multiplicity of experiences extrapolate a broader analysis. Such an approach would help to eliminate meaningless political posturing that is founded on idealised fantasies about aboriginal women instead of on their lived experiences.

4. Gendered Analysis and Aboriginal Rights Jurisprudence

In aboriginal rights jurisprudence, it appears that indigenous women have been erased off both the land and the legal landscape.[50] This is not to suggest that aboriginal rights litigation has not included aboriginal women. Dorothy Van der Peet, for instance, was the defendant in the seminal aboriginal rights case *R v Van der Peet*.[51] However, while she claimed an aboriginal right to sell fish, fishing is still mainly characterised as primarily a male activity across many aboriginal societies.[52] Reliance on the jurisprudence alone might excuse one for concluding that women did not have an important or active presence on the land. The literature and images[53] of aboriginal peoples focus almost entirely on males and their activities—hunting, fishing, and trapping. In this recent mythology, women's role is restricted to dealing with what the men bring home from the hunt.[54]

Consider the following excerpt from the work of historian Sarah Carter:

> But plains people were not solely hunters of buffalo. To rely on one staple resource alone was risky in the Plains environment, as there were periodic shortages of buffalo, and it was mainly the gathering and preserving work of women, based on their intimate understanding of the Plains environment, that varied the subsistence base and contributed to 'risk reduction', a role the immigrant women to the Plains would also acquire. Midsummer camp movements were determined not only by the buffalo but also by considerations such as the ripeness and location of saskatoon berries, the prairie turnip, and other fruits and tubers. Many of the foodstuffs women gathered were dried, pounded, or otherwise preserved and stored for the scarce times of winter. Women fished, snared small game, caught prairie chickens and migratory birds, and gathered their eggs. A high degree of mobility was essential for people effectively to draw on the varied resources of the Plains.[55]

[50] See generally G Van Woudenberg, 'Placing Gender in the Mediation of Aboriginal Resource Claims and Conflicts' (2004) 34(3) *Recherches Amérindiennes au Québec* 59.

[51] *R v Van der Peet* [1996] 2 SCR 507.

[52] See, eg, I Altamirano-Jimenez, 'The Politics of Aboriginal Nationalism and Women, Mexico and Canada: A Comparative Perspective' (PhD dissertation, University of Alberta, 2006).

[53] The images in the offices of many aboriginal organisations (and now many websites) are most often of male warriors and hunters. The rare images of women are usually of very young, beautiful maidens or very old elders.

[54] L Peers, 'Subsistence, Secondary Literature, and Gender Bias: The Saulteaux' in Miller and Chuchryk, above n 15, 41.

[55] S Carter, '"We Must Farm to Enable Us to Live": The Plains Cree and Agriculture to 1900' in RCA Maaka and C Andersen (eds), *The Indigenous Experience: Global Perspectives* (Canadian Scholars, 2006) 221. See also S Carter, 'First Nations Women of Prairie Canada in the Early Reserve Years, the 1870s to the 1920s: A Preliminary Inquiry' in Miller and Chuchryk, above n 15, 51.

Aboriginal women were and are on the land (as well as everywhere else).[56] What is important about women's activities is that they show how women managed the harvesting of foods, medicines, and other resources, including (1) access (who can harvest and where), (2) sharing information about the location of the resources, (3) distributing and sharing the harvest, and (4) managing conflicts arising from interpretation of the rules and carrying out the activities. The variable factors that women consider in interpreting and applying these rules include availability, location, and types of resources, as well as relationships within the community. These guidelines form the basis for indigenous resource law. They originate in people's interactions and activities over time, and are maintained by continued social interaction.[57]

Since these are the key functions of women's role with regard to the land, indigenous women were (and still are) involved with law at every level, including its source, interpretation, application, and recording. Yet around the world, indigenous women are erased from the land both legally and politically. The consequences for women are serious, including loss of access to land and resources, of property rights, and of authority in reconstituted governance structures.[58] Recently in Australia, these issues have become more explicit because of the gendered division of knowledge and aspects of culture in some of the indigenous societies. The controversial issue of gender-specific evidence has been raised in numerous claims involving women-only sacred sites or ceremonies.[59]

One of the best-known gendered controversies involved the Hindmarsh Island Bridge in South Australia, where developers successfully challenged the Minister's decision to protect the site under the Aboriginal and Torres Strait Islander Heritage Protection Act 1984 (Cth).[60] The case involved Ngarrindjeri women providing confidential evidence about 'women's business' at Hindmarsh Island, which they considered sacred. According to their indigenous law, they could not divulge this evidence to men, and so they submitted it in sealed envelopes.[61] The

[56] For a powerful example of Gwich'in women on the land, see B Parlee, F Berkes and the Teetl'it Gwich'in Renewable Resource Council, 'Indigenous Knowledge of Ecological Variability and Commons Management: A Case Study on Berry Harvesting from Northern Canada' (2006) 34 *Human Ecology* 1.

[57] See generally: LL Fuller, 'Human Interaction and the Law' (1969) 14 *American Journal of Jurisprudence* 1.

[58] There is extensive scholarship on these questions. See, eg, M Rugadya, E Obaikol and H Kamusiime, 'Gender and the Land Reform Process in Uganda: Assessing Gains and Losses for Women in Uganda' (Associates for Development Land Research Series No 2, Oxfam GB, 2004); R Hitchcock, M Johnson and C Haney, 'Indigenous Women in Botswana: Changing Gender Roles in the Face of Dispossession and Modernization' in R Hitchcock and D Vinding (eds), *Indigenous Peoples' Rights in Southern Africa* (International Work Group for Indigenous Affairs, 2004); A Manji, 'Commodifying Land, Fetishising Law: Women's Struggles to Claim Land Rights in Uganda' (2003) 19 *Australian Feminist Law Journal* 81; A Manji, *The Politics of Land Reform in Africa: From Communal Tenure to Free Markets* (Zed Bbooks, 2006).

[59] See generally A Keely, 'Women and Land: The Problems Aboriginal Women Face in Providing Gender Restricted Evidence' (1996) 3(87) *Indigenous Law Bulletin*.

[60] H McRae *et al*, *Indigenous Legal Issues: Commentary and Materials* (3rd edn, Lawbook, 2003) 131.

[61] *Ibid*.

Federal Court criticised the Minister for delegating the women-only evidence to a female staff member for her assessment of its implications. Instead, the Federal Court directed, the Minister should have read the material personally or arranged for a female minister to review it. In effect, the court decided that, if the Ngarrindjeri women wanted protection under Australian law, they would have to do so on the law's terms.[62]

The Hindmarsh Bridge case generated much heated debate and accusations of 'cultural fabrication' on the part of the Ngarrindjeri women. In fact, a Royal Commission agreed that the Ngarrindjeri women had fabricated their claim, under Ngarrindjeri law, of a sacred 'women's business' connection to the disputed land.[63] The gendered division in this case resulted from aboriginal women being excluded from early anthropology and contemporary legal processes involving their connection with the land. Such treatment caused one aboriginal woman to ask, 'What about that land rights? They going to let women talk for land too, or is just for men'?[64]

Consider the following observation on exclusion of women's voices generally:

> To our knowledge, guidelines for the inclusion of gender and indigenous concerns in natural resource management activities are not yet available in a comprehensive manner within NGOs, indigenous organisations and government structures.[65]

This means that, for the most part, women's knowledge of the land and resources remains unacknowledged politically and legally. Since men and women often have different traditional knowledge of natural resources in relation to 'habitat, conservation, management, use, storing, and processing', women's knowledge can, and does, disappear.[66] This includes knowledge relating to access to, and control and use of, natural resources, which are basic elements of indigenous law. Without the thoughtful and deliberate inclusion of aboriginal women, the aboriginal discourse will continue to be impoverished, incomplete, and therefore profoundly flawed.

C. Authenticity and Identity: Case Study of a Small Community

The absence of political and legal remedies to contest the injustices faced by Aboriginal Peoples has contributed to their unacceptable socio-economic status within a generally prosperous society. As a result of this treatment, Aboriginal Peoples became 'uncertain

[62] *Norvill v Chapman* (1995) 133 ALR 226 (FC).

[63] McRae *et al*, above n 60, 134.

[64] *Ibid*, 210.

[65] E Kiørboe *et al*, *Integrating Indigenous and Gender Aspects in Natural Resource Management: Guidelines for Practitioners* (WWF-Denmark, IWGIA, KULU, Nepenthes, 2006) 5, www.iucn.org/themes/spg/files/DK%20IGARM.dk.

[66] *Ibid*, 11.

citizens', loosely associated with the Canadian political community but denied the institutions, rights and/or resources necessary to meaningfully participate in the life of the country, either collectively or as individuals. As a result, Aboriginal Peoples have not enjoyed social cohesion, political stability and civic peace in their relationships with other Canadian citizens.[67]

1. Authenticity

Within aboriginal discourse, there are underlying and pervasive conflicts about authenticity. Who qualifies as an authentic aboriginal person, and who has the authority to make this determination? Often these conflicts are implicit, obscured in the language of identity, collectivity, difference, culture, colonialism, decolonisation, and rights. We must ask: How does gender factor into decisions about who is 'in' and who is 'out'? Who has power? Whose voices are heard? Power does not exist in a vacuum, but is relational—it can only exist inside relationships between people. In these relationships, authenticity has become a divisive currency of power among indigenous peoples, one that has been and still is supported by the state through legislated racialisation (for example, the Canadian Indian Act).

The ongoing conflict about authenticity derives mainly from contested access to state benefits and revenues, state-recognised power, and control of land and resources. Much of this conflict is gendered, and those with less power—often women—lose their access to benefits and land. In the case of some very wealthy aboriginal groups, there appears to be a flat refusal to share the wealth, though the issue is never so baldly stated.[68]

For example, in *Sawridge*, three bands in Treaties 6, 7, and 8 challenged amendments to the Indian Act[69] that reinstated aboriginal women who had lost their status (that is, registration as Indians under the Indian Act) when they married non-status men (that is, men not registered as Indians under the Indian Act). These bands claimed they had a 'woman-follows-man' custom. This meant that female band members who married non-band members left the band. The bands argued that this custom was an aboriginal right that was protected by s 35 of the Constitution Act 1982,[70] and the Indian Act amendment requiring the reinstatement of female band members was a violation of their custom. In an interlocutory proceeding, Hugessen J ordered the band to comply with the Indian Act:

> [W]hatever inconvenience the plaintiff may suffer by admitting 11 old ladies to membership is nothing compared both to the damage to the public interest in having Parliament's laws flouted and to the private interests of the women in question who, at

[67] J Borrows, 'Measuring a Work in Progress: Canada, Constitutionalism, Citizenship and Aboriginal Peoples' in Walkem and Bruce, above n 35, 225 (footnote omitted).

[68] *Sawridge* 1996, above n 43. See *Sawridge v Her Majesty the Queen* 2008 FC 322 (hereafter *Sawridge* 2008).

[69] An Act to amend the Indian Act, SC 1985, c 27, referred to as 'Bill C-31'.

[70] Constitution Act, 1982, above n 3.

> the present rate of progress, are unlikely ever to benefit from a law which was adopted with people in their position specifically in mind.[71]

The latest *Sawridge* trial which began in 2004 ended abruptly in January of 2008 when the plaintiffs, alleging among other complaints, apprehension of judicial bias, informed the court that they would not be calling any further evidence and were instead closing their case. Furthermore, the plaintiffs advised the court that they would be proceeding with an appeal to the Federal Court of Appeal. In concluding his 137-page reasons for judgment, the Honourable Mr Justice Russell dismissed the plaintiff's case 'because there is no case for the Crown to answer'.[72]

With the recent British Columbia Supreme Court decision in *McIvor v Canada (Registrar, Indian and Northern Affairs)*,[73] the legal landscape will soon be experiencing an earthquake. Plaintiffs Sharon McIvor, aboriginal feminist lawyer, and her son Charles Grismer successfully argued that the Indian Act, as amended in 1985, violates s 15(1) of the Canadian Charter of Rights and Freedoms.[74] Madam Justice Ross wrote:

> I have concluded that s 6 of the *1985 Act* violates s 15(1) of the *Charter* in that it discriminates between matrilineal and patrilineal descendants born prior to April 17, 1985, in the conferring of Indian status, and discriminates between descendants born prior to April 17, 1985, of Indian women who married non-Indian men, and the descendants of Indian men who married non-Indian women. I have concluded that these provisions are not saved by s 1.[75]

Consequently, Ross J held that s 6 of the Indian Act is of no force and effect insofar as it authorises this discriminatory treatment of Indian men and women.

However, at least while the legal landscape is being reshaped by the current litigation regarding membership, the issue of authenticity remains at the heart of many paralysing and oppressive conflicts among aboriginal peoples. While the Indian Act does not contain provisions for either general or gender equality, the *McIvor* trial decision clearly signals that it will be subject to the Charter.[76] For example, consider how the *McIvor* decision will impact membership codes that bands have established for themselves under the Indian Act. At the very least, if the McIvor decision stands at the Supreme Court of Canada, many bands will find that their membership codes contravene the Charter, thereby generating further internal conflicts, basic confusion, and local legal challenges—much of this mirroring the effects of the original 1985 amendment, C-31.

Since all legal decisions have direct and widespread political ramifications, how might these issues play out for aboriginal women in local power dynamics? Arguably, some of the early anthropological constructs and methodologies have

71 *Sawridge* 2003, above n 43, 8.
72 *Sawridge* 2008, above n 68, 135.
73 *McIvor*, above n 44.
74 Canadian Charter of Rights and Freedoms, Part 1 of the Constitution Act, 1982, above n 3.
75 *McIvor*, above n 44, para 343.
76 See also *Corbiere v Canada (Minister of Indian and Northern Affairs)* [1999] 2 SCR 203.

been major contributors to the creation and continuation of this conflict both internally (within aboriginal groups) and externally (in relationships with the Canadian state and third parties).[77] In recent years, the courts have waded into the conflict arena with aboriginal rights decisions that reflect and perpetuate the concepts of authenticity that serve to sustain the dynamics of colonialism.[78]

A deeper analysis of this issue requires locating this conflict within its political, legal, and historical context. Aboriginal people have been forced to defend themselves against relentless land theft and marginalisation by a colonial regime. Now, aboriginal people are engaged in ongoing struggles to reclaim land and resources, self-government, identity, and language. These circumstances have resulted in many aboriginal people relying on colonially imposed constructs that are now voluntarily maintained. Aboriginal groups are defensively drawing around themselves boundaries based on exclusive definitions of 'aboriginal', such as blood quantum, Indian Act membership formulas, and so on. Audra Simpson recalls the following remark made at a community event in Kahnawake:

> His mother wasn't Indian and his father was barely Indian, he is lucky if he is even 30 per cent! Look at him in that 'Warriors' jacket—who the hell does he think he is?! He's not even an Indian and he's got his jacket on, walking around here like that.[79]

These issues are often cloaked in a deflective covering, such as 'sacred'[80] or 'cultural'. In the case of *Sawridge*, membership exclusion wears a 'traditional' cloak (woman follows man). Kenyan lawyer Celestine Nyamu-Musembi suggests that when an oppressive cultural practice is identified, the remedy is to first identify the goal of the practice, and then figure out how to meet that goal without oppression. She sets out a three-stage 'critical pragmatic approach':[81]

1. Challenge any legal framework or social process that protects cultural, spiritual, or religious practices from questioning. Create space for diverse voices and challenges to the norms.
2. Gather evidence of varied and alternative local practices to counteract negative, static cultural rhetoric (there are always variations). These could be used to develop new case law within indigenous jurisprudence.

[77] See generally M Pinkoski and M Asch, 'Anthropology and Indigenous Rights in Canada and the United States: Implications in Steward's Theoretical Project' in A Barnard (ed), *Hunter-Gatherers in History, Archaeology, and Anthropology* (Berg, 2004).

[78] *Ibid.* See also N Vallance, 'The Misuse of "Culture" by the Supreme Court of Canada' in Eisenberg, above n 8; JK Cowan, M-B Dembour and RA Wilson, *Culture and Rights: Anthropological Perspectives* (Cambridge University Press, 2001).

[79] A Simpson, 'Paths Toward a Mohawk Nation: Narratives of Citizenship and Nationhood in Kahnawake' in Maaka and Andersen, above n 55, 180.

[80] There is an important distinction between believing that the laws themselves are spiritual and sacred, and outside human control; and understanding that law is founded on its supporting cosmology. Law is fundamentally a culturally bounded enterprise that is based on how we perceive human beings, non-human life forms, and the spirits and the universe.

[81] CI Nyamu-Musembi, 'How Should Human Rights and Development Respond to Cultural Legitimization of Gender Hierarchy in Developing Countries?' (2000) 41(2) *Harvard International Law Journal* 410.

3. Identify concepts of fairness and equality within the culture and apply these principles to issues relating to gender, sexual orientation, ageism, and other imbalances.

I contend that many pre-contact aboriginal societies practised forms of nationhood that were deliberately inclusive in order to build strong nations with extensive international ties.[82] From a pragmatic perspective, had aboriginal peoples practiced the exclusive forms of membership that are in place today via the Indian Act,[83] they would not have survived and North America would have been truly *terra nullius*.[84]

I contend further that the authenticity conflict could be constructively dealt with by rigorously employing the legal reasoning processes contained in aboriginal legal orders and contextualising it within a gendered understanding of aboriginal nationhood and citizenship.[85] And, given the nature of the membership/citizenship issue, the building of future equitable relations in our communities requires a deliberate gendered analysis to ensure that gender discrimination is, in fact, eliminated. Nyamu-Musembi's critical pragmatic approach offers one way to begin this work at the local level.

2. Case Study

> The slow and often bitterly disputed recovery of geographical territory which is at the heart of decolonization is preceded—as empire had been—by the charting of cultural territory. After the period of 'primary resistance', literally fighting against outside intrusion, there comes the period of secondary, that is, ideological resistance, when efforts are made to reconstitute a 'shattered community, to save or restore the sense and fact of community against all the pressures of the colonial system'.[86]

[82] See V Napoleon, 'Extinction by Number: Colonialism Made Easy' (2001) 16 *Canadian Journal of Law and Society* 113.

[83] There are profound differences between western and aboriginal constructs of nationhood, so care must be taken not to impose a western definition. Diverse histories and cultures have produced different ways for large groups of people to define themselves and relate to others, to non-human life forms, to space, and to land. A critical cosmological difference is that, generally, many aboriginal nations make no fundamental separation between the history of humans and the history of the world, and they fuse human power with the power of the land. Another critical divergence between aboriginal and non-aboriginal constructs of nationhood lies in the structuring of social and political regimes (eg, hierarchical vs non-hierarchical and centralised vs decentralised).

[84] On the unjustified application of the concept of *terra nullius* to territories occupied by indigenous peoples, see Borrows and Rotman, above n 45, 6.

[85] Obviously, there is no one aboriginal society, so there is no one understanding of citizenship or nationhood, and no one aboriginal legal order. I am speaking very generally because each aboriginal nation would have to conduct its own analysis of these concepts. However, I think Robert Bee's level of abstraction theory can be usefully applied to broaden the scope of my arguments and analysis, even though I will focus on the Saulteau First Nation herein. See RL Bee, *Patterns and Processes: An Introduction to Anthropological Strategies for the Study of Social Change* (Free Press, 1974) 23.

[86] E Said, *Culture and Imperialism* (Vintage, 1994) 209, including quotation from B Davidson, *Africa in Modern History: The Search for a New Society* (Allen Lane, 1978) 155.

An on-the-ground example of the authenticity conflict can be found in the membership policies of Saulteau First Nation, a small band located in northeast British Columbia.[87] This region is covered by Treaty 8 (1899), which includes a vast tract of land in northeastern British Columbia, northern Alberta and Saskatchewan, and the southern Northwest Territories.[88] Treaty 8 involved negotiations between the federal government and Cree, Dunnezah,[89] and Chipewyan peoples.[90]

Northeast BC is the homeland of the Dunnezah peoples. By 1911, a group of Saulteaux had moved into Dunnezah territories. According to the Saulteaux oral histories, a vision of their spiritual leader, Kahkakokwanis, guided them on a 10-year journey across Canada.[91] In his spiritual trance, Kahkakokwanis saw the 'Two Mountains that Sit Together' (now called the Twin Sister Mountains), so the people travelled until they found these mountains near Moberly Lake.[92] In 1914, the Saulteaux were 'admitted' into Treaty 8 without the negotiated adhesion process having been followed.[93] In 1918, they took up residence at the eastern end of Moberly Lake, where a reserve of 7,646 acres was set out for them.[94]

Today, Saulteau First Nation has approximately 644 members, but fewer than half the members currently reside on the reserve.[95] With the goal of maintaining Saulteaux cultural practices, Saulteau First Nation has structured its election policy around its original five founding Saulteaux families. In 1988, Saulteau First Nation passed a band bylaw pursuant to s 2(3)(a) of the Indian Act that recognises the inherent power of a band to establish custom election procedures rather than

[87] Formerly called Moberly Lake, Saulteau First Nation is the home community of Cree, Saulteaux, and Dunneza peoples. (The people of Saulteau First Nation prefer the spelling 'Saulteau'. The spelling used otherwise is Salteaux.) I am a member of this First Nation. It has become the practice for groups that were formerly called 'Indian Bands' pursuant to the Indian Act to call themselves 'First Nations'. While the original intent of this renaming may have been to emphasise the fact that indigenous nations were in Canada prior to European contact, and so they are the *First* Nations, calling each band a First Nation is problematic. Bands are groups of varying sizes that are usually part of larger nations, and in fact, the larger nation groups have been legally and politically fragmented. See Canada, *Report of the Royal Commission on Aboriginal Peoples: Reconstructing the Relationship*, vol 2 (Ministry of Supply and Services, Canada, 1996) 234–5 (hereafter *RCAP Report*).

[88] Treaty 8 Between Her Majesty the Queen and the Cree, Beaver, Chipewyan, and Other Indians (repr of the 1899 edn, Ottawa, Queen's Printer, 1964) www.ainc-inac.gc.ca. As with the other treaties in Canada, the negotiations for Treaty 8 were precipitated by colonial expansion—in this case, the Klondike gold rush and the advent of non-native settlers. See DFK Madill, *Treaty Research Report: Treaty Eight (1899)* (Indian and Northern Affairs Canada, 1986) at www.ainc-inac.gc.ca/pr/trts/hti/t8/index_e.html.

[89] The Dunnezah were formerly called Beaver by the settlers.

[90] The Cree are part of the Algonquin linguistic group. The Dunnezah and Chipewyan are part of the Athapaskan (Dene) linguistic group.

[91] A Napoleon, *Bushland Spirit: Our Elders Speak* (Twin Sister, 1998) 28–9. According to Saulteau elder Fred Courtoreille, in Napoleon at 32, the Saulteau lived at Moberly Lake for three years before they entered into Treaty 8.

[92] *Ibid.*

[93] Madill, above n 88, unpaginated.

[94] Indian and Northern Affairs Canada (INAC), *Treaty 8 and the BC Indian Reserve Question* (INAC, undated) 1, at www.ainc-inac.gc.ca/pr/trts/hti/C-B/ques_e.html.

[95] *Napoleon v Garbitt* [1997] BCJ no 1250 (BCSC) 4–5. In my work experience with aboriginal communities in BC, I have noticed that this is not an unusual residence ratio. The residents of most reserves range from 10 to 50% of the total membership.

follow the procedures in s 74 of the Act.[96] Basically, the Saulteau First Nation system of custom elections was codified into the Saulteau Indian Band Government Law, containing procedures for each of the five founding families to nominate and elect a 'headman' to serve as a band councillor for the band.[97] In its initial version, the headmen and council of elders elected the chief from among the headmen. This was amended in 1996 to allow the entire band to elect one of the five headmen as chief.[98]

'Headman' is the language of Treaty 8 which has been carried over to present-day band governance policies. While the position of headman is no longer restricted to men, there are serious questions about the reification of the patriarchal family within the Saulteau First Nation. Historically, family groups were highly mobile and fluidly constituted. That is, members were able to move from one group to another as necessary and to avoid conflict.[99] For instance, a person could follow his or her own mother or father's families, or their spouse's mother or father's families, or some other variation. The question must be asked: What are the implications of this patriarchal reification of families for women and the dynamics of the larger community?

There has been extensive disagreement within the Saulteau First Nation about its election procedures, including several acrimonious legal actions.[100] To date, these disputes have been largely procedural rather than substantial. That is, the disputes have not directly challenged the founding family structure, but rather have focused on the legitimacy and interpretation of the amendments to the Saulteau Indian Band Government Law,[101] candidate eligibility requirements, and accountability of the headmen and chief.[102] Nonetheless, I think the procedural disputes are directly connected to the same overall issues raised by the founding family structure.

Turning to the membership policy, Saulteau First Nation passed the Saulteau Indian Nation Citizenship Act[103] in 1986, pursuant to s 10 of the Indian

[96] *Ibid*, 7–9. As required under the Indian Act, the federal Minister of Indian and Northern Affairs approved this bylaw.

[97] Obviously, further thought should be given to custom 'elections' and the implications of adopting this form of representative democracy as custom.

[98] Saulteau Indian Band Government Law (6 October 1996), Saulteau First Nation band office, Moberly Lake, BC.

[99] For discussion of the effects of settlement in fixed locations on another aboriginal people, the Innu, see H Schuurman, 'The Concept of Community and the Challenge for Self-Government' in C Scott (ed), *Aboriginal Autonomy and Development in Northern Quebec and Labrador* (UBC Press, 2001).

[100] See, eg, *Napoleon* v *Garbitt*, above n 95; *Saulteau Indian Band v Totusek* 2002 FCT 132. The latter case was limited to dealing with a request for a summary judgment that was denied. The Band Government Law (above n 98) in place at the time of the *Totusek* action did have a provision to challenge the selection/election of the chief, but it did not have a provision for the removal of the chief from office.

[101] Amendments may be initiated by a minimum of 50 band members or by chief and council. In either case, a process is set out in the proposed amendments for required time frames, notice periods, and 60% approval by band members eligible to vote.

[102] *Napoleon v Garbitt*, above n 95, 8.

[103] This Act was duly approved by the federal Minister of Indian and Northern Affairs. Archived at Saulteau First Nation band office, Moberly Lake, BC.

Act.[104] This bylaw enables the band to determine who is a member,[105] rather than rely on the procedures set out in s 6 of the Indian Act. According to the bylaw, the persons *entitled* to be band members are those who were entitled prior to the April 1985 Indian Act amendments and those born after April 1985 to parents who are both members of Saulteau First Nation. Other persons may *apply* for membership, provided they have one birth parent who is a member of Saulteau First Nation, or are a child under 19 being considered for adoption by a Saulteau First Nation member.

The consequence of this bylaw is that it incorporates the discriminatory practices of the Indian Act prior to 1985—exactly what Sharon McIvor argued against in her s 15 challenge to the Indian Act. Women who were discriminated against by the Indian Act before 1985 were recognised as s 6(2) Indians (that is, second class), not as s 6(1) Indians (that is, first class). This is the negative starting place for the Saulteau First Nation citizenship bylaw. A consequence of these classifications is the extent of one's ability to pass on Indian status to one's descendants. In my family, this means that my mother was reinstated through Bill C-31 as a s 6(2) Indian. Her brothers, who never lost their status by marriage, remained s 6(1) Indians. In the end, my grandsons do not qualify for status whereas my uncles' great-grandchildren do.

The first basic criterion for membership is whether the applicant is a descendant of a member. If the applicant is an adult, the enrolment officer 'shall' consider whether the applicant (1) can speak Saulteaux or Cree; (2) is 'knowledgeable' about Saulteau First Nation customs and traditions; and (3) agrees to a five-year probation period, during which time he or she will acquire knowledge about the community's way of life.[106] Additionally, in the case of either adult or non-adult applicants, the enrolment officer may consider how long the applicant has lived with the Saulteau First Nation and the social and cultural ties that the applicant has with the Saulteau First Nation.[107]

Basically, the Saulteau First Nation is trying to protect itself and its place in a colonial world by determining the authenticity of its members through its leader-

[104] The Indian Act was amended in 1985 to allow Indian bands to adopt their own membership codes (above n 69).

[105] While the bylaw uses the term 'citizen' in place of 'band member', the document still describes a band member, not a citizen.

[106] While there are a number of obvious technical problems in the Saulteau Indian Nation Citizenship Act criteria, these are not the focus of this Chapter. For example, in s 6 the enrolment officer is required to ('shall') consider the list of criteria, but there is no guidance as to how to actually decide membership based on the criteria. How much Cree or Saulteau does an applicant have to know in order to qualify? More importantly, the way the section currently reads, even if the applicant is fluent in either language as well as knowledgeable about Saulteau customs, traditions and 'way of life', there is no requirement that the enrolment officer accept him or her as a member. It is also unclear whether the applicant must meet all three criteria or just one.

[107] The Saulteau Indian Nation Citizenship Act (Saulteau Band Council, November 1986) includes provisions for appeals and amendment processes (at paras 11, 13). To hear appeals, a five-member citizenship committee was established with two elders (minimum 55 years old), one representative of chief and council, and two band members (at para 10).

ship and membership policies. While it would be easy to characterise and dismiss these efforts as essentialist, the community has good cause to want to protect itself, and the members' perspectives deserve consideration.

Unfortunately, what Saulteau First Nation is ultimately protecting is questionable. The fundamental assumption contained in Saulteau First Nation's election and membership policies is that only people directly descended from the five founding families are authentic. This means that the primary requirement of membership and leadership is based on descent and blood ties. In other words, the Saulteau First Nation has attempted to draw a line around itself on the bases of descent and the abstraction of blood.

Furthermore, as of April 1985, the Saulteau First Nation membership policy incorporated all the former band members, including Saulteaux, Cree, and Dunneza as well as non-registered aboriginal women, registered aboriginal women from other bands, and non-aboriginal women who had gained aboriginal 'status' by becoming registered upon marriage to a registered band member. This means that despite the descent-based standards and rhetoric, the Saulteau First Nation's membership code is not really about protecting Saulteaux genetics.

It is important to appreciate that the Saulteau First Nation membership policy demonstrates that the community values other cultural attributes besides descent: the Cree and Saulteaux languages, residency, cultural customs and traditions, a community way of life, and social and cultural ties. All these eligibility requirements are highly subjective and open to a very broad range of interpretations. And although the membership criteria are to be considered by the enrolment officer, there is no guarantee of acceptance. Nor is fulfilment of the membership criteria required of existing Saulteau First Nation members. That is, not all current band members speak Cree or Saulteaux, are knowledgeable of the Saulteau First Nation's customs or way of life, have a long history of residency on reserve, or have close ties with the community. It is therefore arguable that a double standard is being established—no requirements for existing members, but very rigorous ones for new members, even when they have blood connections, unless both their parents are already band members.

The Saulteau First Nation polices have on-the-ground consequences. For example, there is no recognised role for non-member spouses. The descent/blood restriction on membership and leadership creates a group of 'disenfranchised' people who live in the community without a recognised role or kinship group.[108] Yet the practical reality is that given the small size of most aboriginal communities, marrying out is a necessity to avoid family connections. When there is a high

[108] According to Brian Maracle (*Back on the Rez* (Viking, 1996)), this is precisely the situation for the Haudenosaunee on the Six Nations Reserve near Brantford, Ontario. In this matrilineal society, a growing number of band members are born of non-Haudenosaunee mothers, and consequently have no clan affiliation. Without clans, they cannot participate in the traditional governing activities of the community unless they are adopted under Haudenosaunee law.

rate of intermarriage to 'outsiders' in aboriginal communities,[109] whether to non-aboriginal spouses or to spouses from other aboriginal groups, any authentic blood quantum will become negligible over the generations—if it has not already done so.

Arguably, a deeper understanding of aboriginal conceptions of citizenship and nationhood would enable communities such as the Saulteau First Nation to develop broader, inclusive approaches that would further the aboriginal political project. According to legal scholar John Borrows:

> [t]he recognition of Aboriginal law as a vehicle to foster stability and normative order within and between Aboriginal communities and others could be of great benefit to Canada's social structure. It could enable Aboriginal Peoples to become a stronger force in the promotion of certainty and stability throughout the country as they exercise greater responsibility in resolving disputes that lie in their midst.[110]

Borrows argues that citizenship is more than the existence of rights. He advances an interesting argument for expanding aboriginal citizenship to comprise three facets: (1) some formal type of relationship among citizens and groups within the state; (2) the freedom to act with others in any variety of groups not created by the state; and (3) respectful acknowledgement of aboriginal peoples' self-identity, even without state sanction.[111] In addition, Borrows argues that 'citizenship must also concern itself with social cohesion, which includes concerns about social stability, political unity, and civil peace'.[112] This expands citizenship from the individual to the collective and political, concerned with society as a whole.[113] I would add that it is also important for citizenship to be concerned with internal relations of equality, specifically with gender and gender discrimination.

Unfortunately, Saulteau First Nation's membership and leadership policies do not and will not facilitate a larger conception of citizenship that allows for diversity, gender equality, and the assumption of collective political responsibility for society as a whole. Nor do the principles of citizenship of the Saulteaux, Cree, and Dunneza form the basis for the development of a citizenry that is both responsibility-based (as proposed by Borrows), and sensitive to gender equality. Sadly, at the end of the day, the experiences of Saulteau First Nation women are no different from those typically described for aboriginal women across Canada—despite the membership and leadership bylaws.

[109] See S Clatworthy and AH Smith, 'Population Implications of the 1985 Amendments to the Indian Act' (paper, Assembly of First Nations, December 1992) 36–9. According to this study, the anticipated average marriage-out rate for aboriginal persons who are registered under the Indian Act is 25%. According to the late Métis leader, Harry Daniels, after two generations of registered aboriginal people marrying non-registered spouses, there would be no more registered aboriginal people left in Canada. See H Daniels, 'Bill C-31: The Abocide Bill' (paper, Native Women's Association of Canada Conference on Bill C-31, March 1998) 12–13.

[110] Borrows, above n 67, 237.

[111] *Ibid*, 227, referring to the work of Justice GV La Forest, TH Marshall, A De Toqueville and J Tully.

[112] *Ibid*, 229, paraphrasing W Kymlicka and W Norman, *Citizenship in Diverse Societies* (Oxford University Press, 2000).

[113] *Ibid*, 230.

3. Identity

> Indigenous women appeal to protections of their right to ethnic membership in their cultural community in a manner that protects their dignity and control over social reproduction. They challenge the right of the state to assume control over the definitions of identity and the state's power to define identity by race and gender.[114]

'Identity' has been described as a concept of synthesis, integration, and action. 'It represents the process by which the person seeks to integrate his various statuses and roles, as well as his diverse experiences, into a coherent image of self'.[115] According to the Royal Commission on Aboriginal People, identity for aboriginal people is a complex of features that shapes how one understands oneself, and includes belonging to something larger than oneself.[116] This conception of identity includes spirituality, connection to ancestral territory, and social relationships.

The membership and election policies of Saulteau First Nation raise complex issues of power and identity. It is at the community level that the face of colonialism becomes personal. It can be seen in the faces of our families, friends, and neighbours, and it pervades our relationships and the functioning of our entire community. Whose voices are heard? What are the internal power dynamics? It is within these constellations of power that we form our very ideas of ourselves—positive and negative. At the most basic level, when a daughter watches her mother being raped at knifepoint, that little girl's identity is impacted.[117] Similarly, growing up in a community where violence against women is normalised is a formative experience. Finally, when little aboriginal girls learn that there are 500 missing aboriginal women in Canada, what might they think about their country and about their own place in it?[118]

Around the world, women are reconceptualising citizenship, and with it, redefining identity and developing new forms of civic relations.[119] For the purposes of the Saulteau First Nation and this Chapter, identity matters because it has become the fulcrum for trying to reconcile the consequences of colonial history in present-day circumstances. In other words, authenticity and therefore identity have become central features in the current aboriginal political struggles relating

[114] Fiske and George, above n 18, 64, referring to the work of J Bushnell, 'The Responsibilities and Powers of Reproduction' (2001) 4(2) *Indigenous Woman* 23.

[115] AL Epstein, *Ethos and Identity* (Tavistock, 1978) 101, quoted in A Rew and JR Campbell, 'The Political Economy of Identity and Affect' in JR Campbell and A Rew (eds), *Identity and Affect* (Pluto, 1998) 7.

[116] See Canada, *Report of the Royal Commission on Aboriginal Peoples: Perspectives and Realities*, vol 4, (Ministry of Supply and Services, Canada, 1996) 524–5.

[117] Welsh, above n 14. One of the survivors described this experience in the documentary.

[118] Of course, Aboriginal men and boys are also victims of, and witnesses to, sexual abuse, and all these experiences profoundly affect them too. I do not mean to minimise or detract from that, but rather, to focus for a little while on the experiences of aboriginal women. It is a different experience to be the expected object of intimate or general sexualised violence.

[119] Fiske and George, above n 18, 65.

to land, citizenship and membership, and governance.[120] For aboriginal peoples, this is further complicated because contemporary constructs of identity (and culture) are also consequences of our colonial history.

Edward Said wisely suggested that, while groups must preserve what is unique about themselves, they must also strive to preserve some sense of the broader human community.[121] Said was concerned with theories of essentialism and exclusiveness, or with barriers that might 'give rise to polarizations that absolve and forgive ignorance and demagogy more than they enable knowledge'.[122]

My concern here is that identity is not a sufficiently cohesive basis for building a social movement because it cannot hold people together—as the current situation in Canada (and Saulteau First Nation) attests. Rather, identity needs to be combined with a proactive and critical engagement with the larger political project. For the Saulteau First Nation, to focus only on identity without connecting it to the larger political context is to fall into the endless trap of shoring up Saulteau First Nation's authenticity barriers instead of building a strong citizenry.

D. Conclusion

The Saulteau First Nation case study demonstrates how complex and closely woven the issues of gender, authenticity, and identity are. No bright lines separate the issues in the lived experiences at the community level. For example, women are discriminated against by the Indian Act, but women have sons who then are discriminated against by virtue of the discrimination against their mothers.[123]

Even the issues of gender become murky as one realises that aboriginal women are politically diverse locally as well as nationally. This raises other questions that are beyond the scope of this paper, but must be seriously examined as part of the aboriginal political project. For example, how are the larger political dynamics that surround indigenous peoples mirrored by indigenous women at the community level in their relationships with one another? What becomes obvious is that aboriginal women and men are not simply divided politically along gender lines because the issues discussed here (that is, citizenship, leadership, etc) are not

[120] Conflicts about authenticity and identity are an international phenomenon. Regarding similar conflicts in the United States, South Africa, and New Zealand, see, eg, W Churchill, 'The Crucible of American Indian Identity: Native Tradition *versus* Colonial Imposition in Postconquest North America' in W Churchill, *Perversions of Justice and AngloAmerican Law* (City Light Books, 2003) 201; JD Hill and TM Wilson, 'Identity Politics and the Politics of Identities' (2003) 10(1) *Identities: Global Studies in Culture and Power* 1, 1; K Gover and N Blaird, 'Identifying the Māori Treaty Partner' (2002) 52 *University of Toronto Law Journal* 39; R Sylvain, 'Class, Culture and Recognition: San Farm Workers and Indigenous Identities' (2003) 45(1) *Anthropologica* 111; MS Brownell, 'Who is an Indian? Searching for an Answer to the Question at the Core of Federal Indian Law' (2000/2001) 34 *University of Michigan Journal of Law Reform* 275.

[121] Said, above n 86, 32.

[122] *Ibid*, 31.

[123] *McIvor*, above n 44.

straightforward. Rather, these are issues involving various levels of power and privilege, and so the analysis must include questions about whose voices are heard and who benefits from decisions.

How might aboriginal women avoid the political naivety described by Doris Lessing? In this Chapter, I have suggested a dual strategy to bridge the gendered disconnect within the aboriginal discourse. First, aboriginal women's issues must be contextualised within the larger political frames of self-determination and self-government. Second, a gendered and feminist analysis must be applied to the larger political projects of self-determination and self-government. This dual approach must be applied locally at the community level and nationally at the political level. Its development and implementation must be sustained and become an integral part of the political struggle taken up by all aboriginal peoples.

Aboriginal women might consider Nyamu-Musembi's approach to assessing the intellectual processes and social capital that are contained within their indigenous legal traditions. Also, the intellectual processes of law (that is, problem solving, interpretation, and application) could provide a way for indigenous peoples to challenge internal oppression generally, and sexism specifically. Aboriginal women must ask how they might build the intellectual capacity of their families and communities to enable them to take on these challenges.

Identifying and ending sexual oppression in aboriginal societies and in aboriginal governments is the responsibility and work of self-determining peoples for whom the self fully includes women. Without a concerted and sustained commitment, the oppression of aboriginal women is not going to end. The conditions of violence and sexism that make it possible for 500 Canadian aboriginal women to disappear are a part of Canada.[124] And the terrible reality is that these conditions exist not just outside aboriginal communities, but within them as well. The conditions that enable the disappearance of aboriginal mothers, sisters, daughters, granddaughters, aunties, cousins, friends, and grandmothers are the same conditions that have excluded the experiences and perspectives of aboriginal women from the definition of self-determination. Basically, how aboriginal women are impacted by these conditions depends on where they are on the spectrum of power that exists both inside and outside aboriginal societies. At one end of this spectrum, where aboriginal women are disposable, are sexual oppression and violence. At the other end of the spectrum are the more benign forms of oppression such as the gendered membership codes in aboriginal communities. The full spectrum of power is rarely understood or appreciated, and even more rarely acknowledged. In the spectrum of our political consciousness, this must change.

[124] Indigenous women are also disappearing elsewhere, such as in Mexico. (Prof Isabel Altamirano-Jimenez, personal communication, University of Alberta, 20 June 2007.)

10

Judicial Treatment of Indigenous Land Rights in the Common Law World

KENT MCNEIL

A. Introduction

After the so-called 'discovery' of the Americas by Christopher Columbus in 1492, the dominant powers of Europe participated in a competitive rush for colonies that eventually encompassed most of the world. The initial pre-eminence of Spain and Portugal in this colonial enterprise was later overtaken by the ascent of France and Great Britain, with Britain emerging as the dominant empire-builder at the end of the Seven Years War in 1763. After World War II, this process was reversed by the decolonisation of much of Asia and Africa, where former colonies became independent and joined the international community as nation-states. In other parts of the world, colonies generally known as 'settler colonies' also achieved independence. In these former colonies, European settlers had arrived and reproduced in such numbers that they became the majority of the population. Achievement of nation-state status by these colonies did not result in restoration of the independence of the Indigenous peoples who lived there when the Europeans arrived. Instead, the European settlers remained in control after asserting independence from their mother country. In some cases, this was the result of unilateral assertion, as occurred when the Thirteen Colonies in British North America rebelled in the 1770s and created the United States of America. In other instances, there was a gradual evolution from colonial status to independent nation-state: Canada, Australia, and New Zealand are the leading examples from the British Empire.[1]

Transformation of settler colonies into settler states therefore did not mean decolonisation for Indigenous peoples. They continued to be subjected to the

[1] See generally WR Louis (ed), *The Oxford History of the British Empire*, 5 vols (Oxford University Press, 1998–1999); A Calder, *Revolutionary Empire: The Rise of the English-Speaking Empires from the Fifteenth Century to the 1780s* (rev'd ed, Pimlico, 1998); JH Elliott, *Empires of the Atlantic World: Britain and Spain in America 1492–1830* (Yale University Press, 2006). On the independence of Canada, Australia and New Zealand, see KC Wheare, *The Statute of Westminster and Dominion Status* (3rd ed, Oxford University Press, 1947).

domination of the Europeans who had come to their territories.[2] Politically, the settlers claimed sovereignty, externally against other nation-states and internally over the territory and people of the settler state. They exercised this sovereignty—and continue to do so today—through government institutions that were modelled on, or adapted from, the European institutions to which they were accustomed.[3] Canada, Australia and New Zealand accordingly remained parliamentary monarchies, whereas the United States, in keeping with its rejection of British aristocratic traditions, opted for a republican form of government. Given their historical foundations, geographical extent, and regional diversity, Canada, Australia and the United States also chose federal systems of government, whereby sovereignty is divided internally between a central government (which also exercises external sovereignty) and various states or provinces. However, only the United States acknowledged the internal sovereignty of the Indigenous peoples—the Indian tribes or nations—living within its borders.[4] Canada, Australia and New Zealand all relied on the British constitutional doctrines of unity of the Crown and parliamentary sovereignty to deny official acknowledgement of even the internal sovereignty of their Indigenous peoples. Only recently have cracks begun to appear in this colonial edifice, as Indigenous peoples in Canada in particular have asserted their inherent right of self-government and obtained begrudging, limited acceptance of this right from the Canadian state.[5]

European legal systems—including the law of nations (now international law) developed in Europe to regulate relations among nation-states—distinguish between sovereignty and property rights. Sovereignty involves the exercise of governmental authority over a territory by a polity that asserts and maintains (in principle, if not always in practice) its independence. Externally, sovereignty includes the capacity to enter into relations with other polities that exercise sovereignty over other territories. Internally, it can be equated with jurisdiction, or the authority to make and enforce laws and government policies. Property rights, on the other hand, involve rights in relation to things (corporeal and incorporeal), including land, that arise under and are regulated by domestic laws that generally originate from either practice (customary law) or enactment (positive law). This distinction is vitally important in colonial contexts because acquisition of

[2] See Chapters by Jennifer Clarke, Jacinta Ruru and Mark Walters.

[3] However, the drafters of the American Constitution were also influenced by Indigenous forms of government, particularly that of the Haudenosaunee (Iroquois Confederacy): see DA Grinde Jr, *The Iroquois and the Founding of the American Nation* (Indian Historian Press, 1977); BE Johansen, *Forgotten Founders: Benjamin Franklin, the Iroquois and the Rationale for the American Revolution* (Gambit, 1982); DA Grinde Jr and BE Johansen, *Exemplar of Liberty: Native America and the Evolution of Democracy* (American Indian Studies Center, University of California, 1991).

[4] See Benjamin J Richardson's Chapter on US Indian Law. For judicial affirmation, see *Cherokee Nation v Georgia*, 30 US (5 Pet) 1 (1831); *Worcester v Georgia*, 31 US (6 Pet) 515 (1832); *US v Lara*, 541 US 193 (2004).

[5] See Shin Imai's Chapter, and K McNeil, 'Judicial Approaches to Self-Government since *Calder*: Searching for Doctrinal Coherence' in H Foster, H Raven and J Webber (eds), *Let Right Be Done: Aboriginal Title, the* Calder *Case, and the Future of Indigenous Rights* (UBC Press, 2007) 129.

sovereignty by a colonising European power did not necessarily entail acquisition of proprietary land rights.[6]

When the European colonisers arrived in North America, they claimed sovereignty vis-à-vis other European powers. But they also entered into treaties with Indigenous nations, some of which acknowledged the sovereignty of those nations.[7] Other North American treaties involved acquisition of property rights in land, and so were admissions by the Europeans that the Indigenous peoples had such rights.[8] Similarly in New Zealand, by the 1840 Treaty of Waitangi the British Crown acknowledged the pre-existing sovereignty (at least in the Māori version of the Treaty) and land rights of the Māori.[9] Nonetheless, the British Crown claimed that its own acquisition of sovereignty over a territory included underlying title to all the land, and courts have consistently upheld this claim.[10] The same rule has been applied in Australia, where no treaties have been acknowledged and there was no judicial recognition of Indigenous land rights (apart from statute) until 1992.[11]

This Chapter focuses on the common law land rights of the Indigenous peoples in the United States, Canada, Australia and New Zealand. These former settler colonies share a common British heritage, and all have legal systems that are based on English law. Despite these commonalities, the law in relation to Indigenous land rights has developed in distinctive ways in each of these jurisdictions. The connection between land rights and Indigenous sovereignty has also been dealt with differently. As already mentioned, American law recognised early on that land rights and internal sovereignty are both aspects of Indigenous territorial rights, while the other three jurisdictions have been reluctant to acknowledge this connection.

The discussion is structured thematically rather than geographically. Topics covered are the sources, content and proof of Indigenous land rights, and the ways in which they can be extinguished and infringed. The focus is on judicial treatment

[6] See M de Vattel, *The Law of Nations, or the Principles of Natural Law*, trans of 1758 edn by CG Fenwick (Carnegie Institution, 1916) bk I, c 18, ss 204–5; K Roberts-Wray, *Commonwealth and Colonial Law* (Stevens and Sons, 1966) 99, 625–36.

[7] Eg the Two-Row-Wampum Treaty with the Haudenosaunee: see M Mitchell, 'An Unbroken Assertion of Sovereignty' in B Richardson (ed), *Drumbeat: Anger and Renewal in Indian Country* (Summerhill Press, 1989) 107, 109–11. See also RA Williams Jr, *Linking Arms Together: American Indian Treaty Visions of Law and Peace, 1600–1800* (Oxford University Press, 1997).

[8] See Mark Walters' Chapter.

[9] See Jacinta Ruru's Chapter, and C Orange, *The Treaty of Waitangi* (Allen and Unwin/Port Nicholson Press, 1987); P McHugh, *The Māori Magna Carta: New Zealand Law and the Treaty of Waitangi* (Oxford University Press, 1991); M Belgrave, M Kawharu and D Williams (eds), *Waitangi Revisited: Perspectives on the Treaty of Waitangi* (Oxford University Press, 2005).

[10] See *St Catherine's Milling and Lumber Company v The Queen* (1888) 14 App Cas 46 (PC); *Delgamuukw v British Columbia* [1997] 3 SCR 1010; *Te Runanga o Wharekauri Rekohu Inc v Attorney-General* [1994] 2 NZLR 20, 23–24 (CA); *Attorney-General v Ngati Apa* [2003] 3 NZLR 643 (CA).

[11] By *Mabo v Queensland [No 2]* (1992) 175 CLR 1 (HC Aust). For evidence of an unacknowledged treaty in Tasmania, see H Reynolds, *Fate of a Free People: A Radical Re-Examination of the Tasmanian Wars* (Penguin Books, 1995). On statutory land rights, which will not be dealt with here, see Jennifer Clarke's Chapter.

of these matters, rather than on legislation and negotiated agreements.[12] Comparisons of the law in the four jurisdictions under consideration are undertaken in relation to each of the topics covered. While this comparative analysis is meant to be critical, it nonetheless examines these matters from the perspective of the dominant legal system in each jurisdiction, which is based on English common law. I realise that this involves making a choice of law. This is not intended to reflect negatively on the relevance or validity of Indigenous legal systems.[13] Instead, it is an acknowledgement of the limitations of my own knowledge and expertise as a non-Indigenous academic, and of the fact that, with the exception of tribal and peacemaker courts in the United States, the law of Indigenous rights has been formulated and applied primarily by common law courts.

B. Sources of Indigenous Land Rights

While the existence of Indigenous land rights has long been acknowledged by governments and courts in the United States, Canada and New Zealand, and more recently in Australia, the sources of these rights have not always been clear. One possibility is that these rights arise from the Indigenous legal systems that were in place when the European colonisers arrived. According to established principles of British colonial and international law, when the Crown acquired sovereignty over a territory the land rights of the local peoples under their own systems of law continued, and became enforceable in common law courts, through what is known as the doctrine of continuity.[14] A second possibility is that the common law itself acknowledged that use and occupation of land by Indigenous peoples at the time of Crown acquisition of sovereignty gave rise to real property rights.[15] This alternative should be available to any Indigenous occupants, whether or not they had land rights under their own pre-existing systems of law.[16] Thirdly, Indigenous land rights may have been based on the law of nations, as applied by domestic courts. A fourth possibility is that Indigenous land rights arose after Crown acquisition of sovereignty, through a positive act of creation by the Crown or a legislative body.[17]

[12] For statutory and agreement-based rights, see Chapters by Jennifer Clarke, Shin Imai, Benjamin J Richardson and Jacinta Ruru. Resolution of land claims is dealt with in Michael Coyle's Chapter.

[13] See Chapters by John Borrows and Christine Zuni Cruz, and Borrows' book, *Recovering Canada: The Resurgence of Indigenous Law* (University of Toronto Press, 2002).

[14] See M Walters, 'The "Golden Thread" of Continuity: Aboriginal Customs at Common Law and under the Constitution Act, 1982' (1999) 44 *McGill Law Journal* 711; RL Barsh, 'Indigenous Rights and the *Lex Loci* in British Imperial Law' in K Wilkins (ed), *Advancing Aboriginal Claims: Visions/Strategies/Directions* (Purich Publishing, 2004) 91; Vattel, above n 6, bk III, c 13, ss 200–1; PD O'Connell, *State Succession in Municipal and International Law* (Cambridge University Press, 1967) vol I, 237–50.

[15] See K McNeil, *Common Law Aboriginal Title* (Clarendon Press, 1989) esp 196–221.

[16] *Ibid*, 193–6.

[17] A fifth potential source not discussed here is natural law or fundamental principles of justice: see B Slattery, 'Aboriginal Sovereignty and Imperial Claims' (1991) 29 *Osgoode Hall Law Journal* 681.

In North America, the British Crown purchased Indigenous lands by treaty, a practice that was formalised by the Royal Proclamation of 1763.[18] In its decision in *St Catherine's Milling and Lumber Company v The Queen*[19] in 1888, the Judicial Committee of the Privy Council suggested that the Royal Proclamation was the source of Indigenous land rights in British North America, but in 1973 the Supreme Court of Canada in *Calder v Attorney-General of British Columbia*[20] decided that this was not the sole source. Justice Judson put it this way:

> Although I think that it is clear that Indian title in British Columbia cannot owe its origin to the Proclamation of 1763, the fact is that when the settlers came, the Indians were there, organized in societies and occupying the land as their forefathers had done for centuries. This is what Indian title means.[21]

While this passage indicated that occupation of land can be a source of Indigenous land rights, the words 'organized in societies' implied a further requirement.[22]

The notion that any people could exist without being socially organised attracted considerable criticism,[23] and was notably absent from the Supreme Court's subsequent reassessment of Aboriginal title in *Delgamuukw v British Columbia*.[24] Chief Justice Lamer stated:

> It had originally been thought that the source of aboriginal title in Canada was the Royal Proclamation, 1763: see *St Catherine's Milling*. However, it is now clear that although aboriginal title was recognized by the Proclamation, it arises from the prior occupation of Canada by aboriginal peoples.[25]

He went on to explain that there are two ways in which prior occupation is relevant. First, in the common law physical occupation is proof of possession, which in turn grounds title. He thus accepted the second potential source we identified earlier.[26] But he also suggested another 'source for aboriginal title—the relationship between common law and pre-existing systems of aboriginal law'.[27] However, he does not seem to have meant by this that Aboriginal title is derived from Aboriginal law and the application of the doctrine of continuity. Instead, when elaborating on proof of Aboriginal title, he clarified that both physical occupation and Aboriginal law can be relied upon to establish the exclusive occupation at the time of Crown assertion of sovereignty that is necessary to prove title. Moreover,

[18] See Mark Walters' Chapter.

[19] Above n 10.

[20] [1973] SCR 313.

[21] *Ibid*, 328.

[22] See *Baker Lake v Minister of Indian Affairs* [1980] 1 FC 518 (FCTD), 557.

[23] See, eg, C Bell and M Asch, 'Challenging Assumptions: The Impact of Precedent in Aboriginal Rights Litigation' in M Asch (ed), *Aboriginal and Treaty Rights in Canada: Essays on Law, Equality, and Respect for Difference* (UBC Press, 1997) 38.

[24] Above n 10.

[25] *Ibid*, para 114.

[26] In *R v Marshall; R v Bernard* [2005] 2 SCR 220, the Supreme Court reaffirmed that occupation of land at the time of Crown sovereignty is the source of Aboriginal title. See also *Tsilhqot'in Nation v British Columbia* [2008] 1 CNLR 112 (BCSC).

[27] *Delgamuukw*, above n 10, para 114.

as discussed in more detail below, he regarded Aboriginal title as a generic right that does not vary from one Aboriginal group to another, as it would if it were based on the continuation of rights under vastly different systems of Aboriginal law.[28] However, it is nonetheless conceivable that the Chief Justice meant to leave the door open for Indigenous peoples to claim title on the basis of their own laws, as an alternative to occupation-based title.

The Canadian Supreme Court has distinguished Aboriginal title from more limited Aboriginal rights to harvest resources—such as fish, game and timber for domestic use—from specific lands.[29] These rights stem, not from exclusive occupation of land, but from practices, customs and traditions in relation to harvesting that were integral to distinctive Aboriginal cultures at the time of contact with Europeans[30] (or, for the Métis, effective European control[31]). In this context, customs can include Aboriginal law,[32] but the Supreme Court has not applied the doctrine of continuity as such in identifying and enforcing these land rights.[33]

Turning to the United States, the Supreme Court acknowledged the existence of Aboriginal or Indian title early in the 19th century.[34] In the famous case of *Johnson v M'Intosh*,[35] Chief Justice Marshall regarded occupation as the basis for this title, but not in the way the Canadian Supreme Court did later in *Delgamuukw*. Instead of applying the common law property rule that physical occupation of land is proof of possession and title, Marshall CJ relied on his understanding of the doctrine of discovery in the law of nations.[36] He explained that, on discovering North America, the major European states all wanted to acquire as much of it as they could, but, to reduce conflicts among themselves, they all agreed 'that discovery gave title to the government by whose subjects, or by whose authority, it was made,

[28] See B Slattery, 'A Taxonomy of Aboriginal Rights' in Foster, Raven and Webber, above n 5, 111.

[29] See, eg, *R v Adams* [1996] 3 SCR 101; *R v Côté* [1996] 3 SCR 139; *R v Sappier; R v Gray* [2006] 2 SCR 686.

[30] *R v Van der Peet* [1996] 2 SCR 507. For critical commentary, see J Borrows, 'Frozen Rights in Canada: Constitutional Interpretation and the Trickster' (1997) 22 *American Indian Law Review* 37; RL Barsh and JY Henderson, 'The Supreme Court's *Van der Peet* Trilogy: Naive Imperialism and Ropes of Sand' (1997) 42 *McGill Law Journal* 993; CC Cheng, 'Touring the Museum: A Comment on *R v Van der Peet*' (1997) 55 *University of Toronto Faculty of Law Review* 419.

[31] *R v Powley* [2003] 2 SCR 207. The Métis, who originated as a distinct people from intermarriage between Aboriginal women and European fur-traders, are one of the three Aboriginal peoples (Indians and Inuit are the others) whose Aboriginal rights were recognised and affirmed by s 35 of the Constitution Act 1982, being Sch B to the Canada Act 1982 (UK), 1982, c 11. See PLAH Chartrand (ed), *Who Are Canada's Aboriginal Peoples? Recognition, Definition, and Jurisdiction* (Purich Publishing, 2002).

[32] See *Sappier* and *Gray*, above n 29, para 45.

[33] For critical analysis, see K McNeil and D Yarrow, 'Has Constitutional Recognition of Aboriginal Rights Adversely Affected Their Definition?' (2007) 37 *Supreme Court Law Review* (2d) 177, esp 204–11.

[34] See *Fletcher v Peck*, 10 US (6 Cranch) 87 (1810), 142–3.

[35] 21 US (8 Wheat) 543 (1823). For detailed background and analysis, see LG Robertson, *Conquest by Law: How the Discovery of America Dispossessed Indigenous Peoples of Their Lands* (Oxford University Press, 2005).

[36] See RJ Miller, *Native America, Discovered and Conquered: Thomas Jefferson, Lewis and Clark, and Manifest Destiny* (Praeger Publishers, 2006).

against all other European governments, which title might be consummated by possession'.[37] As a result, the pre-existing sovereignty and land rights of the Indian nations were reduced:

> They were admitted to be the rightful occupants of the soil, with a legal as well as just claim to retain possession of it, and to use it according to their own discretion; but their rights to complete sovereignty, as independent nations, were necessarily diminished, and their power to dispose of the soil at their own will, to whomsoever they pleased, was denied by the original fundamental principle, that discovery gave exclusive title to those who made it.[38]

Indian title thus became a right of occupancy through application of what Marshall CJ considered to be an international principle, which he applied domestically. Indian law was not the source of this title, though in his view this law continued to apply internally within the Indian territories.[39]

Marshall CJ's reliance on the law of nations rather than on the common law of property or Indigenous law reveals a fundamental difference between the United States and Canada. In American law, Indian title is not just a proprietary right to land. It really amounts to title to territory, which includes governmental authority as well as land rights. So the Indian nations have retained residual sovereignty over their territories as 'domestic dependent nations' within the United States.[40] In Canada, land rights and self-government have been treated as separate issues by the Supreme Court,[41] though we shall see later that Aboriginal title does have jurisdictional dimensions that have been acknowledged by the British Columbia Supreme Court.[42]

In Australia and New Zealand, Indigenous law has played a more prominent role as a source of Aboriginal title to land. Prior to the High Court's decision in *Mabo v Queensland [No 2]*,[43] the sole judicially acknowledged source of Indigenous land rights in Australia was legislation, enacted in the Northern

[37] *Johnson*, above n 35, 573. Marshall CJ undoubtedly got this wrong, as there was no agreement among European nations during the colonial period on the requirements for obtaining territorial sovereignty in the Americas: see MF Lindley, *The Acquisition and Government of Backward Territory in International Law* (Longmans, Green and Co, 1926); J Goebel Jr, *The Struggle for the Falkland Islands: A Study in Legal and Diplomatic History* (1927, reissued Kennikat Press, 1971), 47–119; P Seed, *Ceremonies of Possession in European Conquest of the New World, 1492–1640* (Cambridge University Press, 1995); B Slattery, 'Paper Empires: The Legal Dimensions of French and English Ventures in North America' in J McLaren, AR Buck and NE Wright (eds), *Despotic Dominion: Property Rights in British Settler Societies* (UBC Press, 2005) 50.

[38] *Johnson*, above n 35, 574.

[39] *Ibid*, 593. See also the cases cited in n 4 above.

[40] *Cherokee Nation*, above n 4, 17. See also *Worcester*, above n 4.

[41] See *Delgamuukw*, above n 10; *R v Pamajewon* [1996] 2 SCR 821. Compare *Mitchell v MNR* [2001] 1 SCR 911, per Binnie J, and discussion in McNeil, above n 5, 143–52. For critical analysis, see K McNeil, 'Aboriginal Rights in Canada: From Title to Land to Territorial Sovereignty' (1998) 5 *Tulsa Journal of Comparative and International Law* 253, reprinted in K McNeil, *Emerging Justice? Essays on Indigenous Rights in Canada and Australia* (Native Law Centre of Canada, 2001) 58.

[42] In *Campbell v British Columbia* [2000] 4 CNLR 1.

[43] Above n 11. For background and analysis, see PH Russell, *Recognizing Aboriginal Title: The* Mabo *Case and Indigenous Resistance to English-Settler Colonialism* (University of Toronto Press, 2005).

Territory and most states to address the denial of land rights in *Milirrpum v Nabalco Pty.*[44] In *Mabo*, the court reassessed this matter, and concluded that the Indigenous peoples of Australia did indeed have native title (the Australian term for Indigenous land rights) to lands they occupied under their traditional laws and customs at the time the British Crown acquired sovereignty. Applying this conclusion to the Miriam People of the Murray Islands in the Torres Strait, the court declared that they 'are entitled as against the whole world to possession, occupation, use and enjoyment of the lands of the Murray Islands'.[45]

Although there was no evidence of the communal title that the court apparently declared the Miriam People to have,[46] in his judgment Justice Brennan included the following general statement about the source of native title that has become entrenched in Australian law:

> Native title has its origin in and is given its content by the traditional laws acknowledged by and the traditional customs observed by the indigenous inhabitants of a territory.[47]

Despite the evident contradiction between this statement and the absence of traditional laws and customs supporting the communal title declared by the court,[48] the Australian Parliament adopted Brennan J's statement in the Native Title Act 1993 (Cth),[49] which was enacted to validate pre-existing, non-Indigenous land rights and provide a mechanism for resolution of native title claims. Section 223(1) of that Act provides:

> 223. (1) The expression 'native title' or 'native title rights and interests' means the communal, group or individual rights and interests of Aboriginal peoples or Torres Strait Islanders in relation to land or waters, where:
>
> (a) the rights and interests are possessed under the traditional laws acknowledged, and the traditional customs observed, by the Aboriginal peoples or Torres Strait Islanders; and
> (b) the Aboriginal peoples or Torres Strait Islanders, by those laws and customs, have a connection with the land or waters; and
> (c) the rights and interests are recognised by the common law of Australia.

In subsequent judgments, the High Court has relied upon this statutory definition, and required strict proof of Indigenous laws and customs supporting claimed land

[44] (1971) 17 FLR 141 (NTSC). See McNeil, above n 15, 290–7; H McRae *et al* (eds), *Indigenous Legal Issues: Commentary and Materials* (3rd ed, Lawbook Co, 2003) 184–6, 204–30.

[45] *Mabo*, above n 11, Order of the Court, 217.

[46] Moynihan J, the judge who made the factual findings, had 'found that there was apparently no concept of public or general community ownership among the people of Murray Island, all the land on Murray Island being regarded as belonging to individuals or groups': *ibid*, 22.

[47] *Ibid*, 58.

[48] See K McNeil, 'The Relevance of Traditional Laws and Customs to the Existence and Content of Native Title at Common Law' in *Emerging Justice?*, above n 41, 416, 418–22.

[49] Amended by the Native Title Amendment Act 1998 (Cth) and the Native Title Amendment Act 2007 (Cth). For detailed discussion, see McRae, above n 44, esp 247–376; RH Bartlett, *Native Title in Australia* (2nd ed, LexisNexis Butterworths, 2004).

rights at the time of Crown acquisition of sovereignty, as well as proof that these laws and customs have been maintained up to the present day.[50]

In New Zealand, Māori land rights were acknowledged by the British Crown in the 1840 Treaty of Waitangi, the English version of which guaranteed to the Māori 'the full exclusive and undisturbed possession of their Lands and Estates Forests Fisheries and other properties'.[51] Judicial acknowledgement followed soon after, in the 1847 decision of the NZ Supreme Court in the *Queen v Symonds*.[52] In *Nireaha Tamaki v Baker*,[53] the Privy Council approved of the *Symonds* decision, and rejected a contrary opinion expressed by another New Zealand judge that 'there is no customary law of the Maoris of which the Courts of Law can take cognizance'.[54] On the contrary, the Privy Council said that the statutory regime put in place to integrate Māori title into the English landholding system 'plainly assumes the existence of a tenure of land under custom and usage'.[55] This view that Māori land rights have their source in Māori custom and usage (tikanga Māori) has recently been affirmed by the NZ Court of Appeal in *Attorney-General v Ngati Apa*.[56]

The doctrine of continuity has thus been applied in New Zealand, but less rigidly than in Australia.[57] Māori land rights are sourced, not just in traditional laws and customs, but also in practice and usage, rendering bright-line distinctions between law/custom and practice/usage unnecessary.[58] This approach also avoids the problem that Indigenous claimants have faced in Australia of having to prove that they had a normative system prior to Crown acquisition of sovereignty that generated 'rights' cognisable to non-Indigenous Australian judges.[59]

[50] See, eg, *Fejo v Northern Territory* (1998) 195 CLR 128; *Commonwealth v Yarmirr* (2001) 208 CLR 1; *Western Australia v Ward* (2002) 213 CLR 1; *Members of the Yorta Yorta Community v Victoria* (2002) 214 CLR 422. For critical analysis, see L Strelein, *Compromised Jurisprudence: Native Title Cases Since Mabo* (Aboriginal Studies Press, 2006); S Dorsett, 'An Australian Comparison on Native Title to the Foreshore and Seabed' in C Charters and A Erueti (eds), *Māori Property Rights in the Foreshore and Seabed: The Last Frontier* (Victoria University Press, 2007) 59; S Young, *The Trouble with Tradition: Native Title and Cultural Change* (Federation Press, 2008).

[51] Art 2. The Treaty is reproduced in the First Schedule to the Treaty of Waitangi Act, NZS 1975, No 114. For detailed analysis, see works cited above in n 9.

[52] [1840–1932] NZPCC 387.

[53] [1901] AC 561.

[54] Prendergast CJ in *Wi Parata v Bishop of Wellington* (1877) 3 NZ Jur (NS) SC 72.

[55] *Nireaha Tamaki*, above n 53, 577.

[56] Above n 10. See Jacinta Ruru's Chapter.

[57] See Young, above n 50, esp 167–200. For recent application of this doctrine in another common law jurisdiction, see *Cal v Attorney General of Belize; Coy v Attorney General of Belize*, Claim Nos 171 and 172 of 2007, SC of Belize.

[58] See K McNeil, 'Legal Rights and Legislative Wrongs: Māori Claims to the Foreshore and Seabed' in Charters and Erueti, above n 50, 83, esp 87–9.

[59] See *Yorta Yorta*, above n 50. For critical analysis, see McNeil, above n 48; Young, above n 50.

C. Content of Indigenous Land Rights

Indigenous land rights are sui generis—they are different from other interests in land under the common law. There are also variations in the nature of these rights in each of the four jurisdictions under consideration here. These variations are largely due to the different sources of these rights examined in the previous section. The content of land rights rooted in occupation and use is not the same as content stemming from traditional laws and customs. The right of occupancy of the Indian nations in the United States also has unique features arising from American constitutionalism and the US Supreme Court's application of the doctrine of discovery.

In Canada, we have seen that the Supreme Court held in *Delgamuukw* that Aboriginal title arises from exclusive occupation of land at the time of Crown assertion of sovereignty. At common law, exclusive occupation usually results in a fee simple estate, which, apart from Crown title, is the largest permissible interest in land.[60] However, given its unique source in occupation pre-dating Crown sovereignty, and other *sui generis* aspects (such as inalienability and communal nature, to be discussed below), the court declined to equate Aboriginal title with a fee simple estate. But despite arguments by counsel for the Crown, the court also refused to limit Aboriginal title to traditional uses. Chief Justice Lamer stated:

> I have arrived at the conclusion that the content of aboriginal title can be summarized by two propositions: first, that aboriginal title encompasses the right to exclusive use and occupation of the land held pursuant to that title for a variety of purposes, which need not be aspects of those aboriginal practices, customs and traditions which are integral to distinctive aboriginal cultures; and second, that those protected uses must not be irreconcilable with the nature of the group's attachment to that land.[61]

This means that Aboriginal title includes the natural resources on and under the land, including standing timber and oil and gas, regardless of whether the Aboriginal titleholders used these resources in the past.[62] It also means that they have the right to prevent third parties from trespassing on their land.[63]

Chief Justice Lamer's second proposition placed an inherent limit on the uses Aboriginal titleholders can make of their lands that was intended to preserve the land for future generations. Elaborating, he said that lands subject to aboriginal title cannot be put to such uses as may be irreconcilable with the nature of the occupation of that land and the relationship that the particular group has had with the land which together have given rise to aboriginal title in the first place'.[64] As

[60] See McNeil, above n 15, 6–9, 198.
[61] *Delgamuukw*, above n 10, para 117.
[62] *Ibid*, para 119–24; *Tsilhqot'in Nation*, above n 26, para 971–81.
[63] See K McNeil, *Defining Aboriginal Title in the 90's: Has the Supreme Court Finally Got It Right?* (Robarts Centre for Canadian Studies, York University, 1998) 8–11.
[64] *Delgamuukw*, above n 10, para 128.

examples of situations where this limit might apply, he suggested that Aboriginal titleholders might not be able to strip-mine their traditional hunting grounds or convert a ceremonial site into a parking lot.

Although well-intentioned, the inherent limit the court placed on uses of Aboriginal title land was without precedent, and could seriously impede beneficial economic development by Aboriginal communities. It is also paternalistic, shifting authority to protect Aboriginal lands from communities to Canadian judges.[65] Given the long history of exploitation of Aboriginal lands and removal of natural resources for the benefit of colonial interests, one has to wonder who is better placed to ensure the protection of these lands for future generations.[66]

In addition to this inherent limit and Aboriginal title's unique source in occupation prior to Crown sovereignty, Chief Justice Lamer identified two further *sui generis* aspects: inalienability and communal nature.[67] In each of the four jurisdictions under consideration, courts have consistently held that Aboriginal title cannot be sold or otherwise transferred to anyone other than the Crown, or, in the United States, the American government.[68] This is a matter of both law and policy.[69] Various reasons have been given for this inalienability, including protection of Indigenous peoples from exploitation, incapacity of private persons to acquire title other than by government grant, and a need for government control of settlement. While each of these explanations has some validity, I think a more fundamental reason is that, unlike private property interests, Aboriginal title has jurisdictional dimensions that cannot be transferred to private persons, and so only another government can acquire the title.[70]

In *Delgamuukw*, the Supreme Court took a distinctly propriety approach to Aboriginal title, without explicitly considering its jurisdictional dimensions. Although the Gitksan and Wet'suwet'en peoples who brought the action had asked the court for a declaration of their right of self-government as well as of their title, the court regarded self-government as a separate matter, and decided not to deal with it directly.[71] Significantly, however, in reference to the communal nature of Aboriginal title, Chief Justice Lamer observed:

> Aboriginal title cannot be held by individual aboriginal persons; it is a collective right to land held by all members of an aboriginal nation. Decisions with respect to that land are also made by that community.[72]

[65] For critical discussion, see K McNeil, 'The Post-*Delgamuukw* Nature and Content of Aboriginal Title' in *Emerging Justice?*, above n 41, 102, 116–22.

[66] See Benjamin J Richardson's Environmental Governance Chapter.

[67] See K McNeil, above note 15, 221–35; K McNeil, above n 65, 122–35.

[68] See, eg, *Johnson*, above n 35; *Symonds*, above n 52; *Mabo*, above n 11.

[69] The Royal Proclamation of 1763 prohibited private purchases of Indian lands in British North America, and the 1840 Treaty of Waitangi affirmed the Crown's right of pre-emption of Māori lands in New Zealand: see Chapters by Mark Walters and Jacinta Ruru.

[70] See K McNeil, 'Self-Government and the Inalienability of Aboriginal Title' (2002) 47 *McGill Law Journal* 473.

[71] *Delgamuukw*, above n 10, paras 170–1.

[72] *Ibid*, para 115.

In addition to attributing legal personality to Aboriginal nations,[73] this brief passage does contain an indirect acknowledgement of the jurisdictional dimensions of Aboriginal title. As recognised by Justice Williamson of the BC Supreme Court in *Campbell v British Columbia*,[74] where title is held communally by an Aboriginal group that has decision-making authority, there must be a political structure for exercising that authority. In other words, communal title and decision-making authority necessitate self-government, at least in relation to Aboriginal title land.[75]

Before discussing the other three jurisdictions, mention needs to be made of the content of Aboriginal land rights in Canada apart from title. In a number of cases, the Supreme Court has held that Aboriginal peoples can have site-specific rights to harvest resources, even though they do not have title to the land itself.[76] In *Sappier* and *Gray*,[77] for example, the court held that the Maliseet and Mi'kmaq peoples in New Brunswick have an Aboriginal right to harvest wood for domestic purposes, such as constructing houses and making furniture for themselves. The content of these resource-use rights is determined by practices, customs and traditions that were integral to the distinctive culture of the people in question at the time of contact with Europeans.[78]

Turning to the United States, the Supreme Court's approach to Aboriginal title has never been strictly proprietary. Ever since *Johnson v M'Intosh*[79] was decided in 1823, Indian title has been inseparable from Indian sovereignty. In the two Cherokee Nation cases in the early 1830s,[80] Chief Justice Marshall affirmed that, after European colonisation and subsequent incorporation of their territories into the United States, the Indian nations retained not only their lands, but also their internal sovereignty. Indian title therefore has jurisdictional dimensions that make it more akin to title to territory than to title to land: Indian nations exercise jurisdiction over their tribal lands in the same way other sovereigns exercise jurisdiction over lands within their territories.[81] It follows that Indian nations have a plenary, collective interest in their lands that includes all surface and subsurface rights.[82]

[73] This is an exception to the common law rule that unincorporated collectivities are not legal persons and so cannot hold property: see K McNeil, above n 65, 122–5.

[74] Above n 42, paras 137–8.

[75] See K McNeil, above n 5, 139–43.

[76] See cases cited above in n 29, and K McNeil, 'Aboriginal Title and Aboriginal Rights: What's the Connection?' (1997) 36 *Alberta Law Review* 117.

[77] Above n 29.

[78] See *Van der Peet*, above n 30, and the articles cited in that note.

[79] Above n 35.

[80] *Cherokee Nation* and *Worcester*, above n 4. See J Norgren, *The Cherokee Cases: The Confrontation of Law and Politics* (McGraw-Hill, 1996).

[81] See V Deloria Jr and CM Lytle, *The Nations Within: The Past and Future of American Indian Sovereignty* (Pantheon Books, 1984); DE Wilkins and KT Lomawaima, *Uneven Ground: American Indian Sovereignty and Federal Law* (University of Oklahoma Press, 2001); C Wilkinson, *Blood Struggle: The Rise of Modern Indian Nations* (WW Norton, 2005); NB Duthu, *American Indians and the Law* (Viking Penguin, 2008).

[82] See *US v Shoshone Tribe*, 304 US 111, 115–18 (1938); *US v Klamath and Moadoc Tribes*, 304 US 119, 122–3 (1938); *Otoe and Missouria Tribe v US*, 131 F Supp 265, 290–1 (1955), *cert* denied 350 US 848 (1955); *US v Northern Paiute Nation*, 393 F 2d 786, 796 (1968); *US ex rel Chunie v Ringrose*, 788 F 2d 638, 642 (1986).

Moreover, in exercising their sovereignty they can make laws providing for the creation of individual and other property rights within their territories, but the restriction on alienation mentioned above prevents them from selling their lands so that they would be removed from their territory and hence their jurisdiction, unless the purchaser is the United States.[83] Furthermore, unlike Aboriginal title in Canada, Indian title is not subject to an inherent limit restricting the uses Indian nations can make of their lands.

The US Supreme Court's jurisdictional approach to Indian land rights has had a down-side for the Indian nations. In *Tee-Hit-Ton Indians v United States*,[84] the court held that Indian title that has not been legislatively or executively recognised by the United States is not a property right compensable under the Fifth Amendment to the American Constitution.[85] Instead, it is a mere 'right of occupancy [that] may be terminated and such lands fully disposed of by the sovereign itself [the United States] without any legally enforceable obligation to compensate the Indians'.[86] Although this decision has been justifiably criticised,[87] the jurisdictional dimensions of Indian title and the political nature of the relationship between the Indian nations and the United States may help to explain it.[88] Justice Reed, in his majority judgment, remarked that the Tee-Hit-Ton claim 'was more a claim of sovereignty than of ownership'.[89] As discussed in the introduction to this Chapter, sovereignty is distinct from property, and numerous decisions of the Supreme Court have held that Indian sovereignty is subject to the plenary power of Congress.[90] Nonetheless, it is more in keeping with the territorial nature of

[83] However, from 1887 to 1934, the General Allotment Act, 24 US Stat 388, allowed for creation and sale of individual allotments and distribution of 'surplus' Indian land to homesteaders: see DS Otis, *The Dawes Act and the Allotment of Indian Land*, edited by FP Prucha (University of Oklahoma Press, 1973); FP Prucha, *American Indian Policy in Crisis: Christian Reformers and the Indian, 1865–1900* (University of Oklahoma Press, 1976) 227–64; CF Wilkinson, *American Indians, Time, and the Law: Native Societies in a Modern Constitutional Democracy* (Yale University Press, 1987) 8–9, 19–20; and Benjamin J Richardson's Chapter on US Indian Law.

[84] 348 US 272 (1955).

[85] 1 US Stat 21. The Fifth Amendment provides, among other things, that private property shall not be taken for public use without just compensation.

[86] *Tee-Hit-Ton Indians*, above n 84, 279.

[87] See, eg, JY Henderson, 'Unraveling the Riddle of Indian Title' (1977) 5 *American Indian Law Review* 75; NJ Newton, 'At the Whim of the Sovereign: Aboriginal Title Reconsidered' (1980) 31 *Hastings Law Journal* 1215; SJ Bloxham, 'Aboriginal Title, Alaskan Native Property Rights, and the Case of the Tee-Hit-Ton Indians' (1980) 8 *American Indian Law Review* 299.

[88] See K McNeil, above n 15, 259–67. For a political analysis of the decision, see K McNeil, 'How the New Deal Became a Raw Deal for Native Americans: The *Tee-Hit-Ton* Alaska Decision and the Denial of Fifth Amendment Protection to Indian Land Title', paper delivered at the Western History Association's 40th Annual Conference, San Antonio, Texas, 11–14 October 2000 (on file with author).

[89] *Tee-Hit-Ton Indians*, above n 84, 287.

[90] See, eg, *Lone Wolf v Hitchcock*, 187 US 553 (1903); *US v Wheeler*, 435 US 313, 323 (1978); *Cotton Petroleum Corporation v New Mexico*, 490 US 163, 192 (1989); *South Dakota v Yankton Sioux Tribe*, 522 US 329, 343 (1998). For critical commentary, see V Deloria Jr, *Behind the Trail of Broken Treaties: An Indian Declaration of Independence* (University of Texas Press, 1985) 141–60; Wilkins and Lomawaima, above n 81, 98–116. See also the concurring judgment of Thomas J in *Lara*, above n 4, questioning the plenary power doctrine.

Indian rights, and with earlier American case law, to regard these rights as both jurisdictional *and* proprietary.[91]

In Australia, reliance on traditional laws and customs and the doctrine of continuity has had a very negative impact on Indigenous land rights.[92] Contrary to the all-encompassing native title of the Miriam People declared by the High Court in *Mabo,* in subsequent cases Indigenous claimants have had to prove rights in relation to land by reference to specific laws and customs at the time of Crown acquisition of sovereignty. The content of their rights is therefore defined by their laws and customs.[93] So even if they were in exclusive occupation of land at that time, they would not, for example, have any rights to minerals if they did not have laws and customs in relation to those resources.[94]

Post-*Mabo*, the High Court has thus taken a particularised approach to native title, treating it as a divisible bundle of rights, each arising from specific laws or customs. As a result, a right to take estuarine crocodiles is as much a native title right as a right to exclusive possession.[95] So Australian law contains no equivalent to the fundamental Canadian distinction between Aboriginal title and other Aboriginal land rights. Moreover, the High Court has adamantly refused to envisage continuation of rights other than in relation to land. The doctrine of continuity has therefore been applied selectively, eliminating the possibility of an Indigenous right of self-government.[96] On the positive side, this means that native title rights and interests can co-exist with non-exclusive third party interests, such as some pastoral leaseholds, though in the event of conflict the third party interests generally prevail.[97]

While the doctrine of continuity has also been applied in New Zealand, it has not had the negative impact seen in Australia. This is mainly because Māori land rights are based on tikanga Māori, encompassing both custom and usage.[98] Rights that were not otherwise extinguished have mostly been converted into common law interests by the Native Land Court (now the Māori Land Court).[99] But as recently affirmed by the NZ Court of Appeal, Māori land rights based on tikanga Māori can still exist, usually as exclusive interests equivalent to fee simple estates, or, less commonly, as more limited interests.[100] Although the matter has not yet been conclusively decided, it appears that exclusive Māori interests include rights

[91] See text accompanying nn 35–40 above.

[92] For detailed discussion, see McNeil, above n 48; Strelein, above n 50; Young, above n 50.

[93] See esp *Ward* and *Yorta Yorta*, above n 50.

[94] *Ward*, above n 50, esp para 382.

[95] *Yanner v Eaton* (1999) 166 ALR 258 (HC Aust).

[96] See *Walker v New South Wales* (1994) 182 CLR 45; *Coe v Commonwealth* (1993) 68 ALJR 110; *Thorpe v Commonwealth (No 3)* (1997) 71 ALJR 767; *Yorta Yorta*, above n 50.

[97] See *Wik Peoples v Queensland* (1996) 141 ALR 129 (HC Aust); K McNeil, 'Co-Existence of Indigenous Rights and Other Interests in Land in Australia and Canada' [1997] 3 *Canadian Native Law Reporter* 1. Compare *Anderson v Wilson* (2002) 213 CLR 401 (HC Aust).

[98] See text accompanying nn 57–58 above.

[99] See DV Williams, *'Te Kooti Tango Whenua': The Native Land Court 1864–1909* (Huia Publishers, 1999), and Jacinta Ruru's Chapter.

[100] See *Ngati Apa*, above n 10, esp per Elias CJ, para 46; Young, above n 50, 167–200.

to standing timber and mineral resources, a conclusion that follows from their equivalence to fee simple.[101]

D. Proof of Indigenous Land Rights

When Indigenous peoples seek judicial acknowledgment of their land rights in the courts of the nation-states that have asserted sovereignty over them, they have the onus of proving their rights in accordance with tests and standards that are usually set by the judiciary.[102] These tests and standards vary from one jurisdiction to another, depending on the source of the title and other factors, but the burden of proof is always onerous. The difficulties Indigenous claimants face are compounded by the fact that their traditions were generally oral, and courts tend to place greater weight on written documents in determining historical issues arising beyond the limits of living memory.

The Supreme Court of Canada has acknowledged these difficulties, and has sought to alleviate them to some extent by directing trial judges to admit oral histories as evidence and to accord them appropriate weight. In *Delgamuukw*, for example, the court overturned the trial judge's decision and ordered a new trial, in part because he had not given sufficient credence or weight to the oral histories of the Gitksan and Wet'suwet'en claimants. After acknowledging that the hearsay rule, for example, could act as a barrier to the use of oral histories in court, Chief Justice Lamer stated that 'the laws of evidence must be adapted in order that this type of evidence can be accommodated and placed on an equal footing with the types of historical evidence that courts are familiar with, which largely consists of historical documents'.[103] Nonetheless, judges still retain considerable discretion regarding the weight to be given to any evidence, including oral histories.[104] Moreover, in Australia there appears to be an ongoing tendency to give more weight to the written evidence of settlers than to the oral histories of Indigenous peoples.[105]

[101] See *New Zealand Maori Council v Attorney-General* [1989] 2 NZLR 142 (CA); *Tainui Maori Trust Board v Attorney-General* [1989] 2 NZLR 513 (CA), per Cooke P, 527–30; and discussion in Young, above n 50, 180–82.

[102] For critical analysis in the Canadian context, see K McNeil, 'The Onus of Proof of Aboriginal Title' (1999) 37 *Osgoode Hall Law Journal* 775, reprinted in *Emerging Justice?*, above n 41, 136.

[103] *Delgamuukw*, above n 10, para 87. See also *Van der Peet*, above n 30, para 68; *Mitchell*, above n 41, paras 27–39; *Benoit v Canada* [2003] 3 CNLR 20 (FCA), leave to appeal refused, SCC, 29 April 2004. For discussion, see J Borrows, 'Listening for a Change: The Courts and Oral Traditions' (2001) 39 *Osgoode Hall Law Journal* 1.

[104] *Mitchell*, above n 41, para 36.

[105] See, eg, *Members of the Yorta Yorta Aboriginal Community v Victoria* [1998] FCA 1606, aff'd [2001] 110 FCR 244, (2002) 214 CLR 422. Compare *De Rose v South Australia (No 1)* [2002] FCA 1342, rev'd on other grounds (2003) 133 FCR 325 (Full FC), and *Neowarra v Western Australia* [2003] FCA 1402, where oral histories figured more prominently. In the United States, the Indian Claims Commission, though given a broad mandate that included authority to hear and determine 'claims based upon fair and honorable dealings that are not recognized by any existing rule of law or equity' (Indian Claims Commission Act of 1946, 60 Stat 1049, s 2: see Michael Coyle's Chapter), generally

What Indigenous peoples actually have to prove to establish their land rights depends largely on the source of these rights. In Canada, where Aboriginal title is based on occupation, Aboriginal peoples have to prove that they were in exclusive occupation of the claimed land at the time of British assertion of sovereignty.[106] As discussed earlier, the requisite occupation can be established by proof of physical presence and use of the land, and by evidence of Aboriginal law. In *Delgamuukw*, Chief Justice Lamer explained:

> . . . the source of aboriginal title appears to be grounded both in the common law and in the aboriginal perspective on land; the latter includes, but is not limited to, their systems of law. It follows that both should be taken into account in establishing the proof of occupancy.[107]

Regarding physical occupation, Lamer CJ said it 'may be established in a variety of ways, ranging from the construction of dwellings through cultivation and enclosure of fields to regular use of definite tracts of land for hunting, fishing or otherwise exploiting its resources'.[108] Factors to consider in deciding whether the occupation was sufficient to establish title include 'the group's size, manner of life, material resources, and technological abilities, and the character of the lands claimed'.[109]

Somewhat surprisingly, when the Supreme Court next considered proof of Aboriginal title in *R v Marshall; R v Bernard*,[110] Chief Justice McLachlin emphasised the importance of physical occupation, and virtually ignored the evidentiary role of Aboriginal law. She also seems to have raised the threshold for establishing occupation by deciding that proof of occupation of specific sites rather than of a broader territory is required.[111] She suggested as well that nomadic peoples may not have been in sufficient occupation of at least some of their territories to have title. In contrast, Justice LeBel (Fish J concurring), in a separate judgment concurring in result, thought the Chief Justice's physical occupation approach was 'too narrowly focused on common law concepts relating to property interests', and might preclude establishment of Aboriginal title by nomadic or semi-nomadic peoples.[112] Moreover, in his trial decision in the *Tsilhqot'in Nation* case in 2007, Justice Vickers of the BC Supreme Court found that *Marshall* and *Bernard* differed

regarded oral histories as too vague and self-serving to be relied upon: see, eg, *Pueblo of Taos v US*, 15 ICC 688, 694–5 (1965). For commentary, see G Stohr, 'The Repercussions of Orality in Federal Indian Law' (1999) 31 *Arizona State Law Journal* 679.

[106] *Delgamuukw*, above n 10, para 144.

[107] *Ibid*, para 147.

[108] *Ibid*, para 149.

[109] *Ibid*, quoting B Slattery, 'Understanding Aboriginal Rights' (1987) 66 *Canadian Bar Review* 727, 758.

[110] Above n 26. For critical commentary, see K McNeil, 'Aboriginal Title and the Supreme Court: What's Happening?' (2006) 69 *Saskatchewan Law Review* 281.

[111] Compare the more territorial approach taken by Cromwell JA of the NSCA and Daigle JA of the NBCA: *R v Marshall* (2003) 218 NSR (2d) 78, esp para 183; *R v Bernard* (2003) 262 NBR (2d) 1, esp para 85.

[112] *Marshall* and *Bernard*, above n 26, para 110, 126.

from the claim before him because in that case 'the persons accused both attempted to prove Aboriginal title at specific sites' to defend themselves against charges of violations of provincial forestry legislation,[113] whereas in the Tsilhqot'in claim for a declaration of Aboriginal title the evidence ranged 'over tracts of land'.[114]

Marshall and *Bernard* also addressed the requirement that the occupation be exclusive. After noting that factual evidence of acts of exclusion might not be available, Chief Justice McLachlin concluded that

> evidence of acts of exclusion is not required to establish aboriginal title. All that is required is demonstration of effective control of the land by the group, from which a reasonable inference can be drawn that it could have excluded others had it chosen to do so.[115]

In connection with exclusivity, in *Delgamuukw* the court briefly addressed another issue, namely, whether two or more Aboriginal groups can have joint title if they occupied land to the exclusion of other Aboriginal groups. Chief Justice Lamer suggested that shared exclusivity could result in joint Aboriginal title,[116] as recognised by the US Supreme Court in *United States v Santa Fe Pacific Railroad.*[117] While this issue has not, as far as I know, received further judicial consideration in Canada, several American decisions have acknowledged that joint title can exist where two or more Indian nations amicably occupied land to the exclusion of other Indian nations.[118]

As discussed earlier, Canadian law distinguishes between Aboriginal title and other land rights, which generally involve rights to harvest particular resources from specific lands. Proof of the latter involves meeting the test created by the Supreme Court in the *Van der Peet* decision: Aboriginal claimants must show that the activity they claim a right over was 'an element of a practice, custom or tradition integral to [their] distinctive culture' at the time of European contact[119] or, for the Métis, effective European control.[120] Applying this test in 2006 in *Sappier* and *Gray*, Justice Bastarache said that '[f]lexibility is important when engaging in the *Van der Peet* analysis because the object is to provide cultural security and

[113] In *Marshall* and *Bernard*, *ibid*, paras 142–3, LeBel J also expressed reservations over deciding Aboriginal title in a quasi-criminal prosecution. See S Imai, 'The Adjudication of Historical Evidence: A Comment and an Elaboration on a Proposal by Justice LeBel' (2006) 55 *University of New Brunswick Law Journal* 146.

[114] *Tsilhqot'in Nation*, above n 26, para 582.

[115] *Marshall* and *Bernard*, above n 26, para 65.

[116] *Delgamuukw*, above n 10, para 158.

[117] 314 US 339 (1941).

[118] See *Iowa Tribe of the Iowa Reservation v US*, 195 Ct Cl 365, 394–6 (1971); *Turtle Mountain Band of Chippewa Indians v US*, 490 F 2d 935, 944 (1974, Ct Cl); *US v Pueblo of San Ildefonso*, 513 F 2d 1383, 1394–5 (1975, Ct Cl); *Strong v US*, 518 F 2d 556, 561–2 (1975, Ct Cl), *cert* denied 423 US 1015 (1975); *Uintah Ute Indians v US*, 28 Fed Cl 768, 785, 787 n 21 (1993). For discussion, see MJ Kaplan, 'Proof and Extinguishment of Aboriginal Title to Indian Lands' (1979, updated 2003) LEXSEE 41 ALR Fed 425, heading 3b, '"Exclusive" use or occupancy; joint aboriginal title'.

[119] *Van der Peet*, above n 30, para 46, 73.

[120] *Powley*, above n 31.

continuity for the particular aboriginal society'.[121] Regarding the 'integral to the distinctive culture' aspect of the test, he clarified:

> What is meant by 'culture' is really an inquiry into the pre-contact way of life of a particular aboriginal community, including their means of survival, their socialization methods, their legal systems, and, potentially, their trading habits. The use of the word 'distinctive' as a qualifier is meant to incorporate an element of aboriginal specificity. However, 'distinctive' does not mean 'distinct', and the notion of aboriginality must not be reduced to 'racialized stereotypes of Aboriginal peoples'.[122]

On the basis of the evidence presented, the Supreme Court accordingly held that the Pabineau and Woodstock First Nations of the Mi'kmaq and Maliseet peoples have an Aboriginal right to harvest wood for domestic uses on Crown lands traditionally used by them for that purpose.

In the United States, there is no equivalent to the distinction between Indian title and other Indian land rights found in Aboriginal rights law in Canada.[123] The explanation appears to be that American courts have defined occupation more broadly, so that virtually any Indian use of lands can give rise to Aboriginal or Indian title.[124] As early as 1835, Justice Baldwin expressed the opinion of the Supreme Court that Indian occupation 'was considered with reference to their habits and modes of life; their hunting-grounds were as much in their actual possession as the cleared fields of the whites, and their rights to its exclusive enjoyment in their own way and for their own purposes were as much respected'.[125] So while Indian title, like Aboriginal title in Canada, is based on exclusive occupation, American courts have taken a distinctly territorial approach to its geographical extent. In *Santa Fe Pacific Railroad*, Justice Douglas said:

> If it were established as a fact that the lands in question were, or were included in, the ancestral home of the Walapais in the sense that they constituted definable territory occupied exclusively by the Walapais (as distinguished from lands wandered over by many tribes), then the Walapais had 'Indian title'.[126]

The same territorial approach has been taken in other American cases, including decisions of the Court of Claims on appeals from the Indian Claims Commission, which had been established in 1946 to resolve outstanding Indian claims against the US government.[127] Even tribes described as 'nomadic' have been held to have Indian title to lands they used on a regular basis in accordance

[121] *Sappier* and *Gray*, above n 29, para 33.

[122] *Ibid*, para 45, quoting J Borrows and LI Rotman, 'The *Sui Generis* Nature of Aboriginal Rights: Does it Make a Difference?' (1997) 36 *Alberta Law Review* 9, 36.

[123] While Indian resource rights can exist off their lands in the United States, this is usually the result of treaties: see Duthu, above n 81, 99–109.

[124] See FS Cohen, 'Original Indian Title' (1947) 32 *Minnesota Law Review* 28.

[125] *Mitchel v US*, 34 US (9 Pet) 711, 746 (1835).

[126] *Santa Fe Pacific Railroad*, above n 117, 345.

[127] See I Sutton (ed), *Irredeemable America: The Indians' Estate and Land Claims* (University of New Mexico Press, 1985), and Michael Coyle's Chapter.

with their own ways of life.[128] Moreover, title extends to 'seasonal or hunting areas over which the Indians had control even though those areas were only used intermittently'.[129]

Another important distinction between Canadian and American law in relation to proof is that Indian claimants in the United States do not have to prove occupation of land at the time of British, or even American, assertion of sovereignty. Instead, proof of occupation 'for a long time' is sufficient.[130] In *Confederated Tribes of the Warm Springs Reservation of Oregon v United States*, Justice Durfee explained:

> The time requirement, as a general rule, cannot be fixed at a specific number of years. It must be long enough to have allowed the Indians to transform the area into domestic territory [so that the court is not] 'creating aboriginal title in a tribe which itself played the role of conqueror but a few years before'.[131]

This means that Indian nations could acquire title from one another (especially if by peaceful transfer) or by occupying vacant lands after American assertion of sovereignty,[132] and eases the burden of proof by shortening the timeframe for establishing the requisite occupation.[133]

Finally, while American courts have held that the occupation required for Indian title is a matter of fact,[134] what has to be established is not so much physical occupation as control of territory. In *United States v Seminole Indians of Florida*, Justice Collins said that

> the Government leans far too heavily in the direction of equating 'occupancy' (or capacity to occupy) with *actual* possession, whereas the key to Indian title lies in evaluating the manner of land-use over a period of time. Physical control or dominion over the land is the dispositive criterion.[135]

Proof of native title in Australia is another matter entirely. What is required is not evidence of exclusive occupation or control, but rather of a connection to the land through traditional laws and customs.[136] This requirement originated from

[128] *US v Kagama*, 118 US 375, 381 (1886); *Cramer v US*, 261 US 219, 227 (1923); *Northwestern Bands of Shoshone Indians v US*, 324 US 335, 338–40 (1945); *Tee-Hit-Ton Indians v US*, 120 F Supp 202, 204 (1954, Ct Cl), aff'd above n 84, 285–8.

[129] *Confederated Tribes of the Warm Springs Reservation of Oregon v US*, 177 Ct Cl 184, 194 (1966). See also *Delaware Tribe of Indians v US*, 130 Ct Cl 782, 789 (1955); *Spokane Tribe v US*, 163 Ct Cl 58, 66 (1963).

[130] *Sac and Fox Tribe of Indians of Oklahoma v US*, 161 Ct Cl 189, 202, 205–7 (1963), *cert* denied 375 US 921 (1963); *Confederated Tribes of the Warm Springs Reservation*, above n 129, 194; *US v Pueblo of San Ildefonso*, above n 118, 1394; *Seneca Nation of Indians v New York*, 206 F Supp 2d 448, 503 (2002, WDNY).

[131] *Confederated Tribes of the Warm Springs Reservation*, above n 129, 194, quoting *Sac and Fox Tribe*, above n 130, 206.

[132] *Turtle Mountain Band of Chippewa Indians*, above n 118.

[133] In *US v Seminole Indians of Florida*, 180 Ct Cl 375 (1967), 58 years was held to be a sufficiently long time to acquire title. In *Alabama-Coushatta Tribe v US*, 28 Fed Cl 95 (1993), 30 years sufficed.

[134] See *Santa Fe Pacific Railroad*, above n 117, 345, quoted in text accompanying n 126 above; *Pueblo of San Ildefonso*, above n 118, 1394; *Six Nations v US*, 173 Ct Cl 899 at 910 (1965).

[135] *Seminole Indians of Florida*, above n 133, 385–6 (emphasis in original).

[136] See *Ward*, above n 50, esp paras 89–93.

Justice Brennan's judgment in *Mabo*.[137] As we have seen, it was given statutory force by incorporation into the definition of native title in section 223(1) of the Native Title Act 1993,[138] which, as interpreted by the High Court, makes it necessary for claimants to prove that they have maintained a connection with the land through substantially uninterrupted acknowledgment and observance of their laws and customs from the time of Crown assertion of sovereignty to the present.[139] This requirement makes proof of native title especially difficult for Indigenous peoples in more populated areas whose connection to the land and observance of traditional laws and customs have been severely interfered with by settlers. Particularly disturbing is the pronouncement by the Full Federal Court in 2008 that the cause of loss of connection and observance is irrelevant.[140] Apparently, even illegal squatting—a historically common way of taking Indigenous land in Australia—could have resulted in loss of native title because it would have severed the necessary connection with the land.

The Australian High Court's approach to native title claims also necessitates proof of specific laws and customs relating to particular uses of lands and resources.[141] It is not enough for claimants to establish they had, and have maintained, a general system of traditional laws and customs in relation to land; instead, they have to prove that their laws and customs provide specific 'rights' that are recognisable as such by common law courts.[142] So, unlike in Canada where historical practices alone can generate rights, Australian law requires proof that practices were engaged in pursuant to traditional laws and customs.[143] Moreover, as mentioned previously, in Australia proof of exclusive occupation does not necessarily result in all-inclusive rights to surface and subsurface resources.[144]

While New Zealand has also based Māori land rights on pre-existing laws and customs, this has not had the negative consequences that reliance on traditional laws and customs has had in Australia. This is because Māori land rights are more broadly grounded in tikanga Māori, which includes both custom and usage.[145]

[137] *Mabo*, above n 11, esp 58–60.

[138] See text accompanying nn 49–50 above.

[139] *Yorta Yorta*, above n 50. See also *De Rose [No 1]*, above n 105 (Full FC); *De Rose v South Australia [No 2]* (2005) 145 FCR 290; *Northern Territory v Alyawarr* (2005) 145 FCR 442; *Bodney v Bennell* [2008] FCAFC 63.

[140] *Bodney v Bennell*, above n 139, paras 96–7, relying on *Yorta Yorta*, above n 50, paras 89–90.

[141] See esp *Ward*, above n 50. For application of the High Court's approach, see *Daniel v Western Australia* [2003] FCA 666; *Sampi v Western Australia* [2005] FCA 777; *Rubibi Community (No 7) v Western Australia* [2006] FCA 459; *Risk v Northern Territory* [2006] FCA 404, aff'd (2007) 240 ALR 75 (Full FC). Compare *Neowarra*, above n 105.

[142] For detailed discussion and criticism, see Young, above n 50.

[143] See *Mason v Tritton* (1994) 34 NSWLR 572 (NSWCA); *Derschaw v Sutton* (1996) 90 A Crim R 9 (Full SCWA); *Dillon v Davies* (1998) 156 ALR 142 (SC Tas). For discussion, see McNeil, above n 48, 454–8; Dorsett, above n 50, 61–6; Young, above n 50, 338–42; A Erueti, 'The Recognition of Indigenous Peoples' Rights to Traditional Lands: The Evaluation of States by International Treaty Bodies' in Charters and Erueti, above n 50, 175, 178–83.

[144] *Ward*, above n 50, esp para 382.

[145] This is a statutory as well as common law approach: *Kauwaeranga Judgment*, Native Land Court, 1870, reproduced (1984) 14 *Victoria University of Wellington Law Review* 227; *Ngati Apa*, above n 10. See Jacinta Ruru's Chapter.

Proof of Māori land rights therefore involves proof of custom or usage in relation to the claimed land at the time of British assertion of sovereignty in 1840. If the claimant group proves exclusive occupation, they have title equivalent to an inalienable fee simple estate, whereas proof of customary rights or uses not amounting to exclusive occupation could result in more limited interests.[146] Moreover, unlike in Australia, it does not appear to be necessary in New Zealand to prove continuous observance of tikanga Māori from the time of British assertion of sovereignty to the present.[147] As in Canada, where title has been established as of that time, apparently it is presumed to continue until shown to have been extinguished.[148]

E. Extinguishment and Infringement of Indigenous Land Rights

In all four jurisdictions considered in this Chapter, Indigenous land rights can be voluntarily surrendered by means of a treaty or other agreement. In British North America, this was specified in the Royal Proclamation of 1763, which forbade private acquisition of Indian lands and stipulated that they could only be acquired by the Crown or a proprietary government at a public assembly of the Indian titleholders gathered for that purpose.[149] The Proclamation continued the pre-existing Crown practice of purchasing Indian lands, resulting in land-surrender treaties in what is now Canada from 1763 to the 1920s, when the Canadian government stopped negotiating treaties. The process recommenced in the 1970s when, following the Supreme Court of Canada's acknowledgment of the existence of Aboriginal title in *Calder*,[150] Canada established the comprehensive claims process.[151] In the 1990s, a similar process was created in British Columbia when the BC Treaty Commission was set up to facilitate the negotiation of land claims in that province.[152]

Extinguishment of Aboriginal title by treaty or other agreement is controversial. Regarding the Canadian historical treaties, questions remain regarding interpretation of the land-surrender provisions, and what the Aboriginal parties understood

[146] See text accompanying nn 98–101 above.

[147] See Young, above n 50, 172–5.

[148] See K McNeil, 'Continuity of Aboriginal Rights', in Wilkins, above n 14, 127. However, the New Zealand Foreshore and Seabed Act 2004, s 50(1)(b), created a statutory exception: see McNeil, above n 58, 92–3, 103–16; Dorsett, above n 50, 71–7; Erueti, above n 143, 186–7.

[149] See Mark Walters' Chapter.

[150] Above n 20.

[151] See Michael Coyle's Chapter.

[152] See C McKee, *Treaty Talks in British Columbia: Negotiating a Mutually Beneficial Future* (UBC Press, 1996); A Woolford, *Between Justice and Certainty: Treaty Making in British Columbia* (UBC Press, 2005); T Penikett, *Reconciliation: First Nations Treaty Making in British Columbia* (Douglas and McIntyre, 2006).

those provisions to mean.[153] In the Prairie Provinces, for example, it has often been contended that the land was to be shared, and that only surface rights to the depth of a plough were being accorded to the government for the purpose of farming.[154] Questions have also been raised over whether Aboriginal peoples had the authority under their own systems of law to alienate their lands.[155] In the modern-day treaty process, extinguishment of rights has been vigorously opposed by Aboriginal peoples, and compromises have been sought to affirm existing rights while meeting government demands for certainty.[156]

In the United States, the federal government continued the British policy of acquiring Indian lands by purchase, though often by applying coercion, especially during the 19th century removal period when many eastern tribes were moved from their homelands to Indian Territory in what later became the State of Oklahoma.[157] Congress also has the authority to extinguish or infringe Indian title unilaterally, without any legal obligation to pay compensation unless the United States had previously recognised the title by treaty, agreement or unilateral government action.[158] The states, however, have no such authority, as the Commerce Clause in the American Constitution gives Congress exclusive jurisdiction over Indian affairs, and the Indian Trade and Intercourse Acts, dating from the 1790s, prohibit state acquisition of Indian lands.[159] In the past, the United States could also extinguish Indian title by conquest,[160] though more commonly military force was used to compel Indian tribes to cede their lands to the government.[161]

[153] See *Re Paulette* (1973) 42 DLR (3d) 8 (NWTSC), rev'd on other grounds (1975) 63 DLR (3d) 1 (NWTCA), [1977] 2 SCR 628; P Macklem, 'The Impact of Treaty 9 on Natural Resource Development in Northern Ontario' in Asch, above n 23, 97; S Imai, 'Treaty Lands and Crown Obligations: The "Tracts Taken Up" Provision' (2001) 27 *Queen's Law Journal* 1.

[154] See Treaty 7 Elders *et al*, *The True Spirit and Original Intent of Treaty 7* (McGill-Queen's University Press, 1996) esp 113–23, 144–5; H Cardinal and W Hildebrandt, *Treaty Elders of Saskatchewan: Our Dream Is That Our Peoples Will One Day Be Clearly Recognized as Nations* (University of Calgary Press, 2000) esp 34–47.

[155] See L Little Bear, 'Aboriginal Rights and the Canadian "Grundnorm"' in JR Ponting (ed), *Arduous Journey: Canadian Indians and Decolonization* (McClelland and Stewart, 1986) 243, 247; Canada, *Report of the Royal Commission on Aboriginal Peoples*, vol 2, *Restructuring the Relationship* (Supply and Services Canada, 1996) 459; S Venne, 'Understanding Treaty 6: An Indigenous Perspective' in Asch, above n 23, 173, esp 192–3.

[156] See *Report of the Royal Commission on Aboriginal Peoples*, vol 2, above n 155, 527–57; M Asch and N Zlotkin, 'Affirming Aboriginal Title: A New Basis for Comprehensive Claims Negotiations' in Asch, above n 23, 208; and works cited in n 152 above.

[157] See FP Prucha, *American Indian Policy in the Formative Years* (Harvard University Press, 1962); RN Satz, *American Indian Policy in the Jacksonian Era* (University of Oklahoma Press, 1975); MD Green, *The Politics of Indian Removal: Creek Government and Society in Crisis* (University of Nebraska Press, 1982).

[158] *Tee-Hit-Ton Indians*, above n 84. See also Kaplan, above n 118, heading III, 'Extinguishing aboriginal title'.

[159] Originally 1 US Stat 137 (1790). See *County of Oneida v Oneida Indian Nation*, 470 US 226 (1985); RN Clinton and MT Hotopp, 'Judicial Enforcement of the Federal Restraints on Alienation of Indian Land: The Origins of the Eastern Land Claims' (1979) 31 *Maine Law Review* 17; GC Shattuck, *The Oneida Land Claims: A Legal History* (Syracuse University Press, 1991).

[160] See *Johnson*, above n 35, 586–92; *Santa Fe Pacific Railroad*, above n 117, 347.

[161] See generally S Banner, *How the Indians Lost Their Land: Law and Power on the Frontier* (Belknap Press of Harvard University Press, 2005).

In theory, British common law restrictions on the authority of the Crown would have prevented the taking of Indigenous lands by conquest in Canada, Australia and New Zealand after Crown acquisition of sovereignty. In practice, however, legal constraints are not always effective: in Australia, Aboriginal peoples were often killed or driven from their lands by force, whereas in New Zealand the wars of the 1860s resulted in substantial loss of life and land.[162] Because Indigenous land rights were not acknowledged (apart from statute) in Australia prior to the *Mabo* decision in 1992,[163] no recognised land-surrender treaties or agreements were entered into there. The Treaty of Waitangi in New Zealand confirmed rather than extinguished Māori land rights, though large areas of Māori land have been lost through conversion of those rights to common law interests and subsequent alienations.[164]

In the absence of constitutional protections for Indigenous land rights, there are no domestic legal impediments to extinguishment or infringement of those rights by legislatures that have constitutional authority over them.[165] Legislative extinguishment has occurred relatively recently in Australia and New Zealand. By the Native Title Act 1993 (as amended),[166] the Australian Parliament validated some past acts, such as Crown grants of land, so that they extinguished or infringed native title rights.[167] In 2004, the New Zealand Parliament enacted the Foreshore and Seabed Act, extinguishing most Māori rights to coastal lands below the high-water mark.[168]

It is, however, essential to distinguish between legislative and executive authority. In parliamentary systems of government established on the British model, the executive branch of government has no authority apart from statute to take away or infringe property rights.[169] As Indigenous land rights in Canada, Australia and New Zealand are proprietary, it should be unconstitutional for the executive branch to extinguish or infringe them without clear and plain statutory authority. While this appears to be the law in Canada and New Zealand,[170] in Australia the

[162] See H Reynolds, *The Other Side of the Frontier: Aboriginal Resistance to the European Invasion of Australia* (Penguin Books, 1982); D Day, *Claiming a Continent: A New History of Australia* (HarperCollins, 2001) 73–88; J Belich, *The New Zealand Wars and the Victorian Interpretation of Racial Conflict* (Auckland University Press, 1987); M King, *The Pelican History of New Zealand* (Penguin Books, 2003), 211–24.

[163] Above n 11.

[164] See Orange, above n 9; McHugh, above n 9, 333–4.

[165] See K McNeil, 'Extinguishment of Aboriginal Title in Canada: Treaties, Legislation and Judicial Discretion' (2001–2002) 33 *Ottawa Law Review* 301, esp 317–27.

[166] Above n 49.

[167] See McRae, above n 44, 341–5; Bartlett, above n 49, 392–402. However, s 51(xxxi) of the Australian Constitution (s 9 of the Commonwealth of Australia Constitution Act, 63 and 64 Vict, c 12 (UK)), provides that the taking of property by Parliament be on 'just terms', and so the Native Title Act 1993 provides for compensation: McRae, 356–7; Bartlett, 402.

[168] See Charters and Erueti, above n 50.

[169] *Entick v Carrington* (1765) 19 St Tr 1030 (CP); *Attorney-General v De Keyser's Royal Hotel* [1920] AC 508, 569 (HL); *Spooner Oils Ltd v Turner Valley Gas Conservation Board* [1933] SCR 629. See JW Ely Jr, *The Guardian of Every Other Right: A Constitutional History of Property Rights* (2nd ed, Oxford University Press, 1998) 13–14, 54–5.

[170] Re Canada, see *Calder*, above n 20, 402 (Hall J, dissenting on the deciding issue); *Guerin v The Queen* [1984] 2 SCR 335, 376; *R v Sparrow* [1990] 1 SCR 1075, 1099; *Delgamuukw*, above n 10, para 113, 180; and discussion in McNeil, above n 165, 311–16. Re New Zealand, see *Nireaha Tamaki*, above n 53.

High Court has held that, prior to enactment of the Racial Discrimination Act 1975 (Cth),[171] native title could be extinguished executively by inconsistent Crown grant or Crown appropriation of the land for its own use, apparently without clear and plain statutory authority to do so.[172] Moreover, no compensation needed to be paid for this unilateral taking.[173] As both the taking and the denial of compensation are inconsistent with fundamental common law principles,[174] it appears that the High Court was driven by political considerations to favour the property rights and economic interests of non-Indigenous Australians over the pre-existing land rights of the Indigenous peoples.[175]

In Canada, Aboriginal land rights have two additional constitutional protections that prevent even legislative extinguishment and infringement in some instances. First, section 91(24) of the Constitution Act 1867 placed 'Indians, and Lands reserved for the Indians', within the exclusive jurisdiction of the Parliament of Canada.[176] As a result, the Supreme Court has held that the provinces have lacked the constitutional authority to *extinguish* Aboriginal title ever since Confederation in 1867.[177] While this should mean that the provinces also lack the authority to *infringe* Aboriginal title,[178] the Supreme Court has suggested otherwise, without adequately explaining how provincial legislatures can infringe rights that are within the core of the exclusive jurisdiction of Parliament.[179] More recently, however, the court has held that treaty rights, which are also within the

[171] This Act of Parliament provides legislative protection against discriminatory actions by the states that would extinguish native title rights: *Mabo v Queensland [No 1]* (1988) 166 CLR 186 (HC Aust). The Native Title Act 1993 provides further protection because valid Commonwealth legislation prevails, due to s 109 of the Australian Constitution, above n 167, over inconsistent state legislation: *Western Australia v Commonwealth* (1995) 128 ALR 1 (HC Aust). See also *Ward*, above n 50.

[172] *Mabo*, above n 11; *Fejo*, above n 50.

[173] *Mabo*, above n 11, 15. The requirement in s 51(xxxi) of the Australian Constitution, above n 167, that taking of property be on 'just terms', applies only to Parliament, not to state legislatures, from the time the Constitution was proclaimed as of 1 January 1901.

[174] See K McNeil, 'Racial Discrimination and Unilateral Extinguishment of Native Title' (1996) 1 *Australian Indigenous Law Reporter* 1, reprinted in *Emerging Justice?*, above n 41, 357. Extinguishment by grant is also inconsistent with American law, as a grantee in the United States generally takes subject to any unextinguished Indian title: see K McNeil, 'Extinguishment of Native Title: The High Court and American Law' (1997) 2 *Australian Indigenous Law Reporter* 365, reprinted in *Emerging Justice?*, above n 41, 409. Moreover, any Presidential taking of Indian land by executive order has to be authorised and ratified by Congress: *Gila River Pima-Maricopa Indian Community v US*, 494 F 2d 1386, 1394 (1974, Ct Cl), *cert* denied 419 US 1021 (1974).

[175] See K McNeil, 'The Vulnerability of Indigenous Land Rights in Australia and Canada' (2004) 42 *Osgoode Hall Law Journal* 271.

[176] Constitution Act 1867, 30 and 31 Vict, c 3 (UK).

[177] *Delgamuukw*, above n 10, paras 172–83. Compare Australia, where Parliament first received jurisdiction over Indigenous affairs by a 1967 amendment to s 51(xxvi) of the Constitution, above n 167: see Jennifer Clarke's Chapter. Because this jurisdiction is concurrent with state jurisdiction, the states are only barred from extinguishing native title to the extent that the extinguishment is inconsistent with federal legislation, such as the Native Title Act 1993: see n 171 above.

[178] See *Tsilhqot'in Nation*, above n 26, paras 1001–49; K McNeil, 'Aboriginal Title and the Division of Powers: Rethinking Federal and Provincial Jurisdiction' (1998) 61 *Saskatchewan Law Review* 431, reprinted in *Emerging Justice?*, above n 41, 249; K Wilkins, 'Of Provinces and Section 35 Rights' (1999) 22 *Dalhousie Law Journal* 185 and 'Negative Capacity: Of Provinces and Lands Reserved for the Indians' (2002) 1 *Indigenous Law Journal* 57.

[179] See *Côté*, above n 29, para 74; *Delgamuukw*, above n 10, para 160.

core of Parliament's exclusive section 91(24) jurisdiction, are immune from provincial laws that would infringe them.[180] Logically, Aboriginal title should have the same division-of-powers protection.[181]

The second protection accorded to Aboriginal land rights in Canada is found in section 35(1) of the Constitution Act 1982, which recognised and affirmed the 'existing aboriginal and treaty rights of the aboriginal peoples of Canada'.[182] The Supreme Court has held that this provision prevents these rights from being unilaterally extinguished, even by Parliament.[183] So, since 1982, extinguishment can only occur (constitutional amendment aside) with the consent of the Aboriginal peoples concerned. The court has nonetheless held that, despite section 35(1), Aboriginal and treaty rights, including land rights, can still be *infringed*, provided the test for justifiable infringement laid down in *Sparrow* has been met.[184] This test requires the government to prove two things: first, a valid legislative objective for the infringement that is substantial and compelling; and second, that the Crown's fiduciary obligations to the Aboriginal people in question have been respected. Depending on the circumstances, the second branch of the test can involve asking the following questions: 'whether there has been as little infringement as possible in order to effect the desired result; whether, in a situation of expropriation, fair compensation is available; and, whether the aboriginal group in question has been consulted with respect to the conservation measures being implemented'.[185] Since *Sparrow*, the consultation requirement has become a major factor in determining whether an infringement is justifiable. The Supreme Court has decided that governments must engage in consultation, and in appropriate situations accommodate Aboriginal interests, where Aboriginal rights, though not yet established, are asserted and supported by some evidence.[186] The scope of the consultation depends on the strength of the case supporting the rights and the seriousness of the infringement.[187]

While government infringement of Aboriginal land rights is still possible in Canada, those rights nonetheless have much greater protection than Indigenous

[180] *R v Morris* [2006] 2 SCR 915. See K Wilkins, '*R v Morris*: A Shot in the Dark and Its Repercussions', forthcoming, *Indigenous Law Journal*.

[181] See *Tsilhqot'in Nation*, above n 26, paras 1021–3; K McNeil, 'The Métis and the Doctrine of Interjurisdictional Immunity: A Commentary' in F Wilson and M Mallet (eds), *Métis-Crown Relations: Rights, Identity, Jurisdiction, and Governance* (Irwin Law, 2008) 289.

[182] Above n 31.

[183] *Van der Peet*, above n 30, para 28; *Mitchell*, above n 41, para 11.

[184] *Sparrow*, above n 170; *R v Gladstone* [1996] 2 SCR 723; *Côté*, above n 29; *Delgamuukw*, above n 10; *R v Marshall* [1999] 3 SCR 533; *Sappier* and *Gray*, above n 29. For critical commentary, see McNeil, above n 175, 286–300.

[185] *Sparrow*, above n 170, 1119.

[186] *Haida Nation v British Columbia* [2004] 3 SCR 511; *Taku River Tlingit First Nation v British Columbia (Project Assessment Director)* [2004] 3 SCR 550. The duty to consult also applies in the context of treaty rights: *Mikisew Cree First Nation v Canada (Minister of Canadian Heritage)* [2005] 3 SCR 388.

[187] *Haida Nation*, above n 186, para 39. For detailed analysis and subsequent case law, see M Morellato, 'The Crown's Constitutional Duty to Consult and Accommodate Aboriginal and Treaty Rights', February 2008, at: fngovernance.org/pdf/CrownDuty_MM_0208.pdf.

land rights in the United States, Australia and New Zealand. The addition of section 35(1) to the Canadian Constitution in 1982 took away the parliamentary equivalent of the plenary power that the US Congress still has over Indian tribes. Unilateral extinguishment has been barred, so that the kind of termination policy pursued by Congress in the 1950s cannot occur in Canada.[188] Nor can the Canadian Parliament enact provisions like those in the Native Title Act 1993 and the Foreshore and Seabed Act 2004 that have extinguished some land rights in Australia and New Zealand. Even parliamentary infringements of land rights have to be justified by a stringent test. The duty to consult and to accommodate asserted Aboriginal rights has also become an effective means for forcing governments to involve Aboriginal peoples in decision-making, especially in regard to resource development on their claimed territories. As consultation must take place with Aboriginal representatives who have the authority to act on behalf of their peoples, the process of consultation itself is an exercise of self-government, and a way for Aboriginal peoples to assert and establish government-to-government relationships.

F. Conclusions

This discussion has revealed that, despite their common British heritage and legal traditions, the United States, Canada, Australia and New Zealand have developed divergent legal doctrines in relation to Indigenous land rights. Differences in the content and requirements for proof of these rights stem largely from differences in judicial opinion over their source.

In the United States and Canada, the courts have ruled that occupation is the source of Indigenous title, but the American approach has distinctly territorial and jurisdictional dimensions, whereas the Canadian approach is more narrowly proprietary. In the United States, Indian nations have both residual sovereignty and land rights in the territories occupied by them. By contrast, the Canadian Supreme Court has determined that Aboriginal title is a property right arising from occupation of land that is separate from governance rights. And yet the court has acknowledged that Aboriginal nations have decision-making authority over their collectively held lands, authority one Canadian judge has concluded is governmental in nature.

In Australia and New Zealand, the courts have decided that Indigenous land rights stem from the Indigenous legal systems that existed prior to British acquisition of sovereignty. Through the doctrine of continuity, these rights became enforceable in common law courts. Unfortunately, in applying this doctrine the Australian judiciary has required strict proof that traditional laws and customs

[188] On this policy, see DL Fixico, *Termination and Relocation: Federal Indian Policy, 1945–1960* (University of New Mexico Press, 1986), and Benjamin J Richardson's Chapter on US Indian Law.

confer specific rights, and that knowledge and observance of the laws and customs have continued up to the present. These requirements have narrowed the scope of claimable rights, and imposed impossible burdens of proof on some Indigenous claimants. In New Zealand, application of the doctrine of continuity has been less problematic, as land rights stem from tikanga Māori, broadly defined as including both custom and usage. Nor is proof of continuous observance of tikanga Māori necessary, except where required by statute.

The authority of non-Indigenous governments to extinguish or infringe Indigenous land rights is dependent on a nation-state's constitution. In the four jurisdictions examined here, these rights are most vulnerable to legislative extinguishment and infringement in New Zealand because the unicameral Parliament has sole authority over them. In the United States and Canada, exclusive federal jurisdiction over Indigenous affairs provides some protection against the states and provinces. In Australia, federalism also provides some protection against the states, to the extent that the Commonwealth Parliament legislates in favour of Indigenous land rights. Only in Canada are land rights generally protected against legislation by a specific constitutional provision.

Ultimately, however, the fate of Indigenous rights depends on the vision of judges, the political will of legislators, and a belief within the larger community that justice requires that these rights be maintained and respected.

11

Indigenous Self-Determination and the State

SHIN IMAI

One of my clients in the mid-1980s was a First Nation located in northern Canada. To get to the reserve, I had to take a two-hour flight from Toronto to a small town by jet, stay overnight, and board a connecting flight on an eight-person prop the next morning. The reserve was located on an island in the middle of the wilderness. There were no roads or railways within hundreds of miles. When the plane landed I could see nothing but a carpet of scrub broken only by the small paved landing strip and a dusty road heading off to the village. An invisible line separated provincial Crown land, where the landing strip was located, from federal Crown land, where the Indian reserve was located.

The elders of the community were concerned about a growing alcohol problem among the youth. Their worries came to a head when a young man was found frozen to death in the woods after drinking. After hearing from the elders, the Chief and Council enacted a law banning liquor on the reserve. There was a straightforward way to enforce the prohibition and stem the flow of alcohol. The only entry into the reserve was by plane, so it would be easy to search the luggage of the passengers, as the plane was unloaded. The First Nation asked the police constable who was stationed in the community to search the luggage of all the passengers and confiscate all liquor.

There was a legal problem with this idea. Because the plane landed on provincial land, only provincial law applied. The police constable, who was appointed by the Commissioner of the Ontario Provincial Police, was told by his superiors that he could search people's personal belongings only if there were reasonable and probable grounds that a crime was being committed. Possessing liquor was legal on provincial land. Therefore, when the person got off the plane, there was no crime, and there were no grounds to perform a search. This meant that a search could only be conducted once the individual set foot on federal reserve land, where the possession of liquor was illegal. But there was a practical problem with this idea. There was no fence demarcating the boundary and there was no easy way to police the crossing of the invisible line between provincial and federal land.

The Chief was frustrated, and decided to appoint his own 'peacekeepers' from the First Nation to search all the passengers as they unloaded their luggage off the plane. Most passengers co-operated with the peacekeepers, but during one of these searches a community member objected to the search. A scuffle followed, and liquor was found in the community member's bag. The liquor was confiscated and destroyed by the peacekeepers. No other action was taken against the individual. The community member, however, was outraged and complained to a legal aid clinic located in the nearest town, which was an hour and half away by air. The clinic lawyer felt that the search was illegal, as the search occurred on provincial land. Therefore, in the eyes of the law, the peacekeepers were no more than private citizens who had no right to search the belongings of other private citizens. The lawyer helped the community member lay a criminal information against the two peacekeepers, and they were charged with assault.

A variety of 'legal' work-arounds were canvassed to address this problem. The most obvious solution was to make sure that the airstrip was located on federal reserve land. The province, however, refused to transfer the airstrip to the federal government, and the federal government would not consider paying for a new airstrip on its own land. Another proposal was for the Band to construct a huge fence around the airstrip and force individuals to pass through a gate. Poets and cartoonists would immediately see the comic potential of constructing such a fence in the middle of a wilderness, to circumvent a problem created by an invisible and meaningless boundary. Some government lawyers, alas, had less of a sense of humour, and actually suggested the fence as an appropriate solution. Unfortunately, or fortunately, neither the federal nor the provincial government would pay for such a fence. In the end, the matter was never resolved. The charges against the individual peacekeepers were quietly dropped. The federal–provincial boundary has not changed, and the challenge of enforcing the prohibition on liquor continues.

Aboriginal communities across Canada have similar stories, featuring laws that are appropriate for urban areas in the south, but are imposed in ludicrous ways in the remote north. For example, Susan Drummond recounts a story of an Inuk youth who was tried by a judge in a city in the south for a violent crime. The judge's solution was to sentence the youth to return to his isolated northern community. The northern community was just as worried about the youth in their community and incarcerated him on his arrival. The southern judge ordered the youth released and threatened to have community members charged with kidnapping.[1]

In the two stories recounted above, the Criminal Code operated in a way that was counterproductive to community protection. In the first story, the Criminal Code helped protect the bootleggers by making prosecution and detection very difficult. In the second story, the mainstream justice system dealt with a problem youth in a southern community by moving him back to his isolated northern community. Exposing the northern community to potential problems protected

[1] S Drummond, *Incorporating the Familiar: Investigating Legal Sensibilities in Nunavik* (Queen's University Press, 1997).

the southern community. More serious, however, was the fact that the application of the Criminal Code in both cases disempowered the leaders of the community and placed the authority and responsibility for dealing with internal issues in the hands of non-Aboriginal people from the south.

I thought of these stories after reading *Citizens Plus: Aboriginal Peoples and the Canadian State*, by Canadian political scientist Alan Cairns.[2] In this book, he criticises Canada's Royal Commission on Aboriginal Peoples,[3] which recommended that governments enter into negotiations with Aboriginal nations in order to increase the Aboriginal land base and to recognise law-making powers in their own communities. Cairns says that these agreements emphasise 'nation to nation' relationships, treaties and a third order of government for Aboriginal nations at the expense of fostering a 'common sense of belonging' through shared institutions with other Canadians. In the two communities described above, I wondered how it could be said that the application of the 'shared' Criminal Code fostered a 'sense of belonging' to Canada? From the point of view of the dominant, non-Aboriginal society, having the same Criminal Code apply on and off reserve may have appeared to strengthen the connection to Canada. From the Aboriginal point of view, however, the 'sense of belonging' may not have been felt as a particularly positive experience and would likely have contributed to a further alienation from Canada.

A. Overview of Self-Determination

1. The Need for Self-Determination

In Australia, Canada, New Zealand and the United States, Indigenous people have survived a very dark century when government policy was aimed at destroying their cultures and taking away their lands.

A low point was reached in Canada in 1969, when the then Prime Minister Pierre Trudeau released the *White Paper on Indian Policy*. This initiative called for the legal termination of Indian status, dismantling of Indian reserves, repeal of the Indian Act, and amendment of the Constitution to eliminate federal jurisdiction over Indians. The *White Paper* referred to Indian claims to land as 'so general and undefined that it is not realistic to think of them as specific claims capable of [legal] remedy'.[4] Trudeau apparently thought that he was doing nothing more than formally announcing what had already happened—the disappearance of the

[2] A Cairns, *Citizens Plus: Aboriginal Peoples and the Canadian State* (UBC Press, 2000) 51–2.

[3] Royal Commission on Aboriginal Peoples, *Report* (Supply and Services Canada, 1996) ('Royal Commission, *Report*'). One of the complaints made by Cairns is that the majority of the seven Commissioners were Aboriginal.

[4] Quoted in P Macklem, *Indigenous Difference and the Constitution of Canada* (University of Toronto Press, 2001) 268.

Indian. Much to his surprise, he was set back on his heels by the angry reaction of First Nations, and by court rulings recognising Aboriginal title. His government had to do an about-face and institute a policy that addressed land claims and Aboriginal title.

Similar changes in government policy occurred in the other jurisdictions. In New Zealand, after years of hostility to Māori, the government enacted the Treaty of Waitangi Act 1975, which provided legislative recognition of the 1840 Treaty and establishment of the Waitangi Tribunal. The Tribunal, which incorporates both Māori and *pakeha* (non-Māori) personnel and procedures, has launched a series of hearings looking into land, resource and cultural rights of Māori.[5] In Australia, a 1967 referendum approved changes to the Constitution which allowed the Commonwealth (federal) government to make laws with respect to Aboriginal people, and ensured that they would be taken into account for calculating state populations. In the 1970s the government began a policy favouring self-determination or self-management,[6] which has continued off and on since that time. The United States began the era of self-determination with President Richard Nixon's speech in 1970, which opened the way for the Indian Self-Determination and Educational Assistance Act in 1975. This Act provided a mechanism for transferring responsibility for federal programs to tribes.[7]

These changes occurred partly because non-Indigenous governments realised that the era of assimilation had not worked. Indigenous people had survived massacres, European diseases, forced removal of their children and mass deportation out of their homelands. The 'Indian problem' had not disappeared: instead, the assimilation policy had exacerbated the problems and governments were left with the prospect of social and economic disaster in Indigenous communities. Indigenous people themselves impelled the change by joining the wave of consciousness that began in the 1960s. In 1966, in Australia, Vincent Lingiari led 200 fellow Aboriginal workers in the Wave Hill 'Walk-Off'. What began as a protest for the same pay as non-Indigenous employees turned into a seven-year strike for the return of Aboriginal lands.[8] In the United States the Trail of Broken Treaties was a caravan that departed from the West Coast in 1972. It travelled to various reservations, gaining support, before finishing in Washington DC, where Indians occupied offices of the Bureau of Indian Affairs.[9] In Canada, a Native Peoples

[5] J Hayward and NR Wheen (eds), *The Waitangi Tribunal* (Bridget Williams Books, 2004).

[6] C Gibson, 'Cartographies of the Colonial/Capitalist State: A Geopolitics of Indigenous Self-determination in Australia' (1999) 31 *Antipode* 45, 47.

[7] See G Nettheim, GD Meyers and D Craig, *Indigenous Peoples and Governance Structures: A Comparative Analysis of Land and Resource Management Rights* (Aboriginal Studies Press, 2002) 32; The Harvard Project on American Indian Economic Development, *The State of the Native Nations* (Oxford University Press, 2008) 20–1 ('The Harvard Project'). For a review of economic development in Canada, see C Beal, 'Aboriginal Economic Development' in G Bailey (ed), *Indians in Contemporary Society* (Smithsonian Institution, 2008) 231.

[8] National Archives of Australia, *Fact Sheet 24*, at www.naa.gov.au/about-us/publications/fact-sheets/fs224.aspx.

[9] V Deloria, *Behind the Trail of Broken Treaties: An Indian Declaration of Independence* (Delacorte Press, 1974).

Caravan travelled across the country in 1974 and they were confronted by riot police on the steps of Parliament in Ottawa.[10] In 1975, Whina Cooper led Māori in the Land March under the slogan 'not one more acre more of Māori Land'. The march began in the northern part of the country and arrived in Wellington with 30,000 supporters.[11]

It is now clear that there are sound economic and social reasons for promoting self-determination. The Harvard Project on American Indian Economic Development conducted a series of studies beginning in 1987, which culminated in the publication of *The State of the Native Nations.* They show that self-determination and economic prosperity are inextricably linked. They reveal that poverty levels dropped on United States reservations exercising self-government powers, at a greater rate than poverty levels dropped in the general population. The studies also found that with greater self-government, leaders are more accountable to the members of the community and that their decisions are more likely 'in tune with the cultural values of the community'.[12] Stephen Cornell, the co-founder of the project, is forthright in his view:

> [T]he US record is clear: if central governments wish to perpetuate Indigenous poverty, its attendant ills and bitterness, and its high costs, the best way to do so is to undermine tribal sovereignty and self-determination. But if they want to overcome Indigenous poverty and all that goes with it, then they should support tribal sovereignty and self-determination, and they should invest in helping Indigenous peoples build the governing capacity to back up sovereign powers with effective governments of their own design.[13]

The social basis for a self-determination policy is also sound. Michael Chandler and his colleagues have conducted a series of interesting studies, trying to understand why some suicide rates on Indian reserves in British Columbia, Canada, were 800 times the national average, and on others, suicide was practically unknown. Their conclusions are remarkable. They find that suicide rates are lower in communities that have retained their own language. In addition, Bands have higher rates of youth suicide when they *lack* measures of self-government over areas such as health, education, child protection, policing, access to traditional lands, and the construction of facilities for preserving cultural artefacts and traditions.[14]

[10] V Harper, *Following the Red Path* (Native Peoples' Press, 1979).

[11] SC Bourassa and AL Strong, 'Restitution of Land to New Zealand Maori: The Role of Social Structure' (2002) 75 *Pacific Affairs* 227, 237.

[12] The Harvard Project, above n 7, 70. For the website of the project, see www.ksg.harvard.edu/hpaied.

[13] S Cornell, *Indigenous Peoples, Poverty, Self-Determination in Australia, New Zealand, Canada the United States* (Native Nations Institute for Leadership, 2006) 28.

[14] D Hallett, MJ Chandler and CE Lalonde, 'Aboriginal Language Knowledge and Youth Suicide' (2007) 22 *Cognitive Development* 292, 292. The first study on cultural continuity was MJ Chandler and CE Lalonde, 'Cultural Continuity as a Hedge Against Suicide in Canada's First Nations' (1998) 35 *Transcultural Psychiatry* 191.

2. What is Self-Determination?

Claire Charters, in her Chapter, discusses the growing recognition of the self-determination rights of Indigenous peoples at the international level. The most recent is the United Nations Declaration on the Rights of Indigenous People, Article 3, which recognises the right to self-determination: 'Indigenous peoples have the right to self-determination. By virtue of that right they freely determine their political status and freely pursue their economic, social and cultural development'.[15]

A wide variety of terms are used to describe the general policy approach described in this chapter. A Māori commentator from Aotearoa/New Zealand says:

> Maori aspiration for greater control over their own destinies and resources is variously described as a search for sovereignty, autonomy, independence, self-governance, self-determination, *tino rangatiratanga*, and *mana motuhake*. There are important distinctions between those terms, though they all capture an underlying commitment to the advancement of Maori people as Maori, and the protection of the environment for future generations. And all reject any notion of an assimilated future.[16]

Agreement on terminology is rendered more difficult because Indigenous and non-Indigenous parties may formulate the problem in entirely different ways. Non-Indigenous governments and courts tend to analyse the issue in relation to relative powers and jurisdictions. What laws will Indigenous people be able to enact? Will Indigenous laws be subservient to federal laws? What institutions will be established to implement policies? Indigenous parties, on the other hand, tend to view the issues in terms of ongoing resistance to the encroachment of non-Indigenous social, economic and political structures.[17] Their approach to self-government may be better understood as a 'bundle of dynamic legal relationships, political aspirations and affirmations of cultural continuity'.[18]

The difference in these approaches may be illustrated by comparing the Canadian government's negotiation policy on self-government, with the approach of Canadian Aboriginal academic John Borrows. The federal government policy recognises that there is an inherent right of self-government and sets out what areas of jurisdiction are negotiable, with whom the government will negotiate, and how negotiated agreements are to be ratified. A major objective is to harmonise laws: 'it is in the interest of both Aboriginal and non-Aboriginal governments to

[15] United Nations Declaration on the Rights of Indigenous Peoples, GA Res A/RES/61/295, UNGA, 61st Session (13 September 2007).

[16] M Durie, *Te Mana, Te Kawanatanga: The Politics of Maori Self-determination* (Oxford University Press, 1998) 218.

[17] See F Barth, 'Preface, 1998' in F Barth (ed), *Ethnic Groups and Boundaries: The Social Organization of Culture Difference* (Waveland Press, 1969, 1998) 7 ('in analysing Indigenous people's political activism, we discussed the shift to seeing such groups as engaged in a social struggle for meaningful change, not the revitalization of an unchanging heritage of aboriginal cultural traits').

[18] S Imai, *Aboriginal Law Handbook* (2nd edn, Carswell, 1999) 116 ('Imai, *Handbook*').

develop co-operative arrangements that will ensure the harmonious relationship of laws which is indispensable to the proper functioning of the federation'.[19] Borrows, on the other hand, in 'A Genealogy of Law: Inherent Sovereignty and First Nations Self-government', recounts his family history going back to the great Shawnee leader, Tecumseh, who fought with the British against the Americans during the War of 1812. Borrows points out that Tecumseh fought as an ally to the British, not as a subject, with the objective of protecting Indian lands. Borrows talks about a great-great-grandmother who was a medicine woman and who kept alive the traditions of her people. He talks about other ancestors who converted to Christianity and signed treaties, and relates this history to the present-day actions of the Chippewas of the Nawash Band Council. Through all this, he shows how the Indigenous people asserted their autonomy in the face of huge pressures. Of his methodology, Borrows says:

> the term 'self-government' does not require a legal or technical definition because I do not refer to self-government as an abstract, futuristic institution. I identify self-government with particular events in which our people have exercised specific instances of control in their internal and external societal relationships.[20]

Of course, the federal policy and the reflections by Borrows are not comparable because they were drafted for different purposes. But that is precisely the point. The parties may come to the negotiating table for very different purposes, making communication a challenge.

The difference between the parties does not lie only in the different expectations of the process. The parties may also conceptualise 'difference' itself in different ways. Non-Indigenous governments generally see this 'difference' as a set of static practices, some of which can continue today and others that are of no relevance in the contemporary world. Much of the current judicial thinking on 'culture' and 'tradition' is also static and judgmental. It is based on the view that cultural practices and beliefs can be taken apart and catalogued into 'integral' and 'incidental' value to the social group. For example, in the Supreme Court of Canada decision, *R v Van der Peet*, Lamer CJ thought that it was reasonable to ask Aboriginal groups to demonstrate that a pre-contact 'practice, tradition or custom was one of the things which made the culture of the society distinctive—that it was one of the things that truly made the society what it was'.[21] He felt that it would be possible to do this while excluding those practices that 'are true of every human society (for example, eating to survive)'.[22] This approach has been criticised by John Borrows for freezing Aboriginal societies in the past:

[19] See 'The Government of Canada's Approach to Implementation of the Inherent Right and the Negotiation of Aboriginal Self-Government' ('federal self-government policy'), at www.ainc-inac.gc.ca/pr/pub/sg/plcy_e.html.

[20] J Borrows, 'A Genealogy of Law: Inherent Sovereignty and First Nations Self-government' (1992) 30 *Osgoode Hall Law Journal* 291, 294.

[21] [1996] 2 SCR 507, para 55.

[22] *Ibid*, para 56: 'The court cannot look at those aspects of the aboriginal society that are true of every human society (eg, eating to survive), nor can it look at those aspects of the aboriginal society that

> Chief Justice Antonio Lamer has now told us what Aboriginal means. Aboriginal is retrospective. It is about what was, 'once upon a time', central to the survival of a community, not necessarily about what is central, significant and distinctive to the survival of these communities today. His test invites stories about the past.[23]

The static view of culture arose at a time when societies were viewed hierarchically with some cultures being more advanced than others—some so low on the scale of human development that they deserved to be enslaved or exterminated. Modern anthropology no longer subscribes to those views. Culture is not a static group of attributes that can be placed in a hierarchical order, but rather a dynamic, ever-changing complex of relationships. Commenting on the *Van der Peet* decision, anthropologist Michael Asch says: 'culture is a system and a process rather than merely items and arrangements. It is inappropriate to attempt to ferret out whether a practice, custom or tradition is "distinctive" '.[24]

This dynamic experience of culture may be why many Indigenous people are attracted to 'self-determination', a concept that refers to the right of a people to decide how it wants to relate to a majoritarian population. As understood in international law, it does not say what form the association will take. Technically both the option of full sovereignty and the option of complete assimilation are open. 'Self-determination' refers to a choice, not a particular institutional relationship. It is dynamic and not fixed on particular arrangements. In the next section, I will discuss four possible *outcomes* from the exercise of self-determination: sovereignty and self-government; self-administration and self-management; co-management and joint management; and participation in public government.

B. The Exercise of Self-Determination

Because self-determination is a choice, it can be exercised in different ways. The 'sovereignty and self-government' option leads to more autonomy for the Indigenous community to control its own social, economic and political development. The 'self-management and self-administration' option leads to greater control of local affairs and the delivery of services within a larger settler government legislative framework. The 'co-management and joint management' model institutionalises Indigenous participation in the management of lands and resources.

are only incidental or occasional to that society; the court must look instead to the defining and central attributes of the aboriginal society in question'. Subsequent cases, including *Sappier v The Queen* [2006] 2 SCR 686, have backtracked a little from this position.

[23] J Borrows, 'Frozen Rights in Canada: Constitutional Interpretation and the Trickster' 22 *American Indian Law Review* 37, 43. A similar observation for the Inuit is made by Drummond, above n 1, 42 ('Fixing Inuit culture at the period of the ethnographer's fieldwork ignores the unceasing dynamism of groups that are constantly forming and reforming in the grip of the contingencies of time. Such ahistorical depictions prevent the Inuit from sharing the present with us').

[24] M Asch, 'The Judicial Conceptualization of Culture after Delgamuukw and Van der Peet' (2000) *Review of Constitutional Studies* 119, 129.

The 'participation in public government' option provides a means to influence the policies of the settler governments through Indigenous-specific institutions. Within each category, there are a number of variations. These options are not mutually exclusive and in some jurisdictions, all four forms co-exist.

1. Sovereignty and Self-government

In no jurisdiction does use of the term 'sovereignty' connote the existence of a separate international state. Rather, the sovereignty and self-government models are characterised by the recognition of an *inherent* Indigenous authority to make laws over a defined territory. These Indigenous governments do not rely on delegated authority from settler government legislation. This does not mean that domestic courts recognise that Indigenous nations have plenary authority. In both the United States and Canada, courts and legislation have imposed limitations on the autonomy of these governments.

(a) The United States

Indian tribes in the United States have the most explicit recognition of their autonomy. Since 1831, the Supreme Court of the United States has described the tribes as 'domestic dependent nations',[25] and recognised their prior possessory rights to their territory. As one notable case explained: '[t]he Indian nations had always been considered as distinct independent political communities, retaining their original natural rights, as the undisputed possessors of the soil, from time immemorial'.[26] This means that the tribes derive their authority independently of the Constitution of the United States, and only Acts of Congress can limit their authority.

> The sovereignty that the Indian tribes retain is of a unique and limited character. It exists only at the sufferance of Congress and is subject to complete defeasance. But until Congress acts, the tribes retain their existing sovereign powers. In sum, Indian tribes still possess those aspects of sovereignty not withdrawn by treaty or statute, or by implication as a necessary result of their dependent status.[27]

The most significant Congressional incursion has been the Major Crimes Act,[28] of 1885, which gives the federal courts jurisdiction over more than a dozen offences such as murder, kidnapping and rape. Other statutes that limit tribal authority include the Indian Civil Rights Act,[29] which gives individual Indians recourse

[25] *Cherokee Nation v Georgia* 30 US (5 Pet) 1, 17–20 (1831).
[26] *Worcester v Georgia* 31 US (6 Pet) 515, 559 (1832).
[27] *US v Wheeler*, 435 US 313, 322–3 (1978).
[28] Major Crimes Act, 18 USC s 1153.
[29] Indian Civil Rights Act 1968, 25 USC ss 1301. This statute is necessary because the sovereign status of tribal governments means that they do not derive their powers from the American constitution. Consequently, the Bill of Rights contained in the American constitution does not apply to tribal governments.

against their tribal governments for violation of their civil liberties; and Public Law 280,[30] which transferred some federal authority to about 16 states in 1953. Nonetheless, the 'doctrine of retained sovereignty' has survived. Therefore, in the absence of Congressional legislation, the tribes can enact their own laws and administer their own justice system. Today, tribal codes cover a wide range of subject matter including criminal offences not covered by the Major Crimes Act, commercial relations, land use, marriage and child welfare.[31] There are about 275 tribal courts in the United States and many tribes have courts of appeal.[32] The extent to which tribal jurisdiction extends to non-Indians has been litigated several times in the Unites States Supreme Court. The current law, in a nutshell, is that in most cases the tribal jurisdictions do not apply to non-Indians.[33]

From the mid 1970s onwards, Congress passed a number of laws that encouraged greater exercise of tribal powers. The most significant, in terms of the recognition of tribal authority, was the Indian Child Welfare Act of 1978. This Act explicitly recognises tribal jurisdiction over Indian children residing on reservations, as well as providing for the transfer of jurisdiction over Indian children living off the reservation from State to tribal courts. In cases where there is no transfer, the statute gives the tribe the right to intervene in the proceedings.[34]

(b) Canada

Prior to 1982, the Canadian government and courts did not acknowledge that Indigenous peoples have inherent government powers. The only authority granted to Indians was through the Indian Act, which established elected Band Councils which could only enact by-laws on local matters. The other two Indigenous peoples in Canada, the Inuit and the Métis, fared even worse as there was almost no formal recognition of their existence as collectivities.

In 1982, Canada amended its Constitution. Among other things, it added a provision recognising rights of the Aboriginal peoples of Canada:

> s 35(1) The existing aboriginal and treaty rights of the aboriginal peoples of Canada are hereby recognized and affirmed.
> (2) In this Act, 'aboriginal peoples of Canada' includes the Indian, Inuit and Métis peoples of Canada.[35]

[30] Pub L 83-280, 67 Stat 588 (1953).

[31] For a description of tribal jurisdiction see DH Getches, CF Wilkinson and RA Williams Jr, *Cases and Materials on Federal Indian Law* (5th edn, West Publishing, 2005) 456–58; and the Harvard Project, above n 7, 37–51.

[32] These courts generally follow American adjudication processes but many are introducing traditional peacekeeper functions. See National Tribal Resource Center, www.tribalresourcecenter.org/tribalcourts/history.asp; and the Chapter in this book by Christine Zuni Cruz.

[33] The leading case limiting tribal criminal jurisdiction over non-Indians is *Oliphant v Suquamish Indian Tribe*, 435 US 191 (1978). For a recent case limiting civil jurisdiction over non-Indians, see *Plains Commerce Bank v Long Family Land & Cattle Co*, 128 S Ct 2709 US (2008).

[34] *Indian Child Welfare Act*, 1978, 25 USCA, s 1911.

[35] Constitution Act 1982, being Sch B to the Canada Act 1982 (UK) s 35.

Although no rights were specifically mentioned, the Royal Commission on Aboriginal Peoples, in its 1996 report, reasoned that a right of self-government was already included in section 35(1).[36] While the Supreme Court of Canada has yet to decide whether this is correct, it has held that assertion of a general right of self-government over reserve land is too broad; instead, self-government rights need to be proven on a specific, case-by-case basis. Nonetheless, the court has decided that, in cases involving Aboriginal title and treaty rights to fish, Aboriginal peoples have some decision-making authority.[37]

In the meantime, the federal government has committed itself to recognising the existence of the inherent right to self-government. Based on the federal self-government policy, negotiations have continued on land claims and self-government. Over a dozen significant agreements have been signed since the mid 1970s, as well as scores of minor settlements for land disputes. The land portions of these agreements range from 136,000 square miles of land for the Inuit of the Eastern Arctic to 2.7 square miles for Tsawwassen in British Columbia.[38]

While all these agreements contain a self-government component, the Nisga'a Agreement of British Columbia is among those that go the furthest, by giving the self-government powers constitutional status. Because the rights contained in the Nisga'a Agreement are section 35(1) 'treaty rights', ordinary legislation cannot derogate from them. They thus enjoy much greater protection than self-government rights in the United States, where Congress has plenary power to derogate from tribal authorities. However, the extent of Nisga'a jurisdiction is considerably more restricted than that of the Navajo in the United States, or even than that envisaged by the Royal Commission on Aboriginal Peoples. Nisga'a authority is paramount over some internal matters, including Nisga'a government and constitution,[39] Nisga'a citizenship,[40] culture and language,[41] Nisga'a property,[42] use of Nisga'a lands,[43] child and family services,[44] education,[45] and cultural

[36] See Royal Commission, *Report*, above n 3, Vol 2 Pt 1, 245–65.

[37] Generally, see K McNeil, 'Judicial Approaches to Self-Government since *Calder*: Searching for Doctrinal Coherence' in H Foster, H Raven and J Webber (eds), *Let Right Be Done: Aboriginal Title, the* Calder *Case, and the Future of Indigenous Rights* (UBC Press, 2007) 129. In *R v Pamajewon* [1996] 2 SCR 821 the court held that holding a bingo without a provincial licence did not fall under a right of self-government, and left open the question of whether such a right could exist. Other cases have suggested that First Nations have authority over Aboriginal title land (*Delgamuukw v British Columbia* [1997] 3 SCR 1010), and treaty rights (*Marshall v Canada* [1999] 3 SCR 533), without specifically finding that a right of self-government existed.

[38] For a more detailed description of some of these agreements, see S Imai, 'Aboriginal Land Claims' in *Handbook of North American Indians*, vol 2 (Smithsonian Institution, 2008) 177–84. See also the Department of Indian and Northern Affairs (www.ainc-inac.gc.ca) and the British Columbia Treaty Commission (www.bctreaty.net).

[39] *Nisga'a Final Agreement* (Canada, British Columbia, Nisga'a Nation, 1998) ch 11, s 34.

[40] *Ibid*, s 39.

[41] *Ibid*, s 41.

[42] *Ibid*, s 44.

[43] *Ibid*, s 47.

[44] *Ibid*, s 89.

[45] *Ibid*, ss 100, 103.

property.[46] In other areas, the provincial or federal government laws are either paramount (for example, health services and intoxicants), or are exclusive (for example, criminal law). As for adjudication of disputes, the Agreement provides for the creation of a Nisga'a court if provincial approval is obtained,[47] but any appeals must be taken to Supreme Court of British Columbia.[48] Finally, the form of government does not look radically different from Indian Act's Band Councils.

(c) Australia and New Zealand

The courts in Australia and New Zealand have traditionally not recognised any sovereignty for Indigenous people. In fact, in 1971 an Australian case, *Milirrpum v Nabalco Pty Ltd*,[49] decided that, as a matter of law, Australia was *terra nullius* when the first settlers arrived. That is, the land was empty. Far from recognising any rights to land or self-government, the court found that the Aborigines did not even exist as people with rights. It was not until 1992 that the High Court in *Mabo* reversed this decision and recognised the existence of native title in Australia.[50] In New Zealand, the existence of Māori sovereignty turns on the meaning of the 1840 Treaty of Waitangi. The Māori version of the treaty states that the Māori retained *tino rangatiratanga* over their *taonga*, which roughly translates to sovereignty over their treasures. The English version of the Treaty states that Māori ceded all their sovereignty to the British Crown. While there was a period when the Treaty was completely ignored, courts and government have now begun to recognise some Māori interests in relation to land and resources.[51] However, in neither country have courts recognised sovereignty in the way that courts in the United States have. As a consequence of the hostile judicial environment, in neither country have land settlements with Indigenous people resulted in the combination of land and jurisdiction that has characterised policy towards American tribes and recent Canadian land claims settlements.

Nonetheless, sovereignty is part of the political vocabulary of Australian Indigenous people and Māori. In Australia, in the late 1980s during the debates on negotiating a modern treaty, some Aboriginal leaders suggested that Aboriginal Australians should seek full independence as a country.[52] This idea does not appear to have gained much traction, but there is interest in looking for a new arrangement within Australia. Will Sanders argues that Indigenous people in Australia have jurisdiction to make their own laws and that they represent 'a

[46] *Nisga'a Final Agreement* (Canada, British Columbia, Nisga'a Nation, 1998) ch 11, s 115.

[47] *Ibid*, s 36.

[48] *Ibid*, ch 12, s 45.

[49] *Milirrpum v Nabalco Pty Ltd* (1971) 17 FLR 141. See also *Coe v Commonwealth* (1979) 53 ALJR 403.

[50] *Mabo v State of Queensland (No 2)* (1992) 107 ALR 1 (HC). See the Chapter by Kent McNeil for a fuller discussion.

[51] See Bourassa and Strong, above n 11.

[52] N Pearson, 'Reconciliation: To Be or Not To Be—A Separate Aboriginal Nationhood or Aboriginal Self-determination and Self-government Within the Australian Nation?' [1993] *Aboriginal Law Bulletin* 12.

repressed third order within Australian government, alongside the State and Commonwealth orders'.[53] Lisa Behrendt suggests that the aspiration of the treaty would be for 'internal self-determination' within the Australian state:

> [t]he rights enmeshed in the concept of 'self-determination' include, I would argue, everything from the right not to be discriminated against, to the rights to enjoy language, culture and heritage, our rights to land, seas, waters and natural resources, the right to be educated and to work, the right to be economically self sufficient, the right to be involved in decision-making processes that impact upon our lives and the right to govern and manage our own affairs and our communities.[54]

Similarly, Andrea Tunks from Aotearoa/New Zealand states flatly, '[s]ecession is not at the forefront of Māori aspirations?.[55] She sees the Treaty of Waitangi as recognising the existence of a parallel Māori law-making authority:

> Minimally, it would enable *hapu* [tribes] and iwi [tribal confederations] to exercise law-making power in respect of their territories, resources and their own members. It may also include an ability for pan-tribal structures to gather separate tribal nations into one decision-making entity so that the relationship with Crown *kawantanga* [governmental authority] and non-Māori can be continually negotiated.[56]

2. Self-administration and Self-management

In these arrangements the Indigenous community does not exercise inherent authority. They derive their powers from, and are limited by, settler government legislation and policies. The most advanced variation of this model includes a land base. These variations usually include powers for Indigenous institutions to make by-laws over local matters. Where there is no land base, there can be a transfer of a government programme and attendant funding to an Indigenous organisation. These self-administration and self-management initiatives have brought significant benefits by way of control over funding and the potential for more appropriate service delivery. However, they have been criticised for being a poor replacement for true self-government or sovereignty.[57]

(a) Self-administration on a Land Base

The Indian Act regulates most Canadian Indians.[58] This statute has the dual purpose of shielding Indians from the settlers, but also promoting eventual assimilation. It set

[53] W Sanders, 'Towards an Indigenous Order of Australian Government: Rethinking Self-determination as Indigenous Affairs Policy', Discussion Paper No 230/2002 (Centre for Aboriginal Economic Policy Research, University of New South Wales, 2002).

[54] L Behrendt, 'Unfinished Journey—Indigenous Self Determination' (2002) 58 *Arena Magazine* 24, 27.

[55] A Tunks, 'Pushing the Sovereign Boundaries in Aotearoa' [1999] *Indigenous Law Bulletin* 69, text at fn 34.

[56] *Ibid.*

[57] See, eg, Cornell, above n 13, 10–11.

[58] Indian Act, 1876, RSC 1985, c I-5.

aside reserves for Indian communities and shields the land from being sold off piecemeal, by requiring that communities consent to the 'surrender' of the land.[59] The Act sets out rules for a wide variety of matters including membership, education, land use, wills and taxation. The Indian Act also gives the government almost complete control over the day-to-day functioning of the elected Band Council. For example, the government has imposed western-style elections on Bands, thereby displacing traditional governance structures. Although the Act gives Band Councils authority to make by-laws, the subject matter is limited to local issues, such as consumption of alcohol and residence on the reserve. Even with this limited jurisdiction, the Minister of Indian Affairs can disallow any Band Council by-law.[60] At the present time, only a small minority of First Nations have succeeded in negotiating the self-government arrangements discussed earlier in this Chapter that have freed them from the Indian Act.

Canada's Métis are recognised as having self-administration powers only in the Province of Alberta where they have a similar type of arrangement to the Indian Act. The Métis Settlements Act established eight communities with governing bodies that can make local decisions.[61]

The Indian Bands and the Métis Settlement Councils receive government funding to administer their reserves and settlements. They are also eligible to receive funds to deliver social services and economic development projects. In this, they are similar to American tribes who administer quite a range of federal programmes through the Indian Self-determination and Education Assistance Act.[62]

In Australia, the Corporations (Aboriginal and Torres Strait Islander) Act 2006[63] permits Aboriginal groups to create their own associations related to business, to land councils and town councils. Over 3,000 entities have been created under this Act.[64] The powers of these associations vary, depending on what state or federal statute provided them with jurisdiction, but in all cases, the authority to make laws is more limited than the authority delegated to Canadian Indian Bands.[65] For example, in the Northern Territory, Land Councils under the Aboriginal Land Rights (Northern Territory) Act 1976 are empowered to consult with landowners and negotiate land issues. The only regulatory powers they can exercise, however, are, with the permission of the appropriate Minister, functions

[59] The land set aside for Indian reserves in a 50-year period beginning in the mid 1800s was minuscule compared to American standards. All the reserves in Canada put together would have been less than one half of the size of the Navajo reserve alone. See Royal Commission, *Report*, above n 3, Vol 2, Pt 2, 422–3. Modern land claims agreements beginning in the mid-1970s, described above, have increased the total amount of land under the jurisdiction of Aboriginal people in Canada.

[60] For a general description, see Imai, *Handbook*, above n 18, chs 8–10.

[61] C Bell, *Alberta's Métis Settlement Legislation: An Overview of Ownership and Management of Settlement Lands* (Canadian Plains Research Center, University of Regina, 1994).

[62] Indian Self-determination and Education Assistance Act, Pub L No 93-638, 88 Stat 203 (1975).

[63] Corporations (Aboriginal and Torres Strait Islander) Act 2006 (Cth); formerly Aboriginal Councils and Associations Act 1976 (Cth).

[64] T Anthony, 'Aboriginal Self-determination after ATSIC: Reappropriation of the "Original Position"' (2005) 14 *Polemic* 4, 6.

[65] See Nettheim *et al*, above n 7, 237–317.

set out in the law of the Territorial government relating to (a) the protection of sacred sites; (b) access to Aboriginal land; and (c) schemes for the management of wildlife on Aboriginal land.[66] Indigenous communities in the Northern Territory can also carry out some local administrative functions if they are approved under the Local Government Act. Under this statute, a Council has power to make by-laws over a very limited number of local issues including alcohol consumption, the destruction of animals and issuing of licences.[67]

(b) Self-administration off a Land Base

Traditionally non-Indigenous people administered social services and economic development projects in Indigenous communities. There are many horror stories from past years, ranging from the indiscriminate 'scooping' of Indigenous children by over-zealous child welfare agencies to the imposition of economic 'development' schemes that only benefited non-Indigenous developers. The decisions taken in the 1970s and 1980s to transfer the administration of these programs to Indigenous people themselves would appear to be a good thing. There are critiques, however, that programmes designed by non-Indigenous people will not necessarily be appropriate or even feasible in Indigenous communities.[68]

An example that shows both the strengths and weaknesses of the self-administration model is the Aboriginal and Torres Strait Island Commission (ATSIC) of Australia. This organisation was established in 1990 in response to the demand for 'self-determination'. It was composed of an 18-member Board of Commissioners who were elected from 35 Aboriginal Regional Councils. It was established to provide advice to the government on issues affecting Aboriginal people and to assist Aboriginal communities.[69] At its height, it provided vigorous advocacy and brought Australian issues to international fora. On the domestic front, ATSIC was involved in the delivery of a variety of funding programmes in the arts, Indigenous rights, housing, economic development and legal services.[70] Although ATSIC played an impressive role in the Australian political landscape, there were problems with the design. Some critics said that ATSIC was too focused on addressing disadvantage of Aboriginal individuals, rather than pursuing self-government goals such as land claims. Other critics noted that federal government control over the organisation and its activities was very tight. The employees were not hired directly by ATSIC, but rather through the federal bureaucracy; for the first decade, the Chair was appointed by the government; and almost all of the programmes were delivered under guidelines provided in Australian legislation. Consequently, in spite of the fact that the leadership of ATSIC was Aboriginal, the organisation itself was criticised for being too 'white'. In addition, there were

[66] Aboriginal Land Rights (Northern Territory) Act 1976 (Cth) s 23(2).
[67] Local Government Act 1994 (NT) ss 182–201.
[68] Imai, *Handbook*, above n 18, 182–3.
[69] Aboriginal and Torres Strait Islander Commission Act 1989 (Cth) s 7.
[70] The ATSIC website is now closed, but some pages are archived at: pandora.nla.gov.au/pan/41033/20060106-0000/ATSIC/default.html.

internal challenges. The elected Board of Commissioners were said to be too involved in decision-making on funding, leading to charges of favouritism. As a consequence, in 2003, the service delivery functions were transferred to the Aboriginal and Torres Strait Islander Services. The political vulnerability of an Indigenous government structure based on delegated authority was illustrated when, in 2005, a conservative Australian government shut down the organisation and transferred the service delivery options to other institutions and government departments.[71]

In spite of these critiques, in urban settings, self-administration may provide a valuable vehicle for Indigenous people. The urban populations are significant. In New Zealand, over 85 per cent of the Māori live in urban centres[72]; in the United States about 67 per cent live off reservations and half in urban centres[73]; in Australia, about 30 per cent of Aborigines live in major urban areas[74] and almost half live in urban areas in Canada.[75] People living in non-Indigenous areas do not have an exclusive land base, and the communities are often fragmented, as individuals have different degrees of identification with their indigeneity.[76] Although there are calls for 'self-determination for urban Indians',[77] such self-determination must result in arrangements that are different from communities with a land base. Rather than beginning with an identifiable community and a geographical location, the project might build up from the services that are used by Indigenous people such as education, community centres, housing, employment training or child welfare. The institutions providing the services could facilitate participation by Indigenous people through reserving seats on the board of directors or establishing liaison or advisory committees. In addition, where numbers warrant, Indigenous people themselves could be funded to run some services. In the city of Toronto, Canada, where there is an Indigenous population of perhaps 60,000, there are many Indigenous-specific services run by Indigenous peoples, including two community centres, a co-operative housing project, an elementary school, a legal aid clinic, a library, a health clinic, a men's residence, a seniors' residence and a child welfare agency.[78] In the best of these models, the Aboriginal people not only deliver the service, they also play important roles in the design and decision-making.

It may be possible to go a step further by co-ordinating all these services under an umbrella organisation. This is the form of self-government suggested by Canada's Royal Commission on Aboriginal Peoples, called 'communities of interest'.[79] In this

[71] See Nettheim *et al*, above n 7, 379–81. See general critiques by Anthony, above n 64.

[72] Durie, above n 16, 55.

[73] Harvard Project, above n 7, 321–66.

[74] From Human Rights and Equal Opportunity Commission, Australia, drawing on 2001 statistics: www.hreoc.gov.au/Social_Justice/statistics/index.html#fn28, drawn from ABS stats.

[75] Statistics Canada: www12.statcan.ca/english/census01/Products/Analytic/companion/abor/canada.cfm#6.

[76] See Durie, above n 16, 95 (discussing alienation of urban Māori from traditional *iwi*).

[77] Harvard Project, above n 7, 359.

[78] Imai, above n 18, 187–8.

[79] Royal Commission, *Report*, above n 3, Vol 4, 519–622.

model, Indigenous people would centralise the delivery of services and provide a structure for advocating for their members. It is similar to the Australian ATSIC model: an elected Indigenous body involved in service delivery and advocacy. To my knowledge, outside of Australia, no group has been able to implement this model for urban self-government.

3. Co-management and Joint Management

The areas of land that are reserved or set aside for the exclusive use of Indigenous people is often not large enough to provide the support necessary for traditional ceremonial and sustenance activities, let alone for modern-day economic pursuits that will provide an economic base for the communities. Indigenous peoples need access to, and control over, the land and resources, not only in their small exclusive use areas, but also in the larger land and resource base that they have traditionally accessed to survive.

It is difficult to measure whether or not there has been 'progress' on the lands issue over the years. Certainly, in Canada, Australia and New Zealand, the situation has improved, in that governments in all three jurisdictions have said that they are committed to addressing issues of land and resources. Kent McNeil's Chapter on land rights shows that there have been advances in recognising title for Indigenous groups, including the recognition in both international law and domestic law that governments must consult with Indigenous peoples before taking away Indigenous access to lands or resources. On the other hand, this is the area where Indigenous people encounter the greatest pressure to assimilate. Mining, gas and oil, forestry, agriculture, hydro-electric power generation, settlement: they can all combine to create a rationale for pursuing a 'public good' that results in the transfer of the ownership and management of lands from the Indigenous inhabitants to the settler governments. Physical confrontations over land continue in Canada, the United States, Australia and New Zealand, resulting in road blockades and land occupations.[80] Gordon Christie is critical of the imposition of a dominant vocabulary on the issues:

> While pre-existing Aboriginal interests may be transformed into proprietary, or quasi-proprietary rights, Aboriginal sovereignty is removed from the scene at the point of the assertion of Crown sovereignty (replaced with, at most, the notion of 'self-government'—another construct within domestic Canadian law). The Crown is charged exclusively with the task of deciding how land is to be thought of, and how this translates into how land is used. Vital Aboriginal interest, those which exist today as 'unsettled' claims, are to be replaced with 'rights' and 'title', constructs essentially unrelated to these vital interests, and distanced from Aboriginal sovereignty. These constructs are grounded in non-Aboriginal visions—state visions—of interests Aboriginal nations

[80] For a thoughtful report following the shooting death of an Aboriginal protester by the police, see Ontario Government, *Report of the Ipperwash Inquiry* (Publications Ontario, 2007).

might have in their lands, non-Aboriginal visions which are directed toward economic/exploitative ends.[81]

The question then, is not only a question of law. In Canada, at least, some First Nations were better off not having any recognised rights in law, but having control and use of their resources in fact. The coming of legal recognition has been accompanied by an invasion of their lands and an expropriation of their resources.

The obligation to 'consult' with Indigenous communities is certainly an improvement over the past, when no consultation was necessary. However, settler governments are loath to acknowledge that Indigenous 'consent' is required. This means that no matter how elaborate the consultation process, courts and governments do not recognise the community's right to say 'no'. Recently in Ontario, Canada, the Kitchenuhmaykoosib Inninuwug were involved in a dispute in the bush hundreds of miles from any road, in an area accessible only by plane and skidoo. The First Nation objected to exploration activity on territory over which it still retained rights to hunt and fish. A court ordered the First Nation to participate in a 'consultation' with the company, Platinex. Throughout the consultation, the First Nation insisted that it intended to follow its own protocols before deciding whether to permit further exploration. After some months had passed, the judge decided that the First Nation's right to be consulted had been fulfilled. When the First Nation continued to block exploration activity, the judge found that the Chief and the majority of the members of the elected council were guilty of contempt of court and he sentenced them to six months in jail.[82] It was the longest sentence that people could remember for a contempt of court arising from protest actions.[83] As for precedents, no examples come to mind of an entire mayor and council of a non-Aboriginal municipality being jailed over a dispute over land use. To exacerbate matters, Platinex was not an innocent, well-meaning resource company. Although the company had received a letter from the First Nation objecting to the exploration activity, in their public listing they said that the Band had verbally consented to the exploration.[84] When the Band physically prevented the exploration activity, Platinex sued for over C$10 billion. That was about C$10 million for every man, woman and child on this isolated reserve.

A softer way for governments to access Indigenous lands is through co-management regimes. In the typical case, a commission or board is established with Indigenous and government appointees. The idea is that this type of structure will facilitate a collaborative relationship that embeds Indigenous participation.

[81] G Christie, 'A Colonial Reading of Recent Jurisprudence: Sparrow, Delgamuukw and Haida Nation' (2005) 23 *Windsor Yearbook of Access to Justice* 17, 46.

[82] *Platinex Inc v Kitchenuhmaykoosib Inninuwug First Nation* [2008] 2 CNLR 201 (Ont Sup Ct).

[83] See *Frontenac Ventures Corp v Ardoch Algonquin First Nation* [2008] OJ 2651 (Ont CA) para 63. In this case, the trial judge had imposed a sentence of six months and a fine of C$25,000 to a former Chief for blocking a uranium mine on disputed land. The Ontario Court of Appeal found the sentence much too harsh and reduced it to a C$1,000 fine.

[84] *Platinex Inc v Kitchenuhmaykoosib Inninuwug First Nation* [2006] 4 CNLR 152 (Ont Sup Ct) paras 23–28. The trial judge's decision was overturned after the leaders of the First Nation had spent over two months in jail: *Platinex Inc v Kitchenuhmaykoosib Inninuwug First Nation* [2008] OJ No 2650 (Ont CA).

Canada uses co-management boards extensively and they are an important feature of all land claims agreements.[85] The jurisdiction and composition of each board depends on the land claims agreement. An example is found in the Nunavut Land Claims Agreement.[86] A number of wildlife management, resource management and environmental boards are established to provide Inuit with a formal role in making recommendations to government decision-makers. These include the Nunavut Planning Commission, the Nunavut Water Board, the Nunavut Wildlife Management Board and the Surface Rights Tribunal. The Boards are generally composed of the same number of representatives from the Tunngavik Federation of Nunavut as from the federal and territorial governments. Since Inuit will dominate the territorial government, the majority of the members of a Board may be Inuit people. For the most part, the decisions of the co-management bodies remain advisory opinions for a government Minister, who will make the final decision. Nonetheless, the Agreement makes it more difficult to ignore the advice of the co-management board. The structured decision-making in the Nunavut Wildlife Management Board is illustrative. The Board is the main instrument for wildlife management in the Nunavut Settlement Area and the main regulator of access to wildlife. The purpose of the Board is to create a system of harvesting rights and priorities and privileges that reflect current and traditional Inuit harvesting. When the Board makes a decision, it is to convey the decision privately to the Minister. If the Minister decides to reject the advice of the Board, the Minister must give his or her decision in writing within 30 days and permit the Board to reconsider its decision. The Board will then reconsider the matter and make its decision publicly. At that point, the Minister is again in a position to accept the decision of the Board or reject the decision of the Board.[87]

In some cases, however, the Boards have more significant authority. The Nunavut Impact Review Board is the environmental assessment agency for the Nunavut Settlement Area. The Board examines the impact of project proposals on the land, air and water, and on the people of the Nunavut Settlement Area. They rely on traditional Inuit knowledge and recognised scientific methods to assess and monitor the environmental, cultural and socioeconomic impacts of proposals. The Board determines whether project proposals should proceed to development and, if so, under what conditions. If the Board decides that a development proposal needs to be reviewed, the Minister is required to refer the matter to a federal environmental assessment panel for socioeconomic and ecosystem impacts.[88]

In Australia, there have been extensive negotiations over joint management of parks. The individual arrangements vary, but they all have two elements in

[85] For a general discussion, see Royal Commission, *Report*, above n 3, vol 2 pt 2, 665–80. For American examples, see E Goodman, 'Protecting Habitat for Off-reservation Tribal Hunting and Fishing Rights: Tribal Comanagement as a Reserved Right' (2000) 30 *Environmental Law* 279.

[86] *Agreement between the Inuit of the Nunavut Settlement Area and Her Majesty the Queen in Right of Canada* (Minister of Indian Affairs and Northern Development and Tungavik, 1993) ('Nunavut Land Claims Agreement').

[87] *Ibid*, Art 5.

[88] *Ibid*, Art 12.

common: Indigenous participation on a board that manages the park, and lease payments to the local Indigenous community. A typical agreement relates to the Uluru-Kata Tjuta National Park. The Anangu were granted title deeds to the park and they leased the land back to Parks Australia for 99 years. The lease agreement 'encourages the maintenance of Anangu tradition through protection of sacred sites and other areas of significance'. The Anangu are to have a majority on the Board of Management, receive annual rental payments, and benefit from training and employment opportunities.[89] A similar initiative exists in Aotearoa/New Zealand, where there have been negotiations over three sacred mountains. Māori have been provided a role in the management of the mountains, although Jacinta Ruru feels it falls short of the type of co-management that exists over some parks in Australia.[90]

The co-management or joint management arrangements can bring benefits to Indigenous people, but usually, the scope of their powers is so limited that they fall well short of recognising Indigenous jurisdiction over their traditional lands.

4. Participation in Public Government

The three models described above involve the creation of institutions that are run by Indigenous people to serve Indigenous people. Self-determination could also take a direction that incorporates participation in the mainstream political system. There are three main variants to this model.

(a) Guaranteed Seats in Parliament

In 1867, New Zealand set aside four seats for Māori in the Parliament. Voters choose whether to be on the 'Māori roll' or on the general roll. Those who decide to be on the Māori roll vote for a representative in one of four Māori districts. In the 1996 elections, a partly Māori party, New Zealand First, took all the Māori seats. The Māori vote was diverse, however, and there were 15 Members of Parliament representing a cross-section of the political spectrum.[91] Nonetheless, there have always been doubts about the extent to which the sitting members represented distinctly Māori interests. This is because the mainstream political parties have run candidates for the Māori seats so that the sitting members owed their first loyalty to the party, not to their constituents. The issue came to a head in 2004,

[89] See Australian Department of the Environment, Water, Heritage and the Arts at www.environment.gov.au/parks/national-parks.html. Generally, see D Craig, 'Indigenous Joint Management of National Parks' [1999] *Australian Indigenous Law Reporter* 46, at www.austlii.edu.au/au/journals/AILR/1999/46.html.

[90] J Ruru, 'Indigenous Peoples' Ownership and Management of Mountains: The Aotearoa/New Zealand Experience' (2004) 3 *Indigenous Law Journal* 111. For a weak version of co-management over other natural resources, see the iwi management plans under the Resource Management Act 1991, at www.rmalink.org.nz/view-subprocess.php?id=21.

[91] Durie, above n 16, 98–110.

when the Labour government enacted legislation that overturned a court decision and purported to extinguish Māori rights on the foreshore and seabed. The measures were strongly opposed by many Māori and there were marches against the legislation. The members sitting in the Māori seats were all members of the Labour party and they were told to vote with the government or face sanctions. One member decided to resign and went on to found the Māori Party. By the 2005 election, changes to the election laws resulted in seven Māori seats. The Māori Party took four of them, with the remaining three going to Labour.[92]

New Zealand is the only country with seats set aside for Indigenous voters. In Canada, the Electoral Reform Commission decided against this model and opted instead to recommend that electoral boundaries be adjusted to create ridings with higher concentrations of Aboriginal people.[93] The federal government did not adopt this recommendation.

(b) Public Government

In Canada's North, the Inuit of the Eastern Arctic succeeded in creating a new Territory called Nunavut. They have opted for a 'public government' model in which all residents of the territory, whether Inuit or not, may vote in territorial elections. Presently, the Inuit constitute a majority in this territory and therefore will have control. However, the government itself is structured as a territorial government exercising powers delegated by the federal government. This means that the Inuit will enjoy the full range of services and jurisdictions available to other territorial governments, but that they will also be bound by conventional institutional structures.[94]

The Inuit in Nunavut have protected their own rights in a separate Nunavut Land Claims Agreement that establishes their ownership to land and ice as well as harvesting rights. I have already described the co-management aspects of this agreement. What you have in the result, is a publicly elected territorial government that is largely Inuit, presiding over land that is partly under the mainstream regime and partly under a land claims agreement that preserves rights for Inuit. If the population balance shifts toward non-Inuit in the future, there may be a danger of diluting the Inuit influence. On the other hand, this model may provide the means for an organic way to incorporate changing demographics.

(c) Elected Indigenous Parliament

The three Scandinavian countries have Parliaments for the Sami people. The Sami are Indigenous people who live in the northern parts of Finland, Sweden, Norway and Russia. They number 75,000–100,000. They have traditionally been associated with reindeer husbandry and it is still an important component for many Sami.

[92] Elections New Zealand, at www.elections.org.nz.
[93] RA Milen (ed), *Aboriginal Peoples and Electoral Reform in Canada* (Dundurn Press, 1991).
[94] Nunavut Act (1993) c 28.

The Parliaments were established first in Finland (1972), followed by Norway (1989) and Sweden (1993). Although they are called Parliaments, the number of elected members is small, consisting of 20–30 representatives. In Norway, the mainstream parties run candidates for the elections whereas in Sweden, there are Indigenous parties who put up candidates. These Parliaments do not have law-making power, but serve to advise government on issues of concern to Sami and have responsibility for some programme funding.

The Scandinavian Parliaments have been criticised for being ineffective. In fact, the Royal Commission on Aboriginal Peoples flatly stated '[s]imply put, the Sami Parliaments lack clout'.[95] The Royal Commission favoured the concept of a separate legislative body for Aboriginal peoples and recommended the establishment of a third chamber of Parliament called the House of First Peoples. Unlike the Scandinavian models, this chamber would have the ability to initiate legislation as well as providing 'advice to the House of Commons and the Senate on legislation and constitutional matters relating to Aboriginal peoples'.[96]

C. Process for Implementation

Up to this point, we have discussed self-determination mostly in the context of the relationship between an Indigenous community and the nation-state in which they live. We have looked at how the models differ, depending on the degree to which the Indigenous community can act independently of state legislation. In this section, I will touch on issues that are important internally for the Indigenous community itself: the process for implementation; what constitutes the community; what accountability mechanisms will control the Indigenous authority; and the importance of addressing the interests of women. The settler governments have a role in ensuring a smooth transition toward the exercise of greater self-determination in all these areas, but must act in a way that respects the autonomy of the community.

1. Community-based Process

One thing that must be clear from earlier Chapters of this book is that imposed solutions concocted by non-Indigenous social engineers will not work. Even the most well-meaning individuals can trigger disastrous social consequences. The only sensible process is one that involves the Indigenous community in the conceptualisation, design and execution of the initiative. It is important for the community to be given the space and time to identify its needs, its priorities and the

[95] Royal Commission, *Report*, above n 3, vol 2, pt 1, 378. For an article on possible reforms, see AJ Semb, 'Sami Self-determination in the Making?' (2005) 11 *Nations and Nationalism* 531.

[96] See recommendations 2.3.51–2.3.54 in Royal Commission, *Report*, above n 3, vol 2, pt 1, 377–82.

way in which it wishes to proceed. The proposals put forward by the community may not fit neatly into the bureaucratic boxes created by government departments. But that is the challenge that progressive governments must take up.[97]

When I worked for the Ministry of the Attorney General, we funded a community justice initiative on an Indian reserve. Some months into the project, the reserve justice committee heard from teachers that children from a particular family were arriving hungry at school. Rather than sanctioning the parents or apprehending the children, the justice committee decided to run a bingo to raise money for a lunch programme for all the children in this school. This caused some consternation within the Ministry because it appeared that the justice project had become involved in areas that should perhaps be in the domain of the Ministry of Family Services or the Ministry of Education. Some bureaucrats wondered whether the Ministry of the Attorney General should continue funding the programme. This may seem like a trivial issue but it is real, as anyone who has worked in government can attest, and the internal bureaucratic dynamics can have devastating impacts on projects on the ground.

For lawyers, especially, the importance of understanding a community-based approach is crucial. Law students are generally given the impression that law is a system of rules and the role of lawyers is to apply those rules with as much precision as possible. The focus is on the rule and what courts or legislatures have said about the rule. But in working with Indigenous communities, the rule-based focus can lead to bizarre results, such as the fight over the provincial–federal boundary in the story that opened this Chapter. In the community lawyering approach, the focus is on how law interacts with the community as a whole. Christina Zuni Cruz makes the connection between community lawyering and self-determination in her work with the Isleta Pueblo:

> Successful community lawyering has just as much to do with process as it does with outcome, and when one values community, process becomes critical. Process is critical because for native peoples, community lawyering is about self-determination, both for the community and the individual, about recognizing traditional norms and practices, and about valuing relationships.[98]

2. Who is the 'Community' or the 'Nation'?

Forced migration, urbanisation and internal social dynamics have splintered Indigenous communities in many ways so that today, many do not conform to historical or 'traditional' groupings. For government, it is sometimes difficult to know who represents what constituency. For communities there is a danger that a purported 'leader' may not be mandated to speak for that community.

[97] Imai, *Handbook*, above n 18, 181–5.

[98] C Zuni Cruz, '[On the] Road Back In: Community Lawyering in Indigenous Communities' (1999) 5 *Clinical Law Review* 557, 563. See also S Imai, 'A Counter-Pedagogy for Social Justice: Core Skills for Community-based Lawyering' (2002) 9 *Clinical Law Review* 195.

The New Zealand Law Commission has addressed this issue in its report, *Waka Umanga: A Proposed Law for Maori Governance.*[99] The two main political units among Māori are the *hapu* (tribe) and *iwi* (tribal confederation), but there are also many urban Māori who do not identify with any particular *iwi*. The law has recognised that Māori collectivities have interests in communal assets, but the legal or social personality of the group holding those assets is not clear. Māori collectivities had been using a variety of existing vehicles, such as corporations and trusts, in order to interact with the mainstream legal system, but these vehicles were an awkward fit. In order to provide more certainty in this area, both for the government and for the Māori themselves, the Commission recommended creating a special corporate vehicle called the *waka umanga*, which would have some of the characteristics of a corporation but which would leave most of the internal arrangements to a charter developed by the Māori collectivity. It is interesting to see the approach the Law Commission has taken to determine how the *waka umanga* would be established. They regarded the *hapu* as the basic unit and suggested that there should be at least 50 members for the group to be viable.

> . . . A viable *hapu* being one that can respectably manage customary requirements in welcoming, feeding and bedding other tribal groups. That probably requires an active and local membership of at least 50, as nowadays all are not available for every event.[100]

The Law Commission recommended that 15 people could propose or oppose the creation of a *waka umanga* and that disputes can be taken to the Māori Land Court, which has expertise on Māori issues. Initially, those that get together to make or oppose the waka umanga determine the membership of the group. Outside of the requirement for the minimum size of a *hapu*, there are no imposed criteria. The Law Commission stated that 'it is the right of a tribe to determine its own membership and membership rules'.[101]

The Canadian Royal Commission on Aboriginal Peoples also turned its mind to the process for the creation of nations that would have a land base and self-governing jurisdiction. In order to move towards a model that was closer to the American situation, Canada's 600 or so Bands created under the Indian Act would need to be reconstituted as larger nations based on traditional affiliations numbering 50–80.[102] These larger nations would hold the inherent right to self-government. The Commission suggested that a charter group, a group of Bands currently recognised under the Indian Act, for example, would hold a referendum to determine whether to proceed towards self-government. This group would then develop a constitution and membership criteria that were inclusive of those historically excluded by the membership criteria of the Indian Act. Membership would not depend on blood quantum. It is contemplated that there would be wide

[99] New Zealand Law Commission (NZLC), *Waka Umanga: A Proposed Law for Maori Governance Entities*, Report 92 (NZLC, May 2006) at www.lawcom.govt.nz.
[100] *Ibid*, para 7.65.
[101] *Ibid*, para 4.50.
[102] Royal Commission, *Report*, above n 3, vol 2, pt 2, 181.

consultation with the larger membership. In order to be recognised the constitution and membership criteria would be presented to a Recognition Panel, composed of a majority of Aboriginal people.[103]

The flexibility suggested by the New Zealand and Canadian reports is important. Stephen Cornell of the United States says:

> the best way to avoid the one-size-fits-all recipe for failure is to let Indigenous peoples decide for themselves who the appropriate self in self-governance is and how self-governing institutions should be structured—and to accept the variety of relationships and governance solutions that will surely result. This is what self-determination means. Furthermore, not only is outsider decision-making in this regard the antithesis of self-determination, but neither collective units nor governing institutions that are imposed by outside authorities are likely to command the respect or allegiance of the peoples on whom they are imposed—which means they will not work.[104]

3. Accountability of Indigenous Government and the Role of Courts

There is some controversy on how to ensure that an Indigenous governing body should be made accountable to its own citizens and how it should adhere to human rights standards. Some Indigenous leaders have expressed concern that merely applying civil liberties law from the common law systems would import a set of criteria based on western individualistic values that are incompatible with Indigenous forms of organisation.[105] For example, the importance of collectivity and communal ownership of land for Indigenous people would be different from the concepts of private property enshrined in the American Bill of Rights. It has been noted earlier that United States Congress enacted the 'Indian Bill of Rights' in the Indian Civil Rights Act because the Bill of Rights in the American constitution did not apply to the tribes. The enactment of this statute was not universally welcome. Domingo Montoya, a Pueblo leader, wanted to be exempt from its application, saying '[o]ur deep concern over the Indian Bill of Rights stems from our fear that it will destroy the traditions—and in doing so greatly weaken our governments'.[106] Nonetheless, in every jurisdiction, there are imposed limits on Indigenous governments. Every self-government agreement in Canada states that the Charter of Rights and Freedoms applies to that Aboriginal government, although there are provisions for ensuring that the impact is softened where the application of individual rights would derogate from Aboriginal or treaty rights.[107]

[103] *Ibid*, 314–20.

[104] Cornell, above n 13, 27.

[105] ME Turpel, 'Aboriginal Peoples and the Canadian Charter: Interpretive Monopolies, Cultural Differences' (1989–90) 6 *Canadian Human Rights Year Book* 3. For a discussion of the impact of the Indian Civil Rights Act, see K McNeil, 'Aboriginal Governments and the *Charter*: Lessons from the United States' (2002) 17 *Canadian Journal of Law and Society* 73.

[106] Quoted in J Wunder, *Retained by the People* (Oxford University Press, 1994) 149.

[107] Constitution Act 1982, s 25 reads, in part: '[t]he guarantee in this Charter of certain rights and freedoms shall not be construed so as to abrogate or derogate from any aboriginal treaty or other rights or freedoms that pertain to the aboriginal peoples of Canada'.

The courts will have an important role to play in the application of individual rights standards to Indigenous governments. In this task, the courts should be sensitive to balancing the interests of individual Indigenous citizens against the importance of the integrity of the Indigenous government and the reality of the context of Indigenous communities. The courts in the United States used the Indian Bill of Rights to make very interventionist decisions in the first five years after its enactment, but have since pulled back to give greater rein to Indigenous sovereignty.[108] Undoubtedly, the task of resolving disputes within an Indigenous community can be challenging for judges. While a mechanical application of rules established in the common law would yield some sort of a *result*, it might not be a result that would be appropriate for the community. In Canada, Federal Court judges have been developing jurisprudence on disputes arising from customary selection of Indian Band leaders. The codes for these elections are created by the Bands themselves and the procedures for their adoption are often contentious, as disputes arise around decision-making 'traditions' or 'customs'. The judges have adapted some general administrative law principles, such as bias and procedural fairness, taking into account the small size of the communities. For example, the strict application of 'conflict of interest' does not make sense when there are so many people related to each other.[109]

4. The Role of Women

Gender relations in Indigenous communities have been greatly influenced by gender relations in the larger settler communities. Consequently, during the time when white women had few rights, the same regime was enforced, directly or indirectly, in Indigenous communities. In Canada, for example, the Indian Act reflected patriarchal attitudes of the 19th century when women lost much of their independence on marriage. White women who married Indian men became Indians. On the other hand, Indian women who married white men lost their status as Indians. When women in the settler society began asserting equality rights in the 1960s and 1970s, the same occurred in Indigenous communities. Canadian Indian women waged a successful campaign to repeal the offending provisions of the Indian Act in 1985.[110]

The right of women to membership is controversial because it can run up against the very self-determination right that is being advocated here. The issue is

[108] Wunder, above n 106, 148–56.

[109] For summaries of court cases on custom elections, see the annotations to s 2(1) 'council of the band' in the annual volumes of S Imai, *Annotated Indian Act and Aboriginal Constitutional Provisions* (Carswell, 2009).

[110] J Silman, *Enough is Enough: Aboriginal Women Speak Out* (The Women's Press, 1987) for interviews with the women who led the fight. Although the amendments to the Indian Act allowed women who lost their status to be reinstated, there is still discrimination against women built into the new scheme: Royal Commission, *Report*, above n 3, vol 4, 37–53. For a general commentary from a Mohawk perspective, see P Monture-Angus, *Thunder in My Soul: A Mohawk Woman Speaks* (Fernwood Publishing, 1995).

illustrated in the case of *Santa Clara Pueblo v Martinez*.[111] The Pueblo tribal law set out that the children of a woman who married out of the tribe lost their tribal membership. In this case, a Pueblo woman married a Navajo man and the family continued to live on the reserve. The mother and a child challenged the law as discriminatory under the Indian Civil Rights Act because the children of men who married out of the tribe retained Pueblo membership. The US Supreme Court held that federal courts lacked jurisdiction to deal with claims under this statute because, imprisonment aside, enforcement of the statute was a tribal matter. Author John Wunder hails this decision as an affirmation of tribal sovereignty.[112] Others see this as toleration of sexism within tribal communities.[113]

One way to address concerns about discrimination against women has been to ensure that settler government documents impose gender equality. The Law Commission report from New Zealand has addressed the gender issue directly suggesting that, while the right to decide membership is to be respected, gender discrimination in the *waka umanga* should not be permitted.[114] In Canada, the Constitution Act 1982 states that Aboriginal and treaty rights are 'guaranteed equally to male and female persons'.[115] Another way to address the concern is to ensure that, in any transitional period toward new structures or new initiatives, the interests of women are taken into account in the process. The Royal Commission on Aboriginal Peoples recommends that all nations 'ensure that the participation of women in the creation and design of justice systems is both meaningful and significant'.[116]

In the end, we must realise that establishing abstract legal standards or creating inclusive processes do not, by themselves, ensure the protection of women. There must be a meaningful way, on the ground, to implement solutions that are effective. The opening story in this Chapter showed how a conflict between the federal and provincial government stymied attempts by the community to control alcohol abuse. In the United States, a jurisdictional conflict affects women who experience domestic violence on tribal lands. Statistics reveal that Indian women experience very high rates of spousal abuse—39 per cent have been victims. Non-Indian men commit 75 per cent of the abuses. As we have mentioned, Indian tribal courts do not have jurisdiction over non-Indians, so they are left powerless. The federal government, which does have jurisdiction, has not committed funds to enforce federal laws on Indian reserves. Only 30 per cent of all federal crimes on tribal land were prosecuted by federal attorneys and within that number, domestic assaults are a low priority. Rebecca Hart and Alexander Lowther argue that the solution lies in placing greater authority in the hands of the tribes: '[t]ribal

[111] *Santa Clara Pueblo v Martinez*, 436 US 49 (1978).

[112] Wunder, above n 106, 153–6.

[113] For a summary of critiques of this decision from the perspectives of women, see Getches *et al*, above n 31, 399–405.

[114] *Waka Umanga*, above n 98, para 4.53.

[115] Constitution Act 1982, s 35(4).

[116] Royal Commission on Aboriginal Peoples, *Bridging the Cultural Divide: Aboriginal People and Criminal Justice in Canada* (Canada Communications Group, 1996) 275.

remedies not only bolster the sovereignty of tribes, they aid Native American women in reclaiming self-determination over their bodies'.[117]

D. Conclusion

In this Chapter we have reviewed a number of forms of governance that could result from the exercise of self-determination. Outright independence apart, the form that gives the greatest autonomy from the settler government is the United States model where courts have recognised tribes as 'domestic dependent nations'. Under the doctrine of retained sovereignty, tribes generally have power to make laws in all areas until they have been overridden by an Act of Congress. In Canada, the recently negotiated self-government agreements, such as the Nisga'a Agreement, recognise that First Nations have an inherent right of self-government. Although the scope of Nisga'a powers is more limited than the powers of tribes in the United States, the laws that the Nisga'a can make in relation to some matters are paramount over federal and provincial laws. Unlike in the United States, the Nisga'a law-making authority is constitutionally protected so that unilateral federal legislation cannot take away those powers.

Self-administration and self-management models are found in all four jurisdictions. Indigenous nations receive delegated responsibilities from federal or state governments to administer services to their constituents. The most advanced form of this model is found in Canada under the Indian Act. Indian Bands have reserves set aside and some power to make local by-laws. Land settlements in Australia and New Zealand have given limited by-law-making authority to Indigenous bodies. Where there is no land base, the most elaborate model was the Aboriginal and Torres Strait Island Commission in Australia, which had nationally elected Aboriginal representatives on its board, and its mandate included advocating for the interests of the Indigenous people. This model for service delivery has advantages, especially for Indigenous people living in urban areas. However, it has been criticised for being too dependent on non- Indigenous design and implementation to be entirely satisfactory.

Ownership and control of lands and resources is crucial to the survival of Indigenous peoples. Some Indigenous communities and nations do own some resources, especially where there is a recognised land base. But ownership is not the only issue. Indigenous control and participation in the stewardship of the resource is also important, and this is most often accomplished through co-management or joint management structures.

Finally, we have reviewed variations on participation in public government. In Aotearoa/New Zealand, the reserved seats for Māori have been a feature of their

[117] RA Hart and MA Lowther, 'Honoring Sovereignty: Aiding Tribal Efforts to Protect Native American Women from Domestic Violence' (2008) 96 *California Law Review* 185.

legislature since 1867. Recently, Inuit of Nunavut have opted for a public government model combined with reserved rights set out in a land claims agreement for Inuit. Institutions similar to Sami Parliaments in Scandinavia have not picked up many adherents in the four countries studied in this reader.

It is difficult, in the abstract, to judge which is the 'best' model. They all have limitations and advantages for certain constituents. It is important to note, however, that a judgment cannot be made simply on whether the institutions or activities 'look Indigenous'. Indigeneity, like non-indigeneity, changes over time. To understand a society, it is not appropriate to take a snapshot that freezes relationships and movement at a particular moment in history. It is more appropriate to think of a video camera that captures shifting patterns, motion, and temporal texture. Indigenous people interacting with the non- Indigenous world are constantly defining Indigeneity, so it is difficult to 'fix' on a particular set of characteristics.

Rather than focusing on outward appearances, it may be more useful to think of criteria that reflect the dynamic nature of Indigenous communities and their relationship with the state. I believe that there are at least three factors to consider in the evaluation of particular choices for self-determination. The first would be to determine the degree to which the Indigenous group participated and consented to the arrangement. I have indicated that wide participation at a community level, including the active participation of women in the decision-making process, is crucial to success. Second, the arrangement could be judged on the degree to which the Indigenous people have autonomy to conceptualise, design and implement their priorities. For example, laws that may work perfectly well within the mainstream society may not be appropriate in the Indigenous context. Third, the initiatives adopted should ensure transparency and accountability within the Indigenous community. This will require a careful balancing between respecting the autonomy of the Indigenous collectivity and ensuring that individuals within that collectivity are treated equitably. To continue the development of Indigenous self-determination, then, would involve increased participation, increased autonomy and increased Indigenous government accountability.

The road ahead is not clear by any means. While there have been some advances in government policies through court decisions, there have also been significant setbacks. In Australia, the recommendation for a national treaty was rejected by the government of the day and the only nationally elected representative organisation for Indigenous people, the Aboriginal and Torres Strait Islander Commission, was disbanded in 2005. In Canada, there has been very little follow-up by governments on the recommendations of the Royal Commission on Aboriginal Peoples.[118] New Zealand enacted the Foreshore and Seabed Act 2004 to vest title in the Crown in order to overturn a court decision that had looked favourably on Māori

[118] Assembly of First Nations (AFN), *Royal Commission on Aboriginal People at Ten Years: A Report Card* (AFN, no date); D Stack, 'Making Aboriginal Policy: A Conference Ten Years After the Final Report of the Royal Commission on Aboriginal Peoples The First Decade of RCAP's Influence on Aboriginal Law' (2007) 70 *Saskatchewan Law Review* 123.

interests.[119] The US Supreme Court has backtracked on sovereignty rights and has severely curtailed jurisdiction of tribes over non-Indians.[120] On the international front, it is important to note that the only four countries to vote *against* the Declaration on the Rights of Indigenous Peoples at the United Nations General Assembly in 2007 were Australia, Canada, New Zealand and the United States.

History so far has taught us two things. First, Indigenous people are not going to disappear. Second, the assimilation policies have been a dismal failure. Studies, such as that of Chandler, that relate self-determination to lower suicide rates, and that of the Harvard Project on American Indian Economic Development, that relate self-determination to greater economic stability, should impel governments to recognise that self-determination for Indigenous peoples is the only viable policy for the years ahead.

[119] See the Chapter in this book by Jacinta Ruru.
[120] See the Chapter in this book by Benjamin J Richardson.

12

Law of the Land—Recognition and Resurgence in Indigenous Law and Justice Systems

CHRISTINE ZUNI CRUZ

A. Introduction

Indigenous knowledge recognises that we live within the 'contexts of flux, paradox and tension'.[1] Man is less significant in the overall scheme of things than we generally think: for example, even though he can divide time in more ways than is necessary, it does not mean he can control it or dictate precisely when everything will happen, though he tries. Man is important, yes, but not always central, not always in control.

There are different types of law in the Indigenous legal tradition, and they are related—natural law or the law of nature, law of the land, law of relationships, spiritual law—ultimately shaping, dictating, and setting the law and course of life for all. Man's law is meant to operate in balance with other laws. The law of nature and spiritual law will and do operate independently, in the same realm, and in their own realm regardless of whether man's law is in balance or opposition to them, because that is the power of these laws.

Not too long ago, the Department of the Interior's Bureau of Indian Affairs employed the slogan 'Tradition is the Enemy of Progress'.[2] This slogan was actually printed and posted in Navajo country. It sent the message that there is no progress in tradition or that tradition never progresses. Certainly, there are legitimate questions about the relevancy and utility of traditional law. Does it change? Can it be used or misused in the contemporary context?

As in all legal traditions, there are reference points that may not change. In the case of Indigenous legal systems, law contained in creation narratives may be

[1] M Battiste and J (Sákéj) Y Henderson, *Protecting Indigenous Knowledge and Heritage: A Global Challenge* (Purich, 2003) 42.

[2] *In the White Man's Image*, PBS, produced by C Lesiak and M Jones, 1991 (documentary contains photograph of sign).

constant.[3] However, like all legal traditions, the Indigenous legal tradition is a living law, it is not static, belonging to some bygone era.

Having worked in this area, I can say my experience with the emerging scholarship on Indigenous knowledge has helped me better understand the paradigm shift required when moving between the Indigenous legal tradition and the common law tradition. Indigenous tradition is embedded in an Indigenous knowledge system that informs a way of thinking that is different from Western approaches to knowledge. Indigenous legal tradition as it is contained within Indigenous knowledge reaches into time immemorial and has continued as an unbroken strand in spite of national policies aimed at completely assimilating Indigenous peoples. It continues to operate in the social consciousness of Indigenous peoples and in their everyday lives, even if it is not recognised as 'law' by the undiscerning.

This Chapter draws from my experience as a judge in tribal courts over the past years, and also builds on my teaching and scholarship on the modern law of Indigenous Nations in the United States (US) and in other countries.[4] I believe that Indigenous peoples themselves must be instrumental in promoting an understanding of Indigenous knowledge. We need to reframe the discourse and the approach to Indigenous legal tradition. In some instances, Indigenous peoples themselves must unlearn the language and legacy of conquest; in others, we must re-learn or learn to trust our own knowledge and our way of thinking about that knowledge. It is in essence an exercise of self-determination.

B. Perspectives on Indigenous Law

Indigenous legal tradition, like other aspects of Indigenous knowledge, has been approached from a Western perspective, and this has produced a certain method of inquiry and study and, therefore, a certain result. Karl N Llewellyn and E Adamson Hoebel wrote the classic in the field of legal ethnography—their study of Cheyenne legal tradition, published under the title *The Cheyenne Way*.[5] They

[3] C Zuni Cruz, 'Tribal Law as Indigenous Social Reality and Separate Consciousness [Re]Incorporating Customs and Traditions into Tribal Law' (2001) 1 *Tribal Law Journal*, available at tlj.unm.edu: 'Traditional law is internal to a particular community, oral, and for the most part, dynamic and not static in nature. There are some who feel that traditional law, such as that contained in creation narratives, for example, can never change. Both these positions can be reconciled.' *Ibid.*

[4] Portions of this Chapter are taken from a conference paper entitled 'Self Determination and Indigenous Nations in the United States: International Human Right, Federal Policy and Indigenous Nationhood', presented at the 2003 Australian Institute of Aboriginal and Torres Strait Islander Studies (AIATSIS) Native Title Research Unit's Native Title Conference in Alice Springs, Northern Territory ntru.aiatsis.govau/conf2003/papers/zunicruz.pdf; and C Zuni Cruz, 'Indigenous Pueblo Culture and Tradition in the Justice System: Maintaining Indigenous Language, Thought, and Law in Judicial Review' in J Anderson (ed), *Land, Rights, Laws: Issues of Native Title*, vol 2, Issues paper no 23 (AIATSIS, 2003) 1–7.

[5] KN Llewellyn and EA Hoebel, *The Cheyenne Way: Conflict and Case Law in Primitive Jurisprudence* (7th edn, University of Oklahoma Press, 1983).

studied cases of trouble, carefully gathered from informants, carefully monitored themselves and their informants and their information for quality-control purposes and arrived at postulates and norms of Cheyenne law. Their approach was meant to improve on the decidedly 'unscientific' method through which prior information on 'primitive law' (their term) was obtained largely through random observation and recordings by individuals in a variety of roles who happened to be in the 'field'. Their methodology relies heavily on a Western approach to Indigenous knowledge. It is both useful and problematic. Useful, in the sense that a clear and reliable picture of law ways emerges from the cases of trouble related to the authors. Problematic, in that the aspect of Indigenous knowledge under study, Indigenous law way or Indigenous legal tradition, is approached from an 'objective', categorical Eurocentric manner premised on 'law' or 'case law' as it exists in Western culture. So does this devalue their work? It simply points out the Western scientific approach utilised in this methodology of study. It was a portal of understanding carved out by employing Western knowledge to access and attempt to understand Indigenous knowledge, in this case their law—some might argue it represents an important or innovative accommodation to better access Indigenous knowledge.

Recently, H Patrick Glenn, a comparative law professor from the US, published a text on the legal traditions of the world.[6] He refers to Indigenous law as 'chthonic' law, because it is the law of autochthonic peoples—peoples 'who live ecological lives by being chthonic, that is, by living in or in close harmony with the earth'.[7] He then describes chthonic law 'by criteria internal to itself, as opposed to imposed criteria',[8] an extremely important methodology when approaching Indigenous subjects.[9] I appreciate two things about his work. First, it recognises the distinct existence of a legal tradition of Indigenous peoples, and places it among seven of the most important and complex legal traditions of the world, including Talmudic, civil law, Islamic, common law, Hindu and Asian legal traditions. Second, it provides a broad understanding of chthonic or Indigenous law in terms of its institutions, its form, and its foundational concepts and methodologies, albeit from an external and general point of view.

Glenn makes a series of general observations on the nature of chthonic law. For example, he notes that it is transmitted orally, in everyday life, and that it is communal in nature.[10] Glenn further notes that this type of law 'does not lend itself to complex institutions' as mainstream law does.[11] Instead, authority lies with elders of the community. Chthonic law lends itself more to dispute resolution processes, which are intended to be inclusive, and aim to foster reconciliation

[6] HP Glenn, *Legal Traditions of the World* (Oxford University Press, 2000).
[7] *Ibid*, 57, citing E Goldsmith, *The Way: An Ecological World View* (Rider, 1992).
[8] Glenn, above n 6, 57.
[9] Battiste and Henderson, above n 1, 41.
[10] Glenn, above n 6, 59.
[11] *Ibid*, 60.

over adjudication. This legal tradition believes in the sacredness of the natural world, and has this belief at the core of its tradition.[12]

Marie Battiste and Sákáj Henderson of the University of Saskatchewan recently published a book on Indigenous knowledge—*Protecting Indigenous Knowledge and Heritage: A Global Challenge.*[13] They write from an Indigenous perspective. If one looks at 'law' through a Western lens, then the Indigenous legal tradition is practically unrecognisable. But if one looks at 'law' from an Indigenous perspective, it is in operation everywhere—even in those places where law is not supposed to be, not expected, because it is intertwined with everything else. That is the nature of Indigenous knowledge, and the Indigenous legal tradition is an aspect of that knowledge. It is there to be found in Indigenous communities, even where it is declared to be non-existent.[14]

The most important aspect of Indigenous knowledge is that it stems from an ecological order, as Richardson explains further in his Chapter in this book. This means that it is rooted and grounded in the land. From our Australian Indigenous sisters we hear that the 'Land is Law'. In the US there is a book on the Apache entitled 'Wisdom Sits in Places'.[15] If Indigenous knowledge stems from an ecological order, this tells us that the law of Indigenous peoples is diverse, because the land and its ecologies are diverse; and while there are 'strands of connectedness', these connections arise from Indigenous thinking 'reflect[ing] a cultural interpretation based on observation of processes inherent in nature'.[16] There are other important aspects of Indigenous knowledge that pertain to the Indigenous legal tradition. According to Battiste and Henderson, Indigenous ways of knowing share the following structure:

i) knowledge of and belief in unseen powers in the ecosystem (Unseen Power);
ii) knowledge that all things in the ecosystem are dependent on each other (Inter/Dependency);
iii) knowledge that reality is structured according to most linguistic concepts by which Indigenous peoples describe it (Indigenous Language);
iv) knowledge that personal relationships reinforce the bond between person, communities and ecosystems (Relational);
v) knowledge that sacred traditions and persons who know these traditions are responsible for teaching morals and ethics to practitioners who are then given responsibility for this specialized knowledge and its dissemination (Sacred/Moral/ Ethical); and
vi) knowledge that an extended kinship passes on teaching and social practices from generation to generation (Generational).[17]

This structure reinforces the knowledge; likewise, movement away from this structure weakens the knowledge.

[12] Glenn, above n 6, 73.
[13] Battiste and Henderson, above n 1.
[14] *Ibid*, 35
[15] K Basso, *Wisdom Sits in Places: Landscape and Language among the Western Apache* (University of New Mexico Press, 1996).
[16] Battiste and Henderson, above n 1, 40.
[17] *Ibid*, 42.

In the next section, I will outline historical and current difficulties in 'seeing' and recognising the existence of Indigenous law.

C. Recognition

There are two levels of recognition of Indigenous legal tradition—external recognition and internal recognition. The external recognition and recording of Indigenous knowledge historically has not been accurate, complete, fair or unbiased. In fact, quite contrary to recognition, the suppression of Indigenous legal traditions was, and in many cases continues to be, a formal policy objective of many nations in their attempts to assimilate Indigenous peoples. While external to the Indigenous community, it has affected how the Indigenous legal tradition has been viewed and treated as a category of law. The internal recognition of traditional law is a completely different matter; nevertheless, it too has been affected by the external view of traditional law and has led in part to the imposition and adoption of external non-Indigenous law in Indigenous communities.

1. External Recognition

When contact first occurred, colonists ascribed little value to Indigenous ways. Indigenous peoples were viewed as uncivilised, unlearned, with everything to gain from the civilising influence of the colonist.[18] So unfamiliar was their legal tradition that by convenience and ignorance it was declared non-existent. All aspects of the way of the people were attacked: religion was outlawed, language, political organisation, dispute resolution, social and familial structure were devalued. Many Indigenous peoples did not survive, but those who did were able to retain and protect aspects of this legal tradition.

In 1934, the US government enacted major legislation aimed at 'assisting' tribes with their governance structures,[19] which were badly affected by the allotment period in which millions of acres of land were taken from Indian reservations,[20] by removal of children to boarding schools,[21] and by other policies of the government

[18] FP Prucha, *The Great Father, The United States Government and the American Indians*, vol I (University of Nebraska Press, 1995) 8. 'There was little doubt in the minds of the European (*pace* those who used the noble savage concepts to condemn evils in their own society) that savagism was an inferior mode of existence and must give way to civility (civilization)'.

[19] Indian Reorganization Act 1934 (Wheeler-Howard Act), 48 Stat 984 (codified at 25 USC 461, et seq).

[20] General Allotment Act 1887 (Dawes Act), 24 Stat 388 (codified as amended at 25 USC 331–4, 339, 341, 342, 348, 349, 354, 381).

[21] R Strickland (ed), *Cohen's Handbook of Federal Indian Law* (Michie Bobbs-Merrill, 1982) 140. (Please note that I have cited the 1982 edition throughout this Chapter. There is a new edition that has been substantially revised with new authors: NJ Newton (ed), *Cohen's Handbook of Federal Indian Law* (LexisNexis Matthew Bender, 2005)

aimed at assimilating Indian people into the white population. As a result of the Indian Reorganisation Act, non-traditional governance structures replaced traditional governance, many of which had already broken down.[22] This displacement was sealed for most tribes through the adoption of tribal constitutions.[23] These constitutions incorporated such concepts as representative democracy, individual rights, elections, voting and majority rule, and the concept of three branches of government—executive, judicial and legislative, interestingly without the separation of powers and checks and balances principles ingrained in the US Constitution.[24] They introduced some ideas and structures unknown in the chthonic legal tradition.

In 1968, Congress enacted legislation known as the Indian Civil Rights Act, which made certain US constitutional Bill of Rights protections applicable to tribal governments.[25] This Act reinforced the concept of 'individual rights' as paramount within tribal governments. The focus on 'individual rights' is problematic because in the chthonic legal traditions, the relation between the individual and collective is not conceived as an opposition between a citizen and a nation-state. This is to be expected, since Indigenous communities were not organised like modern-day nation-states.[26] Nonetheless, American tribes were faced with a prime directive to recognise and enforce individual rights. Chthonic legal tradition in the US has thus been operating alongside US laws that have imposed non-chthonic legal traditions on peoples whose identity and existence are tied to their chthonic legal tradition.

It is interesting to me that the chthonic legal tradition is now being used as the measure of recognition of land rights and use of land in Australia[27] and Canada[28]; and that legal tradition in the past tense is identified,[29] especially since chthonic

[22] See also *ibid*, 238–9 (Indian governments reached their nadir between the 1870s and 1920s).

[23] *Ibid*, 149. Boilerplate constitutions were prepared by the Bureau of Indian Affairs (BIA) based on federal constitutional and common law rather than tribal custom.

[24] F Pommersheim, 'A Path Near the Clearing: An Essay on Constitutional Adjudication in Tribal Courts' (1991–92) 27 *Gonzaga Law Review* 393, 396 (BIA model constitutions omitted protections of Bill of Rights and doctrine of separation of powers, omissions that tribes now are criticised for).

[25] Indian Civil Rights Act 1968, 82 Stat 73, 77 (codified as amended at 25 USC, ss 1301 et seq).

[26] L Sheleff, *The Future of Tradition Customary Law, Common Law and Legal Pluralism* (Frank Cass, 2000) 62–3, quoting P Skalnik, 'Questioning the Concept of State in Southern Ghana' (1983) 9 *Social Dynamics* 11. 'The state is by and large a Euro-Asian invention, whereas the Africans gave the world their systems of chieftainship or their ingenious systems of kinship-based organization': *ibid*, 63.

[27] *Mabo v Queensland (No 2)* (1992) 107 ALR 1 (HC). 'In the result, six members of the Court (Dawson J dissenting) are in agreement that the common law of this country recognizes a form of native title which, in the cases where it has not been extinguished, reflects the entitlement of the Indigenous inhabitants, in *accordance with their laws or customs*, to their *traditional lands*' (Mason CJ, para 2).

[28] *Delgamuukw v British Columbia* [1997] 3 SCR 1010. 'I first consider the source of aboriginal title. As I discussed earlier, aboriginal title arises from the prior occupation of Canada by aboriginal peoples. That prior occupation is relevant in two different ways: first, because of the physical act of occupation, and second because aboriginal title originates in part from pre-existing systems of aboriginal law' (Lamer CJ, para 126).

[29] 'The task of the Court is to identify those laws and customs which regulated the lives of the forebears of the present members of the applicants prior to European settlement which are currently acknowledged and observed': G Neate, 'Three Lessons for Australia from *Delgamuukw v British Columbia*' in L Strelein and K Muir (eds), *Native Title in Perspective, Selected Papers from the Native*

legal tradition is living law. It exists not in the past tense, but in the present tense. In the US, our adherence to chthonic legal tradition is being used to limit our jurisdiction over our territories and the people within those territories.[30] It is used in the negative sense[31] in respect to the unacceptability of traditional law being applied to non-Indians and even to other Indians not of a particular tribe,[32] and there is great concern about what this does to the rights they enjoy as American citizens.[33] In some sense, there is a degree of recognition of the very real difference between the chthonic legal tradition that survives in Indigenous communities in the US and the common law tradition of the country. However, the real problem is that there is not a serious understanding of the chthonic legal tradition. Surface views of deep Indigenous concepts without the context of how Indigenous knowledge systems operate lead to misunderstanding. The US Supreme Court justices write of traditional law as if unknowable rules will be applied to unsuspecting non-Indians in some unjust manner within our tribal court forums as justification for asserting that tribal court jurisdiction does not extend to the non-Indians who live, work and enter our borders. In *Duro v Reina*, Justice Kennedy referred to 'unspoken practices and norms' in reference to legal method.[34] I'm still trying to figure out what this refers to within a chthonic legal tradition, which is characterised by orality. In *Nevada v Hicks*, Justice Souter lamented the unwritten nature of traditional law and the difficultly of sorting out the complex mix of law for outsiders.[35] To me, the characterisation of traditional law as problematic because it is oral and unwritten represents an attack on the continued existence of our legal tradition because the underlying message is that we will gain more power and

Title Research Unit 1998–2000 (Aboriginal Studies Press) 227, citing *Yarmirr and Others v Northern Territory of Australia and Others* (1998) 771 FCA, para 85. See also L Mandell, 'The *Delgamuukw* Decision' in Strelein and Muir, *ibid*, 216–17 (evidence of past laws acceptable as proof of Aboriginal title), citing *Delgamuukw*, above n 28, para 148.

30 *Oliphant v Suquamish Indian Tribe*, 435 US 191 (1978) (tribe had no criminal jurisdiction over non-Indian); *Duro v Reina*, 495 US 676 (1990) (tribe had no criminal jurisdiction over non-member Indian), but see 25 USCA s 1301(2) (congressional enactment in response to *Duro* recognising tribal powers of self-government include 'the inherent power of Indian tribes to exercise criminal jurisdiction over all Indians'); *Nevada v Hicks*, 533 US 353 (2001) (tribe had no civil jurisdiction over non-Indian state officials for excessive action within tribal lands).

31 *Oliphant*, *ibid*, 211.

32 *Duro*, above n 30, 693: 'The special nature of the tribunals at issue makes a focus on consent and the protections of citizenship most appropriate. While modern tribal courts include many familiar features of the judicial process, the unique customs, languages, and usages of the tribes they serve influence them. Tribal courts are often "subordinate to the political branches of tribal governments", and their legal methods may depend on "*unspoken practices and norms*"'. *Ibid*, citing Strickland, above n 21, 334–5 (emphasis added).

33 'We hesitate to adopt a view of tribal sovereignty that would single out another group of *citizens*, nonmember Indians, for trial by political bodies that do not include them. As *full citizens*, Indians share in the territorial and political sovereignty of the United States'. *Duro*, *ibid*, 693 (emphasis added).

34 See above n 32.

35 'Although some modern tribal courts "mirror American courts" and "are guided by written codes, rules, procedures, and guidelines", tribal law is still frequently unwritten, being based instead "on the values, mores, and example from one generation to another". The resulting law applicable in tribal courts is a complex "mix of tribal codes and federal, state, and traditional law", which would be unusually difficult to sort out'. *Nevada*, above n 30, 384 (references omitted).

authority if we assimilate, if our law and our government and justice systems are just like the US's system.[36] In my opinion, it is a great deception. It is also a continuation of the message that our legal tradition is inferior, when in fact it is a legitimate legal tradition: different—yes; less than—absolutely not.[37]

2. Internal Recognition

I have addressed very broadly the problems with external recognition of the Indigenous legal tradition. I now turn to issues related to internal recognition. Internally, the Indigenous legal tradition has been affected and impacted by external factors. I will discuss three ways in which the impact of external factors on Indigenous legal traditions is evident—knowledge, language and process.

(a) Knowledge

Today we have Indigenous intellectuals schooled in Western knowledge, but we have had Indigenous intellectuals steeped in Indigenous knowledge from time immemorial. This gives rise to a complex interplay of both Western and Indigenous knowledge frameworks that operate internally. Sometimes they complement one another, sometimes they clash, and sometimes they sit side by side with no apparent conflict. We are, after all, Indigenous people existing in the same technological age as everyone else. Indigenous knowledge, however, operates in a different manner from Western knowledge, and this is where a critical divergence takes place in respect to recognising the Indigenous legal tradition in operation within Indigenous communities. Indigenous knowledge, which contains the Indigenous legal tradition, has characteristics that require a different approach to respecting, accessing, processing, understanding, valuing and applying it. They are not the same approaches we learn in respect to law in our legal institutions.

The role of elders in the creation, dissemination, and survival of Indigenous knowledge and Indigenous legal traditions is central. Because the chthonic legal tradition builds on accumulated knowledge, and is entrusted to certain individuals who have a responsibility for its dissemination, the experts are those who have been given or taken on the responsibility to pursue Indigenous knowledge, including traditional leaders, elders, and community people. The chthonic legal tradition is contained in language. It is contained in the immutable law, the unchanging law, the origin stories, the journey narratives. But it is also in the everyday social

[36] 'We recognized that some Indian tribal court systems have become increasingly sophisticated and resemble in many respects their state counterparts. We also acknowledge that with the passage of the Indian Civil Rights Act of 1968, which extends certain basic procedural rights to anyone tried in Indian tribal court, many of the dangers that might have accompanied the exercise by tribal courts of criminal jurisdiction over non-Indians only a few decades ago have disappeared . . . But these are considerations for Congress to weight in deciding whether Indian tribes should finally be authorized to try non-Indians'. *Oliphant*, above n 30, 212.

[37] For a discussion of oral tradition evidence before courts, see J Borrows, 'Listening for a Change: The Courts and Oral Tradition' (2001) 39 *Osgoode Hall Law Journal* 1.

relationships that are reinforced as the proper way to live. It is in no one place, but rather everywhere. This is what makes the Indigenous legal tradition a community endeavour. This is also what alienates it from the tribal court system modelled on the common law tradition and presents the challenge for its incorporation.

I have been working in and with the Pueblo judiciary for approximately 20 years. My first appointment to the Pueblo bench was by the Laguna Pueblo Council in 1983, within a year of my graduation from law school. In addition to working with Laguna Pueblo,[38] both as the Chief Judge and as Judge Pro Tem, I have worked with the Santa Clara Pueblo Court, the Southwest Intertribal Court of Appeals,[39] Taos Pueblo Court[40] and presently with my own pueblo, Isleta. I currently serve as an Associate Justice on the newly created Pueblo of Isleta Appellate Court. It is my experiences in this court that form the focus of this Chapter.

In 1999, for the first time in its history,[41] the Pueblo of Isleta Tribal Council delegated its appellate authority to an internal appellate court for land and property disputes and its civil and criminal appeals to a regional court called the Southwest Intertribal Court of Appeals. At the beginning of 2001, the Council placed all civil and criminal appellate authority in its internal appellate court, now known as the Pueblo of Isleta Appellate Court. The Pueblo Council continues to retain appellate jurisdiction over membership issues. In establishing the Appellate Court for Land and Property disputes, the Council wanted to establish an Appellate Court which would apply the traditional law of the Pueblo to land, probate and property disputes. In order to ensure that traditional law would be applied, the Council wanted the court to be comprised of members of the Pueblo, and in particular members of the community knowledgeable of traditional law. This ensured a presence of elders on the bench, but not necessarily lawyers. The Council did agree, however, about the need for lawyers as well, including in both the 1999 and 2001 resolutions that a minimum of three members in a nine-justice bench must be lawyers. The Council then asked selected individuals about their interest in the court. In 1999, the Council appointed seven justices to the bench. I was one of three lawyers appointed to the Appellate bench with four elders. Of these seven original appointees to the Appellate Court for Land and Property, two remain as members of the Isleta Appellate Court.

The experiences that I had while working with the court serve to highlight some of the ways in which Indigenous legal traditions and mainstream law can be in contention.

[38] See KC Iwamoto with F Cerno Jr, 'Pueblo of Laguna Tribal Government Profile' (2001–02) 2 *Tribal Law Journal*, tlj.unm.edu/archives/vol2/index.php.

[39] CP Zuni, 'Southwest Intertribal Court of Appeals' (1994) 24 *New Mexico Law Review* 309. I served as Court Administrator for the Southwest Intertribal Court of Appeals from 1992 to 1993 and as an Appellate Judge in appointed cases.

[40] See E Lujan, *Taos Pueblo Court* (Indigenous Justice Conference materials, 1994) (on file with the author). The Pueblo of Santa Clara and the Office of Indian Affairs in Santa Fe, New Mexico, hosted the 1994 Indigenous Justice Conference.

[41] Under the Pueblo of Isleta Constitution, the Council has appellate authority, which it can delegate. The 1999 delegation was the first time since the adoption of the Constitution by the Pueblo in the 1940s that the Pueblo Council chose to delegate this authority.

From the outset, the elders exposed the attorneys' Western knowledge of the law and procedure as laden with values and concepts in conflict with the Indigenous worldview of the people of Isleta. It is clear that there are two knowledge systems vying for superiority in the development of tribal court systems. Perhaps the appointment of elders and lawyers to the appellate bench was the greatest mechanism for alerting both to this stark reality. The development of rules of procedure for the Appellate Court proved to be an exercise in taking legalese out of procedure and limiting and tailoring rules to the use of the court primarily by lay people as opposed to attorneys. The greatest challenge was explaining the need for certain rules to the elders and obtaining their consensus, as well as anticipating rules necessary to accommodate a type of customary practice expected by the people and envisioned by the elders. Wholesale importation of the State of New Mexico's Rules of Appellate Procedure was not an option. It was here that the indoctrination and influence of a Western legal education was most obvious. The Anglo-American appellate system is designed for use by attorneys, whereas the tribal appellate court system functions with the occasional attorney. While the Anglo-American system is largely impersonal, the Isleta Court system operates for a society that is interrelated and known to one another, and the appellate judiciary is a part of that interrelated society. The procedural rules developed by Anglo-American courts arise from underlying legal principles, which may or may not exist in the Pueblo, either in adopted form or in traditional approaches to the law.

The creation of an Appellate Court comprised of elders and lawyers has had a profound effect on the direction of the court. Had the court been comprised only of lawyers, much of the influence of the elders would have been lost. The Council's acts of delegating its appellate authority and pooling non-lawyers with lawyers on the appellate bench were not the only catalysts that initiated a significant jurisprudential shift; the acts of affirming traditional law and the articulation of the expectation that both lawyers and elders teach and learn from one another were also important. We have only begun the journey.

(b) Language

I like this quote from the Irish Poet Seamus Heaney, recipient of the Nobel Prize in Literature: 'In any movement towards liberation, it will be necessary to deny the normative authority of the dominant language or literary tradition'.[42] A critical beginning point is to consider the meaning of law in the native language. In Tiwa,[43] for example, there are words for law and custom derived from the Spanish

[42] Quoted in F Pommersheim, 'Tribal Court Jurisprudence: A Snapshot from the Field' (1996) 7 *Vermont Law Review* 21, 44. Pommersheim uses this quote in reference to the development of a tribal jurisprudence. He states: 'Although literature is not law, in periods of liberation, law too will confront dominant norms'. The Heaney quote grabbed my attention and I use it in reference to the language spoken in tribal courts.

[43] The Tiwa words and translations used here are from a discussion and interview between Isleta Pueblo member and Tiwa language instructor, Doris Lucero, and the author (14–15 October 2000).

words for both[44]; there is also a word referring to white man's law or the law of the courts,[45] demonstrating the introduction of outside law from two separate sources, but also the distinction such law has from traditional law. The word that comes closest to 'law' in Tiwa is the word for tradition—*keynaithue-wa-ee*, which translates 'this is our way of living'.[46] That way of life is elaborated upon in prayer.[47]

Chief Justice Emeritus Robert Yazzie of the Navajo Nation Supreme Court also considers the Navajo word for law—*beehaz-aani*. Yazzie states:

> The Navajo word for 'law' is *beehaz'aani*. It means something fundamental, and something that is absolute and exists from the beginning of time. Navajos believe that the Holy People 'put it there for us from the beginning' for better thinking, planning and guidance. It is the source of a healthy, meaningful life, and thus 'life comes from it'. Navajos say that 'life comes from *beehaz'aani*', because it is the essence of life. The precepts of *beehaz'aani* are stated in prayers and ceremonies that tell us of *hozho*—'the perfect state'. Through these prayers and ceremonies we are taught what ought to be and what ought not to be.[48]

Language was the first issue to arise in my position on the Appellate Court, and it arose for me in a personal context. All the Justices appointed to the Appellate Court for Land and Property disputes were fluent Tiwa speakers, except for me. At the first meeting I attended, the issue of my fluency arose with the elders. In this meeting they expressed a need to return to the Council and confirm the appointment to the bench of a Justice who was not a fluent Tiwa speaker. The issues regarding the need for fluent Tiwa speakers were two-fold. First, in order to follow the conversation, and second, to appreciate concepts, an understanding of the Tiwa language was necessary. At the Council meeting I undertook the responsibility to learn Tiwa,[49] as the only other alternatives were that English be used or that I be disqualified from serving on the court, and the lawyers agreed to aid in interpretation. With these undertakings, the Council affirmed my appointment and the elders accepted the confirmation.

The Appellate Court for Land and Property disputes conducted its meetings and its court proceedings in Tiwa. The Isleta Appellate Court has continued this practice. My responsibilities to the court now have me immersed in Tiwa. I follow Tiwa through interpretation provided by the other Justices. The end result, that I learn Tiwa, also placed the role of teaching language on others, if only because at

[44] *Na-ley* translates to 'law'. *Ley* is the Spanish word for law. *Na-costumbre* is custom. *Costumbre* is the Spanish word for custom. *Ibid.*

[45] *Na-shachee* translates to white man's law or laws of the court. *Ibid.*

[46] *Ibid.* As Doris Lucero, *ibid*, elaborates: 'Our way of life is good. There was honor among the people. That's why we survived. We helped each other. We cared. We loved each other. That's the way it should be.'

[47] *Ibid. Key-wah-wai-ee* or 'This is the way of life' is connected to *keynaithue-wa-ee*. Detail of that way of life is provided through prayers.

[48] R Yazzie, '"Life Comes from It": Navajo Justice Concepts' (1994) 24 *New Mexico Law Review* 175 (footnotes omitted).

[49] It has not been an easy obligation to fulfil.

the meetings and hearings Tiwa is spoken. Had English become the discursive language of the court or had I been disqualified, the impetus to learn, the opportunity for immersion, and the opportunity to teach would have been lost. The exclusive use of English was never a possibility with the elders appointed to the court. Their language of choice is Tiwa, because English, though all are fluent, is their second language. The Council reminded us that we (attorneys and younger people) had to learn from our elders, and likewise that our elders (non-attorneys and older people) had to learn from us as well. In this respect, we are bridges of understanding to one another. This principle has gone well beyond language.

The emphasis on the use of the language in official meetings of the court and in court proceedings has fostered a truly unique feel to the court. Much appellate practice before the court is by *pro se* or unrepresented parties who prefer to address the court in Tiwa. For parties who are not proficient or who do not speak the language, accommodation is made. For instance, this includes the use of spokespersons to speak on their behalf or to assist in translation, for those who are not Tiwa speakers, and the use of both English and Tiwa by the bench during proceedings involving parties with mixed levels of fluency in Tiwa or with no Tiwa fluency, including non-member Indians and non-Indians.

The use of Tiwa by the Isleta Appellate Court represents a decision wholly apart from federal policy. The court uses it because it is the language of the people. It makes the court accessible to the people in the language they are most comfortable with. It encourages the use of the language and emphasises the importance of the language for both those who are bilingual and those who are not. Given the endangered nature of native languages, the official use and encouragement of the use of the native language by the court is critical. The encouragement of bilingualism (Tiwa and English) over monolingualism (English only) is not lost when official Pueblo business is conducted in Tiwa.

Maintaining native language is of fundamental importance to the continuance of Indigenous knowledge.[50] The Isleta Appellate Court's internal decision regarding the use of Tiwa is in fact supported by Congressional legislation,[51] though support of Indigenous language was not always US government policy.[52] The Native American Languages Act specifically states that '[i]t is the policy of the United States to . . . fully recognize the inherent right of Indian tribes and other Native American governing bodies . . . to take action on, and give official status to, their Native American languages for the purpose of conducting their own business'.[53] Further, the Act states that the 'right of Native Americans to express themselves

[50] Battiste and Henderson, above n 1, 48. See also AM Dussias, 'Waging War with Words: Native Americans' Continuing Struggle Against the Suppression of Their Languages' (1999) 60 *Ohio State Law Journal* 901, 923.

[51] Native American Languages Act 1990, 25 USC s 2903(6).

[52] Dussias, above n 50, 905, noting: 'The US government adopted the policy of eradicating the allegedly inferior Native American languages and replacing them with English in the schools that it established and supported to educate Indian children.'

[53] 25 USC s 2903(6).

through the use of Native American languages shall not be restricted in any public proceeding'.[54]

(c) Process

I want to focus on one particular aspect of process, though there are many to which I could refer. Very early on, as we began deliberating cases before us, the possibility that we might not all agree on an outcome emerged. The Council resolution provided the option to enter majority and minority decisions. The attorneys, familiar with the concept, accepted the possibility that a judge might have to pen a dissent. However, when that possibility actually was encountered, the elders empathically disagreed. The possibility that the majority was in error, and that a lone dissenter was correct and could convince the majority of the correctness of his or her position, had to be seriously considered.

Consensus was established as the preferred method for decision making, not only because of the court's desire to be in agreement or correct, but because consensus is the traditional method for arriving at decisions in Pueblo communities.[55] We would talk the matter over until there was consensus. However, the outgrowth of employing consensus in the group proved to be much more than ensuring correctness. Consensus necessitates the need to hear from everyone, to listen carefully, and to consider positions. It builds group cohesion and generates respect for everyone's opinion. As a result consensus meant that we had to bridge the gap between different generations, between Western-law-trained professionals and non-law-trained lay people, between Western education and Indigenous knowledge. It has proved to be important to the success of building relationships and understanding among the Justices. Majority rule is less democratic than consensus, as forcing the position of the majority on the group can, in fact, be more harmful in small communities where there is a greater need for people to operate out of agreement rather than out of expedience.

D. Resurgence

It is through our legal traditions that we, as Indigenous peoples, know that we have the right to self-determination. It is the chthonic legal tradition that gives us our identity as peoples separate and distinct from other peoples in the world. It is critical to us. Yet it is, in part, why we experience/have experienced the attacks we have endured on so many levels. The suppression of our religion,[56] our language,[57] the

[54] 25 USC s 2904.

[55] Since the creation of the first Appellate Court in 1999, only one case was decided by a majority decision. All the rest were decided by consensus.

[56] Prucha, above n 18, 647, citing 'Rules for the Courts of Indian Offenses, April 10, 1883'.

[57] Strickland, above n 21, 140.

removal from and destruction and taking of our traditional lands,[58] the imposition of political organisation,[59] the physical removal of our children,[60] Western education,[61] all these impact and continue to impact our legal tradition, our identity. Assimilation has been a goal of US federal policy toward its Indigenous population.[62] If we do not begin to see how our legal tradition is of utmost importance in our internal self-determination, we risk assimilating ourselves in the belief we are exercising self-determination. Our chthonic legal tradition—our journey narratives, our origin stories provide the legal basis for our legitimate claim to self-determination. And once you begin with the chthonic legal tradition, everything else that has to do with self-determination (that is, nation-building) flows from it.

My main point here is that Indigenous peoples faced with maintaining chthonic legal tradition within a nation-state structure that imposes non-chthonic legal norms upon them must take special care that their chthonic legal tradition is preserved. As tribes in the US are contemplating 'nation-building', it is imperative that we understand the importance of the chthonic legal tradition to our very existence as we reconsider our governance systems and how we are responding to the imposition of non-chthonic legal norms on our governments. I believe one of the most important steps is to consider what every act toward nation-building we engage in does to our chthonic legal tradition, as well as thinking about nation-building as reinforcing our chthonic legal tradition.

Today, as some Indigenous legal scholars look critically at tribal governance systems, this shift from Indigenous concepts of political and social organisation is seen as a starting point for more severe political crises that tribes are experiencing today.[63] It is no surprise that Indigenous peoples who continue to operate within a chthonic legal tradition encounter problems in trying to operate under governmental systems that are not related to the way they organise the rest of their lives.[64] So, as Indigenous nation-building is discussed in the US at present, there has been a movement to rewrite constitutions to reflect the chthonic legal tradition of

[58] See, eg, LA French, *The Winds of Injustice: American Indians and The US Government* (Garland Publishing, 1994) 45–60 (brief discussion of the removal and allotment policies as they impacted selected tribes).

[59] Indian Reorganization Act 1934, above n 19.

[60] Strickland, above n 21, 140, noting: 'Off-reservation federal boarding schools were founded in 1879. Reformists thought them an ideal method of assimilation, since youth were completely removed from the family and from the barbarism of tribal life'. See also Indian Child Welfare Act 1978, 92 Stat 3069: 'Congress finds that an alarmingly high percentage of Indian families are broken up by the removal, often unwarranted, of their children from them by nontribal public and private agencies and that an alarmingly high percentage of such children are placed in non-Indian foster and adoptive homes and institutions.'

[61] Strickland, above n 21, 139–41.

[62] *Ibid*, 128–9.

[63] See generally R Porter, 'Strengthening Tribal Sovereignty through Government Reform: What are the Issues?' (1997) 7 *Kansas Journal of Law and Policy* 72 (discussing the impact of colonisation on tribal governments); R Porter, 'Strengthening Tribal Sovereignty through Peacemaking: How the Anglo-American Legal Tradition Destroys Indigenous Societies' (1997) 28 *Columbia Human Rights Law Review* 235 (discussing Seneca civil war and the consequences of the transformation of Indigenous dispute resolution associated with the adoption of the Anglo-American legal tradition).

[64] See generally Zuni Cruz, above n 3.

Indigenous nations. Unfortunately, an ever-present concern is how much difference will be tolerated by the federal government, as well as recognising that a degree of assimilation to Western ideas is evident in the very starting point—the re-drafting of a constitution.

Nonetheless, we must remember that those who preceded us kept our traditions alive, even while they were forced to adopt the outer manifestations of imposed European institutions. It is a phenomenon that has been called 'cultural camouflage'. In a historical study of the Creek Indians in the US, Sydney Harring recounts how tribal governments took on the trappings of mainstream American institutions.

> Much of the historical emphasis on these governments focuses on how 'civilized', meaning Americanized, they were: popularly elected chiefs, bicameral legislatures, universal male suffrage, secret ballots, two-tiered court systems, courthouses, high sheriffs, light-horsemen and schools. But a closer look reveals that a good many of the forms that the Americans imposed on the tribes were adopted but much less of the substance. Tribal values and tribal sovereignty lived within institutions that looked American. There can be no question that this was one part of a conscious Creek strategy to protect tribal traditions and sovereignty.[65]

Chief Justice Emeritus Robert Yazzie explains why the Navajo created the courts of the Navajo Nation in 1959 to look like mainstream American courts. He refers to the American system of adjudication as the 'Law Way' and traditional Navajo procedure as the 'Life Way'.

> The [Courts of the Navajo Nation] were created out of a fear of a State take-over of criminal and civil jurisdiction, and as a defense. They were designed to look like justice of the peace courts with the hope that, with the appearance of The Law Way, the state would leave us alone.[66]

Education in our traditional law is crucial, then, to ensure our survival. But Western education is also a necessity in the struggle for self-determination and nation-building. That education is essential to prepare us to engage the outside system, to protect our interests in that system, and to keep abreast and, hopefully, ahead. Nonetheless, it is important to recognise Western education as a double-edged sword. What it represents, in terms of values, approaches and ideas, can be counter to maintaining a chthonic legal tradition within our nations.[67] Here I will use two examples from the legal field.

Chief Justice Emeritus Robert Yazzie, in an address to Indigenous law students, asked them to be careful that the tools they acquired in law school were not used to destroy the home that they returned to.[68] He told them that some of their

[65] SL Harring, 'Crazy Snake and the Creek Struggle for Sovereignty: The Native American Legal Culture and American Law' (1990) 34 *American Journal of Legal History* 365, 369.

[66] Quoted in The Harvard Project on American Indian Economic Development, *The State of the Native Nations* (Oxford University Press, 2007) 48.

[67] C Zuni Cruz, 'Toward a Pedagogy and Ethic of Law/Lawyering for Indigenous Peoples' (2006) 82 *North Dakota Law Review* 863.

[68] R Yazzie, 'Law School as a Journey' (1993) 46 *Arkansas Law Review* 271.

Western education was not going to be useful within Indigenous communities, and that, in some instances, it could be destructive.[69] Robert Porter considers a 1978 study by Linda Medcalf on the impact on Indian tribes of the first generation of lawyers representing Native Americans in his article examining how Anglo-American legal tradition detrimentally impacts Indigenous societies.[70] Porter explains:

> Medcalf concluded that, despite their best intentions, lawyers working on behalf of Indian people failed in their stated mission of strengthening native communities and had contributed to the breakdown of native culture by imposing upon the Indians the full panoply of Anglo-American values, particularly the emphasis on individual rights.[71]

There is Western knowledge and there is Indigenous knowledge. Indigenous knowledge and approaches are crucial in the struggle for self-determination. Western formal education must be informed by Indigenous knowledge within Indigenous communities. Porter explains that Medcalf recognised

> that the tribal lawyers she studied were, in one sense, successful because they were able to assert tribal rights to obtain political and economic power for their native clients. She concludes, however, that American trained lawyers ultimately fail because they do not provide their native clients with a meaningful choice between retaining a distinct tribal existence and adopting a lifestyle indistinguishable from American society.[72]

One way to counteract this tendency is to practise a community lawyering approach for Indigenous communities. Lawyers should not see themselves in the same role they are taught in law school, where they are experts on knowledge and impose their ideas on their clients. Lawyers cannot focus solely on the problems of individuals. They must become aware of the needs of the community and help translate concepts to non-Indigenous tribunals. The role of the lawyer is not only as a zealous advocate, but also, in issues affecting the community, a facilitator for a consensus-building process that will restore balance in the community.[73] In order to practise in this way, lawyers must also be acutely aware of the legal traditions of the community.

Brenda Small, a Cree from James Bay in Canada, captures the issue nicely when she reflects on her experience in law school:

> We cannot study law and go back home and expect that this knowledge will save our people. We cannot pretend that just because we have learned the white man's law, we are

[69] R Yazzie, 'Law School as a Journey' (1993) 46 *Arkansas Law Review* 271.

[70] Porter, 'Strengthening Tribal Sovereignty through Peacemaking', above n 63, 283, citing L Medcalf, *Law and Identity: Lawyers, Native Americans and Legal Practice* (Sage Publications, 1978).

[71] *Ibid.*

[72] *Ibid*, 284–5 (footnotes omitted).

[73] C Zuni Cruz, '[On the] Road Back In: Community Lawyering in Indigenous Communities' (1999) 5 *Clinical Law Review* 557. See also S Imai, 'A Counter-pedagogy for Social Justice: Core Skills for Community-based Lawyering' (2002) 9 *Clinical Law Review* 195; Zuni Cruz, above n 67, 867; J (Sákéj) Y Henderson, 'Postcolonial Indigenous Legal Consciousness' (2002) 1 *Indigenous Law Journal* 1, 53–4.

> in a better position to enhance the survival of our people. In fact, such conclusions are full of a learned arrogance that fails to recognize that the survival of our people has been assured because of our own strengths.
>
> We can be present at the law school but that doesn't mean that we ought to become the instruments or vehicles for the intrusiveness of the white man's law. Instead, we must retain a vision of the world that is based on own ethics and beliefs. In essence, the law we need to know best are those presented to us in the wind, in the river and across the skies.[74]

In his description of the language of the Anishinabek, John Borrows talks about the relationship of the law and the land:

> The Anishinabek people have a number of legal principles that guide their relationship with other living beings in a conservationist mode. Rocks (land) are animate or living in verb-oriented Algonkian languages such as Anishnabemowin. Their active nature means rocks have an agency of their own which must be respected when Anishinabek people use them.[75]

This brings me to a second way in which to counter the tendency for Indigenous lawyers to reproduce Western law: language. Fluency in the native language is crucial to understanding ways of thinking that are important to Indigenous concepts. Because language orders thought, focuses attention, and establishes relationships, its value to law cannot be mistaken. Whether one is seeking to explain and understand either Anglo-American legal concepts or Indigenous concepts, being bilingual assists in one's explanation and understanding. Encouraging bilingualism in native lawyers is an important aspect of preparing them to function well as lawyers in their own communities.[76] The support for acquiring or strengthening native language skill among native law students is not currently part of American Indian legal training. Based on my experience, I believe this is a drawback in preparing native lawyers for work within their native communities. Supporting, facilitating, and otherwise encouraging native students to become fluent in their native language is an important aspect of the skills needed by students to be effective within their own communities. Bilingualism in the native legal community will help prevent the tribal justice system from getting too far away from the community, both by fostering an understanding of traditional law and avoiding over-reliance on Anglo-American concepts embedded in American law and the English language.

[74] Quoted in S Imai, *Aboriginal Law Handbook* (2nd edn, Carswell, 1999) iii. See also Zuni Cruz, above n 67, and Henderson, above n 73.

[75] J Borrows, *Indigenous Legal Traditions in Canada* (Law Commission of Canada, 2006) 38.

[76] Borrows, *ibid* (at 188) makes a point that I feel is crucial: 'Immersion is important: a program would fail to adequately teach Indigenous law if it did not provide learning opportunities outside of law schools. While there is great value in formal classroom instruction, Indigenous law must also be learned in an applied and practical context. Indigenous laws are often the product of specific relationships to land, plants, animals, water, people, etc. To fully appreciate Indigenous law, students need to be immersed with the people whose law they want to more fully understand. This immersion must also be intensive, and focused on one tradition at a time in order to expose students to each tradition's depth and complexity. Students' education in Indigenous law is incomplete if they do not delve deeper into legal traditions of their choice for either three summer terms or one final year.'

In this regard, Borrows is thinking of a creative way of addressing these issues. He proposes developing a four-year degree that will combine a Bachelor of Laws (equivalent to an American JD) with a Bachelor of Indigenous Law. There will be a cohort of 24 students who study in the law school and in surrounding Indigenous communities. They will take many of the courses from the regular curriculum, such as contract, criminal and administrative law, but each course will have an additional Indigenous perspective. Students will be required to spend some terms in the communities, where they will study specific Indigenous laws. For example, near the University of Victoria, students could study Salish Legal Traditions, Salish Language and Law, and Salish Legal Writing and Advanced Legal Research.[77]

I hope reforms in legal education and new approaches to lawyering can feed the resurgence in traditional systems of justice. No other jurisdiction has a system as extensive as the American Tribal Court system that has around 275 tribal courts administering tribal law.[78] However, there are justice initiatives in other countries as well. In Canada, the Indian Act provides for the appointment of Indigenous justices of the peace who have limited jurisdiction to try offences under that Act.[79] Only a few justices of the peace were ever appointed and they did not have jurisdiction to apply Indigenous law. Australia had some Aboriginal courts to try local matters.[80] Queensland, for example, had a court consisting of two Indigenous people appointed as justices of the peace to hear matters relating to the breach of community by-laws.[81] However, this system has been replaced with 'community councils' that can only give advice to regular judges.

More common in Australia and Canada is Aboriginal participation in sentencing of offenders. In these initiatives, when the accused pleads guilty or accepts responsibility for an offence, there are opportunities for members of the community to participate in deciding on the appropriate sentence. Australia appears to be heading in this direction with the establishment of sentencing courts in a number of jurisdictions, including Queensland, South Australia, Victoria, New South Wales and Western Australia.[82] In these courts, the purpose is to 'to make the Court process less alienating and the Orders of the Court more culturally appro-

[77] J Borrows, *Indigenous Legal Traditions in Canada* (Law Commission of Canada, 2006), 177–90.

[78] See the National Tribal Resource Center, www.tribalresourcecenter.org; and DH Getches, CF Wilkinson, RA Williams Jr, *Cases and Materials on Federal Indian Law* (5th edn, West Publishing, 2005) 420.

[79] Indian Act, RSC 1985, c I-5, s 107.

[80] See G Nettheim, GD Meyers and D Craig, *Indigenous Peoples and Governance Structures: A Comparative Analysis of Land and Resource Management Rights* (Aboriginal Studies Press, 2002) 281; Australian Law Commission, *The Recognition of Aboriginal Customary Laws* (Australian Government Publishing Service, 1986) vol 2, 30–52.

[81] The Community Services (Aborigines) Act 1991 (Qld). The court provisions in this statute appear to have been repealed. Under the Aboriginal and Torres Strait Islander Communities (Justice, Land and Other Matters) Act 1984 (Qld), there are now only 'community councils' that can give advice in regular court proceedings.

[82] For an overview, see Law Reform Commission of Western Australia, *Aboriginal Customary Law*, project 94 (Government of Western Australia, 2006), ch 7, 'Aboriginal Courts'.

priate for Indigenous people who come into contact with the criminal justice system'.[83] However, the proceedings are squarely within the larger justice system. The Department of Attorney General of Western Australia makes this clear in its description of the Kalgoorlie-Boulder Community Court, stating that this court 'does not involve different laws or use customary Aboriginal law'.[84]

A variation of this model, called the 'sentencing circle', is used in Canada and some parts of Australia. Typically, the accused, who has taken responsibility for the offence, will sit in a circle with the victim, relatives, the judge, the Crown attorney, the defence lawyer and other community members. The circle will make a recommendation to the Crown about the appropriate sentence. While the Royal Commission on Aboriginal Peoples has reported success with a number of initiatives, the most interesting is a process at Hollow Water First Nation dealing with sexual offenders.[85] Here, the First Nation had to address pervasive sexual abuse in a community where 75 per cent of the residents were victims and 35 per cent were victimisers. A group of residents, mostly women, began developing an approach and took two years of study before developing the process. After the offender acknowledges responsibility and is accepted by the group, the offender is allowed to stay in the community but is subject to a 13-step process that takes five years. The description of the process is important:

> The [Community Holistic Circle Healing] is not a program or project. It is a process with individuals coming back into balance. A process of a community healing itself. It is a process which one day will allow our children and grandchildren to once again walk with their heads high as they travel around the Medicine Wheel of Life.[86]

Sentencing circles can be problematic if they are not established properly, and there have been some criticisms that they can revictimise victims of spousal abuse by exposing them to their assailants.[87]

A very interesting model for addressing disputes between the settler government and Māori people in Aotearoa/New Zealand is the Waitangi Tribunal, established in 1975. The Tribunal has Māori and non-Māori judges as well as Māori elders on its panel, and it has developed a procedure that incorporates Māori practices. The hearings are held on Māori territory, the Māori language is used in parts of the proceedings and Māori protocols are followed:

[83] For an overview of the Murri Court, see A Hennessy, Magistrate, 'Justice for all—Victims, Defendants, Prisoners and Community: Indigenous Sentencing Practice' (presented to the Australia International Society for Reform of the Criminal Law Conference, Brisbane July 2006) 2, at www.isrcl.org/Papers/2006/Hennessy.pdf.

[84] See the website of Western Australia's Department of the Attorney General: www.justice.wa.gov.au/A/aboriginal_court.aspx?uid=6986-7860-4445-5582.

[85] Royal Commission on Aboriginal Peoples, *Bridging the Cultural Divide: Aboriginal People and Criminal Justice in Canada* (Canada Communications Group, 1996) 159–67.

[86] *Ibid*, 169.

[87] E LaRocque, 'Re-examining Culturally Appropriate Models in Criminal Justice Applications' in M Asch (ed), *Aboriginal and Treaty Rights in Canada: Essays on Law, Equity, and Respect for Difference* (UBC Press, 1997) 75–97.

> By holding hearings on *marae*, participating in *powhiri*, listening to *karanga*, *whaikorero* and *waiata*, and immersing itself in a Maori environment, the Tribunal develops context within which to interpret oral and written evidence.[88]

The justice initiatives described above—the sentencing circles, the sentencing courts and the Waitangi Tribunal—face the same challenges as the tribal courts in the US. While they provide for greater participation of Indigenous people, there is a constant struggle to promote the use of Indigenous laws. I hope that, with reforms in legal education and new approaches to lawyering, a new generation of lawyers can shape these institutions to be consistent with Indigenous legal traditions. Nonetheless, it is important to note that even limited justice initiatives can be very powerful. A non-Indigenous defence lawyer attended an Elders hearing in northern Canada conducted in the Cree language, and had this to say:

> As you are aware, I have attended in the Northern Courts as Duty Counsel for the past six or seven years and as such am well acquainted with the various Courts in the Northern communities. I have seen on many occasions the veiled and often open contempt with which the natives hold the judicial system which is obviously viewed by many as a continuing aspect of white supremacy and dominance. This lack of respect for the Court is quite apparent from the demeanor of witnesses, onlookers and Defendants in many of the cases. However, during the Elders Court, it became quite apparent to me that the Elders took their job very seriously. They conducted the Court in a manner that was totally unique and foreign to my experience as an Ontario lawyer. They did not ask for example the Defendants how they pleaded but simply asked them as to whether or not they did what was alleged. This direct confrontation elicited from most what I perceive to be an honest answer (in all the cases that I observed the answer was in the affirmative) and the Elders proceeded to lecture the accused as to how they had embarrassed the community at large, their families in particular and themselves, i.e., the Defendants, even more specifically. The accused obviously held the Elders in respect and certainly displayed shame and remorse that I had not observed in my other experiences in the Courts in the North generally and in this one in particular.[89]

E. Conclusion

Allow me to conclude by reiterating my major point. Our Indigenous legal tradition is central to our claim for self-determination. Our chthonic legal tradition is central to our identity. More of our attention should be focused on this legal tradition and its relationship to all that is proposed, imposed, contemplated,

[88] G Phillipson, 'Talking and Writing History: Evidence to the Waitangi Tribunal' in J Hayward and NR Wheen (eds), *The Waitangi Tribunal* (Bridget Williams Books, 2004) 41. The Māori terms can be translated as follows: *marae*—ceremonial centre of a particular descent group used for public business; *powhiri*—beckoning forward, welcome; *karanga*—call or summons; *whaikorero*—ceremonial speech; *waiata*—song. For an observation that the Waitangi Tribunal process is still very much Western oriented, see R Boast, 'Waitangi Tribunal Procedure', *ibid*, 53–64.

[89] Quoted in Royal Commission on Aboriginal Peoples, above n 85, 107.

envisioned and ultimately accepted by Indigenous peoples. Everything should be reconcilable to our legal tradition. If it is not, we must rethink what it is we are doing.

Law is a dynamic force. Western written law contains Western values, beliefs, and precepts that dictate thinking, behaviour and approach to justice. Once law is adopted, it begins its work.[90] If any law must be written, and applied to us, it should be law we fashion and create based on our own understanding of law, with knowledge of the importance of the relationships critical to our communities. It should also be based on what we know motivates and influences our social structure, with an understanding of our social reality and our separate consciousness as Indigenous peoples.

The challenge of incorporating traditional law lies in doing so in modern tribal societies, where colonialism and imperialism have been internalised and have affected tribal institutions and thought. The challenge lies in negotiating that clash between values and principles embedded in traditional law and those embedded in Western law. Decolonisation is not easily accomplished, whether one is struggling to build a nation-state or exercising self-determination within a nation. There are fears and risks to confront, and through it all the responsibility for mistakes is our own. Perhaps the greatest price to pay, however, is failing to take a risk to break out of colonial patterns because the familiar paths of oppression have made the paths of self-determination and liberation unfamiliar.

Of course there are real issues at stake—jurisdiction, economic development opportunities, federal funding—but these things are not necessarily assured, even if tribes mirror external law. The idea of creating law that is uniquely our own, based on our values, should encourage dialogue, ignite debate, and be tested and explored in practice. I believe the threat to our cultural survival as distinct Indigenous people is real, and we have survived in the face of this threat, but we must do what we can when we see the opportunity to reinforce our way of life. Significant encroachment in the area of internal tribal law has occurred, but it has not garnered the same type of attention that other encroachments have, and, perhaps more significantly, Indigenous nations themselves have facilitated this encroachment, both through their own actions and failure to act.[91] Law is of great cultural significance, and not to be so easily acquired and borrowed. What written law we have should be influenced by our way of thinking.

[90] 'Law is an adjunct of society. When the latter changes, the former must also adjust': MC Lâm, *At the Edge of the State: Indigenous Peoples and Self-Determination* (Transnational Publishers, 2000) 202.

[91] As former Pueblo of Isleta Tribal Court Associate Judge Raquel Montoya-Lewis points out, the basis of this facilitation can be internalised oppression. It can also occur because legal advisors to Indigenous communities lack a vision of the role of tradithat said, it is also important to point out that the primary sources of traditional law are in Indigenous communities, not in the legal institutions.

13

The Ties that Bind: Indigenous Peoples and Environmental Governance

BENJAMIN J RICHARDSON

A. The Issues

Indigenous peoples, at least traditionally, have often been regarded as exemplars of environmentally sustainable living. The impact of their subsistence livelihoods was apparently kept in check by customary laws to ensure they lived by the laws of nature.[1] Today, some people see answers to our environmental crisis in these traditions. The United Nations' pioneering report, *Our Common Future*, proclaimed that: 'these communities are the repositories of vast accumulations of traditional knowledge and experience, [and] larger society . . . could learn a great deal from their traditional skills in sustainably managing very complex ecological systems'.[2] Could it thus be assumed that upholding Indigenous rights and conserving the environment go hand-in-hand? So, while states have often been hostile to Indigenous interests, in times of grave environmental threats there will presumably be peaceful collaboration and the voices of Indigenous peoples will be respected.

Yet, for many reasons, the Aboriginal and environmental agendas often do not coincide. Putting aside the contrary historical record—when European colonisers plundered Indigenous lands, exterminating the herds of buffalo, damming the rivers, and felling the forests—the supposedly heightened environmental-consciousness of modern Western societies has not necessarily assuaged Indigenous peoples. The history of nature conservation in Africa provided one of the first hints that a vast chasm can arise between Western environmental policies and the interests of local communities. When colonial authorities in Africa set

[1] See D Craig, 'Implications of Indigenous Rights and Customary Laws on the Development of Environmental Law for Sustainable Development' in L Sun and L Kurukulasuriya (eds), *UNEP's New Way Forward: Environmental Law and Sustainable Development* (UNEP, 1995); GA Klee (ed), *World Systems of Traditional Resource Management* (VH Winston and Sons, 1980).

[2] World Commission on Environment and Development, *Our Common Future* (Oxford University Press, 1987) 114–15.

aside large territories as game reserves and parks, they evicted the native inhabitants to make way for places that would primarily serve the recreational and scientific interests of outsiders.[3] Areas occupied by subsistence hunters and farmers for thousands of years suddenly were relabelled as 'wildernesses'. These callous policies set precedents that continue today, such as the evictions of the Bushmen of the Kalahari by the Botswana government.[4]

Likewise, modern environmental policy in the West can be the context for bitter disputes between Indigenous and non-Indigenous interests. They arise for many reasons. Sometimes governments' lofty environmental policies are sacrificed to short-term development interests, where the seeming riches of a new mine or logging concession trump any rival values Indigenous peoples or other environmentally minded communities may attach to such lands. Conflicts may also arise in reconciling Indigenous traditional knowledge with the supposed hard 'objectivity' of Western science in environmental decision-making. Also, because of the prevalent belief that nature conservation depends on separating nature from humankind, the presence of Indigenous peoples can be seen as incompatible with the protection of endangered species and their habitats.

This Chapter explores the relationships between Indigenous peoples and environmental governance.[5] 'Governance', defined broadly, means the norms and decision-making processes by which society and its organisations are controlled and co-ordinated.[6] While governance is habitually associated with official regulation by states,[7] scholars in the field of legal pluralism are advancing more nuanced understandings that also emphasise the roles of non-state institutions in the market and civil society in policy-making, norm-setting, implementation, and other aspects of governance.[8] Indigenous scholars such as John Borrows also stress the role of Indigenous communities and their legal traditions as a critical source of social ordering.[9] For this Chapter, therefore, *environmental governance* covers a range of values, norms, institutions and processes, both state- and non-state-

[3] JM MacKenzie, *The Empire of Nature: Hunting, Conservation and British Imperialism* (Manchester University Press, 1988); RA Schroeder, 'Geographies of Environmental Intervention in Africa' (1999) 23(3) *Progress in Human Geography* 359.

[4] C Timberg, 'Eviction of Bushmen Is Ruled Illegal' *Washington Post* (14 December 2006) A20.

[5] It builds on an extensive literature on the interaction between Aboriginal law and environmental law: see, eg, M Blumm, 'Retracing the Discovery Doctrine: Aboriginal Title, Tribal Sovereignty, and their Significance to Treaty-making and Modern Natural Resources Policy in Indian Country' (2004) 28 *Vermont Law Review* 713; D Curran and M M'Gonigle, 'Aboriginal Forestry: Community Management as Opportunity and Imperative' (1999) 37 *Osgoode Hall Law Journal* 711; E Goodman, 'Protecting Habitat for Off-Reservation Tribal Hunting and Fishing Rights: Tribal Co-Management as a Reserved Right' (2000) 30 *Environmental Law* 279; GD Meyers, 'Different Sides of the Same Coin: A Comparative View of Indian Hunting and Fishing Rights in the United States and Canada' (1991) 10 *UCLA Journal of Environmental Law and Policy* 67.

[6] See generally M MacNeil, N Sargent and P Swan (eds), *Law, Regulation and Governance* (Oxford University Press, 2003).

[7] OECD, *Reforming Environmental Regulation in OECD Countries* (OECD, 1996).

[8] S Merry, 'Legal Pluralism' (1988) 22 *Law and Society Review* 869.

[9] J Borrows, 'With or Without You: First Nations Law (in Canada)' (1995) 41 *McGill Law Journal* 629.

based, that shape entitlements to use or benefit from natural resources, and to control their exploitation or protection.

Nominally, the importance of Indigenous involvement in environmental governance is now affirmed in many laws and policies. It is commonplace, for instance, to find references to Indigenous peoples in international environmental declarations, resolutions and policies.[10] Notably, the Rio Declaration on Environment and Development of 1992 declared:

> indigenous people . . . have a vital role in environmental management and development because of their knowledge and traditional practices. States should recognize and duly support their identity, culture and interests and enable their effective participation in the achievement of sustainable development.[11]

Given the attention this topic has acquired, this Chapter has two specific aims. First, it examines the environmental values and practices of Indigenous peoples, primarily in order to assess their implications for the Indigenous stake in environmental governance. As these peoples seek greater involvement in environmental decision-making, it is worthwhile to understand the values that they bring to these processes. For instance, in establishing a national park or conducting an environmental impact assessment of a proposed mine, we should ask what values and knowledge are brought to decision-making when Indigenous peoples are involved. In what ways might resulting land use decisions differ?

Another reason to examine Indigenous environmental values and practices is because the push for Indigenous participation in environmental governance is often not merely grounded in Indigenous rights to natural resources, but also in the societal perceptions of the sustainability of Indigenous livelihoods. They are sometimes said to be more environmentally sustainable than Western lifestyles, thereby justifying giving Indigenous peoples more say in environmental management. Yet, as this Chapter shows, in the scholarly and policy literature, a wide variety of theories and perspectives regarding Indigenous environmental values and practices can be found, not all of which see Indigenous cultures as consistently environmentally benign. We need to be aware of these theories and perspectives, because their legitimacy can influence the voice Indigenous peoples may have in environmental decision-making.

The second aim of the Chapter is to review the legal norms and governance tools that structure Indigenous involvement in environmental management, in order to assess their relative value for Indigenous stakeholders and implications for environmental care. The Chapter focuses on examples in Australia, Canada, New Zealand and the United States (US), where some of the most substantial reforms for Indigenous participation in environmental governance have arisen. Some governance techniques emphasise *access* to natural resources, yet fail to provide a framework for the *management* of those resources. Some institutional mechanisms

[10] See BJ Richardson, 'Indigenous Peoples, International Law and Sustainability' (2001) 10(1) *RECIEL* 1; RK Hitchcock, 'International Human Rights, the Environment and Indigenous Peoples' (1994) 5 *Colorado Journal of International Environmental Law and Policy* 1.

[11] 1992, 31 ILM 876, Principle 22.

for resource management promote Indigenous self-governance, yet fail to resolve how Indigenous peoples can govern environmental impacts that emanate far beyond areas under tribal authority. In other words, governance frameworks based on Indigenous rights and other legal interests may not always be isomorphic with the dynamic properties of ecosystems and the disturbances they face.

The next section addresses the first stated aim of this Chapter, namely to canvass the literature and evidence concerning the environmental knowledge and practices of Indigenous peoples and their contributions to sustainability.[12] At least six major theories or perspectives are present. While the labels given to these perspectives are my own, they reasonably capture the gist of the various arguments and ideas in the scholarship and policy literature. As we review the material, the seminal question that should be borne in mind is this: what are the implications of such perspectives for Indigenous peoples' role in environmental governance?

B. Environmental—Indigenous Peoples' Relationships

1. Ecological Guardians

A common perspective in the literature portrays Indigenous peoples as prototypical environmentalists, living harmoniously with nature without indulging in the profligacy associated with Western culture.[13] The close attachment to the land and the environment is described by some commentators as the 'defining characteristic of indigenous peoples'.[14] A study by a task force of the International Union for the Conservation of Nature (IUCN) trumpeted that Indigenous peoples 'are the sole guardian of vast habitats critical to modern societies . . . [and] their ecological knowledge is an asset of incalculable value'.[15] Other commentators contend that 'commercial consumption, exploitation of natural resources, and notions of enrichment are not part of indigenous cultures'.[16] Thus, they should provide a salutary model for the rest of humanity.[17] This perspective also strongly implies that protecting Indigenous rights should dovetail with those forms of modern

[12] See H Brody, *Maps and Dreams: Indians and the British Columbia Frontier* (Douglas and McIntyre, 1988); D Brokensha, DM Warren and O Werner, *Indigenous Knowledge Systems and Development* (University Press of America, 1980); B DeWalt, 'Using Indigenous Knowledge to Improve Agricultural and Natural Resource Management' (1994) 53 *Human Organization* 123; JD Hughes, *American Indian Ecology* (Texas Western Press, 1983).

[13] See F Berkes, 'Traditional Ecological Knowledge in Perspective' in JT Inglis (ed), *Traditional Ecological Knowledge: Concepts and Cases* (International Development Research Centre, 1993) 1.

[14] SH Davis (ed), *Indigenous Views of Land and the Environment* (World Bank, 1993) x.

[15] IUCN Inter-Commission Task Force on Indigenous Peoples, *Indigenous Peoples and Sustainability: Cases and Actions* (IUCN, 1997) 35.

[16] JP Kastrup, 'The Internationalization of Indigenous Rights from the Environmental and Human Rights Perspective' (1997) 32 *Texas International Law Journal* 97, 114.

[17] Eg, AT Durning, *Guardians of the Land: Indigenous Peoples and the Health of the Earth* (Worldwatch Institute, 1992) 6–7.

environmental governance that stress sustainability. Indeed, the environmental movement often touts Aboriginal peoples as unfailing allies.[18]

Posey highlights several features of Indigenous livelihoods relevant to environmental sustainability, including high levels of social co-operation, local-scale self-sufficiency and concern for the well-being of posterity.[19] One example of the latter outlook in a Canadian Indigenous community is the Haudenosaunee's 'seven generations' principle.[20] It has similarities to the modern international environmental principle known as 'intergenerational equity', requiring nations to ensure that their economic development does not compromise posterity's ability to enjoy a healthy environment.[21]

Another factor cited as contributing to the sustainability of Indigenous cultures is their spiritual veneration of the natural world. Nature is often the wellspring of ancestral and creation stories, such as in the Dreamtime of Australia's Aborigines[22] and the cosmologies of North American Indians.[23] These spiritual values can underpin specific environmental norms. Indigenous communities may protect natural sites that are dedicated to ancestral spirits or deities.[24] In New Zealand, the Māori treat many mountains as 'intensely sacred'.[25] Kenya's Bukusu protect wetlands for their function in holding cultural rites such as male circumcision ceremonies.[26] Wildlife harvesting practices may be controlled by animal totems and the recognition of taboo species.[27]

The ecological guardianship thesis also cites the traditional environmental knowledge (TEK) of Indigenous peoples.[28] They are active environmental managers

[18] Eg, S Schwartzman and B Zimmerman, 'Conservation Alliances with Indigenous Peoples of the Amazon' (2005) 19 *Conservation Biology* 721.

[19] DA Posey, 'Culture and Nature: The Inextricable Link' in UNEP *Cultural and Spiritual Values of Biodiversity* (UNEP, 2000) 1, 4; see also Berkes, above n 13, 4; RE Johannes (ed), *Traditional Ecological Knowledge: A Collection of Essays* (IUCN, 1989).

[20] The principle requires that one consider the effects of decisions on the seventh generation yet to be born. Similar concepts inform many Indigenous legal orders worldwide. See, eg, Indigenous Environmental Network, 'Bemidji Statement on Seventh Generation Guardianship' (2006) at www.sehn.org/bemidji.html.

[21] See GF Maggio, 'Inter/intra-generational Equity: Current Applications Under International Law for Promoting the Sustainable Development of Natural Resources' (1997) 4 *Buffalo Environmental Law Journal* 161.

[22] A Voigt and N Drury, *Wisdom of the Earth: The Living Legacy of the Aboriginal Dreamtime* (Simon and Schuster, 1997).

[23] JD Hughes, *American Indian Ecology* (Texas Western Press, 1987) 81–5.

[24] SA Bhagwat and C Rutte, 'Sacred Groves: Potential for Biodiversity Management' (2006) 4 *Frontiers in Ecology and the Environment* 519.

[25] J Ruru, 'Indigenous Peoples' Ownership and Management of Mountains: The Aotearoa / New Zealand Experience' (2004) 3 *Indigenous Law Journal* 111, 115.

[26] RW Kareri, 'The Sociological and Economic Values of Kenya's Wetlands' in SA Crafter *et al* (eds), *Wetlands of Kenya: Proceedings of a Seminar an Wetlands of Kenya* (IUCN, 1992) 99, 102.

[27] J Colding and C Folke, 'The Relations Among Threatened Species, Their Protection, and Taboos' (1997) 1 *Conservation Ecology* 6.

[28] See MA Altieri and LC Merrick, 'In Situ Conservation of Crop Genetic Resources through Maintenance of Traditional Farming Systems' (1987) 41(1) *Economic Botany* 98; GM Morin-Labatut and S Akhtar, 'Traditional Environmental Knowledge: A Resource to Manage and Share' (1992) 4 *Development Journal of the Society for International Development* 24.

guided by eons of accumulated wisdom and expertise.[29] Berkes defines TEK as 'experience acquired over thousands of years of direct human contact with the environment'.[30] McGregor catalogues three sources of TEK: 'traditional knowledge' (passed from generation to generation through elders, rituals, initiation and storytelling); 'empirical knowledge' (gained from observation); and 'revealed knowledge' (acquired through spiritual origins and recognised as a gift).[31] Traditional knowledge of plants, animals and ecosystems informs specific management practices such as resource rotation to ensure that one favoured species is not unsustainably harvested. In Canada, the James Bay Cree use this method for managing beaver and fish populations.[32] Countless other examples could be given.[33]

The notion of 'traditional', however, can be a mixed blessing for Indigenous peoples, for it can be used as an excuse to deny their involvement in contemporary environmental management to address new threats and issues such as climate change. TEK's relevance to contemporary environmental practice is thus a significant area of research, including its relationship to Western science in environmental decisions.[34]

2. Environmental Architects

Putting an even stronger gloss on the ecological guardianship thesis, related literature portrays Indigenous peoples as architects of benign environmental change through active landscape management over millennia.[35] Durning notes that 'animal and planet populations in most of the world reflect not just the blind logic of natural selection; they also reflect human selection'.[36] This position therefore rejects Western conservation concepts such as 'wilderness', as wrongly implying natural terrain never inhabited by humankind. Indigenous peoples have moulded and shaped the environment through fire burning, selective hunting and gathering, and other forms of husbandry.

In Australia, for instance, repeated seasonal burnings of woodlands and scrub contributed to a mosaic of vegetation that enhanced biological diversity.[37] The

[29] See F Berkes, *Sacred Ecology: Traditional Ecological Knowledge and Resource Management* (Taylor and Francis, 1999).

[30] Berkes, above n 13, 1.

[31] D McGregor, 'Coming Full Circle: Indigenous Knowledge, Environment and Our Future' (2004) 28 *American Indian Quarterly* 385, 388. See also RG Kuhn and F Duerden, 'A Review of Traditional Environmental Knowledge: An Interdisciplinary Canadian Perspective' (1996) 16(1) *Culture* 71, 73.

[32] F Berkes, J Colding and C Folke, 'Rediscovery of Traditional Ecological Knowledge as Adaptive Management' (2000) 10(5) *Ecological Economics* 1251, 1255.

[33] Berkes, above n 29, 61.

[34] HP Huntingon, 'Using Traditional Ecological Knowledge in Science: Methods and Applications' (2000) 10(5) *Ecological Applications* 1270; E Sherry and H Myers, 'Traditional Environmental Knowledge in Practice' (2002) 15(4) *Society and Natural Resources* 345.

[35] BS Orlove and SB Brush, 'Anthropology and the Conservation of Biodiversity' (1996) 25 *Annual Review of Anthropology* 329.

[36] Durning, above n 17, 18.

[37] D Yiburak *et al*, 'Fire Ecology and Aboriginal Land Management in Central Arnhem Land, Northern Australia: A Tradition of Ecosystem Management' (2001) 28 *Journal of Biogeography* 325.

forcible removal of Aborigines from the land by colonial authorities led to the loss of these fire management regimes, and precipitated a catastrophic loss of species that had become dependent on these seared landscapes.[38] Worldwide, many Indigenous peoples continue to deploy fire as a way to manipulate environmental conditions, such as is practised by the Krahô in the savannas of Brazil.[39] A UN report on the subject thus reasoned that there is 'a direct relation between cultural diversity, linguistic diversity and biological diversity and that the quickening pace of loss of traditional knowledge was having a corresponding devastating impact on all biological diversity'.[40]

Another manifestation of the environmental architect thesis is the phenomenon of 'cultural landscapes'. These are natural areas that have acquired special cultural significance from thousands of years of human use, representing the permanent interaction between humans and their environment. The concept of cultural landscapes has been recognised under the World Heritage Convention.[41] New Zealand's Tongariro National Park, a sacred region to Māori, was the first cultural landscape listed under the Convention for international protection.[42] Protected areas management in this country and others, including Canada and the US, is being transformed by the philosophy that in many landscapes the natural and cultural heritage are inextricably bound together and that conservation can benefit from more integration between the two.[43] One governance consequence of this approach is that ongoing management of such sites should involve the people who are most culturally associated with them.[44]

3. Misguided Environmentalists

Some environmental historians and scientists dispute views that Indigenous peoples generally lived in blissful harmony with nature.[45] They indict some communities for environmental degradation, citing historical evidence in areas under Indigenous occupation. While such findings may seem irrelevant to contemporary environmental debates about Indigenous peoples, some of the evidence involves

[38] T Flannery, 'Who Killed Kirlilpi?' (1989) 23 *Australian Natural History* 234.

[39] J Mistry *et al*, 'Indigenous Fire Management in the *Cerrado* of Brazil: The Case of the Krahô of Tocantíns' (2005) 33 *Human Ecology* 365.

[40] This was noted in the Workshop on Traditional Knowledge and Biological Diversity, *Report of the Workshop* (UNEP, 1997) 2.

[41] 1972, 27 UST 37, 11 ILM 1358.

[42] S Forbes, 'Tongariro National Park World Heritage Cultural List "He Koha Tapu—A Sacred Gift"' (Government of New Zealand, 1993).

[43] N Mitchell and S Buggey, 'Protected Landscapes and Cultural Landscapes: Taking Advantage of Diverse Approaches' (2000) 17 *George Wright Forum* 1.

[44] *Ibid*, 43.

[45] LM Shields, 'Are Conservation Goals and Aboriginal Rights Incompatible?' (2000) 10 *Journal of Environmental Law and Practice* 187; AM Stearman, 'Revisiting the Myth of the Ecologically Noble Savage in Amazonia: Implications for Indigenous Land Rights' (1994) 49 *Culture and Agriculture* 2; MS Alvard, 'Testing the "Ecologically Noble Savage" Hypothesis' (1993) 21 *Human Ecology* 355.

more recent transformations such as in the South Pacific,[46] and the research can provide ammunition for those seeking excuses to limit Indigenous environmental rights today.

Several reasons for associating Indigenous peoples with environmental decline are advanced. First, when Indigenous peoples moved into an area unaccustomed to human beings, such as in the arrival of the first people in North America estimated at some 11,000 years ago or the Māori in New Zealand 1,000 years ago,[47] animal species were naive to the hunting threat posed by the newcomers.[48] Indigenous settlers may have lacked awareness of the relative scarcity of unfamiliar natural resources and had not evolved quickly enough the requisite social norms to limit exploitation. Tim Flannery, a scientist who has documented such ecological changes, describes the arrival of Māori hunters as precipitating a 'blitzkrieg extinction' in which some 12 species of moa (giant birds, most larger than ostriches) were exterminated within a few centuries.[49] In North America, the influx of Clovis hunters is cited as an seminal factor in the demise of some 35 primarily large mammals, including mammoths.[50] However, the evidence of such impacts is disputed.[51]

Another factor linking environmental wastefulness to Indigenous peoples relates to the impact of their spiritual systems. Ironically, their deep spiritual attachment to nature may have blinded them to evidence of their real ecological impacts. The great reverence some Indigenous peoples have had for their environment may have fed beliefs that nature, nourished by mystical forces, provided an unlimited bounty. North American historian Dan Flores quotes a 19th-century report regarding bison hunting:

> [e]very Plains Indian family firmly believed that the buffalo were produced in countless numbers in a country under the ground, that every spring the surplus swarmed like bees from a hive, out of great cave-like openings.[52]

Alternatively, some research on other communities doubts that spiritual beliefs were sufficiently potent to cause Indigenous peoples to moderate their behaviour

[46] JBC Jackson *et al*, 'Historical Overfishing and the Recent Collapse of Coastal Ecosystems' (2001) 293 *Science* 630; but see the robust counter-arguments in RE Johannes, 'Did Indigenous Conservation Ethics Exist?' (2002) 14 *SPC Traditional Marine Resource Management and Knowledge Information Bulletin* 3.

[47] These dates are the most widely cited in the literature, but are disputed by many, including by Indigenous peoples.

[48] See J Diamond, *The Rise and Fall of the Third Chimpanzee* (Vintage, 1992); R Edgerton, *Sick Societies: Challenging The Myth of Primitive Harmony* (Maxwell Macmillan, 1992); T Flannery, *The Future Eaters* (Reed Books, 1995); T Flannery, *The Eternal Frontier* (Atlantic Monthly Press, 2001); KH Redford and AM Stearman, 'Forest-Dwelling Native Amazonians and the Conservation of Biodiversity: Interests in Common or in Collision?' (1993) 7 *Conservation Biology* 248.

[49] Flannery, *Future Eaters,* above n 48, 195.

[50] See G Haynes, 'The Catastrophic Extinction of North American Mammoths and Mastodonts' (2002) 33 *World Archaeology* 391.

[51] See DK Grayson and DJ Meltzer, 'Clovis Hunting and Large Mammal Extinction: A Critical Review of the Evidence' (2002) 16 *Journal of World Prehistory* 313.

[52] D Flores, 'Bison Ecology and Bison Diplomacy: The Southern Plains from 1800 to 1850' (1991) 78 *Journal of American History* 483. Of course, the extermination of these bison herds was primarily caused by European hunters.

in response to environmental depletion. Colchester suggests that 'many studies show little correlation between beliefs prescribing certain practices and actual behaviour'.[53] With regard to Amazonian Indians, Colchester notes that many 'have an opportunist rather than conservationist attitude to the environment, and achieve ecological balance because their traditional political systems and settlement patterns encourage mobility'.[54] Low population densities and technological restraints are other factors cited that might have kept the environmental burden of Indigenous peoples unintentionally relatively low.[55]

In sum, these arguments essentially claim that Indigenous peoples, like other human cultures, do not possess some innate ecological wisdom etched in their genes; rather, their environmental relationships and impacts are contingent, depending on the particular customs, values and social practices of a given community. For contemporary environmental governance, the past, however, is not necessarily a guide to the present. While we should be mindful that no human culture is infallible, the contribution of Indigenous communities to environmental care should be assessed on a case-by-case basis and not crudely inferred on the basis of distant, historical evidence.

4. Forsaken Environmentalists

A fourth argument in some scholarship holds that, whatever the merit of claims that Indigenous peoples were ecological stewards or architects, the cold reality is that Indigenous livelihoods have often changed irreparably.[56] Urban living, displacement and migration, technological changes and the influence of the market economy are among the miscellany of factors transforming Indigenous culture. These social and economic changes have removed many Indigenous peoples from the traditional hunter-gatherer lifestyle, thereby weakening the traditional customary laws and norms to control inappropriate environmental behaviour in other contexts.[57] The integrity and relevance of Indigenous communities' environmental values is questioned when their members live increasingly in urban areas outside tribal structures and the traditional, subsistence economy. While it would be grossly naive to contend that Indigenous cultures have remained untainted by centuries of colonialism, we should be careful about implying that they have been ill-fated and lack the will to adapt successfully to changing

[53] M Colchester, *Salvaging Nature: Indigenous Peoples, Protected Areas and Biodiversity Conservation* (World Wide Fund for Nature, 1994) 27.

[54] *Ibid.*

[55] S Krech III, *The Ecological Indian: Myth and History* (WW Norton and Co, 2000) (discussing North American natives).

[56] Eg, DR Lewis, 'Native Americans and the Environment: A Survey of Twentieth Century Issues' (1995) 19 *American Indian Quarterly* 423; R Meher, 'The Social and Ecological Effects of Industrialisation in a Tribal Region: The Case of the Rourkela Steel Plant' (1998) 57 *American Journal of Economics and Sociology* 105; CR Ramirez, 'Ethnobotany and the Loss of Traditional Knowledge in the 21st Century' (2007) 5 *Ethnobotany Research and Applications* 245.

[57] Redford and Stearman, above n 48, 252; Colchester, above n 53, 26.

circumstances, as another scholarly perspective examined later in this Chapter contends.

Nonetheless, some cultural changes, with environmental consequences, have been documented even for Indigenous peoples continuing to subsist on the land. For example, Alaskan natives have been implicated in destructive forestry practices.[58] Even in relatively remote places, such as in the highlands of Papua New Guinea, Flannery found resource depletion pressures from population growth and access to more efficient hunting technologies.[59] These trends may imply that Indigenous people have not yet evolved the necessary new norms to control the pressures posed by increased numbers and new technologies.

These changes to Indigenous livelihoods have sometimes led Aboriginal peoples to tolerate or welcome commercial developments that mainstream environmental groups oppose. For example, a 1991 public inquiry into mining on Aboriginal lands in a conservation zone in northern Australia found that:

> [t]he Jawoyn do not oppose mining per se . . . A number of Jawoyn people are in favour of mining . . . They do not consider [the affected lands] as significant culturally or religiously, although they express concerns about disturbance to certain sites outside the Zone. These pro-mining Jawoyn people appear to be motivated by a desire for personal and community advancement in a context of limited alternative employment opportunities and welfare dependency.[60]

The nature of contemporary Indigenous environmental practices is also being questioned in other contexts. One example is the resumption of whaling. Animal welfare and environmental groups have criticised the International Whaling Commission's rules permitting subsistence hunting by some Aboriginal groups. The stated concerns are the threats to endangered cetaceans and that harvested whale meat is being traded commercially.[61] Another concern is the 'bush meat' crisis in Africa, where civil strife and the breakdown of traditional community institutions has fuelled rampant, unsustainable hunting of wildlife.[62] The primary factors in this crisis, however, are probably not dysfunctional Indigenous management practices per se, but rather the growing intrusion of outside economic

[58] F Cassidy and N Dale, *After Native Claims: The Implications of Comprehensive Claims Settlements for Natural Resources in British Columbia* (Oolichan Books, 1988) 104–7.

[59] T Flannery, *Throwim Way Leg: Tree-Kangaroos, Possums, and Penis Gourds—On the Track of Unknown Mammals in Wildest New Guinea* (Text Publishing, 1998).

[60] Resource Assessment Commission, *Kakadu Conservation Zone Inquiry: Final Report and Summary* (AGPS, 1991) 7–8. Indigenous organisations in the Canadian North have also welcomed and participated in numerous mining, oil and gas ventures: see, eg, R Boychuk, 'The Road from Bathurst Inlet' 124(2) *Canadian Geographic* 40; Inuvialuit Corporate Group, *Annual Report 2002* (Inuvialuit Regional Corporation, 2003).

[61] R Black, 'Greenland Whale Hunt "Commercial"' *BBC News online* (17 June 2008); L Jenkins and C Romanzo, 'Makah Whaling: Aboriginal Subsistence or a Stepping Stone to Undermining the Commercial Whaling Moratorium (1998) 9 *Colorado Journal of International Environmental Law and Policy* 71.

[62] MI Bakarr *et al*, 'Hunting and Bushmeat Utilization in the African Rain Forest' (2001) 2 *Advances in Applied Biodiversity Science* 170.

and social factors associated with commercial forestry and oil exploration, as well as military conflicts.[63]

Whatever the veracity of its claims, the forsaken environmentalist thesis should not be an excuse to deny Indigenous involvement in modern environmental governance. Indigenous environmental rights should not be reduced to a crude calculation of their functional value to wider society. If this standard were adopted, it would also be a reason to rebuff mining companies, fishing businesses and many other economic interests with appalling environmental records. Rather, we need to find ways to allow Indigenous communities to rebuild their ties to the land and, to the extent that there are limitations to Indigenous knowledge, expertise and capacity, to look to cross-cultural approaches to resource management that combine Indigenous and non-Indigenous stakeholders' strengths.

5. Environmental Victims

A fifth perspective in the literature stresses that Indigenous peoples are primarily victims, not perpetrators, of environmental harm.[64] Scholars such as Westra and Howitt highlight the conscription of Indigenous resources into the cash economy through dams, mines and other projects that have had ruinous consequences for native lands and communities.[65] These projects have undermined the economic foundations of Indigenous communities, spawned various public health problems, and fuelled a host of collateral cultural impacts.[66] To the extent that Indigenous communities are complicit in any of these activities, this perspective implies that it would be a context not of their making. Robbed of their lands and denied a viable economic resource base, Indigenous peoples sometimes partake in environmentally problematic developments only as a result of limited options.[67]

Indigenous peoples, of course, have not necessarily been hapless bystanders to the juggernaut of the market economy. They have often fiercely resisted forestry[68]

[63] M Thibault and S Blaney, 'The Oil Industry as an Underlying Factor in the Bushmeat Crisis in Central Africa' (2003) 17 *Conservation Biology* 1807.

[64] Eg, D Brook, 'Environmental Genocide: Native Americans and Toxic Waste' (1998) 57 *American Journal of Economics and Sociology* 105; T Nachowitz, 'Repression in the Narmada Valley, India' (1988) 12(3) *Cultural Survival Quarterly* 23; R Niezen, 'Power and Dignity: The Social Consequences of Hydro-electric Development for the James Bay Cree' (1993) 30 *Canadian Review of Sociology and Anthropology* 510.

[65] R Howitt, *Rethinking Resource Management: Justice, Sustainability and Indigenous Peoples* (Taylor and Francis, 2001); L Westra, *Environmental Justice and the Rights of Indigenous Peoples—International and Domestic Law Perspectives* (Earthscan Publishers, 2007).

[66] LA Lambert, *Keepers of the Central Fire: Issues in Ecology for Indigenous Peoples* (Jones and Bartlett Publishers, 1999).

[67] J Borrows, 'Living between Water and Rocks: First Nations, Environmental Planning and Democracy' (1997) 47 *University of Toronto Law Journal* 417, 424 (discussing Native Americans' involvement in commercial forestry).

[68] P Utting, *Trees, People and Power. Social Dimensions of Deforestation and Forest Protection in Central America* (Earthscan, 1993); L Starke (ed), *Breaking New Ground: Mining, Minerals, and Sustainable Development. The Report of the MMSD Project* (Earthscan, 2002).

and extractive industry[69] projects on their lands. Open-cut mines undertaken by transnational corporate behemoths at Ok Tedi (Papua New Guinea), Freeport (Indonesia) and Jabiluka (Australia) have engendered some titanic conflicts.[70] Big dams have also ignited clashes, such as Quebec's damming of the James Bay River[71] and India's Narmada River dam.[72] The flooding of traditional hunting grounds and the physical displacement of whole communities were a high price to pay in the name of national economic development in both cases. According to the World Dams Commission, large dams in India displaced between 16 and 38 million people from 1950 to 1990, and about 40 per cent of those displaced were tribal people.[73]

Recently, the long-range environmental impacts of 'dominant' societies upon Indigenous peoples have become a cause for possibly greater concern.[74] These impacts include toxic contamination in the Arctic food chain and global warming. Such problems illustrate the cruel irony of Indigenous peoples' situation: not only are those closest to nature the worst impacted by environmental degradation, but Western societies often impose environmental harms on Indigenous societies from afar.

Even seemingly environmentally benign policies can hurt. Most notably, the creation of nature conservation parks can displace Indigenous peoples, removing them from their traditional hunting and foraging grounds.[75] Bernard Grzimek, one of the colonial-era architects of East Africa's extensive network of protected areas, once said: '[a] National Park . . . must remain a primordial wilderness to be effective. No men, not even native ones, should live inside its borders'.[76] This philosophy continues to permeate nature conservation policies in some countries.[77]

The environmental victims thesis has various implications for environmental governance. The two most significant are the need for compensation and other remedies for displaced and injured Indigenous communities and, to address

[69] See RT Libby, *Hawke's Law: The Politics of Mining and Aboriginal Land Rights in Austrailia* (University of Western Australia Press, 1989).

[70] Eg, C Ballard and G Banks, 'Resource Wars: The Anthropology of Mining' (2003) 32 *Annual Review of Anthropology* 287; S Cuffe, 'Global Actors, Mining and Community-Based Resistance in Honduras and Guatemala' (Rights Action, 2005); A Gedicks, *The New Resource Wars: Native and Environmental Struggles Against Multinational Corporations* (South End Press, 1993).

[71] R Niezen, 'Power and Dignity: The Social Consequences of Hydro-electric Development for the James Bay Cree' (1993) 30 *Canadian Review of Sociology and Anthropology* 510.

[72] C Alvares and R Billorey, *Damming the Narmada: India's Greatest Planned Environmental Disaster* (Third World Network, 1988); T Nachowitz, 'Repression in the Narmada Valley, India' (1988) 12(3) *Cultural Survival Quarterly* 23.

[73] World Dams Commission (WDC), *Dams and Development* (WDC, 2000) 104, 110.

[74] DL Brown, 'Toxic-tainted Arctic Animals Passing Poisons on to Inuit' (22 May 2001) *Seattle Times*.

[75] See examples detailed in World Rainforest Movement (WRM) 'Protected Areas: Protected Against Whom?' (WRM, January 2004); E Kemf (ed), *Indigenous Peoples and Protected Areas. The Law of Mother Earth* (Earthscan, 1993).

[76] Cited in JS Adams and TO McShane, *The Myth of Wild Africa: Conservation Without Illusion* (WW Norton and Co, 1992) xvi.

[77] R Poirier and D Ostergren, 'Evicting People from Nature: Indigenous Land Rights and National Parks in Australia, Russia, and the United States' (2002) 42 *Natural Resources Journal* 331.

future threats, to ensure much greater Indigenous voice in environmental decision-making. The emerging international principle of an Indigenous right to 'free, prior and informed consent' is an obvious legal standard to prevent creating more Indigenous victims by allowing communities to veto inappropriate development projects.[78]

6. Environmental Innovators

We should also be aware that some Indigenous communities have successfully adapted to demographic, economic and technological changes, maintaining and innovating robust systems of environmental management that can address contemporary challenges.[79] In this sixth scholarly perspective, Indigenous knowledge is not simply a relic of ancient hunter-gatherer societies, but continues to be relevant and adaptable to modern resource management situations.[80] Through greater Indigenous self-governance, Aboriginal peoples seek a framework to apply their skill and wisdom to natural resources management.[81]

One World Bank report summarised several examples of the contemporary relevance of TEK and social practices, noting that

> [t]he the pastoral peoples of eastern Africa—who for so long have been identified by Western livestock specialists as a major cause of arid and semi-arid land problems—are today recognized as possessing sophisticated knowledge about range and animal management, including strategies for adapting to periodic drought and other natural calamities.[82]

In developed countries, where Indigenous minorities often have endured even greater cultural and economic pressures, there is similarly evidence of a growing appreciation of Indigenous environmental practices. For example, Aborigines' traditional fire management techniques have been reintroduced in some outback national parks in Australia to restore biological diversity that co-evolved in response to periodic burning of the savannah.[83] In Canada, the National Aboriginal Forestry Association drafted the *Aboriginal Forest Land Management Guidelines*, setting 'out a broad and flexible framework for Aboriginal peoples to develop and implement community- and ecosystem-based forest management

[78] JP Rosenthal, 'Politics, Culture, and Governance in the Development of Prior Informed Consent in Indigenous Communities' (2006) 47 *Current Anthropology* 119.

[79] See KK Misra (ed), *Traditional Knowledge in Contemporary Societies: Challenges and Opportunities* (Pratibha Prakashan, 2007); N Turner, *The Earth's Blanket: Traditional Teachings for Sustainable Living* (University of Washington Press, 2005); M Gadgil, F Berkes and C Folke, 'Indigenous Knowledge for Biodiversity Conservation' (1993) 22 *Ambio* 151.

[80] AL Booth and HM Jacobs, 'Ties That Bind: Native American Beliefs as a Foundation for Environmental Consciousness' (1990) 12 *Environmental Ethics* 27.

[81] A Ross and K Pickering, 'The Politics of Reintegrating Australian Aboriginal and American Indian Indigenous Knowledge into Resource Management: The Dynamics of Resource Appropriation and Cultural Revival' (2002) 30 *Human Ecology* 187.

[82] Davis, above n 14, x.

[83] R Kimber, 'Black Lightning: Aborigines and Fire in Central Australia and the Western Desert' (1983) 18 *Archaeology in Oceania* 38.

planning that takes into account multiple forest values'.[84] Countless other encouraging examples could be given.

One worth commenting on is the Centre for Indigenous Environmental Resources (CIER), in Canada. Established in 1994, CIER illustrates the new generation of Indigenous organisations fashioning environmental governance. Using grass-roots approaches, it advises and facilitates communities' involvement in the environmental planning and management. For instance, CIER has initiated projects for 'identifying economic, environmental, social, and cultural solutions and options for First Nations to better adapt to climate change'.[85] It is also supporting the Assembly of First Nations to launch a *Plan of Action for Drinking Water in First Nations Communities.*[86] Its work on legal aspects of sustainability includes a research report on *First Nations Governance Success Stories* and an *Indigenous Laws* project to document the contribution of TEK and customary laws to environmental protection.[87]

The environmental innovation thesis presents one of the most forceful arguments for bolstering the Indigenous voice in the governance of their lands and resources. It coincides with a plethora of scholarship that calls for democratising and decentralising environmental decision-making to community levels.[88]

7. Other Perspectives

While none of the foregoing perspectives in the scholarly literature alone provide a sufficiently plausible account of all Indigenous peoples' relationships to the environment, each appears to hold some truth in some situations, depending on the time, place and community. Indigenous peoples are multi-cultural, with a diversity of values, customs and social practices. Their relationships with the environment therefore vary. Historically, some tribes were hunter-gatherers, while others were partial-agriculturalists; some were nomadic while others more settled, depending on available natural resources. Today, some communities have successfully adapted to new environmental threats and conditions, while others have struggled.

A few further arguments about this topic should be noted, before examining Indigenous participation in environmental governance. First, regardless of their environmental impacts, we should be careful of implying that Indigenous peoples should be held to a higher environmental standard. Industrial societies, with their vastly greater environmental burden, are hardly qualified to pass judgment on

[84] National Aboriginal Forestry Association (NAFA), *Aboriginal Forest Land Management Guidelines: A Community Approach* (NAFA, 1995).

[85] Centre for Indigenous Environmental Resources: www.cier.ca/taking-action-on-climate-change.

[86] See *Plan of Action for Drinking Water in First Nations Communities. Progress Report* (Indian and Northern Affairs Canada, 2008), www.ainc-inac.gc.ca/H2O/prpf/wpr3-eng.asp#bkg.

[87] See www.cier.ca/building%2Dsustainable%2Dcommunities.

[88] EF Schumacher, *Small is Beautiful: Economics as if People Mattered* (Harper and Row, 1973); J Agyeman and B Evans, 'Sustainability and Democracy: Community Participation in Local Agenda 21' (1995) 22(2) *Local Government Policy Making* 35; G Smith, *Deliberative Democracy and the Environment* (Routledge, 2003).

Indigenous livelihoods. Nuclear weapons, toxic chemicals and urban sprawl are some of the appalling legacies of modern society that dwarf even the most damning environmental evidence against Indigenous peoples.

Conversely, we also should be wary of arguments that romanticise Indigenous people as ecological guardians. They can foster harmful stereotypes, implying expectations of Indigenous peoples that are unrealistic in an environmentally depleted world.[89] Stereotyping them as ecological guardians can hurt and hinder Indigenous cultural evolution. Likewise, when we contrast Indigenous environmental values with those of non-indigenous cultures, we should also avoid stereotyping the latter. In fact, within Western environmental traditions there are diverse philosophies and practices, including deep ecologism and animal liberationism.[90]

The following sections canvass the legal standards and rights developed in international and domestic law pertaining to Indigenous peoples and their environments.[91] Legal rights and institutions are critical, because most commentators agree that Indigenous communities are more likely to continue environmentally sustainable practices and to maintain their cultural integrity when they enjoy territorial security and autonomy.[92] Where ownership of the land is in the hands of the traditional owners, they are in a much stronger position to control its environmental management.[93] Yet, because Indigenous self-determination and environmental protection may not always be mutually reinforcing, other institutions are needed to reconcile Indigenous livelihoods (as with all lifestyles) with overarching collective responsibilities to safeguard the planet.

C. Indigenous Environmental Governance: A Typology of Approaches

1. Legal Pluralism and Indigenous Legal Traditions

Before canvassing environmental governance approaches, it is worth noting that they all reflect in some ways a shift towards more pluralistic and eclectic legal

[89] See D Waller, 'Friendly Fire: When Environmentalists Dehumanize American Indians' (1996) 20(2) *American Indian Culture and Research Journal* 107.

[90] See R Eckersley, *Environmentalism and Political Theory: Toward an Ecocentric Approach* (SUNY Press, 1992); M Fox, *Toward a Transpersonal Ecology: Developing New Foundations for Environmentalism* (Shambala, 1990); D Pepper, *Modern Environmentalism: An Introduction* (Routledge, 1996).

[91] Small portions of this discussion draw on the author's previous writings in BJ Richardson and D Craig, 'Indigenous Peoples, Law and the Environment' in BJ Richardson and S Wood (eds), *Environmental Law for Sustainability* (Hart Publishing, 2006) 195.

[92] JB Alcorn, 'Noble Savage or Noble State? Northern Myths and Southern Realities in Biodiversity Conservation' (1994) 2(3) *Ethnoecologica* 7; Posey, above n 19.

[93] See L Burton, 'Indigenous Peoples and Environmental Policy in the Common Law Nation-States of the Pacific Rim: Sovereignty, Survival, and Sustainability' (1998) *Colorado Journal of International Environmental Law Yearbook* 136; JM Glenn and AC Drost, 'Aboriginal Rights and Sustainable Development in Canada' (1999) 48 *International and Comparative Law Quarterly* 176.

regimes, as evident in modern governance generally.[94] Legal pluralism essentially refers to 'a situation in which two or more legal systems coexist in the same social field'.[95] Virtually all societies blend official state-based and informal non-state methods of social ordering.[96] Often legal pluralism is associated with reforms to formally acknowledge a separate space in state law for an alternative legal order derived from other legal traditions. Sack has emphasised that authentic legal pluralism 'is more than the acceptance of a plurality of law; it sees this plurality as a positive force to be utilised—and controlled—rather than eliminated'.[97] Such arrangements are found in Great Britain and Canada (accommodating civil legal systems in Scotland and Quebec respectively), for example.

States are also accommodating Indigenous legal traditions, although rarely to the extent of treating them as of equal status. Discrete areas such as family law and criminal justice are being opened up to Indigenous laws and decision-making customs.[98] A few states have tinkered with more substantial accommodations, including constitutional-level recognition of the distinct status of their Indigenous peoples.[99] In Scandinavia, each country has established a Sámi parliament comprising individuals elected by and among the Sámi. These are advisory bodies primarily responsible for the review of policies and proposed legislation of concern to Sámi. Norway's Sámi Act 1987 obliges 'state authorities to create the conditions necessary for the Sámi to protect and develop their language, their culture and their society'.[100]

As we shall later see, environmental law in some countries is also being infused with Aboriginal values, customs and practices. Sometimes, it appears that Indigenous peoples are offered more control over land and natural resources only on condition that, in the interests of environmental sustainability, they assume responsibility for conserving the few forests or other environmental resources left, and limit their economic aspirations accordingly. Thus, we should be aware that legal pluralism may largely perpetuate 'legal centrism', reinforcing the existing hierarchy of normative ordering, with state-based regulation at the apex.[101]

While Indigenous peoples' assertion of their legal traditions has been tied largely to their conflicts with specific nation-states, some of their initiatives transcend the dominant state-based framework of national and international law. For example, the Inuit Circumpolar Conference brings together Indigenous peoples from across the Arctic regions of several jurisdictions.[102] Indigenous groups are

94 See generally MB Hooker, *Legal Pluralism: An Introduction to Colonial and Neo-Colonial Laws* (Clarendon Press, 1975).

95 S Merry, 'Legal Pluralism' (1988) *Law and Society Review* 869, 871.

96 J Griffiths, 'What is Legal Pluralism?' (1986) 24 *Journal of Legal Pluralism* 1.

97 P Sack, 'Legal Pluralism: Introductory Comments' in P Sack and E Minchin (eds), *Legal Pluralism: Proceedings of the Canberra Law Workshop VII* (Australian National University, 1988) 1.

98 Eg, N Zlotkin, 'Judicial Recognition of Aboriginal Customary Law in Canada: Selected Marriage and Adoption Cases' (1984) 4 *Canadian Native Law Reporter* 1.

99 See DL Van Cott, *Indigenous Peoples and Democracy in Latin America* (St Martin's Press, 1984).

100 The text of the Sámi Act 1987 is set out in (1996) 1 *Australian Indigenous Law Reporter* 286.

101 W Tie, *Legal Pluralism: Toward a Multicultural Conception of Law* (Ashgate, 1999) 162, 167.

102 Inuit Circumpolar Conference: www.inuitcircumpolar.com.

expressing their own environmental agenda in other ways. These include international statements such as the Kari-Oca Declaration[103] adopted at the tribal forum parallel to the 1992 Earth Summit, and the Charter of the Indigenous and Tribal Peoples of the Tropical Forests adopted at an international meeting in Malaysia.[104]

Not only may Indigenous peoples seek to by-pass the state, the state itself is off-loading or losing some of its regulatory responsibilities to the market. In turn, therefore, Indigenous groups must reckon with the power of markets to influence states' law-making activities or to generate their own, rival legal orders. The movement for corporate social responsibility has spawned various codes of conduct and market-based standards for business behaviour. For example, the Equator Principles, a voluntary code of conduct devised by the banking sector for socially and environmentally responsible financing, includes provisions regarding consultation with affected Indigenous communities.[105] The strategies needed to influence private banks are not necessarily the same as those that will sway public governments.

2. Historical Perspectives

Historically, Indigenous peoples secured toe-hold acknowledgement of their hunting and other subsistence activities in treaties imposed by colonial authorities—though at the terrible price of ceding vast swathes of their traditional territories. In North America, the 18th-century treaties were negotiated to maintain peace, trade, alliance and military support.[106] The Canadian Supreme Court in the *Marshall* case interpreted a 1760 treaty between the Mi'kmaq people and the British Crown as guaranteeing their rights to fish for a moderate livelihood in return for their allegiance to the Crown in its war against France.[107]

As European colonisers became more numerous and powerful during the 19th century, treaties served essentially to confiscate and plunder Indigenous lands.[108] The better organised communities that were able to mount armed resistance, such as New Zealand's Māori, usually were best placed to negotiate fairer terms. The Treaty of Waitangi of 1840 provided that the Crown

[103] Reproduced in M Terena, 'The Kari-Oca Conference in Rio' in L van de Fliert (ed), *Indigenous Peoples and International Organisations* (Spokesman Books, 1994) 181.

[104] Charter of the Indigenous-Tribal Peoples of the Tropical Forests, February 1992, Malay, available at homepage of the International Alliance of the Indigenous-Tribal Peoples of the Tropical Forests, at www.gn.apc.org/iaip/chart/char1.html.

[105] BJ Richardson, *Socially Responsible Investment Law: Regulating the Unseen Polluters* (Oxford University Press, 2008) 473–4.

[106] See LG Robertson, *Conquest by Law: How the Discovery of America Dispossessed Indigenous Peoples of their Land* (Oxford University Press, 2005).

[107] *R v Marshall* [1999] 3 SCR 456; see further LI Rotman, '"My Hovercraft Is Full of Eels": Smoking Out the Message of *R v Marshall*' (2000) 63 *Saskatchewan Law Review* 617.

[108] See S Carter, *Aboriginal People and Colonizers of Western Canada to 1900* (University of Toronto Press, 1999).

> guarantees to the Chiefs and Tribes of New Zealand . . . the full exclusive and undisturbed possession of their Lands and Estates Forests Fisheries and other properties which they may collectively or individually possess so long as it is their wish and desire to retain the same in their possession.[109]

Yet, differences in cultural understandings, intentions and assumptions underpinning such treaties often greatly reduced their significance. Notoriously, for instance, in the *Wi Parata* judgment of 1877 the New Zealand Supreme Court dismissed the Treaty of Waitangi

> as a simple nullity. No body politic existed capable of making a cession of sovereignty . . . So far as the proprietary rights of the natives are concerned, the so-called treaty merely affirms the rights and obligations which, *jure gentium*, vested in and devolved upon the Crown.[110]

Consequently, many disputes about the failure to honour treaty obligations linger. Modern treaty negotiations, such as those for comprehensive land claims agreements in Canada, have been pursued with heightened expectations of greater equity and a guaranteed land and natural resources base for Indigenous participants.[111]

In the modern era, a notable trend, particularly in Latin America, is the constitutionalising of Indigenous rights. Constitutional law enunciations have often explicitly acknowledged Indigenous environmental-related rights and interests. The Paraguayan Constitution recognises the right of Indigenous peoples to preserve and develop their ethnic identity; the right to freely apply their system of political, social, economic, cultural and religious organisation; and their right to enforce customary law.[112] The Constitution of Peru, inter alia, allows Indigenous institutions to exercise judicial functions pursuant to their customary law within their territory.[113] The Bolivian Constitution guarantees Indigenous peoples' use and sustainable exploitation of their traditional natural resources.[114] Such provisions, however, sometimes masquerade continuing human rights abuses. Constitutional law precepts can be too vague and non-justiciable to meaningfully accommodate Indigenous legal traditions. Furthermore, enforcement of such provisions has tended to lag considerably in a region where the rule of law often has a fragile status.[115]

Since the 1980s some international legal instruments have also recognised Indigenous legal traditions, which should help to nurture more pluralist environ-

[109] Art 2.

[110] *Wi Parata v Bishop of Wellington* (1877) 3 NZ Jur (OS) SC 72, 78.

[111] BJ Richardson, D Craig and B Boer, *Regional Agreements for Indigenous Lands and Cultures in Canada* (Australia National University, 1995).

[112] Constitución de la República de Paraguay, 1992, Art 63.

[113] Constitución Política del Perú de 1993, Art 149.

[114] República de Bolivia Constitución Política con Texto Acordado en 1995, Art 171.

[115] See J Méndez, G O'Donnell and P Pinheiro (eds), *The Rule of Law and the Underprivileged in Latin America* (University of Notre Dame Press, 1998).

mental law regimes locally. Both the ILO Convention Concerning Indigenous and Tribal Peoples in Independent Countries[116] of 1989 and the UN Declaration on the Rights of Indigenous Peoples[117] of 2007 address rights to territory and natural resources, as detailed further in Claire Charters' Chapter in this book. The Declaration proclaims Indigenous peoples' rights to own, develop and control the use of their traditional lands,[118] as well as the need for Indigenous consent for the approval of any development project affecting native lands.[119] The ILO Convention contains similar standards, including an obligation on states parties to 'respect the special importance for the cultures and spiritual values of the peoples concerned of their relationship with the lands or territories'.[120] To secure these rights and values, the Convention declares that Indigenous peoples have the right to 'participate in the use, management and conservation' of their natural resources. Yet, the effectiveness of such lofty standards is debatable. Few states have ratified the ILO Convention, and Australia, Canada, New Zealand and the US have so far shunned it. Although the UN Declaration fares better, with over 140 signatories, it is a softer law standard than the ILO Convention.

International environmental conventions containing provisions on Indigenous peoples may be more useful, given that many of these treaties enjoy extensive ratifications. The Convention on Biological Diversity of 1992,[121] ratified by some 190 states, obliges states parties to:

> respect, preserve and maintain knowledge, innovations and practices of indigenous and local communities embodying traditional lifestyles relevant for the conservation and sustainable use of biological diversity and promote their wider application with the approval and involvement of the holders of such knowledge, innovations and practices and encourage the equitable sharing of benefits arising from the utilization of such knowledge, innovations and practices.[122]

Still, the protection offered attaches only to 'traditional lifestyles' (reflective of the ecological guardians perspective) and the article dilutes the obligations by relying, in the opening clause (not quoted above), on such dubious qualifications as 'as far as possible and appropriate' and 'subject to its national legislation'. Still, as the following sections show, some national legislation and other legal sources do respect Indigenous traditional hunting and fishing rights.

[116] International Labour Organisation (ILO), Convention No 169 1989, 28 ILM 1382; see further RL Brash, 'An Advocate's Guide to the Convention on Indigenous and Tribal Peoples' (1990) 15 *Oklahoma Law Review* 209.

[117] UN Doc A/61/L.67, Sept 7, 2007.

[118] *Ibid*, Art 26.

[119] *Ibid*, Art 30.

[120] ILO Convention 169, above n 116, Art 13.

[121] 1992, 31 ILM 818.

[122] Art 8(j).

3. Territorial-based Environmental Rights

Indigenous peoples should enjoy the most extensive opportunities to participate in environmental decisions in relation to those territories that they own and occupy. Whether they hold the land under freehold or Aboriginal title, Indigenous landowners in theory can determine how the land is used or protected.[123]

Yet, for any private property owner, Indigenous or non-Indigenous, in most jurisdictions the Blackstonian notion of absolute, unfettered control over land use is a myth. Modern systems of planning law and environmental regulation have long effectively nationalised rights to development, allowing governments to control even the most seemingly trivial activities such as erecting a shed or pruning a tree.[124] Property rights in Western legal traditions are conceptualised as a bundle of rights, in which development and environmental rights are increasingly the prerogative of governmental authorities. Indigenous property can be similarly regulated. Thus, in Scandinavia, Indigenous territories have been opened to mining, logging and other uses without the consent of, and sometimes even consultation with, the Sámi people.[125] Usually only where tribal landowners also enjoy a measure of self-governance can they exercise such prerogatives, as occurs to some extent in tribal reservations in the US, as discussed later in this Chapter.

Even constitutionally protected Aboriginal and treaty-based resource rights in Canada are susceptible to land use regulation by the Crown. The Canadian Supreme Court has held that federal regulations[126] and provincial regulations[127] may restrict Aboriginal hunting and fishing activities so long as the regulation rests on 'valid legislative objectives' that are compelling and substantial, and the limitation itself is compatible with the Crown's fiduciary duty to First Nations.[128] In *Delgamuukw*,[129] Lamer CJ explained what this could mean in relation to developments on lands under full Aboriginal title:

> the development of agriculture, forestry, mining, and hydroelectric power, the general economic development of the interior of British Columbia, protection of the environment or endangered species, the building of infrastructure and the settlement of foreign populations to support those aims, are the kinds of objectives that are consistent with this purpose and, in principle, can justify the infringement of aboriginal title.[130]

[123] Curran and M'Gonigle, above n 5, 716.

[124] See P Booth, 'Nationalising Development Rights: The Feudal Origins of the British Planning System' (2002) 29 *Environment and Planning B: Planning and Design* 129; JC Nicholas, 'State and Regional Land Use Planning: The Evolving Role of the State' (1999) 73 *St Johns University Law Review* 1069.

[125] G Nettheim, G Meyers and D Craig, *Indigenous Peoples and Governance Structures: A Comparative Analysis of Land and Resource Management Rights* (Aboriginal Studies Press, 2002) 219; L Watters, 'Indigenous Peoples and the Environment: Convergence from a Nordic Perspective' (2002) 20 *UCLA Journal of Environmental Law and Policy* 237.

[126] *R v Sparrow* [1990] 1 SCR 1075.

[127] *R v Côté* [1996] 3 SCR 139.

[128] L Dufraimont, 'From Regulation to Recolonization: Justifiable Infringement of Aboriginal Rights at the Supreme Court of Canada' (2000) 58 *University of Toronto Faculty Law Review* 1.

[129] *Delgamuukw v British Columbia* (1997) 3 SCR 1010.

[130] *Ibid*, para 165.

However, the 2007 case of *Tsilhqot'in Nation* reviewed the test for justification of the infringement of Aboriginal rights.[131] The Supreme Court of British Columbia held that the province had failed in its obligations to consult with the Tsilhqot'in and that actions taken by the province under its forestry legislation were unjustified infringements of Tsilhqot'in aboriginal rights.

Even more extensive land use control is exercisable by the Crown where such constitutional protections are absent. In Australia, traditional and non-commercial hunting and food-gathering by Indigenous persons are protected under several laws such as the Native Title Act 1993 (incorporating the *Mabo* judgement of 1992),[132] and some state- and territory-based land rights legislation such as the Aboriginal Land Rights (Northern Territory) Act 1976.[133] However, in the wake of the *Wik* case,[134] the former Howard government watered down some of the statutory protections to make it easier for governments or companies to use Aboriginal lands for various uses contrary to the wishes of the title-holders.[135] The Native Title Act does not allow native title owners to veto mining projects on their land; rather, it merely concedes rights to be consulted and to negotiate with the government and mining company.[136]

In some developing countries, such as Papua New Guinea and the Philippines, Indigenous land tenures are widely recognised.[137] For instance, the Philippines Indigenous Peoples' Rights Act 1997 establishes procedures for confirmation of communal ownership of ancestral land, and some 3 million hectares are now held by Indigenous groups under these provisions.[138] The 'rights of ownership' recognised under the Philippine law include the right 'to negotiate the terms and conditions for the exploration of natural resources in the areas for the purpose of ensuring ecological, environmental protection and conservation measures, pursuant to national and customary laws'.[139] Similarly, in Latin America, some nations have made progress in demarcation and titling of Indigenous lands.[140] The Amazon's Huaorani people received from the Ecuadorian government some 676,000 hectares of Amazon land in 1990, dedicated as a Huaorani ethnic reserve.[141] Government agencies and environmental scientists in the region are

[131] [2007] BCSC 1700.

[132] *Mabo and Others v Queensland (No 2)* (1992) 175 CLR 1.

[133] See RH Bartlett, *Native Title in Australia* (2nd edn, Lexis Nexis Butterworths, 2004).

[134] *Wik Peoples v Queensland* (1996) 187 CLR 1.

[135] Native Title Amendment Act 1998 (Cth).

[136] Subdivision P.

[137] RG Crocombe (ed), *Land Tenure in the Pacific* (University of the South Pacific, 1994); T van Meijl and F von Benda-Beckmann (eds), *Property Rights and Economic Development: Land and Natural Resources in Southeast Asia and Oceania* (Kegan Paul, 1999).

[138] M Colchester, 'Indigenous Peoples and Communal Tenures in Asia', in *Land Reform, Land Settlement and Cooperatives* (UN Food and Agricultural Organisation, 2004) 28, 38.

[139] Section 7.b.

[140] R Plant and H Soren, *Land Titling and Indigenous Peoples*, Sustainable Development Department Technical Papers Series (Inter-American Development Bank, 2001).

[141] JE Brady, 'The Huaorani Tribe of Ecuador: A Study in Self-Determination for Indigenous Peoples' (1997) 10 *Harvard Human Rights Journal* 302.

starting to acknowledge that Indigenous-held land can dovetail with nature conservation goals.[142]

4. Resource Harvesting Rights

Indigenous environmental rights are not necessarily tied to ownership of the land. They may involve usufruct-type rights associated with areas traditionally fished or hunted. For example, 'immemorial' rights of the Sámi people to reindeer herding, hunting and fishing have been recognised by the Norwegian[143] and Swedish courts.[144] In the US and Canada, where the following discussion concentrates, such rights have been recognised on the basis of treaties and custom. While harvesting rights are culturally and economically significant to their holders, they do not alone provide a basis for comprehensive environmental management.

In the US, treaties signed by Native American tribes not only affirmed tribal members' rights to hunt and fish on reservation lands, they also sometimes guaranteed them such rights in their traditional harvesting grounds located outside the reservations.[145] These off-reservation rights have led to intense opposition from state governments and non-Indian hunters and fishers who have sought to make Native Americans subject to state game regulations. The US courts, however, have mostly upheld the off-reservation hunting and fishing rights of Native Americans. In the 1905 case of *United States v Winans*, even such rights over privately owned land were upheld.[146]

The most intense conflicts over off-reservation harvesting rights have flared in the state of Washington, leading to several judicial rulings on the ambit of tribal fishing rights. In a 1942 case, *Tulee v Washington*, the court ruled that tribal members could not be forced to purchase fishing licences because the treaties that their ancestors had signed already reserved the right to fish in the 'usual and accustomed places'.[147] In *Puyallup I*, the court ruled that state authorities have the right, pursuant to conservation policy goals, to regulate tribal fishing activities, so long as they do 'not discriminate against the Indians'.[148] Disputes have also arisen over the apportionment of fish resources between tribal and non-Indian interests; in *United States v Washington*,[149] the court determined that the treaty rights guaran-

142 T Walschburger, 'Delimitación y Manejo de Territorios Indígenas Ecológicamente Equilibrados en Áreas de Selva Húmeda Tropical' in M Cárdenas, HD Correa and M Gómez (eds), *Derechos Territoriales Indígenas y Ecología* (Cerec-Fundación Gaia, 1992) 261.

143 *Altevatn Case*, L nr 42, nr 8/1966 (1966).

144 *Taxed Mountain Case* ('Skattefja Ilsma'l'), NJA 1981 s 1 (1981); see further Nettheim, Meyers and Craig, above n 125, 209–35.

145 Even when hunting and fishing rights were not specifically recognised in treaties, the reserved-rights doctrine holds that tribes retain any rights that are not explicitly abrogated by treaty or statute: JV Royster, *Native American Natural Resources Law: Cases and Materials* (2nd edn, Carolina Academic Press, 2008).

146 198 US 371, S Ct 662, 49 L Ed 2d 1089 (1905).

147 315 US 681, 62 S Ct 862, 86 L Ed 1115 (1942).

148 *Puyallup Tribe v Department of Game*, 391 US 392, 88 S Ct 1725, 20 L Ed 2d 689 (1968).

149 384 F Supp 312 (WD Wash 1974).

teed the Native Americans the right to a certain percentage of the harvestable catch, up to 50 per cent.[150]

In Canada, off-reservation hunting and fishing are also recognised. While such entitlements may be based on customary rights independent of a treaty, and have enjoyed constitutional protection since 1982, governments may still regulate such rights in a manner that achieves similar arrangements as found in the US. In the seminal *Sparrow* case of 1990, the Canadian Supreme Court held Aboriginal fishing rights cannot be infringed without justification on account of the government's fiduciary duty to the Aboriginal peoples.[151] In *Van der Peet*, in denying that the Aboriginal people in question have fishing rights that extend to commercial sale of fish, the court ruled that the practices, customs and traditions must have been an integral part of the distinctiveness of their culture prior to colonial contact.[152] In the *Powley* case of 2003, the courts also found that the Métis peoples (of mixed Aboriginal and European ancestry with a distinctive culture) also enjoyed customary rights to hunt wildlife for food.[153] On the other hand, in 2005 the Canadian Supreme Court, in the cases of *Marshall* and *Bernard*, denied that the Mi'kmaq people held Aboriginal or historic treaty rights to log Crown forests without a permit for commercial gain.[154]

A limitation of Aboriginal harvesting rights in both the US and Canada is that they have not always been interpreted by courts as implying environmental protection of the habitat that supports the wildlife. In order to enjoy Aboriginal harvesting rights there surely must be edible and abundant fish and wildlife populations to support harvesting. Occasionally, courts have recognised implied environmental rights. The British Columbia Court of Appeal in *Claxton* ruled that environmental degradation posed by a government-licensed marina would impermissibly infringe a treaty right to fish.[155] The Canadian Supreme Court in *Mikisew Cree First Nation* recognised that the Aboriginal treaty right to trap and hunt is geographically limited, and it would lose its value without the preservation of the enabling wildlife habitat.[156] US law also recognises some implied water protection rights for the maintenance of on-reservation fishing, based on the *United States v Adair* and *Kittitas Reclamation District v Sunnyside Valley Irrigation District* cases.[157]

[150] This decision was affirmed by the US Supreme Court in a collateral case: *Washington v Washington State Commercial Passenger Fishing Vessel Ass'n* 443 US 658, 99 S Ct 3055, 61 L Ed 2d 823 (1979).

[151] *Sparrow*, above n 126; see further LI Rotman, 'Defining Parameters: Aboriginal Rights, Treaty Rights, and the *Sparrow* Justificatory Test' (1998) 36 *Alberta Law Review* 149.

[152] [1996] 2 SCR 507. Compare to *R v Gladstone* [1996] 2 SCR 723, where the court held that Aboriginal defendants have an Aboriginal right to take and sell certain fish species in commercial quantities.

[153] *R v Powley* [2003] 2 SCR 207.

[154] *R v Marshall*; *R v Bernard* [2005] 2 SCR 220.

[155] *Saanichton Marina Ltd v Claxton* [1989] 57 DLR (4th) 161, 36 BCLR (2d) 79 (CA) (eC).

[156] *Mikisew Cree First Nation v Canada (Minister of Canadian Heritage)* [2005] SCC 69, paras 2, 45. The Mikisew treaty right to hunt in the national park was threatened by the Crown decision to build a road through the area.

[157] *United States v Adair*, 478 F Supp 336 (D Or, 1979); *United States v Adair*, 187 F Supp 2d 1273 (D Or, 2002); *Kittitas Reclamation District v Sunnyside Valley Irrigation District*, 763 F 2d 1032 (9th Cir 1985).

However, in all these cases, the traditional harvesting territory of the tribal group was near the environmental damage. For Aboriginal peoples who harvest migratory species, a much larger habitat area used by the animal would need safeguarding. In many other cases, given the interconnectedness of the natural environment, activities occurring afar may indirectly affect fish and wildlife populations within traditional hunting areas. Adequate proof that a proposed activity would cause harm to wildlife and therefore infringe harvesting rights would be a barrier for some Aboriginal groups in such situations.

One solution, as taken in New Zealand, is to insert into general environmental legislation specific provisions to guard Indigenous interests. The Resource Management Act 1991—the country's principal environmental and land use planning statute—affirms as a matter of 'national importance' the 'relationship of Māori and their culture and traditions with their ancestral lands, waters, sites',[158] as well as the Māori environmental stewardship principle of 'Kaitiakitanga',[159] to which government decision-makers must have regard when administering the legislation.[160] The Act has led to municipal planning authorities usually consulting with Māori *iwi* when considering resource development applications.[161]

Indigenous harvesting rights are also affirmed in some international environmental conventions, which signatory states must respect. Under the International Convention for the Regulation of Whaling,[162] in 1989 the International Whaling Commission approved a small Aboriginal subsistence whaling quota.[163] The prohibition on hunting polar bears imposed by the Agreement on Polar Bears of 1973 does not apply in relation to hunting 'by local people when using traditional methods in the exercise of their traditional rights'.[164] The Convention on Conservation of North Pacific Fur Seals of 1976 exempts Indigenous groups inhabiting certain coastal areas from the ban on sealing when not using specified modern technologies.[165] Limiting the exercise of such rights to traditional hunting methods presumably aims to limit the size of the harvest. Such restrictions, however, overlook that the most important mechanism to limit harvesting is the purpose (that is, subsistence living) rather than its means (for example, modern weaponry).[166]

In the future, intellectual property law appears likely to provide another basis for some Indigenous environmental rights.[167] This trend is best illustrated by the

[158] Resource Management Act 1991, s 6(e).

[159] *Ibid*, s 7(a).

[160] See generally P Beverley, 'The Mechanisms for the Protection of Māori Interests Under Part II of the Resource Management Act 1991' (1998) 2 *New Zealand Journal of Environmental Law* 121.

[161] Ministry for the Environment (MfE), *Case Law on Tangata Whenua Consultation* (MfE, 1999).

[162] 1946, 161 UNTS 72.

[163] The Commission has established a sub-committee to deal with aboriginal subsistence whaling: see NC Doubleday, 'Aboriginal Subsistence Whaling: The Right of Inuit to Hunt Whales and Implications for International Environmental Law' (1989) 17 *Denver Journal of International Law and Policy* 373.

[164] Art III(d), Agreement on Polar Bears 1973, 13 ILM 13.

[165] Art VII, Convention on Conservation of North Pacific Fur Seals 1976, 27 UST 3371.

[166] *Indigenous Peoples and Sustainability*, above n 15, 64–5.

[167] See, eg, T Janke, *Our Culture, Our Future: Proposals for the Recognition and Protection of Indigenous Cultural and Intellectual Property* (Michael Frankel, 1997).

far-reaching claim filed by Māori groups to the Waitangi Tribunal seeking control of knowledge-based uses of New Zealand's entire panoply of native flora and fauna.[168] Reliance on intellectual property law, in addition to territorial-based rights, to protect Indigenous interests in the environment has arisen principally because of the growing commercial pressures to exploit Indigenous knowledge and culture in the fields of biotechnology, agriculture and tourism.[169]

Indigenous peoples remain vigilant about such uses without their consent. The UN Declaration on the Rights of Indigenous Peoples also affirmed their right

> to maintain, control, protect and develop their cultural heritage, traditional knowledge and traditional cultural expressions, as well as the manifestations of their sciences, technologies and cultures, including human and genetic resources, seeds, medicines, [and] knowledge of the properties of fauna and flora.[170]

However, to implement such standards within mainstream intellectual property law is difficult, as copyrights, trademarks and patents are not easily adapted to Indigenous knowledge.[171] They are designed to promote innovation and commercialisation of knowledge, whereas Indigenous communities tend to be more interested in preserving the integrity of existing traditional knowledge. The intellectual property law requirements of authorship and novelty also pose difficulties where traditional knowledge has evolved gradually from generation to generation and is owned collectively. Currently, there are few international or national legal instruments that create specific intellectual property standards tailored to Indigenous knowledge or cultural practices.

5. Indigenous Land Use Governance

Logically, environmental governance should coincide with Indigenous interests most closely in those areas over which Indigenous communities exercise self-governance. Their quest for self-governance, as discussed in Shin Imai's Chapter in this book, has often centred on resource management. In this context, self-governance could mean an Indigenous group asserting jurisdiction over wildlife harvesting, mining, forestry, water extraction and other conceivable land uses in a manner compatible with community preferences. The quality of self-governance depends on many factors, including whether Indigenous authorities have community support, adequate financial resources and technical expertise, as well as the size of the land mass governed, and the extent of jurisdiction over the activities of non-Aboriginal actors.

[168] Waitangi Tribunal, at www.waitangi-tribunal.govt.nz.

[169] F Yamin and D Possey, 'Indigenous Peoples, Biotechnology and Intellectual Property Rights' (1997) 2 *RECIEL* 141; DA Cleveland and SC Murray, 'The World's Crop Genetic Resources and the Rights of Indigenous Farmers' (1997) 38 *Current Anthropology* 477, 483–5.

[170] Art 31(1).

[171] S Patel, 'Can the Intellectual Property Rights System Serve the Interests of Indigenous Knowledge?' in S Brush and D Stabinsky (eds), *Valuing Local Knowledge* (Island Press, 1996).

In the US, with some of the most comprehensive systems of tribal governance such as on the Navaho reservation, courts have long recognised Native American tribes as independent, distinct political entities retaining inherent sovereign powers to the extent these have not been ceded to or taken away by Congress.[172] Thus, tribes enjoy full equitable ownership of timber and mineral resources located on tribal reservations, and can regulate hunting and fishing on their reservations. Importantly, in 2003 the US court ruled that the Sokaogon Chippewa in Wisconsin have the right to regulate water quality on their reservation and to set water quality standards higher than those promulgated by state authorities.[173] While tribes may also possess off-reservation fishing and hunting rights, as noted earlier, these rights would not ordinarily carry concomitant governance authority.[174]

Apart from self-governance powers derived from their inherent sovereignty, tribes may also hold delegated legislative powers. In 1984 the US Environmental Protection Agency adopted a Federal Indian Policy which recognised tribal governments as the appropriate sovereign for setting environmental standards, issuing permits and managing environmental programmes within reservation boundaries.[175] Since then, numerous federal environmental statutes have authorised delegation of regulatory authority to tribes, including the Clean Water Act, the Clean Air Act, and the Surface Mining Control and Reclamation Act, among many examples. Few tribes have been able to take advantage of such powers without additional federal funds and technical support.[176]

A setback for tribal governance has arisen from some US court decisions denying tribes the authority to regulate hunting and fishing on non-Indian fee simple lands within reservation boundaries,[177] or to regulate non-Indian resource use within reservations.[178] These limitations can severely undermine tribes' ability to provide comprehensive land management schemes in reservations containing substantial non-Indian parcels, as many do.

These jurisdictional lacunae are curious omissions, for even under Canada's much-loathed Indian Act 1876, bands' by-law powers apply to everyone within the reservation. On the other hand, the Indian Act gives bands only rudimentary land use powers, such as management of stray dogs and removal of weeds.[179] First Nations and the Canadian government negotiated a Framework Agreement in 1996 to provide an alternative land management regime on reservations. The resulting First Nations Land Management Act 1999 gives bands the choice to opt

[172] See *Johnson v M'Intosh*, 21 US (8 Wheat) 543, 572–88 (1823).

[173] *State of Wisconsin v Environmental Protection Agency et al*, 266 F3d 741 (7th Cir, 2001).

[174] Nettheim, Meyers and Craig, above n 125, 40.

[175] WD Ruckelshaus, *EPA Policy for the Administration of Environmental Programs on Indian Reservations* (American Indian Environmental Office, 1984).

[176] JA Milford, 'Tribal Authority Under the Clean Air Act: How Is It Working?' (2004) 44 *Natural Resources Journal* 213.

[177] *Montana v United States*, 45 US 544, 566 (1981).

[178] *United States v Anderson*, 736 F 2d 1358, 1366 (9th Cir 1984).

[179] See ss 18, 57, 58, 73.

into a different self-governance regime over their reserve land.[180] As of July 2008, at least 35 First Nations had committed to this process, which involves the drafting of a new land management code for each community and negotiation of an individual agreement with Indian and Northern Affairs Canada. The land management codes drafted to date, such as the Scugog Island First Nation Land Management Code, tend to resemble municipal planning codes setting out procedural standards rather than substantive environmental or land use policy goals.[181]

Although Indigenous communities may enjoy significant control over natural resources on designated reserves, the small size of many reserves make long-term, sustainable management approaches impractical. According to the 1996 report of the Royal Commission on Aboriginal Peoples, nearly 80 per cent of the some 600 First Nations reservations in Canada are less than 500 hectares in size.[182] These reservations are probably not viable for comprehensive ecosystem-wide management. For example, in forestry management, many reservations have been found to be too small to allow for traditional rotation methods of log harvesting.[183] A further problem is that natural resources on First Nation lands may be harmed by third-party pollution, emanating from distant places beyond Indigenous control. In the case involving ICI Canada, the First Nation was unable to prevent the company from discharging pollutants into a river that ultimately flowed through their reservation.[184]

The 2000 Nisga'a Final Agreement in British Columbia is a rare example of a framework for an Aboriginal Nation to exercise substantial environmental self-governance over a large area.[185] Covering some 2,000 km^2 of Nisga'a lands, well as some adjacent Crown lands, the treaty gave the Nisga'a Lisims government a primary role in the environmental assessment and protection of project proposals on Nisga'a lands.[186] While federal or provincial law will prevail whenever there is a conflict with Nisga'a environmental laws, the Nisga'a Agreement also provides a key safeguard: '[n]o Party should relax its environmental standards in the Nass Area for the purpose of providing an encouragement to the establishment, acquisition, expansion, or retention of an investment'.[187] By contrast, the other comprehensive land settlements negotiated in Canada in recent years have tended to provide for resource management institutions jointly controlled by Indigenous and non-Indigenous interests, rather than Aboriginal self-governance, as the following section explains.

[180] See T Isaac, 'First Nations Land Management Act and Third Party Interests' (2005) 42 *Alberta Law Review* 1047.

[181] See www.fafnlm.com/content/en/LandCodes.html.

[182] Royal Commission on Aboriginal Peoples, *Report* (Supply and Services Canada, 1996) Part 2(2), 810–11.

[183] Curran and M'Gonigle, above n 5.

[184] *Walpole Island First Nation v Ontario* [1997] OJ No 3768, 35 OR (3d) 113 (Ct J (Gen Div)).

[185] D Sanders, 'We Intend to Live Here Forever: A Primer on the Nisga'a Treaty' (1999) 33 *University of British Columbia Law Review* 103.

[186] *Nisga'a Final Agreement* (2000) ch 10.

[187] *Ibid*, para 18.

6. Joint Resource Management

Indigenous communities may also participate in environmental decision-making through cross-cultural institutions that allow Aboriginal and non-Aboriginal stakeholders to work collaboratively in managing wildlife, forests, water and other natural resources.

Perhaps the leading example is Canada's Comprehensive Land Claims Process (CLCP), which has led to nearly 20 major settlements since it began in the mid-1970s.[188] First Nations and the federal and other governments have negotiated complex agereements for financial compensation, co-management of Aboriginal lands, wildlife management and regional development.[189] Most have involved areas in northern Canada where Aboriginal or Inuit lands were never historically ceded to the Crown. Negotiation of the CLCP agreements has often been precipitated by development pressures; the Inuvialuit Agreement of 1984 was negotiated against the backdrop of the discovery of oil and gas deposits in the region.[190] The Nisga'a Agreement was also shaped partly by disputes over deforestation and control of British Columbia's lucrative salmon fishery.[191]

Each CLCP agreement creates specific institutions for environmental governance that are typically managed jointly by Indigenous and governmental representatives. The Nunavut Agreement of 1993 contains perhaps the most extensive array of governance institutions, including: a Nunavut Wildlife Management Board; a Nunavut Impact Review Board to screen project proposals and to monitor projects that do proceed; a Nunavut Planning Commission to oversee general land use planning; a Nunavut Water Board; and a Surface Rights Tribunal.[192] In each institution, the federal or territorial government representatives have an overriding obligation to ensure sustainable utilisation and resource conservation, but they must also act in accordance with basic constitutional principles on Aboriginal rights.[193] Thus, in *Kadlak v Nunavut* the court considered the legality of a Minister's decision to overrule a recommendation of the Nunavut Wildlife Management Board to allow traditional hunting of polar bears.[194] The court

[188] See Nettheim, Meyers and Craig, above n 125; Richardson, Craig and Boer, above n 111. The Canadian CLCP, however, was inspired by the earlier Alaska Native Claims Settlement Act, Pub L No 92-203, 85 Stat 339 (1971).

[189] Indian and Northern Affairs Canada (INAC), *Comprehensive Claims Policy and Status of Claims* (INAC, 2003).

[190] AJ Black, 'Legal Principles Surrounding the New Canadian and American Arctic Energy Debate' (2002) 23 *Energy Law Journal* 81, 83.

[191] DE Stokes, 'Modern Treaty Making with First Nations in British Columbia' (2000) 8 *Waikato Law Review* 117, 122.

[192] Agreement Between the Inuit of the Nunavut Settlement Area and Her Majesty The Queen in Right of Canada, 25 May 1993; see further C Marecic, 'Nunavut Territory: Aboriginal Governing in the Canadian Regime of Governance' in L Watters (ed), *Indigenous Peoples, Environment and Law* (Carolina Academic Press, 2004) 205.

[193] Canada Department of Indian Affairs and Northern Development, *Federal Policy for the Settlement of Native Claims* (March 1993) 10.

[194] *Kadlak v Nunavut (Minister of Sustainable Development)* [2001] NUCJ 1.

viewed the decision of the Minister as a prima facie infringement of an Aboriginal right that could not be justified under the *Sparrow* test, and the matter was referred to the Minister for reconsideration.[195]

While the Canadian examples of cross-cultural resource management may be faulted for often assigning Indigenous parties only a minority voice, they compare favourably to models in other jurisdictions. In Australia, by contrast, governments have tended to limit the Aboriginal voice to various advisory committees and consultation mechanisms.[196] Such arrangements have been introduced under the Torres Strait Fisheries Act 1984 and the Environment Protection and Biodiversity Conservation Act 1999, for instance.[197]

The joint management of protected areas in Australia provides a more genuine example of cross-cultural resource management.[198] The Kakadu and Uluru national parks in the Northern Territory are among the most comprehensive and successful examples of joint management.[199] They each provide for Aboriginal ownership and lease-back of the land to the government conservation agency, an Aboriginal majority on the board of park management, and financial payments to the traditional owners. Jointly managed national parks have also led to advances in cross-cultural education, training and employment for local Indigenous communities to share in the economic benefits of parks. There are also numerous examples of less formal partnerships for environmental management in Australia. These include the Kowanyama community strategy for joint management of fisheries resources in Queensland's Mitchell River, and the natural and cultural resource management undertaken by the Dhimurru Land Management Aboriginal Corporation in Arnhem Land.[200]

Another distinctive feature of the Australian approach to Indigenous participation in environmental governance is the extensive use of contractual arrangements between Aboriginal organisations, public agencies and developers relating to land and cultural heritage management.[201] One example is the partnership agreements negotiated pursuant to the Indigenous Protected Areas programme under the Natural Heritage Trust of Australia Act 1997, providing for co-operative management of terrestrial and marine areas as protected sites. Another example is the Indigenous Land Use Agreements negotiated under the

[195] *Ibid*, para 170.

[196] Nettheim, Meyers and Craig, above n 125, 393.

[197] D Craig, *Aboriginal and Torres Strait Islander Involvement in Bioregional Planning: Requirements and Opportunities under International and National Law and Policy* (Department of Environment, Sport and Territories, 1996).

[198] S Woenne-Green *et al*, *Competing Interests: Aboriginal Participation in National Parks and Conservation Reserves in Australia* (Australian Conservation Foundation, 1994).

[199] T DeLacy and B Lawson, 'The Uluru-Kakadu Model: Joint Management of Aboriginal-Owned National Parks in Australia' in S Stevens (ed), *Conservation through Cultural Survival: Indigenous Peoples and Protected Areas* (Island Press, 1997).

[200] Nettheim, Meyers and Craig, above n 125, 384–5.

[201] See E Young *et al*, *Caring for Country: Aborigines and Land Management* (Australian National Parks and Wildlife Service, 1991).

Native Title Act, allowing native title claimants to enter into resource management arrangements, such as for biodiversity conservation, in territories under claim.[202]

Negotiated agreements have also been used in New Zealand for joint resource management. The most important settlement is the 1989 and 1992 'Sealords' agreements by which the Crown agreed to transfer a large proportion of the nation's commercial fisheries quota to the newly created Treaty of Waitangi Fisheries Commission to manage on behalf of all Māori, and to provide funding to enable the Commission to purchase the Sealords fishing company.[203] In return, Māori agreed that the settlement would discharge and extinguish all their commercial fishing rights and claims against the Crown.[204] There have been other negotiated settlements for the return of Māori tribal lands, financial compensation and co-management of natural resources, although not as comprehensive as the Canadian examples.[205]

7. Environmental Governance beyond the State

Another governance trend is the growing influence of the corporate sector, including in the areas of environmental policy and Indigenous peoples. Corporate influence in governance has mushroomed in the wake of policy shifts in many countries, particularly in the Anglo-American sphere, to reduce the regulatory role of states while ceding greater responsibilities to markets and private sector institutions.[206] The resulting growth of corporate self-regulation is reflected in the plethora of private sector codes of conduct and voluntary standards, which typically emphasise procedural rather than normative standards.[207] Procedural standards, such as for public disclosure, consultation and reporting, may make stakeholders (for example, non-governmental organisations, local communities and Indigenous peoples) more informed of corporate behaviour, promote a dialogue with companies and enable stakeholders to apply pressure for change.

A paradigmatic example of such process standards is the Equator Principles, designed for the financial sector. Through the long-standing movement for socially responsible investment, the financial sector is under mounting pressure from many stakeholders to promote environmentally sustainable development

[202] D Craig, 'Native Title and Environmental Planning; Indigenous Land Use Agreements' (2000) 17 *Environmental and Planning Law Journal* 440.

[203] HK Guth, 'Dividing the Catch: Natural Resource Reparations to Indigenous Peoples—Examining the Māori Fisheries Settlement' (2001) 24 *Hawaii Law Review* 179.

[204] The customary taking of seafood for subsistence needs is also recognised and preserved in government fisheries regulations: Fisheries (Amatuer Fishing) Regulations, cl 27.

[205] Eg, the Tainui and Ngai Tahu settlements: Nettheim, Meyers and Craig, above n 125, 144.

[206] See C Scott, 'Regulation in the Age of Governance: The Rise of the Post Regulatory State', in J Jordana and D Levi-Faur (eds), *The Politics of Regulation: Institutions and Regulatory Reforms for the Age of Governance* (Edward Elgar, 2004) 145.

[207] See B Krumsiek, 'Voluntary Codes of Conduct for Multinational Corporations: Promises and Challenges' (2004) 109 *Business and Society Review* 503; D Leipziger, *The Corporate Responsibility Code Book* (Greenleaf Publishing, 2003).

and social justice.[208] Socially responsible investors began to acknowledge Indigenous rights in the 1980s, following the lead set by the World Bank and other multilateral lenders that pioneered policies for the special treatment of tribal peoples in development projects.[209] Investors were not principally driven by any ethical belief in the sanctity of Indigenous rights or interests. Rather, they saw a business case for respecting Indigenous interests; the World Resources Institute, for instance, argued that financiers and developers should seek the 'free and informed consent' of affected Indigenous and other local communities if they wish to avoid costly protests and resistance to their economic plans.[210]

These considerations weighed on the international banking community when it formulated the Equator Principles (EPs). The Principles, which were drafted in 2003, provide a voluntary code of conduct for responsible project financing.[211] The EPs are based on the World Bank's International Finance Corporation standards, the Bank's private sector lending arm. Lenders that sign the EPs agree to implement measures to minimise the social and environmental harm of financed infrastructure projects (for example, dams, highways and mines), such as by following procedures for undertaking environmental and social impact studies before disbursing money, and consulting with affected local communities.[212]

The EPs touch briefly on Indigenous peoples specifically. A bank must ensure that its borrower formulates an 'Indigenous Peoples Development Plan' in accordance with the International Finance Corporation standards. They provide, in part:

> [w]hen avoidance [of adverse impacts] is not feasible, the client will minimize, mitigate or compensate for these impacts in a culturally appropriate manner. The client's proposed action will be developed with the informed participation of affected Indigenous Peoples and contained in a time-bound plan, such as an Indigenous Peoples Development Plan.[213]

The EPs do not, however, require borrowers to obtain the free, prior and informed consent of affected Indigenous communities. The lesser standard of 'consultation' does not necessarily require developers to respond to and address their advice or concerns.

Of the approximately 60 banks that had signed the EPs as of mid-2008, few have drafted policies that explicitly address Indigenous peoples. JPMorganChase, with perhaps the most comprehensive policy, commits itself to finance projects only where: free, prior informed *consultation* using customary institutions results in

[208] R Sparkes, 'A Historical Perspective on the Growth of Socially Responsible Investment' in R Sullivan and C Mackenzie (eds), *Responsible Investment* (Greenleaf Publishing, 2006) 39.

[209] GA Sarfaty, 'The World Bank and the Internalization of Indigenous Rights Norms' (2005) 114 *Yale Law Journal* 1791.

[210] S Herz, A Vina and A Sohn, *Development without Conflict: The Business Case for Community Consent* (World Resources Institute, 2007).

[211] See www.equator-principles.com.

[212] T O'Riordan, 'Converting the Equator Principles to Equator Stewardship' (2005) 47(4) *Environment* 1.

[213] International Finance Corporation (IFC), *Performance Standard 7: Indigenous Peoples* (IFC, 2006) cl 7.

support of the project by the affected Indigenous people; they have been fully informed about the project; they have access to a grievance mechanism; and major Indigenous land claims have been appropriately addressed.[214] While the policies of JPMorganChase fall short of best practice, they are comparable to governmental policies.

Apart from such procedural standards, occasionally the private sector commits to more substantial standards in its dealings with Indigenous and other local stakeholders. One example used in Canada is formal agreements negotiated between developers and communities. While the Supreme Court of Canada ruled in *Haida Nation v British Columbia (Minister of Forests)* that resource developers do not owe an independent duty to consult with First Nations, a duty of the Crown that cannot be delegated, some Canadian companies have been acting independently to consult with and reach accommodations with Indigenous resource owners.[215] One mechanism is 'impact and benefit' agreements (IBAs).

Used particularly in Canada's resource economy, IBAs are typically negotiated between resource-sector corporations, Indigenous communities and sometimes governments as well, to alleviate various adverse socio-economic and environmental impacts that can arise from resource development.[216] IBAs operate on a project basis and include provisions covering employment, training, profit sharing, compensation, and cultural and environmental protection. Environmental provisions can include additional impact assessments and environmental monitoring.[217] IBAs do not take the place of official regulation, but may supplement it with additional measures to accommodate the concerns of affected local communities.[218] One limitation of IBAs as used in Canada is their confidentiality; this restricts public access, and therefore does not allow parties entering IBA negotiations to be fully aware of useful precedents and learn from previous negotiations.[219]

D. Conclusions

Indigenous peoples' ties to environmental governance have been shaped by specific legal rights, as well as academic and policy debates about the relative value of Indigenous knowledge and customs to modern environmental management. It is too simplistic, however, to conclude that more Indigenous control will resolve

[214] JPMorganChase, 'Environmental Policy', s 4; at www.jpmorganchase.com.

[215] [2004] 3 SCR 511.

[216] SA Kennett, *A Guide to Impact and Benefits Agreements* (Canadian Institute of Resources Law, 1999); I Sosa and K Keenan, *Impact Benefit Agreements between Aboriginal Communities and Mining Companies* (Canadian Environmental Law Association, 2001).

[217] K O'Reilly, 'Impact and Benefit Agreements: Tools for Sustainable Development?' (2000) 25(4) *Northern Perspectives* 1.

[218] S Gogal, R Riegert and J Jamieson, 'Aboriginal Impact and Benefit Agreements: Practical Considerations' (2005) 43 *Alberta Law Review* 129.

[219] Kennett, above n 216, 2.

both their desires for self-determination and ensure sustainable use of the environment. Even where Indigenous institutions have remained relatively intact, evidence from the South Pacific, for instance, suggests that the maintenance of customary land tenure systems and tribal authorities has not prevented significant environmental decline.[220]

The purpose of this Chapter is not to provide answers to these challenges, but rather to illuminate more fully the complex discourse about Indigenous environmental values and practices, and the governance tools availed to give voice and authority to Indigenous peoples. Yet by understanding these two issues, we should be better placed to evaluate appropriate reforms.

We should be mindful not to assume that there is an inevitable path to reform. While the trend in most jurisdictions has been for more Indigenous voice and authority in environmental governance, setbacks have occurred. Some courts have become less receptive to or ambivalent about Indigenous claims. The US Supreme Court has been 'backtracking on Indian sovereignty',[221] as evident in *Nevada v Hicks.*[222] Tribal governments have seen their jurisdiction chipped away.[223] In Canada, after the ground-breaking *Sparrow* decision, the Supreme Court retreated somewhat in its judgments in *Van der Peet*[224] and *Pamajewon.*[225] In Australia, the euphoria of *Mabo* has abated because of rulings like *Yorta Yorta,*[226] which held that native title claimants must prove continuous acknowledgement and observance of traditional laws and customs in relation to land. Even when courts favour Indigenous claims, such as the crucial decision of the New Zealand Court of Appeal on Māori rights to the foreshore and seabed,[227] governments have intervened to extinguish Indigenous rights given sufficient economic and political stakes. The New Zealand government did so with the Foreshore and Seabed Act 2004, as explained further in Jacinta Ruru's Chapter.

Enduring measures to safeguard Indigenous environmental practices—and thereby their distinctive cultures—are unlikely to be found if the Aboriginal stake is defined narrowly in terms of mere usufruct rights to harvest plants and animals. Even full territorial rights and Indigenous self-government are likely to be

[220] DD Paulson, 'Understanding Tropical Deforestation: The Case of Western Samoa' (1994) 21 *Environmental Conservation* 326, 329.

[221] P McHugh, *Aboriginal Societies and the Common Law* (Oxford University Press, 2005) 330, although there were exceptions to this trend, notably *California v Cabazon Band,* 480 US 202 (1987) (concerning the rights of Indian tribes to operate gaming facilities on Indian reservations), and *US v Lara,* 541 US 193 (2004) (affirming Congressional power under the constitution to recognise inherent criminal jurisdiction of tribal authorities over non-member Indians).

[222] 533 US 353 (2001). In this case the Supreme Court held that state officers could enter an Indian reservation uninvited to investigate or prosecute an off-reservation violation of state law. It further held that tribal courts are not empowered to hear civil rights cases under federal law because they are nnot courts of general jurisdiction.

[223] See D Luckerman, 'Sovereignty, Jurisdiction, and Environmental Primacy on Tribal Lands' (2003) 37 *New England Law Review* 635.

[224] *R v Van der Peet* [1996] 2 SCR 507.

[225] *R v Pamajewon* [1996] 2 SCR 821.

[226] *Yorta Yorta Aboriginal Community v Victoria* [2002] HCA 58.

[227] *Ngati Apu v Attorney-General* [2003] 3 NZLR 643.

insufficient where the land mass is small and there are no rights to influence environmental decisions on a regional or higher scale. Environmentally threatening processes from afar can undermine even the most robust local resource management regimes. In a global economy, the sustainability of Indigenous livelihoods will increasingly be shaped by factors quite distant from Indigenous homelands. Global warming is the gravest threat, while also being the environmental challenge most beyond Indigenous control. Traditional governance approaches that emphasise Indigenous autonomy and self-control will not work very well in the face of such looming disasters.

What could help? The Inuit of the Arctic regions have submitted a petition to the Inter-American Commission on Human Rights seeking remedies from the US for its contribution to global warming.[228] While their petition may help to build recognition of an international human right to maintain cultural traditions, reform must also address mechanisms by which Indigenous communities can collaborate with management institutions at other levels of economic policy-making and development planning. If Indigenous livelihoods that respect the environment are to be sustained, an Indigenous voice in local environmental governance is not enough—it must also be heard in the institutions that shape the global economy, trade, finance and other fundamental causes of environmental pressure.

[228] *Petition to the Inter American Commission on Human Rights Seeking Relief from Violations Resulting from Global Warming Caused by Acts and Omissions of the United States* (7 December 2005).

14

ADR Processes and Indigenous Rights: A Comparative Analysis of Australia, Canada and New Zealand

MICHAEL COYLE

A. Overview

1. The Importance of ADR in Addressing Indigenous Rights

In May 2008, the Ontario Court of Appeal ordered the release of eight indigenous leaders from prison. All had been jailed for civil contempt after opposing mineral developments in violation of court orders. In two judgments released that day the court reaffirmed its strong preference that serious efforts be made to resolve indigenous rights disputes through negotiation and conciliation rather than through the courts.[1] In urging that the complexities of indigenous rights be addressed through other dispute resolution processes, the Ontario court echoed previous declarations of the highest courts in Canada, Australia and New Zealand.[2]

This Chapter will introduce the reader to the out-of-court processes created to address indigenous land rights disputes in each of Australia, Canada and New Zealand. Each of these countries has developed systematic forums for recognising and implementing those rights. These forums are commonly (if misleadingly[3]) referred to as alternative dispute resolution (ADR) processes. This Chapter will describe these processes and compare their approaches and the results they have

[1] *Frontenac Ventures Corp v Ardoch Algonquin First Nation* [2008] ONCA 534; 91 OR (3d) 1, leave to appeal to SCC refused [2008] SCCA No 357, paras 45–6 ('*Frontenac*'); see also *Platinex Inc v Kitchenuhmaykoosib Inninuwug First Nation* [2008] ONCA 533, 91 OR (3d) 18 ('*Platinex*').

[2] *Delgamuukw v British Columbia* [1997] 3 SCR 1010, 1123 ('*Delgamuukw*'); *Haida Nation v British Columbia (Minister of Forests)* [2004] SCC 73; [2004] 3 SCR 511, 521–2 ('*Haida Nation*'). In Australia, see, eg, *Re Waanyi Peoples Native Title Application* (1995) 129 ALR 118, 617 and *North Ganalanja Aboriginal Corporation v Queensland* (1996) CLR 595, 617. In New Zealand, judicial reluctance to intervene in the claims process became commonplace in the late 1990s: PG McHugh, *Aboriginal Societies and the Common Law: A History of Sovereignty, Status, and Self-Determination* (Oxford University Press, 2004) 522.

[3] Pursuing litigation to final judgment is a relatively uncommon method of resolving legal disputes.

achieved. It will adopt a framework for comparison that will focus on the degree of congruence between the nature of each process and the nature of the indigenous grievances it was designed to address. In other words, this Chapter seeks to assess the robustness of existing ADR regimes in addressing the grievances underlying contemporary rights claims. Finally, it will draw on the experience of the now-defunct US Indian Claims Commission as a reference point from which the evolution of current ADR processes might be evaluated.

ADR processes are worthy of attention for a number of reasons. First, as in other areas of legal dispute, the number of indigenous rights claims resolved outside the courts exceeds by a significant margin the number of such disputes that are adjudicated by domestic courts.[4] Indeed, as we shall see, the law in Australia, Canada and New Zealand currently requires that many indigenous land rights disputes be addressed outside the courts.

A second reason for the importance of ADR processes in contemporary conflicts between indigenous peoples and non-indigenous governments is that such conflicts frequently involve disagreements about more than the interpretation of laws currently in place. Other important interests are at stake—such as *whose* laws should be used to resolve the dispute, how the parties should coexist today, and whether non-judicial remedies might be best suited to righting historical wrongs. ADR approaches allow non-legal interests and perspectives of the parties to help shape the outcome of their dispute. This feature is particularly important in the context of indigenous rights, where settler government laws and legal structures often played a major role in creating the grievance in the first place. As such, settler laws are often not accepted by indigenous peoples as neutral standards for resolving such grievances.

Third, even for those who believe that domestic law should play a primary role in guiding the resolution of indigenous rights disputes, establishing non-judicial processes for acknowledging and enforcing rights can be seen as essential to the administration of justice. The law of each jurisdiction recognises some form of indigenous land rights. However, for many years, in each jurisdiction indigenous peoples were effectively prevented from using the courts to recognise and enforce their land rights until long after most of their lands were taken. The accumulated volume of indigenous land disputes, combined with their evidential and substantive complexity, precludes the majority of them from being resolved through court judgments in the foreseeable future. The absence of an effective judicial mechanism for addressing the bulk of these claims in a timely way has led each of the jurisdictions to privilege non-judicial mechanisms for resolving them.

Finally, relying on the court system alone to resolve indigenous land rights disputes seems particularly problematic in light of the colonial history of each

[4] The number of indigenous rights disputes resolved through each country's ADR processes will be discussed later. As for ordinary civil disputes, the proportion resolved through negotiation rather than final judgment is high, sometimes estimated at more than 95%. See DP Emond, 'Alternative Dispute Resolution: A Conceptual Overview' in DP Emond (ed), *Commercial Dispute Resolution: Alternatives to Litigation* (Canada Law Book, 1989) 3.

country. Each saw the widespread dispossession of indigenous peoples, the gradual imposition by settler governments of sovereignty and British common law and the systematic marginalisation of indigenous societies. Adjudication of historical claims by the domestic courts once again involves the imposition of an outcome on indigenous peoples, an outcome determined by settler values and procedures. The use of consensual ADR processes offers at least the promise of a shift away from the colonial paradigm and its historical disrespect for the values of indigenous peoples.

This Chapter focuses on ADR processes that address disputes about historic rights to lands and resources, as this is the area where each of the jurisdictions has moved the furthest to develop formalised, non-judicial institutions to address indigenous grievances. This is so for a number of reasons. In the US, the creation of an Indian Claims Commission seems to have been driven by a desire on the part of the federal government to eliminate outstanding legal obligations to the tribes and pave the way for the tribes' termination as self-governing entities.[5] In Canada, formalised negotiation processes began in the wake of a belated judicial recognition of the enforceability of indigenous land rights and increasingly powerful indigenous protests against developments on their traditional lands.[6] In Australia too, it was the judicial recognition of aboriginal title that led to legislation granting negotiation rights to indigenous peoples.[7] Finally, in New Zealand the force of mass protests by Māori against the non-recognition of the Treaty of Waitangi led the government (this time without judicial intervention) to create a tribunal which has since focused largely on Māori rights to land and resources under the treaty.[8] To understand the significance of the particular ADR processes that developed in each country, it is necessary to reflect on the conceptual basis of ADR processes generally.

2. Situating ADR Processes Relative to Adjudication

This Chapter has already noted the popularity of out-of-court dispute resolution processes in ordinary civil disputes. To some extent, that popularity can be attributed to the promise of cost savings to the disputants through the avoidance of

[5] See HD Rosenthal, 'Indian Claims and the American Conscience: A Brief History of the Indian Claims Commission' in I Sutton (ed), *Irredeemable America: The Indians' Estate and Land Claims* (University of New Mexico Press, 1985) 57.

[6] These included opposition of the James Bay Cree to a massive hydroelectric development planned by the Quebec government. After the Cree commenced litigation, negotiations between the Canadian government, Quebec government and the Cree culminated in the 1975 James Bay Agreement.

[7] The case was *Mabo v Queensland (No 2)* (1992) 175 CLR 1 (HC) (*Mabo (No 2)*) and it led to the Native Title Act 1993 (Cth), discussed below.

[8] As discussed later, the protection of Māori culture, customs and traditional authority has also been an important part of the Tribunal's work. For the political climate leading up to the Treaty of Waitangi Act 1975 (TWA), see C Scholtz, 'Cabinet Decision-Making and Māori Land Rights in New Zealand (1944–1989)' in *Negotiating Claims: The Emergence of Indigenous Land Claim Negotiation Policies in Australia, Canada, New Zealand and the United States* (Routledge, 2006) 73.

lengthy, formalised and adversarial court procedures. In other cases, out-of-court dispute resolution processes have been mandated through court rules in an effort to reduce judicial case loads and speed up the disposition of legal claims. Because ADR processes are often used as substitutes for litigation, it is tempting to examine those processes from a purely legal perspective, comparing their outcomes to the verdicts that the courts might deliver.[9] To adopt such a frame of reference would be to overlook the distinct nature and purpose of ADR processes. The distinctiveness of alternative dispute resolution is that it permits parties to address their interests and the complexities of their dispute in a manner that reliance on legal values and the adversarial system cannot match.

Viewed on their own terms, the promise of ADR processes includes: allowing the parties themselves (rather than an outside decision-maker) to participate effectively in shaping the outcome and, accordingly, to increase the likelihood that the outcome will endure; allowing the parties to collaboratively explore areas of possible consensus rather than being reduced to presenting binary, adversarial positions; permitting the parties to avoid damage to valuable long-term relationships by avoiding the antagonism of adversarial approaches; having the parties themselves determine which procedural values and substantive considerations should influence the resolution; lowering costs by avoiding the formalities of the court process; and permitting the disputants to transcend the limitations of traditional judicial remedies in formulating forward-looking outcomes.

The term 'ADR' encompasses a variety of distinct and independent mechanisms, each of which is designed to achieve a particular subset of the above-mentioned goals. There are three prototypical ADR processes: arbitration (binding or non-binding), direct, unassisted negotiation, and negotiation assisted by a third party (a mediator or facilitator). Arbitration is a process whereby a third party to the dispute examines the merits of the parties' positions in accordance with criteria agreed to by the disputants and issues a ruling or recommendation after receiving submissions from the parties. Unassisted negotiation is a process whereby only the parties determine the agenda and format of the discussions, and the outcome is determined by the ability of each party to persuade the other that a proposed agreement is desirable and preferable to all of that party's alternatives. Finally, negotiations assisted by a third party (that is, mediation or facilitation) have the same characteristics as unassisted negotiation, except that here a third party, with no power to compel a particular outcome, steers the discussions in an effort to enhance the parties' communications and help them move towards agreement.

Each of these processes has its own strengths and limitations. Arbitration allows the parties to obtain an outcome that transcends their individual biases about the strength of their claim. Depending on the rules of the process, arbitration can offer the prospect of a guaranteed outcome, achieved in a process that is less formal and less expensive than court adjudication. Negotiation, on the other hand, privileges

[9] For a discussion of the 'shadow verdict' approach to assessing dispute resolution processes, see D Luban, 'The Quality of Justice' (1988–1989) 66 *Denver University Law Review* 381, 387–8.

the goal of maximising the role of the disputants in determining the nature and outcome of the process. Unlike arbitration, negotiation also offers the potential to achieve flexible and creative remedies, and, because the parties themselves developed the outcome, in principle negotiation increases the possibility that the outcome will be respected by the parties. However, negotiations can be protracted and adopting this process does not guarantee that the parties will achieve a timely and inexpensive resolution of their dispute, or indeed any resolution at all. Finally, while assisted negotiation holds the potential benefits of introducing the creative perspective and expertise of a relatively detached third party, there may be little that such a third party can do to address power imbalances at the table, to ensure that any negotiated agreement meets standards of fairness, or to ensure that the parties reach an agreement.

Recognising the particular strengths and weaknesses of each of these three processes, dispute resolution practitioners have long realised the possible advantages of creating other, 'hybrid' processes. That is, elements of the basic ADR models can be combined in such a way as to address the unique character of a dispute or to advance the particular goals of the parties to that dispute. In this way, parties who wish to take advantage of the strengths of negotiation but need to be assured of a timely outcome might choose a 'med-arb' process, providing for arbitration of some or all issues only if they remain unresolved after a specified period of mediation. Alternatively, parties can begin with arbitration as a preliminary step to determine whether a claim has merit, agreeing in advance that the arbitration outcome will form the basis of any ensuing negotiation. Yet again, disputants who are unwilling to allow a third party to determine their rights might agree to a negotiation process which allows them to obtain the non-binding views of a third party on outstanding issues if their negotiations reach an impasse. By combining process elements in these and other ways, the parties can ensure that their dispute is addressed in a manner that is specifically tailored to their needs, values and goals.

The ADR processes that have evolved to address indigenous rights disputes inevitably reflect the values, goals and power relations of the parties that created those processes. Thus, a process that relies heavily on binding arbitration might be expected if the party that dominated its creation is primarily interested in eliminating outstanding disputes in a final and rapid manner. The use of binding arbitration is also likely to involve the application of prevailing domestic law and to exclude indigenous values in its procedures and substantive rules. In contrast, an ADR process that privileges negotiation to address indigenous rights is more likely to arise where settler governments and indigenous peoples are committed to the respect for both parties' traditions and values. On the other hand, privileging negotiation means that both parties' leaders must be prepared to take political responsibility of the outcome and for the possibility that any consensual outcome may be a long time coming.[10] Finally, the inclusion of mechanisms for resolving

[10] For an interesting discussion of the variables that may affect policy makers in deciding whether to negotiate indigenous claims, see Scholtz, above n 8, 13–34.

impasses in a process dominated by negotiation may be expected where both parties are able to insist on a combination of flexibility and timeliness in the resolution of indigenous rights disputes.

It will be seen that Australia, New Zealand and Canada have each implemented hybrid ADR processes to address indigenous rights disputes. New Zealand has adopted a direct negotiation model, but negotiations begin only after claims are filed with an independent tribunal which has the power to hold hearings and make recommendations about the merits and implications of the claims. Canada has for several decades preferred direct, unassisted negotiation of First Nation land claims, but recently created an independent tribunal with the power to arbitrate in certain cases. For its part, Australia has implemented a model which involves an adjudicative role for the courts overlying mandatory mediation in some cases, and in other cases arbitration by a statutory tribunal if direct negotiations fail. Only the US chose to adopt a 'pure' ADR model, creating a court-like tribunal endowed with the power to arbitrate Indian land claims.

3. A Framework for Analysing ADR Processes that Address Indigenous Rights

How might one meaningfully compare the out-of-court alternatives for addressing indigenous land rights in each of these jurisdictions? The choice of lens is an important one. This analysis will focus on four reference points that address, in turn, the role of negotiation or mediation in the process, the nature of the outcomes produced, its robustness in the face of power imbalances, and the extent to which the process incorporates the various disputants' values. For the reasons that follow, each of these issues is likely to be important in disputes involving indigenous land rights.

(a) Role of Negotiation or Mediation in the Process

The complex and polycentric nature of disputes about historical indigenous land rights suggests that flexibility of process and outcome will be required if both parties are to embrace a proposed method for resolving such disputes.[11] As will be seen, one can expect significant differences between the perspectives of indigenous peoples and settler governments as to the appropriate values for determining the validity of an indigenous claim. This diminishes the likelihood that any predetermined set of discrete criteria that might be applied by a third party arbitrator will suffice to resolve such disputes. Similarly, the interest of indigenous parties in obtaining recognition of ongoing relationships to land and resources, combined with settler governments' preference that any such recognition not disturb existing private property rights, means that outcomes are best determined after careful

[11] In other words, the forum should 'fit the fuss'. See Emond, above n 4, 10–11.

consideration by both parties of the complex 'situation on the ground' and available options for the future. Each of these considerations point to negotiation and mediation as process elements that should be useful in resolving indigenous rights disputes.

Other factors reinforce the suitability of using negotiation or mediation to address indigenous rights claims. The complexity of the historical record, written and unwritten, does not lend itself easily to the evidentiary process of courts. Historic damage to the relationship between the parties is likely better addressed by face-to-face discussions than by the adversarial positioning typical of courts and arbitration processes. Negotiation and mediation also offer the prospect of returning to a tradition of diplomacy rather than relying on a process of colonial imposition similar to the processes that marginalised indigenous peoples in the past.

(b) Outcomes Produced

If, as suggested above, flexibility of outcome is an important factor in recognising the ongoing cultural, material and spiritual ties of indigenous peoples to land and resources, it will be useful to examine whether existing ADR processes, however configured, have in fact produced a diverse range of outcomes. After all, even where negotiation or mediation plays a central role in claims resolution, the parties may have fixed preconceptions about the types of outcomes they would be prepared to consider. In the same vein, it will be useful to examine the number of disputes resolved to date by the process and the timeliness of the process in resolving claims.

(c) Robustness in the Face of Power Imbalances

The use of ADR processes to address legal disputes invariably raises concerns that power disparities between the parties may unduly influence the outcome. This is a particularly significant issue in indigenous rights disputes. Without the guarantee of independent judicial assessment of the facts and the evidentiary protections of the judicial process, the question arises as to how, and indeed whether, a particular ADR process counterbalances the possibility that a more powerful party will be able to impose its will on the weaker. One influential legal analyst takes this concern so seriously that he has argued that negotiation is never an appropriate process for the determination of legal rights.[12] 'Power' in negotiation derives from several sources, including access to resources and the parties' respective access to equally acceptable alternatives to a negotiated outcome.[13] Such factors may place

[12] See OM Fiss, 'Against Settlement' (1984) 93 *Yale Law Journal* 1073.

[13] For a general discussion of power in negotiation, see RS Adler and EM Silverstein, 'When David Meets Goliath: Dealing with Power Differentials in Negotiations' (2000) 5 *Harvard Negotiation Law Review* 1; M Coyle, 'The Dynamics of Power in Negotiation' in C Hanycz, T Farrow and F Zemans (eds), *The Theory and Practice of Representative Negotiation: A Book of Readings* (Emond-Montgomery, 2007) 159.

indigenous groups at a disadvantage in rights negotiations with states, a disadvantage that the addition of a third-party mediator will typically be incapable of removing completely.[14] Accordingly, in the context of the ADR processes considered here, it is worthwhile to consider whether those processes include any elements capable of countering pre-existing power imbalances between the parties.

(d) Values Incorporated by the Process

Last, it is important to consider whether a process created to resolve disputes about indigenous rights recognises and incorporates indigenous values as well as non-indigenous values. This is not simply a question of participant satisfaction: a dispute resolution process can only be effective in resolving grievances to the extent that it addresses the underlying conflict as perceived by the parties themselves.[15] A key challenge in designing ADR institutions relating to indigenous rights is that government and settler society perspectives on the nature of the dispute and the values that should govern its resolution are often very different. As far as *outcomes* are concerned, marginalised indigenous peoples frequently seek ongoing participation in decision-making, not just historical determination of past rights; they often seek recognition and respect (for example, through an apology and public narrative of the wrong done) as much as a financial outcome; they may seek recognition of their ongoing relationship to land (something courts, for example, cannot generally provide) rather than money and termination of their relationship to the land. Finally, they may prefer a *process* that brings together their own values and those of the settler society, not merely the application of settler rules and procedures to the dispute.

In contrast, non-indigenous governments often favour dispute resolution processes that reflect differing values and goals. They may expect as a matter of course that 'the law of the land' should determine the legitimacy of indigenous concerns, and that grievances recognised as legitimate be categorised and evaluated in the same way, without reference to indigenous values or laws. Typically, non-indigenous governments will seek finality ('extinguishment' of indigenous rights) as the appropriate *quid pro quo* for settling indigenous claims. They will prefer outcomes, like cash awards, that do not threaten private property interests. Finally, the non-indigenous public may consider the purpose of the ADR process to be an accounting for discrete misdemeanours in the past, in contrast to indigenous peoples, for whom it may be critically important that the ADR process repair

[14] See M Coyle, 'Defending the Weak and Fighting Unfairness: Can Mediators Respond to the Challenge?' (1998) 36 *Osgoode Hall Law Journal* 625.

[15] Grievances reflect human understandings of and emotional reactions to a perceived set of facts and norms; accordingly, the grievance underlying a legal dispute invariably transcends any legal framework for categorising the conflict. See WLF Felstiner, RL Abel and A Sarat, 'The Emergence and Transformation of Disputes: Naming, Blaming, Claiming . . .' (1980–1981) 15(3/4) *Law and Society Review* 631; and D Kahane, 'What Is Culture? Generalizing about Aboriginal and Newcomer Perspectives' in C Bell and D Kahane (eds), *Intercultural Dispute Resolution in Aboriginal Contexts* (UBC Press, 2004) 28.

systemic legal marginalisation and recognise indigenous peoples as important partners in a pluralistic modern collectivity.

Major differences in goals and worldviews are to be expected, then, in disputes about indigenous land rights. An ADR process that recognises this and accommodates the interests and perspectives of both parties is more likely to be judged as fair by both parties and to produce outcomes that endure.

Before examining the Australian, Canadian and New Zealand ADR processes with each of these perspectives in mind, it is helpful to review the contours of a key predecessor process—that of the US Indian Claims Commission. The now discontinued US process and its outcomes informed each of the other jurisdictions' choice of ADR process. The American model serves as a distinct, and therefore analytically useful, counterpoint to the ADR processes adopted in the other jurisdictions.

B: The United States: The Historic Indian Claims Commission Experience

A famous American legal commentator described the treaty-making process in the US as the 'largest real estate transaction in history'.[16] The period between 1784 and 1894 witnessed some 720 treaties and other agreements involving indigenous peoples and nearly two billion acres of land.[17] The history of American expansion is, of course, a controversial one, and in many cases tribal lands were acquired through forcible relocation, military engagement, settler encroachment and other non-consensual means, as Richardson explains in his Chapter in this book.[18] At the same time, significant barriers were placed in the way of Indian tribes wishing to dispute their dispossession in the courts.[19] By 1946, although most tribal claims involving land could be litigated only through special jurisdictional legislation,[20] a large number of tribal claims were advancing through the courts.[21]

[16] FS Cohen, *The Legal Conscience* (Yale University Press, 1960) 69. Elsewhere, Cohen indicates that a conservative estimate of the total price paid by the United States would place the number somewhere in excess of US$800 million. See FS Cohen, 'Original Indian Title' (1947–1948) 32 *Minnesota Law Review* 28, 36.

[17] The last formal treaty made by the American federal government was ratified in 1868. See Rosenthal, above n 5, 36.

[18] Blumenthal has suggested that 'it would be difficult, indeed, to find a land cession made by the Indians entirely of their own volition': see WH Blumenthal, *American Indians Dispossessed: Fraud in Land Cessions Forced Upon the Tribes* (GS MacManus, 1955) 43.

[19] In 1863 all Indian claims based on treaty violations were excluded from the US Court of Claims. See Rosenthal, above n 5, 38. Thereafter, until the passage of the Indian Claims Commission Act (ICCA) in 1946, treaty claims could be brought to the Court of Claims only by special congressional legislation. See Rosenthal, above n 5, 39–41.

[20] By the 1940s, a total of 142 such acts had been passed: MH Pierce, 'The Work of the Indian Claims Commission' (1977) 63 *ABA Journal* 227, 229.

[21] Indian Claims Commission, *Final Report*, 96th Congress, 2nd Sess, 1978 (House Document No 96: 383) 2–3 ('ICC Final Report').

In 1946, after decades of debate about the merits of creating a special process to expedite the resolution of tribal claims,[22] the US Congress created the Indian Claims Commission (ICC). The Act that gave jurisdiction to the ICC (the 'ICC Act')[23] authorised the ICC to address a wide range of historical claims against the US government.[24] Although the ICC Act primarily focused on legal claims against the government, it also authorised the ICC to hear claims 'based upon fair and honorable dealings' that were not recognised by any existing rule of law or equity.[25] On the other hand, all claims had to be filed with the ICC within five years of the ICC Act coming into force, or be forever barred from consideration by any court, administrative agency or by Congress.[26]

The process created by the ICC Act did not explicitly give negotiation any role in the resolution of Indian claims. The Act empowered the ICC to arbitrate claims, granting parties the right to be heard and to present evidence.[27] Although the Act authorised the ICC to determine the appropriate procedures to be used in resolving claims,[28] the ICC chose to adopt court-like procedures and lawyers came to dominate its proceedings.[29] As a result, ICC hearings proved to be so complex, protracted and adversarial.[30]

While the ICC was not a court, its process scarcely resembled a true alternative. If its process came to resemble that of a complex arbitration that turned outstanding land rights claims into cash awards, this appears to have fit closely with the goals of Congress and the bureaucrats who staffed the ICC. Even the final report of the ICC, issued in 1978, stated that the twin goals of its process involved 'giving the Indian his due' while 'giving him his walking papers'.[31] Hearings were rarely held on Indian reservations and little special effort appears to have been made to address with sensitivity the testimony of elders and oral traditions,[32] or

[22] Indian Claims Commission, *Final Report*, 96th Congress, 2nd Sess, 1978 (House Document No 96: 383) 3–5; SC Danforth, 'Repaying Historical Debts: The Indian Claims Commission' (1972–1973) 49 *North Dakota Law Review* 359, 360–70.

[23] ICCA ss 1–28, ch 959, 60 Stat 1049 (repealed 1978)).

[24] Section 2 of the ICCA authorised the ICC to determine all claims in law or equity arising under the US Constitution, laws, treaties and executive orders, including claims that treaties should be reviewed on the grounds of fraud, duress or mistake and claims for the taking of lands without agreed compensation.

[25] *Ibid*, s 2, cl 5.

[26] *Ibid*, s 12. Claims arising after the ICCA came into force could be brought to the Court of Claims: ICCA, s 24.

[27] *Ibid*, s 17.

[28] *Ibid*, s 9.

[29] For the ICC's view that it should follow court procedures, see ICC Final Report, above n 21, 7.

[30] See Danforth, above n 22, 370–83. Some of the responsibility for delays is attributable to the approach of US government lawyers, who reportedly asked for more than 5,000 time extensions of pleading deadlines between 1951 and 1955: see W Churchill, 'Charades, Anyone? The Indian Claims Commission in Context' (2000) 24(1) *American Indian Culture and Research Journal* 43, 54.

[31] ICC Final Report, above n 21, 14.

[32] See D Wishart, 'Belated Justice? The Indian Claims Commission and the Waitangi Tribunal' (2001) 25(1) *American Indian Culture and Research Journal* 81, 97.

the possibility of any continuing relationship between an Indian tribe and the lands under dispute.[33]

By the time the ICC wound up in 1978 it had issued 274 awards, totalling some US$818 million.[34] It had rejected 204 Indian claims and it had transferred 68 uncompleted claims to the Court of Claims.[35] The majority of filed claims related to takings of tribal land, although the ICC Act itself had not limited the subject matter of eligible claims.[36] The typical ICC file involved a claim for additional compensation for a historic taking of tribal land that occurred without payment that adequately reflected the fair market value of the tribal land at the time it was taken.[37] Other files involved claims that the government had mismanaged tribal funds or had failed to provide other benefits (like annuity payments) stipulated by treaty. In the end, only financial remedies were ever provided to successful claimants.[38] In every case, final determination by the ICC had the effect of barring any future claims against the US relating to the dispute.[39]

While one can debate whether the ICC process delivered financial outcomes in line with what judicial resolution would have provided, it is not debatable that the ICC process left no room for the recognition of indigenous cultural values. The criteria used to determine the validity of claimed rights and the appropriate remedy for rights infringement were imposed by non-indigenous courts. So, too, the processes adopted by the ICC were informed entirely by non-indigenous administrative and judicial procedures. The reduction of potentially valid ongoing land rights claims to *per capita* dollar payments could be (and was) seen as a method of undermining political and cultural integrity.[40] Finally, the blindness of the ICC process to tribal values was reflected in the appointment process for its adjudicators. The latter were appointed exclusively by non-indigenous elected representatives,[41] and the appointment process privileged appointees who were ignorant of the context of indigenous rights claims.[42] In fact, the first indigenous appointment to the ICC did not occur until 1969, 23 years after the ICC was created.[43]

[33] For a critique that attributes this result, at least in part, to the desire of lawyers representing tribes to obtain monetary settlements from which they could be paid, see DH Getches, CF Wilkinson, and RA Williams Jr (eds), *Cases and Materials on Federal Indian Law, Fourth Edition* (West Group, 1998) 280, 283–4.

[34] ICC Final Report, above n 21, 125.

[35] *Ibid.*

[36] Danforth, above n 22, 389.

[37] *Ibid*, 387–95.

[38] For a summary of the awards granted, see ICC Final Report, above n 21, 125. For most of the duration of the ICCA, such awards were provided through per capita payments to tribal members. The average such payment amounted to less than US$1,000: Wishart, above n 32, 100.

[39] ICCA, s 22.

[40] Rosenthal, above n 5, 54–7. Some tribes, like the Lakotas, rejected awards that were premised on severing their relationship to their traditional land: see Wishart, above n 32, 101.

[41] ICCA, s 3(a).

[42] NO Lurie, 'Epilogue' in Sutton, above n 5, 384.

[43] McHugh, above n 2, 554.

Turning to the impact of power relations on the ICC process, it is evident from the exclusion of indigenous values from the structure and processes of the ICC Act that the US government was able to impose its own views on the legitimate criteria for resolving indigenous claims. This in turn reflected the litigation alternatives available in 1946, with tribes being limited both in their access to the US courts for rights claims and in the extent to which their land rights were recognised by the courts. If, therefore, the tribes' judicial alternatives were weak, the effect of the ICC Act in eliminating their recourse to the courts left them weaker still. Finally, the ICC process as implemented did not provide funding for tribes wishing to advance their claims. The tribes were left dependent on lawyers willing to work for contingency fees. In turn, they faced the formidable resources of the US Justice Department—which proved willing to spend an amount equal to one quarter of the value of all claims settlements in resisting the claims.[44]

For all the opportunities to address indigenous rights claims in a flexible and culturally even-handed manner that were missed in the ICC experience, this was the first systematic indigenous dispute resolution process adopted in any of the jurisdictions under consideration here. As we have seen, its limitations were those of an arbitration process created with a view to achieving finality[45] but failing to recognise the values and perspectives of the parties whose grievances were intended to be resolved. As such, the ICC process forms a useful backdrop for analysing whether Canada, Australia and New Zealand have made more effective use of ADR's potential for accommodating indigenous interests and addressing indigenous rights in a manner respectful of both sides' values.

C. ADR Processes in Canada, New Zealand and Australia

1. The Role of Negotiation or Mediation in the Process

We have seen that the incorporation of negotiation or mediation into a dispute resolution process gives parties with divergent perspectives the opportunity to create a process and outcome that reflects both sides' interests and values. It also offers hope that the outcome will be more enduring than an outcome imposed by one side alone, and that the way the outcome is achieved will be consistent with the goal of ending the subordination of indigenous peoples by settler systems of law. Of course, it is the disposition of the parties that will determine whether the

[44] Churchill, above n 30, 55.

[45] In fact, the ICC process did not finally terminate all tribal land claims in the US. The 1980s and 1990s saw a number of special jurisdictional Acts authorising individual tribes to bring additional land claims. Many of these claims have since been resolved through negotiated settlements involving the setting aside of lands as well as compensation. See McHugh, above n 2, 557–9.

process meets that potential. Australia, Canada and New Zealand each have created a space for the negotiation or mediation of indigenous land rights disputes. The next sections will describe the basic elements of the ADR processes in each jurisdiction. In doing so, they will situate negotiation in relation to the overall ADR process for resolving indigenous rights disputes, and identify other elements likely to enhance the effectiveness of negotiations.

(a) Canada

Canada was the first of the three jurisdictions to adopt a nation-wide framework for negotiating indigenous land claims. Hundreds of treaties and land agreements had been negotiated in what is now Canada between 1764 and 1929, as Walters explains in another Chapter in this book.[46] Disputes had arisen about the implementation of those treaties, and in particular about Crown mismanagement of First Nation land and trust funds. Further, vast areas of Canada (including most of British Columbia, the Northwest Territories, the Yukon, Quebec and the Maritime provinces) had never seen the negotiation of a treaty that addressed aboriginal title rights. Still, it was not until the mid-1970s that the federal government took steps to create a process for addressing indigenous land disputes. Various factors contributed to the government's decision, including the mobilisation of Indian organisations to resist a federal proposal to abolish Indian status,[47] the decision of the Supreme Court of Canada in *Calder* recognising aboriginal title,[48] and the issuing of an injunction by the Quebec Superior Court to prevent construction of a massive hydro project in northern Quebec.[49]

Bypassing earlier recommendations to create a binding tribunal to address indigenous land claims,[50] the federal government announced in 1973 that it was willing to negotiate the resolution of those claims. To do so it developed two formal negotiation policies. The 'Specific Claims Policy' authorised the government to negotiate claims that it had breached a treaty promise relating to land, mismanaged First Nations land or assets, or violated a statutory obligation to a First Nation.[51] The 'Comprehensive Claims Policy' authorised the federal government to negotiate claims of unextinguished aboriginal title.[52] Essentially, both policies

[46] OP Dickason, *Canada's First Nations: A History of Founding Peoples from Earliest Times* (2nd edn, Oxford University Press 1997) 248.

[47] The so-called 'White Paper' proposed to eliminate distinct 'Indian' legal status and repeal the *Indian Act*: Government of Canada, *Statement of the Government of Canada on Indian Policy, 1969* (Queen's Printer, 1969).

[48] *Calder v Attorney-General of British Columbia* [1973] SCR 313.

[49] *Kanatewat v James Bay Development Corporation* [1973] QJ No 8 (Que SC), rev'd, [1973] 3 CELN 19 (Que CA), leave to appeal refused, [1975] 1 SCR 48.

[50] Special Joint Committee of the Senate and House of Commons, *Minutes of Proceedings and Evidence*, No 41, 9 July 1947, Recommendation 2; Joint Committee of the Senate and the House of Commons on the *Indian Act, Minutes of Proceedings*, No 16, 30 May–7 July 1961.

[51] Department of Indian and Northern Affairs Canada, *Outstanding Business: A Native Claims Policy* (Department of Indian Affairs and Northern Development, 1982) ('*Specific Claims Policy*').

[52] Department of Indian and Northern Affairs Canada, *In All Fairness: A Native Claims Policy-Comprehensive Claims* (Department of Indian Affairs and Northern Development, 1981; amended 1986).

call for the federal government to negotiate claims if the federal government is satisfied that the claim demonstrated an unfulfilled legal obligation on the part of the government. Because of Canada's federal structure,[53] specific claims negotiations often involve the province as an additional party,[54] particularly where a First Nation seeks the return of Crown lands, or asserts that a province's historical actions have also interfered with its land rights. For its part, the comprehensive claims policy requires that the relevant province or territory participate in the negotiations, and in British Columbia a permanent and distinct tripartite process has been created, under the aegis of a jointly appointed treaty commission. Established in 1992, the BC Treaty Commission (BCTC) assesses the readiness of the parties to negotiate, allocates negotiation funding to First Nations, monitors and reports on the progress of negotiations and, if requested by all parties, may facilitate negotiation meetings or otherwise assist them to resolve disputes.[55]

The past few years have also seen a rapid increase in a third type of formal dialogue across the country between governments and aboriginal groups. These involve ad hoc consultations about proposed government decisions that have the potential to adversely affect claimed aboriginal rights in relation to specific lands or resources. They are the result of the 2004 Supreme Court decision in *Haida Nation*,[56] which ruled that the Crown must consult with aboriginal groups whenever it proposes to take an action that may interfere with existing aboriginal or treaty rights,[57] even where those rights have not yet been finally determined. The result of *Haida Nation* was to increase the urgency that each province and territory, as well as the federal government, develop its own consultation policy that meets the *Haida Nation* requirements.[58]

Until recently, these three formal discussion processes generally unfolded outside the context of ADR mechanisms capable of resolving impasses that might

[53] While the federal government has exclusive jurisdiction over 'Indians and Lands reserved for the Indians' (Constitution Act, 1867 (UK), 30–31 Vict, c 3, s 91, reprinted in RSC 1985, App II, No 5) Canadian provinces own the vast majority of Crown lands, and have jurisdiction over natural resources and management and sale of Crown lands, within provincial boundaries.

[54] Each province's participation is governed by its own independent claims policy.

[55] While federal participation in the BCTC process originates in the comprehensive claims policy, the BC process has some distinct features, quite apart from the facilitative role of the BCTC. See Department of Indian and Northern Affairs Canada, General Briefing Note on the Comprehensive Land Claims Policy of Canada and the Status of Claims ((Department of Indian Affairs and Northern Development, March 2007) 32–5. For a recent independent review of the BCTC process, see Auditor General of Canada, 'Chapter 7, Federal Participation in the British Columbia Treaty Process' in *November 2006 Report of the Auditor General of Canada to the House of Commons* (Minister of Public Works Canada, 2006).

[56] *Haida Nation*, above n 2, paras 35–8, making clear that the duty to consult set out in *R v Sparrow* [1990] 1 SCR 1075 ('*Sparrow*') extends beyond proven aboriginal or treaty rights.

[57] Constitution Act, 1982, s 35, being Sch B to the Canada Act 1982 (UK), 1982, c 11, protects 'existing aboriginal and treaty rights'.

[58] The development of such policies is still far from complete, as demonstrated by the recent imprisonment of eight aboriginal leaders in Ontario and the response of the Ontario Court of Appeal thereto: see *Frontenac* and *Platinex*, above n 1.

arise at the bargaining table.[59] In other words, unassisted negotiation was the norm across the country. The absence of impartial out-of-court mechanisms for resolving claims disputes has been the subject of considerable criticism by independent commentators.[60] Responding to those concerns in the context of the 'specific claims' process, in the summer of 2008, the federal government enacted the Specific Claims Tribunal Act (SCTA).[61] Henceforth, a statutory tribunal will be empowered to make binding decisions about the validity of treaty and other 'specific claims' and the compensation payable under valid claims.[62] The Specific Claims Tribunal has yet to produce a body of decisions. However, it will have no jurisdiction to hear claims where a First Nation seeks the transfer of land or any other non-monetary remedy, or to grant compensation in a single claim exceeding C$150 million.[63] Nor will the tribunal have jurisdiction over aboriginal title claims, or claims to ongoing treaty rights.[64] In all these cases, unassisted negotiation with the Crown will remain the general rule in Canada.[65]

(b) New Zealand

New Zealand has developed a more systematic approach to the review and negotiation of indigenous rights claims. The focus of both parties in those negotiations is the Treaty of Waitangi, entered into by Governor Hobson on behalf of the British and over 500 Māori chiefs in 1840.[66] The Treaty was expressed in separate Māori and English texts. Depending on the text, the Crown acquired either 'sovereignty' or *kawanatanga* (roughly, governorship) over Māori lands, while the Māori chiefs retained *tino rangatiratanga* (roughly, chieftainship) over their lands, properties and *taonga* (roughly, treasures).[67]

As explained further in Ruru's Chapter in this book, the period from 1840 to the 1970s saw widespread disregard for the treaty by non-Māori governments and

[59] As noted earlier, the BC Treaty Commission oversees aboriginal title negotiations in British Columbia, but its mandate is facilitative and to date its direct involvement in ongoing negotiations has been limited. The mandates of two other facilitative claims bodies, the tripartite Indian Commission of Ontario and the federal Indian Specific Claims Commission (ISCC) expired in 2000 and 2008 respectively. At the time of writing it appears that the federal government may re-establish the ISCC to offer mediation services in support of a renewed effort to resolve specific claims. See 'Justice at Last: Specific Claims Action Plan', 6, at www.ainc-inac.gc.ca/ps/clm/scb-eng.asp ('Justice at Last').

[60] See Canada, *Report of the Royal Commission on Aboriginal Peoples: Restructuring the Relationship*, vol 2 (Supply and Services Canada, 1996) 596; GV La Forest, *Report on Administrative Processes for the Resolution of Specific Indian Claims* (Department of Indian Affairs and Northern Development, 1979) 33.

[61] RSC 2008, c 22.

[62] *Ibid*, s 16(1), s 20(1).

[63] *Ibid*, s 15(4), s 20(1).

[64] *Ibid*, s 15(1)(f), (g).

[65] This may ultimately change in relation to specific claims, depending on the degree to which the federal government implements its commitment of 12 June 2007 to make greater use of mediation in the process. See Justice at Last, above n 59.

[66] For a description of the Treaty and its background see Te Puni Kÿkiri, *He Tirohanga ÿ Kawa kit e Tiriti o Waitangi* (Te Puni Kÿkiri, 2001).

[67] For the texts of the treaty, see TWA sch 1.

courts[68] and the dispossession of Māori from most of their lands and resources.[69] Growing Māori anger at the loss of their lands and government indifference to Māori culture and *tino rangatiratanga*, led to the mobilisation of 30,000 protesters in the 'Land March' of 1975,[70] which contributed to the enacting of the original Treaty of Waitangi Act 1975.

The Act created a new permanent commission of inquiry, known as the Waitangi Tribunal, to investigate Māori claims that a government statute, policy, or practice was inconsistent with the principles of the Treaty. In 1985, the Act was amended to extend the jurisdiction of the Tribunal to all such grievances dating back to the time of the Treaty.[71] The Act authorises the Tribunal to hold inquiries into claims made by any Māori that he or she is likely to be prejudicially affected by a government act or omission alleged to be inconsistent with the principles of the Treaty and to issue reports and recommendations to the Crown.[72] Unlike the formal Canadian ADR processes, the Act authorises the Waitangi Tribunal to hear claims that do not directly relate to the loss of land—many claims filed with the Tribunal have focused exclusively on other subjects, including fishing, language and cultural rights. Its recommendations are generally non-binding, although the Tribunal is authorised to make binding recommendations in relation to the return of certain lands to Māori ownership.[73] The Act also grants the Tribunal jurisdiction to examine proposed legislation referred to it by the House of Representatives or a Minister of the Crown for its opinion on whether the legislation would conform to the principles of the Treaty.[74]

The work of the Waitangi Tribunal meshes closely with the negotiation of treaty claims in New Zealand between the Crown and Māori representatives. The Tribunal seeks to group and investigate claims on a systematic basis, often reviewing similar claims together and grouping claims geographically. Current government policy is that all claims must be registered initially with the Tribunal before direct negotiations with the Crown can begin. In general, negotiated claims first go through a Tribunal hearing and report, which serves as the background for negotiations with the Crown.[75] Tribunal hearings have two stages. The first inquires into the validity of the Māori claim. The second stage, which is engaged if the parties are not yet willing to negotiate or if negotiations have failed, involves the Tribunal holding a hearing and issuing recommendations on appropriate

[68] *Wi Parata v Bishop of Wellington* (1878) 3 NZ Jur (NS) SC 72 had ruled the Treaty a 'nullity' under New Zealand law, while the combination of government confiscations in the 19th century and a series of Native Land Acts dramatically reduced the Māori land base.

[69] Today, just under 5% of New Zealand is designated as Māori freehold land. See www.justice.govt.nz/Māorilandcourt/aboutmlc.htm.

[70] See Scholtz, above n 8.

[71] TWA, s 6. The deadline for filing a historical Treaty claim was 1 September 2008: TWA, s 6AA.

[72] *Ibid.*

[73] See the State-Owned Enterprises Act 1986 (NZ) s 27B; Crown Forest Assets Act 1989 (NZ) s 36.

[74] TWA, s 8.

[75] MTW Love, 'The Waitangi Tribunal's Roles in the Dispute Resolution of Indigenous (Māori) Treaty Claims' in C Bell and D Kahane (eds), *Intercultural Dispute Resolution in Aboriginal Contexts* (UBC Press, 2004) 132–5.

remedies for the claim.[76] Finally, independent of the parties' ability to enter direct negotiations, the Act gives the Tribunal the power to refer parties to mediation at any time.[77]

The use of a neutral independent body to act as a gatekeeper and reviewer of indigenous rights claims distinguishes the New Zealand process from Canada, where claims (and particularly specific claims) tend to be reviewed and negotiated in a haphazard order,[78] depending on when they are filed. In particular, the approach of the Waitangi Tribunal in aggregating and consolidating claims by region and subject matter allows claims to be researched and addressed in a more efficient and consistent manner.[79] After the Tribunal's initial recommendations, however, most claims are negotiated directly with the Crown Office of Treaty Settlements in accordance with the Crown's negotiation policies, with little participation by the Tribunal or other neutrals. More will be said about the Crown's policies, and the constraints they place on the outcomes that can be negotiated, in the discussion of 'Power' below.

(c) Australia

The Australian approach to indigenous rights disputes is unique in that it is the only jurisdiction where, depending on the type of dispute, federal legislation *requires* the Crown to enter either negotiation or mediation. Thus, for example, Aboriginal and Torres Strait Islanders have a statutory right to negotiate where a state or the Commonwealth government proposes to engage in certain acts that would affect lands to which they have an aboriginal title claim.[80] As for applications to have aboriginal title confirmed in a specific area, these are subject to mandatory mediation by the National Native Title Tribunal (NNTT).[81] These dispute resolution processes are somewhat limited in scope, however, as the combined effect of Australian case law and applicable federal legislation dramatically restricts the types of land on which aboriginal title might be claimed.[82]

The Commonwealth's Native Title Act 1993 (NTA), which sets out the rules for these dispute resolution processes, was enacted in response to the decision of the

[76] *Ibid*, 134.

[77] TWA, Sch 2, ss 9A–9D.

[78] At least with regard to the progress of negotiations, the treaty process in British Columbia is an exception here, as the BCTC is mandated to determine the readiness of all parties to proceed to the next stage of negotiations.

[79] An example is the Tribunal's commissioning of a comprehensive national overview of the Crown's historical dealings with Māori lands: A Ward, *Rangahaua Whanui National Overview Report*, 3 vols (Waitangi Tribunal, 1997).

[80] NTA, s 25–44. Note that 'aboriginal title' is used here for consistency; in Australia the term used is 'native title'.

[81] NTA, s 86B. The mediation right is subject to certain limited exceptions: NTA s 86B(3). In Australia the term used for aboriginal title is 'native title'.

[82] See the website of the NNTT: www.nntt.gov.au/publications/1036375662_1544.html. In essence, all Crown dispositions of property interests prior to 1994 override aboriginal title to the extent of the inconsistency between the two. For the evolution of the common law and federal legislation with respect to aboriginal land rights in Australia, see McNeil's Chapter in this book.

Australian High Court in *Mabo (No 2)*.[83] That decision had overturned more than a century of Australian jurisprudence to the effect that aboriginal peoples in Australia had no ancestral rights to their land.[84] With the NTA, the Commonwealth government sought belatedly to implement Australia's first nation-wide framework for addressing aboriginal title claims.[85] The framework set out in the NTA was the product of intense consultations among state, federal and aboriginal leaders and representatives of the non-indigenous community.[86] In essence, that framework validated previous government interferences with aboriginal title that could have been questioned pursuant to *Mabo (No 2)*,[87] while in return offering aboriginal claimants the right to be consulted about future governmental actions that might interfere with the exercise of remaining aboriginal title rights.[88]

The NTA created three processes for resolving conflicts over indigenous land rights. First, all claims of unextinguished aboriginal title must be filed with the Federal Court and (subject to passing certain registration requirements relating to the claimant's connection to the land[89]) are generally submitted to mandatory mediation conducted by the NNTT. The NTA requires the parties to the mediation to negotiate in good faith,[90] and allows the NNTT to refer questions of fact or law that may arise to the Federal Court.[91] If the mediation succeeds, a report is filed with the Federal Court, which must approve any agreement to recognise aboriginal title.[92] If the parties fail to reach agreement, the claim returns for a trial and final determination by the Federal Court.[93]

The second process created by the NTA involves applications by a government for permission to engage in certain 'future acts' that may infringe existing aboriginal title. In general, government proposals to grant or renew mining rights or to expropriate aboriginal title interests for the benefit of a third party trigger an aboriginal 'right to negotiate'.[94] Such acts are deemed invalid unless the government has given notice of its intentions as required under the NTA and (if the notice is opposed) has engaged in good faith negotiations aimed at securing the agreement

[83] *Mabo (No 2)*, above n 7.

[84] This conclusion was confirmed as late as 1971 in *Milirrpum v Nabalco* (1971) 17 FLR 141.

[85] New South Wales, South Australia and the Northern Territory had previously legislated to address aboriginal rights, as discussed in Clarke's Chapter in this book.

[86] Scholtz, above n 8, 140–5.

[87] The judgments in *Mabo (No 2)* concluded that legislation, as well as Crown acts in relation to land and resources, were effective to override aboriginal title and generally did not give rise to an aboriginal right of compensation. However, the judgments raised questions about the validity of any such acts that followed the enactment of the Racial Discrimination Act 1975 (Cth).

[88] NTA, s 11 provides that no future government act can extinguish aboriginal title unless the government complies with the NTA, including its 'right to negotiate' provisions described below.

[89] *Ibid*, ss 190A–190C.

[90] *Ibid*, s 136B(4).

[91] *Ibid*, s 136D.

[92] *Ibid*, ss 87, 225.

[93] *Ibid*, ss 86B, 86C.

[94] *Ibid*, ss 25–44. Note that as a result of the 1998 amendments to the NTA, in some cases the right to negotiate is replaced by a lesser right to be consulted, as in the case of certain mining activities: see ss 26A, 26B.

of native title claimants and interested third parties regarding the terms by which the government may proceed.[95] Any party to the negotiations may require that the discussions be mediated by a neutral body.[96] Finally, if the 'future act' negotiations fail to reach agreement, the decision whether to permit the government's act will be resolved through arbitration.[97]

The 'right to negotiate' provisions are subject to three major limitations. First, the aboriginal right to negotiate only guarantees a six-month window for negotiations before the other parties have a right to apply for arbitration by the NNTT.[98] Second, any arbitral decision can be overruled by a State, Territory or Commonwealth minister who considers the proposed act to be in the state or national interest![99] Third, governments may avoid the 'right to negotiate' provisions wherever the proposed act is declared to be in the state or national interest and is not likely to directly interfere with the rights of native title holders, or to involve a major disturbance to the lands or waters affected.[100] On the other hand, the NTA provides a measure of protection to native title interests even where future acts are permitted to proceed, stipulating that in most cases the permitted act will only suspend aboriginal title interests, not extinguish them.[101]

The third dispute resolution process recognised by the NTA involves the negotiation of Indigenous Land Use Agreements (ILUAs). Regardless of the status of any native title or future acts approval processes, aboriginal groups and other interested parties (including mining and pastoral interests) may voluntarily reach agreements at any time on arrangements for the use and management of lands to which the aboriginal groups claim a connection. The NTA allows for aboriginal representative bodies, or the NNTT, to assist in such negotiations on request from the parties.[102]

2. The Impact of Power

We have seen that, unlike the US, Australia, New Zealand and Canada have all placed negotiation (whether assisted by a third party or not) at the centre of their indigenous dispute resolution processes. Reliance on negotiation raises the issue of whether power relations between the parties at the outset of negotiations[103] will

95 The duty to negotiate in good faith applies to the other negotiating parties as well: *ibid*, ss 28, 29, 30A, 31.

96 *Ibid*, s 31.

97 *Ibid*, ss 35–39. Note that the NTA permits the Australian states and territories to opt out of its 'right to negotiate' provisions provided that they satisfy the Commonwealth that they have implemented equivalent procedures: NTA, ss 43, 43A.

98 *Ibid*, s 35(1).

99 *Ibid*, s 42.

100 *Ibid*, ss 32, 237. In the case of proposals by the Commonwealth, this declaration is subject to arbitration by the NNTT: ss 32(4), 42.

101 *Ibid*, s 238.

102 *Ibid*, ss 24BAF, 24CF, 24DG.

103 That is, factors that tilt the balance in favour of one party even before the negotiations begin.

play a role in determining the outcome of the claim. Power in negotiation, defined as the relative ability of one party to influence the outcome, is primarily derived from two sources: the alternatives available to each party outside the negotiation process (taking account of their resources) and the parties' relative preferences in relation to possible negotiated outcomes. Both of these factors can generally be expected to create a systemic risk of power imbalance in negotiations between indigenous groups and the state. First, insofar as it is constitutionally permitted to do so, the state has the ability to legislate to change the parties' respective rights—an option unavailable to indigenous groups.[104] Second, court processes in each jurisdiction have rarely resulted in final orders transferring significant resources to indigenous claimants. Turning to preferences, although all three countries have demonstrated that they are prepared to act on judicial findings that recognise indigenous rights, indigenous peoples are a minority in each country—a factor that may influence governments' willingness to consider a negotiated settlement that will upset politically important non-indigenous interests.

Arguably, one manifestation of a general disparity in the parties' power relations is that in each of the three countries the state will not entertain discussions of an outcome that would displace significant third party property interests, as defined by the dominant legal system. In New Zealand and Canada, this is explicitly provided in applicable government negotiation policies.[105] In Australia, this is due to court judgments that privilege settler interests derived from government grants and licences over aboriginal title interests, and to the cumulative effect of the validating provisions enacted in the NTA. The protection of private property interests may in fact be necessary for the electoral survival of non-indigenous governments willing to negotiate indigenous rights, but the fact that states *can* place such preconditions on indigenous negotiations is due to the relative attractiveness of the states' alternatives to negotiation.

There are significant differences of degree, however, among the three countries in the attractiveness of the parties' negotiation alternatives. In Australia, the absence of constitutional recognition of aboriginal rights, combined with a judicial willingness to privilege settler interests over the incidents of aboriginal title, has allowed the national and state governments' historical actions to override indigenous land rights without compensation. The level of independent judicial protection of aboriginal title is so low in Australia that when it introduced amendments to the NTA in 1998, the national government was not reluctant to make a public pronouncement that its intention was to bring 'bucketloads of extinguish-

[104] Both Australia and New Zealand have chosen to exercise this option in the face of court decisions affirming indigenous rights. As noted, the NTA was enacted largely to limit and clarify the effects of *Mabo (No 2)*. In New Zealand, the enactment of the Foreshore and Seabed Act 2004 (NZ) had a similar intent, as discussed below.

[105] See, eg, *Specific Claims Policy*, above n 51, 31 and Office of Treaty Settlements, *Healing the Past, Building a Future: A Guide to Treaty of Waitangi Claims and Negotiations with the Crown* (Office of Treaty Settlements, 2002) 127 ('OTS Policy').

ment' to aboriginal land rights.[106] Indeed, the NTA generally validates all government interferences with, or extinguishment of, aboriginal title interests prior to January 1994.[107]

In Canada, the constitutional status of aboriginal and treaty rights offers some protection from government interference with those rights, by requiring governments to justify any such interference in court.[108] Also, the *Haida Nation* decision has created a powerful incentive for governments to reach a final resolution of claims, particularly in areas of proposed resource developments where government decisions are likely to clash with unresolved indigenous rights claims. Still, litigation of aboriginal land rights is costly and time-consuming, and a First Nation that actively pursues land claims litigation will see an immediate end to its negotiations with the Crown, and all federal funding of its claims research.[109] Finally, it is worth noting that while the Crown bears the onus of justifying interferences with constitutionally protected rights, the evidentiary burden remains on indigenous groups in court, in negotiations and at the Specific Claims Tribunal, to prove its historical rights, based on whatever evidence remains available.[110]

In New Zealand, as Ruru shows in her Chapter in this book, the Māori do not enjoy constitutional protection of their rights, leaving the government's power to legislate a powerful alternative, which it can exercise to modify Māori land rights even after they have been recognised by the courts.[111] Further, the New Zealand courts have tended to focus on supporting, in a secondary role, legislative recognition of the principles of the Treaty of Waitangi, rather than resolving claims themselves based on the terms of the Treaty texts.[112] The fact that the New Zealand courts have thus far been unwilling to enforce the Treaty as a free standing source of rights means that when the current government policy states that either party

[106] Statement by T Fischer, Deputy Prime Minister, reported in *Sydney Morning Herald*, 28 June 1997, 'Wik Draft Threat to Native Title'. Taken from Aboriginal and Torres Strait Islander Social Justice Commissioner, *Native Title Report—July 1996 to June 1997* (AGPS, 1997) 7, at hreoc.gov.au/social_justice/nt_report/index.html.

[107] NTA, ss 14–20. Many other interferences with title prior to 23 December 2006 are also validated by ss 21–23JA of the Act. The NTA creates a limited right to compensation in a very restricted set of cases, eg where a governmental act after 1975 would have been invalidated because it was inconsistent with the terms of the Racial Discrimination Act. However, no compensation award has been granted to date pursuant to the NTA: Aboriginal and Torres Strait Islander Social Justice Commissioner, *Native Title Report 2007* (Human Rights and Equality Opportunity Commission, 2008) 5–7 ('NTR 2007') at hreoc.gov.au/social_justice/nt_report/index.html.

[108] See *Sparrow*, above n 56, *Delgamuukw*, above n 2.

[109] As a result of Canada's Specific Claims policies.

[110] This is true in all three jurisdictions. In the case of rights based on historical land relations this is not a light burden, nor (in the context of claims for accounting by a fiduciary) is it the inevitable result of the operation of common law and equity.

[111] This was the situation after the New Zealand Court of Appeal recognised the possibility of continuing Māori customary rights to the seabed and foreshore in *Ngati Apa v Attorney-General* [2003] 3 NZLR 643. The national government responded by enacting the Foreshore and Seabed Act 2004 (NZ), as Ruru explains in her Chapter.

[112] See DV Williams, 'Unique Treaty-Based Relationships Remain Elusive' in M Belgrave, M Kawharu and DV Williams (eds), *Waitangi Revisited: Perspectives on the Treaty of Waitangi* (Oxford University Press, 2005) 366.

may withdraw from negotiations at any time,[113] the Māori party is likely to find little solace in its negotiation alternatives. The absence of a litigation alternative for most historical claims renders the Māori more vulnerable than their Canadian counterparts to settlement limitations dictated by the Crown.[114]

On the other hand, Māori are a more significant minority in New Zealand, numerically and politically, than their indigenous counterparts in Canada and Australia. In consequence, the New Zealand government has often inserted references to the Treaty principles and to Māori concepts in legislation over the past 20 years[115] and it has proved willing, in creating the Waitangi Tribunal, to establish the only bicultural indigenous claims body in any of the three jurisdictions. New Zealand is also the only jurisdiction expressly to provide for cultural and spiritual redress for historical violations of indigenous rights.[116]

Space in this Chapter does not permit a detailed examination of the role of power dynamics in each of the jurisdictions, but it is possible to make certain general observations. First, the judicial alternative will generally be unattractive to indigenous groups to the extent that courts in the three jurisdictions are unable to order the transfer of land to them, to the extent that the indigenous groups are inadequately resourced to maintain complex judicial proceedings for extended periods, and to the extent that court judgments tend to make general pronouncements about applicable legal principles rather than issuing final awards in indigenous land claims. Second, because indigenous claimants are often impoverished, they are more likely than their state counterpart to feel pressure to accept an immediate but less advantageous settlement. Third, indigenous groups typically find themselves seeking change to the *status quo* to recognise their rights. If the *status quo* (that is, non-resolution of the claim) is more attractive to the state than to an indigenous group, first principles suggest that the state will be more tolerant of impasses and lengthy delays in negotiation of the claim. If the ADR process contains no independent mechanisms for resolving the many disagreements likely to arise between the parties, such delays in resolution are likely to be common.

The three jurisdictions have each introduced a statutory mechanism capable of addressing impasses in indigenous claims negotiations. The scope and nature of these mechanisms differ considerably. In Canada, the lack of any such mechanism prior to 2008 has been blamed for a claims backlog that had been increasing steadily.[117] The new SCTA promises binding impasse breaking, at least in many

[113] OTS Policy, above n 105, 56.

[114] These currently include limitations on the land and resources available for redress, and on the value of settlements: OTS Policy, *ibid*, 87–94. Although an attempt by the government during the 1990s to impose a cap of NZ$1 billion on the value of all settlements was later retracted, current policy indicates that government settlement offers will be conditioned by its 'fiscal constraints', in light of competing demands on government funds to deliver social, health and other services: see OTS Policy, 87–8.

[115] For examples, see Williams above n 112, 368.

[116] OTS Policy, above n 105, 96.

[117] G St Germain and N Sibbeston, *Negotiation or Confrontation: It's Canada's Choice*, Final Report of the Standing Senate Committee on Aboriginal Peoples Special Study on the Federal Specific Claims Process (Senate, 2006) 9–18.

specific claims, and its role should assist in empowering First Nations where disagreements arise in negotiations. The Canadian model lacks the flexibility of the New Zealand process, however, as the Canadian tribunal can only address disputes about remedy by issuing a final financial award. Thus, once claims negotiations begin, the parties cannot seek direction from the tribunal to resolve an impasse, and then return to the negotiation table to work out the elements of a settlement themselves. For a First Nation, this means that resort to the Tribunal requires it to relinquish any possibility of receiving land or any other creative remedy in its settlement.

The two-track model in New Zealand allows the Waitangi Tribunal to make recommendations on remedy at any time, including after failed direct negotiations between the Crown and a Māori claimant.[118] Such recommendations may urge any government action that the Tribunal considers necessary to give effect to Treaty principles. Further, insofar as the Tribunal is a respected neutral body, its initial findings about the validity and scope of a Māori claim may serve to temper power imbalances in the ensuing negotiations by influencing the parameters for those discussions. The Waitangi Tribunal is generally not empowered, however, to make binding rulings and there have been prominent examples of the government declining to follow its recommendations.[119]

The Australian Federal Court has broad powers to manage aboriginal title applications, including the power to strike out the application, to determine the appropriate parties, to determine whether mediation by the NNTT is appropriate, to determine questions of fact and law at the request of the NNTT, and to decide the claim if mediation fails.[120] Still, the Australian model of managed mediation has faced repeated criticism by independent reviewers that the process, as currently implemented, is too complex, litigious and time-consuming.[121] In the result, aboriginal claimants appear to be disadvantaged by their lack of financial resources and the use of alien concepts to determine their rights.[122]

As for the statutorily mandated 'right to negotiate', as noted above, it is subject to several significant limitations that allow governments to effectively override the aboriginal interests. The result, despite a statute that appears to benefit aboriginal claimants by privileging negotiation and permitting impasse-breaking by an independent party, is a set of ADR processes that the independent commissioner mandated to review the NTA has characterised as failing to fulfil the Act's object

[118] Since 2000 there have been eight Tribunal inquiries directly relating to Crown negotiations already under way: Personal communication from F Cooke, Assistant Registrar, Waitangi Tribunal (13 July 2008). For resource reasons, the Tribunal has not always been willing to allow claimants to return for a remedies hearing if negotiations break down; see McHugh, above n 2, 575.

[119] See Ruru's Chapter in this book.

[120] NTA, ss 80–86D.

[121] For a review of recent judicial criticisms of the complexity of the title scheme, see NNTT, *New Powers and Functions of the National Native Title Tribunal* (NNTT, 26 February 2007) 5–9. See also NTR 2007, above n 107, 11; NNTT, *Annual Report 2006–2007* (AGPS, 2007) 25, 40 ('NNTT Annual Report 2007').

[122] For a review of various Australian studies concluding that the native representative bodies that act for claimants are chronically under-resourced, see NTR 2007, above n 107, 62–70.

of protecting indigenous land rights and tending to humiliate the people it should serve.[123]

3. The Nature and Timeliness of the Outcomes

(a) Nature of Outcomes Produced

Because of the breadth of the Waitangi Tribunal's mandate to review all Māori allegations of government violation of the principles of the Treaty, Māori claims have led to the widest range of outcomes among the three jurisdictions. To date, these have included allocation of a significant portion of New Zealand's commercial fisheries quota,[124] recognition of Māori as an official language,[125] return of tribal lands, recognition of continuing Māori resource management rights and payment of compensation for historical land losses, together with Crown apologies for past conduct. Although Canada's formal land claims processes have been limited to remedying historical interferences with First Nations' and Inuit property, the Canadian negotiation processes have also led to a wide variety of remedies. These have included the provision of replacement lands where reserve lands have been wrongly taken, shared jurisdiction over navigable waterways, compensation payments, and even the creation of a new territorial government in Nunavut with jurisdiction over 1,900,000 km^2 of land.

The number and cumulative value of the indigenous rights agreements negotiated in Canada and New Zealand are significant. In Canada, the comprehensive claims process has yielded 23 final agreements.[126] In addition to land and other rights, these agreements provide for compensation totalling more than C$1.6 billion, resolving aboriginal title rights over 40 per cent of Canada's landmass.[127] For its part, the Canadian specific claims process has yielded negotiated settlements of another 300 claims, with a cumulative value of over C$2 billion.[128] In New Zealand there have been 22 historical settlements between the Crown and Māori groups, providing for compensation payments totalling slightly less than

[123] This conclusion, by the Aboriginal and Torres Strait Islander Social Justice Commissioner, is stated in NTR 2007, above 107, 2, 9.

[124] Treaty of Waitangi (Fisheries Claims) Settlement Act 1992 (NZ); Waitangi Tribunal, *Report of the Waitangi Tribunal on the Muriwhenua Fishing Claim* (Waitangi Tribunal, 1988).

[125] Pursuant to the *Report of the Waitangi Tribunal on the Te Reo Māori Claim* (1986).

[126] As of July 2008, two of these remain to be ratified: www.ainc-inac.gc.ca/al/ldc/ccl/pubs/gbn/gbn-eng.asp.

[127] *Ibid.* Almost all of the land covered by these settlements lies in Canada's northern territories and northern Quebec.

[128] The claims numbers are drawn from Indian and Northern Affairs Canada, *Specific Claims: A Statistical Snapshot*, www.ainc-inac.gc.ca/al/ldc/spc/jal/fet2-eng.asp ('Mini-Summary'). For the cumulative amount of settlement compensation (excluding provincial contributions), see Proceedings of the Standing Senate Committee on Aboriginal Peoples, *The Government of Canada's Specific Claims Policy*, Issue No 3 (13 June 2006), 3:29, online: www.parl.gc.ca/39/1/parlbus/commbus/senate/Com-e/abor-e/pdf/03issue.pdf.

NZ$1 billion.[129] In comparison with Canada, there has been relatively little land provided for in the vast majority of settlements in New Zealand.[130]

In contrast, the Australian NTA processes have not yet produced a single determination that compensation is owed for past governmental acts interfering with or extinguishing aboriginal title.[131] On the other hand, as of 31 March 2008, the NTA's ADR processes had delivered determinations that some incidents of aboriginal title continue to be protected in *parts of* an area covering 785,000 km^2 (combined with declarations of the nature of those rights and the rights of third parties over the same lands) and determinations in half as many cases that aboriginal title did not exist.[132] Australia has also seen the negotiation of a wide range of 'future act' agreements and IULAs, providing aboriginal groups with varying rights of access and resource management in specific regions.[133] It is difficult, however, for the outside observer to evaluate the quality of these outcomes in terms of the benefits they have delivered to indigenous peoples in Australia.[134]

(b) Timeliness of the Processes

Western common law traditions emphasise that 'justice delayed is justice denied'; from this perspective the length of time it takes an ADR process to resolve indigenous rights disputes is an important measure of the effectiveness of the process. At the same time, in the complex, cross-cultural world of indigenous rights disputes, it is important that the parties take the time necessary to review historical evidence and design remedies that respect the present interests of indigenous and non-indigenous neighbours. What the observer might reasonably focus upon, therefore, is the extent to which delays in reaching outcomes are not the necessary consequence of a careful review of the merits of the disputes.

None of the ADR processes under review has proved particularly quick. In Canada more than 800 specific claims were unresolved at the time of writing, a backlog that has steadily increased in recent years.[135] Describing the system's past

[129] Personal communication from B Jones, Senior Communications Analyst, OTS (24 June 2008). This total includes NZ$196 million related to the 2008 Central North Island Forests Settlement, not implemented through legislation at the time of writing.

[130] Most settlements to date have called for the transfer of less than 1,000 hectares (10 sq km) of land. A notable exception is the 2008 Central North Island Forests Settlement which, if implemented by legislation, will provide for the transfer of some 153,000 hectares (1530 sq km) of forest lands to a Māori collective with more than 100,000 members. See Office of Treaty Settlements, 'Summaries of Settlements,' at www.ots.govt.nz.

[131] See above n 121.

[132] Information obtained from the National Native Title Tribunal website, Map 4: Determinations of native title: www.nntt.gov.au/publications/national_maps.html.

[133] 312 Indigenous Land Use Agreements had been negotiated as of early 2008, covering some 12% of Australia's land mass. See G Neate, 'Improving the Claims Resolution Process' in *Informa Negotiating Native Title Conference, Brisbane* (NNTT, February 2008) 7.

[134] The NNTT concluded in both its 2005–06 and 2006–07 reports that native title determinations often deliver few direct benefits to indigenous Australians: NNTT Report 2007, above n 107, 15.

[135] For numbers of outstanding and resolved specific claims, see Mini-Summary, above n 128. A substantial backlog also exists in the British Columbia Treaty Process, where only three final agreements have been reached at 48 negotiation tables in relation to aboriginal title: see www.bctreaty.net/files/updates.php.

failure to resolve many claims more than 20 years after filing, with successful negotiations taking *on average* more than 15 years, the 2007 Ontario Ipperwash Inquiry concluded that lack of a timely and effective land and treaty claims process had recently contributed to a significant rise in confrontations with police.[136] As noted, Canada's new Specific Claims Tribunal (together with a recent federal earmarking of C$250 million per year for specific claims resolution)[137] are intended to address this concern.

In Australia, almost 600 title applications were outstanding at the end of 2007,[138] with almost a quarter of the claims filed during the mid-1990s.[139] If present trends continue, the NNTT estimates it will take 30 years to clear the backlog of title claims in Australia.[140] It appears that much of the reason for delays in processing these applications is the complexity of the law, the number of parties and the adversarial atmosphere of the process.[141] In New Zealand, with 22 settlements reached, several hundred historical claims remained outstanding in 2008. Not all these claims will be judged worthy of settlement and one settlement may resolve many related historical claims. Recent major settlements have taken on average between eight and 14 years from the planning of a Tribunal hearing to legislative implementation.[142] It is difficult, based on publicly available information, to generalise about the factors that have contributed to the time required to resolve Māori claims. The number of separate claims, the challenge of agreeing on who will represent Māori claimants and the workload of Tribunal members all have contributed to past delays. Looking forward, the Waitangi Tribunal has concluded that the consolidation of related claims, greater Crown-claimant co-operation relating to hearings and negotiations as well as adequate resourcing of both the Tribunal and negotiations process, will all be necessary to accelerate the pace of settlement.[143]

[136] The Ipperwash Inquiry noted in its 2007 report that the Ontario Provincial Police had documented more than 100 'aboriginal critical incidents' since a deadly confrontation in 1995: SB Linden, *Report of the Ipperwash Inquiry: Volume 2* (Ministry of the Attorney General, 2007) 19. For an analysis of delays in Canada's claims processes, see the same report, 79–100.

[137] Office of the Prime Minister, 'Prime Minister Harper announces major reforms to address the backlog of Aboriginal treaty claims' (12 June 2007) at www.pm.gc.ca/eng/media.asp.

[138] NNTT, above n 121, 42.

[139] See G Neate, *Improving the Claims Resolution Process: Informa Negotiating Native Title Conference, Brisbane* (28 February 2008) 10.

[140] *Ibid.*

[141] See NTR 2007, above n 107, 40. In the *Wongatha* case, for example, 1,426 objections were made to the expert reports filed in the proceedings: see *Risk v Northern Territory and Quall v Northern Territory* [2006] FCA 404, per Mansfield J, para 456, referring to *Harrington-Smith on behalf of the Wongatha People v State of Western Australia (No 2)* [2003] FCA 893.

[142] Waitangi Tribunal, 'The Waitangi Tribunal and the Settlement of Historical Treaty Claims' (9 December 2005) at www.waitangi-tribunal.govt.nz/news.

[143] *Ibid.*

4. The Extent to Which the Processes Reflect Indigenous Values

Of the three jurisdictions, only New Zealand has developed ADR processes that go a significant way toward recognising and accommodating indigenous values and culture. Only in New Zealand are indigenous claims reviewed by an independent body whose members are required to be appointed with regard to their cultural background and their knowledge of the issues within the Tribunal's mandate.[144] Thus, only in New Zealand is there consistent review of indigenous claims by persons well acquainted with the worldview and Treaty understandings of the indigenous disputants. Further, New Zealand is the only jurisdiction with a wide array of statutes that in referring to Māori rights expressly refer to Māori concepts, even using Māori words and expressions to convey those concepts.[145]

In terms of the everyday protocols of dialogue between the Crown and indigenous claimants, New Zealand's Waitangi Tribunal process expressly incorporates Māori customs. Thus, the Tribunal hears Māori evidence and submissions according to Māori protocols, evidence may be given in the Māori language, cross-examination of elders may be limited by the Tribunal, and hearings are held on the claimant's *marae* (meeting area)—a practice which, among other things, allows the public lamenting of losses in accordance with Māori tradition.[146] All these practices, respecting and incorporating indigenous values, are specifically provided for in the Treaty of Waitangi Act or the Tribunal's guide to procedure. Further, the Crown's negotiation policy expressly provides that redress will be provided for cultural and spiritual losses caused by state actions in violation of Treaty principles.[147] The ADR legislation and official government policies promulgated by the federal governments of Canada and Australia make no equivalent attempt to recognise indigenous customs, values or language.

Perhaps most significantly, only New Zealand has a process that defines, categorises and determines the validity of indigenous land claims in accordance with what is arguably a culturally neutral standard (that is, claims that one party has violated the principles of a treaty agreed to by both). In this regard, the Treaty of Waitangi Act expressly provides that both the Māori and English texts of the

[144] TWA s 4(2A). At any given time about half the Tribunal members are Māori: Waitangi Tribunal, *Guide to the Practice and Procedure of the Waitangi Tribunal* (Waitangi Tribunal, 2007) 2 ('WT Practice Guide'). The statutory provisions governing appointments to the NNTT provide that the Governor-General appoints its members; appointees are not required to be familiar with aboriginal culture, although for members other than the President or Deputy President this is one of four factors to be considered: NTA, ss 110–11. The Canadian SCTA provides that the federal cabinet alone appoints Tribunal members, who must be drawn from the superior court. The SCTA does not require that the cultural background or knowledge of appointees be taken into consideration: s 6 (2) and (3).

[145] Williams, above n 112.

[146] WT Practice Guide, above n 144, 2, 27, 30. The TWA expressly provides that evidence may be given in Māori, and specifically authorises the Tribunal to take into account 'such aspects of *te kawa o te marae*' as it considers appropriate in each case: Sch 2, ss 5(9) and 6(2).

[147] OTS Policy, above n 105, 96. Compare the compensation rules set out in Canada's SCTA, s 20(1)(d), which provides that the Tribunal 'shall not award any amount for . . . (ii) any harm or loss that is not pecuniary in nature, including loss of a cultural or spiritual nature'.

Treaty shall be considered by the Tribunal.[148] By contrast, both Australia and Canada have established ADR regimes for indigenous land disputes that incorporate concepts drawn solely from the dominant settler legal system (for example, the requirements and content of aboriginal title, extinguishment rules, compensation rules that expressly exclude the cultural significance of land, etc). The use of legal rules drawn from the dominant legal system might be explained on the basis that one of the state's overriding goals is to promote equal treatment for indigenous peoples under its own laws.[149] Still, in New Zealand alone can it be said that the definitions of permissible indigenous claims match indigenous understandings of the nature of the disputes between them and the state.

D. Conclusion

The ADR processes in Canada, Australia and New Zealand are significant for the unprecedented access they have given indigenous groups to forums for resolving their land grievances. Collectively, these ADR processes have produced a quantity and variety of outcomes not previously available through the courts in any of the countries. Those outcomes have ensured the acknowledgement of indigenous rights to land and resources of unparalleled value, particularly in Canada and New Zealand. Structurally, each of the processes formally incorporates a major role for direct negotiation between indigenous groups and the state, something that the US claims experience did not provide. In this way, each process allows some freedom for indigenous views and interests to play a role in the resolution of indigenous disputes. Each offers the prospect of a dialogue that mirrors the ideal of treaty diplomacy, recognising indigenous peoples as equals.

In contrast to the process implemented in the US under the ICCA, Australia, New Zealand and Canada have each made room for hybrid ADR processes that make use of third party neutrals. There are significant differences among the countries regarding the intervention points and authority of such third parties. New Zealand's Waitangi Tribunal is able to address the broadest range of indigenous claims, but its general restriction to recommendatory powers balances a flexibility of interventions with recognition that the parties will have the final say as to whether and how each claim is resolved. Australia's neutrally managed negotiation and mediation processes provide assurance of final resolution, but as implemented, have proved costly and unfriendly to indigenous claimants. For its part, Canada only recently introduced national access to neutral arbitration of claims. That access is limited, however, to financial arbitration and to certain non-aboriginal title claims.

[148] WTA, s 5(2).

[149] Assuming that the dominant legal system derived its approach to indigenous property rights on a comparable basis to the property rights of non-indigenous persons. For a contrary view, see McNeil's Chapter in this volume.

A major concern raised in this Chapter has been the efficacy of the ADR processes in responding to power and cultural imbalance. Whether any of the processes adequately protects indigenous claimants from outcomes dominated by the parties' power relations is a question that merits closer investigation. As for the degree to which each process recognises and incorporates indigenous understandings of the dispute and indigenous perspectives on remedy, the Australian and Canadian processes reflect little formal concern for this issue. While this is understandable when viewed purely from the perspective of domestic law, the absence of such recognition creates a risk that the outcomes of the process will not be embraced or, ultimately, respected by indigenous peoples.

Conclusion

15

Physical Philosophy: Mobility and the Future of Indigenous Rights

JOHN BORROWS

You might as well expect all the rivers to run backward as that any man who was born free should be contented penned up and denied liberty to go where he pleases.

Hin-hah-too-yah-lat-kekht (Chief Joseph), Nez Perce[1]

A. Introduction

As the final contributor to this book, I have been asked to consider what the future might hold for Indigenous peoples. There are many issues that could be canvassed: land rights, governance, economic development, the environment, citizenship, language, education and health. In fact, many of these issues have been ably written about in this book and provide helpful guidance as we look ahead. While all of these concerns deserve close attention, I believe *mobility* is one of the major issues Indigenous peoples must successfully address to secure a brighter future.

Mobility has often been used to undermine Indigenous peoples' rights. I have observed that we, as Indigenous peoples, are denied rights if we move too frequently. Conversely, if we move too little we also see others diminish our rights. This result makes it difficult to advance other matters of crucial importance. When Indigenous mobility is at issue, it seems as if we can't win. In most legal systems, Indigenous peoples are characterised as being either too nomadic or too static to protect our most significant relationships. Thus, mobility should be of special concern for Indigenous peoples.[2] Its negative characterisations and consequences undermine the very foundations of Indigenous peoples' ability to sustain themselves in the world.

[1] Hin-hah-too-yah-lat-kekht (Chief Joseph), Chief Joseph Recounts His Trip to Washington, DC (1879) in H Zinn and A Arnove (eds), *Voices of a People's History of the United States* (Seven Stories Press, 2004) 147–8.

[2] For an excellent study of the issue of Indigenous peoples and mobility, see J Taylor and M Bell, *Population Mobility and Indigenous Peoples in Australasia and North America* (Routledge, 2004).

B. Methodologies of Mobility: Physical and Philosophical

Many Indigenous peoples have histories of movement, despite stereotypes to the contrary. Notwithstanding our frequent moves we are not rootless. Our travels usually occur in relationship to territories with which we have long-standing associations. Indigenous peoples are constantly in a state of settled flux. Our perpetual motion co-exists with a persistent and enduring permanence. Ancient homelands remain a pivotal axis around which most Indigenous peoples' lives revolve. We may wander far and wide, but our journeys generally take their orientation from an older sense of our place in the world.

Of course, there are some Indigenous peoples who move less than others due to group or individual pressure, preference, personality and poverty. Yet even in these instances, mobility or the lack thereof is a significant concern. It shapes many of the most important issues Indigenous peoples encounter in the modern world.

Indigenous peoples not only move through physical space—we also move through time. Our communities are not frozen in the past, as courts too often assume.[3] We interact with other societies as we journey through the generations. In the process we accumulate insights and ideas from other cultures. This can lead to significant change, as the past intermingles with the present and transforms our societies.

Yet this view of Indigenous movement also challenges assumptions about Indigenous peoples' cultures. We are too often seen as intellectually stagnant, with unchanging, static views of life.[4] Some consider our ideas to be the product of another age, having little relevance to the contemporary world.[5] They see our philosophies as quaint anachronisms of another time. Others might regard our ideas as intellectually compelling, even correct, but too feeble to prevail in their encounter with the modern age.[6] Thus, Indigenous people and their ideas are often seen as vanishing from the earth.

[3] B Olthius, 'Defrosting Delgamuukw: (or "How to Reject a Frozen Rights Interpretation of Aboriginal Title in Canada")' (2001) 12 *National Journal of Constitutional Law* 385; J Borrows, 'Frozen Rights in Canada: Constitutional Interpretation and the Trickster' (1997) 22 *American Indian Law Review* 37; R Williams Jr, *Like a Loaded Weapon: The Rehnquist Court, Indian Rights and the Legal History of Racism in America* (University of Minnesota Press, 2005); LG Robertson, *Conquest by Law: How the Discovery of America Dispossessed Indigenous Peoples of their Lands* (Oxford University Press, 2005).

[4] For a discussion of this issue in historic context, see H Reynolds, *The Law of the Land* (2nd edn, Penguin Books, 2001). For a contemporary treatment, see the past tense discussion of Aboriginal civilisation in T Flanagan, *First Nations, Second Thoughts* (McGill-Queen's Press, 2000).

[5] A Duff, *Maori: The Crisis and the Challenge* (HarperCollins, 1993).

[6] First Nations culture might be regarded as too weak to enter into ordinary legal relationships: see *Harry v Kreutziger* (1978) 9 BCLR 166 (BCCA); R Means, 'The Same Old Song' in W Churchill (ed), *Marxism and Native Americans* (Southend Press, 1983).

I do not accept these views. I believe we renew and retain our status as Indigenous peoples as we move through time. Unfortunately, these are difficult points for some to grasp because they defy entrenched stereotypes concerning Indigenous peoples.[7] For people with incomplete views, understanding Indigenous peoples' travels through time can be even more challenging than comprehending the complexities of our physical movement through space.

Thus, to address these challenges this Chapter deals with two issues related to Indigenous mobility: physical and philosophical movement. Most readers will probably understand what I mean by physical mobility, which is the ability of people to shift their locale. By philosophical movement I mean to signal the ideological changes that occur within Indigenous cultures as we interact with other peoples in our movement through time.

As noted, our physical orientation to the world occurs in relation to enduring patterns, despite the presence of significant flux. As with our physical travels, so it is with our ideological wanderings: we are not rootless. Our journeys through the world of ideas can take guidance from familiar, time-honoured models. For example, First Nations often try and understand the future by remembering the past. Insight can be derived from such reflection because we often regard time as being cyclical. While we can also view and experience time as linear, many of our most important teachings orient us towards a life that stresses recurrence.[8] In this light the present and the past can almost be co-extensive.

The co-extensive nature of time is apparent when the layered repetitions of similar events are brought into focus. These particular forms of tiered movement can help us holistically understand mobility. Spring turns into summer, autumn gives way to winter, and the cycle begins over again. Babies grow into youth, youth mature and become adults, and adults persevere to become elders, before the circle repeats itself.[9] For my people, the Anishinabek, much of our cosmology is built on this pattern.[10] I have noticed that some other Indigenous peoples follow these cycles in understanding their world.[11] Thus, in this concluding Chapter I will briefly speculate about what the future might hold for Indigenous peoples by also being mindful of the past.

[7] For a judicial expression of these views, see *Sawridge Band v Canada* [1996] 1 FC 3 (FCTD). For judicial censure of them, see *Sawridge v Canada* [1997] 3 FC 538 (FCA).

[8] Though one must be careful not to romanticise this view of time and conclude that Indigenous peoples have no history. This was a problem in the work of C Levi-Strauss, *The Elementary Structures of Kinship* (Eyre and Spottis-Woode, 1969).

[9] J Borrows, 'Fourword/Foreword: Issues, Individuals, Institutions, Ideologies' (2002) 1 *Indigenous Law Journal* 1.

[10] I am intrigued by the Mayan calendar, described in R Wright, *Time Among the Maya: Travels in Belize, Guatemala and Mexico* (Penguin Books, 1989).

[11] T Peacock, *The Four Hills of Life: Ojibwe Wisdom* (Afton Historical Society Press, 2006).

C. Models of Mobility

When viewed in this broader context, Indigenous mobility is not just a future issue; it also has clear parallels to the past. Indigenous peoples have histories that address mobility. These journeys not only changed their territorial residences, but also transformed certain beliefs and practices. Historically, the Māori tell of their journey from Hawaikii to Aotearoa.[12] These voyages led to new understandings of themselves as people.[13] This occurred for other Polynesians too, as they sailed thousands of miles around the Pacific to make their many homes.[14] Indigenous Australians speak of their movements through the Dream-time and the Walk-about.[15] For millennia, the Sami continually moved through what became the countries of Norway, Finland, Sweden and Russia, herding reindeer and teaching one another about what they learned in the process.[16] The Navajo chronicle their migrations around the deserts of the American Southwest, and others talk of their arrival from an indeterminate place in the north.[17] The Hopi relate their journey from inside the earth.[18] The Maya report that they moved through many cycles of creation and destruction to build their societies in Central America.[19] Each of these physical treks also gave rise to important ideological journeys, as new lessons were related to older teachings. Physical and intellectual mobility has long been a defining characteristic of many of our societies.

Indigenous mobility is also much in evidence in more recent time.[20] The peoples of the North American Pacific Northwest 'turned the 1,600 kilometre stretch of coastline between Puget Sound and the Gulf of Alaska into a maritime region'.[21] The great North American prairies hosted a constant flow of Lakota, Cheyenne,

[12] KR Howe, *The Quest for Origins: Who First Discovered and Settled New Zealand and the Pacific Islands* (Penguin Books, 2003) 159–82.

[13] R Walker, *Ka Whawhai Tonu Matou: Struggle Without End* (Penguin Books, 2004) 24–77.

[14] G Irwin, *The Prehistoric Exploration and Colonisation of the Pacific* (Cambridge University Press, 1992).

[15] R Berndt and C Berndt, *The Speaking Land* (Penguin, 1989).

[16] S Pederson, 'The State and the Rejection of Saami Customary Law: Superiority and Inferiority in Norwegian-Saami Relations' in TG Svensson (ed), *On Customary Law and Saami Rights Process in Norway* (Centre for Sámi Studies, 1999) 127, 132–4.

[17] P Zolbrod, *Dine Bahane: The Navajo Creation Story* (University of New Mexico Press, 1984); R Towner (ed), *The Archeology of Navajo Origins* (University of Utah Press, 1996); J Levy, *In the Beginning: The Navajo Genesis* (University of California Press, 1998).

[18] F Waters, *Book of the Hopi* (Penguin Books, 1977).

[19] M Coe, *The Maya* (7th edn, Thames and Hudson, 2005); D Tedlock, trans, *Popol Vuh: The Definitive Edition of the Mayan Book of the Dawn of Life and the Glories of Gods and Kings* (Simon and Schuster, 1996).

[20] A Wrightman, *Indigenous Migration and Social Change: The Forestaros of Cuzco, 1570–1720* (Duke University Press, 2000).

[21] P Raibmon, 'Meanings of Mobility on the Northwest Coast' in T Binnema and S Neylan (eds), *New Histories for Old: Changing Perspectives on Canada's Native Pasts* (UBC Press, 2007) 176, 177.

Cree, Crow and other peoples following the great buffalo herds.[22] The Apaches of the American Southwest occupied territories that spanned the Sonoran and Chihuahuan deserts, and ranged over the intersections of the Sierra Madre and Rocky Mountains.[23] The Iroquois Confederacy could trade, travel and raid from the Great Lakes to the Carolinas.[24] The Algonkian-speaking peoples of the East Coast eventually paddled their way down the Mississippi and across the rivers of Canada to the Rocky Mountains when early European traders and missionaries arrived in their midst.[25] Once again, it needs to be emphasised that in the process their journeys also had significant spiritual and ideological dimensions.

Consistent with these experiences, Indigenous peoples are also highly mobile today—in where they live and through the ideas that guide their lives. Over 50 per cent of First Nations people in Canada live off-reserve. Over 80 per cent of Māori live in New Zealand's urban centres. Australian Aborigines occupy both cities and wide stretches of traditional country, with 30 per cent living in the cities of that continent. Many Indigenous peoples in Mexico have relationships that reach back and forth between North American cities and traditional homelands.[26] In the United States (US) the picture is similar; over 60 per cent of Native Americans live outside their reservations. It should also go without saying that these new living arrangements have led to a variety of patterns of learning, as time accumulates to produce new ways of seeing the world in relation to past experiences.[27] Where we have sufficient resources we increasingly go to universities, colleges and trade schools, while we simultaneously learn in ancient societies, lodges and longhouses. If we are not coerced to relocate or retrench against our will, we take many healthy lessons from the change we encounter around us. The intermingling of the past

[22] H Meredith, *Dancing on Common Ground: Tribal Cultures and Alliances on the Southern Plains* (University of Kansas Press, 1995); P Duke, *Points in Time: Structure and Event in a Late Northern Plains Hunting Society* (University of Colorado Press, 1999).

[23] K Basso, *Wisdom Sits in Places: Landscape and Language Among the Western Apache* (University of New Mexico Press, 1996).

[24] A Taylor, *American Colonies: The Settling of North America* (Penguin Books, 2001) 235.

[25] Eg Marquette, La Salle, La Vérendrye, MacKenzie, Radisson, and Des Groseilliers: see J Marquette, 'Récit des voyages et découvertes du Père Marquette', in *Relations inédites de la Nouvelle-France (1672–1679) pour faire suite aux anciennes relations*, vol II (Éditions Élysée, 1974); H Joutel, *Journal historique du dernier voyage que feu M. de la Sale fit dans le golfe de Mexique [. . .]* (Estienne Robinot, 1713); L Burpee (ed), *Journals and Letters of Pierre Gaultier de Varennes de La Vérendrye and His Sons: With Correspondence Between the Governors of Canada and the French Court, Touching the Search for the Western Sea* (The Champlain Society, 1927); A Mackenzie, *Voyages from Montreal [. . .] to the Frozen and Pacific Oceans, in the Years 1789 and 1793* (R Noble, 1801); A Adams (ed), *The Explorations of Pierre Esprit Radisson: From the Original Manuscript in the Bodleian Library and the British Museum*, modernisation of the text by L Kallsen (Ross and Haines, 1961).

[26] B Castellanos, 'Cancun and the Campo: Indigenous Migration and Tourism Development in the Yucatan Peninsula' in *Holiday in Mexico: Essays on Tourism and Tourist Experience* (Duke University Press, forthcoming). Similar experiences are present with Indigenous peoples in Sarawak, Malaysia: see O Murang, 'Migration in Sarawak: The Kelabit Experience' (1998) 3(1) *Sarawak Development Journal* 1. For further information about traditions of mobility in Borneo (*bejalai*), see P Kedit, *Iban Bejalai* (Sarawak Literary Society, 1993); R Bulan, *Native Title in Sarawak, Malaysia: Kelabit Land Rights in Transition* (PhD Thesis, Australian National University, 2005) 116.

[27] B Lawrence, *Real Indians and Others: Mixed Blood Urban Native Peoples and Indigenous Nationhood* (University of Nebraska Press, 2004).

and present, as we move between our traditional territories and other places, demonstrates the importance of mobility in Indigenous people's lives.

These examples are highlighted by one of the great insights found in recent geographic and demographic analysis of Indigenous living patterns in Canada. It has been shown that many First Nations people retain significant connections to their homelands, even as they congregate in cities in significant numbers. Studies have shown that permanent ghettos of First Nations people in Canadian cities do not exist, as least as we think of that phenomenon in relation to other ethnic groups in the US.[28] While there are identifiable neighbourhoods of Indigenous people in western Canadian cities, the people who live there continually move back and forth between the reserves and cities.

Thus, while Canadian cities may have sections of town that have been occupied by Indigenous people for generations, these sites are not necessarily intergenerational. This means a person could search for a long time to find a family living in the same neighbourhood as their great-grandparents. There are huge flows of First Nations people, resources and ideas between cities and traditional territories. These circulations have great significance for how Indigenous peoples live their lives. The reality of Indigenous mobility and our cyclical orientation to the earth is not being accurately reflected in most nation-states' socio-political and legal regimes. Even our own Indigenous laws might not properly take into account the energy found in our residential and intellectual movements in the present day.

D. Manipulating Mobility: Settled and Unsettled Law

1. Introduction

Despite the reality of our near-constant motion, most legal systems manipulate conceptions of mobility to deny or diminish Indigenous rights. Laws are devised to limit our movements and to foster confinement within ever-diminishing spaces. Such coercion can lead to exceedingly concentrated living arrangements. This system creates perverse incentives to promote our escape into the surrounding society through assimilation. Such laws can contribute to our removal from wider territories and relationships.

At the same time, colonialism promotes the fiction that Indigenous peoples have similar limitations when it comes to their own intellectual horizons. Some of our own people, having forcibly lived through this onslaught, have internalised the view that Indigenous peoples do not move in their philosophical orientation towards the world. They have almost become strict isolationists, who view themselves as almost completely separated from other peoples' practices and

[28] E Peters, 'Three Myths About Aboriginals in Cities' (Breakfast on the Hill Seminar Series, Canadian Federation for the Humanities and Social Sciences, Ottawa, 25 March 2004), [unpublished].

ideas. If lived in for a generation or two, reservations and residential schools can make captivity appear natural to some caught in this web.

The law in every country with significant Indigenous populations is generally supportive of these narrow views of Indigenous mobility. This recruits Indigenous people in the state's troubling boundary patrol if we view ourselves through this lens. In these circumstances, command coincides with control to continue colonialism's forced confinements. The injustice and intolerability of this situation promotes Indigenous assimilation and extinction because many people are forced or feel compelled to flee colonialism's firm grip. Alternatively, many nestle themselves ever more deeply in its grasp by being in a constant reactive mode, setting their identity solely through oppositional politics, which gives colonialism the power to define the scope of their struggle. It is an understatement to say the law inappropriately stereotypes Indigenous residential and cultural patterns. The laws we encounter deny, diminish or extinguish our rights because we cannot meet the artificial legal standards promoted by most nation-states.

2. 'Damned if We Move': The Too Unsettled Thesis

When examining legal regimes one finds that Indigenous rights are often premised on contradictory views concerning our mobility. These manipulations generate an ironic injustice that works against Indigenous rights from opposing directions. On the one hand, there are times when Indigenous peoples are characterised as too physically and philosophically mobile to claim or prove rights. This approach might be called the 'unsettled thesis' because it captures how courts view Indigenous societies as disconnected from their lands because of their ideas and life patterns. Conversely, there are moments when courts find we are too sedentary and unchanging to claim legal protections. I label this view the 'settled thesis' because it illustrates an approach that sees Indigenous peoples as too static in their relationships to land or ideas to claim rights. In the light of these conflicting manoeuvres, I conclude that, as Indigenous peoples, we are damned if we move, and damned if we don't.[29] The judiciary's inconsistent lurching between these two extremes takes place with too little notice or critique. When it comes to issues of mobility, the law is interpreted flexibly to accomplish results that are the most detrimental to Indigenous interests.

For example, Indigenous peoples can face laws that imply we are too unsettled to claim rights. In these circumstances, courts might find Indigenous peoples do not have rights if we move too much. The Supreme Court of Canada has held that, when present possession is relied upon to establish possession prior to Crown assertion of sovereignty, Aboriginal title cannot be proved without a 'substantial maintenance of the connection' between Indigenous people and their lands.[30] The

[29] I employ the word 'damned' in a dual sense: to be punished and stopped or blocked in one's social progress.

[30] *Delgamuukw v British Columbia* [1997] 3 SCR 1010, para 153.

High Court of Australia has decided that the 'tide of history' can wash our rights away if we don't remain securely connected to the land through our laws.[31] The incorporation of practices from other communities can become a justification for finding we have abandoned our laws and lands.[32] Throughout its history, the US has implemented detailed displacement policies, from the Dawes Act of 1887 to the Termination Acts of the 1950s. These Acts were designed to get Indians to move from their territories and thereby facilitate their assimilation.[33]

Similar attempts to get Indigenous peoples removed from their lands for assimilative purposes can be observed in places like New Zealand, Norway, Brazil, South Africa, Malaysia, Chile, and numerous other countries in the world.[34] In all these cases, legal interpretations of mobility can be fatal to Indigenous peoples. If we are forced or choose to leave our reserves, homelands or traditions, our rights and identity are legally attenuated. This creates the risk of being completely severed by the legal regimes of the surrounding nation-states.

Even if we have lived in the same area for centuries, and do not leave our traditional territories, mobility can be manipulated by the law to diminish Indigenous rights. Our lives can be characterised as hyper-mobile within our homelands, thereby allowing others to lay superior claims. In such cases our rights are presumptively reduced because we are labelled as nomadic.[35]

The US Supreme Court accepted this view in the *Tee-Hit-Ton* case, where they held that 'nomadic tribes of Indians' have a form of occupancy that does not amount to ownership.[36] The Supreme Court is not alone in diminishing

[31] *Mabo v Queensland [No 2]* (1992), 107 ALR 1 (HC) para 66. For a US example, see *State of Vermont v Elliott*, 616 AL 2d 210 (1992), *cert* denied 113 S Ct 1258 (1993), which held that grants, historical events and legislative acts, culminating in the admission of Vermont as a US state in 1791, extinguished Western Abenaki Aboriginal title. For commentary, see JP Lowndes, 'When History Outweighs Law: Extinguishment of Abenaki Aboriginal Title' (1994) 42 *Buffalo Law Review* 75; JW Singer, 'Well Settled? The Increasing Weight of History in American Indian Land Claims' (1994) 28 *Georgia Law Review* 481.

[32] *Members of the Yorta Yorta Aboriginal Community v Victoria* (2002) 194 ALR 538, 561 (HC). For commentary, see K Anker, 'Law in the Present Tense: Tradition and Cultural Continuity in Members of the Yorta Yorta Aboriginal Community v Victoria' (2004) 28 *Melbourne University Law Review* 1. For a US example, see J Carillo (ed), *Recalling the Rhythm of Survival: Readings in American Indian Law* (Temple University Press, 1998) 19–50.

[33] F Hoxie, *A Final Promise: The Campaign to Assimilate the Indians, 1880–1920* (University of Nebraska Press, 1984); WE Washburn, *The Assault on Indian Tribalism: The General Allotment Law (Dawes Act) of 1887* (Lippincott, 1975); D Fixico, *Termination and Relocation: Federal Indian Policy, 1945–1960* (University of New Mexico Press, 1986).

[34] N Seuffert, *Jurisprudence of National Identity: Kaleidoscopes of Imperialism and Globalism from Aotearoa New Zealand* (Ashgate, 2006) 11–27; H Minde, 'Assimilation of the Sami: Implementation and Consequences' (2005) 3 *Journal of Indigenous Peoples Rights* 3; L Valenta, 'Disconnect: The 1988 Brazilian Constitution, Customary International Law and Indigenous Land Rights in Northern Brazil' (2003) 38 *Texas International Law Journal* 643; R Hitchcock and D Vinding, *Indigenous Peoples' Rights in Southern Africa* (International Work Group for Indigenous Affairs, 2004) 113–34; G Benjamin and C Chow (eds), *Tribal Communities in the Malay World* (Centre for Southeast Asian Studies, 2003); MC Lucic, 'Challenges in Chilean Intercultural Policies' (2005) 28 *Political and Legal Anthropology Review* 112.

[35] For an excellent discussion of this issue, see J Gilbert, 'Nomadic Territories: A Human Rights Approach to Nomadic Peoples' Land Rights' (2007) 7 *Human Rights Law Review* 681.

[36] *Tee-Hit-Ton Indians v US* (1955) 345 US 272.

Indigenous rights for this reason.[37] It has long been thought that so-called nomadic people do not sufficiently mix their labour with the soil to acquire its underlying benefits. For example, John Locke convinced others to believe this fiction.[38]

Canada's Supreme Court seemingly accepted troubling implications that flow from this dubious line of argument. In *R v Marshall; R v Bernard*, the court ruled that Mi'kmaq people had insufficient connections with specific sites to establish Aboriginal title, despite living in an area for thousands of years before any European ever set foot on their soil.[39] They wrote: 'The common law right to title is commensurate with exclusionary rights of control . . . If the ancient aboriginal practices do not indicate that type of control, then title is not the appropriate right'.[40] These views demonstrate that the concept of physical mobility can be deployed to facilitate assimilation because past relationships with land are interpreted too narrowly.

Thus, the recognition and retention of our rights can sometimes depend too heavily on notions that we are too unsettled. Sometimes we might even sense this tendency amongst our own people. If you are away from the reserve for too long during one of your travels, your Indigenous identity can be questioned. These views can tether us too tightly to *colonially constructed* reserves, and thereby interfere with our freedom to live throughout our own territories, in accordance with our long-standing patterns of movement.

Inappropriate physical or philosophical conceptions of Indigenous mobility should not be used to deny or diminish our rights. In our physical relationship to land, we should not be stripped of rights because we have been forcibly removed or constantly move within our territories. Our territorial relationships should not be conceptualised in the same manner as common law property rights.

In the last century, the Judicial Committee of the Privy Council advised that 'much caution is essential' when interpreting 'the various systems of native jurisprudence throughout the [British] Empire'.[41] They noted that such caution is essential because judges are susceptible to the danger of only recognising property law within Indigenous societies if they find analogies to concepts within English law. The court said 'this tendency has to be held in check' because it would prevent the recognition of beneficial rights that developed under Indigenous systems.[42]

The Privy Council's caution is appropriate when considering issues of mobility. Legal opinions that have stripped land rights through forcible removal or coerced confinement have to be wrong. Cases that remove Indigenous peoples from their territories on the basis of mobility must be overturned. They are inconsistent with

[37] R Williams Jr, *The American Indian in Western Legal Thought* (Oxford University Press, 1990).

[38] J Locke, *Second Treatise, Two Treatises of Government* [1689], ed P Laslett (Cambridge University Press, 1988): Second Treatise, ch 5, para 32, 37 and 41. See also J Tully, *An Approach to Political Philosophy: Locke in Contexts* (Cambridge University Press, 1993) 137.

[39] [2005] 2 SCR 220.

[40] *Ibid*, para 77.

[41] *Amodu Tijani v Secretary, Southern Nigeria* [1921] 2 AC 399, 402–4.

[42] *Ibid.*

emerging international legal norms and do not represent the best in cutting-edge developments we see in comparative jurisprudence.

For example, the *Western Sahara* case from the International Court of Justice precludes a region from being termed uninhabited if so-called nomadic or resident tribes with a degree of social and political organisation are present in the area.[43] The *Awas Tingni* case from the Inter-American Court of Human Rights found that traditional patterns of mobile use and occupation of territory by the indigenous communities of the Atlantic Coast of Nicaragua generated customary law property systems that should be protected as property rights in Nicaragua's Constitution.[44] The *Dann* case from the Inter-American Commission on Human Rights held that general principles of international law included 'the right of indigenous peoples to legal recognition of their varied and specific forms and modalities of their control, ownership, use and enjoyment of territories and property'.[45] This should be interpreted to encompass Indigenous usages that incorporate mobility.

Article 14(1) of the International Labour Organization's Convention 169 also recognises the importance of protecting Indigenous rights to land that arises from mobility. It states that '[t]he rights of ownership and possession of the peoples concerned over the lands which they traditionally occupy shall be recognized [and] particular attention shall be paid to the situation of nomadic peoples and shifting cultivators in this respect'.[46]

Finally, Article 26(2) of the United Nations (UN) Declaration on the Rights of Indigenous Peoples proclaims that 'Indigenous peoples have the right to own, use, develop and control the lands, territories and resources that they possess by reason of traditional ownership or other traditional occupation or use, as well as those which they have otherwise acquired'.[47] If Indigenous peoples traditionally used or owned land in a manner which incorporated elements of mobility, these principles should protect rather than eliminate Indigenous land rights.

In a domestic context, certain countries are beginning to apply these and similar principles to overturn doctrines that denied Indigenous peoples land rights because of their rotational uses. The South African Constitutional Court held that 'racial discrimination lay in the failure to recognize and accord protection to indigenous law ownership while, on the other hand, according protection to

[43] *Western Sahara Advisory Opinion* (1975) ICJ 12.

[44] *Case of the Mayagna (Sumo) Awas Tingni Community v The Republic of Nicaragua* (2001) Inter-American Court of Human Rights, reproduced in (2002) 19 *Arizona Journal of International and Comparative Law* 415.

[45] *Case of Mary and Carrie Dann v United States, Case No 11.140 (Judgment on the Merits)* (27 December 2002) Inter-American Commission on Human Rights No 75/02, para 130.

[46] Convention (No 169), Art 14(1) states that '[t]he rights of ownership and possession of the peoples concerned over the lands which they traditionally occupy shall be recognized. In addition, measures shall be taken in appropriate cases to safeguard the right of the peoples concerned to use lands not exclusively occupied by them, but to which they have traditionally had access for their subsistence and traditional activities. Particular attention shall be paid to the situation of nomadic peoples and shifting cultivators in this respect'.

[47] UN Doc A/61/L.67, 7 September 2007.

registered [non-Indigenous] title'.[48] The Malaysian Court of Appeal cited comparative and international legal principles to find that the 'precise nature of customary title draws upon the practices and usages of each community'.[49] This approach permitted the court to find that customary titles could be permanent, even if the use of the land was territorial and communal.[50] The Belize Supreme Court cited the Malaysian decision with approval, and decided that rotational land uses can be recognised as property rights under the Belize Constitution.[51] This case also built upon a decision of the Inter-American Commission on Human Rights, which came to the same conclusion.[52] The Belize case was also the first judgment in the world to reference the UN Declaration on the Rights of Indigenous Peoples.

As these cases imply, when making legal judgments the choice and agency of Indigenous peoples in their movements must be recognised and affirmed. These points are also increasingly being made in the field of Indigenous studies. There are some excellent novels written by Indigenous writers that explore this phenomenon.[53] It could be said that we have new kinds of seasonal rounds that take us away from and around our territories, before we return.[54] These rounds often replicate our ancient patterns of life and apply them to changing circumstances.

In keeping with the above insights, the best way to ensure that we do not lose rights because of our physical mobility is to recognise and affirm Indigenous patterns of mobility in law, literature and politics. Indigenous communities can bring these examples to other people's attention, while demonstrating why these movements should not be judged by outdated norms. Legislatures, courts, lawyers, academics and the media should be more sensitive to the consequences perpetuated by inappropriate views of Indigenous mobility. Stereotypes must be jettisoned. Every nation-state would do well to apply the legal principles found in recent international customs, cases and conventions. These actions might help others to see us as *Indigenous*, even as we circulate throughout our countries and traditional territories in ways that do not appear to fit outdated perceptions of what it means to be Indigenous.[55]

[48] *Alexkor Ltd v Richtersveld Community* (2003) 12 BCLR 130, para 99.

[49] *Kerajaan Negeri Selango v Sagong Bin Tasi* [2005] 6 MLJ 289, Malaysian CA (Putrajaya) (Gopal Sri Ram JCA), para 12.

[50] *Ibid*, paras 30–33. See also *Adong bin Kuwau and Ors v Kerajaan Negeri Johor and Anor* [1997] 1 MLJ 418, which provided compensation for restricting Indigenous land rights and movement.

[51] *Maya Villages of Santa Cruz and Conejo v Belize* (Claim 171/172 of 2007) (Supreme Court of Belize).

[52] *Maya Indigenous Communities of the Toledo District v Belize Report*, No. 40/04 of 12 October 2004.

[53] W Ihimaera, *The Rope of Man* (Raupo Books, 2005).

[54] B Child, 'A New Seasonal Round: Ojibwe Families and the Great Depression' in D Edmunds (ed), *People of Persistence: American Indians in the Great Lakes* (forthcoming).

[55] It is not the Indigenous peoples who are outdated; it is those who view them in this old-fashioned, stereotypical way.

3. '. . . and Damned if We Don't': The Too Settled Thesis

While Indigenous peoples are told we cannot have rights if we move too much, we are also informed we cannot possess rights because our societies move too little. Caught in these cross-currents, Indigenous peoples face contradictory doctrines that deny legal rights for reasons directly opposed to one another. While the last section described how we can lose rights by being characterised as too unsettled, judges can also deny rights by finding we are too settled, unmoving, intransient and static in our cultural practices. This approach is best illustrated by understanding how courts treat Indigenous peoples as they move through time.

Judges have been loath to view us as contemporary peoples who retain rights when we interact with other cultures. They often view our societies as frozen upon the date of non-native contact or sovereign assertion. They entrench this approach in the law, thus making it difficult for us to travel beyond their assertions. These doctrines are widespread throughout the world. Judicial stereotypes imply that Indigenous political communities are inferior to those that arrived subsequently, because only non-Indigenous states and peoples are given the privilege of moving through time with unfettered power relative to pre-existent societies. Under this approach, Indigenous peoples' interaction with other societies is held to create assimilation and a loss of rights.

For example, if Indigenous peoples in Canada adopt new practices in response to colonial intrusions, these innovations are not protected as rights.[56] Developments that take place subsequent to colonial influence are regarded as not being 'integral to our distinctive cultures'.[57] By this standard, the courts assume that European arrival initiated change that travelled beyond Indigenous peoples' previously inert, 'integral' state. In this light, we are regarded as being too culturally settled at the time of contact to expect new rights to develop from that point forward. In Australia, even if we adapt or reactivate legal, cultural and political traditions, they do not receive protection as Indigenous rights.[58] Once we 'abandon' old ways, we are told we cannot reactivate them.

To allow Indigenous peoples to invent or revitalise tradition would seemingly shatter stereotypical views that imply we cannot be authentically Indigenous if we move beyond our so-called ancient culturally settled state. These views inappropriately depict Indigenous societies as stationary, non-dynamic and invariable before others arrived in our lands. These stereotypes create a hierarchical caste system that places Indigenous societies lower on the scale of social order, relative to

[56] *R v Van der Peet* [1996] 2 SCR 507, paras 55–59.

[57] *Ibid.*

[58] *Yorta Yorta*, above n 32, para 53: 'When the society whose laws or customs existed at sovereignty ceases to exist, the rights and interests in land to which these laws and customs gave rise, cease to exist. If the content of the former laws and customs is later adopted by some new society, those laws and customs will then owe their new life to that other, later, society and they are the laws acknowledged by, and customs observed by, *that later society*, they are not laws and customs which can now properly be described as being the existing laws and customs of the earlier society'.

the creation of subsequent political groupings like nations, states, provinces and municipalities.

This view is echoed in the US, where courts have severely restricted the application of Indigenous jurisdiction over non-Indians because they have found this to be 'inconsistent with their status'. Like their Canadian and Australian counterparts, the US Supreme Court subjectively patrols the borders of colonialism through their ability to control the characterisation of Indigenous rights. In the US context, the court's touchstone for determining the so-called essence of Indian status is whether non-Indians are affected.[59] This interpretive approach has undermined Native American rights in cases involving zoning,[60] taxation,[61] and criminal and civil jurisdiction over non-Indians on reservations.[62] According to this definition, assimilation is appropriate, as long as it only runs in one direction—from the colonising power to the Indigenous society.

In this view it is impermissible for Indigenous peoples to draw others into their cultures, traditions and laws, and expect the courts to protect these activities as rights. This troubling double-standard prevents nation-states from properly recognising and affirming Indigenous peoples' ability to develop through time. Rights are terminated when Indigenous peoples' political journeys take them beyond the point of colonial contact or sovereign assertions of authority. Shutting the gate to these travels constrains Indigenous philosophical and cultural mobility. We are told 'you can't go there' when we want to trek beyond imposed ideological boundaries, which stereotype us as past-tense peoples. The same restrictions cannot be said to apply to non-Indigenous people. When they venture through land or time, they are presumed to carry their rights with them.[63]

The limitations of this approach become further entrenched when judges cannot acknowledge our knowledge as Indigenous if we have incorporated ideas from the surrounding society.[64] In Canada, many of our most respected elders and chiefs have been discredited because they made claims by referencing events that occurred after European arrival.

[59] *Morton v Mancari* (1974) 417 US 535, 554; *Oliphant v Suquamish Indian Tribe* (1978) 435 US 191, 196; *Montana v US* (1981) 450 US 544, 564; *Nevada v Hicks* (2001) 533 US 353, 359–60.

[60] *Brendale v Confederated Tribes of Colville* (1989) 492 US 408, 426–7.

[61] *Atkitson Trading Post v Shirley* (2001) 532 US 645, 649–51.

[62] For an overview of tribal court jurisdiction in the US, see J Richland and S Deer (eds), *Introduction to Tribal Legal Studies* (Altamira Press, 2004); C Garrow and S Deer (ed), *Tribal Criminal Law and Procedure* (Altamira Press, 2004).

[63] G Gall, *The Canadian Legal System* (Carswell, 2004) 35–53; G Alexandrowicz *et al* (eds), *Dimension of Canadian Law: Canadian and International Law in the 21st Century* (Emond Montgomery, 2004) 48; P Hogg, *Constitutional Law of Canada* (Carswell, 2005) 1–28; M McCallum, 'Problems in Determining the Date of Reception in Prince Edward Island' (2006) 55 *University of New Brunswick Law Journal* 3. For an interesting study of the interaction of colonial and Indigenous laws, see P Karsten, *Between Law and Custom: High and Low Legal Cultures in the Lands of the British Diaspora—The United States, Canada, Australia and New Zealand—1600–1900* (Cambridge University Press, 2002).

[64] A Ray, 'Native History on Trial: Confessions of an Expert Witness' (2003) 84 *Canadian Historical Review* 253, 263; R Riddington, 'Fieldwork in Courtroom 53: A Witness to *Delgamuukw v BC*' (1992) 95 *BC Studies* 12.

For example, in *Ontario (Attorney General) v Bear Island Foundation* the Ontario High Court of Justice dismissed an Aboriginal title case because the Temagami Anishinabek understanding of history was influenced by 'a small, dedicated and well-meaning group of white people', who pieced together 'limited pieces of oral tradition'.[65] This view parallels a discredited historiography that regards Indigenous aspirations as inappropriately influenced by outsiders, thus casting doubt on its authenticity as Indigenous.[66] While the Supreme Court of Canada questioned the trial judge's findings regarding historical occupation, it did not explicitly rehabilitate Chief Potts status as a credible Indigenous oral historian.[67]

It seems that Chief Potts had four strikes against him, thereby making his testimony suspect as Indigenous knowledge.[68] First, he had a white mother and a father who was not of 'pure' Indian ancestry. Second, his family purportedly arrived in the territory after the disputed event had taken place. Third, he could not speak Anishinabek (even though his Elders could speak English). Fourth, Chief Potts learned his oral history by reading a short academic memoir about the Temagami in his teenage years and, for the next 20 years, questioning other people about it, including his father. The trial judge said this was 'obviously not oral tradition in the normal sense'.[69]

It is important to underscore what the trial judge found abnormal in Chief Potts' testimony as Indigenous traditional knowledge. He had seemingly travelled too far beyond what courts consider to be authentically Indigenous. The judge's conclusions illustrate how cultural stereotypes about Indigenous peoples' journeys through the world of ideas are inappropriately limited. If one was being

[65] (1984) 49 OR (2d) 353, 372.

[66] For commentary, see H Foster, 'Letting Go the Bone: The Idea of Indian Title in British Columbia 1849–1927' in H Foster and J McLaren (eds), *Essays in the History of Canadian Law: Volume VI: The Legal History of British Columbia and the Yukon* (University of Toronto Press, 1995) 28; P Tennant, *Aboriginal Peoples and Politics: The Indian Land Question in British Columbia, 1849–1989* (UBC Press, 1990) 289.

[67] The Supreme Court quoted the following passage from the trial court judgment: 'the defendants have failed to prove that their ancestors were an organized band level of society in 1763; that, as an organized society, they had exclusive occupation of the Land Claim Area in 1763; or that, as an organized society, they continued to exclusively occupy and make aboriginal use of the Land Claim Area from 1763 or the time of coming of settlement to the date the action was commenced': *Bear Island Foundation*, above n 65, 373, quoted in [1991] 2 SCR 570, 574. Commenting on this at 574–5, the Supreme Court judges said that although they did 'not take issue with the numerous specific findings of fact in the courts below', it did 'not necessarily follow, however, that we agree with all the legal findings based on those facts. In particular, we find that on the facts found by the trial judge the Indians exercised sufficient occupation of the lands in question throughout the relevant period to establish an aboriginal right'.

[68] See *Bear Island Foundation*, above n 65, 369–70. 'Chief Potts, who is thirty-eight years old, has a white mother and a father who is not of pure Indian ancestry, and whose Indian ancestry descended from persons who arrived on the lands about 1901, long after most of the issues in dispute had occurred. It could not be said that his own ancestors had any direct oral knowledge of the events in question. He was therefore merely giving evidence of oral history he had accumulated from other members of the band. He cannot speak the native language and therefore has difficulty in communicating fully with some of the oldest members, although they speak English'.

[69] *Ibid*, 370.

provocative they might even label these views as racist.[70] It is wrongly thought that Indigenous peoples' ideas travel away from authenticity if their ancestry is not pure, their ancestors were physically mobile, Elders and youth communicated with one another in English, and they learned oral tradition prompted by their own literacy and active inquiry about the world. This is another example of the courts inappropriately blocking our journeys through time. The manner in which the court depicted Chief Potts illustrates an exceedingly narrow view of who constitutes an authoritative Indigenous person, and thus what qualifies as Indigenous knowledge. These conclusions constrain philosophical mobility.

Fortunately, the Supreme Court of Canada later chastised judges who undervalued Indigenous oral history and thereby narrowed its reach.[71] In *Delgamuukw v British Columbia*, Chief Justice Lamer stated that the treatment of evidence in Aboriginal rights cases must accord 'due weight to the perspective of aboriginal peoples'.[72] Thus, the courts must 'come to terms with the oral histories of aboriginal societies' by placing them on an 'equal footing with the types of historical evidence that courts are familiar with'.[73]

Unfortunately, despite the court's caution in *Delgamuukw*, and its potential to respect Indigenous knowledge,[74] Indigenous peoples still encounter stereotypes regarding their knowledge and mobility. Thus, the *Delgamuukw* case has not really changed much in judicial practice. In *R v Marshall; R v Bernard*, the Supreme Court affirmed conclusions that Chief Steven Augustine could not be trusted to properly recite oral tradition because of the so-called 'feedback affect' from ideas generated outside his own culture and a product of his own literacy.[75] In *Mitchell v MNR*, the court regarded Chief Mike Mitchell's evidence of Mohawk mobility and trade across the St Lawrence River, which had been accepted by the trial judge, to be 'sparse, doubtful and equivocal'.[76] Chief Mitchell's testimony, which was substantial during the hearing, largely disappeared from the Federal and Supreme Court's opinions.[77] The Supreme Court in particular was unwilling to draw inferences that Mohawk trade would accompany cross-river mobility, despite the finding of 'ample evidence . . . that trade was a central, distinguishing feature of the Iroquois in general and the Mohawks in particular'.[78] It should be noted that

[70] A Hall, 'Where Justice Lies: Aboriginal Rights and Wrongs in Temagami' in M Bray and A Thomson (eds), *Temagami: A Debate on Wilderness* (Dundurn Press, 1990) 223, 237–39.

[71] *R v Van der Peet*, above n 56, para 68.

[72] *Delgamuukw*, above n 30, para 82.

[73] *Ibid*, paras 84, 87.

[74] J Borrows, 'Listening for a Change: The Courts and Oral Tradition' (2001) 39 *Osgoode Hall Law Journal* 1.

[75] [2005] 2 SCR 220, para 62–65. See also V Napoleon, 'Delgamuukw: A Legal Straightjacket for Oral Histories?' (2005) 20 *Canadian Journal of Law and Society* 123.

[76] *Mitchell v MNR* [2001] 1 SCR 911, para 51. In arriving at this conclusion, the court focused on the inadequacy of non-Indigenous experts and inferences drawn from their research.

[77] The one citation Chief Mitchell was given in the Supreme Court judgment is '[a]ccording to our traditions it had always been one of our areas where we did all our planting, we did our fishing and we did our hunting': *ibid*, para 48.

[78] *Ibid*, 41.

Chiefs Potts, Augustine and Mitchell are amongst the most prominent and well-respected Chiefs of their nations. They also have significant reputations as strong First Nations leaders throughout Canada. If these people have trouble convincing courts of the trustworthiness of Indigenous knowledge, one can glimpse the difficulties other Indigenous people will encounter if they adopt insights from their philosophical travels through other cultures.

Furthermore, when Indigenous peoples enter the more explicitly political arena, outside of the courts, they also find that their philosophical mobility is manipulated by being construed as past-tense and backward-looking. For example, when Indigenous peoples look to the future, they often want to secure their objectives through negotiation, agreement and treaties. When Indigenous peoples make these assertions, it is revealing to observe how they are characterised by non-Indigenous politicians.

Non-Indigenous politicians often call for extinguishment, certainty or finality regarding our rights, as if somehow Indigenous peoples and the conflict their presence generates will magically come to an end through a treaty process and settlement.[79] These views illuminate assumptions that regard treaties as largely being about the past. Many non-Indigenous people believe that treaties are about dealing with old, unfinished business. They do not generally see them as creating frameworks for future Indigenous growth and interaction with the nation-state.[80] This leads to the presumption that once treaties are settled Indigenous peoples will generally participate in political life much like other citizens.

For example, the Indian Claims Commission in the US created a settlement process that focused on extinguishment.[81] The New Zealand government has set 2020 as the date for a full and final settlement of Waitangi Treaty claims.[82] Māori people worry that the government's approach makes their political and philosophical aspirations appear anachronistic. Many iwi, hapu and whanua wish to see the Treaty of Waitangi as an intergenerational agreement that guides political philosophies and relationships through time.[83] Unfortunately, many non-Indigenous politicians do not want to travel down this path, and thus impliedly seek to limit Indigenous peoples' ability to move their ideologies into the future.

[79] M Smith, *Our Home or Native Land: What Governments' Aboriginal Policy is Doing to Canada* (Crown Western, 1995) 264–68.

[80] *Ibid.*

[81] M Lieder and J Page, *Wild Justice: The People of Geronimo vs the United States* (Random House, 1997).

[82] Te Puni Kokir, 'Legislative Reform Treaty of Waitangi 1975', www.tpk.govt.nz/en/consultation/reform/treatyofwaitangi.

[83] See generally M Belgrave, M Kawharu and D Williams (eds), *Waitangi Revisited: Perspectives on the Treaty of Waitangi* Chief Joseph Recounts His Trip to Washington, DC (1879) in Zinn and Arnove, above n 1 at 147–8.

E. Conclusion

Indigenous peoples' physical and philosophical mobility must be recognised and affirmed. Doctrines that diminish healthy movement must be denied, and steps must be taken to remove inappropriate restraints on Indigenous peoples' movement through time and space. The recognition and affirmation of Indigenous perspectives and practices concerning mobility are crucial to the future health of Indigenous peoples. When Indigenous peoples can make their own decisions about who they are, where they live, and how they inter-mingle ancient and contemporary ideas, this will facilitate their mobility. Indigenous peoples need a greater degree of control over their own affairs to overcome doctrines and stereotypes that inappropriately bind them in their relationships.

We are not past-tense peoples. We should be physically free to travel through space and philosophically at liberty to carry our ideas through time. I can think of no better conclusion to summarise this Chapter's thesis than to refer once again to Chief Joseph's words which graced the introduction to this Chapter:

> You might as well expect all the rivers to run backward as that any man who was born free should be contented penned up and denied liberty to go where he pleases. If you tie a horse to a stake, do you expect him to grow fat? If you pen an Indian up on a small spot of earth, and compel him to stay there, he will not be contented, nor will he grow and prosper. I have asked some of the Great White Chiefs where they got their authority to say to the Indian that he shall stay in one place, while he sees the white man going where they please. They cannot tell me . . .
>
> Let me be a free man, free to travel, free to stop, free to work, free to trade where I choose, free to choose my own teachers, free to follow the religion of my fathers, free to talk, think, and act for myself—and I will obey every law or submit to the penalty.
>
> Hin-hah-too-yah-lat-kekht (Chief Joseph), Nez Perce[84]

[84] Hin-hah-too-yah-lat-kekht (Chief Joseph), Chief Joseph Recounts His Trip to Washington, DC (1879) in Zinn and Arnove, above n 1, at 147–8.

INDEX

Introductory Note

References such as '178–9' indicate (not necessarily continuous) discussion of a topic across a range of pages. Wherever possible in the case of topics with many references, these have either been divided into sub-topics or only the most significant discussions of the topic are listed. Because the entire volume is about the "indigenous peoples", the use of this term (and certain others occurring throughout the work, notably commencing "indigenous ...", "aboriginal ..." or "native ...") as an entry point has been minimized. Information will be found under the corresponding detailed topics. Although this index does not pretend to fulfil the role of a table of legislation, statutes, treaties and conventions have been listed where they form the subject of a specific section or subsection of the work.

www.ingramcontent.com/pod-product-compliance
Ingram Content Group UK Ltd.
Pitfield, Milton Keynes, MK11 3LW, UK
UKHW020202290926
15471UKWH00005B/1022

9 781841 137957